Simon Wiesenthal

Simon Wiesenthal

A LIFE IN SEARCH
OF JUSTICE

★ ★ ★

Hella Pick

Weidenfeld & Nicolson

LONDON

First published in Great Britain in 1996 by
Weidenfeld & Nicolson

The Orion Publishing Group Ltd
Orion House
5 Upper Saint Martin's Lane
London, WC2H 9EA

A catalogue reference is available from the British Library

ISBN 0 297 81559 8

Typeset by Selwood Systems, Midsomer Norton

Printed and bound in Great Britain by
Butler & Tanner Ltd, Frome and London

To my mother: in memory

Contents

CONTENTS

Illustrations

Queen Juliana of the Netherlands welcoming Wiesenthal, 1970[8]
In Hollywood with Elizabeth Taylor and Rabbi Marvin Hier[9]
With Anatoly Scharansky and Jane Fonda[9]
Wiesenthal with Chancellor Helmuth Kohl, 1991[10]
With Austrian President Thomas Klestil[11]
At the Wiesenthal Center with the Israeli Prime Minister, Menachem Begin
In Poland laying a wreath at the Warsaw Holocaust Memorial, 1994[12]
Receiving the *Polonia Restituta*
Wiesenthal visiting Auschwitz[12]
Receiving his honorary doctorate from Cracow's Jagiellonian Univestiry
A drawing by Wiesenthal
Wiesenthal in his 87th year

[1] Hoffenreich
[2] Pflaum
[3] Leif Engberg, Dagens Nyheter
[4] Alex Izbicki
[5] Kathleen Blumenfeld
[6] J H Dorchinger, IFJ
[7] Udo Lauer, Merlin Press
[8] NFP, The Netherlands
[9] Art Waldinger, Encino, USA
[10] Ronald Glassman
[11] Neue Kronen Zeitung, Austria
[12] Piotr Janos

Glossary

CIC	Counterintelligence Corps
CROWCASS	Central Registry of War Criminals and Security Suspects
FPÖ	*Freiheitliche Partei Österreichs* (Austrian Freedom Party)
ICRC	International Committee of the Red Cross
OAW	*Ostbahn Ausbesserungs Werke* (Eastern Railway Repair Works)
ORT	Organisation for Rehabilitation and Training
OSI	(US) Office of Special Investigations
OSS	Office of Strategic Services
ÖVP	*Österreichische Volkspartei* (Austrian People's Party)
SA	*Sturmabteilung* (Brownshirts)
SPÖ	*Sozialdemokratische Partei Österreichs* (Austrian Social Democratic Party)
SS	*Schutzstaffel* (Himmler's elite guard, in black shirts)
UNWCC	United Nations War Crimes Commission
WJC	World Jewish Congress

Acknowledgments

It is always enlightening to see a public figure at close-up range, but working on Simon Wiesenthal's biography has been an absorbing task and a singular privilege. Without Wiesenthal's co-operation it would have been impossible to write this book. I have had that co-operation in full measure. He has been infinitely patient with me, clearing a busy diary for several days at a time on the frequent occasions when I came to Vienna loaded with questions about his long and eventful life. That alone would be more than enough to earn my gratitude.

However, there is more: he trusted me. He knew that I was not prepared to write a hagiography, but evidently recognised that I was listening, observing, researching, learning and would do my best to produce a fair account of his life. Occasionally, he expressed impatience, asking for evidence that he was not wasting his time and that I was really writing the book. After showing him the first chapter, I stressed that I wanted to finish the entire biography before letting him see any more. He accepted this with good grace, remained available whenever I asked for information, and in no way tried to interfere or even to betray his curiosity. He gave me the kind of trust that normally only exists between confirmed friends. It has been an enriching experience.

It is impossible to thank Simon Wiesenthal without also extending it to Rosemarie Austraat, his invaluable aide and secretary. She has always known where to lay her hands on any document that I asked to see. She helped me to roam through his archives. She was never too busy to deal with my demands on her time, and she even remained good-tempered on the frequent occasions when my clumsiness jammed the office Xerox machine. Rosemarie Austraat's colleague, Trudi Mergili, performed sterling service, staying behind after office hours to transcribe the tapes of many hours of my interviews with 'the boss'.

Mrs Wiesenthal regularly turns down requests for interviews. In my case, she made an exception on one occasion. Perhaps she was curious to meet the person entrusted to write about her husband's life. At any rate, Mr and Mrs Wiesenthal came to my hotel and we were able to talk for a while. Their daughter, Paulinka, soon overcame her reluctance to discuss her father and though we only had one long meeting in Israel, we talked by telephone on several occasions and she became a real source of encouragement.

Beyond Simon Wiesenthal's immediate entourage it is impossible to single out every member of the large cast that has helped me during the close on three years it has taken to complete this book. I am particularly grateful to Lord Weidenfeld for having enough confidence in me to invite me to write this Wiesenthal biography.

A prerequisite for putting Wiesenthal into the context of contemporary history was an understanding of Israel's and Austria's politics. I owe Alena Lourie and her late husband, Norman, a great debt for opening Israeli horizons to me. In researching this biography, Alena also enabled me to talk to several people who might not otherwise have made themselves available.

The introduction describes the help and co-operation extended by Vienna's Kreisky Forum and by the Kreisky Archive Foundation. Dr Oliver Rathkolb, Research Co-ordinator at the Forum and Research Director at the Archive, deserves very special thanks. We had not met before I started this project. But from the moment I contacted him, he allowed me to tap his knowledge quite shamelessly. With Dr Rathkolb's help, I was able to make many short cuts and to avoid some glaring errors. He also made it possible for me to quote from the manuscript of the third volume of Bruno Kreisky's memoirs, which are to be published in October 1996. Dr Kreisky's son, Peter, encouraged my research. Among others in Austria, several of them my long-standing friends, who gave of their time and experience were Chancellor Vranitzki; Heinz Fischer, the President of the Austrian Parliament; Ambassador Ingo Mussi, Kreisky's former press secretary and now Austria's Consul-General in Trieste; Dr Hugo Portisch, television chronicler of Austria's first and second republics, and his wife, Trauti; Dr Hannes Androsch, Kreisky's former Vice-Chancellor and Finance Minister; Mrs Swanee Hunt, US Ambassador to Austria; Colonel Richard Seibel, the US officer who liberated Mauthausen; Ambassador Georg Hennig, Dr Waldheim's former aide and now Ambassador in London; Johanna Heer; Mrs Ella Lingens and her journalist son, Peter Michael Lingens, Wiesenthal's former aide; Georg Hoffman-Ostenhof of the weekly *Profil*; Dr Irene Montjoy of Webster College, Vienna; and Gideon Yarden, ex-Israeli Ambassador to Austria. I also talked with Dr Kurt Waldheim and Friedrich Peter, former leader of the FPÖ.

In Israel, I would not have been able to gather essential information or interview key figures in Wiesenthal's life without the help of my friend and colleague, the journalist Eric Silver. He persuaded a reluctant Isser Harel, the former Mossad chief, both to explain his reasons for dismissing Wiesenthal's role in Adolf Eichmann's capture, and also to let me read the unpublished Harel manuscript on Wiesenthal's role in the search for Eichmann. Eric Silver also interviewed a number of people on my behalf, including Asher Ben-Nathan, Gideon Raphael, Manus Diamant, Tuviah Friedman and Haim Maas, and retrieved archival material from Yad Vashem and the *Jerusalem Post*. Among several others in Israel who went out of their way to help were Professor Yehuda Bauer and Professor Robert Wistrich, both of the Hebrew University; Efraim Zuroff, head of the Wiesenthal Centre's office in Jerusalem; retired Ambassador Michael Elizur, Mehron Medzini, Moshe Arad and Dr Ari Rath. Dr M. Schumert and Pinchas Porath were among a handful of Wiesenthal friends, going back to his school and university days, who received me with open arms. In Israel, there were a number of other important contacts who prefer to remain anonymous.

In the United States, I owe a special debt to Martin Rosen, Wiesenthal's lawyer in New York, and to Mrs Rhonda Barad, head of the Wiesenthal Centre's office in New York. They gave me many insights and opened important doors for me. My thanks are also due to Carlton Sedgeley, Wiesenthal's agent, and to Martin Mendelsohn, Wiesenthal's lawyer in Washington.

In Los Angeles, Rabbi Marvin Hier, Dean of the Wiesenthal Centre, Rabbi Abraham Cooper, Associate Dean, and Dr Gerald Margolies, its Director, were all generous with their time and insights into the history and aims of their ambitious institution and their plans for handling the Wiesenthal legacy.

I am grateful that Elan Steinberg of the World Jewish Congress and Eli Rosenbaum, author of *Betrayal*, formerly of the WJC and now head of the US Department of Justice's Office of Special Investigations, both agreed to meet me. Without these contacts I would not have appreciated the depth of antagonism that Simon Wiesenthal is capable of arousing. Unfortunately, I failed in my endeavours to talk with Edgar Bronfman, President of the WJC, or with Israel Singer, Secretary-General of the WJC.

In Holland, Simon Speyer, head of the Dutch Wiesenthal fund, told me the full story of Dutch endeavours to be of help to Wiesenthal.

In Germany, President Richard von Weizsäcker and Chancellor Helmut Kohl readily received me to discuss the Wiesenthal phenomenon. Willy Brandt was no longer alive when I began to work on this book, but friendship with him had helped me to come to terms with post-war Germany, and remembrance of conversations with him made it easier to grapple with Holocaust issues.

In Poland, my special thanks go to ex-Foreign Minister Vladyslaw Bartoszewski. At his previous post as Poland's Ambassador to Austria, he organised Wiesenthal's 1994 visit to Poland. I am similarly grateful to Dr Emil Brix, then Austrian Consul in Cracow and now head of the Austrian Institute in London; Professor Alexander Koj, rector of the Jagiellonian University, and Mrs Koj; Professor Geozef Gierowski of the Jagiellonian University; Marek Karpinski, aide to ex-President Lech Walesa; and my long-standing friends in Poland, Mira Michalowski, Daniel Passant, Mieczyslaw Rakowski and Mrs Audrey Glover, head of the OSCE (Organisation for Security and Co-operation in Europe) Democracy Bureau in Warsaw.

In Britain, among those who have been exceptionally generous with advice and information are Martin Gilbert, Rabbi Albert Friedlander, Frederick Forsyth, Professor David Cesarani, Martin Goldenberg and the staff of the Wiener Library. The Chief Rabbi, Jonathan Sacks, was kind enough to see me, and Zvi Aharoni, one of the Mossad operatives involved in Eichmann's capture, who now lives in Britain, showed me the manuscript of his account of those events. Prem Tobias, another Mauthausen survivor, who interpreted for Wiesenthal with the Americans in 1945, lent me some of his documents from that period. Tom Bower's advice steered me in directions I might not otherwise have explored. My agent, Mike Shaw, ably backed by his assistant Sophie Janson, has been a constant morale-booster. It has been my good fortune to have Ion Trewin as editor at Weidenfeld. The interest he has taken in this book, and the help that he and his assistant, Cassia Joll, have given, made my task much easier. I am particularly grateful to Linda Osband for the very helpful and courteous way she undertook the copy-editing of my manuscript.

Throughout the adventure of writing this book, a few close friends have encouraged me, have talked issues through with me, and lifted the burden of focusing for so long and in such a concentrated manner on the Holocaust. I have already referred to some, but no list would be complete without Dr Wolfgang Fischer and his wife Jutta, who introduced me to their beloved Ausseerland and have followed the saga of this book from beginning to end. In the United States, Professor Robert J. Lifton and his wife, and another friend of many years' standing, Professor Gillian Lindt, propelled me to look more deeply into the moral and ethical implications of the Wiesenthal phenomenon. Erik Amfitheatrof convinced me that I should tackle this project when I was still extremely doubtful. Hermann and Christa von Richthofen's steady encouragement has been invaluable. Christopher and Pascale Mallaby, Linda Christmas and John Higgins, Richard, Gabriela and Matthew Fyjis-Walker, Paul and Nicola Cheslaw, Ian and Lydia Wright, Ralph and Mary Blumenau, all cheered me on. Colleagues at the *Guardian*, especially Peter Preston, Martin Woollacott, Ian Traynor, and John Gittings, kept a beady eye on me.

Jan Margerison who transcribed many of my interviews in the United States and in Israel, even when she was already seriously ill, has not lived long enough to read my appreciation for all the help she gave me.

Above all, I want to thank my friend Evi Wohlgemuth. She helped with research, read every chapter as it emerged, checked the proofs, made many helpful suggestions – and in the process thoroughly confused me over the use of commas – and was always at the other end of a telephone prepared to lend a sympathetic ear.

Besides Simon Wiesenthal himself, others who read all or part of the manuscript were Mrs Wohlgemuth, Dr Wolfgang Fischer, Baron and Baroness von Richthofen, Eric Silver and Dr Oliver Rathkolb. But responsibility for the text is mine alone.

Hella Pick
London, November 1995

Introduction

Simon Wiesenthal – Nazi-hunter. Mention the name and, nine times out of ten, the other person will respond with this job description. Wiesenthal and Nazi-hunting have become synonymous.

It was only after I had come to know Wiesenthal much better that I understood that the Nazi-hunter's image is far too narrow – in reality, quite secondary to his significance as a fighter for justice and against Holocaust amnesia. To portray him as an avenger is simplistic. To dismiss him as a flawed intellectual is to betray misunderstanding of Wiesenthal's unique character combination of fighter against evil and passionate believer in a democratic society's system of justice.

As Holocaust survivor and moralist, he recognised the seamless web between past, present and future, and became a messenger who has continuously taught that this truism can only be ignored at great peril to democracy and civilisation. If evils have been committed, responsibility has to be acknowledged. Nations and individuals must not turn their backs on the atrocities of the Holocaust, but neither can they be allowed to indulge in the cheap satisfaction of revenge.

Justice has always been Wiesenthal's leitmotiv: justice that goes beyond acknowledgment of guilt and beyond apology. He has put his trust in the courts, even though he recognised that the post-war array of judges and prosecutors in Germany and Austria included some former Nazis, and he has constantly flailed against their efforts to hold up the prosecution of war criminals.

Wiesenthal has been consistent in arguing that punishment has to be individual, never collective, but that those suspected of war crimes must be exposed to the rigours of the law. Punishment can never match the monstrous deeds perpetrated during the Holocaust, and he has been markedly less concerned with the sentences meted out by the courts than with the trials themselves. He has always opposed capital punishment. His emphasis is on the exposure of organised mass murder and the Holocaust as one of the surest means of convincing reluctant nations to deal with their tainted past. Only by such means can the world come to terms with recent history, or even begin to comprehend that ethnic cleansing in Bosnia or Rwanda corrodes civil society and administers incalculable harm not just to the victim peoples, but to all of us.

Of course I had long known of Simon Wiesenthal. But until I received a telephone call from Lord Weidenfeld suggesting that I write Wiesenthal's biography, I had not met Wiesenthal, or indeed followed his activities at all closely. In retrospect, it seems very odd to me that I had not sought him out earlier. As East European correspondent and afterwards as diplomatic editor of the *Guardian*, Austria had long been in my bailiwick. I had written about Austrian politics, covered election campaigns and had come to know the Chancellor, Dr Bruno Kreisky, very well. I had met Kurt Waldheim way back in the 1960s when he was Austria's Ambassador to the United Nations, and interviewed him both as UN Secretary-General and afterwards when he had become Austria's much-disputed head of state. Yet my articles had rarely addressed the conflict between Simon Wiesenthal and Bruno Kreisky, or Wiesenthal's uncomfortable dilemma over Waldheim, and I had never joined the throng of journalists who habitually commune with Simon Wiesenthal.

So when the Wiesenthal project was put to me in the spring of 1993, I knew that I would bring a relatively uncluttered mind to the task. I use the word 'relatively' only to stress that there was enough common background to ease my way into understanding Wiesenthal's motivation and actions, yet not so much that I already had a whole set of preconceived ideas about Wiesenthal's significance.

As a refugee from Hitler's Austria, who had come to Britain as a young child with my mother – the only other survivor from our small family – I had been lucky enough to escape first-hand experience of the concentration camps, but had lost close relatives and done my fair share of agonising about the Holocaust.

I was born into a family that traced itself back on my father's side to several generations of Austrian-born Jews and on my mother's side to Jewish origins in Bohemia. My parents divorced when I was very small, before the *Anschluss* (the annexation of Austria by Germany) in 1938; and my mother brought me up to be a religious agnostic and, as an aware Jew, to be a strong adherent of assimilation. In common with so many Austrian Jews, she always felt that Polish Jews, of whom Wiesenthal is one, were somehow alien creatures, who never wholly integrated into the nations where they settled.

Yet, rather than blinding me to Wiesenthal's qualities and strengths, or exaggerating his faults and weaknesses, I have found that my upbringing and experiences have given me the right mix of understanding, sympathy and detachment to see this singular individual in the round.

I had insisted from the outset that I was not prepared to write an authorised biography with Simon Wiesenthal retaining editorial control. The publishers fully concurred. This meant that before a firm decision was taken to write the book, I went to Vienna to meet Wiesenthal. He had to decide whether he was prepared to co-operate, even though he would have no control over the contents. That first encounter lengthened into several days of conversation – and I knew that a gripping journey of discovery and learning lay ahead.

Very rapidly, I came to see the humanity of the man. Daily, he relives his sufferings, he mourns his family murdered in the Holocaust and weeps too for all the other victims. But there is no self-indulgence. His grieving is the motor that has driven him and has given him the strength and moral support to pursue his essentially lonely quest against Holocaust amnesia. But his persona is by no means all sadness, or driven purpose. Wiesenthal finds relief in humour. His fund of anecdotes is impressive and he derives as much enjoyment from the telling of his jokes as do those who are allowed to share them.

Wiesenthal is a consistent man. The private man is not very different from the public man. What he says to the outside world is much the same that he says within the walls of his modest office or among a convivial group of friends. He makes no attempt to hide his need for public acclaim. Life for him has been a series of battles – for his architect's education before the war, for survival during the war, and after the war to sustain his good name and credibility against assaults from many quarters ranging from Communist governments to Bruno Kreisky and the World Jewish Congress (WJC). He is a supreme individualist, unsuited to teamwork and unwilling to be part of an organisational hierarchy – even if he were to be in charge. As he grows older, Wiesenthal has undoubtedly become more and more passionate to ensure that history will award him a prominent place in the pantheon of Holocaust fighters. He wants to be accepted as an authentic Jewish hero. All this has heightened one of his most obvious character flaws: his tendency to see people and issues in black and white with little room left for shades of grey.

Being sentimental, Wiesenthal relishes occasional reunions with the handful of school and university companions who are still alive. But his need for close friendship – or his ability to give it – is less obvious.

From those who consider themselves his friends, he demands loyalty and wholehearted approbation. This he has from his family, from his secretary, Rosemarie Austraat, and from a handful of people across the globe who speak of Wiesenthal as 'my brother'. For all that, I see him primarily as a one-man band, who applies all his energies to his work and has little need of companionship. His wife, daughter and grandchildren are all important to him. Other relationships pale by comparison.

Wiesenthal has given me endlessly of his time and has exposed the full range of his remarkable memory – remarkable not only because he can dig back into his childhood, but also because he has an aptitude, rare for people in their late eighties, of recalling the immediate past. Besides allowing me to question him on all aspects of his life, Wiesenthal gave me unrestricted access to all his archives and files, and made clear to his family, friends and associates that he wanted them to be helpful. He made certain that the Polish authorities allowed me to accompany him on his first return visit to Poland.

Naturally I did not restrict my research to people who shared Wiesenthal's views or otherwise approved of him. It did not take me long to realise that he cuts a highly controversial figure in quite a few quarters. But I had not been prepared for the jealousies and rivalry between Jewish organisations, or the distasteful battles for ownership of the Holocaust. Most of all, I was taken aback by the vehemence of the anti-Wiesenthal faction in the WJC. Eli Rosenbaum on first acquaintance immediately voiced suspicion that I had been commissioned by Lord Weidenfeld to do, as he crudely put it, 'a whitewash' on a man he thinks of as a congenital liar. Elan Steinberg, the WJC's executive director, also drew a picture of Wiesenthal as a man, driven by vanity, who had drawn up a false prospectus for himself, and could neither be trusted nor taken seriously. These men see Wiesenthal as an impostor and talk about him in absolutes. They made it clear that if I did not represent their view of Simon Wiesenthal, my objectivity in writing this biography would be suspect.

The contrast between the WJC's attitude to my role as Wiesenthal's biographer and the Kreisky Forum's in Vienna could not have been greater. The Forum is a foundation to promote research and discussion on the policies of social democracy, initiated by Bruno Kreisky. After I signalled my interest in its archives, I was overwhelmed by offers of co-operation. Kreisky's son Peter and Margot Schmidt, Kreisky's former secretary who administers the Forum, both encouraged me in my work. But most of all, Dr Oliver Rathkolb, Director of the Kreisky Forum, went out of his way to help me with documents and reference material, and above all to offer me his advice and insight into Austrian politics and Kreisky's actions. Far from trying to safeguard Kreisky's reputation by giving me a one-dimensional view of the battles between Wiesenthal and Kreisky, Dr Rathkolb and his colleagues in the Kreisky Forum have encouraged me to write a comprehensive and unblinkered account of an episode from which neither of the protagonists emerge with great glory.

In tackling the Wiesenthal biography, choices had to be made. The opening chapter, a full account of Wiesenthal's first return journey to Poland fifty years after he was last there as a concentration camp inmate, aims to introduce the man and his credo. Subsequent chapters describe his background and early life. The story of Wiesenthal's survival from the Holocaust is based on his extraordinarily vivid recollections, and explains how it came about that he refused to make a new existence for himself and instead opted for a life that would permanently tether him to the Holocaust.

It would have been impossible to give a detailed account of all the Nazi criminals he investigated. As the Eichmann case accounts for Wiesenthal's early fame and has punctuated his life on various occasions right up to the present, it was obvious that this story had to be told in full. The other 'case histories' I have chosen, including Franz Stangl, Franz Murer, Josef Mengele and Hermine Braunsteiner-Ryan, are all intended to illustrate both the methods that Wiesenthal has used in his search for Nazi criminals and also the difficulties he has encountered, not least from other Nazi-hunters.

Wiesenthal's personal story since 1945 has been intimately bound up with Austria, where he chose to make his home. He focused far more attention on denazification in Austria than in Germany, and his need to see Austrians purge themselves of their Nazi past has driven him to pound on Austrian sensibilities until he was properly heard and understood. His conflict with Bruno Kreisky can only be properly understood in the context of Wiesenthal's overall relationship to Austria, and that is why I have described that in considerable detail.

Wiesenthal's unease with Austria possibly had an even greater bearing on his handling of the Waldheim affair, but the ramifications of that matter went far beyond Austria and brought into question Wiesenthal's world standing. I was very conscious, in trying to piece together the tangled strands of the Waldheim affair, that there were almost as many versions as there were different parties to the dispute over Waldheim's war record. It is probably impossible to take the story from A to Z without inviting correction, but my aim throughout was to be objective.

As an author, Wiesenthal has been prolific. His books have been widely read and translated into many languages. To complement my conversations with him, I have quoted liberally from his two principal books of memoirs, *The Murderers Amongst Us* and *Justice Not Vengeance*, but I have used a separate chapter to give an account of his other books.

If there are only two brief chapters about Wiesenthal's private life, it is partly because he is a very private person and partly because his life is an open book with no scintillating secrets to uncover.

In researching this book, I realised time and again that many people assume, quite wrongly, that the Wiesenthal Center in Los Angeles and Simon Wiesenthal himself are all part and parcel of the same institution. I have therefore told the story of how the Los Angeles Center came into being, what it is all about, why Wiesenthal gave it his imprimatur and why he hopes that it will perpetuate his legacy.

[1]
Poland 1994 – A Survivor's Return

It was a sparkling October day at Birkenau, the crematorium extension of Auschwitz. The sky was a luminous blue. The single-track railway line, overgrown with weeds, was lit up by the autumn sun, its rays casting long shadows over the mass of crumbling chimneys in the adjoining fields. Half a century earlier, the bodies of millions of men, women and children murdered in the gas chambers of Auschwitz had been fed into the furnaces beneath.

The crimes that were perpetrated at Auschwitz, the moral and physical perversions, are beyond comprehension. No monument could ever express the evil deeds that were carried out here between 1942 and 1945. But a handful of stone slabs, bearing the identical inscription in the languages of the main groups of victims, exhorts visitors to safeguard remembrance of the Holocaust: 'Let this place remain for all time a cry of despair, and a reminder to mankind. Here, the Nazis murdered millions, the majority of them Jews, from many countries of Europe.'

An elderly man, of imposing stature, supporting himself lightly with a cane and bearing a simple wreath of purple chrysanthemums, walked slowly, stiffly, up the few steps to the memorial and stood there for a few moments, lost in thought and silent tears.

The date was 20 October 1994, the mourner, Simon Wiesenthal, then eighty-five years old. He needed no reminder of the sufferings of this place. Firm in the belief that mankind can be educated against perpetrating the worst evils, this man had devoted all his years since the end of the last war to making the world remember and grasp the full dimensions of the Holocaust.

Besides, he had been in this place before – almost exactly fifty years ago to the day.

Only then, in 1944, he had been inside a railway cattle wagon, sandwiched with other human beings so tightly that he scarcely knew who was alive and who was dead. For three days they were kept there in a siding at the end of the line, asking themselves only when, and not whether, they were to be decanted into the gas ovens.

One of the camp guards, Pery Broad, described the scene in a report, written soon after the war's end:

> All four crematoria were working at full capacity. On an average, 10,000 men and women arrived daily. Some of them had gone mad on the journey from thirst or fear. Time and again the furnaces burned out, the chimneys split from being overworked. There was nothing for it but starting up the open fires again to burn up the arrears of corpses that lay heaped behind the crematoria walls. Gas chambers were opened when the last groans had barely ceased, bodies barely dragged out before the next living batch was driven in.[1]

Even though the Nazis were still intent on achieving the Final Solution – the elimination of all Jews and of all others deemed as inferior – an unseen camp commandant decided that capacity at Auschwitz to gas and burn human beings had become overtaxed and ordered that the wagons holding Wiesenthal and a few hundred others had to be moved on to be disposed of in another death camp. And so the victims were taken on to Gross-Rosen, and on again in a horrendous Odyssey from camp to camp that finally brought Wiesenthal, more dead than alive, to Mauthausen, a smaller Austrian, but similarly obscene, edition of Auschwitz.

By now the war was drawing to a close and Wiesenthal managed to survive at Mauthausen until his liberation by the Americans in May 1945. Since then, driven on unswervingly by a self-imposed mission to bring the perpetrators of the Holocaust to justice and build a powerful bulwark of understanding and education against its recurrence, Wiesenthal's name has become inextricably linked to the pursuit of the Nazi murderers – of the 'desk murderers' who planned the killings, and of those who carried out these bestial tasks.

On his 1994 return to Auschwitz, Wiesenthal rested momentarily on a rickety chair in front of one of the now sanitised prisoners' huts and summed up his vocation: neither execution nor long-term imprisonment could ever make up for the crime of mass murder on the scale of the Holocaust. The true worth of war crimes trials was to expose the graphic truth and convince post-war generations, who had themselves been spared the direct experience, that these terrible events had really taken place – and must never be allowed to repeat themselves: 'My whole life's meaning is to ensure that the murderers of tomorrow – who may not even be born yet – must know that they will have no peace. Such warnings are vital for future generations.' He was to return to the theme next day, turning it into an inaugural address, when he received an honorary degree from Poland's venerable Jagiellonian University in Cracow.

On this October day in 1994, Simon Wiesenthal remained captive to his past, even though he had come of his own free will as a treasured guest of the Polish Government. He had arrived by motorcade, driving slowly through the Auschwitz arch with its infamous inscription '*Arbeit macht frei*' ('Work makes free'). True, he had a heavy police escort; but this was there to protect him, not to persecute him. He wanted to honour the dead and see for himself how these horror chambers of the Holocaust were being preserved as evidence for future generations of the meticulously prepared and methodically recorded mass killings by the Nazis.

As Wiesenthal surveyed the crowds of curious young people who happened to be visiting on the same day, he noted poignantly: 'For so much that has happened, I am one of the last witnesses. While I remain alive, I can serve as an eyewitness for the young – for people like those around us today. It is more effective than any amount of reading about those terrible events.'

Perennially young, with his computer-like memory for matters past and present unimpaired, he recalled that 'on my seventy-fifth birthday, my wife urged me to give up and to lead a more normal life during the years that remained to us. But to me such normality seemed like betrayal, and I knew there was no alternative but to go on.'

The Auschwitz curators bustling around Wiesenthal gave him a photostat copy of his Mauthausen prisoner's card: 'Number 127,371; Jew; born in Lvov district 31.12.08.' This, in common with millions of other victims' cards retrieved from Nazi documents, has been fed into an IBM computer which Wiesenthal had secured for Auschwitz. The researchers thanked him. The computer made it easier to pursue their work, but it also made it more impersonal. 'Individual lives reduced to signals on a screen,' Wiesenthal muttered to himself.

Yet there was nothing maudlin in the credo he inscribed in the Auschwitz visitors' book. '*Information ist Verteidigung*' – 'Information is Defence,' he wrote – shorthand for his conviction that man is not born evil, but can be conditioned for good or for bad. If that is so, then historical truth becomes an essential deterrent to the practice of evil.

As Wiesenthal moved on from the cavernous room where the visitors' book is kept, his thoughts went out not only to the Jewish victims, but also to the mass of other victims of the Holocaust, especially the Poles and Gypsies – the Roma and Sinti – who had been killed at Auschwitz and elsewhere. Even under obvious stress, as he was that day, Wiesenthal wanted to emphasise that Hitler's drive to exterminate the Gypsies was as ruthless as the extermination of the Jews. It was no accident that two representatives of the Roma were there to greet him.

This brief return to Poland was far more than a mournful pilgrimage to Auschwitz. It combined all the elements of a celebration for Wiesenthal's achievements, and of a vindication for the anti-Semitic insults and mis-representations hurled against him by Poland's former Communist rulers. It prompted him to explain himself and to define his moral values to his compatriots.

For a man incapable of hiding his emotions, Wiesenthal's demeanour also made it obvious that this was a deeply satisfying homecoming, which he savoured not only for the honours and recognition bestowed on him, but also because it surely signified, he said cheerfully, 'a slap in the face' for those of his former Polish Communist tormentors who were still alive.

He was fêted every step of a tiring week of public and private appearances: as if everyone, Jews and Christians, and intellectuals of very different persuasions, had reached the conclusion that this Jew from Galicia, now a citizen of Austria, had to be treated as a national treasure. His international renown deserved to be firmly underpinned by public recognition in his home country – or perhaps more accurately in what would have been his country if the post-war settlement had not shifted his native Galicia out of Poland and, not for the first time in Wiesenthal's lifetime, back to the Ukraine.

Today's Poland claims him as its native son, and Wiesenthal does not demur. He speaks Polish at home and feels no affinity with the Ukraine, even though that country now has his birthplace, Buczacz, firmly within its boundaries. And so it happened that Simon Wiesenthal, born in Galicia when it was in the possession of the Hapsburg Empire, obliged to undertake his architect's studies in Prague because the architectural faculty in Polish universities was closed to Jews, imprisoned in a forced labour camp in Lvov until even worse befell him in Plaszow concentration camp, became the first 'former' Pole to be awarded Poland's highest honour, the Commander's Cross of the Order of *Polonia Restituta*. Three days later, he also became the first Jew in the Jagiellonian University's 610-year-old history to be given an honorary degree, the *Honoris Causa*, for academic achievement.

When Wiesenthal stepped out of the plane from Vienna on 16 October 1994, and set foot in Warsaw's bright new airport, he was apprehensive. The decision to come had not been easy, and he had hesitated long and hard before accepting President Lech Walesa's invitation.

Others might have been deterred by memories of Polish anti-Semitism and of wartime suffering. Wiesenthal's reluctance to come had even more to do with the vicious campaign against him, orchestrated by Polish Communists during the late 1960s. They had accused him of acting as an intelligence agent for Israel, for the CIA, for the Federal Republic of Germany – or, as Wiesenthal described it, 'as spying for almost anyone except maybe the Japanese'.

Wiesenthal, they had insisted, had spawned a network of agents to form 'an anti-Communist alliance', and his office in Vienna had become a 'Mecca for revisionist intellectuals'. Polish propaganda also vilified him for pursuing double standards. Dubbed by the Polish Communists as a Western tool, they accused him of double standards. They had asserted that he had been prepared to turn a blind eye to Nazis who had regained positions of power in post-war West Germany, while at the same time denouncing the East German authorities – without sound evidence – for failing to prosecute the Nazis within their ranks.

Worst of all, they claimed that he had collaborated with the Nazis during the war. Tainted evidence about his relations with the Gestapo had been fabricated. It was an intolerable insult, compounded by the fact that it eventually found its way to Bruno Kreisky's desk. The Austrian leader chose to treat the allegations as authentic and used them during his long, but finally fruitless, campaign to puncture Wiesenthal's reputation and moral stature.

In 1968, Wiesenthal had fought back against his Polish detractors with press conferences and exposures of the personalities who had orchestrated the propaganda directed against him. The conflict with Kreisky rankled most of all. Without Poland's fabrications to muddy the waters, the Austrian Chancellor's private war against Wiesenthal might have collapsed much earlier, and would certainly have been less vicious. As Wiesenthal saw it, injustice had been heaped upon injustice; and the whole sequence had begun in Poland.

In 1988, Wiesenthal had rejected a gesture from the Communist leader, General Jaruzelski, to attend that year's commemoration of the Warsaw Ghetto uprising. Wiesenthal had felt that 'Poland had gone from one slavery to another' and that it was too early to be sure that Poland had changed for the better. He had decided 'to await further developments'.

Now those developments – the end of Communist rule – had duly happened. His Communist enemies had lost power. Wiesenthal was pleased when emissaries from Warsaw came to his Documentation Centre in Vienna early in 1994, declaring that Poland now wished to honour its native son by bestowing its highest medal on him.

At the same time messages came from the Jagiellonian University that, after an improbably long three-year debate, it was approaching a positive decision on the award of an honorary doctorate to Wiesenthal. The Jagiellonian prides itself on the high standards it sets before conferring honorary degrees; nor does it hold with academic gesture politics. So, the official explanation for the long argument over the Wiesenthal degree hinted at doubts over his academic qualifications.

But anti-Semitism too had played a role. Some of the professors were known to have questioned whether a Jew deserved to be honoured by an institution as steeped in Polish learning and tradition as the Jagiellonian University. The final vote in the University's Senate was in favour of the award, but still not unanimous.

Even so, Wiesenthal prevaricated as if seeking more time for mental adjustment. He would come to Poland only on condition that Lech Walesa as head of state would perform the award ceremony of the *Polonia Restituta* medal, and that the Jagiellonian doctorate would be conferred during the same visit. Perhaps too, if he waited a little longer, his wife Cyla might be persuaded to leave the cocoon of their modest home in Vienna and join him on the Polish visit. That hope, he knew, was almost bound to end in disappointment. And so it turned out; she remained behind, not well enough to face the emotional stress, but glued to her television set in Vienna for reports of her husband's progression through Poland.

When all had fallen into place with the dates for the visit finally fixed, a still apprehensive Wiesenthal applied himself to the task of preparing the message he would deliver at the Jagiellonian and elsewhere in Poland. There would be no attempt to gloss over the past, but he would put the emphasis on the values that mattered most to him: justice, fairness and integrity.

It was in character that Wiesenthal's very first remarks in Warsaw carried a message of conciliation that he was to repeat throughout his stay. Even though he had suffered so much at the hands of Poles, he categorically refused to be drawn into wholesale condemnation of the Polish nation. The concept of collective guilt was alien to him. As individuals – yes – Poles could and should be accused of wrongdoing and anti-Semitism. But no one, least of all Jews, who had suffered so much from anti-Semitic generalisations, should ever put a nation, a people or a race into the dock collectively. 'I refuse to categorise a whole people. We must not fall into that trap.'

'I have been severely attacked by the Polish Communist regime,' he reminded a gaggle of journalists, eager to see the former Polish ogre now turned Polish icon. 'But neither do I forget that it was the Polish underground – Home Army units – who ensured my wife's survival during the war.'

The Polish underground – and he did not exclude its Communist groups – counted for him amongst the most important and bravest in Europe. Not only had they sheltered Cyla for at least part of the war, but they had also helped to hide him during a brief period of freedom in 1943 after he escaped from the Janowska forced labour camp at Lvov.

No Jew who survived in Poland during the war, Wiesenthal told his Polish audiences, could have done so without at least some small measure of assistance from a Pole. Even during the hate campaign against him in the 1960s and 1970s, some Polish friends had been courageous enough to show open support for him.

He had come to terms with trials and tribulation. He owed a debt to the dead. 'Everything in life has its price; even survival. And I have been paying that price for the past fifty years.'

Wiesenthal's renown persuaded a great many of Poland's combative intellectuals, even some who would normally refuse to be seen in the same room, to turn up for an overflowing, smoke-filled gathering at Warsaw's PEN club (the international writers' association). Vengeance and prejudice, he tried to make this sceptical group grasp, had never motivated him.

Bitterness has no part of his make-up, and he had come to terms with the fact that neither Eichmann nor any other mass murderer could have received full and just punishment for his crimes. All he had ever sought was to ensure that 'no Nazi murderer, however old he may be, will be allowed to die in peace'. This would continue to be his aim 'even as my life draws to its biological end'.

But surely, asked one of the intellectuals in search of a wholesale condemnation of Polish brutality, he must harbour a deep resentment towards Poland for all the anti-Semitism and discrimination he had experienced from early childhood in his native Galicia, and for his suffering at the hands of Poles during the war years?

'Every country has fools,' was his quick-fire retort.

A guard of honour greeted Wiesenthal's arrival at Warsaw's Koniecpolskich Palace, where President Walesa was to decorate him. It was a brief ceremony, performed in the same chamber where the Soviet Union had corralled its East European satellites into signing the Warsaw Pact Treaty, and where Walesa, in his former, far more renowned incarnation as Solidarity's leader, had participated in the 1989 Round Table talks that brought the Communist era in Poland to a close.

Walesa, still protecting himself against alien spirits with a miniature of Catholic Poland's Black Madonna of Czestochowa pinned on his lapel, had to reach up to the taller, bulkier and solemnly expectant Wiesenthal to bedeck him with the red-ribboned gold *Polonia Restituta* cross. 'Justice means that the innocent go free, but that the guilty are punished. You have followed that principle for fifty years,' Walesa proclaimed, adding that Wiesenthal had had to wait until Poland was restored after Communist rule before Poland was in a position 'to recognise and honour his achievements'.

Wiesenthal, his voice breaking with emotion, accepted his award 'not only on my own behalf, but also to the memory of the millions of innocent victims, irrespective of nationality or religion. As one who grew up in Poland and went to Polish schools, I know what Poles and Jews have always had in common: the pursuit of justice and the commitment to traditional values.'

Moments later, over a celebratory drink, he was again speaking reconciliation – stressing the cultural affinity between Jews and Poles. 'My own education was based on Polish as well as Jewish traditions,' he told Walesa. But he also warned that Poland's young today do not know enough about the bravery and achievements of the Polish resistance. 'When we insist on the crucial importance of freedom we must also speak about those who fight for freedom.'

Wiesenthal had only once before been in Warsaw, and then only for a fleeting couple of hours in the 1930s. But on this grey drizzly day, he displayed little interest in his surroundings as he was driven from the presidential palace to the Ghetto memorial. He had brought a wreath of white daisies and blue irises; and he stood there, a forlorn mourner, momentarily quite oblivious to his surroundings.

But there was little respite. Next it was the turn of the tiny remnants of Poland's Jewish community in Warsaw and Cracow to receive a morale booster from Wiesenthal. He visited the Jewish centres in both cities, promising to use his influence to secure more practical help from Jewish organisations abroad. In Warsaw's struggling Jewish Historical Institute, they showed him a few pathetic cardboard boxes stacked with scraps of archives recovered from the ruins of the country's Jewish communities.

Picking up where he had left off with Lech Walesa, he again put the emphasis on the common heritage between Jews and Poles. Jewish culture had played its share for over a thousand years of Polish history. The museum, which the Jewish Institute wanted to establish in Warsaw, must focus on that history and not concentrate only on the Holocaust and the events that led to it. Poland's Jewry had been 'an intellectual aristocracy', which had been decimated during the war. In its place, 'an aristocracy of money' had emerged. The contemporary world was the poorer for it.

Before the war, Warsaw alone had a population of 350,000 Jews. Now the whole of Poland has only 8,000 Jews, most of whom are elderly survivors, beyond child-bearing age, and dying out. Still afraid of anti-Semitism, virtually no Jewish émigrés have returned to Poland prepared to found a new generation there. A similar situation prevails in Cracow, where a mere 600–700 Jews still make their home. There are no children among them. A Jewish wedding, while Wiesenthal was in the city, was a major event, the first for many years.

Even so, Cracow's Jews were bravely ploughing on to enlarge their 'Research Centre for Jewish Culture', built on the ashes of Kazimierz, the city's former mainly Jewish quarter. Episodes of Steven Spielberg's *Schindler's List* had been filmed there; and Wiesenthal, who had himself been an inmate of nearby Plaszow concentration camp in 1944 – it was from there that he had been transported to Auschwitz – knew only too well how accurate the film's portrayal of the indiscriminate killings had been.

Wiesenthal was back to his twin themes of bridge-building between Poles and Jews, and the dangers of generalisation. 'There was collaboration between Polish Communists and the Soviet Union; but that was directed not just against Jews but also against the whole Polish nation.' And no, 'don't blame any particular group for the crematoria. All of Europe built the death camps, because it remained silent, even after it had been made aware of the facts.'

Indefatigable, he also joked to a packed hall 'that I was not ready to die for Paul Newman'. It was a reference to a fictionalised television series, made some years earlier. Wiesenthal had wanted Paul Newman to play his role, but the American actor had declined, arguing that he never acted to impersonate living people. Fortunately, Wiesenthal was thoroughly pleased with the performance of Ben Kingsley, who did accept the role. 'He really understood me,' he beamed.

A short visit to the cluttered editorial office of *Trygodnik Powszechny*, the Catholic weekly renowned for its bravely independent stance during Communist rule, elicited another cautionary tale from Wiesenthal. Always at his most effective when he uses imagery to illustrate a point, Wiesenthal described the scene at Mauthausen, where he had been dumped in death row, a bundle of brittle bones and close to starvation. Yet on most days a Polish orderly gave him a few extra spoons of the watery soup that was the prisoners' only sustenance.

He had always remained convinced, he said, that this act of generosity saved his life. After the war, he looked for his Polish saviour and traced him to Poznan. When he sent him food parcels, the man was interrogated by Polish security officers and accused of consorting with the enemy. Wiesenthal invited the man to Vienna, but for a long time the Poles refused him a passport. Finally, they relented. Before the man returned home, Wiesenthal offered him a little money. When this was turned down, he told his friend: 'Go to a bank and ask them the value of a few spoonfuls of soup. . . .'

The 21st of October was the climax of Wiesenthal's stay in Poland. It was the day set aside for the award of the honorary doctorate from the Jagiellonian University, an event of even greater significance to him than his medal from the Polish state.

The Jagiellonian's Collegium Maius was founded in 1364. Copernicus had once studied here, and Karol Wojtyla, better known later as Pope John Paul II, taught in the University's faculty of theology. While most of the University's contemporary faculties are housed in the nearby nineteenth-century Collegium Novum, the Collegium Maius, where the University Senate has its seat, also serves as University Museum with a unique collection of old scientific instruments.

In the richly furnished and panelled Aula, the portraits of the University's founders, Wladyslav Yagiello and his consort, Queen Hedwiga, and of other past benefactors and luminaries looked down as the slight figure of the rector, Aleksander Koj, led in the solemn procession of the University's senior academics, robed in black and red gowns and wearing capes of ermine. As they took their places behind their carved sixteenth-century pews, facing invited guests from the Government, church and diplomatic corps, Simon Wiesenthal was escorted in with due solemnity. He had a black gown over his dark suit, leaving just one glint of colour – the gold cross of the *Polonia Restituta* medal he had elected to wear for the occasion.

In a brief commendation, the rector stressed that the

Jagiellonian University wished to pay tribute to the truth and to the tragedy of the Jewish people, who had been destined, under Hitler, for worldwide annihilation. . . . Today we are honouring a man, who has documented uncompromisingly a period of history, which it is essential for future generations to understand. The full enormity of what happened will only be understood through knowledge of the historical truth, to which Simon Wiesenthal has dedicated himself.

The subtext of his remarks had a political note: the doctorate had corrected the personal injustices that Poland had inflicted on Wiesenthal in the 1960s and 1970s.

Now came the *Laudatio*, delivered in Latin by the dean of the University's faculty of history, Professor Maciej Salomon:

Simon Wiesenthal has never been a passive observer when injustice occurs. Evil has to be fought; evil has to be exposed; and the memory of evil must be kept alive, if future generations are to be free of it. ... Wiesenthal encouraged Holocaust survivors to write down their stories, both to create oral history and to testify against the mass murderers. ... His activities, far from alien to us, are a mark of cultural continuity and common heritage between Jews and Poles.

To subdued applause, the parchment roll was handed over and a short blue cape, signifying academic distinction, placed on the new doctor's left shoulder. This was by no means the first honorary doctorate among Wiesenthal's trophies, but it was assuredly one of the most gratifying.

Not accustomed to wearing glasses, he had fretted that the light in the Aula might not be strong enough to allow for smooth reading of his doctoral dissertation. He need not have worried. The light was adequate, and having received special dispensation to sit rather than stand, he perched awkwardly on the edge of his chair.

There was nothing casual or impromptu about this speech. Unlike all his other pronouncements in Poland, this one had been committed to paper. Intending it to be worthy of the academic occasion, he seized the opportunity to address both the historical and the moral context of his Nazi-hunting.

He also wanted to make it a personal testament:

If I have invested my time and strength to fight against forgetfulness and for information and understanding, it is for the sake of passing on to future generations our knowledge and our suffering. For forty years I have fought against amnesia. As I stand before you, I am very conscious that I speak in a country where not only millions of Jews have lost their lives, but also where so many Poles were killed that there is scarcely a family that has not lost at least one member to the Nazis.

A key point, often lost on historians, was to understand the misleading nature of defining mass murderers as 'war criminals', Wiesenthal asserted. The two concepts were not synonymous. The Nazi mass-murder policy preceded the war. To speak of war criminals without studying their pre-war roots was to play into the hands of Nazi propagandists, such as Joseph Goebbels, who coined the phrase in 1941 for their own purposes.

Nazi criminality, Wiesenthal reminded his audience, began six years before the outbreak of war, when the first concentration camps were built. The racist Nuremberg laws, which made legal outcasts of the Jews, were adopted in 1935, the same year as the bonfire of Jewish books and the expulsion of their authors. Three years later came the *Kristallnacht*, on 9 November 1938, when the Nazis went on a rampage against Jewish property and desecrated synagogues in Austria and Germany. By 1940, the Nazis had already drawn up their 'General Plan – *Ost*', which envisaged the creation of 100 million illiterate slaves in Poland, the Ukraine and Russia, and the elimination of everyone else other than the Master Race.

Plans for the Final Solution, the systematic destruction of Jews and other minorities, were refined at the 1942 Wannsee conference. The killing was no by-product of the war, Wiesenthal stressed, but an end in itself. Why else did the trains continue to make the Auschwitz run, even in 1944, when they were desperately needed to ferry weapons to the front-line forces in retreat from the Allied armies?

Why was it still vital in 1994, after more than five decades since the crimes were committed, to bring the guilty to trial, Wiesenthal asked rhetorically. After the respite gained during the Cold War, the perpetrators must not be allowed to die undisturbed. They must be made to fear that even in old age they risk being tried in a court of law. During the worst period of the Cold War, between 1948 and 1960, the logic of events dictated that denazification had to be sacrificed for the sake of defending the West against the Soviet threat. To create an adequate system of deterrence, the Western allies had to have the new Germany's support. Nazi-hunting was low on the list of priorities.

Wiesenthal accepted the logic of Allied policy during the Cold War. But he was emphatic that he would always regret those 'lost' years, when the criminals were allowed to enjoy a peace of mind they did not deserve; and were even helped to escape overseas.

Attitudes began to change with the onset of East–West detente and the Eichmann trial, but it was impossible to recoup what had been lost in the intervening period. Many Nazi crimes were no longer punishable because statutes of limitations had been adopted in many countries. 'The only victors of the Cold War were the Nazis.'

With the passage of time, 'justice has been blindfolded'. Penal codes had not been adapted to deal with the 'desk murderers' – those who organised the killings 'with a telephone call or a signature, thousands of kilometres from where the crimes were carried out'.

Witnesses had dispersed, and the Communist regimes – with Poland an exception – generally refused to yield up witnesses to testify in trials held in West Germany. German experts had estimated that at least 150,000–200,000 persons participated in the depravities of the Holocaust. Only a small number had been caught and brought to trial.

If there is no way of equating punishment with the enormities of the mass murder, why proceed with such trials? 'Because I am convinced that every Nazi trial has its historical and moral justification, and provides an essential education for the young.'

Justice together with equality, freedom and tolerance combined into a fundamental system of human rights. But,

> Our youth, born in freedom, will only understand the value of such rights if they learn about the terrible lack of freedom imposed in the Nazi era. Freedom is like health. We only learn to value it when we have lost it. Freedom is a present from heaven, a valuable property for which we must fight every day.

To conclude the ceremonial, the University choir sang Poland's national anthem. Wiesenthal stood ramrod straight, at last comfortable and proud to be recognised as part of his native land and accorded recognition from this seat of learning.

His imagination was fired by the discovery that the Jagiellonian University had had a faculty for Hebrew Studies for close on 300 years up to the last world war. He would seek funds for its reopening. Perhaps the Israeli Government would be willing to chip in. Perhaps the wealthy Wiesenthal Center in Los Angeles, which bears his name but operates quite independently, might be persuaded to endow a chair. Friends might even see it as an opportunity to leave a permanent memorial in his name – a Wiesenthal professorship at the Jagiellonian University.

In a toast to Wiesenthal a little later that day, Austria's Ambassador Gerhard Wagner said:

> Your price for survival has been to prolong the Holocaust for yourself over the past five decades. You took upon yourself the suffering and the destruction of the spirit of millions of people, because you sought justice for those who died and were dishonoured. You have stood for truth and against forgetfulness. You insist that if the terrible is blotted out from memory, it will recur. You have extracted darkness from our beings and have made the future lighter.

Wiesenthal's response was graphic in its simplicity. His life, since 1947, had been guided by a sacred trust, and this is how it came about: three rabbis had come to him in Linz, where he had taken the first tentative steps towards the establishment of a documentation centre to search for Nazi criminals and find witnesses of their crimes.

> The rabbis told me of a book depot near Villach in Carinthia, where sequestrated Jewish libraries had been stored by the Nazis. You must understand that the

relationship between Jews and their books is like their relationship to old people: it has to be one of respect.

The oldest of the three rabbis said to me that I had to save those books. I had a very small car, and with a driver, the five of us squeezed in. We arrived very late in the village and went to sleep. Next day, we found the house and I explained to its guardian that we wanted to see the interior. Nothing would be removed, we assured him.

Telling a white lie, I said the Americans planned to build a Jewish library and needed to know what was available. Once inside we were amazed to discover that the house was stacked with books from top to bottom. Suddenly, the youngest of the rabbis keeled over in a faint. He was clutching a book so tightly, we could not wrest it from him until he recovered consciousness. The book, in a brown cover, had inscribed on its first page the name of Joshua Seidman.

It was the rabbi's name. And below the name was this scribbled injunction: 'Whoever finds this, give it to our brother. The murderers are amongst us. Soon they will be here. Do not forget us. And do not forget our murderers.' The handwriting belonged to the rabbi's sister.

I was able to take the book away with me. And as we sat together on our return journey, I realised that this message was for us. The three rabbis moved on to other countries, but I have always remembered the message. I have kept the faith.

The last few phrases were spoken with eyes closed and a choking voice. Silence fell around the table.

It was not the first time he had told this tale. It haunts him; and on this Polish journey, so much of it spent on coming to terms with his past, he spoke of it on several occasions, compulsively caught in its emotional grip.

Simon Wiesenthal had arrived in Poland five days earlier, uncertain of his reception; by the end of his visit, all his concerns had been dispelled. The warmth of his reception had taken him by surprise. His relatives had been wiped out in the Holocaust. He had never acquired worldly wealth. 'So, it is my friends who are my family; my friends who are my wealth. And as I return to Vienna, I know that I have become greatly enriched. I am a fortunate man.'

After fifty years, he had rediscovered respect for his country of origin; he had undergone a catharsis. It had been a long, complex and, for the most part, lonely journey of mind and body that had begun in a small Galician *shtetl*, Buczacz, in 1908 and had evolved into a Messianic mission to expose the enormities of the Holocaust and bring the guilty to justice. He had come to see this not as an end in itself, but as one individual's mighty endeavour to influence the future course of history for the better. Mankind had to be shocked into a realisation that organised mass killing, whether it happened in Europe or the remotest spot on earth, destroys the whole fabric of society, and not just the victims themselves.

The tasks he had set himself in the aftermath of the war were monumental and daunting, and he never deluded himself into believing that he could move mountains on his own. But he has always believed passionately in individual commitment and integrity as the motor for change. 'It's individuals; not organisations and machines.'

Wiesenthal has many devoted admirers. But throughout his post-war life, he has also had to contend with fierce detractors eager to destroy his reputation. Controversy has swirled around his combative personality for decades, and his significance and greatness will be debated long after he is gone.

If the visit to Poland was an attempt to define the essential outlines of his testament, it only touched lightly on the experiences, the passions and the unending questioning about the limits of justice and of forgiveness that have conjured up the uncomfortable Wiesenthal phenomenon. It is the story of a wandering Jew, who drew a line under his pre-war life in 1945, and has felt compelled ever since to steer his way as if tethered to the Holocaust. 'I am not a Jewish Don Quixote; only a Jewish survivor.'

Even though Wiesenthal's experiences during the Second World War constitute the defining period of his existence, his background as an East European Jew born into the Hapsburg Empire provides the vital clues to a man of simple tastes and complex character, who has become a household name.

[2]
A *Shtetl* in Galicia

In the world as it emerged after the Holocaust, Buczacz became an inconsequential dot, just one more small Galician township on the map of the Ukraine. Gone, for the most part murdered by the Nazis, were the few thousand Jews who had lived in this *shtetl* when Simon Wiesenthal was born during the closing hours of 1908; and gone with them was the conservative Jewish culture of the miracle-working Hassidic rabbis that had permeated rural Galicia, and spread even to some of Galicia's bigger cities, during more than three centuries of near ceaseless turbulence and of recurring waves of pogroms. The rabbis, who were sages even more than clerics, gave the embattled Jewish communities a framework of justice, and a mystic belief in their right to exist with their own ethical codes and their religious convictions.

Wiesenthal is not a religious Jew in any formal sense and has little interest in the synagogue. Yet, imbued by the Hassidic culture of his surroundings during his early formative years, he has never been tempted into the assimilationist mode that other East European Jews have preferred to adopt. Members of Sigmund Freud's family also stemmed from Buczacz – Wiesenthal's mother-in-law was related to the Freuds – yet the Galician background in no way deterred Freud's absorption into the Viennese environment. Rosa Luxemburg, the personification of Socialist internationalism, came from Galicia, as did Joseph Roth, the novelist, whose portrayal of European Jewry across the whole religious and political spectrum reflects deep understanding and sympathy for assimilation.

If Wiesenthal rejected assimilation, he also remained too much of an outsider to put down roots in the Jewish homeland. He describes himself as a Zionist. Yet unlike another favourite son of Buczacz, Shmuel Agnon, who moved on to become one of Israel's greatest writers, Wiesenthal has never considered emigration to Israel. After his liberation from Mauthausen in 1945, Wiesenthal decided on Austria as his homebase. It made sense, because he had been born a subject of the Hapsburg Emperor, Franz Joseph. Besides, having dedicated himself to seek justice for the Holocaust's victims, he rationalised that Austrians, with their enthusiastic embrace of Hitler, must be forced to acknowledge their guilt.

Galicia occupies a strategic position in the epicentre of the European continent. The early history of the area is obscure. But from East and West, through the ages, the powers that have sought to extend their domination in Europe have played ping-pong with Galicia, often fighting bitter battles on its soil. In the eleventh century, the eastern part of what is now Galicia was shown as the Slav kingdom of Halitsch. Some time during the twelfth century, Catholic influences gained the upper hand, and its name was Latinised to become Galicia. By 1205, the King of Hungary also assumed the title of *Rex Galicia et Ludomeria*. In the mid-thirteenth century, the Mongols overran Galicia. After them came the Tartars.

Ruthenians – Ukrainians – remained in Galicia, even during the subsequent 400 formative years, when the territory was incorporated first into the Polish and then into the Polish-Lithuanian kingdoms. During this period, which was also marked by a gradual extension towards the Carpathians, these lands acquired their predominantly Polish character. With the successive partitions of Poland involving the Hapsburgs, the Prussians and the Russians, which began in 1772, Galicia eventually came under the control of the Hapsburg Empire. Almost a century later, in 1867, the Emperor granted autonomy to Galicia with Lvov (known as Lemberg until 1945) confirmed as the territory's capital.

But even though much of the bureaucracy was Austrian, and German became widely used, Galicia remained essentially Polish. Giving way to nationalist pressure, Polish was made the official language in 1907, even though forty-two per cent of the population was by then Ukrainian.

Galicia's strategic importance was never matched by economic prosperity. A large, but impoverished Polish aristocracy lived alongside an even more impoverished, as often Ukrainian as Polish, peasantry. From the Middle Ages, the Jews began to jump into this cauldron in increasingly significant numbers.

In the twentieth century during the period between the two world wars, most of Galicia was restored to Poland. But after the Second World War, Poland's frontiers shifted westwards and the eastern part of Galicia went to the Ukraine – first as part of the Soviet Union, and then as part of the independent republic of Ukraine. Poland retained western Galicia with its Carpathian mountain range.

If Galicia has always been frontier territory, Buczacz has often been on its cutting edge. Situated on the eastern edge of Galicia, not far from Lvov, it has been tossed backwards and forwards between Poland, imperial Russia, the Ukraine, the Hapsburgs, Germany and the Soviet Union; Ottoman armies have been there, and so have the Tartars, the Cossacks and the Nazi *Schutzstaffel* (SS).

The first recorded mention of Buczacz goes back to 1582. Its first Jewish tombstone is dated 1633. The first wave of killing occurred in 1648, when the Cossacks overwhelmed the region. In 1672, Buczacz made obscure history as the site of a short-lived peace treaty between Turks and Poles, mediated by the Khan of Crimea. Its population then was considerably bigger than it has been in this century – possibly as many as 20,000. The peace lasted less than a year, and Buczacz again became caught up in the strife between the Polish kingdom and Russia to gain control of the Ukraine, and in the fighting between Tartars and Cossacks and their protectors, the Ottomans, who maintained their grip on the region into the eighteenth century.

In 1908, at the time of Wiesenthal's birth, Buczacz, together with much of Galicia, formed an autonomous region within the Austro-Hungarian Empire. In 1941, a few months into the Second World War, Buczacz fell into the hands of the Nazis. In the intervening period, it had seesawed between Poland, the Ukraine and Russia. Even before Wiesenthal was fully adult, his home town had changed masters six times, and for two years, between 1915 and 1917, his family fled from the invading Cossacks and sought refuge in Vienna.

As a child and young man, before having to confront the Nazis, Wiesenthal had already learned the hard way that there was one constant that marked the struggle for territory and influence in Galicia: pogroms had been a regular occurrence in Galicia since the seventeenth century. From then on, the Jews of Galicia remained the universal whipping boy as the great powers fought for control over the territory. In the Buczacz of Wiesenthal's childhood and youth, the warring nations, fighting for territory and influence, shared a common antipathy towards the Jews. The Hapsburgs, being more prepared to accept assimilated Jews, allowed them to be represented in the *Reichsrath* – the federal parliamentary body – but this was largely cosmetic. Among the inhabitants of Galicia, the Cossacks and the Ukrainians were sweeping in their dislike of the Jews. They were always eager to humble the Jews and did so with great physical cruelty.

Trade had initially brought Jews to Poland as it had to so many other parts of Europe. An account of Poland written around 965 by Ibrahim Ibn Ja'qub, a Jewish traveller from Spain, mentions Jewish merchants amongst those engaged in commerce between Western Europe, Ruthenia and the Muslim East. But the first major wave of Jewish settlers began towards the end of the eleventh century and lasted 200 years, bringing into Poland Jewish refugees fleeing from persecution in Western and Central Europe. This was a rare period of tolerance in Polish history. Under the policies of King Kazimierz the Great, Jews were accorded full rights and privileges, even though the Catholic clergy and inhabitants in many towns were often vocal in their opposition to the Jewish presence, and were always quick to blame them even for natural disasters, for maladies and the spread of the plague.

By the end of the fifteenth century, 24,000 Jews had settled in Poland, with growing numbers establishing themselves in Lvov and other *shtetls* of Galicia. The influx reached its peak in the fifteenth century, when Poland became a melting-pot for Ashkenazi Jews forced to leave the Hapsburg lands, and for Sephardi Jews banished from Spain and later Portugal.

This was a golden age – the only period of relative tranquillity for Jews in Poland. The immigrants, for the most part, made their living in commerce, both local and international. Because Christians were forbidden by the Church from engaging in money-lending, Jews established themselves as bankers, currying favour with king and courtiers. During this relatively benign period, the Jews gradually fanned out into business enterprises, building and leasing inns, breweries, mills and distilleries, becoming the link between town and country. They were even permitted to collect customs and tolls.

As their prosperity and their security grew, so their cultural life flourished. Talmudic scholarship and teaching excelled, trickling down to all the Jewish communities, establishing traditions that endured through the hard times that followed, and laying the foundation for generation after generation of notable Jewish thinkers and leaders – albeit often at odds among themselves. There were many centres of learning – *yeshivas* – in the eastern regions, where Jewish scholars made progress in science and medicine. In Cracow, a Hebrew printing house was established in 1534. Many synagogues were built, and developing a respected aptitude for architecture, Jews also designed secular buildings.

A papal envoy in Poland, reporting to the Vatican in 1565, declared that he had encountered

large numbers of Jews who were not despised as was the case elsewhere. They are not condemned to second-class citizenship, and are not restricted to menial occupations. They own land, they are engaged in trade, they study medicine and astronomy. They possess great wealth, and not only count as respected citizens, but also frequently exercise control over others. They do not wear special marks to distinguish them as Jews, and they are even allowed to carry weapons. In sum, they have full civic rights.

A Jewish historian of the period, Natan Hanower, noted that 'never before in the whole of the diaspora, had there been as many Torahs as could be found in the land of Poland'.

This was too good to last. Paradise was lost in 1648. By then the number of Jews in Poland had swollen to half a million, five per cent of the total population. In April that year, the Cossacks swept into the eastern regions over the Dniepr, destroying the Polish armies stationed there and provoking a peasant uprising against their Polish masters. The Tartars from the Crimea, backed by Ottoman fighters, entered the fray. Many thousands of Jews were killed as local fury was vented against Polish landlords and their Jewish agents. The wars, the chaos and the pogroms continued for the best part of 100 years.

But the broader context in which Poland's Jews had lived for 200 years also changed radically in the seventeenth century. In 1656, Poland's King Johann Kasimir II declared the Mother of God to be Queen of Poland. As this merger of secular and religious sovereignty left little space for other faiths, the Catholic church became virulent in its attacks on Jews, frequently accusing them of ritual murder and marginalising every aspect of their existence. Their scope for economic activity and their political rights again became severely circumscribed.

Jewish adversity, not for the first time, provoked rival schools of religious fervour, and among some an even more intense search for Jewish solidarity in the face of anti-Semitism. Three Messianic movements emerged. The first was called Sabbateism, after Shabbetai Zevi from Smyrna, who twice – in 1648 and 1666 – proclaimed himself Messiah. The second was Frankism, led by Jacob Frank from Podolia. He rejected the Talmud and countenanced baptism in the Catholic Church. He provoked much controversy amongst the Polish rabbinate and ultimately settled in Germany, where he found greater acceptance than amongst Poland's Jews.

The third and only movement of lasting significance was Hassidism, which gained rapid ground amongst Poland's bleeding, embattled Jews. It offered a psychological bulwark against persecution and soon became the accepted orthodoxy, especially among the rural, more backward Jewish communities of Galicia.

Hassidism's spiritual inspiration came from Israel ben Eliezer, later named Baal Shem Tov – Master of the Holy Name – who lived from 1700 to 1760. Railing against the established rabbinical hierarchy and its formality, Israel ben Eliezer brought a populist message, urging Jews to express their faith through song and dance and good deeds. Goodness and faith would overcome sin and evil; joyousness, not sadness, should prevail. Each individual Jew, he taught, stood in a mystical relationship to God; but it needed the Zaddikim, the 'wonder' or 'miracle' rabbis, to act as a conduit between God and the rank-and-file Jew. They were the ones who had to draw pictures of everyday life to illustrate and explain the presence of God and the ethics of personal conduct vis-à-vis God and man.

Jewish writers such as Sholom Aleichem, Martin Buber, Elie Wiesel, Isaac Bashevis Singer, Sholem Asch, Joseph Roth and many more have all drawn heavily on Hassidic tales handed down from the *shtetls*. Their writings have helped to transform the image of the simplistic, ignorant Galician Jew into a model for authentic Jewishness, for spirituality and Jewish nationhood.

Much of Hassidic teaching went against the old orthodoxies and was bitterly disputed by the rabbinical establishment. Later the Hassidim also set their face against integration into modern society. Controversy raged powerfully among Jews in Lvov and the other larger towns, where the Jewish bourgeoisie was searching for greater security by identifying itself with the Enlightenment and with the eighteenth- and nineteenth-century struggle for Polish independence. They were more prepared to adjust religious practice to the demands of the emerging civil society. None the less, by the mid-nineteenth century Hassidism had ceased to be a mainly rural movement and had found many adherents amongst the more sophisticated Jewish middle classes.

The 'Jewish question' was never far absent from political debate throughout Poland's turbulent history. After the Congress of Vienna in 1815, when Russia gained sovereignty over the Polish kingdom – minus Galicia – the pressure on Jews to assimilate as a condition for civic rights grew stronger still.

The Congress of Vienna did not disturb earlier partitions which had confirmed Hapsburg sovereignty over Galicia. But the Empire did little to alleviate discrimination against Jews in Galicia, taxing them more heavily, limiting land ownership, withholding full political rights and restricting access to Galicia's high schools and universities. The Emperor Franz Joseph was personally hostile to anti-Semitism and issued an edict awarding full civic rights to his Jewish populations. Even though this was intended to apply to Galicia as much as to the rest of the Empire, the autonomous character of Galicia meant that *de facto* the restrictions against the Jewish population were maintained with impunity. Western Galicia was the scene of terrible pogroms in 1898, and there were repeated boycotts against the Jews throughout the territory.

Poverty and anti-Semitism combined to provoke massive Jewish emigration from Galicia. Between 1891 and 1914, 320,000 Jews arrived in the United States, eighty-five per cent – 270,000 – of whom came from Galicia. Similarly in Vienna, the number of Galician Jews grew from 13,880 in 1880 – eighteen per cent of Vienna's Jews – to 30,325 in 1910 – twenty-three per cent of Vienna's Jews. Others were early converts to Zionism and, against the odds, made their way to Palestine.

Of course there were middle-class Jews in Galicia, who felt more settled and grew wealthy. They were the 'tie wearers', the Jews who opted for assimilation and looked down on their Hassidic brethren. Exploiting their limited opportunities, the more well-to-do joined political parties, or formed their own. One school sought political and cultural autonomy for Jews. In 1897, there was an unsuccessful attempt to set up a Galician section of the Austrian Social Democrats; a few years later, there was a Jewish Social Democrat Party in Galicia. There was also, for a time, a Zionist Labour Party.

But only an insignificant number of Jews involved themselves in the luxury of political activity. At the end of the nineteenth century, Galicia's population numbered approximately 800,000, most of whom were impoverished. They were widely regarded as *Luftmenschen* – people who lived on air, without much education, without job qualifications and without significant earning power.

They were prompted to draw ever more tightly together within the comforting, unifying Hassidic net. Yiddish, already used by Jewish intellectuals in Poland to create a new body of literature, became the chosen language of the *shtetls*, where the men also uniformly adopted distinctive dress by enveloping themselves in their distinctive black kaftans. Rooted in mysticism, their faith gave them strength, a sense of identity and a moral code that could not be dislodged by the antipathy of the world beyond. Jews were so alienated that in the census of 1931, only thirty-one per cent described themselves as Poles, and only 381,000 out of three million Jews in Poland (ten per cent of the country's population) declared Polish as their native language.

Yet this spiritual self-sufficiency also served to reinforce anti-Semitism by creating the prototype hate-figure of the '*Ostjude*' – the Eastern Jew seen as a tentacled weed that refused to merge its identity with the prevailing Christian and civil culture. Antipathy was not confined to Christians. As Simon Wiesenthal was to experience at first hand in the 1970s, Austria's Chancellor, Bruno Kreisky, also a Jew, respected an individual's faith, yet lacked understanding for those who put a premium on their cultural roots and Jewishness.

'I am an Eastern Jew, and our home is wherever we have our dead,' says one of the characters created by Joseph Roth in his novel *Hotel Savoy.* It is a description that exactly mirrors Wiesenthal's feelings. His origins are precious to him, and he has carried them with him always. Into old age, it still always pleased him to recall how his maternal grandparents, deeply religious, steeped in the mores of the 'miracle' rabbis, believed that he would fare better in life if the fact that he was born before midnight on 31 December 1908 was suppressed, so that he could instead be registered as the first-born Jewish boy in Buczacz of the new year, 1909.

This was done, and might have remained so but for the need to correct it twenty-one years later to avoid a charge of dodging military service. To prove that his mother had given birth before the crucial midnight, and not afterwards, Wiesenthal had to find two witnesses. Luck was with him. Neighbours remembered that particular New Year's Eve, because there had been great rejoicing in the Wiesenthal home, and they had been invited to share a bottle of vodka to drink to the newborn's health.

By the time his birth certificate was corrected, his grandmother was no longer alive, but she had had a lasting influence on the little boy. She would take him on visits to the 'miracle' rabbis and have him blessed by them. One of Wiesenthal's outstanding memories as a child was a trip to the rabbi of Czortkov, a sage surrounded by many disciples. Behind the small window of an attic, he noticed a staring man's face. This was 'the silent one', his grandmother said. Elaborating, she told him that this man, in the course of a bitter argument with his wife, had screamed: 'You should burn.' That night, his house burned down and his wife perished. Filled with guilt, the man went to unburden himself to the rabbi. The learned man's ruling was unequivocal: the guilty man must never speak again for the rest of his life, and he must use his time to pray for forgiveness.

Atonement for guilt, and the circumstances that can secure forgiveness, are issues that have nagged Wiesenthal throughout his long life. The 'miracle' rabbi of Czortkov had pointed the way and provided guidelines, but the essentials remained unanswered.

As in many of the other small towns of Galicia, Jews formed a majority of the population in Buczacz during the first decade of the twentieth century. Amid its 10,000 inhabitants there were roughly 6,000 Jews, with the rest made up of 2,000 Poles and 2,000 Ukrainians. But this in no way gave the Jews greater political security or made their lives any easier than in earlier times.

The Buczacz of Wiesenthal's early childhood was a typical Galician *shtetl*: the Jews were not segregated and did not live in a ghetto. But for all that, most of the Jews were concentrated in the centre of the town, while the Poles and Ukrainians, who were generally more affluent, lived on the prettier outskirts. Most of the Jews were artisans and small traders. Wiesenthal's uncle was a baker. His grandfather had an inn a few miles beyond Buczacz at a place called Skala which was a mere 50 metres from the Russian border. As elsewhere in Poland, there were many clockmakers. However, there were virtually no Jews in the professions, and Wiesenthal can only recall one teacher who was Jewish. Poles ran the bureaucracy. Polish was the official language and education was in Polish. The civil servants were almost uniquely Polish.

Yet the Jews of Buczacz had little affinity with Poland. They had no sympathy for Polish nationalism. The capital of the Empire, Vienna, was their lodestar. They were Hapsburg Jews. In the final resort, the Kaiser would look after them. 'We all felt ourselves to be Austrian', is how Wiesenthal remembers his earliest loyalties. 'To us, the Kaiser Franz Joseph was a father figure. We measured everything in distances from Vienna and talked as if it was just round the corner. Legend had it that the Kaiser would open the Hofburg, the Imperial Palace, to the Jews of Galicia if they were forced to flee.'

Wiesenthal has never been able to trace the origins of his family name. As a student in Prague he met three sisters, well-known dancers from Vienna, with the same surname. He recalls that they danced barefoot, and that one of them questioned him about his grandparents and they concluded there might be some distant relationship. Many years later in Vienna, he came across another woman called Wiesenthal. 'I asked her if she was related to Simon Wiesenthal. She didn't know me and retorted, her face red with anger, that the Jews were up to their tricks again, stealing her good Wiesenthal name.'

In his parents' home, the little boy, Simon, lived in traditional Jewish surroundings in relatively affluent circumstances. His father, Asher, was a wholesale merchant trading mainly in sugar. Yiddish was not permitted in public places. They all had to learn Polish. But at home, and with his grandparents, Yiddish was their everyday language; although from his mother, Rosa, he also received his first grounding in German. She had accumulated a wide selection of the German classics. 'Often, when my mother wanted to guide me, she would leaf through one of those books – until she found an apt quotation. And then she would say to me: "I cannot express it as well as the writers. Everything that applies to life, you will discover from great writing."'

The young boy learned languages easily, though his Polish accent is always present. He soon added Russian and, while studying in Prague, acquired the basics of Czech. Decades later, in the 1960s, he taught himself to speak English well enough to lecture in the United States and to give interviews.

Simon Wiesenthal was his parents' first child. Two years later a brother, Hillel, was born. 'One of my first memories of him and of my mother is jealousy of the little one. I felt that my mother was devoting herself exclusively to my little brother,' Wiesenthal confessed many years later in a poignant memoir of his mother, entitled '*Ohnmacht*' ('Powerless'), which hints at a certain distance between them during his childhood. But any reservations he might have had in his earlier years pale behind Wiesenthal's lasting sense of grief over his mother's death in 1942 at the hands of the Nazis. It has remained among the most painful personal blows he has suffered. What happened then, he remembers blow by blow, vividly. It still haunts him in occasional nightmares.

'My early recollections of my mother became almost completely blurred after the Nazis marched into Lvov in 1941.' He was, at that time, still able to work as an architect and was living with his wife in the Galician capital. He had brought his mother to live with them, thinking that it would be safer for her. But with the German occupation, all Jews were forced to move into the ghetto.

'We could only take with us what we could carry. My wife and I were directed into forced labour. So my mother looked after our small household, and she had to sell our few possessions, piece by piece, or to barter them for food. At work, during the day, we were only given a bowl of so-called soup.

'It was the beginning of 1942; and I came home from work to a sight that I can never forget. My mother had prepared a plate of food for me and my wife, and as she brought it to us, she suddenly fainted and I just managed to catch her in my arms. That's when I realised that she had barely eaten for days so as to have food for us. The sight of my mother, unconscious in my arms, has always haunted me.

'That summer the Nazis were rounding up all the Jews in the ghetto who were too old or sick to work. We knew that my mother might be picked up while we were absent at work. Our one remaining valuable was a gold watch; and so I said to my mother on an August morning: "If a Ukrainian policeman comes to take you [the local police were all Ukrainian], then give him the watch, and he will leave you here."

'I had a foreboding that our farewells that morning were for ever; but I did not want to worry my mother and gave her the usual kiss.

'Back from work in the evening, we found the door open, and my mother was no longer there. A neighbour told us that a Ukrainian policeman had come, and that my mother had try to buy her life with the gold watch. But half an hour later, another policeman came. And she had nothing left with which to buy her freedom.

'I stayed awake for a terrible night, certain that she was being sent to her death like so many others before her. I knew that the "superfluous" ghetto inhabitants were being taken by train to the extermination camps. I obtained permission from the railway yard [where he was doing forced labour] to absent myself for a short time, and I ran to the railway station, because Polish workers had told me there were trains already filled with victims and ready to leave.

'I knew my mother had to be on that train. The SS were guarding all the approaches. But I could hear the agonised cries from the trains, stuffed with people. They were begging for water. But nobody could get near. A man told me that two Polish railway workers, who had tried to take a couple of mugs of water to the train, were knocked down brutally by the SS. I remained there for about half an hour. Then I had to go back to work. Next day the train still stood in the same place, and the cries for water were continuing.

'My only hope is that my mother died quickly, before she reached Belzec, the extermination camp to which she was being taken, and that she was spared the march to the gas chamber. She had a bad heart.

'It was 23 August 1942. That date, for me, signifies my mother's death. She was sixty-three.

'Many people have lost their mother – through illness or old age, but by natural causes. Such people can bury their mother and shed tears at the funeral; they can grieve by the grave, and be close to her. The Nazis robbed me of that possibility. My mother's grave has become a part of me.

'I do not even have a photograph of my mother. When I was taken from the ghetto to the concentration camp, everything that I still possessed was taken from me. There is nothing left from my home or my family; not even a handkerchief, and I would give anything to have a picture of my mother.' Worse, there is no grave where he can mourn her.

Simon Wiesenthal cannot talk of his early childhood without leapfrogging the years to that August day in 1942, when he lost his mother. Every other near relative that he and his wife still possessed also fell victim to the Holocaust. The miracles that saved him and his wife did not extend to their families.

But even before Hitler came on the public scene, Wiesenthal had been face to face with violence and war, had lost his father, his brother and his family home, had already known as a small child what it was to be a refugee, and as a young Jew had found himself blocked from studying for his chosen architect's profession in a Polish university. But he had persevered, always finding humour in the midst of grief. Dogged singlemindedness and his survivor's instinct are traits that he developed early. Only before 1939, those traits were directed towards personal ends; towards education, towards marriage with his childhood sweetheart, and towards establishing himself as a fully trained architect.

[3]
The Young Wiesenthal

Simon Wiesenthal was a small, bewildered seven-year-old boy when he first set foot in Vienna, and began a love–hate relationship with the city that was to endure for the rest of his life. It was just before the end of 1915. His father Asher, a reservist in the Imperial Army, had been killed on 14 October at Stanislas on the eastern front of Galicia. Buczacz had been overrun by the Tsar's forces. To escape the marauding, Jew-baiting Cossacks, his feisty mother had taken Simon and his smaller brother to Lvov, where their maternal grandparents were living. There, the small family decided to follow the example of thousands of fearful Galician Jews and make for the greater safety of Vienna.

In common with other East European immigrants, they made their home in the Leopoldstadt, the district where Vienna's poorer, and also more orthodox, Jews were living. The concentration of Jews was so dense that it had become a ghetto, even if without walls, in all but name. Many were unemployed, the Wiesenthals included. There was widespread dependence on welfare and charity. The neighbourhood was a substratum of Viennese Jewry, and the obtrusive presence of their poor brethren was resented by the city's more prosperous and integrated Jewish establishment. Only the narrow Donau Canal separated the Leopoldstadt from Vienna's inner city and its imperial Hofburg Palace. But the two were worlds apart.

Simon and his brother were sent to primary school – the *Volksschule* in the Bäuerlegasse – where the pupils were almost entirely Jewish. They were taught in German, but at home they continued to speak Yiddish. The family had little money and was living in cramped quarters; yet the cultural environment in which they subsisted was not so vastly different from the life the small boys had known in Buczacz.

The Vienna of 1915 was a jumble of nationalities, but it came nowhere close to the metropolis of the imaginings of East European Jewry. They had thought of it as a safe haven, a model refuge and melting-pot, where the benign, all-powerful Emperor Franz Joseph, who had raised the status of Austria's Jews, would also welcome the presence of his loyal Jewish subjects from the Hapsburg Empire's far-flung lands. Such a model had in any event always been far more the product of wishful thinking than of experience grounded in reality.

Notwithstanding the Enlightenment and other periods of more generous attitudes towards Jews, the history of anti-Semitism in Austria was almost as long as in Galicia. Now, even though the First World War had not yet reached its half-way mark, the whiff of defeat, of the end of monarchy and empire, and of the emergence of German nationalism was already tangible.

Wiesenthal was too young to understand the harsh political undercurrents feeding Austrian anti-Semitism at that time. But later in life, memories of that childhood experience reinforced his critical perceptions of Austrian society. The Vienna that Wiesenthal encountered in 1915 bore the anti-Semitic imprint of Karl Lueger, the city's long-serving Mayor, who had died in office in 1910. As leader of the radical right Christian Social Union Party, Lueger had turned anti-Semitism into a popular political force. The seeds of Nazism had already been well and truly planted and had taken firm root in young Adolf Hitler's mind.

Hitler was an obscure army conscript during the period when Wiesenthal was at school in Vienna. But Hitler, as a young loner from the Austrian provinces, already had behind him a six-year period in Vienna which had turned him into a convinced pan-German and anti-Marxist, and had fuelled his anti-Semitism powerfully enough to provoke his search for of racial purity at any price. Hitler was born in 1889 at Braunau-am-Inn, not far from Linz, and close to the German border. His early ambition was to become an artist, but he failed the entrance exam to Vienna's Academy of Fine Arts. He came to Vienna in 1907 and, during the next six years, led an impecunious, aimless existence, living for most of the time among the dregs of Vienna's poor in a men's hostel.

He earned just enough to survive by painting copies of postcards. He remained in Vienna until 1913. He lacked the means, but above all the inclination and curiosity, to dip into the artistically and intellectually exciting and extraordinarily creative world of the city's cosmopolitan elites and the creators of the Secession and Jugendstiel movements – writers, artists and musicians such as Arthur Schnitzler, Karl Kraus, Ludwig Wittgenstein, Theodor Herzl, Sigmund Freud, Gustav Mahler, Arnold Schönberg, Gustav Klimt, Egon Schiele, Otto Wagner, Adolf Loos and Kolo Moser. Many among them were Jewish, but by no means all.

Hitler gradually convinced himself that the cultural ferment around him amounted to a Jewish conspiracy against the German nation, whose tentacles reached throughout society. As Hitler saw it, the business community, the media, the arts – and, at the political level, the Social Democrats – were all infested with Jews, plotting and positioning themselves to prevent the emergence of a German nation out of the ruins of the Hapsburg Empire. The World Zionist Movement was yet another sinister manifestation of the Jewish race.

He came to see life as a struggle; most of all a struggle for the German *Herrenvolk* – master race – who had what he saw as the divine right to extend their living space, and to safeguard their imperial future, by eliminating the biologically impure. German rebirth, he concluded, demanded the eradication of Jews, Marxists, homosexuals and others that he classed as deviants.

In sum, Hitler's experiences in Vienna gave him what he called the 'granite basis' of his ideology, a mixture that included pan-German nationalism, anti-Semitism, biological racism and Slavophobia. By 1925, when *Mein Kampf* was published, Hitler already dismissed the Jews as 'living corpses', as a '*Rassenkonglomerat*' – a racial conglomerate – condemned to destruction. He described them as a fatally flawed, degenerate, decadent race. The sight of the Hassidic Jews in Leopoldstadt, in their traditional black garb, had confirmed his worst prejudices. They were dirty to the extent of putrefying the air, he claimed.

Hitler became an embittered anti-Semite within a few months of living in Vienna. But the image of the Jew who is responsible for all the ills of the world only became set in cement in his mind during his last three years in Vienna, when he was reduced to living in the Mannerheim refuge for the homeless. He blamed Jewish capitalists for exploiting the German poor, the '*Lumpenproletariat*'. 'In Vienna, I learned to hate the Jews. Any licence given to them is tantamount to an increase in the number of destructive parasites,' Hitler wrote in *Mein Kampf*.

Two politicians, who preached and pursued anti-Semitism, influenced Hitler deeply: Georg von Schönerer and Karl Lueger. Hitler went to Lueger's political rallies, and learned much about the language and bearing of the effective political demagogue. And he saw how warmly Vienna's citizenry responded to Lueger's assertions that the Jewish capitalists were to blame for their woes.

As Mayor of Vienna, Karl Lueger campaigned on an anti-Semitic platform from 1895 onwards, when he was first elected to this powerful post. Enthusiastic majorities re-elected him six more times, so that he remained the continuous occupant of Vienna's prestigious *Rathaus* – City Hall – until his death in 1910. 'The Big Karl' knew how to win the support of Vienna's electorate. On three occasions Emperor Franz Joseph refused to confirm Lueger's re-election, but after street crowds had assailed Franz Joseph as 'Emperor of the Jews', he yielded and allowed Lueger to occupy the *Rathaus*. Lueger then used his extensive powers of patronage in the capital to discriminate against Jews; although, in characteristic Viennese manner, he refused to be didactic. In response to allegations that he was acting against principle by employing a Jewish lawyer, for a time working with a Jewish Deputy Mayor and occasionally accepting Jewish hospitality, Lueger produced a classic retort: 'Who is a Jew will be determined by me [*Wer ein Jud ist bestimme ich*].'

Lueger's party vehicle to secure his conquest of Vienna was the Christian Social Union. It attracted the disaffected white-collar classes – artisans, small businessmen, the lower ranks of academia. It was anti-liberal and anti-Semitic, pro-monarchy but also populist in character. In the first Austrian republic, after the collapse of the Hapsburgs, the Christian Social Union expanded into a wider national party, conservative, Catholic and receptive to the message of the emerging Nazi movement.

Hitler learned from Lueger that anti-Semitism was politically popular, that it was widespread and cut across class, age and economic standing. He admired Lueger's techniques and tactics, but thought that in their application he allowed too many exceptions and was not firm enough in wholesale implementation of the anti-Semitic doctrines he was refining. Hitler took Georg von Schönerer as a more consistent role model. As he saw it, here was a convinced racist and pan-German, who combined strong anti-Slav views with deep-felt, powerfully reasoned anti-Semitism. Von Schönerer, persuaded that the multi-national Hapsburg monarchy was fatally flawed, had been calling since the 1880s for its replacement by a closer union between Austria and Germany.

In 1882 von Schönerer founded the *Deutschnationalen Verein* – the German National Club – and launched a pan-German platform, which became known as the Linz Programme because it was first published in that provincial capital. The programme's main focus was on closer treaty-bound ties between the Hapsburgs and Germany, including a customs union. However, in its original form the programme did not fully reflect von Schönerer's anti-Semitism. That element was brought to the Linz Programme in 1885, and has subsequently always been seen as its most crucial, and also most offensive, aspect. The new Point Twelve of the Linz Programme stipulated that 'the achievement of the reform programme requires the removal of Jewish influences from all aspects of public life'.

When Hitler first seized on the Linz Programme, he was probably unaware that two of von Schönerer's co-authors of the 1882 document had been of Jewish origin. They were Viktor Adler and Heinrich Friedjung. They backed von Schönerer's pan-German policies because they had concluded that Germany was more progressive than the Hapsburg regime and that Austria would benefit from association with its German neighbour. They were no longer practising Jews (Adler had been baptised) and in 1882 they turned a blind eye to von Schönerer's anti-Semitism, even though it must have been apparent that this was bound to become the key element in his political strategy. At one stage, as if to confirm the rift between Vienna's assimilated Jewish establishment and the immigrants from the East, Adler and Friedjung even backed von Schönerer's proposal to ban the immigration of East European Jews. That initiative failed. But as a phenomenon, the lack of fellow-feeling and antipathy between the two sets of Jews continues to this day to bedevil relations between Jews in Austria.

Adler and Friedjung themselves lost their place in the pan-German movement in 1885, when von Schönerer secured the anti-Semitic addition to the Linz Programme. Jews were no longer welcome in the German National Club.

In the remaining years before the break-up of the monarchy, Lueger's Christian Social Party partly eclipsed von Schönerer's political activities, but he remained the conduit for the most virulent form of anti-Semitism until his death in 1921. In 1887, von Schönerer formed the 'United Christians' party as a coalition against Jewish political activism. Its first manifesto was rabidly anti-Semitic, demanding sanctions such as the elimination of Jews from the civil service, the officer corps and the judiciary, a reduction in the number of university places available to Jewish students and a prohibition on Jewish immigration.

Increasingly, politically active Jews turned to the Social Democrats, the only party prepared to offer them a political home – and also the only party with a substantial number of Jewish supporters. Jewish intellectuals and Austria's working class alike each felt rejected by the bourgeoisie. Socialist internationalism, Marxism, seemed to be the only positive response – especially to those Jews who could see no meaningful sense in Zionism and the pressure for a Jewish national home.

By joining the Social Democrats, the Jewish intelligentsia was also registering a protest against the dominant Christian establishment which had rejected them and which, besides, appeared to have Fascist tendencies. Viktor Adler, after his flirtation with von Schönerer's pan-German movement, underwent a political catharsis and emerged as leader of the Social Democrat Party.

During the inter-war period, the Social Democrats endowed themselves with a succession of leaders of Jewish origin. They repeated this after the Second World War, when Bruno Kreisky was able to fight his way to the leadership. This in no way meant that the party became a vehicle in defence of Jewish interests. On the contrary, in the period before 1938 most of Austria's Jewish Social Democrats preferred to keep silent in the face of the anti-Semitic barrage from the political right. And when Kreisky became party leader in 1967, he certainly saw it as no part of his mission to give special consideration to the Jewish victims of Nazi persecution. The road to political power, even in the Social Democrat camp, has always demanded at the very least a non-committal attitude towards anti-Semitism. It was a habit that the SPÖ (*Sozialdemokratische Partei Österreichs*, the Austrian Socialist Party) found difficult to shed, even after Hitler came to power and the persecution of Austria's Jews took a far more violent turn. Many party critics, Simon Wiesenthal included, argue that it had always been thus.

Even Wiesenthal's elders in the Leopoldstadt probably did not fully understand the finer points of Social Democrat tactics during the First World War years. But during the inter-war period, as Wiesenthal became an adult and grew more experienced, he became convinced that the Social Democrats, supported or even encouraged by the Jewish intelligentsia, failed to grasp the realities of the dangers facing Austria's Jews. As he saw it, the Jewish Social Democrats were making quite unjustified compromises that were likely to rebound against the Jewish community, themselves included.

Wiesenthal has always clung to the analysis that the events of the Second World War did not bring about a fundamental reappraisal of the Socialist Party's attitudes towards the Nazis. There is ample evidence that the SPÖ, even with the experience of the Holocaust behind it, was not averse to co-operating with some of the far-right politicians of the post-war period.

Wiesenthal was determined to expose these fault-lines. The true dimensions of his violent confrontation with Bruno Kreisky in the 1970s and 1980s have to be seen against the SPÖ's flirtation with the far-right FPÖ (*Freiheitliche Partei Österreichs*, the Freedom Party of Austria), which was founded after the war and became the natural political home for many former highly placed Nazi Party members. In his old age, and after he had made his home in Vienna for more than thirty years, Wiesenthal still explained that he had remained in Vienna because 'the best way to keep an eye on the murderers was to live amongst them'.

Wiesenthal's first encounter with Vienna lasted from 1915 until 1917, when the Russians were forced to withdraw from Galicia and it seemed safe to return. His grandfather had died in Vienna in the spring of that year. His mother, like many of the other refugees eking out a difficult existence in the city, was eager to find out what could be salvaged from their former existence in Buczacz. The family decided that the widowed grandmother should stay behind for the time being and take care of the younger grandson, while in October Rosa and her older son, Simon, boarded a train bound for Poland and then on to Buczacz. Their old home had been preserved. But the Wiesenthal commodity stores in Buczacz had been burnt out, and his mother 'fought singlehanded to rebuild a modest living for her family'. She had little time for her son, and Simon felt lonely and miserable. Now eight years old, he missed his schoolfriends and his grandmother in Vienna. As he recalled eight decades later: 'I was alone in Buczacz without friends. I had nobody, while my mother was busy with the business.' He begged her to let him go back to Vienna.

To his astonishment she relented and entrusted him to a soldier who was travelling to Vienna. 'He was a medical orderly with a large dog, a Saint Bernard. He was given a sheet of paper with my name and the address in Vienna written in large capital letters. The soldier had his place on a military train; and with a great deal of persuasion they allowed me to get on too. The journey took between twenty-five and thirty hours. And for much of the time the dog had his head on my lap.' The octogenarian had a small child's satisfied smile as he recalled the scene. 'I couldn't move at all.'

'When we arrived in Vienna, I had a small amount of cash left over after I bought my tramway ticket to the Leopoldstadt. When I got off, I realised that my money had been stolen. But at least I was back with my grandmother.' Six months later, with the Hapsburg Empire in ruins and Austria in the growing pains of its first republic, his mother came to take them all back home to Buczacz. That seemed to be the end of Wiesenthal's life in Vienna. He never dreamed that he would return to make his permanent home in the city.

Under the armistice agreement, eastern Galicia had been given independence and named the Western Ukrainian Republic. But the independent state turned out to be a transitory phenomenon, lasting a mere three months. Then the Poles decided to reaffirm that they were the rightful owners of the country and moved in with their forces. Wiesenthal's education continued in Polish and, although born a subject of Austro-Hungary, he was now counted as a Polish citizen. From that time on, for better or worse – even though the Communists ranked him a traitor – the Poles have considered Wiesenthal one of their own: no matter that Poland's hold on eastern Galicia during the inter-war period turned out to be tenuous, and that it had to give it up to the Ukraine for good after the Second World War.

After 1918, Poland's grip on western Ukraine lasted less than two years until war broke out with the Soviets. The Bolsheviks invaded Galicia. The Poles, fighting to avoid retreat, recruited the support of the Ukrainian Petlyura cavalry – marauding bands of soldiers who were, if anything, even more brutal than the Bolsheviks. Wiesenthal, speaking about this period, is hard placed to put dates upon the constant changes of authority in Buczacz. 'We would get up without knowing what regime was in power,' he says with only a minor degree of exaggeration. At school they would look at the picture on display behind the teacher's desk: if it was a Polish leader, then it had to be assumed that Poland was in control. If it was a Bolshevik leader or a Ukrainian, it signified that Buczacz had found new, self-styled 'protectors'.

There is nothing vague about Wiesenthal's recollection of the depredations of the Petlyura. 'You must understand. It was a pogrom. Sometimes, I can still see it as vividly as if it happened yesterday. One day they demanded 100 litres of Schnapps to be delivered before nightfall. If it was not produced, they threatened, the town would be burned down. Well, who amongst us had 100 litres of Schnapps? Nobody. So there were two Jews pushing a small cart with a barrel on it, who went from house to house. Everybody who had Schnapps, or some similar alcohol, poured it into the barrel. ... The Petlyura stayed for quite a while, and we were virtual prisoners in our houses. We couldn't buy food, and my mother managed to signal a woman on the other side of the street that she would send me across to get flour from her so that we could bake bread. She thought a child could safely run across the street. I crossed over without trouble. She gave me flour.

'Suddenly a Cossack, riding a horse, appeared on the scene. I stood still on the pavement. I don't know whether he was drunk. But at any rate, he rode straight at me, pulled out his sabre and stabbed me. It was my good fortune that he drove the tip of the weapon into my leg and not my heart. I fell. People screamed from all the houses around. The Cossack disappeared. Someone ventured into the street and carried me home. Avoiding the streets, and making his way through gardens and courtyards, a doctor managed to reach me. The wound was right down to the bone. The doctor dressed it. The scar remained, and as I grew bigger, the scar also grew bigger.' Wiesenthal does not resent this. On the contrary, for him the scar is the first in a chain of evidence that he has long been protected from violent death by an unseen power that wanted him kept alive for a purpose.

But the Ukrainian-inflicted scar also serves as a reminder that the Nazis did not possess a monopoly on wanton cruelty.

This incident took place in 1920, just before the Bolsheviks took a turn at 'liberating' Wiesenthal by capturing Buczacz. The new occupiers were no less cruel than the Petlyura, but they made little distinction between Jews and non-Jews. Besides territorial conquest, their main target was the middle classes, the bourgeoisie. Wiesenthal's mother fell within the category. She was made to clean the school buildings and perform similar menial tasks. The Russians stayed for about half a year, then the Poles returned.

Throughout this time, Wiesenthal's mother kept the family business going and even launched herself into new activities. 'She was a business-woman, and I saw little of her,' he says sadly. By 1923, now aged fifteen, Wiesenthal had gained admission to the *Gymnasium*, the secondary school in Buczacz. Three-quarters of the children were Jewish. One of the other pupils in his class was a pretty girl, unusual for a Jew because she was very blond. Her name was Cyla Müller. They became friends. She was to be his future wife.

But 1923 also stands out for Wiesenthal because that was the year his brother had the terrible accident that led to his death a few months later. He remembers Hillel as a child 'who was lively, even though he was no daredevil. One day he was playing, running and, stumbling, fell from a height of about ten metres. His back was broken. My mother decided to take him to a children's specialist, a Professor Lorenz, in Vienna, leaving me and my grandmother behind in Buczacz.'

At that juncture the Bolsheviks made another appearance in the town. Communication with Vienna was cut. For six months Wiesenthal was out of touch with his mother. Then the Poles recaptured the town. Rosa was able to return with Hillel. The boy was paralysed and beyond help. At the very least, he should be allowed to die in his home surroundings. Before the year was out, the boy was dead.

Wiesenthal is always close to tears when he recalls these events. Yet unlike the irreparable loss he feels for his mother, who disappeared without trace and is therefore without a grave, Wiesenthal has the comfort of knowing that something at least has remained of his brother: 'The cemetery in Buczacz was desecrated during the war, but my brother's gravestone survived. I have a photograph of it.'

During the inter-war years, Wiesenthal's family life shrunk further. First his grandmother, whom he had loved so dearly, died. And then, early in 1926, his mother remarried. His stepfather, who was of Viennese origin, had a brick factory in Dolina, a little country town in the foothills of the

Carpathians. It meant that Rosa moved away from Buczacz. Wiesenthal was content to spend holidays there, but wanted to stay behind in Buczacz to complete the *Gymnasium*. His mother agreed, and arranged lodging for him with Cyla Müller's parents.

Simon and Cyla were both just over seventeen years old. They now saw much more of each other. They were still in the same class at school. Yiddish was prohibited, so they practised Polish with each other to prepare for their exams. 'Cyla passed her *Matura*, but I failed the exam the first time and had to take it again the following year, in 1928.' Cyla, listening to this version, explains that he failed the first time round not because he was lazy or inept, but only because he often played truant from school, preferring to stay at home and concentrate on his drawing. He had also been eager to learn the piano, but there was never enough time.

Wiesenthal was well-versed then in Jewish culture and traditions and could speak a good smattering of Hebrew. This he had learned from the rabbis and from his family. But where his broader education is concerned, he considers himself largely self-taught. He thinks of himself as 'a child of the streets', but is convinced that his rigorous commitment to the concept of justice, and his resistance to generalisations about criminal behaviour, stem from his upbringing within Galicia's Jewish culture.

Still at school, Cyla and Simon were so close that it was virtually taken for granted that they would eventually marry. But it was also accepted by those involved that before there could be any serious talk of marriage, Simon would have to complete his studies.

What profession should he choose? 'I had been drawing for ever. I wanted to study art, but my mother and my stepfather insisted that I had to do something practical. Through my stepfather and his brick factory, I knew a little about house building.' The combination of these two factors led to the decision to study architecture.

But where? Lvov was close and had the educational facilities. It was the obvious choice – except that in Lvov, at this period under Polish rule, the *numerus clausus* regulation was being applied against Jews, restricting their access to university. Only ten per cent of available places could be allocated to Jews. And even then, only certain faculties were open to them. Philosophy and law were sometimes more accessible, but architecture and medicine were closed altogether.

If he wanted to persevere with architecture, Wiesenthal would have to go abroad. Prague, with its more liberal outlook, was prepared to take him. His first term there was spent at the German Technical College. The teaching was in German, which made it easy for him.

However, home in Buczacz during the vacation, his friends convinced him that it would be difficult for him to practise later if he earned his diploma at the German rather than at the Czech Technical College. There was another, even more compelling reason for switching away from studies in German: Hitler was already straining for power. Wiesenthal recalls that 'The Sudeten Germans in Czechoslovakia were completely besotted by him. I remember a day when Hitler was making a big speech. I was in Reichenberg, and the Sudeten Germans all opened their windows, turned on their radios as loud as they could, and the whole town echoed with Hitler's words.' He also cites 'the *Germania*, a German academic house not far from Wenceslas Square in Prague. We were warned not to walk past the building, because among its student population, there were many who took great enjoyment in attacking the Jews.'

Even though he has not forgotten these symptoms of incipient Nazism, these were only minor scars on a thoroughly happy time. Prague's artistic wealth overwhelmed him with its beauty and variety. As a child in Vienna, he had been too young to appreciate its architecture or tour its galleries. Now in Prague he was old enough to understand and carefree enough to feast on its offerings. But the wonders of Prague went deeper. Here in this city, Simon Wiesenthal came out of his chrysalis and began to adapt to new and wider horizons beyond the narrow reaches of Galician Jewry.

Wiesenthal had never before lived such an unrestricted life. The behaviour of the police in Prague was a revelation. They were so benign compared to everything he had ever known at home. 'Can you realise what it meant to a Jew from Poland to see policemen who merely carried harmless-looking batons, and were not intent on beating people up?

'It was a new world for me. There were more than 30,000 foreign students.' There were Jews and non-Jews; and among the Jewish students, there were far more whose first language was German or Czech than Yiddish. 'Living at close quarters with such a mixed group was an entirely novel experience. It was exhilarating.' He learned the meaning of freedom, but given his background it was always a freedom allied to responsibility.

Wiesenthal had left behind the Hassidic ways of his Galician environment, as well as the all-pervasive, oppressive anti-Semitism he had always known. For the first, and possibly only, time in his life, he felt a surge of personal liberation, where he could revel in his surroundings and do what he most enjoyed: read, study art and architecture, draw and indulge his gift for caricature and humorous writing.

'The Czech Technical College was better equipped for architectural studies than its German counterpart. We drew, we painted, we had sculpture classes. Once they even took us to Barandov, where the Czech film industry had its studios, and we worked on film decor. It was all quite wonderful.'

Wiesenthal was tallish, handsome and fun-loving. He had already discovered his gift for memorising and telling humorous stories. He was poor, but he was popular and made lasting friendships. Even in his eighties, Wiesenthal still laughs as he recalls the stories he and his friends would tell each other during the train journeys going home to Poland for vacations. The journey was long, the seats were hard, but if they were exhausted on their arrival, it was only because they had swapped jokes all the way; eighteen hours of laughter, his mother always said when she welcomed him back to Dolina.

Wiesenthal's memories of the four student years spent in Prague are rose-tinted, and he glosses over the fact that many of Czechoslovakia's Jews were suffering from an acute identity crisis and were uncertain of their place in the post-Hapsburg republic. The Kafkaesque agonising and navel-gazing over assimilation that gripped so many Czech Jews made little impact on Wiesenthal, who felt secure in his identity.

For a while he became caught up in the Zionist fervour of some of his fellow students. Already back in Buczacz he had joined *Hashomer*, a Zionist youth organisation. But the group, while committed to the concept of a Jewish national home, proved too left-wing for him. It was leaning overly close to Communism, he felt. In Prague, he had had his initiation into the works of Karl Marx and decided that Marxism was not for him. It did not require much reflection: 'In Galicia we had had too much first-hand experience of Communism.' Besides, he was not seriously interested in emigration to Palestine. 'I had a childhood sweetheart; my future wife. She had to work because her father had died in the war, and her brother was a composer, a dreamer. If I had gone to Palestine, I would have been forced to give her up.'

Among his new friends in Prague were members of the right-wing Revisionists, the group founded by Vladimir Jabotinsky, and for a while Wiesenthal joined them. Their aim was the emigration of all Jews from Eastern Europe and the establishment of a fully independent Jewish state straddling both sides of the River Jordan. Jabotinsky despised the *shtetl* Jews and argued for a no-holds-barred approach to secure a modern, secular Jewish nation. His politics were corporatist, and he alienated left-wing Zionists.

Wiesenthal, never quite at ease with the militancy of the Revisionists, stayed with them for two years, but he became increasingly disaffected. 'They were arrogant and behaved as if they had a monopoly on the truth.'

He had no difficulty leaving the Revisionists when the Prague group splintered. He now became a founder member of a new grouping, the *Judenstaatspartei* – Jewish State Party – which adopted a more moderate approach. It was also closer to Wiesenthal's conviction, already formed then, that Jews, however badly persecuted, must never take the law into their own hands.

Wiesenthal remained a member until 1939. That was the last time he belonged to a political grouping. He denies that he has strong political leanings, or that he became a closet supporter of Austria's Conservative party, the ÖVP (*Österreichische Volkspartei*, the Austrian People's Party), after he settled in Vienna in 1961. 'I vote for individuals, not for political parties.' But while he claims that on social issues he has always been on the left of the political spectrum, it has been obvious since his Prague days that he has felt more comfortable with right-of-centre politics.

The Prague idyll ended in 1932. He was twenty-four years old. He had passed the '*absolutorium*', but still needed a Polish diploma to practise as a fully qualified architect. He went back to Poland, not to Buczacz, but to Lvov. At long last the Technical University was prepared to let him study there – on sufferance and with constant reminders that Jews were not welcome in the university. At the same time, he secured a job with a local building firm, and was soon given commissions to design houses for some of the wealthier among Lvov's Jews. This left little spare time.

Even so, already deeply conscious of the danger signals from Germany, Wiesenthal edited a Jewish student magazine, *Omnibus*. Its thrust was satirical, focusing primarily on the Nazis and their anti-Semitism. It was always sailing close to the wind. Wiesenthal's pseudonym for Hitler was 'Musso-Lenin'. He caricatured him in the illustrations he drew, and particularly remembers a 'Heil Hitler' cartoon which showed the *Führer* trampling on Jews. Wiesenthal cites this as evidence that he correctly grasped from the beginning that Hitler had all-encompassing designs against the Jews. Another cartoon, entitled 'The world has a headache', had a man's head with a swastika precariously balanced on it. After Austria's *Anschluss* in 1938, *Omnibus* published a Wiesenthal cartoon of Vienna's Schönbrunn Palace, which carried a one-word description: 'Confiscated'. Frequently, officialdom censored these cartoons, and *Omnibus* would appear with a blank frontispiece.

'You must understand, I always had good political antennae,' Wiesenthal says. *Omnibus* closed for lack of funds after two years, but some of the cartoons are preserved in Poland's National Library.

In September 1936, Wiesenthal felt that he was sufficiently well advanced in his studies and established in his work to marry Cyla Müller. A few days before the wedding, the chief architect in his firm called Wiesenthal into his private office. 'Yesterday was Yom Kippur, the Day of Atonement, and yet I saw you walking arm in arm with a *Schickse* [a woman who is not a Jew].' Wiesenthal smiled and replied, 'The blonde girl with the grey-blue eyes is my bride.' The wedding was performed not in Buczacz but in a rabbi's house in Lvov on 9 September 1936.

Lvov is a handsome city, typical of the provincial capitals fostered by the Hapsburgs. For a while Wiesenthal had lodgings in Janowska Street, not far from the small Kleparov railway station which the Germans later used for the departure of the trains that took their victims to the extermination camp at Belzec – Wiesenthal's mother included. The whole Janowska district was to become notorious under the Nazis, and for two years was the scene of Wiesenthal's wartime Calvary. At one end of the road the Germans built the Janowska concentration camp, where both Wiesenthals became inmates.

Even the happiness of the pre-war early married days was overshadowed by the growing Nazi menace and by the increasingly militant anti-Semitism manifesting itself in Lvov. In 1935, Hitler's Germany had adopted the Nuremberg laws, the precursor of the Final Solution. Under the ordinance, Jews were deprived of the ordinary rights of citizenship, excluded from the civil service and prohibited from marrying German Aryans. The law makers proclaimed that 'the purity of the German blood is a precondition for the continued existence of the German people' and promised that they were 'filled with the inflexible determination to make the German nation secure for all time'. A year later, Jews were denied the vote, and Jewish children were forced to add either Israel or Sarah to their names.

In the years up to the Second World War, Lvov belonged to Poland, and Germany's writ did not – yet – apply. But the reverberations from Nuremberg fell on to fertile ground in Poland, and anti-Semitic attitudes grew stronger. The Technical University, a neo-classical structure in terracotta and yellow, was in Sapiehy Street. It was dubbed 'street of doom' by Jewish students, who often had to brave barriers of anti-Semitic demonstrators armed with razor blades fastened to the tip of their sticks. In the mid-1930s, Polish universities instituted the practice of 'Jew-free days'. Frequently held during examination periods, it served the twin purpose of keeping Jewish students off the premises and delaying their efforts to obtain diplomas and degrees. The academic staff, for the greater part anti-Semitic, overtly supported the campaign against the Jewish students.

Among the Jewish community, Wiesenthal's reputation as an architect grew, and he won particularly welcome family praise for a large villa in

Dolina, built for his stepfather in 1937. Wiesenthal remembers it as a very handsome house. He likes to recall that of all the houses the Red Army Commander in Dolina might have selected for his headquarters, he chose the Wiesenthal-designed villa. Even the Communists recognised good quality and design. The villa survived the war, and lawyers have told him that he could probably recover it. 'But,' he says, 'I don't even want to know who lives there now. That chapter of my life is over.'

Even though he was becoming a sought-after architect, Wiesenthal, hampered by the university's discriminatory treatment of Jews, made only slow progress towards his diploma. It was not until the end of 1939 that a tuberculosis sanatorium constructed under his direction was accepted as evidence of academic adequacy, and he was allowed to qualify as an 'architectural engineer'. It was too late to make any difference to his professional life because the Holocaust was very nearly upon him. But at least it has served him in Austria, where titles are still essential to establish social standing. In Vienna, Wiesenthal is always addressed as '*Herr Ingenieur*', even though he never again worked as an architect, or an engineer.

In 1939, Hitler and Stalin signed their non-aggression pact, under which Poland was partitioned. Galicia, with Lvov remaining its capital, was transferred to Soviet sovereignty, so that in mid-September Wiesenthal experienced yet another 'liberation'. On this occasion it was the Red Army accompanied by the NKVD, the security police, which set about arresting 'bourgeois' Jewish merchants together with doctors, lawyers and teachers. Wiesenthal's stepfather was among the first to be arrested and died in a Soviet prison soon afterwards. His stepbrother was also arrested, but stayed alive until 1941, when he was shot by the Russians during their retreat from the advancing German army.

Any bourgeois Jews left at liberty had their status and movements severely restricted. They were formally designated second-class citizens and were issued with identity cards that prohibited them from living in the larger cities or within 100 kilometres of the frontier. Under this edict, Wiesenthal would have been obliged to leave Lvov, but luck of sorts was on his side. He managed to bribe an NKVD official and secured regular passports, without domicile restrictions, for himself, his wife and for his widowed mother, who had come to live with them. Not long afterwards most of the Jews on whom the restrictive identity cards had been imposed were deported to Siberia, where many of them died.

This was the 'phoney war period' for Simon Wiesenthal, when he retained a modicum of control over his life – though there were premonitions of far worse to come. He still managed to go to the university often enough to complete his courses and obtain his architectural engineer's degree. But he could no longer work in his 'bourgeois' profession and was lucky to earn some money by working in a factory, making duvet bed covers filled with down and chicken feathers.

An Israeli intelligence report on Wiesenthal, written in 1952 and stored in the file that the CIC (the US Counterintelligence Corps) had kept on him, claims that after the Russians occupied Lvov, Wiesenthal spent a prolonged period in Soviet hands. The report says that

> Wiesenthal was taken into custody by the Soviets and transported to the Russian interior. After several months in a labour camp, he was put to work as an engineer in a pen factory in Odessa. Later he advanced to the position of chief engineer. In some instances he was used as a technical advisor to the Ukrainian Ministry of Industry.

Wiesenthal maintains that this is pure invention.

In 1952, Israeli intelligence had not functioned long enough to build up its formidable capacity for intelligence-gathering. Much of their reporting was based on rumours, and often unwittingly influenced by Communist-bloc disinformation. Israeli sources, who acknowledge that mistakes were made, now discount the accuracy of their 1952 report on Wiesenthal. Its credibility is further thrown into doubt by the summary of his activities between 1941 and 1945, where the Israelis omitted most of the essentials and built up a grossly distorted picture. The report says: 'After the German invasion of Russia, Wiesenthal joined the partisans and was later promoted lieutenant. In 1944, without being recognised as a partisan officer, he was taken prisoner by the German army and put into a concentration camp from which he was freed by the Americans in 1945.' All this seems to have been distilled from the transcript of a 1948 CIC interrogation, whose accuracy Wiesenthal disputes as an almost unrecognisable distortion of the real facts.

Wiesenthal's own account of his visits to Odessa is entirely different. He explains that his boss in the bedding factory in Lvov was a Jew from Odessa, who sent him to the Black Sea city on several occasions to work on architectural plans to rebuild the Lvov factory. He remembers Odessa with considerable fondness as a beautiful, vibrant city. He denies that he was taken into custody by the Soviets, or that he was ever in a Soviet labour camp, and says that everything he observed in the Soviet Union convinced him that his 'aversion to Communism as practised in the Eastern bloc was surpassed only by aversion to Nazism'.

On 22 June 1941, Hitler invaded the Soviet-occupied part of Poland.

Four days later, the Ukrainians once again proclaimed a national government in Galicia and wrote to Hitler, expressing their support and respect for him. But Hitler's armies advanced, regardless, and the independent republic only lasted three days. On 28 June, the *Reichswehr* and the SS marched into Lvov.

The agony began.

[4]
The War Years –
The Miracles of Survival

Holocaust survivors believe in luck, in miracles. Certainly Simon Wiesenthal, forever unable to comprehend how his life came to be spared when all around him was only unspeakable cruelty and senseless killing, has no other explanation and can see no other justification. But who or what was at hand to perform those miracles? The childhood lessons absorbed from Galicia's wonder rabbis seemed irrelevant in the face of such enormities. Of course there were many victims whose faith remained unshakeable, and who took comfort from the belief that they would receive their just rewards in heaven. Wiesenthal did not experience the luxury of such certainties. His doubts expressed themselves in the phrase that 'God must have been on leave during the Holocaust', which he quotes in what he considers his most important book, *The Sunflower*. Had God been present, surely the Nazis would have been struck down before they could have organised an industrial machine for the purpose of killing millions of men, women and children?

Miracles without a God to perform them are among the imponderables that began to nag at Wiesenthal during the first pogroms in Lvov in 1941. Considering himself an 'uncomfortable philosopher', he has never been able to resolve the dilemma sufficiently to give him peace of mind. All the more reason, he concluded, to dedicate his life to the victims, to those untouched by the miracles that allowed him to survive.

Experience has shown that most death-camp survivors carry a sense of guilt that they emerged from the camps alive while so many others perished. Even given miracles, or just luck, the mere fact of survival makes them question whether they did not somehow betray their dead companions.

The unrelenting search for answers to these troublesome riddles will continue as long as mankind seeks to understand the existence of the death factories of the Holocaust. Wiesenthal's preoccupation with guilt has been a constant. He has always been more of an activist, a doer, than an intellectual. Even so, all his activities, and that includes a great deal of writing, reflect an unceasing search for answers to systematically organised mass murder, and how to deal with the perpetrators.

While others may have been able to construct moral certainties for themselves, Wiesenthal, having ruled out revenge and questioned for-giveness as a way of cleansing the soul, was left with a dilemma that he has never been able to resolve to his own satisfaction. How to attribute guilt? How to secure justice and punishment, or to deal with redemption, responsi-bility, revenge, compassion and forgiveness?

The horrors, the miracles – and the questioning – began for Wiesenthal on a summer Sunday afternoon, on 6 July 1941. Breaking the non-aggression treaty with the Soviet Union, the Germans had invaded the Soviet-con-trolled part of Poland eight days earlier. During their last days in Lvov, the Soviets, in a classic display of animosity towards the Ukrainians who had also fought over these lands, herded 3,000 of them into the KGB headquarters compound and shot them dead. But this did nothing to rid the Jews of their Ukrainian tormentors. As the Russian troops turned tail, the first German uniforms appeared in Lvov. They were worn by Ukrainian auxiliaries, collaborators who had fled to Germany in 1939, after the Soviet Union annexed western Ukraine and occupied Galicia. The Ukrainians celebrated this new 'liberation' of the Galician capital with a three-day pogrom. At least 6,000 Jews were killed. They also took two groups of Jewish students from the nearby Jewish High School and forced them to take the corpses out of the KGB building and pile them up in the street. Several of the young Jews were then killed by the Ukrainians, chanting 'Bolshevik killers' and denouncing them as KGB accomplices.

Behind the Ukrainians, worse was on the way. The *Einsatztruppen*, the SS troops under the command of Reinhard Heydrich, came in with their orders to execute the Bolshevik intelligentsia – meaning especially the Jews. They took the names and addresses from the telephone directory, where the Wiesenthal name was listed.

Memory plays tricks even under ordinary circumstances. Not surprisingly the trauma of the Holocaust experience multiplies the distortions of remem-brance. Some survivors took years and years before they were able to speak about what had happened to them; some have remained silent. Survivors have rarely been entirely consistent in telling their stories – and later accounts have sometimes been more accurate than the initial ones. Some events may not have happened in the way that memory portrays them; some are imagined, parables of actual experience.

Wiesenthal has never had inhibitions about telling his wartime saga – on the contrary, they have been an essential tool in his mission to keep alive the memory of the Holocaust – and he has always singled out events that he felt had bordered on the inexplicable – the miraculous – and on happenings which inexorably positioned him to dedicate his life to the exposure of Nazi criminals and anti-Semitism, and to the battle against Holocaust amnesia. But as with other survivors, some aspects of the story have been distorted in the remembrance.

Much of it Wiesenthal has told many times over and, not surprisingly, with occasional variations. He rarely talks to an audience without illustrating his points with some reference to what happened to him during the war. His own books are laced with reminiscences. He has encouraged film makers to portray his wartime experiences and has rarely demurred even if they have overdramatised or oversentimentalised the scene. Inevitably the skeletal Wiesenthal who explained himself to his American liberators in 1945 still lacked the distance and detachment to call up, let alone evaluate, the seminal events of his wartime Odyssey.

Wiesenthal soon grasped that some time must be allowed to lapse to give him a true perspective. His first attempt to give a full account was not made until 1961 when Wiesenthal was in Jerusalem for the Eichmann trial. Then he co-operated with Yad Vashem, Israel's Holocaust centre, to provide an oral history of his war years. This contains a wealth of vivid detail, which Wiesenthal intended to be published only after his death. The material was recorded by Haim Maas, a respected Israeli journalist, who later persuaded Wiesenthal to write an account of his involvement in hunting Adolf Eichmann. Maas, recalling Wiesenthal as he was in 1960, spoke of his 'phenomenal memory for names and circumstances, even dates', and noted that in those days, 'Wiesenthal was more modest and not as egocentric as he seemed after he became famous'.

In two semi-autobiographical books – *The Murderers Amongst Us*, written with Joseph Wechsberg, and *Justice Not Vengeance*, with Peter Michael Lingens – Wiesenthal has described the wartime incidents that have made their deepest impression on him. In 1994, at the age of eighty-five, Wiesenthal talked himself through the war years once more for the purposes of this biography. But use has also been made of his earlier accounts, especially of his file in Yad Vashem's archive.

As an octogenarian, he still recalled vividly how narrowly he had escaped death right at the beginning in 1941, during the first pogrom in Lvov. He had been hiding in the cellar of his house, playing chess with a Jewish friend. A Ukrainian auxiliary found them and took them to the Brigidki prison. In the courtyard were about forty Jews, lawyers, teachers, doctors – members of the hated bourgeoisie. They were ordered to form a row facing the wall and to put up their arms behind their necks. Next to each man stood a wooden crate. Then the shooting started; beginning at the left side of the row, each Jew in turn was shot in the neck. After each shot, time was left for the body to be thrown into the crate and removed. Wiesenthal's turn was just about to come when church bells rang out.

A Ukrainian shouted, 'Enough. Evening Mass,' and the shooting was interrupted for the day. The twenty Jews who remained were led off to two cells, where their shoelaces and belts were removed to prevent suicide attempts. Wiesenthal dozed off, only to be woken by a flashlight and a Polish voice expressing astonishment at finding him among the victims due to be shot in the morning. The voice turned out to belong to a Ukrainian construction worker called Bodnar, for whom Wiesenthal had once secured a flat in one of the houses he had built. 'He was a decent, honest man,' Wiesenthal recalled, and so it proved again that night. The man offered to help Wiesenthal and his friend to escape by telling the Ukrainians that he had found two Russian spies among the Jews. He predicted that they would be beaten, but that they would then be put into his custody for delivery to the Ukrainian Army Commissar for questioning. The two men were indeed beaten up. 'The Ukrainians were rushing through the cells. The noise was much like a cowboy film scene, with a stampede of wild steer.' Wiesenthal lost two front teeth. But Bodnar managed to take him and his friend out of the prison, and after a long night of adventures in the streets, and afterwards at the Commissar's quarters where their life hung in the balance, the two Jews summoned enough audacity and bravado to make their way back to their own homes.

The respite did not last long. A week later he was rounded up again – not for immediate killing this time, but to do forced labour for the occupation forces. He was assigned to the OAW – the *Ostbahn Ausbesserungs Werke* (the Eastern Railway Repair Works) – but for the time being was allowed to return to his home at night, exhausted from carrying heavy, sharp-edged armour plates and oxygen bottles. They worked without breaks, and the German soldiers made short shrift of anyone who collapsed from fatigue. Wiesenthal was lucky – there were vacancies for signpainters; he pushed hard to be accepted and succeeded.

But the overall situation for Jews was deteriorating rapidly. The Germans ordered the Jews to ring-fence the area around Zamarstynovska Street. This was to be the ghetto, where all of Lvov's Jews were compelled to move. The three Wiesenthals were at home when an SS man arrived with a prostitute. The flat was to her liking. The Wiesenthals were given an hour to clear out, taking only the few possessions they could carry to the ghetto.

They had to share rooms in Block 2 with another family, called Segel.

Life became a day-to-day struggle to survive. Yet Wiesenthal and his fellow sufferers in the Lvov ghetto still had no real inkling of the enormity of the evil that the Nazis had decided to unleash. Their world had drastically shrunk. It took until early 1943 before they knew for sure that Belzec, the camp where Wiesenthal's mother had been taken, was an extermination establishment complete with gas chambers and crematoria. Even so, they did not realise that Belzec was but one of scores of similar killing-fields. They were unaware that, on 31 July 1941, Field Marshal Hermann Göring had signed the order instructing the SS leader, Reinhard Heydrich, to examine how the 'Final Solution' of the Jewish question could be achieved. Heydrich was to submit, as rapidly as possible, a 'comprehensive plan to include the organisational, executive and material requirements' for this task. Hitler wanted all of Europe's Jews killed.

The Nazis realised that it would be far too slow to kill the victims individually, and that an industrial process was required. On 3 September, the first experiments with Zyklon-B gas were carried out at Auschwitz. Several hundred Soviet prisoners of war were successfully killed. Auschwitz was a prime site, already used as a concentration camp supplying slave labour to Siemens, IG Farben and other enterprises engaged in war materials production. An extermination camp was a logical addition, because of its excellent railway connections with Eastern and Central Europe, where the Jews were being rounded up.

It took less than five months for Heydrich to produce a detailed blueprint for the establishment of extermination camps, the infrastructure required to kill millions and make Germany safe for Aryans. On 20 January 1942, at Wannsee in Berlin, Hitler's minions worked out the mechanics of implementing the death warrant of Europe's Jews. Adolf Eichmann, note-taker at the Wannsee conference and Heydrich's trusted collaborator, was put in charge of devising cost-effective machinery designed to exterminate the Jews in Germany and German-occupied territories in their entirety. The construction of death camps would be speeded up. Chelmno was already working. Belzec was ready by March. Sobibor and Treblinka followed soon afterwards. Auschwitz was enlarged.

Concentration camps had existed since the mid-1930s. The inmates were used as slave labour. They were so badly fed that few survived more than three or four months, and many were arbitrarily killed. By 1940, Western governments were fully aware of the existence of these camps, and Winston Churchill declared in 1941 that 'retribution for these crimes must take its place among the major purposes of this war'.

Indisputable confirmation of the plan to kill all Jews in Europe, and to that end to construct the extermination camps, did not however reach the outside world until August 1942. Gerhart Riegner, the Geneva-based representative of the WJC, had sent a message to London declaring that he had received 'an alarming report'. A plan had been discussed in the *Führer's* headquarters, Riegner wrote,

> according to which all Jews in countries occupied or controlled by Germany, numbering three and a half to four millions, should, after deportation and concentration in the East, be at one blow exterminated, in order to resolve once and for all the Jewish question in Europe. Action is reported to be planned for the autumn. Ways of execution are still being discussed – including the use of prussic acid.

Riegner added that he could not confirm the exactitude of his report, but stressed that his informant had close connections with the highest German authorities. In fact, construction of the death camps was already far more advanced than Riegner realised, and Jews in ever more massive numbers were being sent to the gas chambers. But in any event, both the US and the British Governments professed scepticism. Appeals from Riegner to the Vatican to speak out against the Final Solution fell on deaf ears. Jan Kozielewski, working for the London-based Polish government-in-exile, smuggled himself into the Warsaw ghetto and into a concentration camp. But even his first-hand reports failed to convince. They went so far beyond the norms of brutality that even US Supreme Court Judge, Felix Frankfurter, responded to Kozielewski with the remark: 'I am unable to believe you.'

In London in November 1942, Sidney Silverman, a Labour Member of Parliament and a Jew, handed over to the Foreign Office details about Auschwitz and at least three other death camps. But (Sir) Frank Roberts, then still a middle-ranking diplomat, advised the Government against becoming involved. He feared that public condemnation would 'irritate Herr Hitler, who was in a difficult mood about the British prisoners of war'. There was an added consideration: Britain wanted to keep down Jewish emigration to Palestine. If the Government acknowledged that Europe's Jews were at risk and facing wholesale death, then it would have to relax its immigration policies in Palestine. The US administration, gripped by internal divisions on the issue, also hesitated to speak out.

This ostrich-like attitude was rapidly becoming untenable. The New York-based WJC had compiled a detailed dossier, demonstrating that a blueprint for extermination existed in Germany. At last, in December,

Churchill issued a dramatically phrased declaration that had the endorsement of the United States and Soviet Governments:

> Jews are being transported in conditions of appalling brutality and horror to Eastern Europe. In Poland, long the principal Nazi slaughterhouse, the ghettoes established by the German invader are being systematically emptied of all Jews, except for a few highly skilled workers required for war industries. The able-bodied are slowly worked to death in the camps. The infirm are left to die of exposure or starvation or are deliberately murdered in mass executions. . . . The Government condemns in strongest political terms this bestial policy of mass extermination.

Still, the Allies refused to follow the pleas of those who called for more than verbal condemnation and were proposing carefully targeted bombardment. Instead, the killing went on, even accelerated, right to the closing stages of the war, with the extermination camps phased down only to destroy evidence for the advancing Allied armies.

About two months after Göring had signed the decree for the Final Solution, the SS came for Simon and Cyla Wiesenthal and took them to the Janowska concentration camp on the western outskirts of Lvov. They were separated into the men's and women's sections of the camp. Their rations were minimal; the huts overcrowded. Prison guards were routinely taking potshots, arbitrarily killing prisoners. The camp was being enlarged, and the prisoners had to quarry and carry stones. They also had to dig huge pits, the Sands, where the ever-growing number of dead bodies were dumped. The remains of at least 140,000 bodies were dug up from the pits in 1943 by a special 'Blobel' commando of prisoners, who were forced to build huge wood pyres and burn the skeletons. (After the war, the Soviets used the Janowska site as a prison for convicted criminals, and one of the pits became a training ground for sniffer dogs.)

The Wiesenthals had been taken into the Janowska camp in October 1941. Wiesenthal counted amongst the earliest inmates, and was given the number 504. Within weeks, a mini-miracle occurred. They were transferred to a small labour camp — a considerable upgrade from the brutalities of the concentration camp — which had been established at the important OAW. There was room for 300 prisoners, needed to supplement the regular Polish workforce employed at the railway repair works. The Germans in charge of this repair yard had apparently found it wasteful to train the prisoners sent up daily from the Janowska camp, only to find that many of them soon dropped out — having been shot or beaten up, or dying from starvation. By housing their prisoners on site, work at the yard could be organised more smoothly.

Cyla's job was to polish brass and nickel. Simon resumed his signpainter's job. The camp was not large; the atmosphere was more relaxed. Those in charge displayed quite unexpected decency and sought to protect the prisoners from the long arm of the Janowska camp commandant.

Wiesenthal's adamant rejection of the concept of collective guilt owes a great deal to his time in the railway camp, and to his dealings with the Nazis who ran the railway repair yard. Their behaviour towards the prisoners, but especially towards him and his wife, remained a constant reminder that people, including Nazis, had to be judged as individuals. The proposition that the exception proves the rule, and that individual goodness is no argument against collective guilt, carries no weight with Wiesenthal.

There were no SS guards in the OAW labour camp, only railway guards. Wiesenthal saw Cyla almost daily. Occasionally – that is, until his mother was taken away to Belzec in August 1942 – they were allowed to spend the night in the ghetto with his mother.

Wiesenthal takes up the story, and improbable though some aspects of Wiesenthal's experiences at the OAW may seem, a German lawyer, who researched wartime conditions there, concluded that there was no justification for doubting Wiesenthal's accuracy. At the OAW there were many locomotives, captured from the Russians; Wiesenthal describes how, as a signpainter, he 'had to replace the Soviet insignia with the swastikas. My supervisor gave me tracing papers with the new inscriptions and the swastikas – we dubbed them "*Pleitegeier*" [bankrupt eagles]. After a while, the painting became so routine that I could do it without first having to trace the pattern. One day, the head of the railway repair works, Heinrich Günthert, walked past and, observing my work, asked me about my schooling. Knowing that the Nazis had put Jewish intellectuals at the top of their hit lists, I replied that I had no special training.

'But a Polish worker, overhearing this, said that I was a well-known architect from Lvov. Günthert, accusing me of lying – a punishable offence – ordered me to his office.

'For a second time he demanded why I had lied about my training. I asked whether he wanted the truth or an apology. "Tell me the truth." So I told him that I was an architect, but as the intelligentsia was under constant threat, I had not disclosed my qualifications.

'Günthert walked up and down. Then he called Adolf Kohlrautz, his deputy. They decided to give me work as a draughtsman and took me into a large hall, where about twenty Polish and ethnic German engineers were at work on extensions to the railway works. It was 1942, and the Germans assumed that the occupation of Poland would last in perpetuity. Kohlrautz explained what needed to be done, and I got down to work.

'Next morning Kohlrautz was waiting for me at the gates and said, "Those damned Poles. Last evening they sent a delegation to protest that they could not work with a Jew in the same room. I'll have to find you somewhere else to work." He did. He put me into a hut, installed a telephone, and said that I could sleep there too instead of going back to the camp. Every morning he brought me the instructions for my drawings, and at the end of the day he would collect the work. Cyla was allowed to join me, and no longer had to sleep in the women's barracks.'

Wiesenthal's Yad Vashem memoir has the most vivid description of his time at the OAW. He describes how he reached a tacit understanding with Kohlrautz: he did all the works plan drawings and Kohlrautz signed them. Wiesenthal became indispensable to the German, and in return he had Kohlrautz's protection. During the months before his mother was taken to her death, Kohlrautz even occasionally went to the ghetto to bring her food.

> I had long conversations with Kohlrautz. We formed something approaching a friendship. He was not a member of the SS, but only of the SA (the less malign arm of the Nazi power structure). One day, he told me of his suspicions that various building firms, working for the repair yards, were defrauding him. He wanted me to check all the bills. This meant that I could move freely around the yards.

Wiesenthal had access to all the archives and secret plans of the strategically important OAW. He was allowed to deal directly with the Polish workers, and this enabled him to identify and establish contact with members of the Polish underground. They belonged to the non-Communist AK (*Armja Krajowa*) home army, which was under the control of the Polish government-in-exile in London. He gave them detailed plans to enable them to blow up key railway points. In return, he wanted help to get his wife out of the camp to safety.

It was early in 1943. With her blonde hair and grey-blue eyes, nobody would suspect Cyla of being Jewish. There would be little risk if the partisans helped her out of the camp and found her a lodging. Before long one of the builders offered to smuggle her out to friends in Lublin, who would take care of her.

The Yad Vashem memoir continues:

I told Kohlrautz that I wanted to save my wife. His response was to tell me to take one of the identity card forms, which were normally given to the employees of building firms. 'Choose any pseudonym for your wife that comes into your head. Fill it in, and as you already know my signature well, you should have no difficulty in writing it in.' Now that I could provide Cyla with papers, the builder was able to spirit her away to live with an architect's family in Lublin. There, for a while at least, she was safe, looking after the man's children.

Years later, when Wiesenthal was under attack from Poland's Communist regime, the grandson of Cyla's rescuers turned up in his office in Vienna. He wanted him to know that his grandmother, who was still alive, had never forgotten those few months in 1943 when Cyla sheltered with the family. It was good to be reminded that there had always been Poles prepared to take risks for Jews.

It was not the family's fault that Cyla had not been able to remain in Lublin safely for very long. One day, in June 1943, one of the railway guards called Wiesenthal to the railway works' perimeter fence:

The guards had respect for me by then, because they saw that all the top people came to my office. My wife stood outside the fence. She told me what had happened: that she had fled from Lublin because the Gestapo were rounding up everybody who was not domiciled in the town. Cyla had given out that she was the wife of a Polish officer, taken prisoner by the Russians. She realised that she would not be able to convince the SS with her story, and she also knew that the women who had been taken to the SS ahead of her had been sent straight to the Majdanek concentration camp. She decided to attempt to make her way back to Lvov. She had spent the previous two nights with the women's lavatory attendant at the railway station.

For a second time Wiesenthal asked his underground contacts for help to bring his wife to safety:

An hour later, they came back to tell me that my wife should take a certain train to Warsaw. In a corner of the arrival hall, she would find a woman contact who would give her false papers and lodgings. It all happened as the partisans promised. She adopted the name of Irena Kowalska, sleeping in a kitchen where rabbits were also kept. The destruction of the Warsaw ghetto had begun in April 1943, and when Cyla arrived in the city in June that year, the Nazis were still hunting for Jews. Once she was questioned, but they let her go. Nobody was allowed to know her Jewish identity; not even another Jewish woman, using the same hiding-place, who was the wife of the Polish poet Jerzy Lec. Cyla found a job in a radio factory.

For a few weeks after Cyla had reached Warsaw, she and her husband were able to communicate — and not just by courtesy of the Polish underground. Wiesenthal even had enough freedom to telephone her from his office in the railway yard. Then, after he too escaped from the camp, they lost contact and he became convinced that she was dead — killed during the 1944 Warsaw uprising, when the street, where he knew she had lived, was blown up during the fighting. In fact, the Germans, not recognising that Cyla was a Jew, had rounded her up with other Polish women in Warsaw to work in a machine-gun factory in Solingen, where she remained until 1945.

Wiesenthal did not learn of his wife's survival until a few months after the war's end. Their reunion was one of life's great miracles. But for that to happen, it took a long series of other miracles, or extraordinary escapes from death, for Wiesenthal himself to remain alive. He experienced the crassest brutality at the hands of the Nazis. And yet there were other Germans whose actions convinced him that it would always be wrong to tar every Nazi with the brush of collective guilt.

Brick by brick as the Holocaust gathered momentum, Wiesenthal experienced seemingly miraculous escapes from death, and often help came from the least expected Nazi quarters. Hitler's fifty-fourth birthday — 20 April 1943 — was one such occasion. Cyla was already out of the camp, and Wiesenthal thought her safe in Lublin. The Germans at the OAW wanted a big birthday celebration for the *Führer* and Wiesenthal, who had temporarily been put back to his old job of painting Nazi emblems, was making posters for the birthday party. Suddenly an SS officer arrived and demanded that Wiesenthal and two other Jews be taken back to the Janowska concentration camp. More Jews, thirty-eight men and eight women, were rounded up inside the camp and were marched to the '*Schlauch*' — the hose — a narrow corridor leading to the Sands, the pits where the SS shot their victims and smothered the bodies with sand, creating layer upon layer of skeletons. They were all told to undress and stand in a row. Wiesenthal thought back to the first time he had faced being shot — that day in 1941, when the Nazis had arrived in Lvov. Then a friendly hand had rescued him, but now hope had gone.

Wiesenthal felt certain that he was about to die. The bodies were already falling. His turn to be shot was edging closer. Suddenly there was a commotion. His name was being shouted out. In his nakedness, Wiesenthal was told to stand to attention. He heard an SS officer tell the executioner to continue shooting the others, but to let Wiesenthal go, because he was needed elsewhere.

The instinct for survival was so great in the camps that Wiesenthal, like most inmates, felt no compunction about leaving the others behind in firing range. That seems to have come later when he omitted this particular escape from death in the oral history he gave to Yad Vashem in 1961. Afterwards, when Wiesenthal had a wider perspective on his war years, he was again able to talk and write about it. He recalled how, on that April day, he was allowed to put on his clothes again and was taken back to the railway works, where Kohlrautz was waiting. 'We need him to finish the posters for the Hitler birthday celebrations,' he told the SS officer. Wiesenthal was then detailed to paint an outsize poster with the swastika and the inscription – in white letters against a red background – which read: '*Wir danken unserem Führer* [We thank our leader].' This was the one and only occasion when Wiesenthal had a minuscule, momentary spasm of gratitude for Hitler.

Back in greater safety at the railway works, Wiesenthal worked ever more closely with the underground. He was now making considerable sums of money by accepting bribes from building firms who looked to him to influence Kohlrautz in the award of contracts. In the Yad Vashem memoir, Wiesenthal described this very frankly: how he used money to look after a young boy, Olek, whom the underground brought to him one day, and how he helped two or three other families in the ghetto; how he used his telephone to call underground contacts in the ghetto and elsewhere; and how he even managed to smuggle a few arms to the inmates in Janowska camp, where they were hidden in the barracks where the camp orchestra was housed. For himself, he acquired two revolvers, which he kept hidden in his desk.

Compared to his fellow prisoners Wiesenthal's existence was now oddly privileged. Obviously it could not last. The builders were bribing him with food as well as money, and so he was well fed. He had money and with it came power, and he had influence because he had both. But he never suspected that the Communists would later use this to accuse him of collaboration with the Gestapo, and worse still that Austrian Chancellor, Bruno Kreisky, would seize on such black propaganda to make similar charges.

Kohlrautz proved his concern for Wiesenthal on one more occasion. In September 1943, Kohlrautz was told that the railway works would, in future, have to function with Jewish forced labour. The Jews would be taken to the concentration camps. 'What are you waiting for?' Kohlrautz asked Wiesenthal, hinting that he was prepared to let him escape.

Since the events on Hitler's birthday, Wiesenthal had felt that the railway works camp was the only opportunity he would ever have to attempt escape. Now here was Kohlrautz virtually inviting him to act. And act he did. He already had his connections with the underground partisans. He would need shelter, and he therefore asked a young Polish girl, Danuta, who worked in the railway works, whether her parents could hide him in their small house at Kulparkov, a village close to Lvov. Kohlrautz had often allowed him to go into Lvov, accompanied by a guard, to buy supplies for the railway works. Now again he asked Kohlrautz for permission to go to the town, and made it plain that he and another Jewish prisoner, Arthur Scheimann, married to a Ukrainian woman, a dressmaker, would give their guard the slip. While Kohlrautz went out to fetch a guard, Wiesenthal took the pistols which he knew were in the desk drawer.

'We didn't embrace,' Wiesenthal notes as he tells of his last encounter with Kohlrautz. (His Nazi friend was killed on the Russian front in 1944. But Günthert survived; Wiesenthal found him after the war, met him on several occasions and even invited him to his daughter's wedding in 1965. On Wiesenthal's eighty-fifth birthday, Günthert sent him a long letter of congratulations complete with an appreciation of his achievements.)

Wiesenthal escaped from the OAW on 6 October 1943. 'Just before one o'clock, I took the tram into Lvov. We told our guard, a Ukrainian, who didn't know the town, that we needed about twenty minutes in the station-ery shop, and he should wait outside. He didn't know there was a back exit. We used it and took another tram to the place where we had arranged to meet Danuta. She took us to her home, and her parents hid us in their attic for about a month.' After a week, Scheimann's wife collected her husband, and Wiesenthal remained alone in his hiding-place. But ten days later, his hostess raised the alarm. The village was surrounded by Ukrainians; he should flee. 'I hid under the straw with both my revolvers, ready to sell my life dearly.' But when two Ukrainians approached, 'I lost my nerve, used both pistols simultaneously, but only managed to wound one of them in the arm.' The Ukrainians fled in one direction; Wiesenthal also fled and succeeded in making his way to the Scheimann house. Even in old age, he still has a vivid sense of the claustrophobia that gripped him in the clothes closet where Mrs Scheimann hid him and her husband. The closet was where she also kept the clothes waiting to be tried on by her customers. It was so uncomfortable, and the air was so putrid, 'that even the concentration camp might have been preferable'.

After four days in the closet, Wiesenthal decided that he could stand no more. In the Yad Vashem memoir, he described how he took his two revolvers, a little food, a blanket and a compass, and thought he might be able to reach Ukrainian territory. It was now November 1943. Everything was covered in snow. Hungry and exhausted after eight days in the woodlands near Lvov, he lay there only half-conscious. When he at last became fully aware of his surroundings Wiesenthal realised that he had managed to reach a motley group of partisans. There were a few Jews, a Polish priest and several other Poles, some French and Belgian prisoners of war who had escaped, and a sprinkling of Russians and Ukrainians.

Their survival was precarious. The advance of the Red Army decided them to leave the woods in pairs. Wiesenthal managed to contact Olek, the Jewish boy with the AK whose life he had helped to save while he was at the railway repair works. Wiesenthal and his friend were led to an AK 'safe flat', occupied by two women. The visitors dug themselves a hide-out under the floorboards, and a carpet and a table were placed on top. It seemed like a coffin. But at least Wiesenthal had paper and pencils, and passed the long hours compiling lists of SS officers whose names he could recall, and of the crimes he had witnessed. On the assumption that the Soviet forces were close to recapturing Lvov, Wiesenthal also drew maps of partisan emplacements to provide helpful intelligence for the Red Army liberators. 'I had to do something useful with my time.'

The bunker period came to an abrupt end on 13 June 1944. In a neighbouring house, there had been a drunken brawl and a senior inspector of the German Railways had been beaten up. This provoked a house-to-house search for weapons. Tapping the floorboards in the house where Wiesenthal was hidden, the Germans discovered the hollow under the floor. They forced it open and found Wiesenthal lying there, and without room for manoeuvre to use his pistols. There were two Poles with the German search party, and they snatched Wiesenthal's two weapons before the others noticed. But the Germans did find Wiesenthal's partisan drawings and over a hundred sketches of the Lvov ghetto and the Janowska camp, which he had drawn during the six months of his escape.

Wiesenthal was beaten up and, with the others, was bundled off to the police station. Immediately he thought of suicide. In his Yad Vashem memoir, he explained that even though the Germans had not found his revolvers, he was convinced that he would be interrogated about his period with the partisans, and about the documents he had on his person. He was sure he would be tortured and doubted that he would be able to remain silent. Since he knew the dispositions of the partisans, and feared that he would betray them, he felt it was his duty to do away with himself.

He told a woman, Lola Friedman, who had been hidden with him, what he planned to do. She protested, telling him that he still had plenty of time to die. They were taken to the Janowska concentration camp. As a former inmate, he still had his original – low – prisoner number, 504: 'I felt like a museum piece.' For a few days the SS ignored him. Then a sudden instruction came for him to get into a prison car. Together with some other prisoners, he was taken to the Gestapo headquarters in Lvov. A notorious SS officer, Oskar Waltke appeared, gleefully declaring how he relished the prospect of finding out how tough Wiesenthal was. It was obvious that torture lay ahead. Wiesenthal still had a razor blade on him and cut his wrists. By the time they reached the prison yard, he had lost consciousness and was bleeding heavily.

'You lost 2,800 grams of blood,' the prison doctor told him, and he very nearly died. Since Jews were almost never given treatment, Wiesenthal was surprised when he was taken to the prison's hospital cell, and a real effort was made to save his life. He believes this happened because the Germans had discovered the partisan maps he had drawn and wanted to interrogate him further.

He was in the hospital for almost five weeks. Wiesenthal is still haunted by the memory of 'Waltke, who was chief of the SS's Jewish Affairs section in Lvov. He came every day, warning that he was only waiting for my health to improve so that "we can talk better". I knew that he had been responsible for hanging the whole of Lvov's *Judenrat*, one of the Jewish councils which the Nazis had set up to supervise the ghettoes in Polish cities. Waltke even made the Jews pay for the ropes. I have the evidence — receipts which I managed to unearth after the war.' Wiesenthal succeeded in tracing Waltke after the war and had him arrested. He was tried and given an eight-year sentence.

Waltke's prison visits were so sinister that Wiesenthal made two more suicide attempts. The first time he managed to steal a bottle of pills and swallowed all one hundred of them, without knowing what they were. 'I just assumed that so many pills would have the desired effect.' He still laughs when he recalls that the supposedly deadly drug turned out to be saccharin. However, taken in such quantities, even saccharin could be a killer. But before they could be absorbed, the pills made him sick, leaving him only with a bitter aftertaste. One more little miracle that proves to Wiesenthal that he was meant to survive.

The second time he tried to hang himself. It was now mid-July 1944. He had twisted his trousers into a kind of rope and had stood on a chair to fasten it to the window-frame of his tiny skylight. Then he tried to put a sling around his neck and kick the chair away. But he was too weak. 'My veins had not yet mended, and I just fell down.' He had fainted before he could have a second try. After that incident, his hands were handcuffed together and he was immobilised.

While Wiesenthal had been in the prison hospital, the Soviet offensive was gathering momentum and Soviet forces closed in on Lvov. On 19 July – as it turned out, a week before the Red Army took Lvov – the prison inmates, including those in the hospital, were brought to the prison yard, where the SS and the Gestapo were waiting for them. Waltke was amongst them. 'It was eleven o'clock in the morning. Suddenly, Soviet planes swooped overhead. Bombs fell, throwing up a great cloud of dust. Papers scattered. In the general mêlée, the Gestapo took shelter. I darted across to the small group of Jews.'

In his Yad Vashem account, Wiesenthal spoke of his overwhelming feeling that day that, if he had to die, he longed to be in a mass grave with Jews and not with Russians, Ukrainians or black marketeers. As the Gestapo were sorting out their victims, he remained with the Jewish group. They were first pushed back from the Gestapo prison yard inside the building. Then there was another bomb alert. A police car with sirens drove around. After an hour the alert was over. The Jews were ordered to return to the yard and were transported back to the Janowska concentration camp.

With the Soviets now so close, the camp was being closed and installations destroyed. Most of the prisoners had already been killed, or else dispatched to other concentration camps. Wiesenthal, with his apparently detailed knowledge of the underground, did not believe he would be allowed to leave Janowska alive a second time. He urged the camp commandant, Friedrich Warzok, to shoot him at once. 'Jews cannot choose when to die,' was the response.

A group of sixteen or seventeen Jews, with Wiesenthal as leader, thought that they might be able to organise an escape during the nightly bombardments by the Russians. During those raids, the SS guards went into shelters and turned off power. This gave the prisoners cover to cut through the perimeter fence undetected. On the chosen night, some were already through when the guards began to shoot. Wiesenthal and the rest still inside the camp were lined up to be shot. They had to undress and stand naked on planks laid across a ditch, the idea being that they would fall, as they were shot, straight into a mass grave. After two and a half hours, Warzok reappeared. He had saved their lives, he declared. To escape from the Russians, they would all soon be leaving Janowska and they would experience the end of the war together.

That night bombs fell around the camp. Next morning Warzok took the prisoners to the camp store. They could take anything they wanted. They felt punchdrunk, Wiesenthal remembers. 'Some took cabbages, others bread, someone took a barrel of salt, another a large wooden box full of butter. I had just picked up a crate of sweets, when one of the SS guards poured a can of petrol over it and said that now I was welcome to eat them.'

After that incident thirty-six prisoners, all that seemed to be left of Lvov's Jews, were marched to the Kleparov railway station. They could clearly hear the artillery fire of the oncoming Soviet forces. At the station the captives, with Ukrainians and Poles now also amongst them, were herded into a freight car. Were they about to be consigned to the gas chambers? Wiesenthal thought not. The reason? Because a canary and a dog had been brought to the freight car with an admonition from an SS orderly that if any harm came to the bird, the prisoners would be made to suffer. Faulty logic perhaps, but Wiesenthal was proved right.

In one of those surreal situations that developed when German defeat had come to look inevitable, Warzok's SS detachment had decided to use the Jews as a way of delaying their own dispatch to the front. As long as they could claim to be guarding prisoners, they could stay clear of the fighting. So for a while the Jews became a shield for the SS. Decanted from the train at Przemysl, the SS told them that they now belonged to 'Organisation Todt', which was responsible for building fortifications for the army. They had now been designated 'non-German forced labour'. Warzok warned that anyone who admitted to being a Jew would be summarily shot.

Wiesenthal recalls the irony of being instructed to hide that they were Jews, and to take off their yellow stars. They were even given cigarettes and Schnapps. The SS guards and their captives moved on by foot, retreating from the Russian advance, seeking hiding-places in the woods. The Russians were so close that the SS whipped the prisoners to make them move faster. They caught up with a detachment of *Wehrmacht* regular soldiers, also in retreat, who protested to the SS against the whipping of the Jews. They screamed that there had been enough persecution of the Jews. It was high time that the SS experienced the real war and went to the front to fight.

Next they came across a group of fleeing ethnic Germans. Warzok confiscated their horse carts, so that now they could stop walking. Each cart had two Jews and one SS guard. Then the SS decided that they needed more prisoners to justify their claim that they had to guard prisoners rather than fight on the front. So they surrounded a church at Dobromil and took more people. Now there were five hundred of them.

Approaching Sanok, Warzok's motley band found themselves competing for priority across a bridge with a contingent of *Wehrmacht* tanks. Warzok drew his pistol and told the commanding *Wehrmacht* officer, a major, that the horse carts had priority. The Russians were less than a mile away. The

SS and their prisoners went ahead; the bridge, having been mined, was blown up by Warzok when all were safely across. The tanks were on the wrong side, already being overwhelmed by the Russians.

Wiesenthal admits that this must seem stranger than fiction, but says his story was corroborated after the war during the interrogation of one of the SS guards involved in these events.

It all became still more surreal. The group pitched camp near Grybow, about thirty-five miles away from the front. A large field was designated 'SS building site Venus', and Wiesenthal was told to paint a suitable sign board. Nobody knew what this was supposed to signify.

It was September now. One afternoon Wiesenthal was taken aside by an SS corporal, whose name was Merz. Together they went scavenging for food and found two sacks of potatoes. Then Merz suggested that they should rest for a moment and there ensued one of those exchanges that left an indelible mark on Wiesenthal. He recalls it with the same urgency – though not the same anguish – as his discovery soon after the war of the book with the 'Do not forget us. And do not forget our murderers' message from the rabbi's sister who knew she was about to be killed by the Nazis. Now, at Grybow, Merz said to Wiesenthal: 'Suppose you were taken on a magic carpet to the United States, what would you tell them? How it was in the concentration camps? How they treated the Jews?' Wiesenthal hesitated. If he gave the wrong response, he might be shot on the spot. He opted for frankness. 'I believe I would tell the truth,' he said.

Merz replied: 'They would think you are crazy. They would never believe you.'

There and then Wiesenthal made up his mind that, if he survived, he would make sure that the world would know, and would be given proof, that the Nazi atrocities really had taken place; that there would be no revision of history.

The group was again on the move. Warzok was trying to reach Slovakia. He could no longer prevent some of the Jews from escaping. Wiesenthal decided against escape. He calculated that at this juncture he was probably safer with the SS than roaming around on his own. On the way to Zakopane, Warzok took the prisoners to a remote clearing and instructed them to build anti-tank defences – no matter that they were working on a dead-end road, where the Russians were unlikely to pass. To the SS, it seemed a good enough subterfuge to keep them away from the fighting. They remained there for about two weeks.

So far in the war Wiesenthal had not had first-hand experience of death camps and only knew by rumour about the killing machines in the extermination camps. This lacuna was now about to be remedied.

Still seeking to distance themselves from the Russians, the SS had moved the group on again, edging closer to Cracow. Here Warzok's subterfuge was finally exposed on 15 September 1944. SS officers from Cracow found Warzok with his men and his prisoners. They immediately recognised what was going on and they removed the Jews. Some were shot straightaway. The rest, Simon Wiesenthal included, were taken to Plaszow concentration camp, which still held several thousand Jews. This notorious camp was in every way as brutal as has been depicted in Steven Spielberg's *Schindler's List*, but in the autumn of 1944, with the area about to be taken by the Red Army, the SS was trying to erase evidence of some of the worst excesses. Wiesenthal was detailed to work in a special commando that had to dig bodies out of mass graves and burn them. They built pyres, alternating bodies and layers of wooden planks. Their sleeping quarters were close by. The stench was so terrible that sleep was impossible.

On 15 October, the Jewish inmates who were still alive at Plaszow — men, women and children — were all loaded into trains bound for nearby Auschwitz. After three days of waiting for space to dispose of them in the gas chambers, they were moved on to Gross-Rosen, a concentration camp near Wroclaw, close to a large stone quarry.

'There was no work for us there. So we became a so-called "*Steh-Kommando*". That means we had to stand still in front of a barrack, all day long. Inside the barracks at night, there was no space for us. We had to sleep sitting hunched up, leaning against the legs of the person behind us. Then I was detailed to peel potatoes. So I could eat a few raw potatoes — and still I had to be careful that nobody would notice. On the way back to the barrack, I noticed an onion on the ground. I hate onions. But I took it all the same. And the next day, I ate it with a tiny piece of bread . . . yes, such are memories. . . .'

During his potato-peeling, Wiesenthal encountered a newly arrived prisoner, who had been brought from Warsaw. This was just after the Warsaw uprising and Wiesenthal asked the man if he had known any of the people in Topiel Street (where Wiesenthal's wife was hidden) and whether he had met 'Irena Kowalska', who lived at number 5. The answer was brutal: he did not recognise the name, and, in any event, the whole street had been blown up by the Germans; nobody could have survived. The street had to be a mass grave. From that moment on, Wiesenthal says, he assumed that his wife was dead.

'Then they decided to punish me, because I had looked at an SS man and failed to greet him. He wrote down my number, and that same evening

I was assigned to the punishment brigade to work, barefoot, in the quarry. This was usually made up of 100 prisoners. When we set out in the morning, the guard at the gate to the quarry shouted out: "Ninety-nine will be returning." At first I didn't understand what that meant. The man next to me explained: "It means that one of us has to be killed." Then I heard a scream. Now we were the required ninety-nine. On the fifth or sixth day, they said that only ninety-six should return at the end of the day. So several of us would have to be killed.

'And now there was another miracle. I felt instinctively that I was to be the next victim. My executioner was behind me, poised to smash my head with a rock. I turned around, and the man, surprised, dropped his stone. It crushed my toe. I screamed. That saved my life, because there was some kind of an inspection – I think by the International Red Cross – and they were told there had been an industrial accident. A stretcher appeared, and I was taken to the first aid station. The doctor there was one of the prisoners. I looked for him after the war, but never managed to discover whether he survived. He told me that my toe would have to be amputated, but that he had no anaesthetics.

'So they laid me down on a table; tied me to it. Two people sat at either end to hold me still. They put some tissue paper under my foot, and then he just cut off my toe.

'Then they put me into a room with many other sick people. Next day I developed a high fever. The pain was terrible. The doctor came back, and saw that I had a septic blister on the sole of my foot. So they cut it open, and the gangrene spurted all over the room. ... But now comes the evacuation: One of the Kapos [orderlies co-opted by the Germans to act as their auxiliaries and "rewarded" with minor privileges, often drawn from the criminal elements among the camp's inmates, but some of them Jewish], his name was Granitsch and he came from Vienna, came to us and said, "Dear friends, they have already mined the first aid station (to destroy it before the Red Army reached Gross-Rosen). Those capable of walking should get dressed." And Granitsch turned to me with the sleeve of an old coat, which he wrapped round my foot with wire. It passed for a shoe over my bad foot. Somebody else, I don't remember who it was, brought me a broomstick, and so I managed to hobble out.

'From Gross-Rosen – it was either 7 or 8 January – we went in the direction of Chemnitz. Each day we covered around twenty miles. We slept in the snow, and during a march that lasted four to five days all we had by way of sustenance was one kilo of bread each. There were 6,000 prisoners at the outset of the march. Only 4,800 were left by the time we were loaded into open railway wagons. We had neither food nor water. People died, frozen into statues. We tried to throw them off; or else we used the bodies as benches to sit on them. That's how we arrived in Buchenwald. There they took us to the so-called "small camp", where there was only straw. They put us down on to it. We lay there for about a week.'

The war was now in its final phase. German defeat was certain, with US and British forces advancing on Germany and Austria from the west and racing against the Red Army advancing from the east. And yet, even though Auschwitz and several over death camps had already fallen to the Russians, the Nazis continued the killing in the camps that remained in their control.

On a bitterly cold day, 3 February 1945, with the Red Army close, the prisoners from Buchenwald were again piled on to open rail trucks and moved slowly on. Their destination, for those who would survive, was Mauthausen. This notorious camp in Austria, built soon after the *Anschluss*, had initially housed political prisoners; afterwards it was expanded as a concentration camp to supply slave labour for the war effort and was later equipped with gas chambers and crematoria. The last consignment of prisoners arrived at Mauthausen railway station on 9 February 1945. Wiesenthal was amongst them, the tattered foot bandages put on a month earlier at Gross-Rosen still serving him as makeshift shoes.

A count was made on reaching Mauthausen; now there were only 1,100–1,200 left of the original Gross-Rosen 6,000. They were starving. It was three in the morning when the train decanted them. The snow lay thick on the ground. Everything else was pitch-black. They could not see the fortress-like Mauthausen camp sited high up on the hill above. A perilous two-and-a-half-mile march up a narrow, winding path lay ahead. Prisoners were ordered to move in groups of five, and were surrounded by camp guards and snarling dogs.

'Shots were constantly ringing out around us. Those who stumbled and fell were simply killed. About 180 died on that march from the railway station to the camp entrance. I owe it to another prisoner, Count Radziwill, that I was kept on the move. He was at my side, holding me up, hectoring me to ignore the pain and keep moving. After a while, I was just too tired to go on. We sat down to rest. An SS guard, seeing us down, sent a shot flying between us.'

The pair dozed and would undoubtedly have frozen to death but for another fortuitous happening. A lorry from the Mauthausen crematorium, on early morning duty to collect the dead, spotted Wiesenthal and Radziwill, picked them up for dead and delivered them to the crematorium. Just in time, the two unthawed. In his Yad Vashem account, Wiesenthal said that the two managed to make their way to the building next door, the bathhouse. There Wiesenthal finally took off his makeshift bandage. His badly swollen foot was blue-green, badly infected right up to his knee. A Yugoslav prisoner, a doctor, saw the emaciated figure and marked Wiesenthal's chest with the symbol used at Mauthausen to indicate that a prisoner was dying and ready for dumping in the camp's death block to await the end.

And so it was that Wiesenthal arrived in Room B of Block vi. The crowded barrack was filled with the smell of death, but Wiesenthal was too ill to take it all in. To the extent that he was still capable of thought in his hungry, befuddled state, he did not imagine that he had many more days of life in himself. And he certainly had no way of knowing that he would still be around three months later when Mauthausen was at last liberated.

[5]
Liberation

Mauthausen is close to Linz in upper Austria. The landscape is gentle, lush and green. Once a hiker's paradise, under the Nazis it became the '*Totenberg*', the mountain of death. When General Patton's forces reached it on 5 May 1945, it was the very last extermination camp to be liberated.

The camp was on high ground above the fruit orchards on the north side of the Danube. Like Auschwitz, had Category 3 classification, the top-grade extermination camp classification, and had four sub-camps nearby at Gusen, St Valentin, Gunskirchen and Ebensee. Mauthausen provided slave labour for a Messerschmidt arms factory and for the Wienergraben granite quarries, which had traditionally supplied Vienna with its paving stones, but was designated by the Nazis as an SS property to supply granite for the monumental buildings that Hitler wanted for his future metropolis, Linz. Enfeebled prisoners had to stagger down 138 steps merely to reach the quarry. Anyone seen stumbling was beaten, often killed. At one end of the Mauthausen perimeter, there is a cliff reaching to the quarry below, where countless prisoners, their physical strength exhausted, were hurled to their death down 'parachutists' wall'.

Mauthausen was divided into several stations. Red triangles were worn by political prisoners; yellow by the Jews. Other categories of prisoners in the camp included 'ordinary criminals': Gypsies, homosexuals, Jehovah's Witnesses and Spanish Republicans. Towards the end of 1944, Adolf Eichmann dispatched 10,000 Hungarian Jews to Mauthausen, who were housed in tents. In the bitter cold, there were no trousers, only shorts for them to wear.

Himmler had personally chosen the site in 1938. To mark one of his visits, 1,000 Dutch Jews were thrown down 'parachutists' wall'. Eichmann and other leading Nazis also took a close interest in Mauthausen and came on inspections. It became a show-place, a model way of using and disposing of slave labour. The first furnaces began operations in 1941, but there were also many killings by shooting, even by axe, and some victims were thrown down to the quarry while still alive. Mobile gas vans, known at the time as 'gas mines', and later replaced by gas chambers, were used in Mauthausen from 1942. That year, the *Sunday Times* and the *Daily Telegraph* both carried reports of tortures there, but the full import of what was happening was not understood in Britain and no serious attention was paid to the allegations.

In any event, at that stage outsiders were unaware that the camp also had close links with nearby Renaissance Schloss Hartheim, one of the Nazi 'euthanasia' establishments where horrific human experiments and pilot projects on mass extermination were carried out under the guise of mercy killing. Its gas chambers, though relatively small-scale, could be used to dispose of prisoners when Mauthausen itself ran out of capacity. No prisoner ever emerged alive from Hartheim. However, in December 1944, as part of the Nazi effort to eradicate evidence of their euthanasia experiments, Mauthausen prisoners were brought to restore Hartheim to its former appearance, and by the time the Allies arrived, this notorious place had been turned into a children's home.

While the Nazis had attempted in other extermination camps to destroy at least some of the traces of their activities before the Allied forces reached the sites, in Mauthausen the killing continued unabated right up to the arrival of the Americans. During the last chaotic months of the war, as more prisoners arrived from the concentration camps in the east, bodies were piled outside the blocks and even inside the huts. Plans were made to drive the 30,000 prisoners at Ebensee into underground tunnels already packed with explosives and to blow them up. But the prisoners, sensing that relief was close, refused to enter. The SS guards, more eager now to save their own skins than to kill still more prisoners, abandoned the tunnel scheme.

Even so, more than 30,000 deaths were recorded by the SS in Mauthausen between January and May 1945, and the Americans, when they reached the camp, were horrified to count at least 10,000 bodies in a communal grave. During the whole history of Mauthausen, only one child out of the hundreds that were brought there is known to have survived.

In February 1945, when Wiesenthal became a Mauthausen inmate, the gas chamber was working round the clock at full capacity. Day and night there was a great cloud of smoke from the crematorium. The inmate of Block VI, the death block where Wiesenthal had been put, were too sick to be capable of work. They had only one task: each day to remove the dead to make space for newcomers.

Wiesenthal believes that yet again luck was on his side. 'The block had been built to house animals, not human beings. It was so overcrowded that the bunks on which the prisoners had to exist were in three layers. It was worst for those who had to sleep on the bottom tier. The stench was terrible. But I was put on the top bunk next to a window, and so at least there was a little fresh air. The SS did not bother with us as they expected us to die anyhow. All they wanted was to find out each day how many had died. Every morning, a Kapo came in to make the count. The "blockwriter" gave him the information. During March, out of 1,500 in the block, 930 died. They were replaced with new arrivals.

'The daily diet was a bowl of watery soup, and a small piece of bread that was usually already stale and mouldy. The hunger was almost unbearable.' Occasionally, they were allowed a short time outside the huts and they would throw themselves on the ground tearing up the odd blades of grass they could see. They devoured them like cattle.

'I had virtually given up all hope of staying alive. And then, one morning, a food-bearer came in and asked whether there was anyone among us who could draw. I was lying on the plank I shared with three others – there was so little space that we had to sleep in turns, two at a time – and I answered with a weak voice that yes, I could draw.'

The man – his name was Eduard Staniszewski – moved further into the block to identify the voice and told Wiesenthal that he needed a beautiful drawing with a special dedication as a birthday presentation for the 'Ober-Kapo', the head Kapo. This was another life-saving miracle, Wiesenthal asserts. In a camp whose inmates were kept at starvation level, Staniszewski gave him a little extra food; not much, but enough to sustain him so as to be able to draw. By way of advance payment for the birthday commission, Wiesenthal was given a large piece of bread and, luxury of luxuries, a piece of sausage. Then Staniszewski moved him to a better sleeping space, where he only had to share with one other man. When that man died, Wiesenthal was allowed to keep the plank for himself.

Staniszewski kept on returning with more orders for birthday and name-day drawings, and paid for them with food. Even though Wiesenthal's big frame had deteriorated into a weakened bag of bones, that little extra, combined with his determination and refusal to give up, was enough to ward off death. When Wiesenthal visited Poland in 1994, he spoke eloquently of the debt he owed Staniszewski, a debt he would never be able to repay.

As Wiesenthal languished in the death bunks, he managed to persuade one of the guards to give him some scraps of paper and Staniszewski even brought a few old magazines. One of the camp doctors, who occasionally ventured in to survey the human wreckage, gave him pencils. Wiesenthal now embarked on a series of gruesome concentration camp cartoons and collages. Some of these he managed to save for publication after the war. One depicted the guard towers at the entrance to the camp, the entire walls stuccoed with skulls; another entitled 'Diabolical symphony of Mauthausen' has an SS officer with whip instead of conductor's baton, which he is pointing at prisoners, strung up on the music lines. Yet another, of an almost benign-looking mask of Hitler, with beneath it the SS death-head, its prominent teeth snarling with menace, was used for the cover of the Italian edition of Wiesenthal's book, *The Murderers Amongst Us*.

Wiesenthal drew several more Mauthausen cartoons soon after the camp's liberation. Some were at the request of the American soldiers who wanted 'souvenirs' of the horrors they had found in the camp. But he assembled the most telling cartoons, and improved on the collages, for a slim volume, *KZ Mauthausen*, published in 1946. Wiesenthal has always denied allegations that, far from drawing cartoons while he was still a Mauthausen prisoner, he plagiarised photographs taken for *Life* magazine after the war's end. He says that such claims are all part of the character assassinations orchestrated against him from certain quarters in the United States.

The cartoons have a startling immediacy of concentration camp suffering and of the victims' bitterness. They certainly demonstrate Wiesenthal's solid ability as a draughtsman and satirist. But it was virtually the last time that he exercised those gifts. In tandem with his refusal to return to his architect's profession, he also denied himself the satisfaction he had always derived from satirising the cruelties of an anti-Semitic world.

Wiesenthal no longer knows the whereabouts of the originals of his Mauthausen cartoons. But he is aware of at least one American who tried to peddle three of his cartoons to the Wiesenthal Centre in Los Angeles for $20,000 each. Alerted to this, Wiesenthal was upset; his concentration camp cartoons were not to be desecrated as market investments. A friend afterwards acquired them for the Centre, but for much less money: 'I wanted something of all this to survive.'

During those weeks as a prisoner at Mauthausen, Wiesenthal lost track of time and often of all reality outside his dreadful surroundings. And yet he tried to discipline his mind and memory, and to chronicle the excesses he had experienced or witnessed and list the rank and names of their perpetrators. He had done this before, when he was with the partisans. Even though weak and far more debilitated, his exceptional memory remained in good working order. He could not have known that the list in his mind's eye was to be his passport to the US War Crimes Office and to his new life in quest of Nazi criminals.

Lying on his bunk, Wiesenthal's thoughts wandered back over his life, and especially over the tribulations of the last four years. He saw most of it as through a haze. At times he must have hallucinated. One prophetic happening stood out above all else: an encounter, which he thought had occurred during his time at the Janowska concentration camp, with a dying, blinded SS officer. The man's head was swathed in bandages, and only his eyes were visible as he gave his name and his mother's address, and confessed to Wiesenthal with graphic detail how he had gunned down Jews fleeing from a house set on fire by his SS unit. He told this to a stranger because he wanted to be forgiven by a Jew. Without an answer, the SS officer said that he could not die in peace. 'I have longed to talk to a Jew and beg forgiveness of him,' Wiesenthal remembered hearing. 'Only I didn't know whether there were any Jews left. I know what I am asking is almost too much for you, but without your answer I cannot die in peace.'

Wiesenthal, who had not witnessed this man's crimes, and had not personally suffered at his hands, walked away from the hospital bed without responding. He could not ease the dying man's last hours. He had felt unable even to consider an act of forgiveness.

But was his reaction determined, he asked himself over and over again, by the precepts of his Jewish teaching, which, in sharp distinction to Christianity, dictates that forgiveness is generally reserved for God alone and not for humankind? Even where there is recognition of wrongdoing, Jews believe that man is not entitled to act alone, or on God's behalf, to grant absolution – the only exception being forgiveness by a victim to the actual perpetrator. It could not be administered by proxy. Even so, Wiesenthal tortured himself with the thought that his refusal to give absolution reflected a desire for revenge. Were the Nazi crimes so heinous that any notion of forgiveness had to be automatically dismissed? Would forgiveness have been possible if the SS man had not been dying, and could have been made to atone for his sins? Had he, Wiesenthal, shown a lack of compassion? But should compassion even be allowed to enter the equation? Why is there no general law of guilt and expiation? Has every religion its own ethics, its own answers?

Much later in life, Wiesenthal could only guess whether it all happened precisely the way it registered with him at Mauthausen, but he never doubted that an encounter with the German officer, and a challenge of the kind he recalled, had taken place. What matters is Wiesenthal's perception of a single unique happening that humbled him and persuaded him to question the moral imperatives that had guided him so far. It was about the relationship between perpetrator and victim, about the nature of forgiveness, about faith and about loss of hope, about contradictions and confusion.

He had memorised the officer's name and, in 1946, he even sought out the officer's mother in Stuttgart. In the 1960s, prodded by the prevailing debate about forgiveness, Wiesenthal decided to write about his strange wartime encounter. In 1969, his book, *The Sunflower*, was published, where the deathbed scene becomes a parable for a moral dilemma that Wiesenthal found impossibly hard to resolve for himself. Written in one burst, Wiesenthal has always considered it his most important book; both because of the questions that it poses, and because it seeks to demolish what he sees as a 'widespread perception of the Jew as a hater. I set out to show that if Jews do not forgive, it is because they are not empowered to do so, because forgiveness, they believe, is for God alone to decide. ... In writing *The Sunflower*, I followed my instinct, rather than any long-drawn-out reflections,' Wiesenthal explains. The book was translated into several languages, including French, German, Italian and Japanese, and has remained in print.

The sunflower itself is part of the tale's symbolism: marching with other prisoners in Lvov between concentration camp and workplace, he saw the sunflowers growing over by the graves of Lvov's military cemetery:

> My gaze wandered from the sunflower to the grave. It seemed to penetrate the earth, and suddenly I saw before me a periscope. It was gaily coloured and butterflies fluttered from flower to flower. Were they carrying messages from grave to grave? Were they whispering something to each flower to pass on to the soldier below? Yes, this was what they were doing; the dead were receiving light and messages.
>
> Suddenly I envied the dead soldiers. Each had a sunflower to connect him with the living world and butterflies to visit his grave. For me there would be no sunflower. I would be buried in a mass grave, where corpses would be piled on top of me. No sunflower could ever bring light into darkness, and no butterflies would dance above my dreadful tomb.

Christians believe in the resurrection, but for a Jew, the grave is his last and also his perpetual home. That is why Wiesenthal always stresses that, for a Jew, the significance of his sunflower image is so important.

The sunflower theme recurs when Wiesenthal writes of the deathbed scene. The SS man tells him that he comes from Stuttgart and is just twenty-one years old.

> I stared at his bandaged head. I didn't know (yet) what he wanted to confess, but I knew for sure that after his death a sunflower would grow on his grave. Already a sunflower was turning towards the window, the window through which the sun was sending its rays into the death chamber. Why was the sunflower already

making its appearance? Because it would accompany him to the cemetery, stand on his grave and sustain his connection to life. And this I envied him. I envied him also because in his last moments he was able to think of a mother, alive and able to grieve for him.

In the book, Wiesenthal describes a picnic in the hills near Linz. About a year had gone by since the war's end. 'As I looked around I suddenly saw behind me a bush and behind the bush a sunflower. I stood up and slowly walked towards it. I saw other sunflowers there and at once became lost in thought. I remembered the soldiers' cemetery in Lvov, the hospital and the dead SS man on whose grave the sunflower would now be growing.' Those sunflowers revived his preoccupation with that 'haunting episode in the hospital at Lvov'. He asks, 'Had I anything to reproach myself for?', and determines to go to Stuttgart to the man's family. At the back of his mind once again was the question whether he could or should have dispensed forgiveness in response to the dying man's pleas. Would he find an answer by meeting the man's family? Should he tell them about the encounter?

Wiesenthal reacted to the man's mother with a certain pity, and in his book, he describes how he could not bring himself to shatter the old woman's illusions about her dead son's inherent goodness. So, for the second time, he remained silent:

And how many bystanders kept silent as they watched Jewish men, women and children being taken to the slaughterhouses of Europe? There are many kinds of silence. Indeed, it can be more eloquent than words, and it can be interpreted in many ways.

Was my silence by the bedside of the dying Nazi right or wrong? This is a profound moral question that challenges the reader of this episode just as it once challenged my heart and my mind. There are those who can sympathise with my dilemma and so endorse my attitude, and others who will be ready to condemn me for refusing to ease the last moments of a repentant murderer. The crux of the matter is, of course, the question of forgiveness. Forgetting is something that time alone takes care of, but forgiveness is an act of volition, and only the sufferer is qualified to make the decision.

Can crimes against humanity be allowed to rest quietly, perhaps forgotten, beneath the sunflower?

With that, Wiesenthal throws it open to his readers to change places with him and ask themselves the crucial question: 'What would I have done?'

Before publishing the story, he sent his manuscript to some of the more eminent thinkers of the time, those who were preoccupied by the moral and ethical issues raised by the Holocaust. These included Primo Levi, Albert Speer, Salvador de Madriaga, Herbert Marcuse, Hannah Arendt, Léopold Sédar Senghor, Canon John Östreicher, Jacob Kaplan and Friedrich Torberg. But Eli Wiesel, who has written so extensively on the theme of forgiveness in the context of the Holocaust, did not respond to the request to comment, Wiesenthal says.

Those who did respond to Wiesenthal's request took the sunflower tale seriously as a parable that posed fundamental issues in a memorable, accessible form. It also helped to place Wiesenthal in the forefront of those who were determined to raise awareness of the Holocaust and its significance for contemporary politics.

The replies, incorporated in *The Sunflower* as a symposium, offer a rainbow of views on the book's challenges. Most of the contributors, including some prominent Roman Catholics, for a variety of reasons felt that Wiesenthal had acted correctly and should not have responded with forgiveness to the dying soldier's plea. Even had he done so, it would have been a lie, Primo Levi asserted. But the responses also suggest a general feeling that no one should presume to put his or her person in Wiesenthal's place under the circumstances he had described. Only he could solve his dilemma.

Wiesenthal has sought to deal with it by circumventing the issue of forgiveness with the precept of 'justice not vengeance', which he maintains has guided his actions and his attitude throughout his pursuit of Nazi criminals.

At the beginning of May 1945, unaware that the Americans were already close, Wiesenthal hardly dared to imagine that he could still emerge alive. Repeatedly he dreamed about the SS officer with all those bandages enveloping his head. Waking up once, he saw a man, his head bandaged, lying next to him in the bunker. Wiesenthal began to shake. The other man, a Christian, demanded to know why. So he told him the sunflower story. The response was unequivocal: 'You have committed a great sin. The SS man showed remorse, and you did not forgive.' Wiesenthal replied that as a Jew, who had not been directly harmed by the SS man, it was surely understandable that he had hesitated to forgive. Long afterwards, even in his old age, he still regrets this 'eternal dispute between the religions'.

Wiesenthal weighed a mere 99 lbs when, on 5 May 1945, US Colonel Richard Seibel led units of the 11th Armoured Division into Mauthausen. The area had been destined for the Soviet zone, but the Americans reached the concentration camp just ahead of the Red Army and stayed in possession for five weeks. Then, as part of the four-power division of Austria, the Mauthausen area was transferred under the jurisdiction of the Soviet zone of occupation. Wiesenthal's life would surely have gone very differently if he had been liberated into Soviet hands. It is doubtful that the Russians would have acted as the Americans did to restore his health, or that he would have been allowed to participate in the search for Nazi murderers.

Colonel Seibel found the camp 'in bedlam' with prisoners running amok. A Russian camp inmate, a major, was in the commandant's seat, insisting that he had taken over command and had established a tribunal for the execution of certain Kapos. A pistol had to be pointed at the major's head before he was persuaded to leave for the Russian lines behind Mauthausen. It was not until dusk that Seibel could turn his attention to the chaos confronting him, and it was only next morning that he realised just how awful, how harrowing the situation was.

The horror, for which nothing had prepared Seibel, has never left him. Though his Californian background had nothing in common with that of Wiesenthal's, he has carried with him throughout a long life the same sense of urgency to make the world understand the crimes perpetrated by the Nazis. Before his demobilisation, when he saw the beginnings of concerted efforts to play down the Holocaust, even to question whether mass extermination had occurred, the Colonel acted 'to clarify certain confusion regarding the capture and liberation of Mauthausen'. He set out for his army superiors 'the highlights' of the scenes that so shocked him and his troops. This eyewitness document alone should be enough to silence Wiesenthal's critics, who assert that he has grossly exaggerated the brutality of Mauthausen, and who use this argument to build up their allegations against Wiesenthal as a liar and a hypocrite. Seibel wrote:

> Here were thousands of people who had been starved, beaten and cruelly tortured, suddenly free. They had no food, no sanitation, clothing or electricity. The tension that existed was unbelievable and erupted the next day with a riot in which four Kapos were executed by having their throats cut by the prisoners. ... After we were able to bring some order to the camp, it was found there were approximately 18,000 prisoners representing 20 nations ... but 1,500 were beyond help and died in the first few days.

Seibel described how they slowly fed the survivors with thin soup and bread to prevent their digestive systems from 'going into shock'. The German commandant of Mauthausen, Franz Ziereis, had tried to escape, but was caught by the Americans and later executed. 'Throughout the interrogation he denied any wrongdoing.' But Seibel added that,

> the crematoria did in fact exist, as I personally viewed them and could not believe

man's inhumanity to man where prisoners would be sprayed with firehose in winter and left to die from exposure. I viewed the gas chambers where people were packed so tightly they couldn't move and little children were thrown on top of their heads before they were gassed. I saw the dissection rooms and the cooling rooms where the bodies were stacked like planks of wood, awaiting dissection or cremation. I viewed the private execution rooms where prisoners were hanged or shot by the commandant. I saw the highly charged electric fences where prisoners, who could no longer endure the suffering, threw themselves for a swift death. I saw the bunkheads in the barracks, bunks made for one man, where prisoners so emaciated could sleep three to a bed. And I saw the people and what had been done to them and realised the severity with which they had been mistreated.

Mauthausen did exist. Man's inhumanity to man did exist. The world must not be allowed to forget the depths to which mankind can sink lest it should happen again.

To quell any remaining doubts, Seibel added as a footnote that the 'US War Crimes Commission stated that the size of the camp and the atrocities committed there were the worst they had investigated'.

Colonel Seibel is one of Simon Wiesenthal's heroes – not just because of the way he set about restoring some sense of humanity to the motley, disoriented survivors he found at Mauthausen, but above all because he restored Wiesenthal's sense of dignity and convinced him that there was purpose to his life. Wiesenthal has written movingly of Seibel in two of his books – *The Murderers Amongst Us* and *Justice Not Vengeance* – and he often speaks of him with undiminished gratitude as the man whose actions taught him that right and justice were alive and well.

Wiesenthal has always remained in touch with Seibel and made sure that he was invited as a guest of the Austrian Government to the fiftieth anniversary of Mauthausen's liberation. Seibel did indeed come, surrounded by his children and grandchildren. The place where he had once come face to face with all those heaps of skeletons and near dead was alive not merely with dignitaries but with more than 30,000 people eager to pay their respects to the survivors. It was a warm summer's day, disturbingly incongruous with the occasion's sombre memories. Seibel spoke of the Holocaust briefly in strong voice. He emphasised how unprepared he had been for the inhuman conditions he had found at Mauthausen. It remained as inexplicable to him fifty years on as it had been on that May day fifty years before. Like his friend Wiesenthal, he urged the young never to forget.

Certainly Wiesenthal has 5 May 1945 etched for ever in his consciousness.

The skeletal Wiesenthal had been lying in his bunk, surrounded by corpses that had not been removed because the SS had fled and the crematoria were at last at a standstill. He stumbled outside into the sun-drenched yard and saw a big grey tank with the American flag waving from the turret. He wanted to touch it, but he was so weak that he crumpled up in a faint and was carried back to his bunk. When he regained consciousness, the block had been cleaned, the bodies removed, the old stench replaced with the smell of disinfectant. And there was an American soldier with soup – real soup, not just coloured water.

'Two days after the liberation I was told that you could get passes to go out of the camp and return. The man with the passes was one of the Polish prisoners who had become camp auxiliaries. He was Kazimierz Rusinek, who later became President of the Polish Council for Culture, and held other functions in the Communist regime. Slowly, slowly I crossed the few yards to Rusinek's office and knocked on the door. He was well nourished compared to us. He looked at me and called me "you damned *Muselman*" – that's the word they had for the prisoners who were about to be consigned to the furnaces. When I asked him for a pass, he retorted that I would have been dead if the Nazis had still been there. Then he beat me and threw me out into the courtyard.

'I am free and yet I am beaten up? Next morning I told an American doctor that I wanted to be taken to the US commandant. The doctor said that I was too weak, but I told him that he and a second person must help me. So they half carried me to Colonel Seibel. He spoke no Polish, and I no English; but he had an interpreter [another Mauthausen prisoner, Prem Tobias, who became a devoted Wiesenthal friend], and so I learned that the Americans were already interrogating suspected war criminals. They were using the former commandant's office, and they brought me there.'

Colonel Seibel has retained a haunting image of Wiesenthal's appearance that day. He remembers him as 'a skeleton supported by two men; a skeleton on which hung striped pyjamas. A man who could however speak with his eyes.'

Wiesenthal found a vacant chair in the interrogation room and slumped down. 'There were two uniformed Americans, and one in civilian dress, and they brought in a number of chained SS men and questioned them. This was the US War Crimes unit at work. SS men came and went, and I was so absorbed, I completely forgot that I had come to complain about Rusinek. After a while, a German-speaking lieutenant asked me why I was there, and I explained. The American's name was Abbie Mann, and he told me that Rusinek would be fetched next morning to answer for his action.

'I asked the lieutenant whether I could stay a little longer in the interrogation room, because what I had just witnessed was the stuff of dreams, something that I would never have thought, during all the years in the camps, could happen in real life. Believe me [Wiesenthal said forty-nine years later], I still don't know how I brought myself to leave that room and go back to my bunk.

'That evening several Poles, among them a future Polish Prime Minister, Josef Cyrankiewicz, and Count Radziwill, who had all been prisoners at Mauthausen, begged me not to go ahead with my complaint against Rusinek. They didn't dispute that he had behaved badly; but surely a man who had spent years as a Mauthausen prisoner did not deserve to be lumped together with the SS people and brought before the War Crimes unit. They all said that I should be looking for Nazis, not for fellow victims.

'Next morning the desire to go back to witness the interrogations was stronger than the desire to seek Rusinek punished. I found someone to help me back, and I sat down in the same chair. Abbie Mann saw me and asked whether I had come back because someone else had beaten me up. On the contrary, I told him, I want to withdraw my accusation. The lieutenant was not amused. Do you think we are children here, playing games about wars and tribunals, he asked. I explained that so many Poles had urged me not to be vindictive against a fellow sufferer.

'Lieutenant Mann then decided that Rusinek must, at the very least, be made to give me a public apology. After half an hour he led me out to the yard. It was full of survivors, sitting in a semi-circle. I was taken to the centre, Rusinek was brought, said that he had been under great stress and this explained his actions. He apologised. The Americans asked us to shake hands. I was prepared to accept the apology, but I could not shake hands because I had no way of knowing whether he had not beaten many others. Years later, Rusinek was among the Polish Communists who mounted the slander attacks against me.

'Every day I went to watch the interrogations, and every day I asked them to let me come and work for the War Crimes unit. The Americans kept on asking me how much I weighed, and I always replied 55 kilos (about 120 lbs). They laughed. I was nowhere near that weight. I found a scrap of mirror and saw what they meant. I was as white as sugar. But, just to get rid of me, they gave me pen and paper, and said write down all you know, and then we'll think again. Back in my bunker, I listed the camps where I had been, and the names of Nazis I remembered with their rank and number and their crimes. I wrote in Polish and addressed it to Colonel Seibel. I was too tired to make a copy for myself.'

Years later, Abbie Mann, by then a scriptwriter for an American television film about Wiesenthal, went to the US National Archives in search of material and discovered the original of Wiesenthal's 1945 list. It contains ninety-one names, and Mann was told that the document was unique, no other person having been able to produce a similarly long list of Nazi criminals. Wiesenthal quotes this testimonial with exceptional pride: 'My memory in those days was excellent.'

It remained so, as did his inquisitive instincts. 'Wiesenthal's most important archive is his memory,' one of his close collaborators in Vienna maintains. Camp inmates, who had encountered him during the war years, also recall how Wiesenthal had constantly quizzed them for information about the SS killers around them. At the time, they could not understand why he was so interested. Why, at times when death seemed imminent, had he wanted to memorise the names of Nazis and their victims around him? Later they understood his passion for names and fact-finding.

Wiesenthal's Mauthausen list is dated 25 May 1945. A covering letter shows that Wiesenthal had already made up his mind that he wanted to dedicate himself to the task of bringing Nazi criminals to justice, even though he had not yet quite abandoned the thought of an eventual return to Poland. Wiesenthal wrote:

Having spent a number of years in thirteen Nazi concentration camps ... and desirous to be of help to the US authorities in their effort to bring the Nazi criminals to account, I take the liberty of submitting the following:

1 – As all the camps where I was confined are located in the zones taken by the Soviet armies, it is my conviction that those responsible for the atrocities are not to be found in the Eastern part of Europe but should be sought either in Southern or Western Germany.

2 – I enclose a brief list of those I have seen in various camps and whom I can recognise on sight. Many of these have caused incalculable sufferings to myself and my fellow inmates. Many of these I have personally seen commit murder phantastic both in number and method. As shown, some of them either had homes or relatives living in localities now under Allied occupation.

3 – With all the members of my family and of my nearest relatives killed by the Nazis, I am asking your kindness to place me at the disposal of the US authorities investigating war crimes. Although I am a Polish citizen and would like to return to my homestead, I feel that the crimes of these men are of such magnitude that no effort can be spared to apprehend them. I also feel that it is my duty to offer my services either for the purpose of furnishing the description of their misdeeds or as an eyewitness in case identification is needed.

The following is a brief list of SS men and Gestapo agents as well as Nazi Party members whom I had the opportunity of seeing to partake in murder and other crimes against human life. They are classified in this list into two groups – those who were in Galicia and those of camp Cracow-Plaszow.

In a series of one-liners, the list adds up to a profile of brutality, all the more startling because it was compiled when Wiesenthal still felt so close to these events and had not yet become acclimatised to the fact that an end had been put to the torturing. Top of the list is SS Major-General Katzmann, described by Wiesenthal as 'responsible for the death of at least one million people'. Or take Gestapo Kommissar Shöls: 'Timekeeper and schedule maker for mass killing throughout Galicia.' He names Friedrich Warzok, the Janowska camp commander, who used Wiesenthal and fellow camp inmates as a shield in the retreat from the Red Army. The document describes him as 'a beast who liquidated at least 60,000 Jews and used to burn prisoners alive in their barracks'. Amon Göth, the Plaszow camp commander, was the 'greatest killer of all. His victims ran into thousands. Master of cruelties', and Leo John, another from Plaszow, whose 'speciality – killing women and children. Victims ran into thousands.'

Wiesenthal's Plaszow listings further include SS guard Hujar, 'winner of numerous wagers by sending one bullet through two heads at a time'; another called Lied, who was a 'degenerate collector of his victims' skulls'; and Becher, who was a 'killer of the sick in hospitals'. A few guards are simply described as 'sadists'.

However, even at this juncture Wiesenthal was already anxious to put on record the names of Nazis who had behaved well. The 1945 document lists two men at the OAW at Lvov, who had shown Wiesenthal such decency during his time spent under their regime. One is Adolf Kohlrautz, who did so much to help Wiesenthal to survive, and the other is Werner Schmidt, whom he knew from the same period. 'These two men were our friends and were of great assistance in preventing many cruelties,' Wiesenthal wrote in his memorandum.

A few days later, Wiesenthal again asked Mann whether they were at last prepared to accept him to work as part of the War Crimes unit. The reply was in the affirmative. He was assigned to Captain Tarracusio, in civilian life a professor of international law at Harvard University, and together the two scoured the surrounding country in search of Nazis. In those days Nazi-hunting was easy. They were thick on the ground, and Wiesenthal was soon able to score up dozens of successful catches. It was never again going to be so straightforward.

[6]
Reunion with Cyla

'For me, there was no home to return to. Poland was a cemetery, and if I wanted to make a new life, I was not going to make it in a cemetery, where every tree, every stone reminded me of the tragedy which I had barely survived. Nor did I want to meet those who bore the guilt for our sufferings.' Still traumatised, Wiesenthal wanted to remain with his liberators in Austria.

That was his response to Colonel Seibel and Lieutenant Mann, and to anyone else who suggested that he should return to Lvov, during those first few days at liberated Mauthausen, when he was slowly recovering his physical strength and adjusting to the reality of recovered freedom. His new American friends, impressed by his camp drawings, elicited from him that he had been an architect in his previous existence. Just as the US military were counting the days before they could return home, they took it for granted that Wiesenthal would want to go back to his former home as soon as possible to pick up his life and his profession where he had left off in 1941.

Wiesenthal saw it very differently and was not to be dissuaded. He told them that his whole family had been murdered by the Nazis, and that he believed his wife had been killed during the Warsaw uprising. Galicia no longer had any meaning for him, other than menace and death and the destruction of any illusions he might once have harboured that Jews could rank there as equal citizens. It would certainly have been open to him to practise elsewhere as an architect, but he no longer had any interest in his former profession. Intuitively, he felt that he could not turn the clock back. For Wiesenthal, there was never any other option except to make good on the promise he had made to himself to concentrate on the capture and exposure of the Holocaust's perpetrators.

During those late spring days in 1945, all this was still somewhat incoherent. The shock of freedom was hard to absorb. Everything around him was in disarray. Improvisation was the order of the day among the Allied forces. The liberated camps constituted a dismal twilight-world full of human beings who were not only displaced but also disoriented, of people uncertain where to turn for their future existence. Survivors adopted many different ways of coming to terms with what they had suffered and the terrible events they had witnessed. Most of them just wanted to distance themselves physically and mentally and put the terror behind them. Many saw their salvation in Palestine, soon to be Israel.

Wiesenthal stood out as one camp inmate who knew for sure what he did not want to do, and had a good inkling of what he did want. But if anyone had asked him that summer in 1945 precisely how he envisaged his future Nazi-hunting activities, or where he would live after the American safety blanket was gone, he would certainly not have been able to give a clear answer.

First things first. He had made a start by attaching himself to the US War Crimes Office and, for the time being, he was content to go out with Captain Tarracusio in search of SS guards fleeing from Mauthausen. By origin, Tarracusio was an aristocrat from (Soviet) Georgia, who had come to the United States as a child in 1918. The two men liked and respected each other. Tarracusio understood how important it was to Wiesenthal to be allowed to make some arrests on his own. Still weak and easily exhausted, Wiesenthal had considerable difficulty in walking up the two flights of stairs of a small village house in order to arrest an SS guard from Mauthausen – only a minor figure of torment, yet never to be forgotten because he was Wiesenthal's first trophy.

The Wiesenthal–Tarracusio team turned out to be a temporary partnership. It lasted a mere three weeks, until Mauthausen was transferred to the Soviet zone and the US forces moved out. But the Americans did not abandon Wiesenthal. They allowed him to come to Linz and transfer to the OSS (the Office of Strategic Services), the American wartime intelligence group that was the precursor of the CIA (the Central Intelligence Agency). The Americans were committed to a policy of denazification and to the search for war criminals. But the OSS had also been given the task of recruiting counterintelligence agents with links to the Soviet Union and Eastern Europe's Communists. Simultaneously, the CIC (the US Counter-intelligence Corps) was trying to locate information about Nazi weapons projects and scientific developments.

As a result, even in the immediate post-war period, when denazification was still officially a top priority for the four wartime allies, the search for Nazi criminals had to compete with a hidden agenda of recruiting intelligence informants, as well as key German scientists to work in the West and prevent the Soviet Union from securing their expertise.

Wiesenthal had no direct knowledge of these other pursuits when he went to work for the OSS, but he concluded very quickly that it would be mistaken to place too much reliance on the Americans. There was both need and also room for private initiative in gathering evidence about war crimes, and tracing survivors to reunify families; he would have to organise his own network, even while he remained with the Americans. Together with a few other former Mauthausen inmates he set up a Jewish Committee of Survivors, which in turn recruited others to tour the displaced-persons camps, where the former inmates were being cared for pending resettlement. One objective was family reunification.

But Wiesenthal was also keen to document as much evidence of war crimes as possible while memories were fresh and, above all, before witnesses dispersed. So, as the Jewish Committee's members toured, they made lists of survivors and urged them to identify their Nazi tormentors and describe their crimes. People milled in and out of the two rooms in Linz where the Jewish Committee had set up shop, searching through the lists for relatives and friends, and adding new names to the lists.

And that was how once again miracles, or call it luck, worked for Simon Wiesenthal, and he discovered that his wife had survived after all and that he could trace her whereabouts. Certainly the story of their reunion is the stuff of fiction. Yet it has to be remembered that in those confused post-war months, the improbable was an everyday occurrence, with people finding each other through a series of accidental encounters that could not have been planned or even envisaged.

He had already asked his American friends if they could help find out what had happened to her. Then one evening, sifting through a list of Cracow survivors, Wiesenthal noticed the name of a lawyer, a Dr Biener from Buczacz, whom he had known before the war. On impulse Wiesenthal wrote a letter asking him to go to Warsaw to Topiel Street, where Cyla had lodged, and try to find out whether her body might still be lying beneath the ruins of the building. Then he could at least give her a burial, could plant a sunflower on her grave.

Postal services had not yet been restored, but there were plenty of smugglers and black-market dealers prepared to act as couriers. The routes to Poland were circuitous, often via Hungary and Czechoslovakia, with cigarettes, leather, weapons, gold and other valuables being traded along the way. Wiesenthal's letter reached Cracow in October 1945. Two or three days later, there was a knock on Dr Biener's door. He opened it a crack and there, pale, dishevelled but still unmistakably Cyla, was the woman whose remains he had just been asked to find in Warsaw. Taken aback, the lawyer mumbled to Cyla that she was supposed to be dead; after all, he had just received a letter from her husband telling him that, in all probability, she was under the ruins of Topiel Street.

Cyla could hardly believe what she was hearing. Just as Simon had been told by a survivor from the ghetto uprising that she must have been killed, Cyla had been told before the war's end that her husband, having disappeared in Lvov, was presumed dead. She was trying to make her way back there, to what was now the Soviet Union, for one last trawl to find out what had really happened since that day when she bade him farewell across the perimeter fence of the OAW.

Wiesenthal takes up the story, telling it in 1994, with the essentials unchanged, but with some minor variations on the version in one of his earlier books, *The Murderers Amongst Us*.

Soon after he had dispatched his letter to Dr Biener, he had persuaded one of the farmers outside Linz to let him ride a horse. 'As a young man, I had been a passionate rider. Now I weighed only around 50 kilos. I just wanted to sit on a horse for ten minutes and to discover whether I could still ride. The farmer was dubious, but sent his son for a saddle. I said that I didn't need a saddle, swung myself up and I was off. Moments later, the horse threw me and I had a broken ankle.

'My leg was set, and I was immobilised, in bed. And then suddenly, there was this totally unexpected surprise, a letter from my wife. It turned out that the Germans had rounded up some of the people in Topiel Street before they blew up the buildings. My wife's papers, given to her by the Home Army underground, were good enough to convince the Germans that they were authentic and that she was Aryan. She and other women were taken as forced labour to Solingen in Germany, where she had to work in a weapons factory. Solingen was liberated by the British early in 1945, while Mauthausen was still under SS control.

'There were several hundred Polish women in the Solingen camp. Among them were six with false papers, and they included my wife. So, these six decided they would have to make their own way back to Poland. There was no transport. They walked and hitchhiked; and just imagine, at one point they were quite close to Linz where I was. But of course, they could not have known that I was alive, let alone that I was there. In fact, before she was taken to Solingen, while she was still in Warsaw, Cyla had been told by one of the partisans to stop writing to me as he had learned I had been killed.

'But one of the Polish women kept on telling Cyla not to give up hope. If Simon was still alive, he is surely still in Lvov, my wife reasoned. So that was where she was going, when she reached Cracow in the first post-war autumn of 1945. The city was under Soviet occupation. She was told there would be a train for Lvov in four hours, and so she left her bundle of possessions at the railway station and went for a walk. Suddenly she heard her name being called out. It was a dentist she had known in Lvov. He told Cyla, that yes, he knew that Simon was dead, but was unaware of the circumstances.

'Normally, he might have been able to find out from his Home Army contacts exactly what had happened. But being considered undesirable bourgeois, the Soviets were trying to track down all the Home Army elements, and my wife's dentist friend did not dare to get in touch with them. He advised her to go to Dr Biener, who might know more. He gave her the address, and as there was no transport, she trudged across the city to find the house.

'Once Dr Biener had overcome the shock of finding Cyla alive, he showed her my letter. But she continued to assert that I was dead, and even said that she couldn't recognise the handwriting as mine. Dr Biener told her to forget about her belongings at the station and remain with him until matters could sort themselves out. Together they wrote a letter and sent it, again by courier, to the Jewish Committee in Linz.

'I was still nursing my broken ankle when the letter arrived. I could barely move, but I managed to go down and call Captain O'Meara, my superior at the OSS office. I told him that I had to get to Poland; but of course I was hampered by my physical condition. The Captain's solution was to suggest that I find someone who was anyhow travelling to Poland and could bring my wife the entry permit into the US zone and other documentation that she would need to join me.

'I knew a Dr Weissberg, a man who had lost his wife in Auschwitz and who was intent on returning to Poland. I told him that I had a little money to help pay his travel costs. There were still no trains to Poland, and he hitchhiked on a lorry. Weissberg was warned that the Soviets usually made very thorough searches at their control posts to the Soviet zone. Only a few days earlier, another man, who had been travelling with English documents, had been arrested as a spy. So with the exception of his personal travel documents, Weissberg tore up all the papers he was carrying. Cyla's US zone entry pass was destroyed, along with Cyla's Cracow address.

'As it happened, Weissberg was not searched; he was just waved through and arrived in Cracow unharmed, but no longer knew how to find Cyla.

Next day, he went to the Jewish Committee in the town and put up a notice asking for the whereabouts of Mrs Wiesenthal, whose husband was in Linz and was searching for her to rejoin him.

'A few weeks later, in December, Weissberg returned to Linz. He came to see me, alone, told me the saga of the lost address and said that three women had come forward in response to his advertisement, each claiming to be Cyla Wiesenthal. The promise of getting to Austria must have seemed a deliverance to them, an opportunity to get away from Poland and perhaps go on to the United States. Weissberg told me that he had decided to bring one of the trio. He had chosen the one he liked best; so that if she turned out not to be my wife, he would perhaps marry her.

'I asked him where the woman was. Downstairs, was the reply. So I asked Weissberg to bring her to my room. And as soon as I saw her, I told Weissberg that he would have to find himself another wife. This one was mine.

'So that was the end of another chapter of my life. Miracles and more miracles; perhaps more than any human being deserved.'

Simon was almost thirty-seven years old and Cyla a few months older. They had not had a child before the war. Now they were determined to have one before it was too late. Their daughter Paulinka was born in September 1946. After their tribulations and their long separation, the child seemed like another miracle. It was one from which each of them has drawn great and lasting happiness.

Simon would have liked another child, but Cyla was opposed. Paulinka's birth had not been easy. Besides, his wife wanted to follow the ways of most of the survivors around them who were putting the Holocaust behind them and establishing a new normalcy in their lives. But her husband would not hear of it. Simon had glimpsed his vocation and was not prepared to give it up, even though he realised that Cyla felt unable to give him her active support. She loved him and could not change him. But it always felt as if she was trapped, forced against her will and inclination to live with the Holocaust in perpetuity.

Sharing life with Wiesenthal, there was no escape for Cyla from the demons of the war years except to insulate herself from his work and escape into some small world of her own. Cyla concentrated her energies on maintaining a peaceful home and on bringing up and protecting Paulinka. But unhappiness over the circumstances of her life, and fear that Wiesenthal's enemies would do physical harm to the family, often manifested itself in ill-health. This became even more pronounced in later years, after the family had moved from Linz to Vienna and Wiesenthal had stepped up his activities in defiance of a constant stream of both verbal and also physical threats. 'Of course I know that I am not an easy person to live with,' Wiesenthal acknowledges. He quotes his wife as declaring that 'I am not married to a man. I am married to thousands, or maybe millions of dead.'

Gradually the marriage acquired the appearance of an empty shell, or so at least it seems to Wiesenthal's friends. Yet, paradoxically, the couple's fierce devotion and loyalty, and their mutual dependence, remained undiminished. From the beginning, Wiesenthal had decided that he must not take his cases, or indeed any of his problems, home to his wife. He did not want to burden her, and she did not really want to know. 'I have never discussed with her what goes on in the office – whether it's positive or negative,' Wiesenthal admits. 'But it was tough to carry this load on my own, especially in the early days, and it caused me constant sleepless nights.'

As his fame and acclaim grew, Cyla's pride in his achievements was undeniable. His enemies became her enemies. When her husband's good name was under attack by Austrian Chancellor Kreisky, she responded with the same deep animosity as Simon himself. But often she also saw enemies where there were none.

Mrs Wiesenthal is only rarely prepared to demonstrate her solidarity by joining him at public functions. She always refuses to give interviews, because she suspects the motives of the journalists. Few friends are invited to their home. Pleading ill-health, she has only travelled with him on rare occasions and hardly ever accompanies him even in Austria. After Wiesenthal refused to give way to his wife's pleas to retire on his seventy-fifth birthday, she became still more reclusive, more plagued by ill-health and more dependent on him. Outside observers see them as if linked to each other by an umbilical cord, never doubting their deep mutual love – and yet incapable of giving much substance to their relationship.

Simon and Cyla do not discuss their marriage with outsiders – probably not even with each other. Nor is their daughter, Paulinka, prepared to let others intrude on the privacy of the family. She is far too loyal and devoted for indiscretions, and shares her parents' view that only Simon's public life is of interest to others and deserves to be scrutinised. Paulinka lives in Israel with her husband and grown-up children, but keeps in constant touch with her parents, telephoning almost daily and meeting them three or four times a year.

Wiesenthal has always chosen to idealise his love for his wife. He does not express criticism, never even hints that he might have preferred a more fulfilling relationship. He shows perpetual concern for her ill-health and gives the impression that life without her would be too empty for him to bear. He has always insisted that he dropped his controversial libel action against Bruno Kreisky in 1975 mainly because Cyla was close to a nervous breakdown. 'I could have gone on with the fight, left on my own. But I could not fight, with my wife at home having to be treated against depression. She refused to go and stay with our daughter, who was then still in Holland. So I had no alternative but to drop the action against Kreisky.'

When Cyla had to undergo a lengthy operation in her eighty-fifth year, her husband said the wait to know the outcome seemed as if three hours had turned into three days and more.

The nearest Wiesenthal comes to conceding that there might be something missing in his marriage is when he occasionally comments sadly how little communication is left between them. In place of meaningful partnership, the marriage only seems to have accentuated the loneliness of Wiesenthal's self-imposed mission.

It is impossible not to wonder, as some of his close friends certainly do, how Wiesenthal's work and character would have developed with a more actively involved partner as his wife. Few people know Cyla intimately, or have sought to penetrate the deeper recesses of the couple's relationship, but enough of it is visible to question whether its apparent limitations have bruised his persona. Would he have been less combative, less single-minded? Would he have been less concerned to nurture his public image? Would he have been more trusting? Less emotional? Would he have been as much of a crusader?

Or had the mould already been so firmly set during the war years that Wiesenthal was impervious to any disappointment which his marriage might have generated?

Women have always found him attractive both for his physical appearance and for the myths that have grown around him. He responds with warmth and old-world courtesy. But there has been no gossip about him: no suggestion that he has sought, and still less found, solace elsewhere. In the hothouse atmosphere of Vienna, where public figures find it impossible to preserve privacy, there have been no salacious rumours about Wiesenthal.

But then, Wiesenthal's true passion, as it developed after his reunion with Cyla and his work with the American war crimes investigators in the early post-war years, was to search for the enduring cement that would keep the memory of the Holocaust alive for the generations to come. His private life was of little consequence compared to the giant task of creating enough awareness of evil to put an end to genocide.

The First Documentation Centre

It took Simon Wiesenthal about eighteen months to transform himself from concentration camp inmate to founder of an independent institute, 'The Historical Documentation Centre' in Linz. Its purpose was to search for war criminals and to collect evidence against them from the survivors in the displaced-persons camps. In the interim period, he worked on similar tasks with the Americans and became active in Jewish organisations; he also liaised with the *Brichah* (escape), the secret operation to organise the illegal emigration of Jews to what was then still Palestine.

From the moment he regained his freedom, Wiesenthal was groping for ways of promoting his goal of bringing Nazi criminals to justice, and he understood the urgency of compiling evidence before the survivors dispersed around the world. He knew that he was committed to a life-long task, although in those early days he still responded to his wife's pleas to stop with reassurances that the work would be done within two or three years. As for emigrating to the Jewish homeland, he was sure that he did not wish to go, but was still Zionist enough to urge others to emigrate there.

Wiesenthal was energetic, highly motivated and sensed that his work could ease his wartime trauma. He found that he possessed an instinct for networking and building contacts in sensitive places. Even in those early days, he displayed a grasp of the importance of using the media to promote his causes. He saw himself as a natural leader and did not yet understand that he would always be more at ease working on his own without the encumbrance of organisational ties.

Hyperactive, Wiesenthal found himself in a deeply disturbed political environment. Austria was an occupied country. He had no illusions, as he sought to give new meaning to his life, that he was a minnow in rough waters. Truth, trust and integrity were scarce commodities. Groping for ways of establishing the principle that the hunt for Nazi murderers had to be more than a temporary mopping-up phase in the aftermath of war, Wiesenthal was never comfortable with the compromises that had to be made to keep afloat and promote his cause. Steadily growing in self-confidence, outspoken and often aggressive, the circumstances of the time made it inevitable that, as Wiesenthal began to attract attention, he also became a magnet for controversy. Sometimes it was clash of temperament, or rivalry with other Nazi-hunters, that left behind a bitter legacy of animosity. But often there were principles at stake: he collided with American colleagues when he began to realise that they were losing interest in denazification and war crimes trials.

Without an appreciation of the political context in which Wiesenthal's work evolved, it is impossible to understand the factors that bred his fierce independence and led him to establish his Documentation Centre in Linz. Austria was a very different place from today's prosperous and stable democracy. In 1945, it was unimaginable that, fifty years later, the country would count amongst the wealthier members of the European Union and would finally, after decades of prevarication, accept responsibility for its Nazi past.

As with Germany, the transformation has been so far-reaching that it is very hard for those who did not experience the physical devastation at the end of the war to fathom the currency of everyday life that followed Hitler's defeat: the extent of the physical damage, the millions of displaced people in search of relatives and a new hold on life, the confusion and improvisation, the political manoeuvring, the strains between the four Allied occupation forces even before the parameters of the Cold War had emerged, the corruption, the black-marketeering, the prevalence of intrigue and the espionage. Austria's wounds and scars, after its spell of fellow-travelling as Nazi Germany's *Ostmark*, went far deeper than those caused by the country's loss of empire at the end of the First World War. Erecting the second Austrian republic on sounder foundations than the first was a marathon task.

The wartime Allies were agreed that Germany's 1938 *Anschluss* of Austria was null and void, but they had reached no decisions on how Austria should now be governed, how much political activity should be allowed, which parties should be legalised, how far to take denazification and what the constitutional arrangements should be. However, on 29 April 1945, the Austrian Socialist Party leader, Karl Renner, at the head of a provisional government, was permitted to proclaim the birth of the second republic from the bomb-damaged parliament building in Vienna. Much of the capital lay in ruins; people were despondent and hungry, there was no public transport and little clean water. The Red Army controlled the city; heavily armed Soviet soldiers surrounded the parliament and were packed inside with almost as many Red Army officers sitting on the parliamentary benches as there were Austrian politicians present.

The Western Allies assumed that Stalin was intent on making Austria a Communist preserve, and suspected that Renner would turn out to be malleable, a stooge, in Stalin's hands. They soon realised that they were wrong on both counts: Renner was determined to rebuild democracy in Austria; and Stalin's main objective in 1945 was to claim its industries as war booty, bleed the Austrian economy dry and prevent the country from threatening Soviet interests by forming links with southern Germany or its Danube neighbours.

Stalin's goal of enfeebling Austria might have been achieved if he had succeeded in having the country placed solely under Soviet occupation. This almost came about when President Roosevelt briefly considered proposals to halt the US advance on Austria to leave his forces free to concentrate on northern Germany. But in the end, all four Allied armies converged on Austria to occupy zones, whose lines were only settled after the war's end in July 1945. The four-power occupation lasted until the 1955 peace treaty, which the Soviet Union ratified on the basis of an Austrian commitment to neutrality.

At the war's end, Austria immediately set out to distance itself from the Nazis and to deny that it willingly embraced Hitler's take-over of the country in 1938. Austrians wanted to be treated by the occupying powers as Hitler's first victims, who had been liberated, and not as an enemy country which had acted as Hitler's accomplice and which must therefore come to terms with its Nazi past. Wiesenthal found this reprehensible and was shocked by Allied equivocation on such a fundamental question of fact.

The wartime allies were in fact divided in their response to the Austrians. Britain and the United States would have preferred to give priority to denazification and delay the establishment of national government structures until democratic parties, purged of Nazis, were firmly in place. The French position was different. It wanted to have Austria treated as a friendly state, and saw the Austrians more as victims than as sinners. Denazification was less urgent that the re-establishment of a sovereign nation. Stalin, being more concerned to lay his hands on Austria's industrial assets, did not care one way or the other.

French and Soviet strategy was similar: to be less preoccupied with denazification than with the installation of friends in key government positions in Austria – the difference, of course, being that the French wanted a pro-Western democracy, and the Soviets a government docile enough to serve their interests.

Britain and the United States did not hold out long against the establishment of a national government for Austria. All four allies joined in recognising the provisional Renner Government in October 1945. National elections followed, and on 20 December Renner was accepted by the occupying powers as Austria's legitimately elected head of state. Though the occupying powers retained a watching brief, responsibility for denazification was transferred to the Austrian authorities. In practice, this meant that the process was slowed down and many Nazis survived in positions of influence.

With the first stirrings of the Cold War, denazification in Austria, as in Germany, became secondary to the East–West race to secure access to Nazi weapons technology and to recruit key scientists and industrial personnel. In Austria, the treasure-trove of expertise was nowhere near as significant as in Germany. Yet the Western Allies, like the Soviet Union, had little compunction about shelving their wartime commitment to impose and ensure denazification of Austria's political and economic power structures. Wiesenthal was profoundly disillusioned. He had expected better, at least of the Americans, whom he had come to know and admire. No longer sharing the same purpose, a gradual parting of the ways became inevitable.

Wiesenthal owes it to the Americans in the OSS that he only had a brief spell in a displaced-persons camp. In June 1945, when the OSS agreed that he should work for them, he was moved to a makeshift camp in school buildings in Leondig, a small town near Linz. Camp beds had been set up in a classroom, and for a few days, Wiesenthal slept close to a window that overlooked the small house that had been the home of Adolf Hitler's parents. The view disturbed him, and instead he was given a small furnished room that ranked as an annexe to the camp. When Wiesenthal's wife rejoined him, they found larger accommodation in nearby Uhlandgasse, and this remained his base until the move to Vienna in 1961.

But Wiesenthal also quickly differentiated himself from other survivors by displaying an individualistic, militant streak, working to expose Nazi atrocities and turning himself into a self-appointed spokesman for the Jews caught up in Austria's American zone.

Wiesenthal was out and about with OSS agents, collating information and arresting SS personnel, until the end of 1945, when the OSS closed its office in Linz. As early as 27 August 1945, Captain O'Meara, the commanding officer of the OSS in Linz, issued Wiesenthal with a *laissez-passer*, which states that he 'is working on confidential investigative work for this organisation (the OSS). Kindly let him move freely in American-occupied Austria.'

When the OSS handed some of its tasks over to the CIC, Wiesenthal transferred to the CIC where he remained for several months still doing the same work. Throughout the period with the OSS and the CIC, Wiesenthal was given power to arrest. Many of the approximately 2,000 'cases' which he estimates he has helped to expose refer back to those early post-war months, when the SS prey was still relatively easy to find. 'It was like running after a fly. If I pursued one Nazi, I would pick up three others on the way. I would meet people, who told me stories about their neighbours. After rainy Sundays, when people remained at home, I would receive heaps of letters with information, most of them sent anonymously.' To his great disappointment, most of those he arrested were only briefly detained and few were brought to trial.

The CIC was bringing in new personnel from the United States and Wiesenthal saw that this was leading to a fundamental change in attitude to the whole war crimes agenda. 'Those who had fought in Europe understood us, the former camp inmates. Their successors, who had no first-hand knowledge of the war, were different,' Wiesenthal remembers. 'They didn't really understand our attitude towards the Nazis. They would say, "Oh yes, there are some Nazis and some anti-Nazis here just as there are Republicans and Democrats in the US." They couldn't see the fallacy of drawing such parallels.'

That was not the worst of it. The denazification process and the search for war criminals was becoming increasingly incoherent. Americans now had four separate organisations with overlapping functions, but lacking adequate co-ordination – the OSS, the CIC, the War Crimes group and the Military Intelligence group. Wiesenthal believed the left hand didn't know what the right hand was doing. Besides, he was becoming increasingly frustrated because he had failed to persuade the Americans to mount an intensive search for Adolf Eichmann, whom he suspected of hiding in the US zone of Austria. Wiesenthal had begun to build up a picture of Eichmann, and though in 1946 he did not yet know the full extent of Eichmann's responsibility for the organisation of the Final Solution, he knew enough to recognise him as a major war criminal and argued that the resources of the Americans were needed to track him down.

'The Americans were intrigued to see that, on most days, I was already in the office when they arrived and stayed long after they left in the evening, and they often asked me why I didn't at least accept some cigarettes from them. I told them that I didn't want any kind of payment for my work.' Strains reached breaking-point one day, when Wiesenthal's CIC superior, an American of German origin, urged Wiesenthal to emigrate to the United

States. 'Why should I go, I asked? The reply was succinct. "With your ideas and your energy, even though you are still weak, you can go far. You should realise that in America, traffic is regulated by red and green lights. Everything else is controlled by the Jews."'

That short exchange was a red warning light for Wiesenthal. He interpreted his superior's remark as a reflection of deep anti-Semitism. Even if it was a joke, as the American officer claimed, it was a joke in unacceptable taste. 'Tomorrow, you must look for a substitute,' Wiesenthal said in his rudimentary English. 'If people like you, who are supposedly working to root out Nazism, can make jokes of this nature, then our work is not in good hands.' Other CIC officers tried to dissuade Wiesenthal from leaving, 'But I was not to be held.'

There had been further instances of friction. Fraternisation between the Americans and the Austrians had brought women on to the scene. On a number of occasions Wiesenthal arrested a Nazi suspect, only to find that a wife or daughter had pleaded with a friendly CIC officer to secure his release. Wiesenthal would then have to go to one of the other US agencies to authorise a rearrest.

Wiesenthal did not go lightly. He recognised how much he had learned from the Americans and told them that he would never do anything against their interests. 'But I said that it was our, the survivors', obligation to carry on with the work on our own.'

That same evening Wiesenthal talked with the members of the Jewish Committee of Survivors, and told them that he would select a number of young people to set up a Jewish Historical Documentation Centre. 'I asked who among them wanted to work with me. Naturally all of them put up their hands. I was popular, and they believed in our work. I selected twenty-eight, and two more pressed so hard that our group became thirty strong.

'I had no experience. I used the same approach to map out an organisational structure as I had formerly done to draw up building plans. I knew that there were still between 150,000 and 200,000 people in the displaced-persons camps in Austria, Germany and Italy. I went to the camps, or wrote to them, and in every camp I selected one or two people. I gave them questionnaires, and they sat day and night, taking down the oral histories of the survivors, where they had been, whom and what they had witnessed. And six months later I collected the questionnaires and we had a list of a thousand places where crimes had been committed for which we had witnesses. I sent all this to the Allies, and nobody questioned whether we had been authorised to do this. As Jews we had a moral right to do it. And after a while, the Allies came to us and asked us whether we could produce witnesses for such and such a war crimes trial. . . .

'We had nothing, not one *Groschen* [the lowest Austrian currency denomination]. So, I went to see the *Landeshauptman* [Governor] of upper Austria, Dr Heinrich Gleissner, and told him that I was leaving the Americans and that I needed two office rooms. I told him it was for a Documentation Centre, but only gave him a partial description of what we planned to do. He told us that all the national delegations dealing with refugee problems had been installed in Goethestrasse 63, and he said that space would be made for us there.

'Many people, who were only partly Jewish, had been offering help to our Jewish Survivors' Committee. Now I said to one of them, an Austrian called Polaczek, that we needed chairs, tables, the bare essentials of office furniture. He secured them for us without asking for money.'

Wiesenthal paints a telling portrait of himself at the time when he went independent. In his book *I Hunted Eichmann*, he records that,

Among the Jews, I had become well-known. They knew about my work, and I was continuously receiving information from Jews in the US zone, and later also from the rest of Austria. I collated all this information, brought order to it and passed it on to the relevant institutions, including the CIC. Gradually, the officials became used to me, even though I was constantly in conflict with them – usually over minor matters. I was often unwise in the way I was handling myself and made enemies, even though I afterwards regretted my intransigence. I considered that my self-appointed task was holy, and my determination became the more pronounced, the more I learned how Jews had been abused. I had ceased to be the shy man who had stood outside the war crimes office in Mauthausen, and had felt that someone was doing me an immense service by allowing me to share in their work. My self worth had greatly increased.

It was now close to the end of 1946. Money remained short. More would have to be raised before the Documentation Centre could properly begin work. Wiesenthal knew of another Pole, a lawyer named Adolf Silberschein, who was living in Geneva and had formed Relico, a small organisation to aid Jewish intellectuals. Wiesenthal wrote to him appealing for financial help. Silberschein was prepared to authorise small sums, because, as he wrote to Wiesenthal, he valued 'both the work you do and the methods you employ'. But the same letter also insisted that Wiesenthal had to produce a far more carefully itemised budget than he seemed to think was necessary.

Finally, it was agreed that Silberschein should subsidise the Historical Documentation Centre with a monthly sum of $50, which continued until

Silberschein's death. The sum covered telephone and postage bills. The rest had to be scraped together. Though it helped that most of Wiesenthal's co-workers were still living free in the displaced-persons camps, the pattern was set for the future: Wiesenthal would always work on a shoestring, would remain largely dependent on small voluntary donations, and would turn to writing books and newspaper articles to raise income for his living expenses. Aside from secretaries, he would never be able to afford a professional staff.

As head of the Documentation Centre, Wiesenthal was on the side of those survivors who insisted that Jewish collaborators should not be protected against prosecution. Others argued that Jews had suffered enough, and that a blind eye should be turned to those who had worked as SS auxiliaries. Even though Wiesenthal knew well enough that many Jews had been coerced into working for the SS in the concentration camps, he adopted a compromise to exclude any Jewish Kapos, who had worked for the SS as go-betweens with the camp inmates, from membership of any Jewish committees and organisations concerned with the resettlement of the displaced persons in the US zone of Austria. To prove that candidates for committee memberships were 'clean', Wiesenthal ruled that they must produce a minimum of two witnesses to testify that they had not held any function under the SS. This became known among the survivors as 'Lex Wiesenthal'.

'It does not require much imagination to understand that this made me many enemies,' he comments. It does, however, say a great deal about his forceful character that Wiesenthal nevertheless succeeded in remaining a key figure in Jewish politics in the American zone of Austria, and was recognised as such by the Americans.

Wiesenthal's activism and the rigidity of the ethical credo that informed his attitudes were always bound to attract extreme reactions. Those who knew him either approved or disapproved, but were rarely indifferent. He had his fervent admirers among other survivors and among some of the US officers, who saw him as a resourceful, intelligent and courageous operator with a surprising commitment to secure the due process of law even for the worst perpetrators of the Holocaust. They saw in him a single-minded individual so possessed by his task that he remained largely uncontaminated by the freewheeling, murky environment of the time. Integrity was at a premium, and Wiesenthal appeared to possess it. 'He is a brother to me; I could see he would be a great man,' Prem Tobias always maintains when describing Wiesenthal's activism after the liberation.

Wiesenthal's close association with the Americans had continued after his formal parting with the CIC at the end of 1946. Even though he became progressively more and more disillusioned with US policy weaknesses in dealing with denazification, he accepted an offer to act as adviser on 'persecuted minorities' to the US military government in their zone in upper Austria. But they did not pay much attention to the facts that he gave them. The Americans seemed deaf to the information he was amassing about the emergence of neo-Nazi organisations and the immunities that leading Austrian Nazis continued to enjoy. Wiesenthal swore to fight a private war against their resurgence in Austria's political life.

After the Documentation Centre opened its doors early in 1947, Wiesenthal began to receive threatening letters. He suspected that this was in response to newspaper articles in local papers, where he named those who had been, he contended, wrongly freed. The threats prompted him to ask the US authorities for permission to carry a rifle or tommy-gun 'for the protection of my home'. The request was granted, and he often shows his gun permit with great pride – not because he has ever fired a weapon, but as evidence of the trust that the Americans placed in him.

At Wiesenthal's prompting, Lieutenant-Colonel W. I. Wright, the US commander in charge of the CAC, gave him a testimonial to establish his credentials in his capacity as chief of the Documentation Centre:

To whom it may concern: this is to testify that Mr Simon Wiesenthal, President of the members of the International Concentration Camp Organisation, has given invaluable assistance to this organisation in securing evidence for the Mauthausen Concentration Camp case. Mr Wiesenthal has given up much of his free time to facilitate the work of this organisation in Austria, and has also effected expeditious liaison with other groups for the rapid consummation of our mission here. Mr Wiesenthal has proven himself to be honest and sincere at all times and is definitely deserving of any assistance rendered him in the furtherance of his work in Austria.

Wiesenthal had become a busy man. The American reference to his involvement with Jewish organisations goes back to 1945, when he had formed the Jewish Committee of Survivors, which later became the Jewish Central Committee for the US zone in Austria. He was named Vice-President and promoted collaboration with a sister organisation formed in Germany. In June 1946, Wiesenthal was also elected to the Presidency of the Paris-based International Union of Concentration Camp Survivors, which grouped together eleven national committees.

Wiesenthal spent periods at the Nuremberg trials, mainly engaged in researching the war crimes archives, assembled by the prosecution, for evidence that might be used in other trials. In 1946, he also published his first book, the collection of his Mauthausen cartoons.

He was a delegate at the first post-war Zionist Congress, held in Basle in 1946, where he came to the attention of Gerhart Riegner, the Geneva-based head of European operations of the WJC. Riegner may have concluded that the WJC should keep Wiesenthal at arm's length. The WJC's President was Nahum Goldmann. Riegner was one of his closest collaborators. His assessment of Wiesenthal's character and of his political attitudes to the Zionist cause may lie at the origin of the deep feud that later developed between the WJC and Wiesenthal. Even in 1994, when Riegner was in his eighties, mere mention of Wiesenthal's name still aroused deep anger – but also a refusal to explain its cause. He exclaimed to a friend: 'I am too old to cope with the emotions that recollections of Wiesenthal arouse in me. All I want to say is that difficulties with him did not begin with the Eichmann case. They began began much earlier, in the late forties.'

Wiesenthal himself only has vague recollections of a meeting with Riegner at the Basle Zionist Congress, and says that he is personally convinced that Riegner's anger against him stems from much later events in 1991, when Riegner briefly became directly embroiled in the bitter dispute between the WJC and Wiesenthal over the history of events that had led to the capture of Adolf Eichmann in 1960. Riegner apparently caused great anger at WJC headquarters with a letter in the *Jerusalem Post* that appeared to confirm one of Wiesenthal's key assertions about his dealings with Nahum Goldmann. There were rumours that Riegner's WJC pension may even have been briefly under threat. At any rate, a few days later, Riegner dispatched another letter, rescinding his earlier statement – and decided that Wiesenthal, where he, Riegner, was concerned, was a closed chapter.

As if the plethora of Wiesenthal's activities during the early post-war period was not enough, he also co-operated for a time with the shadowy *Brichah* organisation, whose main purpose was to smuggle Jewish refugees into Palestine. There were tens of thousands of displaced persons in Austria and many more in Germany. Fresh pogroms in Poland and growing concern that Eastern Europe would be incorporated into the Soviet bloc made the displaced Jews reluctant to return to their former homes. Many wanted to go to Palestine; but Britain, still set against the creation of the Jewish homeland, remained determined to keep down Palestine's Jewish popu-lation. Immigration quotas set by Britain remained minuscule. The situation prompted the *Haganah*, the future Israel's embryo intelligence service, using the *Mossad Le'Aliyah Beth* (Institute 'B', illegal immigration), to send operatives to Austria to set up the *Brichah*. Austria became a vital transit route to smuggle refugees out of Europe. From 1944 until the establishment of Israel in 1948, at least 200,000 Jews were brought out by the *Brichah*, using the Austrian route.

But *Brichah* agents were also involved in a far more controversial and highly secret operation to identify and liquidate SS officers responsible for Nazi atrocities. Israel has acknowledged that summary executions of suspected Nazis were undertaken in Europe after the war, but has maintained silence on everything connected with these actions. The only pointer to the scale of what might have taken place is the disappearance of middle-ranking Nazis, unlikely to have had access to Nazi escape routes to Latin America, whose fate has never been established. In any event, Wiesenthal objected to liquidation – even in the semi-anarchic conditions of the early post-war period, he was insisting on the due processes of law for mass murderers.

The *Brichah*'s command in Austria operated from Vienna with branches in Salzburg, Linz, Graz and Innsbruck. A young man in his twenties, Asher Ben-Nathan (who used the name Arthur Pier during his period in Austria), was in charge of the illegal exodus of refugees from 1945 to 1947 with Gideon Raphael and Ehud Avriel, both experienced undercover agents, as his aides. All three men later became senior Israeli diplomats. Another operative was Tuviah Friedman, who remained in Vienna until 1952 running a small Documentation Centre similar to Wiesenthal's Linz operation. (Friedman later moved to Israel, working initially at Yad Vashem in Jerusalem; he then moved to Haifa, where he set up another, little-known Documentation Centre. For a while the two men were friends, but they later fell out over their respective contributions to the hunt for Adolf Eichmann.)

Ben-Nathan and his co-workers in Vienna reacted coolly to Wiesenthal's activism in Linz, even though Wiesenthal only recalls amicable co-operation with them. In Palestine, there were sharp divisions over the strategy and tactics to secure the establishment of the Jewish homeland, Israel. Ben-Nathan and his colleagues were mainstream members of the *Haganah*; they assumed that Wiesenthal was a Revisionist, a Jabotinsky follower, and even suspected him of secret support for the militant *Irgun Zvai Leumi* organisation, the military arm of the Revisionist Party. This meant that they had an inbuilt distrust of him. This was reinforced by concern that Wiesenthal was too close to the Americans. In at least one intelligence report, filed in US archives, there are hints that the *Brichah* people suspected Wiesenthal of having furnished information on their operations to the CIC.

Looking back on those times, Ben-Nathan says now that he had no doubt, even in 1946, that Wiesenthal had to be taken seriously as 'a Jewish personality' among the Jews in Austria. But it was a personality that did not enthuse him. The same held true for Gideon Raphael and Ehud Avriel.

Personal jealousies, never far absent in the miasma of Jewish organisations, may have played a part; but Wiesenthal insists that he developed a principled objection to *Brichah* when he became aware that SS criminals were being liquidated. However, he cannot understand why they should have believed – quite erroneously – that he had any links, or even sympathised, with the Revisionists. His brief pre-war flirtation with them no longer had any meaning or significance for him; though he does acknowledge that he protested to the *Brichah* people that 'you cannot just take *Mapai* people [members of the Zionist Socialist party] to Palestine. In facilitating illegal emigration, you must not discriminate among the displaced persons.'

Wiesenthal prefers a more personal explanation for the cool feelings that developed between him and Ben-Nathan. He asserts that they fell out over a Jew who had defrauded the Jewish Agency while buying arms for the organisation in Prague. Wiesenthal argued that the man should be prosecuted. Ben-Nathan decided otherwise, and the outcome was that the two men did not speak for many years.

Asked in 1994 how he remembered Weisenthal, Gideon Raphael, who later became Director-General of the Israeli Foreign Office, recalled an encounter at the Bindermichel displaced-persons camp near Linz in 1946: 'I went there with Ben-Nathan. We were asking the DPs where they wanted to go, hoping to find overwhelming opinion in favour of going to Palestine. The spokesman for the DPs was Engineer Simon Wiesenthal. It appeared he was the leader of the camp and was known as an ardent Revisionist. Addressing the DPs in my presence he made an enthusiastic speech saying that everyone had to go to Palestine.

'As he spoke, I didn't detect any reservation on his part that he might be the kind of Zionist who collects money from one Jew to send to another Jew in Israel. It was all "we, we. . . ." He never spoke about "you". He was ardent, very activist.'

In a letter written after this meeting, Raphael thanked Wiesenthal for 'the important work' he had carried out with the *Brichah*, and hinted at future collaborations.

Yet like Ben-Nathan, Raphael also concluded that Wiesenthal was very definitely leader material, but rejected close involvement with him. Raphael decided against using him as a contact man in the displaced-persons camps or otherwise involving him in the *Brichah*'s activities. 'I didn't make any recommendation about using him for anything. He wasn't important until he made himself important.'

With the wisdom of hindsight, Raphael in 1994 described Wiesenthal as 'a hitchhiker who took over the driver's seat, and then ran away with the car'. Wiesenthal, surprised by this harsh assessment, dismissed this as 'an old man's distortion'.

The most plausible explanation for such mutual unhappiness lies in the way that paths divided after the confused and difficult early post-war period. Ben-Nathan, Raphael and Avriel all became part of the elite establishment that built up the State of Israel. Wiesenthal stayed away, preferring to beaver among the entrails of the Nazi Party and search for mass murderers – with his eye already on the prize object: Adolf Eichmann.

[8]
The Search for Eichmann Begins

Simon Wiesenthal's name has become inextricably, but also highly controversially, linked to Adolf Eichmann's. He is convinced, and so are his admirers, that without his persistence during the late 1940s and the early 1950s, the search for Eichmann might easily have been abandoned around 1948 or 1949, and Israel, preoccupied with building the new state, might not have resumed the hunt for Eichmann in 1957. And without the Eichmann trial, and the horrors it confirmed, the full dimensions of the Holocaust might never have been fully understood, and its remembrance might even have been allowed to fade away.

Wiesenthal prides himself on having prevented Vera Eichmann from having her husband declared dead in 1947, a move which he believes might have halted the hunt. He also deduced correctly in 1953 that Eichmann had fled to Argentina. This was five years before the Israeli Intelligence Service, the Mossad, received the tip-off from Frankfurt Prosecutor, Dr Fritz Bauer, that Eichmann was in Argentina. Indeed, Wiesenthal remains persuaded that if his information had been pursued, Eichmann could have been captured in the early 1950s.

Without doubt, the origins of Wiesenthal's fame and of his legend as an intrepid hunter of Nazi criminals stem from the Eichmann case. But so also do the attempts to discredit him with question marks over the extent of his contribution to Eichmann's eventual capture by the Mossad in 1960. His detractors, principal among them the WJC, say that Wiesenthal has made a career out of Eichmann and interpret his claims as proof that the whole gamut of his activities is full of blemishes.

One man in particular, Isser Harel, former head of the Mossad and leader of the Israeli team that spirited Eichmann away from Argentina in 1960, bitterly resents the acclaim that Wiesenthal has gained from the Eichmann case, and has fought to prove that Wiesenthal had no role in Eichmann's capture and no right to take any credit for tracing him to Argentina. Another

Israeli, Tuviah Friedman, who was marginally involved in the search for Eichmann in the early post-war period, has taken public issue with Wiesenthal. He charges Wiesenthal with overstating his own role and, much worse, failing to acknowledge Friedman's.

If it were not for the WJC, Harel's fulminations and Friedman's yearnings for greater recognition could be read as an interesting but relatively unimportant fallout from the tortuous road that led to the capture of one of the twentieth century's most demonic killers. But Harel has also found a ready audience at the New York headquarters of the WJC. There, his arguments have been welcomed as useful ammunition against Wiesenthal and have been used to inject still more bitterness into the WJC campaign to disparage Wiesenthal over his refusal to tar Kurt Waldheim as a war criminal. Having once thought of him as an heroic figure, the current leadership of the WJC would prefer to have the world see him as a charlatan.

Harel's refusal to acknowledge Wiesenthal's role can be more readily understood in terms of jealousy and the prejudices of an elderly man, whose career in the Mossad for a multitude of reasons took an irreversible dive soon after the Eichmann capture from which he never recovered: he had to leave the Mossad over sharp policy disagreements involving Israel's handling of the challenges posed by German rocket experts in Egypt. Friedman too has suffered from many personal frustrations over his failure to make a greater mark on the community of Nazi-hunters. But the attitude of the WJC is much harder to justify.

Eichmann was a participant and wrote the minutes of the 1942 Wannsee conference, where the Nazi leadership adopted the Final Solution for the extermination of Jews from the German Reich. He subsequently became the ultimate 'desk murderer', who turned mass killing into an organised industry, and prided himself on the millions gassed, or shot, or beaten, or starved to death. To find this monster, and deliver him to a court of law, became an obsession with Wiesenthal, which began soon after the war's end and did not cease until Eichmann's capture in Argentina by the Mossad. Afterwards, he became similarly obsessive in justifying the significance of his personal contribution to the unearthing of Eichmann.

To some extent, Wiesenthal laid himself open to attack with his 1961 book, *I Hunted Eichmann*, whose title encouraged the widespread belief that he was responsible for finding Eichmann's hide-out in Argentina. He also collaborated on several film projects which glamorised and distorted his personal contribution to Eichmann's capture. In fact, *I Hunted Eichmann*, with its meticulous detail about Wiesenthal's world between 1945 and 1960, unambiguously acknowledges that his involvement was limited to the identification of the early pieces of an intricate jigsaw puzzle that had to be put together before Eichmann's specific whereabouts could be identified. Wiesenthal had nothing to do with the Mossad's search for Eichmann in Argentina, which began in 1957 and culminated in Eichmann's capture in 1960. A later, briefer account in *The Murderers Amongst Us* is equally emphatic that Wiesenthal was but one of many who helped to track down Eichmann.

As with most real-life cloak-and-dagger stories, there are murky areas over who did what and when in the Eichmann case. Its minutiae have been raked over again and again. Not surprisingly, there are discrepancies and differences of emphasis and interpretation. One of the most contentious issues concerns the dossier of evidence, including clues to Eichmann's presence in Argentina, that Wiesenthal had accumulated and which he sent to Nahum Goldmann, President of the WJC in 1954, at his request. Goldmann never directly acknowledged receipt of this correspondence, and Wiesenthal has always been convinced that the WJC President rebuffed him because he was not prepared to work with a man who was determined to remain independent rather than work directly for the WJC. Goldmann is no longer alive, and his successors at the WJC also contend that Goldmann never took Wiesenthal seriously, suspecting that he was merely seeking financial help from them. He may have harboured misgivings from way back in 1946, when his close associate, Gerhart Riegner, had apparently formed a poor opinion of Wiesenthal.

In any event, the WJC argues that it was never set up to be a Nazi-hunting organisation and would, therefore, have been the wrong address for Wiesenthal to seek support in the hunt for Eichmann. The WJC asserts that it cannot find any trace of Wiesenthal's communications in its meticulously kept archives. This is all the more curious since there are copies of the correspondence in Israel's Central Zionist Archives.

The search for Eichmann began before the last of the concentration camps had been liberated, and before the full extent of his role in organising the extermination of millions of Jews and other 'undesirables' was properly understood. He was among the names on the 'most wanted' list of 'instigators and perpetrators of crimes against Jews', which the Jewish Agency for Palestine had drawn up. Representatives of the Agency had first come across Eichmann in Vienna in 1938, when mass murder was not yet Hitler's preferred way of ridding the German Reich of its Jews. At that time, Nazi policy was still focused on the seizure of Jewish property and the promotion of Jewish emigration. Eichmann had been recruited to the Nazi ranks as early as 1932. After the *Anschluss*, he was installed in the Palais Rothschild

The 15-year-old Wiesenthal, who has always refused to wear uniform, with his group of boy scouts in Buczacz. Taken in 1923, and sent to Wiesenthal after 1945, this is Wiesenthal's only pre-war photograph still in his possession.

October 1945. Simon and Cyla, soon after their reunion, celebrating with other survivors and their new US friends.

1947. Wiesenthal at a meeting of Displaced Persons in Linz, urging them to emigrate to Palestine. The Hebrew banners underline the message 'we call you'.

1948. Wiesenthal awaiting his turn to speak at a Displaced Persons rally in Linz to mark the Declaration of Independence of the state of Israel.

Cyla Wiesenthal poses for a rare photograph. Taken in 1947, it illustrates why she was able to survive during the war by passing herself as an Aryan.

Wiesenthal in Israel at funeral ceremonies for unknown death camp victims whose ashes he had accompanied to the new Jewish state.

'If stones could speak ... everything in the Third Reich has to be beautiful; even the Concentration camp, the "sanatorium of the underworld" has to be architecturally perfect. The beautiful facade must cover up the beastly interior ... every stone is a human life ...'

Wiesenthal's 1945 drawing of the watch tower guarding the horrors of Mauthausen concentration camp.

'The play is over ... the mask falls ... "Hitler" is death with all its terrors ... "Hitler" signifies death and destruction and the use of unspeakable sadism.'

Wiesenthal's drawing is entitled 'without mask'.

'Our horizons were narrow and fearful ... when the slave labour laboriously dragged its way from the stone quarries back up to Mauthausen, our heads, bent down with fatigue could only see the SS boots, the pistols and the whips of the slave drivers ... we were too tired to raise our heads ... besides, it would have been pointless.'

Wiesenthal's drawing of a Mauthausen inmate's perspectives.

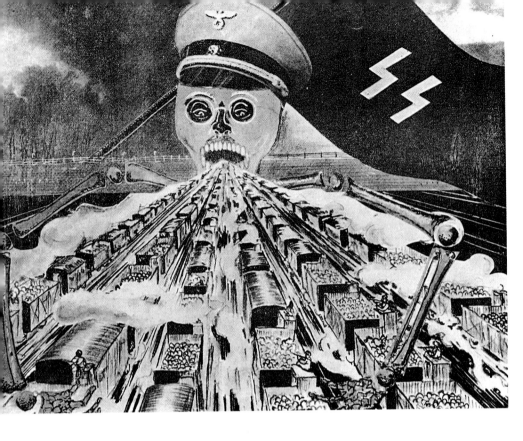

Wiesenthal's project for a Mausoleum in Israel to house ashes taken from all of Hitler's concentration and extermination camps. He drew detailed plans for such a memorial in 1948, the only occasion after the war when he used his architect's training. It was not built.

Left: 'Will anyone believe it or even grasp it, we asked ourselves ... weeks wedged inside a closed animal wagon or an open coal wagon, without food, water and sanitation, in unbearable heat or in biting cold ... In February 1945, 6000 inmates were taken from Gross Rosen concentration camp ... on May 5 1945, Liberation day, only 32 of us were still alive.' Wiesenthal sums it up in this drawing, which he called 'Transports'.

Every year in May on the anniversary of the Liberation of Mauthausen, Wiesenthal returns to the concentration camp site for a survivors' reunion. This photograph was taken in 1963.

By 1965, Wiesenthal's reputation was solidly established. Here he is caught in a typical pose: Wiesenthal explains, declaims, holds forth.

During a brief visit to London in 1975, Wiesenthal stands on the South Bank with Big Ben and the Houses of Parliament in the background.

Wiesenthal has learned to become a man of patience in his search for mass murderers. Here a photographer caught him unawares as he waited for an appointment in a bare Stockholm corridor on a cold winter's day in 1975.

in Vienna as head of the office handling Jewish affairs. Ehud Avriel, then still using his original name of Überall, was working for the Jewish Agency, helping to organise illegal Jewish immigration into Palestine and negotiating the evacuation of Jewish children on the 'Kindertransports'. He never forgot the coldly clinical personality that Eichmann displayed, in his black SS uniform and black boots, whip in hand.

In the later stages of the war, when more and more evidence emerged about the Final Solution, Eichmann's name frequently occurred as one of the key figures. More evidence about his high place in the Nazi hierarchy emerged during the last few months of the war, after the Allied refusal to accept his 'merchandise for blood' proposal to sell the freedom of one million Hungarian Jews in exchange for 10,000 trucks and other commodities for the German war effort. Eichmann, stationed in Budapest, then proceeded to implement a streamlined operation to send Hungary's Jews to their death at Auschwitz.

Wiesenthal first heard Eichmann's name from Hungarian prisoners while he was in Mauthausen's death block. It did not mean much to him then. Even a month after his liberation, and already working for the Americans, he dismissed a query from a member of the *Brichah* office in Vienna who asked if he had heard of Eichmann. He retorted that he was more interested in the war criminals whose actions he had personally witnessed.[1]

However, curiosity had been aroused, and he asked to see what information on Eichmann was stored in the US war crimes files. There were few specifics. He was described as an SS *Obersturmbannführer*, who had been active in Austria, Czechoslovakia, France, Greece and Hungary, but the files contained no detailed job description and no photograph.

Soon afterwards, in July 1945, Wiesenthal went on his first post-war trip to Vienna, where he met Ben-Nathan and Avriel in the *Brichah* office. They knew much more about Eichmann's role. Their intelligence reports suggested that Eichmann had been born in Sarona, the German Templar colony of Palestine, and that he spoke fluent Hebrew and Yiddish as well as German.[2] In fact, Eichmann was born in Germany in Solingen, had grown up in Linz, had only spent two days in Palestine, had been in Sarona for a few hours, and had only a smattering of Hebrew and no Yiddish. But he studied Jewish affairs, and before the *Anschluss* had made himself one of the Nazis' leading experts on Jewry.

Later, when it could all be pieced together, it became clear that Eichmann was only thirty-two years old when he was put in charge of the Central Office for Jewish Emigration in Vienna. A year later, in 1939, following Hitler's occupation of Czechoslovakia, Eichmann was sent to Prague, and after war broke out he was transferred to the German Reich's Centre for Jewish Emigration in Berlin. One of his tasks there was to work on the Machiavellian project to transplant some four million Jews from Poland and elsewhere in Central Europe to Madagascar. This never materialised, and by mid-1941 Nazi policy had taken a decisive shift: Jewish labour would be exploited while they remained fit, with mass extermination as the ultimate aim. Eichmann was promoted, transferred to the Gestapo and made head of Section IV-B-4, the Jewish desk. His boss was Reinhard Heydrich, who informed him that 'The *Führer* has ordered the physical extermination of the Jews.'

After Wiesenthal's encounter with Ben-Nathan, it was not long before he became firmly hooked on the search for Eichmann. Gradually, he built up a picture that enabled him to understand the horrific dimensions of Eichmann's involvement in the Final Solution. This man had to be brought to account as surely as the Nazi leaders, who were being tried by the Nuremberg War Crimes Tribunal. But where was he? He was to prove far more elusive than the Nazi leadership, whose orders he had carried out with such application and enthusiasm.

Back in Linz, Wiesenthal's superior officer, Captain O'Meara, gave him the meagre US-compiled Eichmann dossier with orders to intensify the search for information about his Nazi activities and his present whereabouts. Wiesenthal is adamant that he was the first to discover that Eichmann grew up in Linz and that family members were still living there after the war. From that, it was not difficult to deduce that traces of the missing man might be found in the area.

It was another of life's coincidences that Wiesenthal found the Eichmann family living virtually under his nose. The OSS had given him a room a few doors away from its office in Landstrasse 36. Walking between the two buildings, he had to pass an electrical ware shop at number 32, whose owner's name, Adolf Eichmann, was boldly displayed. 'I didn't think this could be a very common name. And I kept on doodling with the name. One day, my landlady, Frau Sturm, brought me some tea and noticed the name on my writing pad. "If you are looking for Eichmann, that's only a few houses away from here," she said. I said no, that's not the one I am looking for. I was still under the impression that the Eichmann family was in Palestine. But Frau Sturm went on to tell me that these Eichmanns had one son, who had been a high-ranking animal in the SS. "I am sure of it; look into it," she urged.'

Wiesenthal asked Captain O'Meara to let him take a military police patrol to search the Eichmann premises. 'When we reached the house, suddenly I couldn't even touch the door handle. It was abhorrent to think that the man responsible for millions of dead Jews might have had his hand on it. I am too emotional; I had to leave the military police to go in ahead of me. I asked them to search the house, and I waited. When they returned, they said that they had spoken to the father, who said that his son had not returned from the war and that the family had no news of him.

'The family also told the military police that they had no photograph of him, not even a childhood picture. Asked where their son had been when they last heard of him, they said Prague, adding that they had surmised he would have been arrested by the Russians. But the military police extracted at least one significant piece of information: the father confirmed that his eldest son had indeed also been called Adolf.' This suggested they were on the right track. 'But I was still not absolutely certain that the Eichmann we were looking for came from this family.'

Wiesenthal has frequently asked himself whether Eichmann could have been tracked down there and then, if he had applied himself more vigorously, and personally questioned the man's family and their neighbours. There is no way of knowing, although Eichmann was at that stage still quite close, moving around in Bavaria under a series of false identities. But Wiesenthal has also always maintained that Eichmann would have been swallowed up in the war crimes trials, and that the extraordinary responsibility which he bore for the Holocaust might not have been exposed to world opinion in the way that was achieved by his trial in 1960.

On 1 August, an OSS informer, who had all along insisted that the wanted man was from Linz, arrived in Wiesenthal's office greatly excited. He had been told that Adolf Eichmann was in hiding in the village of Altaussee. He even knew the house: number 8, Fischerndorf. Linz was over a hundred miles away, so Wiesenthal asked the CIC, who had by then established an office at Bad Aussee, to search the Fischerndorf house. The CIC in turn asked the Austrian police to undertake the search. They found another wanted SS officer, Anton Burger, who had worked with Eichmann – but no Eichmann. However, they had gone to the wrong house, to number 38. Wiesenthal asked the CIC to try again. This time, rather than leaving it to the Austrians, the Americans went to number 8 and found Frau Veronika Liebl and her three sons. Frau Liebl admitted to being Eichmann's ex-wife, claiming that she had divorced him in Prague in March 1945 and had had no news of him since then.

A few weeks later, Wiesenthal himself went to the Ausseerland in the Salz-kammergut – the region of Austria known as the 'salt estates', because its ubiquitous salt mines used to provide a steady source of income for the

Hapsburgs. He wanted to find out more about this isolated alpine land, where Eichmann's wife and children could apparently lead an undisturbed life in a community where no awkward questions were asked.

Altaussee itself is a small village on the southern edge of a darkly shimmering, almost perfectly rounded lake, with mountains rising steeply from the greater part of its shoreline. Fischerndorf, which is part of the village of Altaussee, is made up of a group of simple, traditional wooden houses built on a hillside. Number 8, Haus Wimmer, is one of the smallest houses, the last building on a steeply winding narrow road. Veronika Liebl and her children had to share the house with its owner, Frau Wimmer. It had the strategic advantage that it was easy to survey the approaches to the house. And of course, if Frau Liebl had an eye for her surroundings, she would have been able to feast on the view from her windows.

The Ausseerland is cut off by mountains from the city of Salzburg and its nearby lakes. Its remoteness and beauty attracted some of the greatest German-language writers in the early part of this century. Theodor Herzl's *Judenstaat*, his concept for a Jewish national home, took shape during repeated holidays in Altaussee. Richard Strauss came to visit Hugo von Hofmannsthal while he spent summers there and wrote several of his librettos for Strauss's operas. Sigmund Freud sometimes joined his friends in Altaussee. A telling caricature has been preserved in the local museum, which has Jakob Wasserman, von Hofmannsthal, Raoul Auernheimer and Arthur Schnitzler sitting around the lake, each dipping his quill into the dark water, their 'inkpot'.

The *Anschluss* changed all that. The Ausseerland became a Nazi preserve, which Hitler designated as the '*Alpenfestung*' – alpine fortress – when military defeat approached in 1944. He imagined that his elite troops could be regrouped in these mountains and moved out again to resurrect the Third Reich.

Joseph Goebbels's wife and children occupied a large lakeside villa not far from Altaussee on Grundlsee during the last years of the war until they left for Berlin, where the family committed suicide. The present owners still have a photograph of Frau Goebbels surrounded by her six small children posing in the garden.

Hitler's scientists were deployed in the area to develop the first anti-submarine missiles. Millions of counterfeit British pound notes, the product of a Nazi scheme to destroy the British economy, were sunk into Lake Toplitz, where there had also been a marine research station. It is widely thought that the Nazis buried large amounts of valuables in these mountains and also hid a list of Swiss bank accounts detailing the Nazi signatures required to gain access. The fake money was found. Local legend has it that some of the real treasure has yet to be unearthed.

It is fact, not legend, that deep inside the salt mines of the mountains above Altaussee the Nazis hid some of the world's greatest works of art, which they had confiscated from Jews or captured during the war. Hitler earmarked his favourite artists for eventual display in a grandiose museum in Linz, his birthplace, which he planned to turn into a city to outrival Vienna. The works of Rubens and Michelangelo, Titian, Dürer, Cranach and many more masters were stacked on the salt shelves.

This treasure only just escaped destruction in 1945. With the US forces fast approaching, the Nazi *Gauleiter* for the region, Adolf Eigruber, laid mines inside the mountain to blow up its contents. The art curators, backed by the mineworkers anxious to preserve their workplace, appealed to Ernst Kaltenbrunner, the Nazi security chief in Austria who was visiting a mistress in Altaussee, to prevent this sacrilege. A furious row broke out between the two Nazi chieftains. One ordered the dynamite to be removed; the other to have it taken back inside. In the end, either the mineworkers or Austrian resistance fighters blew up the entrance to the saltworks and blocked access until the American forces arrived.

Many prominent Nazis found themselves in the Ausseerland at the moment of defeat. One prominent SS officer, Wilhelm Höttl, still lives there undisturbed. Höttl had known Eichmann in Budapest. He bought himself freedom by testifying against the Nazi leadership at Nuremberg, and afterwards maintaining a shadowy relationship with the CIC as an informer. Wiesenthal had some contact with Höttl, but never trusted him.

Eichmann himself passed through Altaussee briefly at the end of the war, when the Nazi leadership was already in full flight. Local legend has it that he spent a few days hidden in an isolated hut at a remote end of the lake, which can only be reached on foot or by boat. He was certainly familiar enough with the area to assume that his family would be able to live there without risking betrayal.

Wiesenthal was to come to the Ausseerland on several occasions. But already during his first visit, he was given information that reinforced his impression that Frau Liebl (Eichmann) was being economical with the truth about her husband's movements, and that her assertion that she had not heard from him since they parted in Prague was a lie. At the Parkhotel in Altaussee, Wiesenthal was told by the proprietor, Maria Bucher, that Frau Eichmann had stayed there in May 1945, and that Eichmann himself had turned up in uniform, had stolen a suit and had disappeared in the direction of the Blah Alm – a nearby mountain restaurant situated on a trail that he could have used to walk out of the Ausseerland. The Blah Alm was a staging-post for Nazis on the run, as its proprietors were prominent Nazis from Linz.

Three months later, in December 1946, Wiesenthal was a delegate to the first post-war Zionist Congress in Basle. There he talked to Dr Reszo Kastner, the former chairman of the Budapest Rescue Committee, who had met Eichmann face to face in 1944 during the abortive negotiations to save the lives of Hungarian Jews in exchange for goods required for the failing German war effort. Wiesenthal pumped Kastner for even the smallest detail he could recall about Eichmann.

Soon afterwards, Wiesenthal was in Nuremberg, summoned there as a 'friendly witness' to tell what he knew about Nazi crimes in Lvov. The main trial of the Nazi leadership had been concluded the previous September. He spent every spare minute searching through the vast stack of Nazi archives that had been gathered for the trials. Much of his research was directed at securing more information about Eichmann's extermination machine, and about the men and women who worked with him. This was more important to him than sitting in on the proceedings of the War Crimes Tribunal. 'The prosecutors were always telling me that surely it must give me great satisfaction to see that these criminals were being brought to justice. But they didn't understand me. Those who were already on trial didn't interest me. I am only interested in those who are still at liberty, and if the Nuremberg archives could help me find them, that's where I had to be.'

At the Linz Documentation Centre, Wiesenthal's fixation with Eichmann was becoming well known. Survivors from the extermination camps told of the suffering they had endured at Eichmann's instigation; reports of sightings and clues to Eichmann's whereabouts were sent to Wiesenthal, and there were quite a few wild-goose chases. One of them netted another wanted man, Franz Murer, but also led to Wiesenthal's brief detention by the British military authorities. The incident began late one night, when three men, one of whom he knew, came knocking on Wiesenthal's door, saying that they had heard of a very important Nazi working on a farm, Gaishorn, near Admont in the British zone. They thought it could be Eichmann. Wiesenthal immediately decided to go with them.

When they arrived in the neighbourhood, it became clear that the farm belonged to Murer, 'the Butcher of Vilna', who is blamed for the death of as many as 80,000 Lithuanian Jews. It was soon apparent that it was he, not Eichmann, who had been spotted. He was living quite openly, under his own name. In the displaced-persons camp at Admont, there were several women from Poland who had direct experience of Murer's torture and had witnessed some of his murders. Armed with their testimony, Wiesenthal obtained Murer's arrest. But he was outraged that the British had tolerated this man's freedom for so long. They must have known he was there. In his usual forthright manner, he decided to talk with the British Field Security Service (FSS) representatives in Admont. Wiesenthal was not unknown to them. The officer who received him listened without much interest and then proceeded to question him about the illegal transports of Jews from Austria to Palestine. 'I had come to talk about Murer, and about nothing else,' Wiesenthal insists. But the officer went on. He thought Wiesenthal could help with information about the activities in Austria of the radical *Irgun Zvai Leumi*. The British may have suspected that he was associated with them. However, Wiesenthal repeated that he had a single agenda that day: to discuss Murer.

The hours went by; the questions were repeated. But word had reached the Admont displaced-persons camp that Wiesenthal was being detained. Hundreds of its inmates converged on the FSS's premises, demanding his freedom. After the brandishing of guns and much shouting, the British allowed him to leave. The demonstration elated him; but the behaviour of the British was depressing and convinced him that Britain was far more interested in fighting a rearguard action against the establishment of Israel than in bringing the mass murderers to justice.

Having accidentally found Murer, Wiesenthal was determined to prevent the British from releasing him. He successfully mobilised his friends, high and low, to have Murer tried for war crimes. But though sentenced in the Soviet Union to twenty-five years in jail, Murer was returned to Austria in 1955 and was able to resume the tranquil life of a respected member of Admont's farming community. The story of Wiesenthal's persistent efforts to consign Murer back to prison belongs to a later period, when his reputation as a Nazi-hunter had been established through his contribution to Eichmann's capture in 1960.

But to return to the search for Eichmann in the late 1940s: in Vienna, Ben-Nathan and his colleagues were as keen as Wiesenthal in Linz to track down the major Nazi criminals; above all to find Eichmann. To acquire official status, Ben-Nathan joined the Central Committee of Jews in Austria, where Wiesenthal had already emerged as a prominent activist. Ben-Nathan also set up a small Documentation Centre to act as a front for the *Brichah*'s activities and put Tuviah Friedman in charge. They recruited a small group of young people, mostly Polish Jews studying in Vienna, to work in the Documentation Centre. 'It was a search team, not a hit team,' Ben-Nathan emphasises. But many who were found were handed over to the Polish authorities, who made short shrift and executed them without bothering much about the due process of law.

During the summer of 1946, Friedman, having been dispatched to Linz to compare notes with Wiesenthal – whom he liked to describe as a freelancer – proposed that Frau Eichmann and her three children should be kidnapped from Altaussee. This might persuade Eichmann to come out of hiding. But Wiesenthal wanted nothing to do with such a scheme. Friedman recollects that Wiesenthal told him: 'I can't do it. I live here. Go to Arthur [Asher] Ben-Nathan and give him the idea. If the *Haganah* want to do it, OK. But I don't believe the *Haganah* will adopt the methods of the Gestapo.' Wiesenthal had judged correctly. Where such major war criminals were concerned, Ben-Nathan told Friedman, 'We use the English method. Eichmann has to be caught and put on trial; and we can't arrest his wife and children.'

Searching for Eichmann was hard enough; searching without even knowing what he looked like made it worse. It was imperative to find a photograph. In Wiesenthal's early accounts of how a good likeness was finally secured, he has suggested that he was closely involved in the project. However, Ben-Nathan, Friedman and Manus Diamant – another Polish survivor and the operative who did the fieldwork – all insist that Wiesenthal had nothing directly to do with this exploit, and, discussing it in 1995, he agreed that his part was largely limited to being kept closely informed of what was going on.

The scheme had taken shape when Ben-Nathan went to Bratislava prison, where Dieter von Wisliceny, one of Eichmann's lieutenants, was awaiting execution. Ben-Nathan had no official standing, but the Advocate-General in Bratislava was a Jew and arranged for him to interrogate Wisliceny. He didn't know where Eichmann was, but he knew a fair amount of Eichmann's strategy for escape. He also pointed to one of Eichmann's drivers, in prison in Vienna, who would be able to identify a former mistress of Eichmann's – one of several – who lived near Linz.

Next, Ben-Nathan interrogated the driver and discovered that the woman was called Maria Mistelbach and that she lived at Urfahr. He decided that Diamant should be sent to ingratiate himself with the lady in the hope that she had a photograph of Eichmann. Diamant was twenty-four, blond, handsome and not likely to be recognised as a Jew. Ben-Nathan provided the funds and sent him off 'to woo the woman'. Diamant introduced himself as a Dutch SS man, who couldn't get back to Holland. He had a Dutch passport in the name of van Diamant and he spoke German. (Diamant says that he is annoyed that a television mini-series about Wiesenthal's life, made in co-operation with Wiesenthal, portrays him as a young German, whose father had been in the SS and who takes the photograph to spite his father. 'This is pure fantasy.')

The mission took six months. As Diamant described it in 1994, he 'became Maria's lover. It was hard. I always carried a camera and said my hobby was photography. One day she showed me her photo album, pointed to a particular photograph and said "That's my Adolf." I went straight to the police. They raided her home and took away the album.'[3] Copies were made of the photograph, taken some twelve years earlier, which were passed on to Ben-Nathan. The album was returned intact to the woman, so that she would suspect nothing. Diamant is adamant that 'Wiesenthal had nothing to do with the discovery of the photograph'. According to Diamant, he followed his usual course of reporting directly to Ben-Nathan and says that, at the time, he was under the impression that Wiesenthal belonged to the Revisionists, perhaps even the *Irgun*. Ben-Nathan and his *Brichah* friends all belonged to the more moderate *Haganah*, and Diamant surmises that the *Brichah* operatives and Wiesenthal could never have been close because 'there was war between the two groups'.

Nevertheless, Diamant came to know Wiesenthal quite well, and they often discussed Eichmann. Wiesenthal likes to think of Diamant as his protégé. Diamant spent about two years on the Eichmann search, and was sent by Ben-Nathan to Bad Aussee to befriend Frau Eichmann in the hope of finding a clue to her husband's whereabouts. 'I lived with a friend of Eichmann's wife. Through her I got to know Frau Eichmann. I went hiking with the family. I visited them, dandling the children on my knee. I brought them chocolate. Frau Eichmann claimed that her husband had fallen during the war. Everything I learned, I passed on to Arthur.

'There was one time we heard that Eichmann was in the mountains. A squad of people came in and kidnapped a German and killed him. They said he was Eichmann; but he wasn't. I didn't like this; nor did Arthur. It did a lot of damage when people came in from the outside like that.'[4]

After a while, Diamant concluded that Frau Eichmann didn't know where her husband was, and Ben-Nathan recalled him from Altaussee. Wiesenthal maintains, on the contrary, that Diamant only had to be taken off the job because he was under growing stress at Altaussee.

In *I Hunted Eichmann* and *The Murderers Amongst Us*, Wiesenthal embellished his dealings with Diamant beyond what really took place. In the books he describes close co-operation with Ben-Nathan in the use that was made of Manus Diamant. He claims that the young man never became acquainted with Frau Eichmann, but that the strain of ingratiating himself with her friends and children became so great that at one point Wiesenthal had to talk Diamant out of doing something terrible to the Eichmann children. He says that Diamant came to him once 'saying that when he reflected on all the children that Eichmann had killed, he could strangle the Eichmann children'. Wiesenthal wrote that he subsequently persuaded Ben-Nathan to relieve Diamant of his Altaussee duties and that, together, they found Eichmann's girlfriend and sent Diamant off to get the photograph. In contradiction to Diamant's account, Wiesenthal also wrote that when Diamant found the photograph, he 'jubilantly brought it to me'.

Ben-Nathan now says that Wiesenthal's account is distorted: 'His memory is failing him', adding that, 'Wiesenthal makes too many claims about Eichmann. He is a great enough man without invading other people's territory.'

With so many egos engaged in the search for Eichmann's likeness, everyone involved has put their own emphasis on this exploit. What matters is that they finally had a photograph which might help to identify Eichmann – even though it had been taken when he was a much younger man. Whether it had really been worth the effort to secure it is another matter: soon afterwards the Germans in Nuremberg tracked down Eichmann's SS file, and found in it two much more recent photographs of him in uniform. At last, they had an almost up-to-date face to the name.

But even this very nearly became irrelevant, had it not been for Wiesenthal's quick thinking. That at least is how he sees it. Late in 1947, Wiesenthal discovered that Frau Eichmann, still presenting herself as Veronika Liebl, had gone to the district court at Bad Ischl to obtain a declaration of death of her divorced husband, Adolf Eichmann. As proof, she had submitted an affidavit by a Karl Lukas in Prague, which stated that he had witnessed Eichmann's death during the fighting in Prague at the end of April 1945. Once declared dead, Eichmann would be removed from the 'wanted' lists and his case would be closed. He would be safe. Wiesenthal had never believed the story of Eichmann's death, and he was all the more convinced that it was a carefully prepared ruse. Wiesenthal knew that Wilhelm Höttl had testified under oath in Nuremberg that he had seen Eichmann alive in Altaussee on 2 May 1945.

Moreover, shortly before he learned of Frau Eichmann's move to have her husband declared dead, Wiesenthal had again visited Nuremberg. There he had been shown the record of an interrogation of a German informant, Rudolf Scheide, who had described details of Eichmann's movements since his disappearance. This proved that Eichmann had still been alive on 30 June

1945, well after the day on which Frau Eichmann claimed he had been killed.

With the help of an American intelligence officer, Wiesenthal succeeded in delaying action on Frau Eichmann's request, until he could discover more about Karl Lukas. A week later he had enough information to convince the local judge that Frau Eichmann's declarations were worthless. Lukas turned out to be married to her sister, and correspondence between Lukas and another sister all pointed to a family conspiracy to help Eichmann's escape.

There was no death declaration. Eichmann remained on the 'wanted' list. Wiesenthal has said time and again that the single most significant contribution he made to Eichmann's eventual capture was to destroy the legend that Eichmann was dead. The ruse might have worked and the search for Eichmann halted. Wiesenthal believes that far too many SS criminals had themselves falsely declared dead, and thus evaded pursuit, living safely under assumed names. He will never be able to prove this, except in as much as a death certificate might have deterred him personally from keeping up the campaign to find Eichmann – and, knowing his persistence, that seems unlikely.

Wiesenthal's most determined detractor, Isser Harel, rubbishes the abortive death declaration as much as he rubbishes everything else that Wiesenthal has described about his involvement in the Eichmann hunt. He questions whether the whole incident ever happened and suggests that Wiesenthal invented it later to enhance his standing in the Eichmann affair. In his unpublished manuscript, 'Simon Wiesenthal and the capture of Eichmann', Harel argues that it is nonsense to think that, in 1957, the Mossad would have been deterred by an Eichmann death certificate from resuming the search for Eichmann. 'I would not have been bothered as to whether someone in Austria in the late 1940s had declared Eichmann dead.'

But this, of course, only begs the question whether, in the late 1950s, Israel would have been stung into action to reactivate the search for Eichmann, if the story of his death in Prague in 1945 had been sealed by a death certificate.

9

Eichmann Escapes to Argentina

Eichmann was alive. Somehow, he was able to keep in touch with his wife in Altaussee; probably also with his family in Linz. But where was he hiding? The Allies were searching for him; so were the Austrians and the Jews; perhaps also some of his former Nazi associates, who suspected him of access to Nazi treasure which had been secreted away before the Nazi defeat.

All of Wiesenthal's waking hours seemed to be consumed by the need to know more about Eichmann and to bring him to account. It was as if a monster had invaded him. He could hardly sleep. He talked to survivors from the death camps; he asked anyone who had ever met Eichmann to describe him; he read everything that had been made available to the Nuremberg trials. He made several more trips to Nuremberg, piecing together every iota of information that had been dredged up about Eichmann. It mattered hugely to Wiesenthal to comprehend why a seemingly ordinary bureaucrat had become a mass exterminator. Such knowledge certainly helped to build up a picture of Eichmann's habits. In an unpublished document, *Meine Suche nach Eichmann* (1961) he has written that he realised that Eichmann, 'he who had allowed millions of children to be murdered, was very fond of his own children, and so I calculated that sooner or later, his wife and children would put us on his trail'. Above all, his researches persuaded Wiesenthal that his obsession with Eichmann was justified, and that he must not allow himself to make a return to a more normal existence.

Towards the end of 1947, Wiesenthal was in Paris for a conference organised by the French *Centre de Documentation Juive Contemporaine*, which reviewed the research that was being undertaken in various parts of Europe about the Holocaust. In his contribution, he was his usual combative, independent self. He argued that the importance of documents 'could only be judged if the criminals were arrested. It required trials in a court of law to build up an objective picture of events, and the background in which they took place.' He respected the work done by the Paris *Centre*:

> But their academic researches did not suit my temperament or my restlessness. I stood for active documentation, which is to say that priority had to be given to the punishment of war criminals, not to the writing of academic treatises. After all the Jewish people had not yet died out, and the circumstances were not yet such that they already had to be eternalised in book form.

He never doubted for a moment that the arrest of mass murderers was 'the fundamental condition and the basis of moral restitution for the Jews'. Neither did he doubt that this had to remain his life's principal task.

By the beginning of 1948, Eichmann had been put on to Austrian and German 'wanted' lists. Jews across the world now wanted him found. In 1949, Wiesenthal went to Israel for the first time. As one of the survivors from Mauthausen, he took part in commemorative ceremonies for the concentration camp's victims. But he also passed on to an Israeli intelligence agent some of the information he had collected about Eichmann's life. In recognition of his work, he was given an Israeli *laissez-passer* to make it easier for him to travel around Europe and pursue his researches.

The Eichmann hunters, Wiesenthal included, had been able to put together their quarry's movements during the first couple of years after the war, but then the trail had gone cold. Eichmann and his immediate staff had definitely been in Altaussee in May 1945 – Höttl and Wisliceny had each said so in their testimony during the Nuremberg trials. Subsequently in 1945 and 1946 he had apparently spent time in the American zone in Germany, using false papers and voluntarily staying in a succession of three internment camps for Nazi suspects. On each occasion, he moved on when he thought his true identity might be uncovered. This was apparently followed by a spell as a farmworker in Bavaria and as a forestry worker in Lower Saxony, and there were indications that he had gone further north in Germany. But the Eichmann hunters could not pinpoint him and did not even know what, if any, alias he was using.

Veronika Eichmann, having been traced to Altaussee late in 1945, was being intermittently watched, with her letters intercepted by the CIC and the telephone tapped in the Haus Wimmer. The Eichmann family was not spending much money and the children were poorly dressed, but they obviously had financial resources. On at least one occasion a mystery man, wearing a trench coat and driving a black Mercedes, was seen at the house. Wiesenthal was convinced that sooner or later, Eichmann, anxious to see his wife and children, would reappear in Altaussee; indeed, there were many reports from the vicinity of sightings of a man matching Eichmann's description. Some informants even had an alias for him: Alfred Veres. But Wiesenthal was never wholly convinced until suddenly, one cold December day in 1949, an Austrian police official presented himself at the Documentation Centre in Linz. He told Wiesenthal that there was good reason to think that Eichmann was hiding somewhere in the scattered houses around Grundlsee, a fifteen-minute drive away from Altaussee.

The police official returned the following day. The police believed that they had accurate information pointing to a New Year's Eve visit by Eichmann to his family in Altaussee. They planned to raid the house. Wiesenthal was invited to join them and was warned to maintain absolute secrecy. Normally discretion is second nature with him. It is part of his trade. On this occasion he may have slipped up. In his books, and the way he remembered it later, Wiesenthal describes a young Israeli, in Europe on an 'educational trip', who was a frequent visitor to the Linz Documentation Centre. Wiesenthal says that he let out to his young friend that before long he expected to have Eichmann in the net. Then, after Wiesenthal mentioned the imminent expedition to the Ausseerland, the Israeli pressed to be taken along.

There is another Wiesenthal version of this incident. In an unpublished account, sent to a friend in Paris in 1960, he wrote: 'I had with me an Israeli friend. It was our intention to take Eichmann and bring him to the American authorities. We feared that something might go wrong if we left it to the local Austrian authorities to arrest him.'

In any event, Wiesenthal and the Israeli checked into the Hotel Erzherzog Johann in Bad Aussee, the 'capital' of the Ausseerland. The Israeli was asked to keep a low profile, and above all not to talk to anyone, while Wiesenthal went off to discuss the arrangements for intercepting Eichmann. Austrian police had stationed themselves in the small inns on the road from Grundlsee to Altaussee. On New Year's Eve, in the late afternoon, they telephoned Veronika Eichmann, hoping she would give away that she had a tryst with her husband. When she picked up the phone, they said nothing; but Wiesenthal says that his Austrian contact heard her whisper: 'Tell me, are you really coming?'

As the evening advanced, Wiesenthal and the Austrian went off to make sure all was in order. But already at the first inn, the policeman warned them that the locals all seemed to know that an Israeli was staying in Bad Aussee. And they soon discovered that word had spread like wildfire. Wiesenthal's friend had been out drinking and had casually dropped his provenance, and had described the attractions of Israel. In 1949, Israelis were not exactly thick on the ground in this isolated part of Austria. He instantly became an object of suspicion.

Therefore, if Eichmann was indeed in the area, he was likely to have received a tip-off. One of the policemen reported that, late at night, he had seen two men on the road at Grundlsee, when a third, running fast, caught up with them and whispered to them; all three turned around and walked away. The policeman thought that he had been within yards of Eichmann, but had done nothing to intercept the three figures. Nobody was arrested that night and Eichmann, if indeed it had been him, vanished into the winter snows.

Wiesenthal was bitterly disappointed. He had been convinced that Eichmann really was in the vicinity; that he had found himself within a few hundred yards of his quarry. In fact, there had really only been the flimsiest circumstantial evidence to suggest that Eichmann was at Grundlsee, or that he would make an attempt to visit his family that winter. It was not until Eichmann's arrest in 1960 that it became apparent that the person who had been spotted in the Ausseerland in the late 1940s was in reality Eichmann's brother, Otto, who closely resembled him. Eichmann himself was in northern Germany at the end of 1949, living under an alias, Otto Hendiger, and was making preparations to escape with the aid of the clandestine SS organisation, *ODESSA* (*Organisation der Ehemaligen SS-Angehöringen*), that was helping Nazis to escape from Europe.

Perhaps Wiesenthal has harped so much on the 1949 New Year's Eve expedition – writing about it in conspicuous detail in *I Hunted Eichmann*, repeating it in *The Murderers Amongst Us*, encouraging the scene to be incorporated in television films about his life, and talking about it in lectures and interviews – because he wanted to show that the Austrian authorities respected him as a key figure in the quest for Eichmann.

However, on New Year's Eve 1949, all he felt was that the search appeared to have reached yet another dead end. 'The shock of failure depressed me for years and endured until I received the news that the Israeli authorities had captured Eichmann.'[1]

Wiesenthal shifted focus and concentrated on learning more about the escape measures which the Nazis were taking to secure their freedom. He built up his knowledge of the monies they had secreted away to finance their escape from Europe and to start them off in their new lives. What startled him most was a document of the minutes taken at a 1944 meeting of leading German industrialists in a Strasbourg hotel, the *Maison Rouge*. The group agreed that Germany's defeat was looming. It was decided to organise the secret transfer abroad of blueprints, patents and, above all, funds, and to invest some of the money in legitimate businesses. The minutes said:

> The Party leadership expects that some members will be convicted as war criminals. Thus preparations must now be made to place the less prominent leaders as 'technical experts' in various key German enterprises. The Party is ready to supply large amounts of money to those industrialists who contribute to the post-war organisations abroad.[2]

When the US Treasury surveyed the scene in 1946, it discovered that at least 750 companies had been set up by Germans abroad since the end of the war. How much money was actually sent out has never been fully established, although estimates put it at up to $1 billion (at 1945 values). It also remains unclear how much by way of money, jewellery and gold the Nazis really managed to secrete in the Ausseerland. The Americans found at least one list with startling statistics of what had been brought to Altaussee. The French also discovered camouflaged gold bricks embedded in the roof of a farmhouse in the Tyrol. And Wiesenthal believes the story of a group of men who arrived at Altaussee on a June day in 1950, said that they were French, put on diving gear and later departed with twelve iron boxes. They later turned out to have been German. There have been several other reports of mystery divers, and Wiesenthal speculated that the master list was sunk in Toplitzsee and has since defied searches. He was also convinced that Eichmann had either been able to lay his hands on a significant amount of gold, or at the very least knew where it was hidden.

Fact and fiction are hard to separate. Much of all this is in the realm of mythology. What is undeniable is that the Nazis possessed the organisation and the funds to help them escape and refashion their lives. Wiesenthal also suspected that money was available to them for the defence of accused war criminals, and to promote neo-Nazi causes in Germany and Austria.

Wiesenthal amassed extensive, at the time still highly confidential, information about the organisations – variously known as *ODESSA* and *SPINNE* (Spider, or Association of German Soldiers) – which the Nazis had managed to set up to their funnel people away from Germany and Austria. They were elaborate, sophisticated, well-oiled organisations and were operating under the noses of the occupation forces. Wiesenthal drew a map of the routes that *ODESSA*, the principal escape organisation, was using. To his surprise, some of them coincided with the routes that the *Brichah* had used for the illegal emigration of Jews. Both used the 'B–B' (Bremen–Bari) line, straight through Germany, Austria and Italy, as their main artery. On occasion Jews and Nazis may even have been lodged in the same inn, without knowing of each others' presence. Wiesenthal learned that *ODESSA* only used Bari for those Nazis who were going to the Middle East. This group received help, especially their vital travel documents, from the Egyptian Red Crescent, which had people working with the International Committee of the Red Cross (ICRC) in Geneva.

Those whose destination was South America were brought to Rome and put under the protection of members of the Vatican *Curia*. A committee set up by the German bishop in Rome, Alois Hudal, took care of them, hiding them in monasteries and in many cases providing Vatican travel documents, until they could be put on to ships bound for Argentina, Brazil and elsewhere in Latin America.

Wiesenthal received information from contacts in American and British intelligence; from his friends in the government of Upper Austria; and from individual informants. He learned that many drivers, employed by the Americans, were in reality couriers for *ODESSA*, using US vehicles that were immune from searches to transport escaping Nazis, and sometimes to bring in neo-Nazi literature. He gave the Americans the names of two drivers, who were arrested. This did not greatly inconvenience *ODESSA*.

However, Wiesenthal did not suspect – or perhaps his pro-American loyalties did not allow himself to suspect – that the Americans were themselves involved with *ODESSA*. He says that he did not know until it emerged in the 1980s that American intelligence services were facilitating the escape of many prominent Nazis – but not of Eichmann – sometimes as a reward for acting as informers on Soviet activities and at other times because it involved scientists whose know-how had to be kept out of Communist reach. Wiesenthal is philosophical about the Americans, and sees their complicity in Nazi escapes more with sadness than in anger as a logical extension of the Cold War.

But he has never been able to find even the slightest justification for the Vatican's actions, or for those of the ICRC, who made it possible for the Nazi murderers to make their escape. Wiesenthal points to Pope Pius XII, whose ambivalent attitude towards Hitler's persecution of the Jews has caused so much controversy. During his Papacy, the Vatican refrained from denouncing Nazi atrocities, even though incontrovertible evidence from the Polish church had reached Rome in 1942 that Jews were being slaughtered in Poland. Pius XII saw Hitler as a bulwark against Bolshevism. But he also thought that the greater interests of the Church dictated that Hitler must not be provoked into retaliation against Germany's Catholics; besides, many Church leaders in Germany supported Hitler, and the Pope did not want to alienate them.

Any validity such arguments might have had during the war, none remained after Hitler's defeat. Yet the evidence of senior churchmen in the Vatican helping Nazis to escape to the Middle East and Latin America is beyond question. Bishop Hudal, who was rector of the Anima, the German Roman Catholic Foundation in Rome from 1923 until 1955, was at the heart of this endeavour, which must have been undertaken in close liaison with the shadowy *ODESSA* organisation. He also successfully enlisted the help of the ICRC, which provided him with Red Cross passports that were handed out to the escaping men. In its defence, the ICRC has argued that it is after all an aid agency, not a detective agency; that it was making out as many as 500 *laissez-passer* passes daily in Italy during the post-war period; that many of them would have been given to perfectly *bona fide* refugees; and that it was in no position to identify the names of wanted criminals.

It is a matter of dispute as to what extent Pope Pius XII was aware of Bishop Hudal's activities. Among the senior members of the Vatican hierarchy there were some who asserted that he was a major influence on the Pope, and that Hudal's arguments in support of Nazi Germany found a ready audience with the Pontiff.

Others claim that the Vatican did not take Hudal very seriously. A senior Vatican archivist told Gitta Sereny, while she was researching her book, *Into that Darkness*, on the trial of Franz Stangl, the camp commandant of Sobibor and Treblinka, that

Hudal was not at all close to the Vatican ... and certainly not to the Holy Father. ... He was slightly suspect, not taken seriously. He was not a Nazi, but as an Austrian he lobbied for federation with Germany. Eventually he went a step further; he thought there was a possibility of collaboration between the Church and the Nazis; and that he might become the means – the liaison man – to achieve this collaboration.

Whatever the truth of Hudal's standing in the Vatican, there can be no doubt about Hudal's own perverted political beliefs, which motivated him to help men like Eichmann and Stangl, and possibly also Josef Mengele and several other prominent architects of the Holocaust, to escape overseas. He stands condemned by his own writings, which explain his extremist, Hitlerian belief in the greater German nation, and by the accumulated evidence of his actions to help SS personnel, Ukrainians and others to avoid arrest by helping them to escape to safety in Latin America and the Middle East.

Hudal was always a combative and controversial figure. Though he professed himself an opponent of the racist ideology behind national socialism, he frequently wrote disparagingly of Zionism and of Austria's Galician Jews as evil forces undermining the German state and the church. He belonged to the faction of the Roman episcopate which advised two successive Popes, Pius XI and Pius XII, that they should recognise Hitler's legitimacy, and that Nazi Germany had to be supported as a bulwark against the menace of Bolshevism.

Wiesenthal is convinced that Hudal masterminded the last, Rome stage of Eichmann's escape to Argentina. By his own admission, Eichmann passed through Rome in 1950 and was sheltered in a Capuchin monastery by one of Hudal's priests, Father Anton Weber of the St Raphael Society. There he was furnished with a Vatican passport, which allowed him to travel to Argentina as Ricardo Klement. Very likely, Frau Eichmann and the three children used the same route, when they joined him three years later.

1950 was an unhappy year for Wiesenthal. He could barely bring himself to look at the Eichmann dossier. But the threats which had been sent ever since his name had come to be associated with the Eichmann hunt continued to arrive at the Documentation Centre in Linz. 'Death to the Jew, signed "Eichmann"'' was typical of the leaflets that landed on his desk.

The Centre was still collecting testimonies from displaced-persons camps, was still involved in reuniting families, in searching for war criminals, in trying to alert the occupation forces to manifestations of neo-Nazism and in pressing for more urgent attention to the denazification process. It had become a race against time. The displaced-persons camps were emptying as people secured visas to emigrate and were happy to disperse. With the declaration of the State of Israel in May 1948, Jews were finally free to go there without subterfuge. Wiesenthal's own team in Linz was slowly beginning to break up as these young men too were drawn to make a new existence for themselves.

Wiesenthal was under pressure from his wife to face the new realities, to move on too. Obstinately, he continued to say 'No.' But he grew more depressed by the day. The Eichmann obsession never left him. There were all kinds of unsubstantiated rumours that Eichmann had been spotted in the Middle East. Wiesenthal could never judge how much was misinformation, but in the first half of 1951 he thought he had two reliable clues that Eichmann had gone to South America. The first came from a German contact who was close to the *ODESSA* organisation. He had found out that Eichmann had been seen in Rome the previous year, that he had been helped by Ante Pavelic, the leader of the wartime Croatian Government and a Nazi collaborator, and that he had been given a Vatican identity that would have enabled him to go to South America.

The second clue came from an unexpected source, the Grand Mufti of Jerusalem, a confirmed Nazi supporter who had had close links with Eichmann. Wiesenthal viewed the Grand Mufti as a singularly sinister and dangerous figure, who had undermined Allied interests during the war, and remained a danger to Israel and to the wider peace. In 1947, he tried to focus greater attention on him with a short biography entitled *Gross-Mufti: Grossagent der Achse* (*The Grand-Mufti: Grand Agent of the Axis*).

Wiesenthal's friends, knowing of his preoccupation with the Grand Mufti, ensured that he was shown a letter, written by the Grand Mufti to a Turkish friend in Munich, Dr Ibn Ajsma Bey Bigi, which asked for news of Eichmann. 'This was an obvious pointer that Eichmann was not to be found in the Middle East.' Wiesenthal asserts that he was tempted to go off to South America to look for Eichmann, but that required substantial funds, which he did not possess. As always, he was impecunious, with barely enough to keep his family, let alone to undertake costly sleuthing in distant countries.

In the autumn of 1951, to earn some money, he sold a series of articles about the mysteries of the Ausseerland and its hidden treasures. This triggered an interesting visit from a middle-aged man of obvious military bearing, who introduced himself as Heinrich von Klimrod. He explained that he represented a group of former SS officers from Vienna, and that they had a proposition for Wiesenthal. If he would help them to find the gold that Eichmann had hidden, they would help with finding the man himself. To prove that the group he represented was familiar with Eichmann's escape, Wiesenthal's visitor described the Rome route that Eichmann had used and said that they had many former comrades in South America who would be able to track him down there.

Without hesitation, Wiesenthal said 'No.' The mere idea of doing a deal over gold that might have been wrenched from the fingers or the teeth of Eichmann's victims was abhorrent to him. It would have been a Faustian compact with the devil. Moreover, it was obvious from his exchanges with Klimrod that the motives of the SS men in seeking Eichmann had nothing whatever to do with repentance for the crimes that had been committed. Wiesenthal believes his response would have been the same even if Klimrod had been in a position to take him directly to Eichmann, but it would have been a terrible dilemma. Perhaps it is as well that he was not put to the test.

A few months later, around Easter 1952, news reached Wiesenthal that Veronika Eichmann and the children had left Altaussee. It turned out that the German consulate in Graz had given her a passport in her maiden name of Liebl, and it was thought that she had gone to Germany. From various indications that the children had given to their friends, he deduced that they might have gone to northern Germany. Later he discovered that the family had spent six months in Odenwald, where Veronika Liebl's mother lived, and had then left for an unknown destination.

In search of clues, he found them in the children's school records. No request had been made for them either before they left or afterwards. Knowing that it would be impossible to secure school admission in Germany or Austria without presenting school records, he concluded that the family must have left Europe. 'I knew enough about educational practices in Europe, combined with the fact that two of the children were of school age, that I was now certain that the family was no longer in Europe.'[3]

Another year on, late in 1953, Wiesenthal believed he had finally found his target. He was able to establish to his own satisfaction that Eichmann was in Buenos Aires. It came about by pure coincidence during a meeting with an Austrian baron in the Tyrol. To combat insomnia, his doctor had advised Wiesenthal to take up stamp collecting, and he had become an enthusiast. It fitted in with his whole approach to information-gathering: widespread contacts and painstaking gathering of facts, photographs and statistics to read clues and paint the larger canvas.

Stamp collectors hear of each other. Wiesenthal was invited to meet Baron Mast to look at his stamps. Mast knew something of Wiesenthal's activities, and they talked about this for a while. Looking through a sheaf of envelopes to show Wiesenthal some of his rare stamps, the Baron produced a letter he had just received from a former *Wehrmacht* friend in Buenos Aires. The writer said that he had met several mutual acquaintances from their old regiment. 'But a few more are here whom you have never met. Imagine whom else I saw ... that dreadful swine Eichmann who commanded the Jews. He lives near Buenos Aires and works for a water company.'[4]

Wiesenthal recalls the sudden thrill he felt all those years ago, as if it had been yesterday. He memorised every word, and wrote it down as soon as he returned to his hotel. He also wrote a letter, dated 24 March 1953, to the Israeli Consul-General, Arie Eshel, in Vienna to bring the Israelis up-to-date on his knowledge of Eichmann's whereabouts. Wiesenthal remains convinced that he was the first to have pinpointed Eichmann in Argentina and reported it to the Israeli authorities. Wiesenthal told Eshel of Baron Mast's month-old letter, which said that Eichmann 'was often seen among the German colony in the Argentine capital'. Wiesenthal offered to pursue the matter further, but wanted to wait until he knew Eshel's reaction to this intelligence. Wiesenthal's letter also refers to earlier communications with the Israeli consulate about Mrs Eichmann's disappearance from Altaussee, and confirms that Wiesenthal had remained in touch with the police chief in the Ausseerland, who was keeping a close eye on Eichmann's family and had discovered letters sent from South America to Veronika Eichmann's sister.

Elation at discovering his quarry's whereabouts was rapidly succeeded by depression. Wiesenthal remembers the sober reasoning that followed when he began to reflect on his next step. 'My work was at an end,' he wrote in his books and private accounts of his part in the Eichmann hunt. This might seem puzzling, given that years of dedication had finally brought him close to solving the mystery of Eichmann's location. Isser Harel, in his unpublished strictures, argues that Wiesenthal's credibility was fatally undermined because he did not immediately act on the Baron's information.

But as Wiesenthal saw it in 1953, Eichmann's successful escape to Argentina put the whole affair beyond his reach and resources. Austria's director of security services told him a few weeks later that he too had indications that Eichmann was in Argentina, but they did not know what alias he was using.

The search for Eichmann in Europe had now become a closed chapter. Wiesenthal recognised that it would require organisational resources far beyond his means to identify Eichmann in Argentina and pinpoint his precise position; and that the involvement of governments would be essential to secure his extradition. At this juncture, all that was left for him to do was to go through his Eichmann dossier and put it together in the expectation that it would be useful to those who would now have to pursue the case.

Perhaps Wiesenthal would have felt less defeatist if his Documentation Centre had still functioned in the way it had done in its heyday, but by the close of 1953 it was practically defunct. It had few resources. His benefactor in Switzerland, Mr Silberschein, had died and his widow had stopped the payments to the Documentation Centre. However, money was the least of his problems. The Cold War had been in full swing since the Berlin blockade in 1948. The East–West division of Germany and Austria, and of Europe, had hardened. The Western Allies needed the new Federal Republic of Germany – West Germany – as a bulwark against the Russians. Allied interest in the pursuit of war criminals had evaporated. Austria and Germany needed viable government structures, and if this meant employing Nazis, so be it. 'The West kept the Nazis going after the war: they believed that no schools, no courts, no police force could function without them,' Wiesenthal observed. It was now up to the German and Austrian Governments to take up war trials and make themselves responsible for denazification. Wiesenthal had no illusions: Austria was not the least eager to take up the cudgels.

In Nuremberg, the Americans were packing up their archives. The officer in charge of them told Wiesenthal: 'Europe cannot be defended against the Russians without the Germans. We must rebuild the German army, and we cannot do this if the German officer class is in prison.' And if the West recruited former Nazis for their intelligence-gathering, that was because they needed information 'for the future, and not information on the past'.

Wiesenthal said such remarks, of which he heard many similar ones, left him devastated. That was how he absorbed the bitter lesson that 'the Nazis had lost the war, but we lost the post-war period'. Yet he still did not understand the full enormity of what was going on – the large-scale recruiting of Nazis as intelligence agents; the recruitment of scientists to go west; the deals that were done to let Nazis escape from Europe. 'I did not have the clarity then that I have about all this now,' he said many years later. However, in 1953 he already knew enough to conclude that the 'post-war phase of Nazi-hunting was over', and that the Linz Documentation Centre had to be wound up.

Wiesenthal had still not quite made up his mind what to do with the Eichmann dossier – the account of his hunt for Eichmann together with the photographs and files that he had accumulated about him – when he received a telephone call from Arie Eshel in Vienna. Dr Nahum Goldmann, President of the WJC, who was on a visit to Austria, wanted to discuss the Eichmann case. Now he knew where to send the Eichmann dossier.

10

Six Years in the Margins

Simon Wiesenthal rarely loses his buoyancy and self-confidence, but the beginning of 1954 was very definitely a low point. With the Linz Documentation Centre closing down, how was he to continue with his search for Nazi criminals? More to the immediate point: how was he to earn enough money to support his family? And who would carry on with the Eichmann hunt?

The first two questions only answered themselves gradually: for close on six years he remained in Linz, earning his living partly as a freelance journalist with articles that drew attention to neo-Nazi activities. He also worked for various Jewish agencies, including ORT (the Organisation for Rehabilitation and Training). His task was to arrange vocational training and language teaching for displaced persons and for the new waves of Cold War refugees from Hungary and elsewhere in Eastern Europe, who were moving on from Austria to new permanent homes.

The Eichmann question answered itself almost immediately – or so he thought at the time. He already knew Arie Eshel, but was surprised when Eshel unexpectedly came to see him in Linz with a request from Nahum Goldmann. Information about Eichmann's hiding-place had reached Goldmann, and this had made the President of the WJC curious to know what Wiesenthal could tell him. Goldmann was therefore asking Wiesenthal for a report on the work that he had done. Eshel however does not appear to have made clear to Wiesenthal that Goldmann's own sources were still convinced that Eichmann had escaped to the Middle East; so that Wiesenthal, in his response, made no attempt to explain why he had already rejected the Middle East thesis some time earlier.

It cheered Wiesenthal greatly that the formidable Nahum Goldmann was involving himself in the search for Eichmann. Here was the head of an institution with worldwide backing apparently prepared to put his muscle behind the drive to bring to justice this exterminator of world Jewry.

Moreover, Wiesenthal seems to have been under the mistaken impression that Goldmann also headed Israel's powerful Jewish Agency. He had the resources and connections that Wiesenthal did not possess to continue the Eichmann hunt. It was only later that Wiesenthal realised that the WJC is a far more limited, and less representative, organisation than its name suggests.

As soon as Eshel left, Wiesenthal sat down to write a four-page letter to Goldmann. He summarised what he had been able to confirm about Eichmann's early life, described his own part in the search for Eichmann, and explained his reasons for assuming that Eichmann was living near Buenos Aires and had been joined by his family. The letter, written on 30 March 1954 in German and addressed to Dr Goldmann in New York, concludes with this passage:

> Based on the material described, I cannot of course guarantee one hundred per cent that Eichmann is in Argentina now, or was there in 1953. However, all the information which I have quoted, convinces me of the likelihood of Eichmann's presence in Argentina.
>
> I attach, dear Mr President, Eichmann's personal file, including his curriculum vitae in his own handwriting (extremely important as a specimen), his photographs in uniform and as a private person – though for the year 1934 – and photographs of his wife. I only hope that the person whom you will put in charge of this matter will have better luck than I have had. In any event, if it is of interest, I am fully prepared to contribute further to the work. Respectfully, Simon Wiesenthal.

In his book *I Hunted Eichmann*, Wiesenthal wrote that 'A great load fell off my shoulders when Nahum Goldmann, President of the World Jewish Congress, took the case over. He would hand it over to a suitable person.' He added: 'I felt full of hope and courage. I waited patiently for confirmation that my letter had arrived, and then for the reply.' He gave a copy of the letter to the Israeli Consul-General and assumed that there would be a response from New York in a matter of days. He thought that the WJC President would ask him to check out and contact the German officer in Buenos Aires who had written to Baron Mast about Eichmann.

No such request ever came. Far from welcoming the information that Wiesenthal had sent, or accepting his offer of co-operation, Goldmann did not even send a reply. At the time that was disappointment enough. But there were no bounds to Wiesenthal's bitterness when, many years later, in 1991, the very existence of Wiesenthal's letter was questioned by Nahum Goldmann's successors at the WJC.

Triggered by the Waldheim controversy, the WJC had engaged itself in a campaign to blame Wiesenthal for failing to cast Austria's President as a war criminal. If it wanted to destroy Wiesenthal's reputation as a Nazi-hunter, it was useful to deny that the WJC had seen Wiesenthal's 1954 letter, which showed that he had deduced Eichmann's presence in Argentina several years before the Mossad reached the same conclusion. So at least it appeared to Wiesenthal in 1991, when Elan Steinberg, Executive Director of the WJC, expressed doubts that it had ever been sent and said that it could not be found in the WJC's files. He has stood by this, maintaining that all Goldmann's correspondence would have been scrupulously filed. According to Steinberg, this meant that if the Wiesenthal letter could not be found, Goldmann could not have received it. He also casts doubt that Goldmann would ever have approached Wiesenthal for information.[1]

But unless the WJC can prove that the correspondence in Wiesenthal's own archive (with copies in the Central Zionist Archives and elsewhere) are all forgeries, it is absurd to argue that Goldmann had neither asked for nor received Wiesenthal's Eichmann dossier. The correspondence also confirms that Goldmann passed the Wiesenthal letter on to others. More-over, Goldmann himself disclosed in a newspaper interview that he had given a copy to the US intelligence services, asserting that this had been done at Wiesenthal's request.

Two months after he had sent the dossier, Wiesenthal did in fact receive an acknowledgment. It came not from the WJC President, but from Rabbi Kalmanowitz, President of the Mirrer Yeshiva Central Institute in New York. Wiesenthal had never heard of him even though the Mir Yeshiva, as the Institute is generally known, was already then a major centre of Talmudic learning whose membership consisted of survivors from Eastern and Central Europe. In a letter dated 21 May 1954, the Rabbi says that Dr Nahum Goldmann had passed Wiesenthal's letter on to him because he too was 'interested in the apprehension of this criminal'. It would be helpful to have some additional information. Did Wiesenthal know the exact present whereabouts of Mrs Eichmann, and the pseudonym she was using? That would be important, 'since Wiesenthal had omitted to name Adolf Eich-mann's address', the Rabbi wrote. And in a reference to the ill-fated tryst at Grundlsee in the winter of 1949, when Wiesenthal believed that Eich-mann was forewarned of a trap to arrest him, Kalmanowitz wanted to know whether Wiesenthal had actually set eyes on the man. 'This is of great importance, as we have no reliable witness that Eichmann has been seen since the end of the war.'

Kalmanowitz went on to say that Goldmann had received information a few days earlier indicating that Eichmann was in Syria. He admitted that the source of this intelligence 'was not reliable', even though it came from a former US intelligence officer and would be passed on by the Rabbi to the State Department.

Wiesenthal's response was studiously polite, though he saw it as a snub that in place of the WJC, he was having to deal with a Rabbi of whom he knew nothing, and who seemed all too unfamiliar with the Wiesenthal dossier. Kalmanowitz seemed to have misunderstood Wiesenthal's report to the WJC President if he naïvely assumed that Wiesenthal already possessed Eichmann's address in Argentina. In his reply to Kalmanowitz, Wiesenthal confirmed that Eichmann had been seen by several people since the war, and that one of the principal witnesses had been Wilhelm Höttl. He added that he personally doubted that Eichmann could be in Syria.

Wiesenthal again declared himself convinced that he had been close to Eichmann's person that night at Grundlsee, but does not say that he had actually seen him. In an attempt to explain why no move had been made to capture and arrest the figure lurking in the shadows, Wiesenthal makes a suggestion here – one which he has not made elsewhere – that the Austrian police were less interested at that time in taking Eichmann than in discovering more about the plans of a Nazi underground movement and the identity of the people involved in it.

Wiesenthal told Kalmanowitz that he did not know Mrs Eichmann's address, but he thought he might be able to find it with the help of a retired police officer from the Ausseerland. It would require $500 to oil the wheels of such an investigation. Wiesenthal had in mind that his man would have to go to Argentina, and his fare and travel expenses had to be met. 'If you think that your Institute, or some other organisation, is willing to invest this sum, I would be prepared to organise this research,' he wrote on 12 June.

Kalmanowitz's reply indicates that this correspondence had turned into a dialogue of the deaf. On 25 June, the Rabbi underlines that he is 'most interested in *definite* proof of Adolf Eichmann's whereabouts, as that is the only information upon which our Government will act'. He does not respond to the request for money to find Mrs Eichmann. Instead, he stresses that he was 'only interested in Eichmann's wife, if through her you are able to learn where he is hiding'. And even though he had earlier said that he gave little credence to Eichmann's reported sighting in Syria, he suggests that Wiesenthal should follow up the report.

Wiesenthal's response on 30 June was a terse five-point letter; no more niceties to the Rabbi. The gist of it was Wiesenthal's belief that Eichmann had been in frequent touch with his wife since the war and that to locate her would lead to him. 'May I therefore ask you to respond to my request [for funds] so that we can take the steps to secure Mrs Eichmann's address.'

No money came, and the correspondence petered out. On 21 September 1954, Wiesenthal wrote once more to Nahum Goldmann. Adopting a friendly tone, he did not upbraid the WJC President for inaction over Eichmann, but drew his attention to a Reuter news agency report that 'the former SS-General, Adolf Eichmann, is reported to have been found in a wood near Linz, murdered by a Jewish revenge group'. Wiesenthal said that this was clearly part of a deliberate disinformation campaign, and that the report had already been firmly denied by the Austrian authorities.

Wiesenthal added that, after exchanging several letters with Rabbi Kalmanowitz, he had reached the conclusion that the Rabbi was 'unable to give any help whatsoever' in the matter of finding Eichmann. There was no reply.

If Wiesenthal's writing tone had been polite, in reality, he had become profoundly disillusioned about Nahum Goldmann. 'He was not a friend,' Wiesenthal concluded. It might have been different, he thought, if he had been willing to go and work within the WJC's organisational framework. But as long as he remained independent, Goldmann appeared to have no use for him. Wiesenthal believes that Goldmann had little interest in tracking down the Nazi killers; nor did he want others, acting independently, to take on the task. Wiesenthal assumes that Goldmann's attitude was that, 'If he needs money, he should work under the WJC.' Judging by what Elan Steinberg says now, Wiesenthal is not so far from the truth. It was an irreconcilable clash of one ego with extensive resources behind him, and another ego with equally supreme self-confidence, but bereft of funds to back it.

In *I Hunted Eichmann*, Wiesenthal has painted a poignant picture of his mood. He asked himself:

> Have I been chasing after a phantom, possessed by an *idée fixe*? I thought of all the insults, remarks and accusations against me during these past years. Perhaps those people were right after all. All this upset me so deeply; yet I had nobody with whom I could discuss it. At home, I acted as if nothing disturbed me, because I did not want to burden my wife with my worries and disappointments. But did the Eichmann chapter really deserve to peter out in this manner? I could not and would not allow this to happen.

Wiesenthal's Nazi-hunting was now in limbo. He was depressed, but felt unable to talk to his wife about his frustration over the WJC's behaviour. At home, he gave off a semblance of cheerfulness that he did not feel. Not for the first or last time, there was no one to share his stress. Had he spent nine years chasing a chimera, a ghost? The depression grew worse; he had a physical collapse. A doctor ordered complete rest: more time for reflection, for dark thoughts. But he reached one decision: he would send all the files that had been assembled in the Linz Documentation Centre to Yad Vashem in Israel.

The archive weighs several hundred kilos, contains material on 365 war criminals, and takes up ten metres of shelving at Yad Vashem. Obviously the Wiesenthal material is only part of a much larger archive; but Shmuel Krakowski, who was archivist at Yad Vashem from 1978 to 1993, said that 'it was a valuable resource, especially as many of the documents are originals. The Wiesenthal material was of great help in preparing the prosecution for the Eichmann trial. At that time there was much less available from other sources than there is now.' The Wiesenthal archive includes survivors' accounts of conditions in the extermination camps and also correspondence and telegrams within the German bureaucracy dealing with the Final Solution. The archive and the painstaking work it represented was one reason why Yad Vashem and the Israeli authorities singled Wiesenthal out as a key figure in the Eichmann case.

The Linz archives were dispatched to Israel in 1955. The Documentation Centre had closed its doors; most of Wiesenthal's friends from the post-war era had dispersed. But he could not bring himself to give up the thought of returning to his quest for justice. The year 1955 also saw the fall of the Peron regime, which had protected the German immigrants in Argentina. Wiesenthal speculated that Peron's successors would be less keen on sheltering the Nazi émigrés and would be prepared to co-operate in tracing the wanted men and authorising their extradition to face war crimes charges, but he lacked the means to test this out. And there was no sign that the Germans and Austrians, or indeed even the Israelis, were interested in tackling Argentina on the matter of Nazi war criminals. The Cold War overshadowed everything and Wiesenthal was without support from the Western Allies. To his bitter disappointment, he realised that for the time being he could not count on Israel either.

Rationalising the situation, Wiesenthal recognized that Israel had other priorities. The massive influx of refugees arriving in the country had to be absorbed. The country had to build a military apparatus powerful enough to deter the Arab enemy. During the 1948 war of independence, Egyptian forces had come within fifteen miles of Tel Aviv. Terrorist attacks were commonplace. Israel's fledgling intelligence services were preoccupied with terrorism and the Palestine Liberation Organisation (the PLO), and with the Nazi scientists in Egypt who were helping to develop missile systems against Israel. Looking back on it in 1994, a key member of the Mossad team that captured Eichmann in Argentina reflected that Israel's Prime Minister, David Ben-Gurion, displayed 'tremendous courage in 1957 to divert scarce Israeli intelligence resources from their prime task of protecting Israel from the enemies that surrounded the new state, and to focus as well on the search and capture of Eichmann. He had a far greater sense of history than most of us.'

Israel's overwhelming concern in the 1950s was with present and future dangers, with survival; most Israelis, unsurprisingly, felt that the past could wait – all the more so since there was then a widely held view in Israel that the Holocaust's victims had gone to their slaughter blindfold; that they could and should have resisted more forcefully. Ben-Gurion was amongst only a handful of Israeli leaders who understood that the long-time Jewish settlers in Israel had to be confronted with the kind of evidence that only an Eichmann trial could provide before they would be able to accept that the Jews of Europe, far from behaving in a cowardly manner, had been up against a superior force which no amount of courage could have overcome.

Ben-Gurion had judged correctly. It was only during the Eichmann trial that Israelis accepted how wrong they had been, and came to see it Wiesenthal's way: that the Holocaust's victims never had a chance against the Nazi extermination machine, that the survivors had emerged from the camps against all the odds and were traumatised, and that the memory of those who suffered must not only be honoured but also preserved as a lesson for future generations.

For the first and last time in Wiesenthal's post-war existence, he allowed himself to become deeply involved in the administrative work of a middle-sized organisation. By all accounts, he did it with considerable skill. ORT, a widespread Jewish organisation promoting vocational training, had set up courses in Vienna to help displaced persons and refugees to adapt more easily to work and living conditions in the countries where they planned to emigrate.

'A Mr Goldmann from ORT (not to be confused with Nahum Goldmann) came to me in Linz with the suggestion that I should organise training facilities in Linz close to the displaced-persons camps. He pointed out that I knew the conditions in the camps; I knew the problems of the emigrants; I could speak their languages – Polish, Czech, Yiddish. I agreed to do it and drew up a pilot project for Linz. But then there was the 1956 Hungarian uprising, which swelled the number of refugees by at least 180,000, and soon I was organising courses throughout virtually all Austria, wherever there were refugees. My salary was paid by ORT, but it was the Americans who were financing the whole project. The majority of the refugees were in Linz and Salzburg and Innsbruck. ... After a six-month course, these people could earn a diploma, signed by the Director of the vocational school. I must have signed about 6,000 diplomas, and in later life, during my travels, I often met people who came up to me and reminded me that I had helped them on their way. I could see I was involved in something very positive.'

It was a different kind of activism. But Wiesenthal does not see it as a divorce from his previous, or from his future, work. Like the Holocaust survivors, these people, who were being helped on their way by ORT, had also become refugees as a consequence of Nazi actions. Wiesenthal rationalises: 'Hitler had given Stalin the appetite to conquer new lands; Hitler was responsible for drawing the Red Army into Central Europe. Hitler gave Stalin the Baltics, invited him to divide Poland and gave him part of Romania. Soviet imperialism was the direct consequence of the Hitler–Stalin pact ... the refugee problem was one of the consequences.'

At one point during this period, around the end of 1956, Wiesenthal went to a conference in Paris, where Nahum Goldmann was another participant. Wiesenthal, introducing himself, told Goldmann that he was the person who had, two and a half years earlier, sent him the dossier about Eichmann. But the great man's eye was already on the next person and he moved on. He had no time for Wiesenthal.

From time to time during his work with ORT, Wiesenthal visited Israel. His wife would have liked to emigrate, but he continued to resist. 'I felt I could do more for Israel from outside than if I lived there.' Even though he was now working in a responsible and satisfying capacity within a Jewish organisation, he knew that this life had no lasting attraction for him. His aims had not changed. He wanted to realise the commitment to the Holocaust victims which he had promised himself, and needed to be his own master. Wiesenthal could not see himself working within the disciplines that a transfer to Israel would have meant, even if he could find work within his chosen vocation. He preferred to remain in Austria, even if it meant feeling permanently rootless.

The fact that so many Nazi criminals, above all Eichmann, remained at liberty cast a perpetual shadow over his work for ORT. He was closely watching how the German and Austrian Governments handled denazification and war crimes issues. It was not a good scene. War crimes trials had all but ceased; arrests were few. More and more people with a Nazi past were installed in key administrative and judicial positions, and gaining membership of mainstream political parties; Nazi industrialists were able to rebuild their factories with the help of Marshall Aid.

There were still a few people in Aussee and in Linz who fed him titbits of information about the Eichmann family. There were rumours that Veronika Liebl had remarried, had a new but unknown name, was still living in South America, and that her relatives in Linz had not heard from her since she had acquired a new husband. Wiesenthal could not bring himself to tell his informants that he could no longer make any use of such intelligence.

Wiesenthal had no idea that in Israel there were stirrings in the Eichmann case. Late in 1957, the Director-General of the Israeli Foreign Office, Walter Eytan, learned that the Public Prosecutor in Frankfurt, Dr Fritz Bauer, believed he could confirm Eichmann's presence in Argentina and had his exact address. Only his alias was lacking. Israel decided to investigate, and the chief of the Mossad, Isser Harel, was put in charge of the mission. The information had come from a blind, half-Jewish German, Lothar Hermann, in Argentina, whose daughter had become friendly with a young man he believed was Eichmann's son. Bauer, himself a Jew and inevitably keen to find Eichmann, was unsure whether he could trust German diplomats in Buenos Aires to pursue the search, so he had decided to pass his information on to the Israelis.

The Mossad contacted Hermann, sent out undercover missions to probe his statements, gave him money, but failed to turn up conclusive evidence about Eichmann's presence in Argentina. By the beginning of 1959, 'nothing remained of the high hopes we had pinned on him [Hermann] at the beginning', Isser Harel writes in his book, *The House on Garibaldi Street*, his account of how Eichmann was finally located and captured. Another senior Mossad operative, Zvi Aharoni, who was sent to Buenos Aires to spearhead Eichmann's capture, was sharply critical of Harel. In his own, unpublished version of the Mossad quest for Eichmann, 'Operation Eichmann', Aharoni asserts that 'Isser had already decided that the whole thing wasn't worth following up'. He describes how Bauer came to Israel in the autumn of 1959 and complained that the Mossad had made a 'big mess' of the Eichmann probe, and persuaded the Israeli authorities to intensify the search. That was when Aharoni first became involved. That was also when Wiesenthal learned that Israel was in earnest in searching for Eichmann in Argentina.

Aharoni wants to 'set the record straight' and says that Harel has 'embellished' his story of Eichmann's capture, but has not responded to his criticism because the former Mossad chief 'does not react to the statements of lower level beings'.[2]

A few months earlier, in April 1959, one of the local Linz newspapers had carried a death notice of Adolf Eichmann's stepmother. As is customary, the announcement was made in the names of all the close relatives. Wiesenthal saw that Adolf's name was missing, but Veronika Eichmann was listed among the mourners. That appeared to make nonsense of her reported remarriage. Wiesenthal thought this significant and concluded that the story of the remarriage was a deliberate fabrication. But given what he believed to be Israel's lack of interest, he did not bother to pass the information on.

In August, he and Cyla went to Switzerland on holiday. One day the telephone rang in his hotel room. It was a journalist from Linz, who wanted Wiesenthal to know that Eichmann had been sighted at Bad Aussee. Cyla saw no reason to interrupt their holiday. Wiesenthal thought otherwise. He had to investigate for himself, but also wrote to the Israeli Ambassador in Vienna, Yecheskel Sahar, to inform him about this new rumour. Wiesenthal made his enquiries. It was a wild-goose chase. The man who had been seen, he later concluded, must once again have been Eichmann's brother. But Ambassador Sahar wrote to Wiesenthal, emphasising 'how greatly Israel valued the help he had provided'. He added that, 'according to Israel's latest information, Eichmann was in Argentina. His wife was acting as if Eichmann was dead, and she was now married to another German. But all the indications are that this marriage is fictitious and designed to "confuse the enemy".' This merely confirmed what Wiesenthal had been saying for so long. But there was one surprise in the letter – a very pleasant one: the Ambassador's letter showed that Israel was at last in hot pursuit of Adolf Eichmann.

There had just been a fresh flurry of rumours that Eichmann was in Kuwait. It had originated with a letter from Dr Erwin Schüle, head of Germany's newly established war crimes investigation unit in Ludwigsburg, to Tuviah Friedman in Israel. Acting quite independently of the Israeli authorities, Friedman had taken it upon himself to publicise the story in Israel, and the Israeli press had run big headline stories, awakening interest in the Eichmann hunt. Dr Schüle quickly intervened to say that he had been misquoted, and that the Kuwait rumour was an old one, long since discarded. No matter, public pressure in Israel was mounting. Ben-Gurion felt that he could not let sleeping monsters lie peacefully in exile. Israel's Prime Minister decided that Eichmann had to be found.

A special Mossad unit to concentrate on the Eichmann case was set up. Two Mossad operatives came to Austria – partly to investigate the rumours of the Eichmann sightings, but also with a great many questions for Wiesenthal of a kind which show that the Mossad at that time regarded him as an Eichmann expert. They invited his help to find out more about the Eichmann family's contacts with Argentina, and in particular about Veronika Eichmann's activities. They wanted, for example, a copy of Veronika Eichmann's 1947 application for a death certificate for her husband Adolf, and details of the travel documents she had obtained to leave Austria in 1950. Over the next few weeks, there were protracted contacts between Wiesenthal and the two Israeli agents. He was given questionnaires that required considerable research, and he met with the operatives on several occasions.

Isser Harel later dismissed as useless any help that Wiesenthal provided, but the intelligence which his agents in Austria sent back to Israel suggests otherwise. Harel has used extracts from his agents' reports in an unpublished, highly critical study of Wiesenthal's own story of his Eichmann hunt. It transpires from the Mossad accounts that early in 1960, Wiesenthal was deemed sufficiently useful for the Israeli agents to keep coming back for more assistance. In one telling report, dated 19 February 1960, and quoted by Harel, the Mossad men said that,

> In every conversation, Wiesenthal reiterates the need for the Israeli Government to declare a large monetary reward for any revelation as to Eichmann's whereabouts. He is convinced this will be useful and will quickly advance us to our goal. There are, he claims, a number of Nazi groups that were conned by Eichmann and would be glad of the reward.

Wiesenthal had discovered that Frau Eichmann's file in the German consulate in Graz, where she had been given travel documents, had been emptied. The Mossad agents reported that,

> All Wiesenthal's efforts with the German consulate – he used pressure and threatened to have the affair published – proved fruitless, and the files are still as empty as before. This proves that Eichmann's wife enjoyed wide-ranging assistance, not from an individual but from a long-armed ramified group. The prospects of discovering anything are poor, since it is known that the whole German civil service still employs a large number of Nazis, who sabotage any search or investigation relating to any Nazi. And since the headmaster of the school where Eichmann's children attended is a rabid Nazi, there was no prospect of our obtaining a sample of the son's handwriting or a photograph. Wiesenthal would none the less try to do something about it.

Wiesenthal knew that the Mossad had established that Eichmann was living in Argentina under the assumed name of Ricardo Klements, but he was under no illusion that they were briefing him fully on the other aspects of their search for Eichmann. He certainly had no knowledge of the plan to kidnap him, and was still assuming that, once found, either Israel or Germany would apply for his extradition.

According to the Mossad report,

In the course of a recent conversation, Wiesenthal expressed himself as follows: Just as there are things that you know and I don't know, so there are things that I know and you do not know. We stressed that we were speaking openly and concealing nothing and that we hoped for the same attitude from him.

They did not record his reply.

The Mossad report continued:

I cannot say whether this was mere boasting, or whether it had some basis. In any event, whenever we offered to reimburse his expenses such as travel, telephone or photography, he refused, saying he would submit his final account at the end, once the goal had been achieved.

In this Mossad report, there is also a reference to the funeral of Adolf Eichmann's father in Linz on 9 February 1960. Wiesenthal had hit on the idea of having the mourners photographed, just in case Adolf Eichmann turned up. He did not. 'He claimed the photography had cost him 600 schillings; but when we offered to cover the cost, he refused as in similar instances in the past.' When Wiesenthal studied the photographs, he realised that Otto Eichmann had an identikit resemblance to Adolf, and deduced that all the numerous so-called sightings of Adolf must really have been his brother, Otto. In a confidential memorandum prepared for the Eichmann trial, Wiesenthal stated categorically that Eichmann had not set foot in Austria since 1945. But because of the likeness between the two brothers, he gave the photograph to the two agents, and apparently had the impression that they were mightily pleased with his achievement.[3]

That is not in Harel's version of events. He cites a final report from his operatives in Vienna, which suggests that by March 1960 the two Mossad agents had grown impatient with Wiesenthal. They suspected him of an indiscretion: that he had hinted to an informant of the Israeli Government's interest in finding Eichmann. He had been under express instructions to maintain total discretion. Wiesenthal denied that he had given anything away. According to the Harel version, the Mossad report, dated 3 March 1960, concludes that 'we again found Wiesenthal to be avoiding full and sincere co-operation, although he is prepared from time to time to feed the [Israeli] Ambassador crumbs of information. ... As decided, we did not assign him [Wiesenthal] any mission. We parted from Wiesenthal very coldly.'

Eichmann was kidnapped on 11 May. The Mossad kept him in a 'safe house' in Buenos Aires for nine days. On 20 May, he was spirited away on a special El Al flight that had brought an Israeli delegation to Argentina for the 150th anniversary of the country's independence. On 23 May, Israel's Prime Minister, David Ben-Gurion, told the world that Eichmann was being held in a prison in Israel.

It was the first that Wiesenthal knew of the Eichmann capture. He had in no way been privy to the fact that Eichmann's hiding place had been pinpointed and that a kidnapping plan had been made. No matter: 'My prayer had been answered . . . my work had not been in vain.'

Hours later a telegram arrived in Linz from Yad Vashem: 'Warmest congratulations on your brilliant success.' It was a recognition to be savoured then – and for ever afterwards to be brought out in evidence against anyone who questioned Wiesenthal's right to be accepted among those who had participated in the Eichmann hunt.

Yad Vashem was not fully briefed by the Israeli authorities about the circumstances that led to Eichmann's capture. They were honouring Wiesenthal for the Linz Documentation Centre archive, which he had given to them in 1954, and which had given them an understanding of the lengths to which he had gone, in targeting Eichmann, since 1946. Their appreciation led to an invitation to come to Jerusalem to describe the years he had devoted to the search for Eichmann. Five months after Eichmann's incarceration in Israel, Wiesenthal was in Jerusalem as the Holocaust centre's guest. He was widely fêted and, for the first time, he savoured fame. He loved being centre-stage. It was a vindication of all the delays, disappointments and slights he had suffered in pursuing his cause.

Wiesenthal's elation blinded him to the frustrations that Isser Harel and others in the Mossad must have felt. He could guess that the Mossad had been responsible; but he had still not been fully briefed and did not know the identity of those who had been involved in ferreting Eichmann out of Argentina. The Mossad itself was sworn to silence: a fifteen-year gag had been imposed on Harel's team by the Israeli Government. For obvious reasons, Ben-Gurion feared the damage to the country's international standing, and to its relations with Latin American states, if the Mossad's role in Eichmann's kidnapping was made public. This was not the time to claim glory for exploits well accomplished. Ben-Gurion's tactic was to pretend that it had all been a freelance action, and that it had not been ordered by the Israeli Government. Wiesenthal was warned that he must not even divulge that he had used the Israeli Embassy in Vienna as a channel of communication about Eichmann. Any mention by him of the Mossad was taboo. Even had he wanted to speculate publicly about the role of Israel's intelligence agency, he would have been breaking the rules.

Unlike the others, Wiesenthal, being independent, was free to describe what he had known about Eichmann's movements since 1945, and to explain his own contributions towards tracking him down. If he was not averse to being received as an hero, he did nevertheless take precautions to stress that many others had shared in the Eichmann case. At a Jerusalem press conference, given under the auspices of Yad Vashem, Wiesenthal said:

> Eichmann's seizure was in no way a single person's achievement. It was a collaboration in the best sense of the word. It was a mosaic, especially during the last decisive phase, when many people, who for the most part did not even know each other, all contributed small pieces. I can only talk about my own contribution, and I do not even know if it was particularly valuable.

With that last phrase, Wiesenthal took modesty too far. It was not even in character. He had all along been convinced that his role, even though he had not taken part in the final stages, had been of great value; and he had felt grossly underestimated until the arrival of that Yad Vashem telegram. He had not just been a bit player in a deadly serious enterprise, but an indispensable protagonist.

Among the journalists present at Wiesenthal's press conference was Haim Maas. He stayed on afterwards and invited Wiesenthal to his home. 'I was very impressed by Wiesenthal and asked him whether he had thought of writing a book about the hunt for Eichmann,' Maas recalls, adding that the idea at first did not appeal at all to Wiesenthal and that he did not anticipate that such a book would make him an international celebrity. Wiesenthal also emphasises his reluctance to write the book: 'I didn't want to do it, because so many people had been involved whom I did not even know. And besides I had never been to Argentina and had had nothing to do with his actual capture.'

But Maas's view prevailed, and Wiesenthal went back to Austria to write. With his packed memory, the words just came pouring out, Wiesenthal says. Maas says that 'he sent me a chapter at a time, written in German, and I translated it into Hebrew and English'. Maas was also looking for a publisher in Israel. 'Finally I found a small Hebrew publisher, Weiss. But the book was badly produced and it was a flop. At the same time, quite unexpectedly, Moshe Pearlman published his book on Eichmann. It contained whole chapters based on the material that Wiesenthal had sent through the Israeli Embassy in Vienna for transmission to the Mossad. Pearlman had used Mossad material. Wiesenthal was very sour about it. So was I.'[4]

Wiesenthal, proprietorial, now felt strongly that his version of the story had to be told. He therefore persuaded the German publishing house, Bertelsman, to publish the book. It tells a great deal about Wiesenthal's background and experiences during and since the war, and brings the Eichmann story up to the point where his personal involvement ended. He cannot be accused of indiscretion, barely hinting at a Mossad role, and making no attempt to describe Eichmann's kidnapping, or even to say how Eichmann was brought to Israel. The book was dedicated to his daughter Paulinka, 'so that she will better understand why her father had so little time to devote himself to her during her childhood days'.

I Hunted Eichmann was published in 1961, while Wiesenthal was back in Israel as the Government's guest to observe the proceedings of the Eichmann trial. 'I have never forgotten the first day of the trial,' Wiesenthal says. 'When the judge asked Eichmann whether he considered himself guilty, the reply was "No". I whispered to my neighbour that the judge ought to be putting the question six million times.'

Wiesenthal is proud that during the Eichmann trial he was able to hand over to government prosecutor, Gideon Hausner, a set of authentic notes written by Eichmann while he was in Argentina. Standing by his rule of confidentiality, Wiesenthal refuses to say how he secured these handwritten notes which Eichmann had evidently prepared for the notorious 'Sassen' interview given in Argentina in 1955. Willem Sassen was a Dutch journalist, who had joined the SS during the war and had been condemned to death *in absentia* in Belgium as a war criminal. Sassen turned up in Buenos Aires, mingling with the German Nazi colony and persuading Eichmann to give him a lengthy, virtually book-length, account of his life and deeds. Eichmann was a compulsive talker, but Sassen edited and greatly shortened the taped material. He first tried to sell some of it in 1956 to the *Time-Life* correspondent in Buenos Aires, without telling him the name of his source. Anyone knowledgeable enough about the extermination camps should have been able to guess from the manuscript that Eichmann was in Argentina.

But this intelligence either did not reach the Israelis, or they were not yet sufficiently interested in capturing Eichmann. Extracts from the Sassen interviews were eventually published under Eichmann's name after his arrest in 1960, first in *Stern* magazine and later in *Life* magazine. However, the original material, Eichmann's own version – whose accuracy he confirmed – before Sassen edited it, has not been published in its entirety. A photocopy of the transcripts with handwritten notes by Eichmann remains in Wiesenthal's office in Vienna.

At a press conference to mark publication of his own Eichmann book, Wiesenthal made a point of complaining that Nahum Goldmann had failed to pay adequate attention to the information about Eichmann he had furnished in 1954. He never regretted that he had publicly expressed his resentment over Goldmann's behaviour, but it inhibited him when, at about the same time, he came to hear of an apparent plan by Alois Brunner and some of Eichmann's other associates to kidnap Goldmann. Brunner had calculated that the kidnapping of a prominent Jewish personality, such as Goldmann, could be used to secure Eichmann's release, or at the very least might prevent his execution. As it turned out, the plot was abandoned. But Wiesenthal made no attempt to inform the WJC of it until 1962, when one of Austria's newspapers carried a report about the abortive conspiracy. He had not written at the time, he explained, both because he already knew that it would not be pursued, but also because he feared that Goldmann would take any further communication from him as 'interference from a busybody'.[5]

In Germany, *I Hunted Eichmann* made Wiesenthal famous overnight, and the legend of the intrepid Nazi-hunter was born.

This did not endear him to Isser Harel – or to Tuviah Friedman. Each, separately, had been unhappy and resentful from the time of Wiesenthal's Yad Vashem press conference. Friedman was under the firm impression – a false one – that he had been the first, in 1959, to discover that Lothar Hermann in Argentina knew of Eichmann's whereabouts and that the Mossad only found Eichmann as a result of the information he had passed on to the Israeli authorities. Because the Mossad was involved, Friedman was not permitted, in 1960, to voice his claims. But he felt all the more strongly that his contributions to the earlier stages of the search for Eichmann in Austria deserved far more recognition than Wiesenthal had attributed to Friedman.

Wiesenthal, determined to defend his patch, reacted angrily with a letter to the Israeli Ambassador in Vienna, Yecheskel Sahar. In June 1960, he wrote:

Tuviah Friedman says that he was involved with the Eichmann search in Austria. But this is absolutely wrong. If anyone else had an involvement it was Asher Ben-Nathan. True, Friedman had worked for Ben-Nathan. But – and I am quite certain of this – he never contributed one iota to the Eichmann search while he remained in Austria.

This was, to say the least, a distortion of the truth which Friedman cannot forgive. 'He [Wiesenthal] is an egotist, who can write books and say I do not exist,' Friedman says. 'He can give a speech to 200 people, and I can be sitting there, and he will say nothing about me. He did a great job; all I want is recognition and that he mentions my name.'

Zvi Aharoni, much more generous in his judgment of Wiesenthal, insists 'that we must give him the credit for having been the only person to persist with the search for Eichmann even when others had given up'.[6] Another member of the Mossad team, who has discussed the Eichmann case with Wiesenthal, has 'no doubt that whatever Wiesenthal says about his role in the search is true. I have never understood why it was necessary to belittle Wiesenthal. Isser Harel just ignored the facts.'[7]

Harel, however, remains a frustrated Eichmann warrior, and he gives no plaudits of any kind to Wiesenthal. Harel had the leading role in the Eichmann kidnapping, planning the entire complex operation of seizing Eichmann, keeping him hidden in Buenos Aires until he could be smuggled on to an El Al plane, and safely delivering him to Israel. He had picked his team, had briefed them, had gone into Argentina with them and had lived through that extraordinarily dangerous mission.

Having achieved all that, he had to stay silent while Wiesenthal was free to talk up his own exploits, and went on to establish himself as a moral authority on the Holocaust and world figure on Nazi-hunting. Harel had to wait until 1975 to publish his own account of Eichmann's capture, *The House on Garibaldi Street*. By then, he had long ceased to be Mossad chief and was living in obscurity in a suburb of Tel Aviv. Harel's publisher asked Wiesenthal for a photograph of Eichmann, but Wiesenthal is never once mentioned in the book. The mystery of 'who did what and when to find Eichmann and bring him to trial' remained far from resolved and was acrimoniously whirring on to haunt the old age of men who had once shared a common passion in preventing a deadly killer from escaping justice.

[11]
Wiesenthal Moves to Vienna

After sixteen years spent in Linz, Simon Wiesenthal, Cyla and their fourteen-year-old daughter Paulinka uprooted themselves and moved to the Austrian capital, Vienna. It was the autumn of 1961. Adolf Eichmann's trial in Jerusalem with its shocking exposure of evil deeds had been followed avidly far beyond the borders of Israel. It had revived waning remembrance of the Holocaust; not least in Austria, where Eichmann, in charge of the Central Office for Jewish Emigration after the *Anschluss* in 1938, had laid the foundations for his future career as arch-exterminator of millions of human beings. Wiesenthal calculated that the political climate for exposing Nazi criminals had become more propitious. He also held very strongly that Austria had to be shamed into bringing more of them to trial. Austria's political leadership was turning a blind eye to the growing number of Nazis in positions of influence; indeed, even helping to advance their political fortunes. With his supreme self-confidence, Wiesenthal felt that he was virtually predestined to turn the tide.

Austrians, learning about the Eichmann capture after the story broke, became increasingly familiar with Wiesenthal's name. With the Israeli authorities still maintaining a discreet silence over their own decisive role in the Eichmann saga, Wiesenthal's Yad Vashem press conference had been one of the few authoritative accounts of the search for this 'desk murderer'. Wiesenthal's prominence multiplied by leaps and bounds when *I Hunted Eichmann* was published soon after the Eichmann trial verdict. In Germany, the book became an instant best-seller, and Austria did not lag far behind. He was now known well beyond the small number of aficionados involved in Nazi-hunting.

It was time, Wiesenthal felt, to leave to others the retraining of refugees – his principal occupation for the last few years – and to re-enter the Holocaust capsule, where he could give his undivided attention to the task of keeping alive the memory of the victims and bringing the murderers to justice. So far, only the two extremes of the Nazi criminal machine had been called to account: the Nazi leadership at the Nuremberg War Crimes Tribunal; and, in a series of other trials, the more easily caught lower orders of the SS. Nuremberg had been high drama, but the other trials generally failed to attract wide public attention. In any event, the camp commandants, and a whole host of other 'desk murderers', had not even been tracked down. The Eichmann trial had drawn attention to Mengele and Stangl and to so many other major Nazis who remained at liberty. The time had come to step up the pressure on governments to act.

There was no point in trying to reopen the Documentation Centre in Linz. The displaced-persons camps, and with them the eyewitnesses to atrocity, were gone. The town itself, with the occupation forces long since departed, had again become a political backwater. If he wanted to remain in Austria, Wiesenthal knew that he must establish his base in Vienna. But he lacked funds. Once more Cyla urged him to make a clean break and move to Israel. There, the small family would find the liberation from the past, she argued, for which she yearned. He had been invited to the Eichmann trial at the Israeli Government's expense, which proved that her husband was highly respected. She never doubted that he would be offered worthwhile, satisfying work in Israel.

But Wiesenthal was not to be moved. He assumed that in Israel, he would have to work for Yad Vashem or the Mossad or some other official or semi-official institution. Inevitably, he would be sucked into a bureaucracy; he would have to sacrifice his independence and would lose his freedom of action. That would be one sacrifice too many. Cyla would have to carry on in Austria. She had no alternative but to agree. But she was full of foreboding. She was convinced that life would for ever be full of hidden dangers; that the demons would never be far away; that her husband would continue to love her, but that his passion would be devoted to the Holocaust's victims.

So Vienna it was. They took an apartment in the unfashionable tenth district. Wiesenthal could not afford to set up his own office, and he decided to accept an offer from the organisation of the Jewish community in Vienna – the *Israelitische Kultusgemeinde* – to open a revamped Documentation Centre within its offices. It gave him a part-time secretary and contributed to his expenses. His status was unclear: he became a quasi-employee, which made him ineligible for election to the organisation's highly politicised council.

In the first newsletter, reporting on the activities of the new Documentation Centre from its foundation on 1 October 1961 until the end of March 1962, Wiesenthal explained that he was assuming three intertwined tasks:

to represent Austria's Jews in combating anti-Semitism, neo-Nazism and anti-Jewish manifestations, by presenting documents, research and historical material; to collaborate with the Austrian and German judicial authorities, and with Jewish organisations throughout the world involved with clearing up the question of war criminals; and to undertake research with the aim of setting straight the historical record.

Wiesenthal added that the Documentation Centre's top priority would be 'to throw new light on the still hidden processes that led to the destruction of Austria's Jews, and to bring those who bore the responsibility to justice'. He expressed optimism that Austria would follow Germany's example in setting up a central bureau to co-ordinate the search for war criminals and the preparation of trials, and that the two bodies would be able to co-operate. He mentions that among 100,000 suspects on the books of Germany's Central Office at Ludwigsburg, there were an estimated 15,000 Austrians. He had been able to convince a senior Austrian Justice official to visit Ludwigsburg, and had given him the names of a further 200 Austrian suspected war criminals.

By the time he published his next newsletter, six months later, Wiesenthal had lost all confidence that the Austrian authorities would act as energetically as the Germans. He wrote that it had become clear to him that each individual case would have to be meticulously prepared, and that the Documentation Centre would have to collect its own evidence before there was any prospect of interesting the authorities in judicial proceedings. From then on, he regularly listed cases which he had prepared and forwarded to the Austrian Ministry of Justice.

Wiesenthal's presence at the *Kultusgemeinde* was not a happy arrangement: 'I have always suffered from the jealousies among Jews, and this was no exception.' There was an instant clash between the traditionalist Galician Jew, secure in his Jewish culture and deeply conscious of Austrian anti-Semitism, and the assimilationist Viennese Jewish establishment figures who dominated the *Kultusgemeinde* and who were content to tie their mast to Austria's Socialist Party, the SPÖ. It was not quite the Vienna of 1915 revisited, when Wiesenthal was there as a child refugee, but it was close enough to rekindle all the mutual suspicions between the immigrant Jew from the east and the Vienna sophisticates.

Wiesenthal insists that he is not opposed to social democracy and that his political views were not at issue. His acutely critical attitude towards Vienna's Strongly politicised Jewish community stems from the fact that it continued to back the SPÖ in the face of well-founded speculation that the Socialists were flirting with the far right, Nazi-infiltrated, FPÖ Party. Encouragement of the FPÖ was becoming part of the SPÖ strategy for tilting the balance of power away from the governing conservative People's Party, the ÖVP.

Wiesenthal had constant arguments and unhappy disagreements with his quasi-employers at the *Kultusgemeinde*. He could not accept the logic of their preference for the SPÖ. Viennese Jews had bitter memories of the Fascist bent of the conservative Christian-Socialist Party – the ÖVP's forerunner – during the inter-war period and could not forget that earlier, Karl Lueger, Vienna's Lord Mayor at the beginning of the century, had been passionately anti-Semitic and the harbinger of national socialism: they found it hard to trust the ÖVP and were reluctant to give its leadership their backing.

During the 1930s, the Socialists had established a markedly better record towards the Jews than the political right. After the war, the small number of survivors from the powerful old Jewish establishment of Vienna remained convinced that the Socialists would be more constructive in helping them to integrate into the second Austrian republic. In fact, there was little difference between the SPÖ and the ÖVP when it came to dealing with denazification, or with restitution of Jewish property. But Wiesenthal was not only unhappy with the *Kultusgemeinde*'s political leanings. He was equally critical of the weight given to the effort to secure compensation for Jewish material losses under Hitler. He argued that this was a diversion. It should be giving absolute priority to the drive for comprehensive denazification in the civil service and public life, and pressing much harder for judicial proceedings against the Nazi murderers. Wiesenthal was right in his instinctive view that the restitution campaign was a waste of time and effort: cabinet minutes published many years later have shown that in 1949, ÖVP Chancellor Leopold Figl presided over a cabinet meeting of his ÖVP–SPÖ coalition which endorsed the views of the Interior Minister, the SPÖ's Oskar Helmer, that any settlement of the restitution issue 'should be dragged out for as long as possible'.[1]

Wiesenthal, still emphatic that he has never been motivated by political sympathy for the ÖVP, was infuriated by what he considered to be the *Kultusgemeinde*'s shortsightedness. He was convinced that all the political parties were quietly conspiring to play down the role of the Nazis in the extermination of Jews, but pointed to the Socialists as the worst offenders. He warned Vienna's Jewish community that the Nazis had political leverage in post-war Austria, while the Jews, few in numbers and of no electoral significance, had virtually none. There were endless arguments. Nerves were frayed. Wiesenthal's aggressiveness, spurred on by justified frustration, mounted. Mutual respect evaporated. 'I was constantly blaming them for giving away and wasting the assets of the Jewish community,' Wiesenthal admits.

There were many unhappy confrontations, but Wiesenthal remembers one epic quarrel with particular relish. The Jewish community owned a plot of land next to the old Jewish cemetery. 'The SPÖ manoeuvred to have the land declared as a preservation site where building would not be permitted. The *Kultusgemeinde* then sold it to the Socialists at a peppercorn price for around 50,000 ÖS [Austrian schillings]. Once they had acquired it, the site was redesignated and a fourteen-storey block was erected. I created such fuss', Wiesenthal says, 'that they had to pay the *Kultusgemeinde* compensation to the tune of 500,000 ÖS.'

To strengthen his hand in countering the *Kultusgemeinde*'s policy, Wiesenthal formed the *Bund der Jüdischen Verfolgten des Hitler-Regimes* – the Association of Jewish Victims of the Nazi Regime. Its membership was small, but Wiesenthal was its President, and this enhanced his status. He could now dispatch his missives on notepaper with an eye-catching heading. In the 1963 elections to the *Kultusgemeinde*'s board, his group won six seats out of twenty-four. 'A respectable result,' Wiesenthal felt. But now that he had formed a kind of official opposition party in the Jewish community's governing body, the Documentation Centre had to find another home. Wiesenthal puts it succinctly: 'I stormed out.'

He found a small apartment on the Rudolfsplatz in the heart of Vienna's garment industry not far away from the *Kultusgemeinde* and still in Vienna's inner city. It was a dingy place. This was to be the new incarnation of Wiesenthal's Documentation Centre. The place quickly became overloaded, stacked high with books and reference material on makeshift shelves, with barely enough room for Wiesenthal's desk and for the two secretaries and the occasional helpers who worked with him. There was no central heating – only an oil stove that had to be wheeled around from one cold spot to the next. The floor was covered with tatty, worn-out linoleum; the view from Wiesenthal's desk was into a dark well between buildings. The sun never reached into the room. In short, it was the very antithesis of the outsiders' perception of a throbbing, ample headquarters, suitable for running a big Nazi-hunting organisation with its tentacles stretching into many lands. The Rudolfsplatz Documentation Centre was even more modest than the premises which Wiesenthal had occupied in Linz. And the political environment in which he was now working in Vienna was far less congenial.

Austria in the early 1960s was struggling to rebuild its economy and to assert its international standing as a small, independent and neutral nation. The wartime Allies were gone. With the 1955 State Treaty, Austria – unlike Germany – had secured a formal peace accord. The country was required to make extensive reparations payments to the Soviet Union, and pay the other three Allies for their occupation costs. Austrians however were left free to portray themselves not as a defeated country, but as a country that had been victimised by the Nazis, was liberated in 1945, and which had now finally regained freedom and democracy. Far from acknowledging their enthusiastic embrace of the *Anschluss* in 1938, they preferred to deny all co-responsibility for Hitler's policies.

Officially, the country was committed from the first days of the new republic in 1945 to pursue denazification with great vigour and to purge public and private institutions alike of the numerous prominent Austrians associated with the Nazi regime. But the two big parties, the SPÖ and the ÖVP, were intent on playing down the magnitude of the crimes committed by the Nazis against the Jews. Wiesenthal was beating a lonely path against what amounted to a virtual conspiracy by the mainstream political parties to suppress guilt. Old wounds had to be healed and a clean slate had to be created for the renewal of democracy, Austria's politicians declared. But they were also driven by cynical political calculations: they were well aware that there was a sizeable number of former Nazi Party members who clung to their old beliefs. These people had their voting rights restored in 1949, and it was generally assumed that they commanded as many as 500,000 votes, numerous enough to hold the effective balance of power in the early post-war elections.

Both the big parties were engaged in a race to win the far right's support and were therefore careful to avoid actions capable of alienating the former Nazis. In the early post-war years, the ÖVP and SPÖ each searched for strategies to win their votes. The Americans, and to a lesser extent the British and the French, tolerated and even encouraged these moves as a way of minimising the Soviet and the Austrian Communist parties' influence in Austria. America's CIC was recruiting former Nazis as anti-Communist informers, but also used them to keep abreast of developments in Austria's domestic politics.

The Americans were certainly aware of a secret meeting, held at Oberweis near Gmunden on 28 May 1949, where the ÖVP's top echelon held talks with a group of former senior Nazi Party members to discuss how the 'National German' electorate could be persuaded to vote for the conservative ÖVP. The negotiations foundered because the conditions posed by the Nazi group were deemed to be unacceptably high.

This left the field wide open to the SPÖ and its leadership was not averse to exploiting it. One reason was the Socialist Party's need to fill the intellectual gap created by the loss of their pre-*Anschluss* Jewish membership; it was therefore prepared to recruit from the professional classes on the far right of the political scene. Electoral considerations were even more important. The Socialists were obviously not content with remaining the junior coalition partner, and calculated that the far-right vote could be exploited to tilt the parliamentary balance to the SPÖ's advantage. Unlike the ÖVP, the Socialists did not consider programmatic concessions to attract the former Nazis' vote. It would have been too controversial with sections of the SPÖ; especially with the large SPÖ membership in Vienna, whose Mayor had campaigned on the slogan: 'Prisoners of war come home; Nazis to Siberia.'

The left's preferred tactic – initially only discussed surreptitiously – was to encourage and strengthen the far right's own political parties as a way of splitting the conservative vote and breaking the stranglehold of the ÖVP. This, some of their leaders calculated, might reverse the balance of power between the mainstream parties and eventually open the way to an absolute majority for the Socialists.

The first move came during the 1949 election campaign, when the SPÖ's Oskar Helmer secretly channelled help in kind, such as paper supplies for election literature, but no money transfers, to the *Verband der Unabhängigen* – the Union of Independents known as the VdU – which openly displayed its Nazi Party leanings. Wiesenthal, through his contacts with the CIC, had heard hints of Helmer's moves, but lacked both influence and proof to speak out about them. The Allies, although reluctant in the immediate post-war period to recognise the VdU, had not prohibited its activities. Though it was a hotly disputed matter between the US military establishment and the State Department, there was even some CIC financial support for the VdU.

In 1955, the VdU was transformed into the *Freiheitliche Partei Österreichs*, the FPÖ, and though the new party was deliberately designed to attract a wider, more liberal range of conservative supporters, its core membership still consisted of former Nazis and Nazi sympathisers. One of its declared purposes was to break up the pattern of two-party, ÖVP–SPÖ coalition governments, which had ruled Austria since 1945.

Actually, the two-party coalition was not broken until 1966; and even then the tactic of encouraging the FPÖ backfired against the Socialists. For in 1966, the ÖVP, in its best post-war election result, won an overall majority, enabling the conservatives, for the first time since 1945, to form a government on their own. This lasted for four years, until the next election. From 1970 to 1983, the Socialists under Bruno Kreisky won four successive elections and were able to govern without coalition partners. The FPÖ itself did not make it into a coalition government until 1983, when the Socialists failed to win an outright majority and turned to the FPÖ as a junior partner under Chancellor Fred Sinowatz.

Rumours of Socialist money behind the FPÖ had circulated in Vienna almost since the party's launch, but became more frequent in the early 1960s. It was one of the reasons why Wiesenthal objected so strongly to the Jewish community's support for the SPÖ. But he did not know the significant lengths to which the Socialist leadership had gone to advance the FPÖ's political fortunes. Such intelligence has only come to light recently through revelations by two of the leading figures involved in the secret deals: the Socialists' Franz Olah and the FPÖ's former leader, Friedrich Peter, who no longer has any inhibitions about revealing the history of his dealings with the SPÖ. Much to Wiesenthal's satisfaction, the insiders have confirmed that the Socialist Party's intrigues with the FPÖ were even more extensive than he had suspected at the time of his battles with the *Kultusgemeinde.*

In his memoirs, *Die Erinnerungen,* Olah has confirmed that the first contacts between the Socialists and the FPÖ took place in 1959, when the two parties agreed on a five per cent clause for elections to the Vienna municipality, a measure that enabled the FPÖ to gain a foothold in the capital's government. But there was also a secret agreement under which the Socialists halted any support for fringe groups that might otherwise join the FPÖ, and there was a small money transfer of 150,000 schillings to help meet the FPÖ's expenses in elections that year to the *Arbeiterkammer* (the Chamber of Labour).[2]

The next stage of SPÖ–FPÖ collaboration came in 1962. Friedrich Peter, the FPÖ's leader from 1958 until 1983, waited until 1994 to describe his side of the secret deals with SPÖ leaders, and how they all began in the run-up to the March 1963 general election, when the FPÖ found itself financially strapped. Peter is the same man whose SS past in 1975 transformed an already simmering feud into a major confrontation between Bruno Kreisky and Simon Wiesenthal.

The former FPÖ leader recalls how he agonised over finding the much needed one million schillings – a sizeable amount at that period's value of the Austrian currency – for his 1963 election budget, and how, after sleepless nights, he suddenly had the idea of going to Franz Olah, then head of the Austrian trade union movement, which was intimately linked to the Socialist

Party. Peter explained his predicament. In his memoirs, Olah spells out his reply to Peter: 'If the FPÖ remains neutral in the election, the party can count on our financial help.'

Not long afterwards, Peter says he received from Olah

> two savings bank books; one with the codename 'Edelweiss', the other code-named 'Enzian', each with a credit of 500,000 ÖS. They required no signatures. Olah told me to use the money 'for the good of democracy' and I replied that 'the money would be used to promote a democratic opposition party'.

According to Peter, Olah was emphatic that the Socialists were not trying to buy the FPÖ; they did not want satellites, but partners. But Olah's memoirs tell a somewhat different story and show how far the SPÖ was prepared to bargain: Olah writes that he told Peter if the conservatives were to invite the FPÖ into a coalition by offering them two ministerial posts, the Socialists would always be prepared to go one better and offer three posts. Olah suggests that he was acting on 'the need to know principle', but that Kreisky and other senior Socialist Party leaders were being kept closely informed of his dealings with Peter, and that the party was very content with the FPÖ's behaviour in the election campaign. As a result of having bought off the FPÖ, 'our party's backs were clear'.

Peter says that he refrained from asking Olah who had authorised the money, but he was convinced that authority for the one million schillings had come from the Socialist Party, and had not simply been a trade union move. At the time, both men understood that strict silence would be observed over their deal. But secrets are hard to keep in Austria, and rumours about the 'Olah million' surfaced soon afterwards. Peter came to the rescue of the Socialists by issuing staunch denials that money had passed between the two parties. But now that he feels free to talk, he has also confirmed that regular money lines were opened between the FPÖ and the SPÖ, with one of his deputies in charge of working out the details with Socialist Party headquarters. In 1964, the Socialists produced another million schillings, he says, and he hints that there was considerably more from the same quarter.

Olah has disclosed in his memoirs that altogether 'financial injections' worth six million schillings were made from Socialist coffers to the FPÖ during the 1960s. He also describes how the SPÖ endorsed the appointment of FPÖ members to a number of important public positions and confirms that regular policy discussions within a bi-partisan 'contact committee' were established in 1963. Bruno Kreisky, who had already developed a friendly personal relationship with Peter, was a member of this liaison group. Peter says that informal promises were made by SPÖ leaders to reform the electoral system in the FPÖ's favour, but that nothing was done before 1970 to implement the commitment.

Wiesenthal bitterly despised the opportunism of the SPÖ, but he was always less concerned with the details of what passed between the Socialists and the FPÖ than with the impact their machinations had on the wider ramifications of the influence the Nazis were able to sustain in Austria. He found it shocking that they could operate with far greater impunity in Austria than in Germany. This led him to collate evidence about the extent to which the Nazis – he always resisted labelling them as neo-Nazis – had progressively re-entered all areas of public life, and how so many war crimes trials had ended with pardons or 'not guilty' verdicts. At the same time, of course, he was pursuing the slow, painstaking search for his prey, for the mass murderers, sifting titbits of information for clues of their whereabouts, and, once located, pressing for their extradition and trial. Topping his list of targets were Josef Mengele, Franz Stangl, Hermine Braunsteiner, Eric Rajakovich, Martin Bormann and Franz Murer, but he sought many others who were less prominent, not least his drive to identify and find the policeman who had been responsible for Anne Frank's arrest.

Inevitably, Wiesenthal's activities continued to attract threats, abuse and enmity. In Linz, he had received plenty of threatening letters, and this continued in Vienna. As far as his own person was concerned, he was not afraid. 'If I suffered from fear, I could never have done my work. But I have always derived strength from what I was doing for the dead and for the living.' It was different for his wife. Knowing that she does not possess the same inner resources that have helped him, he has continuously feared for her safety. Nothing brought that home to him as clearly as an incident in 1963.

He had been in Milan in search of one of Eichmann's lieutenants. On his return, he was met at Schwechat, Vienna's airport, by his secretary, who told Wiesenthal that Cyla had received a threatening telephone call during the previous night. An unknown voice had warned her that their daughter would be killed unless her husband halted his activities. Cyla's response had been a nervous collapse.

'After she improved, we had a long talk.' She resumed her plea to move to Israel. 'She told me: "You must reply. When the life of our child is involved, you cannot simply dismiss it as an idle warning." My reply was to suggest that my wife should take our daughter to Israel. There, they would be safe and I could stay here; and then I would not be betraying the dead. A few days later my wife said to me that, "Where you are, I shall remain." '

'Moral Duties Have No Terms'

Robert Kennedy

Austrians wanted to forget, and here was that uncomfortable man, Simon Wiesenthal, constantly reminding them of their complicity in Nazi atrocities. Nothing illustrated the duel between a nation and its unwelcome conscience better than the case of Franz Murer, the 'Butcher of Vilna'. Murer had been Deputy Commissar of the Vilna district in Lithuania, where at least 80,000 Jews had lived before the war; at the war's end, only 250 remained. The failure to convict and jail him after his trial in 1963 was a dramatic illustration of Austrian reluctance to punish war criminals. Murer's 'not guilty' verdict persuaded Wiesenthal that Austrian juries were so packed with former Nazis that no amount of eyewitness evidence would persuade them to send one of their own to prison. The Murer saga, he felt, typified the hollowness of the Austrian leadership's commitment to denazification. It was also a personal setback for years of effort by Wiesenthal to see Murer end his life behind bars.

Wiesenthal had accidentally found Murer back in 1947, when he had been led to a farm near Admont in Styria on the mistaken assumption that the 'big fish' living there might be Adolf Eichmann. Wiesenthal had convinced the British military to arrest him. Murer pleaded that it was a case of mistaken identity. Anxious to forestall any British move to let him go, Wiesenthal persuaded officials at the International Military Tribunal at Nuremberg to insist that Murer remain in custody as a potential witness at the war crimes trial. Murer was eventually handed over to the Soviet Union – because the Soviets had annexed Lithuania during the war, he fell under their jurisdiction – and was tried in Vilna in 1948; he was sentenced to twenty-five years' hard labour for murdering 'Soviet citizens'.

That seemed like a case of just punishment, and Wiesenthal thought that here was one Nazi criminal he could strike off his list of wanted men. He was wrong. In 1955, after the Austrian State Treaty, the Soviet Union agreed to return Austrian prisoners of war, including war criminals who were to be retried by the Austrian courts. The treaty however stopped short of a general amnesty, and left loopholes that Moscow could exploit if it wanted to hold on to any particular person. Wiesenthal had not noticed that Murer's name was on the list of those who had been repatriated after the State Treaty was ratified. This is not surprising as it coincided with the period when he was working on the vocational training of refugees, and did not involve himself so intimately with the fate of the Nazi criminals.

His curiosity about Murer revived only after Eichmann's capture. That was when he discovered that, far from having died or languishing in a Soviet prison, Murer was alive and well, back at his Admont farm. He had been returned quietly in 1956 and had been able to resume life with a clean sheet. He was locally prominent as a member of the ÖVP and had been elected chairman of the District Agricultural Chamber. He was a popular public figure, often wheeled out when prominent politicians from Vienna visited the area.

Once Wiesenthal saw what had happened, he decided to leave no stone unturned to expose Murer and shame the Austrian judiciary to put him on trial. After all, Austria was in principle committed to retry all convicted war criminals who had been sent back by the occupying powers. Wiesenthal's first step was to write to the Austrian Minister of Justice to enquire when and how he intended to act against Murer. Asked to forward relevant material, Wiesenthal sent thirty-two affidavits. After several weeks and numerous telephone calls, he was told that this testimony could not be used since it had already been submitted to the earlier Soviet trial at Vilna. Wiesenthal changed tack and argued that Murer had only served seven years of his Vilna sentence. Back came the argument that Soviet prisons were three times as hard as Austria's, and Murer could therefore be reckoned to have done twenty-one years – and that was surely adequate.

The Austrian judiciary did not yet know Wiesenthal well enough to understand that he could not be put off by such specious arguments. He was not after vengeance, but after justice, he insisted. The letters and telephone calls continued until exasperated officials told Wiesenthal that he would have to obtain fresh evidence before a further trial could be contemplated. A new batch of witnesses would have to be found after all these years; and, still more problematical, such survivors would have to be persuaded to relive their dreadful experiences, possibly even to the extent of appearing in court and submitting to cross-examination from unfriendly defence lawyers.

Undaunted, Wiesenthal searched through the register of the Documentation Centre, identified survivors from Vilna and, to his surprise, secured a convincing response with eyewitness accounts of atrocities committed by Murer. It was the all-too-familiar tale of women and babies being indiscriminately shot, of men being hanged – and if not killed the first time, being strung up for a second time. The evidence was submitted to the Justice Ministry, but there was no reaction. This was early in 1961. Wiesenthal was still something of a novice with press conferences, but his instinct told him to search out the media – especially the foreign correspondents in Vienna. The press was invited to the *Kultusgemeinde*, ostensibly to hear Wiesenthal talk on the theme of 'The murderers amongst us', but in reality to hear him expose the Murer case as a typical example of the Austrian disease of feigning blindness to evil.

Soon afterwards, at the Eichmann trial, evidence was given about the Vilna ghetto, and Murer's name inevitably came up. This was reported in the Austrian media. Murer was ceasing to be an obscure provincial politico. Articles and editorials were written in Austria and abroad questioning the leniency shown towards him. Finally, the authorities acted and arrested Murer, charging him with seventeen specific murders. The move provoked vociferous protests from the right.

It took more than a year before the trial began in Graz. Wiesenthal was in court. One of the witnesses, he says, had come with the clear intention of revenging himself on Murer by killing him. Wiesenthal cajoled and argued and finally dissuaded the man, arguing that Jews could not accuse others of murder and then commit murder themselves. The administration of justice had to be left to the courts. But Wiesenthal was uneasy. The atmosphere felt wrong. Sympathy was with the defendant. The trial lasted a week and several members of the jury, as an expression of nationalist anti-Semitic sentiment, made a point of wearing traditional *Trachten* (loden) suits. No amount of evidence was capable of persuading the jury that they had before them a man who had committed vile war crimes. After four hours of deliberation, they pronounced Murer 'not guilty'. There were cheers in the court, and the prisoner was showered with flowers.

However, the verdict also provoked protests that it had been a scandal; and there was a degree of concern in Vienna that such blatant disregard of evidence would harm Austria's good name. Groups of Catholic students in Vienna demonstrated, calling for Murer to be tried again. The Public Prosecutor appealed against the verdict. But though the Supreme Court reversed the acquittal, there were no further moves against Murer. Wiesenthal continued to press for a retrial. Year after year he continued to find new evidence against Murer and regularly publicised it, as well as passing details on to the judicial authorities. But they could not be provoked into action. Wiesenthal's efforts against Murer were quite simply ignored.

Such ambivalence towards Austria's Nazi past fuelled Wiesenthal's distrust of the country's post-war leaders. It increased his determination to expose the Nazis sheltering in positions of responsibility. Equally important, Wiesenthal campaigned against the prevalent view in Austria that too much time had already elapsed for further war crimes trials to be staged.

Given that Wiesenthal was born a subject of the Hapsburg Empire, he felt justified in acquiring Austrian citizenship. Yet it often seemed to him as if he had pitched tent in enemy territory. A far higher percentage of the Austrian population than of Germany's had joined the SS and occupied key positions in the Nazi hierarchy. 'And for that matter, Hitler was no Eskimo.' Weisenthal has no sympathy with the argument that Austrians are compulsive 'groupies' and often join associations, clubs, even political parties, without much thought of what is involved. He asserts that even allowing that some Austrians didn't know much about the Nazis when they became party members, they would soon have found out – and would have gone on with enthusiasm to recruit more.

Austrians would have preferred to forget such unpleasantness. Wiesenthal would not allow it. Austria had to purge itself of its guilt, and must acknowledge its true history, he trumpeted. With the example of the Murer verdict burning in his mind's eye, Wiesenthal went to work with a vengeance, setting the scene for more than a decade of fighting with Bruno Kreisky, which began in 1970 and did not end until Kreisky's death in 1986. Characteristic of his thoroughness in marshalling his facts before going on the attack, Wiesenthal spent three years, from 1963 to 1966, collecting data on Nazi penetration in Austria, and trying to put quiet pressure on ministers and officials to act.

However, his representations led nowhere. His next step, in October 1966, was to address a carefully documented memorandum to the Austrian Chancellor, Dr Josef Klaus, entitled 'Guilt and atonement of the Nazi perpetrators from Austria' ('*Schuld und Sühne der NS-Täter aus Österreich*'). After this too failed to elicit a response, Wiesenthal called a press conference, winning widespread coverage in and outside Austria. The facts, figures and arguments that he put forward shocked some Austrians and caused deep resentment among others. But either way, Wiesenthal's paper became a frequently quoted mini-classic used to demonstrate how far Austria still had to travel to restore its good name.

The Wiesenthal 'equation' was stark. Austrians had formed 8.5 per cent of the population of 'Greater Germany', yet 'I have extensive proof that Austrians were responsible for the death of three million Jews [out of the estimated six million killings]'. He conceded that this was an approximation.

But what was beyond doubt was the fact that the number of prosecutions of Austria's war criminals was woefully inadequate, and that the judiciary was not only grossly understaffed, but in many instances was employing former Nazis, who were deliberately impeding the course of justice. He pointed out that there was no comparison between the batteries of prosecutors handling war crimes investigations in Germany and the few over-worked individuals in Austria attempting to do the same work.

Wiesenthal had discussed these issues with Austria's Ministers of Justice and of the Interior. He acknowledged that they recognised the problem, but argued that they failed to respond with the necessary measures. He called for a substantial enlargement of the legal units dealing with war crimes, for an increase in their budget to enable them to look for witnesses abroad, and for the same generous resources to be made available as their counterparts received in Germany. He also demanded more prosecutors. Above all, he urged judicial reform to exclude all former Nazis from jury service in war crimes trials. Their bias was self-evident. 'This is not just a domestic Austrian problem. It has much wider implications because the Nazi victims belonged to many different nationalities. An observant world is following the conduct of the trials, and Austria's international standing is at stake.'

In his letter to Chancellor Klaus Wiesenthal also asserted that during his lecture tours and visits abroad, he was frequently confronted by 'painful questions about the sad situation in Austria. Rightly so, my questioners always stress the international implications of Austria's behaviour.' Austria had a duty to press on with war crimes trials. 'If this problem is not resolved, Austria will be guilty of leaving an empty space in its history, and this will leave a stigma on its standing for all time.'

All this was followed by chapter and verse on the involvement of Austrians in Nazi crimes, and the failures of post-war Austria to prosecute them, and ended with this exhortation:

> Only rapid and energetic measures can re-establish Austria's already weakened international standing. Only an unequivocal attitude by the representatives of our country can reawaken the public conscience; only the unqualified commitment to justice can silence those who are pressing for transparent reasons for a general amnesty for all Nazi crimes.

It took almost three decades before an Austrian Chancellor, Franz Vranitzki, took steps to end Austrian equivocation about the country's Nazi past – and in the process elevated Simon Wiesenthal into a living icon, heaping honours on him and expressing the nation's gratitude for reawakening the Austrian conscience.

But such plaudits came much later; certainly not in the 1960s, when Wiesenthal was ploughing a lonely furrow. He was in his prime throughout that decade, working with all guns blazing. The world in which he found himself now was no longer the compact community of the first Linz Documentation Centre, where hunters and hunted, witnesses and prosecutors were all still closely bound by the immediacy of past brutality, and in many cases by physical proximity. Victimisers and victims had dispersed to many corners of the globe; collegial attitudes between Nazi-hunters, never very pronounced, had evaporated; the moral impetus behind denazification had weakened. The wartime Allies had largely lost interest in war crimes trials, and were reluctant to pressurise Germany or Austria to adopt more vigorous denazification measures – the German Federal Republic was now the pivotal point of NATO's defences against Soviet expansionism, and the country's integration into the European Economic Community (as the EU styled itself then) was far more important than any reckoning with its past. Austria, for its part, had to be propped up as it established its neutrality on the edge of the brittle Balkan and Central European faultlines. Like Tito's Yugoslavia, Austria was needed as a bulwark against the Soviet Union. This became all the more relevant after Soviet intervention in 1968 destroyed the Prague Spring's reform of communism and Leonid Brezhnev pronounced his doctrine of limited sovereignty for the Warsaw Pact countries.

Almost alone, Wiesenthal was bent on convincing the international community that no amount of contemporary tensions could be allowed to obliterate the past. History had not begun with the Cold War. Countries could only tackle present dangers by also confronting the perils of the past. The list of his quarries, the Nazis he sought, lengthened; his network of contacts and informants was widened; he refined his knowledge and analysis of documents; he travelled in Western Europe and the United States – though never in Latin America, where so many of his prey had settled; he produced countless articles and cultivated the press; he published a biannual newsletter; he touched innumerable consciences with his most widely read book, *The Murderers Amongst Us*; he bombarded governments with pleas to instigate deportation proceedings against Nazi criminals whose whereabouts had been traced, and with arguments to prevent the adoption of statutes of limitations under which prosecutions would be halted because supposedly too much time had elapsed since the crimes were committed.

Wiesenthal, reading vociferously and learning from practical experience, was building up his expertise, brick by brick. His architect's training, he says, stood him in good stead. But there was more: instinctively, he understood the importance of generating political pressure and publicity through judicious use of the media. He is a born communicator. In another incarnation, Wiesenthal might have been a populist politician or a leading light of the public relations and advertising world. He made himself a reliable source for key journalists and developed an excellent sense of timing, so that his frequent press conferences would score maximum impact.

As he was writing a great deal for German and Austrian magazines and newspapers, Wiesenthal held a press card, which he occasionally used at press conferences to discomfort controversial personalities with awkward questions. He always knew how to illustrate his points with vivid imagery that attracted interest. And though he was passionate and emotional, he established his credibility and integrity through fairness of approach and a tenacious belief in the law and in justice. All this combined to compensate for his lack of funds and helped to make of him a larger-than-life figure – an image that he relished because it advanced his cause, but also because it boosted his sense of self-worth.

Wiesenthal's greatest handicap during the 1960s was his shortage of money for the Documentation Centre. The family's personal money worries had been eased because he now benefited from the pension scheme, under which the German Government had agreed to provide basic incomes, compensation for ill-health, for concentration camp survivors, irrespective of nationality. But Wiesenthal lacked the means to transform the Vienna Documentation Centre into a well-staffed and well-equipped organisation. There were no more subsidies from the *Kultusgemeinde*. The move to the Rudolfsplatz meant independence, but also new expenses. Then he gave an interview to the *New York Times*, which was published with the memorable headline: 'A sleuth with six million clients'. It produced a welcome dividend in the form of $3,000 in unsolicited donations. It was useful both in itself and as an example of the by-products of publicity.

But of course it was not enough; and in any case, Wiesenthal still had to meet the office running costs: rent, secretarial wages, postage, telephone, a battered car, travel. In the main, he was dependent on income from his publications and on the small donations that came in response to his newsletters, to his lectures and the publicity that surrounded him. From 1965 onwards, Wiesenthal also received a modest, but steady annual donation from Holland, where admirers had set up a foundation in his name. Two years later, a similar body was set up in New York, able to cover some of the Documentation Centre's expenses for their searches outside Austria, but with no spare money to transfer to Vienna. Israel neither offered, nor was asked, to give any material help to the Documentation

Centre. Wiesenthal was far too independent-minded for such arrangements. Jewish organisations often promised money, but, says Wiesenthal with considerable bitterness, they never gave anything.

Adding to his financial worries, the *Allgemeine Wirtschaftsbank*, the Austrian bank where the Documentation Centre's meagre reserves were deposited, collapsed in 1974. It was only towards the end of the 1970s, when the new Los Angeles-based Wiesenthal Center – over which Wiesenthal himself has no control – decided to fund part of the Documentation Centre's running expenses, that its hand-to-mouth existence eased a little. The emphasis has to be on 'little'; contrary to assertions by Wiesenthal's critics in the WJC, who like to claim that Wiesenthal is sitting on a pile of gold, he has never known real affluence.

With the wisdom of hindsight many years later, Wiesenthal cites his failure to apply himself more vigorously to fundraising after he installed himself in Vienna as one of his greatest mistakes. He thinks he should have set up his own foundation rather than rely on others. He was always fretting about small sums, even about paying travel expenses or telephone bills, but never really devised any strategy for establishing a secure financial base. Explaining that he would have felt it wrong to pay the customary hefty commission to professional fundraisers, he made little attempt to tap potential donors in the United States. 'We could have done so much more in the wake of the Eichmann case, during the 1960s when so many Nazi criminals could still have been caught with relative ease,' he laments. Yet, though he now thinks he could have been more effective if he had had more money, he has never been an empire-builder in the sense of seeking to control an army of helpers. Nor has he been keen to share or delegate authority. It went against the grain of his character make-up. He knows that he is best working on his own, taking his own decisions. He was never made for collegial work. In the 1960s, he was rather taken with his Don Quixote image, which he evidently enjoyed and cultivated. But a bigger operation would not, in any event, have been able to exploit his particular gifts. He carries so much information in his head that it has always seemed easier for him to do his own research. And, as happens regularly with larger-than-life personalities in their confidential dealings with the Documentation Centre, people only wanted to talk to him and not to any assistants.

Then as later, there have been occasional aides and always a couple of secretaries. Invariably they are treated with considerable warmth as friends, and in return they respond with uncommon loyalty and fierce devotion to him. In the 1960s, Wiesenthal recruited as his principal secretary a young man, Peter Michael Lingens, who later became one of Austria's most prominent journalists and through the columns of the weekly, *Profil*, led the crusade to defend Wiesenthal's good name against Bruno Kreisky's efforts to destroy his reputation. There was a natural affinity between them. Lingens, not a Jew, is the son of Dr Ella Lingens, who was incarcerated at Auschwitz, and was much admired by Wiesenthal for her work in support of the camp's survivors and her writings about the Holocaust.

Peter Michael Lingens describes the atmosphere in the Rudolfsplatz office:

> It was like a letter-box: queries would come in from newspapers; strangers would write in, if they thought they had found a suspect; others would send eyewitness accounts of their experiences. People wrote to Wiesenthal because they knew his name, or because they trusted him more than public institutions. If anything seemed important, he would forward it to Yad Vashem or to Ludwigsburg (where Germany had established its Central Office of *Länder* (Justice Departments). At other times, he would write to contacts, whose names he never divulged to us, to check the *bona fides* of the person who had sent him information.[1]

Lingens and the other secretaries learned to judge which letters they could answer without showing them to Wiesenthal. But when there was anything interesting, 'he would scream for a file. If we couldn't find it in the disorder around us, he was angered – and invariably found the file instantly.' The anger never seriously bothered them: 'We knew he didn't really mean it.' Even in those early days he acted like a computer, creating his information network in his own mind. 'He had a photographic memory; but over and above that he could make the connections. He possessed all the attributes of the classic criminal investigator.' Lingens stresses that Wiesenthal rarely made snap judgments. Wiesenthal always listened, informed himself and reflected before he made any charges against people; and though Lingens is by no means uncritical, and singles out Wiesenthal's conceit and tendency to exaggerate his own importance, this former collaborator sums up Wiesenthal as an outstanding figure, a 'fanatic for justice, who was incapable of dishonesty, and possessed warmth and sincerity to an uncommon degree'.

Simon Speyer, who became Wiesenthal's friend and benefactor in Holland around the same time that Lingens was working in the Vienna Documentation Centre, reached very similar conclusions about the physically imposing, vigorous and dedicated man he first met in 1964. Speyer is a Dutch textile trader, not exceptionally rich or prominent; but a man in the mainstream tradition of Dutch tolerance and liberality, strongly imbued with the national virtue of commitment to morality in political behaviour.

Wiesenthal had come to Holland with a dual purpose: the first was to find out the identity of the policeman who had arrested Anne Frank; the second was to appeal for funds. He was desperately worried over the prospect that Germany would implement its statute of limitations, with 1965 as the cut-off date for war crimes trials. He needed to step up his investigations, so that more war criminals would be brought to trial before the axe fell. He also needed funds to support his campaign to extend the time-limit within which trials could be held. He had a receptive audience in Holland.

Speyer went one better. He had admired Wiesenthal from afar. When he was introduced to him, Wiesenthal pulled out a picture of Franz Stangl, the commandant of the Sobibor and Treblinka extermination camps, and said that he needed $7,000 to track him down in South America. Speyer, eager to help on a more enduring basis, proposed a foundation dedicated to helping Wiesenthal financially and politically. He approached the Dutch association of former political prisoners and also spoke to a number of Dutch journalists who had stimulated interest in Wiesenthal with their coverage of his activities. This led to a one-hour radio programme about Wiesenthal, accompanied by a phone-in number for donations. In one fell swoop they raised 400,000 guilders, a massive sum by the money values of the time, and enough to endow a foundation that was able to provide Wiesenthal from 1964 onwards with a monthly income of $7,000. Gradually, it became harder to raise enough funds to maintain such payments and the sum had to be reduced to $5,000 monthly, which is now worth less than half of what it would have been back in the 1960s. Even so, 'It is a unique foundation,' Speyer points out, 'because it has absolutely no running expenses.' He looks after its affairs free of charge, issues regular bulletins and also funds the occasional research project. He has also ensured that Wiesenthal has access to the research facilities of the Dutch State Institute for War Documentation, an amenity which has frequently saved Wiesenthal time and money.

The Dutch have also made themselves fierce guardians of Wiesenthal's good name. The Netherlands Foundation for the Fight against Anti-Semitism has shown great dedication in defending him against attacks on his integrity, especially if they came from Jewish quarters such as the WJC. Its President, Richard A. Stein, has conducted a voluminous correspondence with Wiesenthal critics. Eventually, in 1992, Stein put together *Documents Against Words*, a volume of documentary material on Wiesenthal's conflict with the WJC.[2] Wiesenthal believes that Stein's volume provides convincing evidence for his side of the argument both with respect to Eichmann and to Waldheim.

Speyer is proud of Holland's devotion to Wiesenthal. 'Here in Holland, we had the moral fibre and persistence to back Wiesenthal. We recognised him as a man of conviction, who was dedicated to proving that the world must not live with the murderers amongst us,' he emphasises. The Wiesenthal he first knew was a man of considerable charisma and charm. Like Lingens, he also points to conceit and love of public acclaim among the flaws in Wiesenthal's character. 'Yet, if he did not believe in himself, he could not have done what he has achieved.' And like Lingens, he also singles out Wiesenthal's kindness and the modesty of his lifestyle. Speyer has a philosophical explanation for the fierce criticism that Wiesenthal has always attracted from some quarters: 'high peaks attract a lot of wind.'

Led by the late Queen Juliana, and now by her daughter Queen Beatrice, Wiesenthal has become an heroic figure in many Dutch eyes. They share his values and respect his endeavours. His daughter married a Dutchman, and even Wiesenthal's wife, who only travels reluctantly, feels comfortable in Holland and made occasional trips to visit her daughter's family while they lived there before moving to Israel.

Wiesenthal has been honoured with the country's prestigious Erasmus prize, handed over personally by Queen Juliana, who was, Wiesenthal always tells the Dutch, 'one of my real loves'. Dutch schoolchildren regularly visit his Vienna offices, and Wiesenthal is at his most comfortable and relaxed during his visits to Holland. It is his fall-back country; the one European nation where he knows that his work is understood and appreciated, and where children are taught about the Holocaust as a way of preparing them for their adult lives.

In Holland, where Anne Frank's diary is required school reading, its authenticity always went unquestioned. The same did not apply in Austria and Germany. Wiesenthal first understood the long arm of Holocaust revisionism in 1958, when a performance of a play based on the diary of Anne Frank in Linz was interrupted by anti-Semitic demonstrators, all of them children in their teens, high-school pupils, shouting 'swindle' and booing loudly. The Anne Frank story was all a fraud, they remonstrated. A couple of days later, Wiesenthal overheard a conversation, in which a young student expressed regret at having missed the demonstration. The youth went on to argue that there was no evidence to prove that Anne Frank ever lived, and went on to assert that the diary was most likely a forgery. Without proof, it could all be a big lie. 'Nobody will believe you unless you find the man who arrested her,' one boy challenged Wiesenthal.

Wiesenthal interpreted such remarks as proof that a new generation was being fed lies and deceptions by its teachers and parents anxious to obliterate the past. He had to find the SS man who had arrested Anne Frank and had sent her on to Bergen-Belsen concentration camp, where she had died.

It took him five years. Dutch schoolchildren always listen with rapt attention when he tells them the story of his search. At the start, the only clue he found was in the appendix to the Anne Frank diary, where Paul Kraler, an employee of the Frank family business, records how he had tried to intercede with the Gestapo after the Franks' arrest. He failed, but mentioned that he had spoken with the officer who had made the arrests. He was, Kraler said, an Austrian SS man, the first half of whose name was 'Silver'. That could not have been right since Silver is an English word, unlikely to occur in a German-speaking country. But perhaps, Wiesenthal reasoned, the policeman's name had been a combination of 'Silber', a common enough name in Austria. Wiesenthal checked through the people of that name listed in the Vienna telephone directory and in the directories of some of the Austrian provinces. It was like looking for a needle in a haystack. He was able to identify eight 'Silbernagels', who had been members of the Nazi Party or of the SS, but none fitted the policeman's profile.

Wiesenthal says that he was tempted to contact Otto Frank, Anne's father, who had survived and was living in Basle, but he was clearly afraid of being accused of unwarranted interference in private grief. Mr Frank had already declared his readiness to forgive and his desire for reconciliation. Wiesenthal, who opposed forgiveness and wanted the guilty punished, feared that Mr Frank might urge him to give up the hunt for the arresting officer.

During a visit to Amsterdam in 1963, Wiesenthal talked about the continuing search for various prominent members of the Gestapo in Holland during the war, and as a parting present one of his new Dutch friends gave him some reading material for his return flight, a copy of a 1943 directory of SS personnel in Holland. When the plane took off, Wiesenthal scanned the names. It was a soporific, and he became sleepy. But suddenly he sat up, startled. His eyes had lit upon a page headed 'ivb 4 *Joden* [Jews]'. It listed the personnel involved in rounding up Jews. There were four names including that of 'Silberbauer'. That had to be his man, but where was he now? There were numerous Silberbauers in the Vienna telephone directory alone. Even the textile shop on the Rudolfsplatz was called Silberbauer.

Wiesenthal asked for help from a friendly Austrian Ministry of the Interior official, Dr Josef Wiesinger. The Ministry soon identified the man, who was now an inspector in Vienna's police force. Silberbauer was suspended from his duties. But acting on instructions from senior Interior

Ministry quarters, where Wiesenthal's activism had become anathema, Wiesenthal was kept in ignorance. The first he heard about Silberbauer's suspension came from the Austrian Communist Party's newspaper, the *Volksstimme*, which claimed a scoop with a story that Karl Silberbauer had been suspended, pending investigation and possible prosecution for his role in the arrest of Anne Frank. Moscow radio and the Soviet party paper *Izvestia* followed up with claims that Austria's resistance fighters and 'vigilant comrades' had uncovered Anne Frank's captor. Wiesenthal was angry: the Interior Ministry had kept bad faith with him, to put it at its mildest. He would repay in kind. He invited a friendly Dutch journalist and recounted how he had traced Silberbauer's identity. The story was given great prominence around the world. Anne Frank's father does not appear to have appreciated Wiesenthal's intrusion. Otto Frank reacted to the publicity with the assertion that he had long known his daughter had been arrested by a policeman called Silberbauer. Wiesenthal has always doubted that Frank was being truthful. He remarks scathingly that Anne's father rebuffed suggestions that the man should be prosecuted by using the classic apologia that Silberbauer had only done his duty.

This was also the excuse adopted by Silberbauer himself, and by the Austrian authorities who decided that the arrest of Anne Frank did not warrant Silberbauer's prosecution as a war criminal, because there was no evidence that he had also been responsible for her deportation. Wiesenthal thought that perhaps he could raise the stakes by building up popular pressure to insist on a trial. He called another press conference. Next day he looked for headlines in the Austrian press, but for once there were none. A far more important event had occurred: President Kennedy's assassination.

In Wiesenthal's report on the activities of the Documentation Centre during the second half of 1963, he gave top billing to the endeavours to unmask the man who had arrested Anne Frank. He wrote that the search must continue for more evidence to make out a viable case against Silberbauer. There was always a chance that a reader might have incriminating information. Apparently none was found, and Wiesenthal accepted that there was no alternative but to abandon the campaign for Silberbauer's prosecution. At least, he felt, his principal objective had been met: the man had been found and the world now had living proof of Anne's arrest. The authenticity of her diary was secure. Wiesenthal was satisfied that at last 'the neo-Nazis stopped questioning the authenticity of her diary to support their denial of the Holocaust'.

However, in *The Murderers Amongst Us*, Wiesenthal hints at his frustration that Silberbauer was never held to account before the law: 'Of course, he doesn't matter at all. Compared to other names on my list, he is a nobody, a zero. But the figure before the zero was Anne Frank.'

The Murderers Amongst Us, one of Wiesenthal's most significant books, was first published in the United States in 1967. The project had begun in 1965 after Wiesenthal had a visit from Charles Ronsac of the French literary agency and publishing house, Opera Mundi. 'He said to me: "Mr Wiesenthal, in your Eichmann book you were constrained by the Israeli secret service to restrict yourself to events in which you directly participated. Since then you have experienced so much more, achieved so much. The time has come to write about all that." I was advised that *The Murderers Amongst Us* should initially be published in English for the US market. So I sketched it out in German.' He told about some of his wartime experiences, about his search for Eichmann, Josef Mengele and Franz Stangl, and about the euthanasia experiments of Schloss Hartheim. The horrors of the Holocaust were translated into stories that read as parables with Wiesenthal's unerring commitment to justice emphasised with inescapable vigour and logic.

Then the American writer, Joseph Wechsberg, was brought in. His name appears on the frontispiece as 'editor and collaborator'. In fact, Wechsberg was far more. The book has a longish profile of Wiesenthal, of which Wechsberg was the outright author, and a series of vividly drawn incidents from Wiesenthal's life and encounters with the murderers, adapted by Wechsberg from Wiesenthal's notes to 'make them more readable', as Wiesenthal acknowledges. Combined with Wechsberg's profile of Wiesenthal, *The Murderers Amongst Us* brought home to the reader the reality of the Holocaust in an accessible, highly readable form as few books had achieved until then. It made Wiesenthal's name in the United States, opened doors for him at the highest levels of government and turned him into a celebrity much in demand on the US lecture circuit. But the book was also published in at least a dozen languages and has never been out of print. When it was translated back into German, Wiesenthal was 'pleasantly surprised to read the Wechsberg version of what I had said. He invented nothing and kept to the facts as I had put them down. But he gave it a good literary form. He was a wonderful man.'

Wiesenthal went to the United States to promote the book, where, he says, it created a 'sensation'. He could barely speak English, and used Yiddish with his American Jewish friends. But with his gift for languages – though not for pronunciation – he rapidly improved his English, and even if he speaks more slowly and with a pronounced accent that betrays both his Polish and his Yiddish mother tongues, he has become fluent and has no problems with giving lectures and interviews.

Wiesenthal's treasured family

Paulinka, as a small child, and grown up in Israel.

Wiesenthal with his two grandsons in Israel after the award of the Jerusalem Medal by the city of Jerusalem in 1980.

In 1967, Wiesenthal travelled to the US to promote his book, *The Murderers Amongst Us*. This was one of the few occasions when his wife, Cyla, accompanied him on a working trip.

In Wiesenthal's Documentation Centre

Wiesenthal in his office: behind him the crowded bookshelves; beside him his desk heaped with so many papers that there is barely space to work. Displayed on the wall are some of the citations and awards that have been given to him.

Wiesenthal in his small library talking with one of the many groups of young students who are among the most welcome visitors to his Documentation Centre.

Wiesenthal in 1983 at the end of a working day standing in the narrow corridor of the Documentation Centre.

Show Business

Wiesenthal in his office poses happily with a poster for *The Murderers Amongst Us*, the TV biography starring Ben Kingsley. Even though there was only superficial physical similarity between the two men, Wiesenthal was thoroughly content that Kingsley had understood him and portrayed him with accuracy and sensitivity.

The 1994 Vienna premiere of Schindler's List. Wiesenthal, who had been an inmate of Plaszow, the death camp depicted in the film, was among the guests of honour at the premiere. Here he is with the film's director, Steven Spielberg, Swanee Hunt, the US Ambassador to Austria and the book's author, Thomas Keneally.

With the great and the good

In the White House Oval Room with President Ronald Reagan.

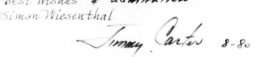

best wishes & admiration
Simon Wiesenthal.
Jimmy Carter 8-80

At the White House in 1980 after President Jimmy Carter has handed Wiesenthal the Congressional Gold Medal. Spontaneously, Carter added his 'admiration' when he signed this photograph for Wiesenthal.

Wiesenthal and the Dalai Lama exchange their philosophies. (1993)

Queen Juliana of the Netherlands welcoming Wiesenthal during a reception in 1970 for the International Association of Resistance Fighters.

Wiesenthal in Hollywood; here with Elizabeth Taylor and Rabbi Marvin Hier, Dean of the Los Angeles Wiesenthal Center.

In Hollywood with Anatoly Scharansky and Jane Fonda.

More of the great and the good

Wiesenthal with his good friend, German Chancellor Helmuth Kohl. They meet informally during Mr Kohl's vacations in Austria; but this photograph was taken during an official dinner in 1991.

With Austrian President, Thomas Klestil, who regards Wiesenthal as a national icon.

At the Wiesenthal Center with the Israeli Prime Minister, Menachem Begin.

The return to Poland

President Lech Walesa toasts Wiesenthal after awarding him Poland's highest medal, the *Polonia Restituta*.

October 1994, on his first return to Poland after 50 years. Wiesenthal has laid a wreath at the Warsaw Holocaust Memorial.

Wiesenthal strides into Auschwitz, not as a prisoner but as a free man surrounded by a respectful throng.

Wiesenthal, displaying his Polish medal during the ceremony to receive his honorary doctorate from Cracow's Jagiellonian University.

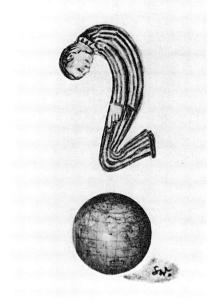

'World, give your response: Perhaps you too bear some of the responsibility?'. With this admonition, Wiesenthal ended his drawings and cartoons from the hell of 'KZ Mauthausen'. His constant message has been that mankind must not close its eye to evil, and that awareness is vital to the fight against injustice.

WELT, GIB ANTWORT!

VIELLEICHT BIST DU AUCH MITSCHULDIG?

Wiesenthal in his 87th year.

Wiesenthal's growing fame in Europe had not preceded him to the United States, but he was fortunate in the early friendships that he formed there. Hy Katz, a wealthy New York businessman, knew of Wiesenthal and admired him. He went to Vienna to meet him and decided to set up a small foundation to give Wiesenthal occasional financial help with his projects. He came with his tax-lawyer, Martin Rosen, who has become Wiesenthal's close and trusted friend and guards Wiesenthal's interests and reputation in the US. After the establishment of the Los Angeles Wiesenthal Center, Rosen also kept in close touch with its activities and has been known to act behind-the-scenes to resolve the occasional difference between Wiesenthal and the Centre. 'We are brothers' is how each of them speaks of their mutual bond.

Carlton Sedgeley, one of America's leading lecture-circuit agents, became another of Wiesenthal's close friends. Like Rosen, he is very protective of his client-friend. He first became aware of Wiesenthal when one of his aides reported that he had been deeply moved listening to Wiesenthal lecture on his Holocaust experiences when he was promoting *The Murderers Amongst Us*. Sedgeley offered to organise his future lecture tours to ensure that he would have a wider and more profitable hearing. 'I am not a Jew. But he always speaks to me, because he emphasises that the Holocaust was not a uniquely Jewish tragedy, but also affected many other peoples, races and creeds. He was not only concerned with anti-Semitism; he was a human rights activist. Over the years, he was one of the rare individuals authentic enough to make the Holocaust come alive for people who had no direct experience of the suffering in Europe.'[3]

Success did not come overnight. Initially the invitations to speak were from smallish survivor groups. Bookings were few and the fees were nominal. But with growing fame and improved fluency in English, Wiesenthal became a much-sought-after speaker in the US, especially on university campuses. Sedgeley always accompanies him, 'because he needs his friends around him' on these fatiguing lecture tours. Even so, with growing age, Wiesenthal has become too tired to accept the US invitations that come his way, and cancelled a country-wide tour that Sedgeley had booked in 1994.

America has a special place in Wiesenthal's heart. Back at Mauthausen in 1945, Americans had ended Wiesenthal's wartime ordeal and had given him his first opportunity to search for Nazi murderers. These actions combined to give him both a second lease of life and a new sense of hope and purpose. But there is more to his love of America. The US tendency, so much more pronounced than in Europe, to give politics a moral dimension is much closer to his way of thinking. Its open society had an instant appeal for him. Through his books, his media contacts and his friends, he soon gained access to the famous and influential. He enjoyed it most of all because it boosted his self-confidence and reassured him that his dedication to Holocaust remembrance and human rights was recognised. He also recognised that he could use his access to influential members in Congress and the administration to gain support for his causes.

Robert Kennedy, recognising that 'moral duties have no terms' was an exceptionally useful connection for Wiesenthal. Later he came to know Presidents Carter, Reagan, and Bush, and all have testified to their admiration of Wiesenthal's achievements. But his crowning recognition, which he probably values above all his other awards, came in 1980, when President Carter handed him the Congressional Gold Medal as 'a national symbol of appreciation for his vital contribution to the advancement of human freedoms'. Senator George McGovern and Representative Christopher Dodd had been the moving spirits behind this gesture.

Wiesenthal however is not universally admired in the United States. There are influential voices in Jewish organisations, and among Jewish intellectuals, who regard him as an interloper with pretensions he has never earned. Wiesenthal can be easily hurt or offended by the slights – real or imagined – inflicted from these quarters. He also has vicious opponents among neo-Nazi émigré groups in the United States, who distribute vitriolic articles and pamphlets against him. These he ignores as outpourings of sick minds. They have lost any capacity to touch him and he never bothers to respond.

During Wiesenthal's periodic visits to the United States, letters pour in from people claiming to be related to him. On one occasion he invited all the people on a list he had compiled. Eighty turned up and were asked to sign a visitors' book explaining their relationship. 'Feeling mischievous, I said that if I had approached them penniless and asked "my relatives" for donations, I wonder how many of them would have come.' Sheepishly, most conceded that they only belonged to the Wiesenthal admiration society. There were among them a few first and second cousins, but he had not found any close relatives. They had perished in the Holocaust.

[13]
The Sleuth at Work

The bulging box files at the Documentation Centre on Vienna's Rudolfs-platz held the names of more than 22,000 men and women, mostly members of the SS, suspected of active involvement in the Holocaust. Less than 1,000 names on these lists have had to face arrest; still fewer have been found guilty. But then Wiesenthal never believed that all of them would be found, and still less that many of them would ever be prosecuted. Even if he could make the suspects feel uneasy, hunted, unable to feel safe, it was better than allowing them a peaceful old age, he rationalised. He used the Documentation Centre's newsletters to appeal for information and eyewitness accounts to strengthen his hand in urging action against these people.

He peppered the Austrian authorities with the dossiers of alleged war criminals, but his information seemed to be falling on to deaf ears. There was no appetite for war crimes trials. In Germany, attitudes towards the prosecution of Nazi criminals were patchy. The 1964 appointment of Adalbert Rückerl as head of Germany's Central Office for the investigation of Nazi crimes in Ludwigsburg was a propitious development. Rückerl was more of an activist than his predecessor, Edwin Schüle. Wiesenthal felt that at last with Rückerl at Ludwigsburg, he had an ally in a position of considerable influence, who was dedicated to the cause and who was, moreover, prepared to pay attention to the expertise and the information that the Vienna Documentation Centre was able to provide. But throughout the German Government Nazis had been restored to positions of influence. Rückerl, like Wiesenthal, found himself up against regional (*Länder*) govern-ments reluctant to conduct further war crimes trials and intent on delaying tactics to bring them to their conclusion.

With his own reputation on steadily firmer ground, the 1960s were a period where Wiesenthal maintained reasonably cordial relations with the WJC in New York. But even though they exchanged information, it was more of a one-sided relationship, with Wiesenthal urging them to mobilise pressure to tackle the thorny issue of Nazi war criminals sheltering in the United States. The WJC rarely approached him for help.

Wiesenthal focused much of his prodigious energy on the big names, including Mengele, Stangl, Alois Brunner, Hermine Braunsteiner and Martin Bormann (until 1973, when Wiesenthal 'unquestionably' accepted new evidence that Bormann had been dead since 1945). But no name was too obscure for Wiesenthal to consider whether that person rightfully belonged to those who should be accused of war crimes. Many people came to him with information, or wrote to draw his attention to Nazi criminals. But his most important source material came from two rare documents. He had one of only fifty copies of a complete register of SS officers, including those belonging to the murderous *Einsatzkommandos*; moreover, he had the advantage of understanding how to read and interpret the document. And after Wiesenthal was asked to authenticate it, he was also one of the first to have access to the notorious SS *Kriegstagebuch* (war diary), which recorded the activities of Hitler's *Einsatz* division, '*Das Reich*'.

In Wiesenthal's pantheon of Nazi criminals, Franz Stangl ranks almost as high as Eichmann. Wiesenthal has always claimed that Stangl's arrest in Brazil, his extradition to Germany, and his trial and conviction, owe more to his endeavours than to anyone else. It certainly is a classic example of the methods that Wiesenthal has employed to end the sojourn of war criminals in South America and to confront them with their accusers before a court of justice. Even though it took a long time to catch up with Stangl – all the more surprising since Stangl took far fewer measures to hide his identity than other Nazis – once Wiesenthal knew that he was openly living and working in Brazil, he did not let go until his quarry was safely behind bars in Düsseldorf. It was a perfect opportunity to do what he does best: to organise private and public pressure to bring a Nazi criminal to justice.

'This was the greatest criminal case in the history of the German judiciary, and with the exception of the Eichmann trial, the most important trial against an individual criminal,' Wiesenthal wrote in the Documentation Centre's newsletter early in 1971, soon after Stangl was sentenced to life imprisonment.

Unlike the controversy swirling around the Eichmann hunt, he believes that his reputation with respect to the Stangl case is secure. When Wiesenthal assesses his work, he cites Stangl as one of the Nazi hunts that instils him with pride: 'In contrast to Adolf Eichmann, Stangl was brought to court entirely as a result of my research, and my intervention to secure his extradition.' Without Wiesenthal, Stangl might have been left to end his days a free man.

Stangl had lived under his own name in Brazil since 1951. At that time, Wiesenthal was already aware of Stangl, but his Linz Documentation Centre was deluged by more immediate problems. Even after he resumed his Nazi-hunting in 1961, when Stangl was high on his list of priorities as a major war criminal, it took until 1964 to pinpoint Stangl's address. The delay not only exposed a major weakness in his research methods, but also shows how much his work was hampered by a perpetual shortage of funds. However, the governments which had Stangl on their 'wanted' lists were no better at tracing him, though it should have been easier for them to discover that Stangl was registered with the Austrian consulate in São Paulo for some time before he was finally identified.

Stangl is in the cast of malefactors mentioned in Wiesenthal's first report on the work of the Vienna Documentation Centre in 1962. At that time, Wiesenthal already knew that Stangl had been commandant of the Treblinka extermination camp and that he had been involved with the euthanasia programme at Schloss Hartheim. He did not yet know that Stangl had received a commendation as 'the best camp commander in Poland', and that he had been a classic 'desk murderer', rarely going near his 'cargo', as Stangl described the victims whose deaths he had to organise. He was just working a system, he said, and because it functioned well, it was 'irreversible'.

In Wiesenthal's 1962 newsletter, he gave little hint of the enormity of Stangl's crimes. He only noted that Stangl came from Linz, was the last commander of Treblinka, was arrested after the war, but escaped in 1948 and fled to Damascus, where he was joined by his family. He said that Stangl was 'of interest' to the Austrian authorities in connection with the euthanasia programme at Schloss Hartheim.

Wiesenthal had come across Stangl's name in 1948, when he was shown a list of decorations awarded to senior SS officers. Against his entry for the War Cross of Merit for 'bravery beyond the call of duty', he noticed a pencilled remark: 'Top secret – for psychological stress'. He knew how to translate this. It meant that Stangl had received the decoration for high-quality work in mass murder at the extermination camps. Here was a man who must eventually be singled out for intensive investigation and pursuit.

Another document he saw about the same time, a report by Stangl to his chiefs in Berlin, revealed in numbing detail how Stangl ran Treblinka, between October 1942 and August 1943, as a factory where human beings were brought in as chattel to be killed, while their valuables, their hair, their gold teeth and anything else of use were assembled and dispatched to his designated customers. The able-bodied were given temporary leave from death and used as slave labour until exhausted. While Stangl was commandant, up to 800,000 people were gassed at Treblinka. The place had been 'Dante's inferno come to life', Stangl himself told Gitta Sereny in a series of interviews in prison after his conviction in 1970.

The booty list from Stangl's Treblinka that Wiesenthal saw included items such as 25 freight cars of women's hair, 145,000 kilos of gold wedding rings, 100 freight cars of shoes, several thousand pearl necklaces and several millions of dollars, Polish zlotys and pounds sterling.

Towards the end of Stangl's tenure at Treblinka, when he was already running out of victims, measures were taken to camouflage the camp against the advancing Red Army. A fake petrol station was erected with flowers planted around it, even a small zoo installed. But there was still time to devise new ways for burning the dead at Treblinka. Bodies were put on racks in layers, with children wedged between the adults. The last transports arrived in mid-August 1943. Then the order was given to close the camp and obliterate the worst traces. Buildings were demolished; flowers and young pines were planted; a farm was built with bricks taken from the dismantled gas chambers.

The Austrian authorities had first noted Stangl's name on a staff list of Schloss Hartheim in Upper Austria, not far from Mauthausen. Hartheim was one of four 'sanatoria' where the Nazis conducted experiments with mentally retarded or terminally sick people – those considered 'useless eaters' – and ran pilot projects for mass extermination. Hartheim was also used as a 'training site', where the personnel learned their technical know-how and were conditioned psychologically before their posting to the death camps. Stangl claimed that he was at Hartheim as police superintendent and had nothing to do with the killings. In fact, he was one of the trainees under the sadistic Captain Christian Wirth, the man in charge of the euthanasia institutions. When Stangl was moved on, he was promoted to work at Chelmno and Belzec, where some of the first gas chambers were installed. In 1942, he was made commandant of Sobibor extermination camp before being promoted a few months later to run Treblinka.

After Treblinka, Stangl was transferred to the Yugoslav front, where the fighting was bitter, and Tito took no prisoners. Stangl however survived, returned to Austria and rejoined his wife. He did not hide his identity. The Americans, apparently aware that he had been at Sobibor and Treblinka, put him into a detention camp at Glasenbach, but, knowing little about him, readily handed him over to the Austrian authorities in 1947, who only had him on a 'wanted' list as a former Austrian police officer at Schloss

Hartheim. Little was known then about the evil significance of that place. Stangl was held under relaxed conditions in the semi-open prison of the Linz provincial court. The prisoners were taken to work each day outside the camp, and he had little difficulty in making his escape in May 1948.

The Austrians were not greatly concerned by Stangl's disappearance and did not report his escape to the American occupying command. Wiesenthal, who was then running his embryo Documentation Centre in Linz, and was in close touch with senior officials in Upper Austria as well as with the Americans, did not discover for several months that Stangl had made a get-away. Had he known, he would have raised the alarm; he already suspected that Stangl had been a profoundly sinister figure: enough had emerged about the killings at Sobibor and Treblinka for Wiesenthal to understand that Stangl deserved to be classified as a major Nazi criminal.

Stangl's escape route from Austria was via Rome to Syria. In Damascus, he first found a job in a textile mill, and later as a mechanical engineer with the Imperial Knitting Company. His wife joined him in 1949, travelling under her own name. In 1951, the family moved to Brazil, where they again did not bother to adopt an alias. Mrs Stangl claimed that her husband's escape from Austria was improvised, and that the move to Brazil occurred after a chance encounter with an old Nazi friend.

However, Wiesenthal is wholly convinced that the escape was carefully planned. 'What nonsense to claim that he just walked out of Austria. It's all lies. He obviously had papers issued by the Nazi helpline, *ODESSA*. Once in Rome, he was provided with shelter by Bishop Hudal, who also secured Stangl a Red Cross passport to enable him to sail from Genoa to Syria.' Hudal must have known of Stangl's record, since he took care to procure Red Cross *laissez-passer* papers on Stangl's behalf, reasoning that if Stangl had to queue himself, he might be recognised by survivors also waiting for their ICRC papers.

Stangl, always several steps ahead, eluded Wiesenthal until 1966. Frau Stangl had already left for the Middle East when Wiesenthal discovered her earlier Austrian address. Neighbours told him that she had gone either to Beirut or Damascus. But with no friendly contacts in those countries, he was stymied and had to bide his time.

By 1959, Wiesenthal says that he knew for certain that 'Stangl had left the Arab countries and was living in South America. But I lacked anything more specific about his whereabouts.'

The breakthrough only came in 1964 with the arrival at the Documentation Centre of someone who claimed that he could provide Stangl's address in exchange for a ransom. In his books, Wiesenthal draws an exciting picture of the encounter with his informant, characteristic of the way he knows how to dramatise every incident. In *Justice Not Vengeance*, Wiesenthal wrote that 'an evil-looking, unkempt type' called at his office a day after Wiesenthal had given a press conference about the killings at Hartheim and the other euthanasia institutions. In his earlier book, *The Murderers Amongst Us*, Wiesenthal said that a 'seedy-looking man' came to see him in February 1964, hours after an agitated woman had appeared in his office, saying that she had read one of his declarations about Stangl and could not bear to think that her cousin Theresa was married to such a man. She let slip that Theresa was in Brazil.

Wiesenthal still has a vivid memory of the ransom bargaining that ensued. The informer said that he wanted $25,000 before he would furnish Stangl's address. Where Wiesenthal was concerned, he might as well have asked for the moon. Wiesenthal explained that he had no such funds at his disposal. Eventually, they settled for $7,000 – 'a bargain with the devil: one cent for every person killed at Treblinka.

'I had three possibilities: to throw the man out, to strangle him, or to deal with him,' Wiesenthal wrote in a letter to the *Suddeutsche Zeitung* on 20 March 1967. 'I chose the third option, because I felt that the arrest of a mass murderer justified such a payment.' So Wiesenthal took one of his visiting cards and wrote on it: 'I shall pay the bearer $7,000, if on the strength of the information given to me, Stangl is arrested in Brazil.' His informant then told Wiesenthal that Stangl was working at the Volkswagen factory in São Paulo.

Wiesenthal has never revealed the identity of his caller. The informer had demanded an undertaking that no attempt should be made to identify him. 'I kept my word, even though I think I know who it was,' Wiesenthal asserts. He scoffs at speculation that Stangl's disgruntled son-in-law, Herbert Havel, was behind the disclosures, and cites a letter he sent to a lawyer in Canada, where Stangl's son-in-law had moved, 'to assure him that I did not suspect him'. Wiesenthal refuses to say whether this was merely a tactic in fulfilment of his promise to the mysterious visitor. Certainly Frau Stangl was not convinced. She told Gitta Sereny that she believed Havel was involved. According to her, Havel had threatened to destroy the Stangl family, unless his wife Renate (the Stangls' daughter) agreed to return to him. Frau Stangl claimed that Havel had threatened, somewhat improbably, to send a Jewish uncle to see Wiesenthal with the Stangl family's whereabouts. Just after Stangl's trial ended, in December 1970, the *Daily Express* also published a story claiming that Wiesenthal had paid Stangl's son-in-law £3,000 for information.[1] Wiesenthal countered by denying all connections with Havel: he had never met him, never received any information from him and never offered to pay any reward to him.

Once Wiesenthal knew Stangl's refuge, he wanted to go to Brazil in person, but says he failed to raise enough money to cover his travel costs. However, this did not prevent him from pulling out all the stops: press conferences, letters and talks with the legal authorities in Germany and Austria, requests for evidence from governments, for testimony from survivors in Israel and Holland, contacts with Brazilian politicians, and eventually use of senior US politicians, most notably Robert Kennedy, to reinforce pressure on Brazil not only to arrest, but above all to extradite, Stangl. Poland rebuffed Wiesenthal, telling him that it had no evidence against Stangl – although by 1970, when the trial took place, East–West relations had eased and Poland, concerned enough to show a more co-operative spirit, submitted its own searing indictment against Stangl.

Three big obstacles were left before Stangl could be brought to trial. First, Brazil had to be convinced that the arrest should be made; second, Wiesenthal thought it essential to organise the arrest with the utmost discretion – if the secret slipped out, he feared, the long arm of ODESSA would reach out to hide Stangl beyond the grasp of the police; and third, the Brazilian authorities had to be persuaded to extradite Stangl instead of pleading that the country's statute of limitations had already put him beyond a court trial.

Austria and Germany were demanding his extradition, but would they press hard enough? Brazil had never extradited a Nazi criminal; and there was reluctance to place too much pressure on Brazil's shaky democracy. Germany had issued an arrest warrant in 1960. Austria had put Stangl on to a 'wanted' list in 1961, which had been circulated to all Austrian embassies and consulates, but although Stangl had registered with the consulate in São Paulo – initially as Paul Franz Stangl, though after being asked to produce his birth certificate, he had altered it to the correct Franz P. Stangl – no connection had been made with the name on the 'wanted' list. Whether this was deliberate, or mere incompetence, remains a mystery.

When Wiesenthal entered the fray to have Stangl arrested and extradited, he assumed that it would be a slow process, but never imagined that it would take close on three years. Among others, he enlisted the help of a Jewish lawyer in Rio de Janeiro as well as that of a member of the Brazilian Senate. Letters in his archives suggest that various payments were made to defray the Senator's 'expenses', although Wiesenthal later said that the Brazilian Senator's role was 'marginal'.

Stangl was finally arrested on 27 February 1967. Even then, it remained uncertain whether he would be extradited. Wiesenthal concluded that more public pressure had to be mobilised. He contacted friends to organise demonstrations outside Brazilian embassies. Fearing that Austria, even if it secured Stangl's extradition, would delay his trial, he pressed for a more vigorous extradition *démarche* by the German government. And when he travelled to New York to promote his book, *The Murderers Amongst Us*, he asked to see Senator Robert Kennedy. Wiesenthal prepared a three-page brief to explain the importance of securing Stangl's extradition, which 'he read and absorbed in thirty seconds'. Kennedy's response was to weigh in with a plea to the Brazilian authorities that this was a unique opportunity to gain friends by ensuring that Stangl was brought to justice. This was also enough to convince Wiesenthal that Robert was the greatest of the Kennedys.

On 8 June, the Brazilian Supreme Court finally ruled that Stangl should be extradited to West Germany with the way left open to Austria to stage a second trial later. On 22 June 1967, Stangl was flown to Germany. Soon afterwards, Wiesenthal had a call from a notary in Germany. This lawyer held Wiesenthal's promissory note to pay a reward for Stangl's whereabouts. Wiesenthal informed his New York friend, Hy Katz, who transferred the money to the notary.

The Stangl trial was three years in preparation, finally opening on 13 May 1970. On the eve of the trial, Wiesenthal wrote to a number of television stations alerting them that a major event, second only to the Eichmann trial, was about to take place in Düsseldorf, adding that he would be present on the initial two days of the trial. He would be available for comment. The story that unfolded more than matched the testimony at the Eichmann trial, possibly because Stangl had consistently been in the midst of the killing machine and had streamlined his expertise even while he could see, hear and smell the agony of death around him.

On 22 December 1970, Stangl was sentenced to life imprisonment. Next day, Wiesenthal tore up Stangl's photograph which he had carried around for years. Wiesenthal thought that Stangl would 'probably be pardoned to a limited punishment' and, since he was already sixty-two years old, 'we assume that his later trial in Austria will never take place'. He was right. Stangl died in his German prison in 1971.

Wiesenthal was philosophical about the brevity of Stangl's spell in prison. After all, there could never have been any adequate punishment for a criminal on Stangl's scale. As with the other mass murderers, Wiesenthal's purpose had been fulfilled when Stangl stood up in court and his accusers were at last able to bring his crimes, in all their stark reality, to the world's attention. The testimony brought out the enormity of it all; the prison interviews with Gitta Sereny, her articles and subsequent book, *Into that Darkness*, combined to produce graphic accounts of Hartheim, Sobibor and Treblinka. As Wiesenthal sees it, the main purpose of the Stangl trial, as of all the other war crimes trials, has been to set the historical record straight and, with its account of unspeakable events, to provide source material convincing enough to counter those who would deny the Holocaust. Put in such terms, the Stangl trial was pre-eminently successful.

Wiesenthal has always taken a special satisfaction from his involvement with the Stangl case. He says he is convinced that, 'If I have done nothing else in my life but bring this wicked man to trial, I will not have lived in vain.'

The search for Stangl had been long-drawn-out, but had led to a worthwhile conclusion. Wiesenthal cannot say the same about the much more extended search for Dr Josef Mengele, the 'Angel of Death'. The Mengele case is noted more for the jealousies and friction between various Nazi-hunters than for their perspicacity. It is further complicated by widely divergent accounts of the search for their quarry.

Wiesenthal found himself at the epicentre of these rows, perhaps not least because Hollywood chose to portray him as an heroic figure battling against the odds, and with the most meagre of means, to vanquish an evil conspirator. The popular film based on Ira Levin's book, *The Boys from Brazil*, with Laurence Olivier playing the Wiesenthal character (in the film he was called 'Liebermann'), was based on a dramatic science-fiction yarn in which Mengele seeks to perpetuate his genetic experiments by establishing a race of identikit Aryans. In the film, Wiesenthal-Liebermann finds out at the twelfth hour about Mengele's designs, and it concludes with a fight to the death between Wiesenthal and Mengele, in which the doctor sets ferocious dogs on his hunter, but ends by himself being bitten and torn to death. Wiesenthal-Liebermann emerges bloodied, but victorious. The film was designed to intrigue the popular imagination, and however preposterous the plot, it undoubtedly helped to confirm Wiesenthal's image as an intrepid sleuth and Nazi-hunter supreme. But this was hardly calculated to increase his popularity amongst competing Nazi-hunters. Wiesenthal was embarrassed by Hollywood's portrayal. He was shown an early draft of the film script and crossed out large sections. And 'when Olivier came to see me,' Wiesenthal recalls, 'I told him to play the fictional character, Liebermann, and not to base it on me.'

In real life, Mengele was never caught. But the search for him was intense, and he was still assumed to be alive years after he had in fact drowned off the Brazilian coast, with the body recovered and buried, and even after a team of medical experts from the US, Germany and Brazil had concluded that the remains dug up from a grave at Embu cemetery were incontrovertibly Mengele's. Wiesenthal has never quite forgiven himself – or the other Nazi-hunters – for the failure to find Mengele during his lifetime. The revulsion that Mengele aroused brought Wiesenthal to the verge of contradicting himself on one of his basic tenets: here was one mass murderer where Wiesenthal appears to have felt a profound need for vengeance.

He admits that he made mistakes in looking for Mengele. Time and again he has also pointed to his shortage of funds, arguing that this precluded him from following up clues in South America. But it is also obvious that he has never had any great urge to venture personally into the jungle of Latin America's Nazi satellites.

Nazi-hunters frequently blamed each other for bungling attempts to capture Mengele. There were countless false trails. Wiesenthal is held responsible by Isser Harel for foiling Mossad hopes of capturing him in Buenos Aires during the 1960 foray to take Eichmann; Wiesenthal blames Harel for using him to cover up some of his own failings. Zvi Aharoni, one of the Mossad agents involved in the Eichmann capture, believes that Harel sent them on a wild-goose chase for Mengele that might have endangered Eichmann's abduction to Israel, and that two years later, in 1962, Harel suddenly halted a Mossad operation led by Aharoni, who was convinced that he had tracked Mengele to Brazil. Harel diverted the Mossad team, including Aharoni, to Europe to pursue the search for a kidnapped eight-year-old child, Yossele Schumacher.

Beate Klarsfeld, the Paris-based German Nazi-hunter, further muddied the waters when she tried her hand at smoking out Mengele by using her routine technique of mounting provocative public protests against the authorities she suspects of sheltering her quarries. Wiesenthal complained that her demonstrations in Paraguay only made matters more difficult and further complicated the search for Mengele.

Much later, in 1984, the Los Angeles-based Wiesenthal Centre, acting with Wiesenthal's support, mounted a campaign for an official US investigation into reports that the US military authorities in Germany had actually held Mengele in 1946 but had released him soon afterwards. This led to a massive manhunt by the US, West German and Israeli Governments, ending with the discovery of Mengele's remains in 1986, seven years after his death. Efraim Zuroff, who is now in charge of the Wiesenthal Center's office in Israel, has written with derision about Wiesenthal and the other individual hunters for Mengele. In his book, *Occupation – Nazi-Hunter*, he asserts that once the US Government weighed in, 'what had been reduced during the previous twenty years to a totally unsuccessful competition between private Nazi-hunters, suddenly became a multi-government effort to launch an exhaustive search for the person who had become the most notorious Nazi criminal thought to be alive'.[2] Such arguments inevitably raise the question why governments did not act sooner, and whether they would have intervened at all if the cause had not been initiated by the private Nazi-hunters.

Mengele was the dreaded camp doctor, the specialist in genetics, at Auschwitz, whose passion was both to select the victims destined for immediate dispatch to the gas chambers, and also to 'save' twins, especially the young ones, for genetic experiments of the greatest bestiality. Handsome, at times deceptively urbane, he disposed of life and death, revelling in his opportunity to use an unlimited supply of human beings in pursuit of research for the perfect Aryan specimen. Survivors among the twins were so traumatised that it took many years after the war before they were able to recollect and talk of their experiences. Some felt unable to talk about it for the rest of their lives.

Wiesenthal believes that Mengele's name was more widely known at the end of the war than Eichmann's or Stangl's, but that there was little awareness of his experiments. In 1946, Ella Lingens, herself a doctor, who had been a relatively privileged prisoner at Auschwitz and had observed Mengele at close quarters, published a book, *Prisoners of Fear*, that described Mengele's depredations in graphic detail. Wiesenthal read it, and has never ceased to be haunted by the man's callousness. But Lingens's book did not gain much attention and, because so few of the twins were talking, it took longer to comprehend Mengele's importance than was the case with other architects of the Final Solution.

While Wiesenthal was still in Linz, he joined Hermann Langbein, head of the International Auschwitz Committee, in the search for Mengele. They believed that Mengele had lived unmolested in Germany until 1950, and that he had then used the *ODESSA*–Vatican route to go to South America, but they had no specific details. By 1954, Langbein believed that he had Mengele's address in Buenos Aires and persuaded the Germans to ask for his extradition. Argentina said that they could not find him. In 1959, Wiesenthal was given two Buenos Aires addresses, which he passed on to the Israeli Government as well as to Yad Vashem. He also wrote to a friendly lawyer in Buenos Aires, asking him to investigate further and adding that 'the information must not, for the time being, be passed on to the press'.

The matter was, he said, very delicate and very difficult, but Mengele was so important that it would be worth the effort. Afterwards, Wiesenthal was to claim that 'the first news about Mengele's whereabouts in Argentina originated from our Office [the Vienna Documentation Centre]'.[3]

For the second time Bonn asked for his extradition, but it was again refused – this time on the grounds that Mengele's alleged crimes were political, not criminal. This coincided with the time when Israel's Mossad was embarking on preparations to capture Eichmann in Argentina. Wiesenthal saw Mengele as a test-case. Had Argentina been willing to extradite him, a precedent would have been set and Israel, rather than kidnapping Eichmann, would have been able to have him extradited. 'I can reveal,' he wrote in *The Murderers Amongst Us*, 'that Eichmann would not have been abducted if Mengele had been arrested.' Abductions have never belonged to Wiesenthal's strategy of bringing people to justice.

Isser Harel interpreted Wiesenthal's move quite differently. 'The malignant outcome [of the extradition demand] was that Mengele was served unambiguous warning, and decamped a few weeks before we reached Buenos Aires at the final stage of the operation for the capture of Eichmann,' Harel has written in his unpublished manuscript about Wiesenthal and the Eichmann case. 'This put paid to the plan to capture Mengele and bring him to Israel with his close friend, Adolf Eichmann.' Other Mossad sources say that Mengele's capture had to be ruled out on the grounds that all efforts had to be concentrated on the Eichmann capture.[4]

Zvi Aharoni, in his manuscript, suggests that Harel was wrong in his decision. He asserts that 'Mengele's name meant absolutely nothing to Harel', when the Mossad began planning for the Eichmann operation. 'By pure coincidence, the name had come up in conversation between Harel and the head of Shin Bet [the Israeli internal security service] just a few days prior to Harel's departure for Buenos Aires. ... Until the actual kidnapping of Eichmann, Harel kept the subject of Mengele on the back burner.' But once they had Eichmann hidden in a 'safe house', Harel instructed his Mossad team to make the search for Mengele a top priority, so that he could also be captured and taken to Israel in the same plane with Eichmann. There was no enthusiasm for such a commando raid, because the others felt that it would imperil the Eichmann operation. 'But Harel stubbornly persisted.'

Aharoni, who was one of Eichmann's interrogators while he was in the Israeli 'safe house' in Buenos Aires, says that Eichmann admitted to meeting Mengele in Argentina, but denied all knowledge of his address. Harel refused to believe Eichmann. 'Finding Mengele had become an obsession,' Aharoni says. Yet when Aharoni, two years later, actually caught sight of Mengele 'on a jungle trail twenty-five miles south of São Paulo', Harel suddenly called off the hunt and ordered his operative to switch to the Schumacher case, which had become top priority for the Mossad.

Harel left the Mossad in March 1963. Aharoni had no further involvement with the Mengele case. But for a few months more, other Mossad agents tried to penetrate Mengele's new hide-out in a predominantly German community in Paraguay. One agent even became engaged to one of the German girls in the hope that Mengele would emerge at the engagement party. But he did not appear. The Mossad agent was not prepared to go through with the marriage on the flimsy expectation that this time Mengele would show up. The Mossad team was withdrawn and the Mossad search for Mengele was abandoned. 'Not every Mossad operation has a successful ending,' according to the source who has revealed this little-known episode.[5]

Wiesenthal, working independently, had also concluded that Mengele was in Paraguay, and he persuaded Bonn to make two extradition demands – in 1962 and in 1964. Both were unsuccessful. In 1962, Wiesenthal also received tips of two possible meetings between Mengele and his wife. The first was to have taken place at Kythnos, and he persuaded the German weekly, *Der Spiegel*, to send a reporter to the island. When the journalist arrived, he was told that a German and his wife had left twelve hours earlier. There is no hard evidence that this couple really were the Mengeles.

The other piece of intelligence in 1962 was a suggestion that Mengele planned to visit his wife in her house on the outskirts of Zurich. Wiesenthal asked the Swiss authorities to watch her. Instead, Switzerland ordered her extradition. Nobody will ever know whether Wiesenthal had been right in thinking that Mengele would otherwise have turned up.

Then, in 1963, there was the curious incident of a group of Auschwitz survivors, who told how they had gone to a Hotel Tyrol in Paraguay, in the belief that they would find Mengele and seize him in time to join the other accused mass murderers in the trial of Auschwitz camp personnel due to begin in December 1964 in Frankfurt. They failed to find him, and Wiesenthal has always thought that their intentions were rather better than their plan.

Wiesenthal was on more solid ground when he discovered in 1964 that Mengele had been in regular touch with Hans Sedlmeier, a long-serving confidential clerk in the Mengele family's agricultural machinery business in Günzburg in Germany. But when Dr Fritz Bauer, who had been promoted to become the Federal Republic's Attorney-General, ordered a raid on Sedlmeier's home, they found nothing. Sedlmeier, it transpired, had been given an advance warning of the raid by a member of the local police force. Wiesenthal mistakenly assumed that the Germans would keep Sedlmeier under observation as the most likely link to Mengele. Sedlmeier, however, was left undisturbed.

Uncertainty over Mengele's whereabouts continued. Wiesenthal says he learned that Sedlmeier was looking for a housekeeper for Mengele. He tried to plant a woman who would act as an informant. This failed, and Wiesenthal again suspected that elements of the German police had foiled the plot.

Wiesenthal, in his report of the Vienna Documentation Centre for the year 1967, wrote that Mengele 'is constantly changing his domicile and it seems he fears for his life. We consider this fact at least as a small part of the punishment he deserves.'

In 1969, a German investigating judge was put on to the Mengele case. Sedlmeier was interrogated and this time admitted to having met Mengele. Wiesenthal assumed that now at last Sedlmeier would be kept under observation, but he was wrong again.

Throughout the 1960s and 1970s, Wiesenthal did everything he could to keep the Mengele case alive. He urged Israel and Germany to involve themselves more closely, following up clues that were beyond the Documentation Centre's means. He also sought to sustain public pressure to step up the search for Mengele by giving press conferences and interviews, and writing articles about him. Israel's response was unenthusiastic: the government felt that it had done its duty to alert the world to the evils of the Holocaust with the capture and trial of Adolf Eichmann. Israel's first priority now was to give undivided attention to its survival as a nation. In any event, there were limits to the Mossad's resources: they had the problem of German scientists developing missiles in Egypt; and they had to deal with Arab terrorism, which became even more dramatic after the PLO outrage against the Israeli team at the 1972 Munich Olympics. Mengele was less important to Israel's vital interests.

The Germans, for their part, were ambivalent. Although undoubtedly keen to try Mengele, their investigations were endlessly delayed by Nazi sympathisers determined to protect Mengele.

So the private Nazi-hunters laboured on without much government support. In 1977, Wiesenthal learned that Mengele's son, Rolf, was to travel to Brazil. Wiesenthal wanted to have him shadowed, but could not afford the fee. When he suggested to a Dutch paper that it cover his expenses in exchange for exclusive rights to the story, he was turned down and told that the risk was not worth the expenditure of $8,000. Rolf later admitted that he had met his father in 1977.

Gradually, interest ebbed. 'Wiesenthal sat in his stuffy office, piled high with his files, his safety watched over by ill-tempered Austrian police and dreamed that one day, he would be able to bring the Angel of Death to account,' wrote one of the Auschwitz survivors.[6] 'I had a strong, almost irrational need,' Wiesenthal says, to find him alive, to have him tried, to have the evidence brought out in court. In *Justice Not Vengeance* he wrote: 'The thought that a mass murderer simply lives on after the war, that he grows old and eventually passes away peacefully, is intolerable ... they must suffer their just punishment; then they can be allowed to die.'

He felt this still more deeply after a 'Mengele hearing', a symbolic trial, held in Jerusalem in January 1985, and organised by Yad Vashem in conjunction with the Vienna Documentation Centre. Wiesenthal, much praised for keeping the cause alive, served on the Praesidium. Thirty pairs of twins, who had survived Mengele's experiments, testified. The accounts of their suffering rekindled interest; all the more so since it coincided with the Los Angeles Wiesenthal Center's discovery of an old letter indicating that the American authorities in Germany had briefly held Mengele in 1946. The writer, Benjamin Gorby, a US intelligence officer in Germany in 1947, had reported that Mengele had been held and afterwards released in Vienna. The Wiesenthal Centre, exploiting its find, insisted that if the US had indeed once had Mengele within its grasp, then it had an even greater obligation now to put its resources behind the effort to find and try him. This tactic paid off, even though thorough research by Efraim Zuroff, then an official of the US Office of Special Investigations (OSI), the bureau charged with the search for Nazi criminals, led to the conclusion that Mengele had never been under arrest.[7] Zuroff's investigation took time. But in the intervening period, the US, German and Israeli Governments at last rallied to establish the truth of what had happened to Mengele. Germany offered a reward of one million marks for information. The OSI pulled out all the stops.

Nobody realised that it was all too late because Mengele was already dead. Certainly not Beate Klarsfeld, who appeared on the scene in Paraguay in May 1985. She had been there once before, in 1979. Like Wiesenthal, she assumed that Mengele was in Paraguay, living under the protection of President Stroessner. Unlike Wiesenthal, she travelled to Asunción to demonstrate, demanding that the authorities reveal Mengele's whereabouts. Then she unfurled a banner: 'President Stroessner, you lie when you say you don't know where Mengele is.' She was invited to pack her bags and leave the country.

Wiesenthal describes Klarsfeld as 'fixated on Mengele'. The same can be said of him. However, while he believes that his way of handling the search had the potential for success, he is convinced that her efforts were counterproductive. 'At first I was pleased to have another Nazi-hunter on the scene.' But he quickly became disenchanted and condemned her as a 'publicity hunter' without any understanding of the complexities of the job.

Certainly there is no love lost between Wiesenthal and Beate Klarsfeld and Serge, her French husband. Wiesenthal judges that their preferred method of attracting public attention was counterproductive and that incidents such as the occasion when Beate slapped German Chancellor Kiesinger at the 1968 CDU Congress, shouting 'Kiesinger, you Nazi', undermined the painstaking effort to make Germans understand that they must come to terms with their past. Beate Klarsfeld and her husband argue the reverse. They probably think that Wiesenthal is jealous of the successes they have scored on forcing a number of former German Nazis out of office. They have also made plain that they see Wiesenthal as an egomaniac who brooks no competition in Nazi-hunting. At any rate the exchanges between Wiesenthal and the Klarsfelds became increasingly bitter. All contact ended after Wiesenthal seized on allegations in the German press, after the unification of Germany, that Beate Klarsfeld and her husband had allowed themselves on occasion to be used by the Stasi, the East German intelligence services.[8] The Klarsfelds do not accept any aspersions on their good faith. But Wiesenthal, when he speaks about Beate Klarsfeld, now always portrays her as a deeply flawed figure.

Ironically, only a few days after Beate Klarsfeld's May 1985 demonstration in Paraguay, the German Government received a further hint that the way to Mengele lay through Hans Sedlmeier. Another search was carried out in his house. Instead of the whereabouts of the living Mengele, a notification of his death in Brazil seven years earlier, in 1979, was found. His son confirmed that he was dead and revealed his burial place. A post mortem on his remains by an international commission concluded that it was indeed Mengele's body.

'For us the case is concluded,' Wiesenthal wrote in his Documentation Centre's report, dated 31 January 1986. But it was not quite so. During the ensuing months, he vainly sought to convince the German authorities to use the reward money they had offered for finding Mengele to compensate some of the survivors among the twins. And in *Justice Not Vengeance*, published in 1988, he wrote that he saw inconsistencies in the reports surrounding Mengele's death: 'I have come to the conclusion that there are sound rational grounds for such doubts. ... I shall continue my search for him.'

This illustrates Wiesenthal's frustration with the failure to find Mengele alive. In reality, he sensed that the search was over. But he only conceded that Mengele must have died after the public prosecutor in Frankfurt sent him the results of a blood test made on Mengele's son. It belonged to the same group as the body's which had been disinterred in Brazil. There were also further bone tests in April 1992, and Wiesenthal declared himself 'finally satisfied' that the Mengele hunt could be called off for good.

Wiesenthal had less difficulty in accepting an expert finding that the remains of a skeleton found in Berlin in 1973 were Martin Bormann's, and that this was conclusive proof that Hitler's deputy had committed suicide on 2 May 1945. In the Documentation Centre's annual report for 1973, Wiesenthal confirms that there was a lengthy correspondence with the Frankfurt Prosecutor's office, concerning the 'clarifications and verifications. At last Mr Wiesenthal agreed that Bormann would be declared dead and the files closed.' Wiesenthal announced at a press conference in Frankfurt that he was now fully satisfied that the skeleton was the genuine article. Recent claims, that Winston Churchill in 1945 had Bormann spirited to Britain and had given him a new identity, hold no credibility for Wiesenthal.

However, he also tried to explain to himself why he had spent years following up clues and rumours about Bormann's movements and had never entertained doubts that Bormann was alive and had succeeded in reaching South America. His answer was largely self-serving. He concluded that he and others had been used by Nazis, who calculated that Bormann's name would serve as a rallying-point for organising the return to power they still envisaged. It was therefore necessary to encourage the idea that Bormann was alive. Wiesenthal also assumed that the Communists, by portraying Bormann as a fugitive, thought it would strengthen their propaganda campaign of painting West Germany as a revanchist power bent on protecting the Nazis.

But Wiesenthal conceded that he must have made mistakes and been slipshod in his investigations. Bormann had such a typical German face that those, Wiesenthal included, who claimed to recognise him from photographs could easily have been wrong. For once, too, there had been a role reversal between Wiesenthal and the media. Instead of Wiesenthal alerting them to a story, he had all too readily thought there was substance to the welter of sensational reporting about Bormann's alleged whereabouts. Yes, he had been very wrong, but he had not been alone; he had been in good company.

Over the years there had been frequent reports of sightings from many different sources, often followed up in the media. However, Wiesenthal had begun to interest himself in Bormann only after Eichmann's capture. At that point, he tried to reconstruct what happened after Bormann supposedly left Hitler's bunker on the night of 1 May 1945, and Wiesenthal asked himself whether Bormann could indeed have survived. His doubts were recorded in *The Murderers Amongst Us* but he weighed them against the fact that from 1960 onwards, the Vienna Documentation Centre had received numerous, convincing-sounding reports of sightings of Bormann. Informants would give him chapter and verse on Bormann's supposed escape from Germany; another said he had seen Bormann and Mengele together fishing in Paraguay. A woman came to Wiesenthal claiming that Bormann had bought land in Chile, close to Bariloche, the Argentine resort where other former Nazis had settled. So it continued. Wiesenthal did not feel the same passionate need to find Bormann as had happened with Eichmann and Mengele; possibly because Bormann had been less intimately involved with the extermination industry, but perhaps also because there was always that nagging doubt whether the man was really alive.

After Bormann's death had been authenticated, Wiesenthal was prominent in the campaign to prevent his remains from being handed over to the family and given a burial that could be used as a rallying-point for neo-Nazis. It was one of the rare times when Wiesenthal was in contact with Willy Brandt. The two men never met. But on this occasion, Wiesenthal had appealed to Brandt, as Federal Chancellor, to intervene, even though legally the family was entitled to claim Bormann's bones. Brandt agreed. It was decided to keep the skeleton under seal in Frankfurt's Forensic Institute.

By no means all the fugitives sought by Wiesenthal and his Documentation Centre were men. One of his most significant cases concerned Hermine Braunsteiner-Ryan, a former concentration camp guard. Though she was not a mass murderer on the scale of an Eichmann or a Mengele, the case confronted Wiesenthal with new challenges and widened his horizons.

Having traced Braunsteiner-Ryan to New York without too much difficulty, the campaign to secure her extradition taught Wiesenthal a great deal about lobbying the great and the good in the United States, and gained him new friends in high places. It also exposed the fact that the US was sheltering numerous war criminals and led to the establishment of the OSI as an offshoot of the Department of Justice, to address the problem more effectively. And when Braunsteiner was finally tried, Wiesenthal broke with his normal practice of distancing himself from the proceedings. He attended the trial at Düsseldorf on numerous occasions, because he believed that the court was biased in favour of the defendant. Public opinion had to be alerted, and he was there to prod the media into action.

Braunsteiner, an Austrian, had been a guard at Majdanek concentration camp in Poland. Her cruelty had become a by-word even amidst the general bestiality that had prevailed. Those who had survived her whips and bullets could never forget her. During a visit to Israel in 1964, Wiesenthal was accosted by three women who wanted to know what had happened to 'Kabyla' – Polish for 'mare' – as Braunsteiner had been dubbed because she was always kicking the women around. He had to confess that he was not all-knowing; that he could tell them nothing because he had never even heard of her.

However, the bait had been cast. He would make it his business to find out; all the more reason because his wife Cyla had only narrowly escaped being consigned to Majdanek. His first move was to search the list of the accused at the Majdanek trial, which the Poles had staged in October 1944, soon after Majdanek had been liberated by the Red Army. Braunsteiner's name was not among them.

Next, Wiesenthal looked at the list of people that had been sentenced for Nazi crimes in Austria. To his surprise, he found that she had been tried in 1948 for her rough treatment of prisoners at Ravensbrück, a small concentration camp near Berlin, and given a mild three-year sentence. Majdanek was not mentioned in the charges. Because she had been detained while awaiting trial, she was released soon after her conviction. There was no indication of what had happened to her since then. But Wiesenthal had established that she was a Viennese. This led him to the city's register, where he found her former address. The sleuthing continued: Wiesenthal went to the place, talked to one of the old women who still lived in the building and was able to tell him that relatives of Hermine were living in a village in Carinthia.

Wiesenthal doubted that he could personally get the family to talk. But he had a young friend, who occasionally helped out in the Documentation Centre, and he sent him on a charm offensive. It worked. Braunsteiner had married an American construction worker, Russell Ryan, and was living in Halifax, Canada. A letter to a contact in Toronto, an Auschwitz survivor, produced the information that the Ryans had moved to New York, where they had just bought a small house in Queens.

Extradition and trial were next on the agenda. But Wiesenthal did not yet know his way around the legal complexities of US procedures, and he decided to take the media route. He turned to the Vienna correspondent of the *New York Times*, Clyde Farnsworth, who had already written a feature about Wiesenthal for the *New York Times* magazine, which had described him, much to his gratification, as 'The sleuth with a million clients'. Farnsworth, told about Braunsteiner-Ryan, scented a good story. The *New York Times* sent one of its reporters to Queens to talk to the Ryans. He happened to be Jo Lelyveld, now the editor of the *New York Times*. On 14 June 1964, the paper carried the story: 'Former Nazi camp guard now a housewife in Queens'. Lelyveld had found a 'large-boned woman with a stern mouth and blonde hair turning grey'. She was wearing pink and white shorts and a short-sleeved blouse and was painting the walls of the small sitting-room. She spoke with a heavy German accent, admitted that she had been a guard, but insisted that she had served her time in jail. Lelyveld then mentioned that he wanted to know not only about Ravensbrück but about Majdanek. She burst into tears: 'This is the end, the end of everything for me.'

But it was far from the end. Just how Mrs Braunsteiner-Ryan was able to live a free, if embattled life in the United States for another nine years is testimony to the checks and balances within the American justice system. But it also fuelled suspicion that high-placed German Nazi scientists, brought to the US after the war to work on weapons development, intervened with the US authorities on her behalf.

Mrs Braunsteiner-Ryan became a US citizen in 1963, and this gave her a significant advantage in the fight against deportation. Her citizenship would have to be revoked before she could be ordered out of the country. Under US federal law, citizenship can only be cancelled if the Department of Justice proves in a federal court that it had been obtained illegally or fraudulently. Having failed to disclose her Austrian conviction when she applied for citizenship, it should have been easy, on these grounds alone, to disqualify her from citizenship. However, the case was up against a bureaucratic maze. The Immigration and Naturalisation Service (INS) requested the Austrian authorities for confirmation of the war crimes conviction against Braunsteiner, but war criminals and denaturalisation suits were not within its brief. It took over a year before Austria formally confirmed the Braunsteiner conviction. Then, in June 1965, the INS sent Braunsteiner-Ryan's papers to the Justice Department with the recommendation that she should be deported. Six months later, the Justice Department returned the papers to the INS, calling for more information about her wartime activities.

Wiesenthal's name cropped up instantly. The mighty INS turned to him to ask whether he could find more witnesses. The old routine was set in motion, even though he questioned why the Americans needed more eyewitness accounts. After all, they were not going to try the woman. Wiesenthal wrote to all the survivors' associations, enclosing a photograph of Braunsteiner. He found two witnesses in Yugoslavia and two in Poland, who were prepared to go to the US to testify.

He also wrote to Senator Hugh Scott on 7 May 1965, urging him to intervene to speed up the proceedings against Braunsteiner. After explaining who Braunsteiner-Ryan was, Wiesenthal wrote in his still imperfect English:

> We know that the INS is leading an investigation into that affair; but we do not know how things are standing now. We suppose the American authorities did not know about her guilt while she was getting American nationality. We can hardly imagine that a country, which fought for the purpose of delivering the world from barbarity, can allocate his nationality to an usufructuary of that barbarity.

This had little effect. The merry-go-round of legal reviews continued.

In 1966, the INS sent the file back to the Justice Department, enclosing the eyewitness reports that Wiesenthal had obtained. The Justice Department returned it again, asking whether charges were pending against Braunsteiner-Ryan in Austria. There were none. Seven months later, on the third anniversary of the *New York Times* article, the file travelled back again to the Justice Department.

Another year passed before the Justice Department made a move. This time the papers were sent to the US Attorney in Brooklyn. On 23 August 1965, he filed charges in the federal court on Long Island, alleging that Braunsteiner-Ryan had entered the country illegally and that her citizenship should be revoked. 'This was due to your help,' Wiesenthal's New York friend, Hy Katz, said in a cable to Vienna. But still the case lay dormant in the courts, untouched for three years, until 28 July 1971, when Braunsteiner finally agreed to sign papers relinquishing her US nationality voluntarily without trial.

Now she was an alien, and the INS was at last able to investigate officially whether she deserved deportation. Some officials were opposed to the investigation. As she had already been tried in Austria, why punish her twice? It was illegal, they argued, because of the 'Woody' rule – a law designed to protect aliens who had been convicted of minor crimes and had subsequently married US citizens. However, a small group of dedicated INS investigators worked on, sometimes ignoring orders from their superiors to stop or slow down.

After the initial splash made by the *New York Times* revelation, public interest in the case had flagged. Little public attention had been paid to the tortuous process, and the Ryans had continued to live an unremarked life. In February 1972, the INS opened public hearings. Some of the witnesses that Wiesenthal had found were present. Graphic accounts were given of the cruelties suffered at Braunsteiner-Ryan's hands. But the hearings were intermittent; between October 1972 and March 1973 there were no hearings at all.

Meanwhile, Wiesenthal had been burrowing at the other end, in Austria and Germany. Since Braunsteiner was Austrian, he thought that the Austrians should demand her extradition. But after three years of trying to prove his case, he gave up with the Austrians and turned to the Germans. His nudging helped to persuade the Federal German authorities at long last to request Braunsteiner's extradition so that she could join the accused in the Majdanek trial that was under preparation. Now the shillyshallying on the US side had to end. On 1 May 1973, Judge Jacob Mishler finally signed a deportation order. Braunsteiner's appeals against the deportation order failed and on 6 August she was finally put on a plane to Germany. But while she waited for the trial in Düsseldorf to begin, she was able to secure bail. The 'Hermine Ryan Defense Fund', set up in the US, had enough money to meet the $17,000 bail set by the German court authorities, and in addition to engage top lawyers for her defence. Already earlier that year Wiesenthal had written to the WJC urging them to find out 'with what forces we have to reckon'.[9]

The Majdanek trial was the last of Germany's major war crimes trials. It was also one of the longest, continuing for five years and seven months. Wiesenthal argued that two of the defence lawyers were so compromised as former Nazis that they should be excluded from the proceedings. One of them, he said, was shielding a wanted war criminal. His interventions were ignored at the time; but there was a public reminder of his objections after the controversial Majdanek verdicts were delivered in 1981. The trial had taken far too long to prepare; it had taken too long to be completed, and the verdicts were far too lenient: of the nine defendants, one had been acquitted, seven received sentences of under twelve years, and only Braunsteiner received a life sentence.

Wiesenthal was angry. 'For me, the sentences are a clear sign of the devaluation of human life,' he declared. And he called for 'a far-reaching exchange with those responsible for the administration of justice in Germany. One has to ask whether it makes sense to continue to co-operate with a system of justice that punishes involvement in countless murders with sentences more usually meted out for robbery and assault.' The German legal community, with a few honourable exceptions like Adalbert Rückerl, was far too riddled with former Nazis, Wiesenthal had reluctantly concluded. Where Germany was concerned, it was, for Wiesenthal, an unhappy end to the inexcusably slow-moving Braunsteiner-Ryan saga.

But with an unerring eye for self-promotion, the overall balance-sheet that Wiesenthal draws from the Braunsteiner case is positive. 'With my discovery of Braunsteiner in a New York suburb, I pushed open a door in the US. She was living with her husband. Nobody knew who she was. I publicised the case, and because of the popularity which I have gained with my lectures in the US, President Carter agreed to set up the OSI, staffed it with fifty lawyers and gave it a big budget.'[10] Of course, there are many others – Jewish organisations and members of Congress, such as Elizabeth Holtzman – who deserve credit for the establishment of the OSI and the acceptance that the United States must investigate the presence of war criminals in its midst. The Braunsteiner case started it all off – and Wiesenthal was the trigger that vaulted the guard from Majdanek into criminal prominence.

[14]
The Two R's –
The Red Cross and Restitution

Simon Wiesenthal lost all respect for the Geneva-based International Committee of the Red Cross after learning how it had deliberately turned a blind eye to the Holocaust. Although Gerhart Riegner of the WJC had in 1942 confronted them with evidence of the Final Solution, the ICRC had waited until 1944 before making any attempt to appeal against the continuing mass of deportations to the concentration camps. After the war, national Red Cross societies, loosely linked to the ICRC, further blotted the record by acting in collusion with Bishop Hudal in the Vatican and providing travel documents for Nazi criminals escaping to the Middle East and South America.

But even though Wiesenthal was thoroughly disillusioned with the Red Cross, he was still taken aback when he accidentally discovered in 1967 that the Austrian Red Cross was actually issuing warnings to wanted Nazis to help them avoid arrest. Soon he learned that the German Red Cross was also involved, and surmised that well-placed German officialdom must be the source of the names. He had stumbled upon another can of worms; 'yet another list of marked men still at liberty,' he sighs, recalling his Red Cross find.

True to form, he would anyhow have gone into high gear with protests to those involved in such misuse of Red Cross societies. But what made him even angrier, and more aggressive than usual, was his belief that the Red Cross warning had foiled the arrest of Alois Brunner, one of Eichmann's most notorious aides. Brunner had operated in Austria, Czechoslovakia, France, Slovakia, Greece and Hungary – wherever there were Jews to be packed off to the extermination camps. Almost as evil in its impact, Wiesenthal felt, Brunner had invented the invidious Kapo system, which used intimidation to corrupt a sizeable number of Jewish prisoners into betraying their fellow victims by assisting the SS with the deportations and with work in the concentration camps.

Brunner had succeeded in escaping to the Middle East and was living in Damascus under an assumed name, Georg Fischer. But he made little attempt to hide his identity. In France, he had been tried *in absentia* in 1954 and condemned to death for his part in the massacres and deportations of French Jews. Indeed, there were French as well as German arrest warrants out for him.

Late in 1967, Wiesenthal learned that Brunner apparently planned to come to Switzerland for an eye operation. With his friend, Adalbert Rückerl at Ludwigsburg, Wiesenthal tried to organise Brunner's arrest after the operation. But this was never put to the test. There is no way of proving that Brunner would really have risked the trip to Europe. In any event he had been forewarned and continued to live in Syria. In 1994, at the age of eighty-two, he was reported to have moved on, belatedly taking the classic Nazi route for Latin America, and very likely hiding in Argentina.

But the incident of the Red Cross warning has never ceased to jar Wiesenthal. Brunner was a major war criminal. Yet almost alone among the principal architects of the Final Solution, he has been able to live on, undisturbed, into old age. Wiesenthal always remembers how startled he was that day in 1967 when he first saw the Red Cross travel alert in black and white. Scanning the *Linzer Turm*, a war veterans' publication, Wiesenthal found on page three of its February 1968 issue a notice headed: 'A warning from the Austrian Red Cross'. Beneath he read the following: 'for political reasons, the following members of the German *Wehrmacht* are urged not to set foot in France, as they would have to reckon there with difficulties!' Among the ten named persons was Alois Brunner. By way of a footnote, the *Linzer Turm* explained that the Red Cross did not know the whereabouts of these men, but 'if any of the comrades had any information, the editor would pass it on to the Red Cross'.

Wiesenthal immediately contacted the head of the Austrian Red Cross Society, Hans Sefcik. His explanation was that the German Red Cross had given him a list of thirty Austrians with a request to trace them and warn them against going to France. The list had apparently detailed the SS rank of the men involved and the sentences they had been given. But Sefcik claimed that the names meant nothing to him. He failed to find the families of ten of them and this led to the notice in the *Linzer Turm*. Wiesenthal was not satisfied. He believed the warnings did not just concern France, but other countries where the men were wanted. He suspected a conspiracy.

He decided on what he calls a 'multi-track' operation. He wrote to the Austrian Minister of Justice calling for an investigation; he requested clarification from the German Chancellor, Georg Kiesinger; he laid a legal complaint with the German Federal Minister of Justice and the prosecutor in Hamburg for 'succouring' criminals; he informed the Dutch and US Red Cross societies about their two sister organisations in Europe with the aim of having them blackballed; and he launched a postcard campaign, directed at Willy Brandt, then German Foreign Minister, to put a stop to the Red Cross warnings. He also informed the WJC in New York. And, second nature to him, he called a press conference to inform the public that the Red Cross was operating a 'warning service' for war criminals and to argue that the Red Cross was betraying its calling.

'Wiesenthal now against the Red Cross' was one headline. Another said that 'an unbelievable affair' has been uncovered. The Austrian Government ordered an enquiry. In Bonn, the Foreign Ministry admitted the existence of the warning list, but claimed that it had acted properly in seeking the help of the Red Cross to warn Germans convicted *in absentia* in France of the risk of arrest in that country. These were people who had been convicted without adequate evidence, and Germany had a right to warn them. The Red Cross had been asked to undertake measures that were fully compatible with its search services, Wiesenthal was told by the Hamburg prosecutor's office. The ICRC was not in breach of any law.

The German authorities refused to accept Wiesenthal's arguments and blocked his attempts to secure legal redress. 'Naturally, there had been no intention to shield Nazi criminals from their just punishment,' Wiesenthal was told in a letter from the Chancellor's office. 'Even though it is possible that a few names were included in the lists of people who had committed major crimes in France, it is hard to imagine that any of these would have risked setting foot in France, with or without warnings. Your concern that there has been a conspiracy to warn Nazi criminals is unfounded', and that far from impeding their prosecution, the German authorities were doing everything possible to bring to justice those who had escaped from German jurisdiction. Germany's intention in asking for the list of those convicted in their absence had been to forward the French dossiers to Ludwigsburg. Yet, the list had been handed to the Red Cross.

The WJC also told Wiesenthal that he would be wiser not to pursue the matter any further. The Red Cross warnings touched on delicate matters involving Franco-German relations. It was also possible that the French themselves had caused the warnings to be issued in order to avoid war crimes trials that might antagonise their Arab friends.

Discussing the Red Cross affair years later, Wiesenthal also pointed at the French and speculated that they had been the real culprits behind the warnings to Brunner and his comrades. But back in 1968, Wiesenthal was reluctant to accept that there could have been quite as much deviousness and double-dealing. He refused to be placated and made one further attempt, early in 1969, to file a legal complaint in Bonn. It was ignored. 'I realised I was flogging a dead horse.' He had no alternative but to admit defeat.

Where the matter of restitution is concerned, Wiesenthal's interventions can best be described as a draw. But this has never been an issue that has greatly stirred him, and there was only one period, in the 1960s, where he tangled, inconclusively, with the Austrian authorities over Jewish property seized by the Nazis. His personal lack of interest in possessions only partially explains his lukewarm concern for restitution. He has always been cynical that the Austrian authorities would delay for so long to make provisions for compensating the Jews that most of them would be dead before the necessary decisions were taken. Above all, he felt that the search for compensation and repossession of property was an unnecessary diversion from the need to bring the Nazi criminals to justice.

The German term for restitution, '*Wiedergutmachung*', translates literally into 'making good again'. Wiesenthal argues that this is an inept word: 'There is no way of fully restoring all that has been taken from us, least of all the intangibles.' All that could ever be achieved is partial compensation.

He acknowledges that German restitution measures, and the monthly pension that he receives for his term in Hitler's concentration camps, have ensured minimal security for himself and his wife. 'If I had had to depend on Austria, I would have received far less.'

He had come to that conclusion early on when he first settled in Vienna, and his Documentation Centre was housed in Vienna's *Kultusgemeinde*. There he had been able to observe the Jewish community's negotiations over restitution. The Austrian authorities had been tight-fisted even where compensation for the destruction of Vienna's synagogues was concerned.

Israel had been wrong, he argues, to press Germany to inject large funds into the Jewish state by way of restitution. Similarly, Jewish communities in Europe should not have made restitution one of their top priorities. Germany acted promptly and generously. But, Wiesenthal insists, this was only accomplished at the expense of a loss of momentum in German denazification and the search for Nazi criminals. In Austria's case, the denazification record was anyhow poor, and the impulse for generosity towards the Jews was largely non-existent. It took until 1995, fifty years after the war's end, for the Austrian government and parliament to decide on a compensation fund; and even then they continued to prevaricate over the conditions for making financial awards.

Given his views on restitution issues, it was uncharacteristic of Wiesenthal to respond to pleas from an elderly Austrian refugee in New Zealand, for help in finding some treasured paintings that had been taken by the Nazis when they seized possessions from her flat in Vienna in 1939. She had written to various Austrian officials, but was no nearer a satisfactory answer. She told Wiesenthal in the letter she sent in 1964 that 'an acquaintance is prepared to buy my missing paintings. I am old and need to pay bills. It would be such a help to me to know what has happened to the paintings.'

Wiesenthal is no connoisseur of art. But through his pursuit of Eichmann in the Altaussee region, he had become interested in the treasures which the Nazis had hidden there in the salt mines. And he knew that the Allies had handed back to the Austrian authorities the 'ownerless' paintings which were formerly the property of Austrian Jews. The Austrians were supposed to return them to their owners within eighteen months, and sell the rest for the benefit of Jewish welfare organisations. Many works were reclaimed. The rest were stored at a secret location, which was later revealed to be Mauerbach, a Carthusian monastery near Vienna.

Wiesenthal remarks: 'People think I am a miracle worker; I am constantly receiving the most unlikely requests for help on matters where I can do nothing at all.' But, of course, it is all very flattering. The letter from New Zealand, which arrived on his desk early in 1965, tempted him to do more than send a sympathetic reply.

Wiesenthal went to work. At first he was rebuffed by officialdom, being told that anything which remained unclaimed at the end of 1968 would become state property. He was again rebuffed when he suggested that a catalogue should be drawn up, so that the former owners would have the opportunity to claim. 'There remained only an appeal to the highest authorities.'[1] Bruno Kreisky was Foreign Minister, Wolfgang Schmitz the Finance Minister. Both received letters from Wiesenthal urging them to have a catalogue made, available for inspection in Austrian embassies and consulates. He sent copies of his letters to the press, stressing that the wider public seemed unaware of the existence of the ownerless art works. But, unusually for a Wiesenthal cause, this created no immediate stir.

Although Kreisky replied in support of Wiesenthal's proposal – this is one of the few occasions where the two men concurred on an important matter – it took almost six months for the government to make a formal response. But it was positive – at least that is what Wiesenthal thought at the time. In a press release, he said that the government had decided to adopt a law, setting a new deadline for claimants, and making it obligatory to publish a list of the stored objects. 'The action of the Documentation Centre has therefore assured complete success,' he stated with pride.

Wiesenthal's confidence was misplaced. Yet he is convinced that without him even the little movement there has been would not have taken place, and the art works would have become state property long ago. Another three years went by, but finally the law was passed and the list published. It filled thirty-four pages of the official government publication, the *Wiener Zeitung*, and comprised 657 oil paintings, more than 300 watercolours and drawings, and numerous tapestries, silver, porcelain and other objects. The claim period was extended until 1995. Thousands of claims arrived in Vienna, but Austria demanded such detailed proof of ownership that ten years later only 100 objects had been handed back to former owners. (Wiesenthal's acquaintance in New Zealand was not among the lucky ones; she died without retrieving her paintings.) 'The Austrians were behaving as if the owners, dragged from their homes by the Gestapo, had been allowed time to measure their pictures and write down other details to help with future identification,' Wiesenthal complained to journalists. In his archives, there are dozens of letters from claimants, with bitter complaints against the red-tape treatment they were experiencing from Austria's bureaucrats. 'Some officials were waiting for the time when the last survivor was dead; because later nobody would claim the property, and it would come under the ownership of the state.'

In 1984, an American art magazine, *Art News*, exposed the story of Austria's ownerless art in a long article entitled 'Testament of Shame'. Stung by such international repercussions a new law was passed, and it became easier to establish claim to the art works. More than 400 were returned in the decade that followed. Many more remained; most of them by minor artists. The Austrian Government decided in 1995 that they should be auctioned, with the proceeds going to Jewish organisations. No date was set. Instead, there was a new hitch. An announcement that everything was to be put on exhibition before the auction was countermanded soon afterwards. If they could be inspected, the explanation went, all manner of unjustified claims might suddenly be put in by unscrupulous pretenders.

Wiesenthal summed it all up with this phrase: '*In dubio contra ebreum*' ('When in doubt, find against the Jew'). It had been an unsatisfactory, seemingly unending encounter with the 'gallery of tears'.

Unfortunately, it was also characteristic of the indecisive and reluctant manner in which Austria has approached all aspects of restitution to the Jewish victims of Nazi rule. There have been endless delays. Weisenthal's view is that: 'They will still be debating restitution until the last victim is dead.'

[15]
Attack and Counter-Attack

Even when he was still a hobbling skeleton in liberated Mauthausen, Simon Wiesenthal grasped that it would be a battle against time to bring the Nazi criminals to justice; and he was not just worrying about old age and their eventual death from natural causes.

Immediately after the war ended, the challenge was to catch fleeing SS personnel before they could escape arrest. Not long afterwards this expanded into concern that the witnesses to war crimes would disperse before they could record their accounts, and that vital evidence for war crimes trials would be lost. Then came the realisation that the commitment to denazification was waning, and that former Nazis were in positions where they could delay, or even block, war crimes trials. The Federal Republic of Germany, and even more so Austria, accommodated people of experience, irrespective of their Nazi past, in senior posts to run the machinery of government, including the judiciary and educational services. Many of those who had given orders in the Third Reich were doing the same again in the post-Nazi era. Though the Communists always denied it, the German Democratic Republic's regime was, if anything, even more riddled with Nazis.

As East–West relations deteriorated, the war crimes trial scene became still more muddied. The Western allies allowed themselves to be further distracted from the task of searching out the Nazi criminals as fear grew over the Soviet Union's intentions. Besides, as more facts became known about the immense scale of killings in the Soviet Union under Stalin, revisionist historians began to argue that the Holocaust was dwarfed by the tragedies of the Soviet Union.

Communist bloc countries, for their part, were reluctant to co-operate with the judicial authorities in the West and became unwilling to provide evidence in their possession required for war crimes trials in the West. Their own war crimes trials were mostly perfunctory. While long sentences were often handed out, the guilty were soon released and absorbed into the Communist Party apparatus.

The Hallstein doctrine, with its prohibition on any dealings with East Germany, meant that Bonn could not request evidence – or demand the extradition of suspects – from the GDR or from any other country that recognised the Communist regime there. This became a major handicap for the Ludwigsburg Central Office in their investigation of German War Crimes committed in German-occupied countries. Ludwigsburg was trying to build up dossiers on the role of individual Germans in the concentration camps in Poland and elsewhere in Eastern Europe. But because the Warsaw Pact countries all recognised the GDR, Ludwigsburg could not ask them for help even if they were willing to give it.

As a private person, Wiesenthal was not bound by the Hallstein doctrine, but this made little difference. Individual enterprise, especially of the kind he was practising, would anyhow have been suspect to the Communists. Natural suspicion was compounded by Wiesenthal's close association during the immediate post-war period with US intelligence personnel in the American zone in Austria. East European regimes might try to use him – as they had when recruiting him to join other experts to authenticate documents which the Czechs claimed they had found in boxes sunk in one of their lakes – but they were never going to trust him, or help him in good faith to build up the dossiers against war criminals.

All this combined to teach Wiesenthal that patience, and therefore much time, were the vital ingredients for preparing the case for prosecution against Nazi criminals.

Yet time was in danger of running out on those who were working hardest to build up the dossiers against war criminals. They were bound by the statutes of limitations in the Federal Republic and in Austria, which dictated that all prosecutions for wartime crimes, including mass murder, had to be initiated within twenty years of the end of the war. For Germany this was May 1965; for Austria it was 29 June 1965. Wiesenthal was certain that many of the major authors of the Holocaust would escape justice unless these statutes were scrapped, or at the very least that the time-limit was substantially extended. By the early 1960s, it had become obvious that many of the worst criminals had escaped beyond German or Austrian jurisdiction. As he knew so well from personal experience, those who had reached South America, or the Middle East, were hard to trace. Once found, it could still take years before they were arrested, extradited and tried.

Wiesenthal, as usual, did not brood in silence. He brought into play his genius for political lobbying and produced a dazzling variety of strokes to secure his aim. He started in 1964 by talking and writing to Ministers of Justice in the Federal Republic and in Austria, to convince them that they owed it to the victims to lift legal bars to the prosecution of mass murderers. In Bonn, he found that there was more interest in the restitution of property to Nazi victims (moves that were not bound by time-limits) than in punishment of the Holocaust's perpetrators. In November 1964, the German authorities confirmed that they had no plans to extend the statute of limitations. In Vienna, Wiesenthal met with similar indifference.

Others might have abandoned the cause, but not Wiesenthal. As he wrote in *Justice Not Vengeance*, 'I realised a fight would be necessary.' His strategy now was to reach for the intellectual heights to generate support in high places. A list was drawn up of 369 eminent people, mainly in German and Austrian public life – academics, lawyers, writers, clerics and musicians. A few émigrés, including Golo Mann, were also asked for their views, but politicians were deliberately omitted. Each received a letter from Wiesenthal urging them to oppose the statute of limitations as it applied to the Holocaust. To allow implementation, he wrote, would be 'an unprecedented injustice towards the millions of victims of Nazi barbarity. Besides, it would be a lasting shame and a danger for many peoples.' If the mass murderers knew themselves to be out of danger of prosecution, they would lose all inhibitions against 'joining with the enemies of democracy to spread their propaganda and poison the minds of the young'.[1]

Almost everyone replied, and though some expressed reservations, nine out of ten endorsed Wiesenthal's views. A German publisher was recruited, and 200 of the replies selected for a booklet, *Verjährung-Nein*, a slogan against allowing the statute of limitations to lapse. This fusillade was promptly dispatched to ministers and members of parliament in Germany and Austria. Wiesenthal organised press conferences to publicise his action. And going one step further, Wiesenthal recruited an eminent American supporter for the cause: Robert Kennedy, who sent him a five-word telegram: 'Moral duties have no term.'

This phrase was adopted as the campaign's motto. But to Wiesenthal, it meant much more. In a nutshell, it expressed everything that Wiesenthal believed. He treasures Kennedy's dictum way beyond the cause that had prompted it, and talks about Robert Kennedy with a fervour that he reserves for few others: 'None of the other Kennedys possessed Robert's finesse and intelligence. Of all the many people I have encountered in my long life, I have never met anyone more impressive.'

Naturally, Wiesenthal's high profile publicity campaign was only one element in a diffuse, often angry, political debate about denazification, which finally persuaded Austria as well as Germany to abandon the twenty-year limit on the prosecution of war criminals. Wiesenthal is uncharacteristically modest about his role on this occasion, claiming only that his campaign 'helped to change the climate' of debate.

Wiesenthal's tactics probably had more of an impact in West Germany, where his image as 'Nazi-hunter' was already well-established and had gained him considerable moral authority. Besides, the Ludwigsburg lawyers and a number of public prosecutors in the German *Länder* shared Wiesenthal's views and added to the pressure on Germany's political leadership; as did the promptings of several eminent international lawyers and human rights advocates. The upshot was that the *Bundestag*, the German parliament, voted to extend the limit by a further five years – and in 1969 went on to extend it until 1979, even though the Federal Minister of Justice, Ewald Bucher, had put his weight behind those who insisted that Germany had already prosecuted the majority of Nazi criminals. After the 1965 defeat, he resigned.

Austria took until 1966 to decide the issue, when it made a clean break and abolished the statute of limitations altogether. But this came about not because arguments for more vigorous pursuit of Nazi criminals had suddenly come to prevail. On the contrary, the law was dropped after an abrasive debate over the dominant role of former Nazi members and Nazi sympathisers among Austria's judges. Their presence, together with the political amnesty granted after the 1955 Austrian State Treaty, made it unlikely that the prosecution of war crimes would continue. With the statute of limitations virtually meaningless, there was little point in holding on to it.

Anyone who imagined that Wiesenthal would be content to leave a time-limit for the prosecution of war crimes on Germany's statute books misjudged his single-minded determination. The further extension in 1969 was voted without great difficulty; but when 1979 loomed, Chancellor Helmut Schmidt sensed that public opinion wanted to see an end to war crimes trials. Wiesenthal thought otherwise. In 1978, he decided to go into high gear to have the statute of limitations finally scrapped outright. Nazi criminals simply must not be freed from fear of prosecution.

In this round, Wiesenthal believes his intervention proved decisive. This time he chose the populist approach: in 1978, a worldwide postcard campaign was launched, directed at the address of Chancellor Schmidt. To publicise it, press conferences were held to generate maximum media impact. The postcard had a photograph of a smiling SS officer standing astride one of his victims, with two more dead men strung up on trees. On the reverse side the card read:

Over 11 million men, women and children – Russians, Poles, Slavs and Gypsies as well as 6 million Jews were murdered by the Nazis. ... One of the murderers is the man shown on this card. He has not yet been found. He and thousands of other Nazi war criminals are free and waiting for 31 December 1979, after which, if the Statute of Limitations is enacted, it will not be possible to bring them to trial. As Simon Wiesenthal says – Justice for crimes against humanity must have no limitations.

Half-a-million cards were printed in German, English, French and Dutch. The Wiesenthal Center in Los Angeles, in existence since 1977, helped with the cost of the postcard campaign and publicity in the United States, but Wiesenthal insists that he remained in charge of the operation. His own files contain numerous requests from private individuals supporting his views and requesting batches of postcards to pass on to others to send to Helmut Schmidt. In the US, he was strongly supported by Representative Elizabeth Holtzman. Her view was that the US Government had been slow to investigate suspected Nazi criminals in the United States. If any were now identified and deported back to Germany, they would nevertheless escape prosecution unless Bonn extended the statute of limitations.

At the same time, Elizabeth Holtzman successfully persuaded Congress that the search for Nazi criminals in the US must be given a higher priority. This led to the establishment of the Office of Special Investigations as a bureau within the Department of Justice. Its first director, Neal Sher, has estimated that 10,000 Nazis entered the US between 1948 and 1952, but that only fifty-two individuals have been stripped of their naturalised citizenship and that up to 1995 only forty-four were deported.

Though pressure from the United States had helped to convince the German government that it must not put a legal time-limit on war crimes prosecutions, the decision had to be ratified by the *Bundestag*. Wiesenthal claims that he made a crucial intervention, which secured a narrow majority vote to postpone the statute of limitations indefinitely. He points to his eleventh-hour meetings with German parliamentarians, and above all a two-and-a-half-hour talk with Franz-Joseph Strauss, the powerful Chief Minister of Bavaria, who wanted the war crimes trials to end. It followed that his party's *Bundestag* members, together with their CDU (Christian Democratic Union) partners, would vote against any further extension of the statute of limitations.

As Wiesenthal tells it, he asked his publisher friend, Axel Springer, to contact Strauss on his behalf. Then he flew to Munich for what he had been told would be a perfunctory thirty-minute meeting. 'Our conversation began with a mutual cannonade. Strauss said that everyone wanted to forget the Nazi horrors. I retorted that I could not accept the statute of limitations, especially since we lost twelve years of war crimes persecutions during the Cold War. He flung at me the memory of all the ordinary German soldiers killed during the war. I challenged him to tell me how many Jews had killed Germans, and to deduct that figure from the six million dead Jews.'

'Strauss had no answer,' Wiesenthal recounts with satisfaction. 'I reminded him that he and I certainly shared one view: anti-Communism. And I pointed out that the Communist bloc media were no longer campaigning against time-limits to Nazi crimes; a sign that they were against further prosecutions. If they adopted that position, then surely there was something wrong with it.'

This obtuse logic apparently impressed Strauss. He promised to brief his CSU (Christian Socialist Union) members in the *Bundestag*; and twelve of them voted against the statute of limitations. Happily this corresponded to 'just the number of votes we needed'. And if the shared antagonism towards Communism really helped to clinch the argument, then here was added satisfaction for Wiesenthal.

He had decided for himself decades ago, during his student days, that Marxism had no appeal for him. But his anti-Communism had become far more pronounced after the war. Awareness of Stalin's gulags and his mass killings was one factor. Another was deep resentment over the Cold War's negative impact on Nazi-hunting, and what made it even worse was evidence that the Communists were turning a blind eye to the Nazis in their midst while attacking the West for failure to denazify or prosecute.

None of this stopped Wiesenthal in 1964 from accepting an invitation from the Czech authorities (the official Czech news agency, CTK) to join a group of experts asked to inspect – and authenticate – the contents of four chests, which the Czechs claimed had been recovered from Cerne Jezero – Black Lake – near Budweis in southern Bohemia. He guessed that the Czechs were seeking authentication so as to be able to sell the documents for hard currency. He was flattered, but not all that surprised that he should have been included in the group, being 'one of the few established experts at that time'. For Wiesenthal, it was a treasure-trove. The papers included the *Kriegstagebuch* of one of Hitler's killing machines, the SS-division 'Das Reich'. There were also lists of Gestapo agents in various European countries, details of the successful assassination plot against Austria's pre-war Chancellor Dollfuss, documents about the activities of the German spymaster, Otto Abetz, in France, and the diary account of Fürst von Hohenlohe's daughter's affair with Lord Runciman.

Wiesenthal and the other experts concluded that the documents were genuine, but that the Czechs had deliberately misled them with their account of how they had been found. The subject-matter of the papers was so disparate that they could not have come from the same archive, Wiesenthal argued. The *Kriegstagebuch* itself would have come from Berlin, but he was not convinced that the rest of the documents had all come from Berlin or had been piled together into the boxes allegedly retrieved from a Czech lake. He gave this as his reason for refusing to sign the authentication certificate. The *Kriegstagebuch* was sold to the Austrian *Europa Verlag* and published the following year.

But the timing of the emergence of these documents, Wiesenthal and his colleagues agreed, was very likely determined by considerations to do with the West German debate on the statute of limitations on war crimes. Wiesenthal for once found himself on common ground with the Communist regimes. Both were seeking to deter Bonn from implementing the statute of limitations and from calling a halt to the prosecution of Nazi criminals. But their motives were radically different. Wiesenthal was seeking more time to find the perpetrators and collect evidence – not least behind the Iron Curtain. The Communists wanted to use the cache of documents to underscore West Germany's war guilt and their responsibility to deal more thoroughly with the Nazi legacy. The whole thrust of the propaganda was to create the impression that they had cleaned the slate in their own countries, while Western capitalism continued to shelter Nazi criminals. Extension of the statute of limitations in West Germany would serve their purposes in two ways: a continuing stream of Nazis in the dock would produce new revelations capable of being used for Communist propaganda purposes. If, on the other hand, war crimes trials dried up, it could be used to show that the West was protecting the Nazis in its midst.

It is fair to assume that when the Czechs invited Wiesenthal to Prague, the Communists had not yet decided to make him the object of the hate and disinformation campaign which they launched against him in the late 1960s in retaliation for his exposure of influential Nazis in prominent positions in East Germany and Poland.

It was obvious to all those familiar with the GDR that denazification had scarcely been more thorough there than in the Federal Republic. But because of Wiesenthal's high public profile in the West as a human rights activist, it touched raw nerves in the Communist bloc when he decided to confront the East German authorities with names, figures and examples of how they had adapted the old Nazi propaganda slander methods to suit the purposes of their Communist regime. He had long been outraged by the distortions of Communist propaganda and the attempts to use denazification as a cudgel against the Federal Republic. He wanted to warn the world against falling prey 'to the preachers of morality in East Berlin, who were insisting that they had a clean Berlin in contrast to the muddied waters of Bonn'.

More immediately, he was prompted into this venture by the avalanche of anti-Semitic diatribes from East European capitals, triggered by the 1967 war between Israel and Egypt. Over several months, he closely monitored East European and especially the East German media, and researched the Nazi past of some of their leading journalists.

Then on 6 September 1968, he called a press conference in Vienna to present his findings. Afterwards they were set out in a paper entitled: '*Die Gleiche Sprache – Erst Hitler, dann Ulbricht*' ('The same language – first Hitler, then Ulbricht'). He named thirty-nine former Nazi Party members, who had worked under Joseph Goebbels and were now active in the East German media. His credentials, Wiesenthal said, entitled him to claim that his overall analysis was sound: 'I know most of the East European languages, and am familiar with their terminology – I spent two years in the Soviet Union, I was in Poland, studied in Czechoslovakia.'[2] This enabled him to recognise how similar the phraseology was then and now. Substitute 'Jew' for 'Zionist', or 'National Socialist' for 'the Socialist camp', and the writings are virtually identical, he argued.

He had been ready to publish in August 1968, but decided to bide his time until the immediate impact of the Soviet intervention in Czechoslovakia had worn off. This made sense, he thought, because he might otherwise have laid himself still more open to Communist allegations that he was using the Documentation Centre on behalf of Western intelligence services as a Cold War weapon. The sole aim of publishing his information about the GDR was to expose the regime's propaganda distortions. He went public on 6 September 1968. Given the restricted access to information in the GDR, the list was inevitably incomplete, he told the Vienna press corps when he launched his campaign to expose the GDR's true record on denazification. He then turned to the GDR hierarchy, and during the weeks that followed he pinpointed 244 former Nazi Party members who, he claimed, had become members of the East German Communist Party and occupied senior positions in the economy, in academia, in sports and in the media. He identified twelve GDR ministers who had been Nazi Party members and fifty members of the *Volkskammer*, the GDR's pseudo parliament.

After German unification, two Stasi agents described how the GDR regime reacted to Wiesenthal's disclosures:

Facts never disturbed our disinformation campaign; not even when the internationally known Nazi-hunter, Simon Wiesenthal, proved during the 60s how
the ex-Nazis had made their careers in the GDR. .... The party leadership had
no intention of putting an end to this disgrace. Instead they gave the green light
to slander Wiesenthal through disinformation. He was 'unveiled' as a Mossad
and CIA agent.[3]

Poland was quick to join the GDR with its own campaign of character
assassination against Wiesenthal. But he was ready for it, and came out, still
in 1968, with a long inventory of allegations against the Polish United
Workers Party – the country's Communist Party. As with the GDR, he
accused the Polish party of recruiting members who were Fascists and anti-
Semites. He declared that Communists had perverted the media, were
ousting Jews from senior posts and were driving the small remnants of
Poland's Jewry out of the country.

In a pamphlet entitled '*Judenhetze in Polen*' ('Campaign against Jews in
Poland'), twenty Poles were named as 'pre-war Fascists and collaborators'
and a further twenty-eight were described as 'leading anti-Semites in Communist Poland'. Both groups, Wiesenthal alleged, had joined to 'build the
Polish way to socialism' through the promotion of anti-Semitism; though
he also stressed that 'the majority of the Polish people are behaving honourably, and are reacting negatively to this new wave politics'. At a press
conference in Vienna, Wiesenthal said that the Communist regime in
Poland had placed known anti-Semites in high positions in the Party, even
though some of them had been imprisoned immediately after the war as
Nazi collaborators. 'What had been beyond the powers of Nazism is being
accomplished by the Polish government today: namely to cleanse Poland of
Jews.' In his book *Justice Not Vengeance*, he wrote that, 'I regard it as my duty
to demonstrate who the men responsible for this vicious campaign really
are. I owe all this to those Poles who opposed Nazism and thereby perished
in prisons and concentration camps.'

The GDR's policies, and the venom directed at him, obviously disturbed
Wiesenthal greatly. But where Poland was concerned, he felt it all the more
passionately since this after all involved the land of his birth. He was speaking
out with the experience of Polish anti-Semitism absorbed during his childhood and youth in Galicia. Neither war nor change of political system
seemed capable of eroding the Polish antagonism towards Jews. Even the
handful of Jews who had been admitted to the Communist Party after the
war and had risen to posts of responsibility were no longer welcome: they
had lost their jobs and were purged in 1967 in protest against the Six Day

Arab-Israeli war. And Wiesenthal's old foe, Kazimierz Rusinek, the Pole who had hit out at him in Mauthausen just after his liberation, had become Minister of Culture, and in that capacity had claimed that Israel had won the war only because it had employed former SS and *Wehrmacht* officers to advise the Israeli army.

Wiesenthal reinforced his attacks against Poland's Communists with an angry broadcast on Radio Free Europe. That was an unwise move. RFE was always seen in the Communist bloc as an arm of the CIA. The broadcast provided Poland and East Germany with ammunition to claim that Wiesenthal was working as a US agent. No matter, he was determined to press on with his denunciation of the Polish Communist Party's anti-Semitism.

Two lines of retaliation were open to Poland and the GDR: to dig into Wiesenthal's past in search of incriminating material; or to disregard fact and undermine his credibility. A neutral account of his life and work, found in Wiesenthal's Stasi file, suggests that the Communists were unable to find any hard facts to substantiate the venomous charges that were levied against him in propaganda material, largely written in Warsaw, but also translated into German and used in articles published against him. Eventually, the Poles compiled a book entitled *Das Netz von Simon Wiesenthal* (Simon Wiesenthal's Network), with 210 pages of innuendoes and denunciations, written in the strident style reminiscent of the Nazis' anti-Semitic tracts.

The smear campaign against him ranged from deep-seated prejudice displayed in numerous articles and broadcasts to allegations of espionage on behalf of the United States, Israel and the Federal Republic of Germany. Worst of all, the Communists claimed that Wiesenthal's account of his wartime sufferings was largely fabricated, and that he could not have escaped with his life from many of the situations he describes, if he had not become a Nazi collaborator. One article, headlined 'Wiesenthal pursued the path of espionage and treason', makes several cryptic allusions to witnesses and documents capable of proving that Wiesenthal benefited from special dispensations 'that saved him during a period when the huge numbers of Jews, Poles and other Europeans were barbarically tortured to death by the Hitler Fascists'. Having compromised himself during the war, it claimed, he moved on seamlessly in 1947 to spy for the US intelligence services.[4]

The Polish–East German propaganda material also made a big meal out of Wiesenthal's connections with a private detective agency in Vienna run by an ex-Austrian police officer, Johann Ableitinger. Wiesenthal's name was found in the agency's files, after Ableitinger was charged with espionage. It turned out that Wiesenthal had once used his services briefly, but the affair caused a major scandal in Vienna and a special parliamentary investigation was ordered. Ableitinger claimed that Wiesenthal had introduced him to the West German and Israeli secret services, and hinted darkly at alleged wartime contacts with the Gestapo. Wiesenthal repudiated everything that Ableitinger said or inferred, and has always insisted that the man had told a pack of lies about him. His dealings with the former policeman had been on a strictly contractual basis to help with investigations into a handful of alleged Nazi criminals. Austria's Socialist Minister of Justice, Christian Broda, nevertheless seized on the allegations against Wiesenthal and stored them away, together with the material that the Poles had put together to discredit Wiesenthal. The Ableitinger affair fitted neatly into the profile of Wiesenthal which his enemies in Eastern Europe had fabricated. Several years later, in 1975, Chancellor Bruno Kreisky would turn to this material to support his attacks on Wiesenthal's good name.

A Polish memorandum on Wiesenthal, found in the Stasi files, points out that the Ableitinger disclosures 'leave no doubt that Wiesenthal was a joint organiser of an espionage ring in Austria, and a linkman to the West German and Israeli information services'.[5] In a reference to the parliamentary investigation into the Ableitinger affair, the Polish paper also refers to allegations that Wiesenthal had collected 'intimate and piquant' personal information on Austria's politicians, which led to the conclusion that he was 'misusing Austrian hospitality'.

The effort to drive a wedge between Wiesenthal and the Austrians was relentlessly pursued: 'Vienna has become a nest for Wiesenthal's agents and the CIA collaborators close to them',[6] and 'dirty tricks performed by the people from the Vienna Centre included falsification and manipulation of documents'.[7]

Naturally, Wiesenthal was not indifferent to this barrage. Had it come from Western sources, he would have sued for defamation. As such a recourse was not available in the Communist bloc, the best way of dealing with his accusers was to use his access to the Western media for further exposures of Warsaw's and East Berlin's hypocrisy. But until his first open clash with Bruno Kreisky after the 1970 elections in Austria, he did not realise the extent to which the East European smears had rubbed off on the SPÖ, and had reinforced the Austrian Socialist Party's prejudices against him.

Of Books and Films and Fame: Fact and Fiction Meet

Frederick Forsyth's *The Odessa File* was an instant best-seller when it was published in 1972, and was afterwards made into a popular film. The book, a thriller, successfully mixed fact and fiction about *ODESSA*, the SS's '*cosa nostra*' that helped Nazi criminals to escape from Europe. Its chief villain was a real person, Eduard Roschmann, a wanted SS officer, second in command of the Riga ghetto, who had escaped to South America along *ODESSA*'s 'ratline'. In Forsyth's book, Roschmann also survives; however, in the film version, Roschmann is killed. Nevertheless, when the film played in Argentina in 1978, its plot helped to smoke the real Roschmann out of hiding.

Forsyth's hero, a journalist turned amateur sleuth in search of Roschmann and the elusive *ODESSA* plotters, is a fictional figure called Peter Miller. But Miller's own hero, the man to whom he turns for advice in Nazi-hunting, is Simon Wiesenthal, a figure drawn true to life by Forsyth. This is how Forsyth portrays Miller's first meeting with Wiesenthal:

He was bigger than Miller expected, a burly man over six feet tall, wearing a thick tweed jacket, stooping as if permanently looking for a misplaced piece of paper. The office was small to the point of being cramped. One wall was lined from end to end and ceiling to floor in shelves, each crammed with books. The wall facing was decorated with illuminated manuscripts and testimonials from a score of organisations of former victims of the SS. The back wall contained a long sofa also stacked with books, and on the left of the door was a small window looking down on to a courtyard. The desk stood away from the window, and Miller took the chair in front of it. The Nazi-hunter seated himself behind it and re-read Lord Russell's letter.

'Lord Russell tells me you are trying to hunt down a former SS killer,' he began without preamble.

'Yes, that's true.'

'May I have his name?'

'Roschmann, Captain Eduard Roschmann.'

Simon Wiesenthal raised his eyebrows and exhaled his breath in a whistle.

'You have heard of him?' asked Miller.

'The Butcher of Riga. One of my top fifty wanted men.'

In real life, Forsyth had gone to Wiesenthal in search of turning vaguely formed ideas into a gripping SS manhunt. The empathy between them was such that Forsyth was soon working out a detailed plot with Wiesenthal. The collaboration intrigued Wiesenthal even before he knew that he would be written into the book as one of its characters. Wiesenthal wanted to use the plot of Forsyth's book for his own purposes. Forsyth obtained a solidly portrayed villain, Roschmann, with carefully documented detail on his wartime crimes and detailed insights into *ODESSA*. Wiesenthal, for his part, calculated that exposure of *ODESSA* and portrayal of Roschmann might help to trace the man. Once he realised that he would be portrayed in the book, Wiesenthal was street-wise enough to realise that it was likely to enhance his public profile as Nazi-hunter supremo.

Wiesenthal never asked for a fee in return for the advice he gave Forsyth. But after *The Odessa Files*'s success was assured, Forsyth decided to make over to the Documentation Centre a small percentage of his first year's royalties.

Forsyth always bases his thrillers closely on contemporary events. In 1970, he had already written *The Day of the Jackal*, based on a plot to assassinate General de Gaulle. The success of that book convinced him that there was a good market for story lines involving a manhunt. He describes how he came to decide that the new book should be centred on Germany and how *The Odessa File* plot was brewed: in his former incarnation as the Reuter's correspondent in East Berlin, he had read enough GDR propaganda to know that they were constantly discrediting the Federal Republic by declaring that it was full of Nazis engaged in subversion. And in the West German press, there were disclosures about a secret escape route for prominent Nazis and how informers had been found murdered, hanged on their own belts or with leather straps. There was one further element that struck Forsyth: in the 1960s, because the Holocaust was a virtually taboo subject in Germany, young people knew nothing about it.

These elements combined to give him the genesis of a new story, and he decided that his hero-sleuth would be a Gentile, a David confronting Goliath, who would learn about the Holocaust while hunting for the SS villain. But he still had no profile and no name for the villain. 'At this point

I turned to the obvious address: Simon Wiesenthal. I wanted his advice on constructing my villain.' Thoroughly briefed about Wiesenthal, Forsyth presented himself in Vienna with a letter, not as in the book from Lord Russell of Liverpool, the eminent war crimes trial lawyer and historian, but from Fred Zinnemann, the American film director who had made *The Day of the Jackal*.

As Forsyth recalls, 'Wiesenthal didn't know who I was, and had not heard of *The Day of the Jackal*. He had no particular reason for giving me of his time. But he was delighted when he realised that I could speak German – his English then was still very halting – and he became very animated when I outlined my plot line.

' "Why use a fictional character?" Wiesenthal asked. He had 200 names on his files who might fit my bill, and argued that a commandant from one of the concentration camps in Eastern Europe would be best. He discarded the best-known names and said it would be better to take someone relatively obscure, but nasty. He proposed Roschmann.'[1]

The initial one-hour interview turned into three days of intensive talk. Between researching the book in Germany and Israel, Forsyth came back to Wiesenthal twice more. Forsyth liked him. He was impressed with Wiesenthal's 'terrific energy and bounciness'. The hunter had plenty of reason to harbour hatred, yet 'he has no hate in him'. Instead, Forsyth thought he recognised a kind of resignation in Wiesenthal, a sense that he had already seen too much horror and that he could no longer be shocked. He had reached a state of 'boredom with horror'.

Wiesenthal helped Forsyth with graphic detail about the Riga ghetto, and Roschmann's behaviour and killings. He gave him the names of survivors from Riga, some of whom Forsyth interviewed, writing their stories into the book. He advised him to talk to the helpful lawyers at Ludwigsburg, and warned him that he would find closed doors if he sought information from the prosecutors in Hamburg. As Wiesenthal remembers it, he thinks that it was he who gave Forsyth the idea of inventing a scene where Roschmann kills a *Wehrmacht* officer to secure a place in an evacuation ship destined for safer ports during the chaotic scenes of German retreat and death marches at the end of the war. But Forsyth says that this was a true incident recounted to him by one of the survivors. When he told Wiesenthal of this discovery, 'he became very excited, and urged me to write it into *The Odessa File*'. Wiesenthal had immediately deduced, rightly, that an account of this shooting would be a time bomb, causing resentment among *Reichswehr* comrades aware of Roschmann's whereabouts, and that they would betray him.

This is what actually happened – though not as a result of the book, but only after the film was made. At first there were some comic false trails to Roschmann. Maximilian Schell had been given the role; and Wiesenthal received several messages that Roschmann had been spotted by people who had in fact seen men resembling Schell! But then the posters announcing the film went up in Buenos Aires. There were quite a few Germans who knew Roschmann was in hiding in Argentina and on 1 July the Argentine police, having received a tip-off, arrested him. Germany immediately filed for extradition. Instead, Roschmann was released and ordered to leave Argentina. He went to Paraguay, where he died a few days later of a heart attack. Local journalists sent Wiesenthal the dead man's fingerprints. They were identical to prints taken from Roschmann when he had been briefly arrested in Graz after the war. Wiesenthal was satisfied beyond doubt that one more name could be struck off his 'most wanted' roll-call.

The Odessa File was unique in that it not only fired the popular imagination but also became a tool for tracking down a war criminal. In *The Boys from Brazil*, a novel by Ira Levin, which was later filmed, Simon Wiesenthal was portrayed as an heroic figure. Unlike Frederick Forsyth's work, this thriller was almost entirely fiction and had no purpose other than to entertain. Wiesenthal had no direct hand in it; so the fact that he was portrayed in it as the man who vanquishes Mengele in the final scene illustrates the extent to which he was established in the public imagination as the archetypal Nazi-hunter. Wiesenthal did not think very highly of the book, written before he had accepted that the real Mengele was dead. But he was flattered when the 'great [Laurence] Olivier' came to see – and study – him, before embarking on the role, and he attended the Hollywood premiere in 1987 since it was in aid of the Wiesenthal Center in Los Angeles.

Wiesenthal has lost count of the television films that have been made about him. His favourite by a long way is the biographical *The Murderers Amongst Us*, made for Britain's Thames Television in 1988. Loosely based on incidents Wiesenthal described in his book of the same title, the film uses actors to recreate several horrific wartime experiences together with formative scenes from his post-war life. Inevitably, there are some distortions, some economies with the truth, but Wiesenthal has never ceased to praise Ben Kingsley for the perceptive way he portrayed him. Kingsley had turned out to be far closer to the way Wiesenthal sees himself than he had dared to expect from any actor.

Other television biographies followed, but most of them have eschewed actors and have used interviews with Wiesenthal to illustrate documentary material. He has lost count, but rarely turns down such requests. The more exposure, the better to nurture his cause of remembrance, but also his public image. Interviewers have generally been able to have him for free, but when the wealthy American or German television networks turn up; he sees no objection to demanding a fee.

Journalism from the beginning, lectures and books later on, have been his chief source of personal income for much of his post-war life. They have been essential to supplement his modest German pension. During the first ten years or so after the war, he could barely have survived financially without the articles he wrote. 'Just to pay the telephone bills, I wrote for the *Oberösterreichische Nachrichten* and other local papers in Upper Austria.' Later he went much wider afield, and when he set up the Documentation Centre in Vienna, he also launched a quarterly newspaper, *Ausweg*, on Jewish affairs related to his own activities, which he has continued to publish.

Most of Wiesenthal's journalistic output addressed concerns of the moment: protests against specific manifestations of neo-Nazism or anti-Semitism; the campaigns against the statutes of limitations; the behaviour of the judiciary; war crimes trials – the same topics that took up his press conferences and were outlined in the Documentation Centre reports. But in his twelve books, Wiesenthal has nearly always sought to portray a more profound and more enduring expression of his ideas and the experiences that have driven him. They fall into three main categories: the autobiographical, written either as memoirs or as novels; historical research of relevance to Jews; and political tracts to underpin his campaigns. One book, on Soviet black humour, published under a pseudonym, fits none of these categories. Ghost-writers, acknowledged in some cases but not in others, were involved in several of the later books; but there is no doubt that the themes and story lines have always been entirely Wiesenthal's and that outside writers were used primarily to improve the books stylistically.

His first book, *KZ Mauthausen*, was locally published in Linz only a few months after he was freed from the concentration camp. This was the collection of the pencil drawings he had made on odd scraps of paper while he was still on death row, with a few added soon after his liberation. Among them was a self-portrait, a gaunt face precariously balanced on a long, bony neck, his inmate's number 'J 127371' pinned on striped pyjamas, and his clenched hands pointed revolver-like with the inscription: '*J'accuse*'. By way of dedication, Wiesenthal wrote a page-long poem to the victims who did not survive, and promised that, 'We will never forget you, for we were always together.'

Few copies of the Mauthausen book were printed, and almost all have disappeared, as have the original plates. However, Wiesenthal himself has held on to one copy, which made it possible to mark the fiftieth anniversary of Mauthausen's liberation with a reissue in a handsome edition and with a new title: '*Denn sie wussten was sie tun*' – 'Because they knew what they were doing' – taken from the Holocaust 'prayer': 'Oh God, do not forgive them, because they knew what they were doing.'

Next, in 1947, came *Gross-Mufti: Grossagent der Achse*, his short, polemical book directed at the Western allies who were protecting the Grand Mufti of Jerusalem, even though well aware that he had been an ardent Nazi supporter. Described as a 'documentary account', it had obtained the necessary publication permit from the US military authorities. The book set out to show how closely the Mufti had been identified with the perpetrators of the Final Solution. The frontispiece of the book is a photograph of the Mufti in Sarajevo, and among the other illustrations are pictures of the Mufti with Hitler and a newspaper cutting announcing 'The Grand Mufti with the Bosnian volunteers of the *Waffen* SS'. There is an undoubted connection between the Fascist Grand Mufti's links with Sarajevo and Wiesenthal's reluctance, decades later, to become over closely involved with the Bosnian cause.

Wiesenthal's early ventures into authorship made little impact. But in 1961 he produced the Eichmann book. It was an intimate, densely packed account of the trails he had followed; it laid bare his motivation, his disappointments, his hopes and ambitions. Published so soon after the Eichmann trial, the reviews and publicity surrounding *I Hunted Eichmann* combined to accord Wiesenthal a hero's dimensions.

The Eichmann book earned him both fame and also much-needed royalties. His next publishing venture in 1965, *Verjahrung-Nein*, his tract to support his campaign against the statutes of limitations on war crimes prosecutions, was a political, but not a popular success. It helped the cause, so it did not worry Wiesenthal that its circulation was minimal.

Besides, three years later, with his next book, *The Murderers Amongst Us*, Wiesenthal scored a major success, with translations into twelve languages. The book is not a conventional memoir. It is gripping, accessible storytelling with a purpose and a moral, each chapter a self-contained personal account of Wiesenthal's search for mass murderers. It not only reflects his origins among Galicia's 'miracle' rabbis and their tradition of expressing truths through homespun tales of the ordinary and extraordinary, but it also confirms his gift for dramatic illustration and for self-promotion. The book includes an account of Wiesenthal's wartime exchange with his SS guard, who boasted that nobody would believe Wiesenthal if he were free to tell Americans the truth about the Final Solution. Though this story is used as the conclusion to *The Murderers Amongst Us*, Wiesenthal says that was the first he wrote. 'Everything else in the book flowed from that.'

In 1969, Wiesenthal decided to write *The Sunflower*, a personal memoir written in the form of a novella, which serves to address his long tussle with the concepts of collective guilt and forgiveness. Encouraged to write it by his French agent and publisher, Charles Ronsac of Opera Mundi, the book was first published in French and only afterwards in English, German and seven other languages. Wiesenthal wrote the original by himself in German, but says that some stylistic improvements were made by the French translators, which were afterwards incorporated in the German edition. *The Sunflower* was chosen as 'Book of the Year' in France, and was serialised in *Figaro Littéraire*. Wiesenthal felt that he had conquered an important bastion of the intellectual establishment.

It encouraged Wiesenthal to embark on his most ambitious excursion into academia: a book on Christopher Columbus, *Sails of Hope*, whose first version was published in 1973. The book addresses the controversial theory that Columbus might have been a *converso*, a Jew converted to Christianity to avoid persecution, whose voyage was financed by wealthy Spanish *conversos* in search of a safe haven in India, where they thought the Promised Land and the lost tribes might be. Many historians have made the connection between Columbus and Spain's embattled Jews. Wiesenthal wanted to know more.

Wiesenthal has no pretensions as an historian, but he was itching for a chance to test his academic skills, having always considered research to be one of his great strengths. It is largely irrelevant, he says, whether he is working on a subject with which he is already familiar, or breaking new ground. 'My research is founded in a mixture of history, legal knowledge, morality, my relationships and experience of life.' He read widely, visited Spain and the Vatican, consulted archives, and contacted Salvador de Madriaga and other historians who had done work on the life and times of Christopher Columbus. Wiesenthal claims that he found new material to strengthen the argument that Columbus was of Jewish extraction, but when he wrote the book, he left the question open.

He was attracted to the theme because he wanted to study the roots of anti-Semitism, and to learn more about the parallels between the persecution of Jews in Spain and Portugal during the Inquisition and, hundreds of years on, in Hitler's Third Reich. 'I knew that the Nazis had not been the first to have policies directed at the extermination of Jews. I knew too that there were many gaps in my knowledge, and that I should look to Spanish history for answers to my questions,' Wiesenthal explains. 'I went to Madrid, to

Seville and to Granada. I saw the papers given to Velázquez to certify him as an Aryan, and saw that such certificates had been the practice then, just as Hitler imposed them in his time. I learned about the Inquisition. I read the story of Ferdinand and Isabella and saw that they had coined the phrase "Spain belongs to us and then the rest of the world" – shades of Hitler: one parallel after another.

'I looked over Columbus's books and documents, and was fascinated by the notes he had made. Just to hold them in my hands thrilled me. I counted at least eighty remarks about Jews, and saw that he often referred to the Book of Prophets, and had even copied a passage from a rabbi who explained his conversion to Christianity. Now I was hooked, and the idea of the book took firm shape in my mind.'

The more Wiesenthal read, the more he became convinced that cause and effect in both periods was very similar, and that anti-Semitism in the Catholic Church was endemic. It was like a long thread, running through the centuries, with the Church treating Jews as heretics outside the fabric of human rights and unworthy of the protection of Church and state. It confirmed him in his judgment that Bishop Hudal, the German cleric in Rome who had helped escaping Nazi leaders, had not been an aberration, but must be placed in the mainstream of Catholic tradition. The Church, he writes bitterly in *Sails of Hope*, had fanned anti-Semitic hatred for 2,000 years.

His studies for the Columbus book also reinforced his long-held view that assimilation was incapable of protecting Jews from anti-Semitism. The *conversos* of the fifteenth century were only tolerated as long as they were useful, and were no more trusted or integrated into Spanish life than those who had chosen to remain Jews. It is not hard to see that Wiesenthal was also thinking of contemporary parallels and had in mind Jews like Bruno Kreisky and many other less prominent Austrian Jews who had chosen assimilation.

Sails of Hope fell distinctly short of critical acclaim, or of popular success, when it was published in 1973. To the extent that any note of it was taken in Spain, it was dismissed as insignificant. In France, a number of historians, who had themselves written books on Columbus, took Wiesenthal to task for lack of scholarship. He comments that 'they regarded their own findings as holy grail, and could not admit new thinking'.

However, Wiesenthal, who had spent more money than he could afford on his research, decided that the book should be revised and republished. Several people were asked to rewrite Wiesenthal's drafts; eventually the Austrian author, Hans Habe, helped to write a new version of *Sails of Hope*, which was published in 1991. This sold much better and was translated into more than a dozen languages.

Wiesenthal is well aware that academics will always be reluctant to accept the book as a significant addition to the literature on Columbus or on the Jews of Spain. But he knows that his own intellectual life was enriched by the research and reading he undertook for the book. Besides, one of his favourite magazines, the German *Der Spiegel*, gave it a generous review, and Wiesenthal says that Jews in the United States reacted to the publication of the book there 'by telling me only half-jocularly – that in future they would have to observe three, instead of two Jewish holy days: Rosh Hashanah, Yom Kippur and – Columbus Day'.

There is a strong connection between the Columbus book and Wiesenthal's other leap into Jewish history: *Every Day a Remembrance Day*, first published in 1986 in a French version by Laffont and reissued by Ullstein in 1990. He took each day of the calendar year and summarised Jewish anniversaries, highlighting Nazi excesses, but also going back in some instances over a thousand years. It is not meant to be a reference book in conventional terms and was intended for a general audience; it has been published in English, German, French and Dutch, but not in Hebrew.

Wiesenthal calls it a 'chronicle of Jewish suffering' and exhorts Jews to understand that 'Jews will live as long as they remember. There is no greater sin than to forget.' He cites the Jewish poet, Layser Aychenrand, who escaped from an Auschwitz transport and reached the Swiss border. The Swiss border guard asked his age and was told, 'I am two thousand years old.' 'This is no conventional calendar,' Wiesenthal wrote in the preface to the book. Instead, 'it is a memorial to horror, it is the story of Jewish martyrdom, of suffering; it is a document to illustrate what man can commit against man.'

While writing his 'calendar', Wiesenthal concluded that there was a pattern to persecution, with the same six elements always recurring: hatred, dictatorship, bureaucracy, technology, crisis or war, and with a minority available as human material for genocide. The only factor that distinguished Nazism from previous genocide was the superior technology of the twentieth century, which made it possible to organise the Final Solution on an industrial scale. In most other respects, his book, he says, unhappily only served to illustrate that history was constantly repeating itself.

When Wiesenthal proposed the Remembrance Day book, he was surprised that nobody had done it before him. He had also assumed that there would be blanks in his calendar – days where there was no suffering to record. 'But no; it was the opposite. Scrutinising the centuries, I found at least three events of an anti-Semitic character for every single day of the year. From old and contemporary documents, and a variety of archives, I established some, previously unknown dates. And there is obviously much more, not yet identified; especially during the period of the "dead centuries" between the 4th and the 11th centuries, when very little is known about Jewish history.'

During one of his early visits to New York, Wiesenthal had an interpreter, who told him the story of Krystyna Jaworska, a young woman in the Polish resistance, who knew about the Soviet involvement in the Katyn massacre, and was caught and shot by the SS. The story became the basis for the first of his three 'docu-novels'. He researched the book by consulting the archives of the Polish resistance in London. Published in 1975, he called it *Krystyna: die Tragödie des Polnischen Wiederstands* (Krystyna: The Story of the Polish Resistance).

He used the story to illustrate the extent of wartime collusion between the Gestapo and the KGB, and although Warsaw and Moscow were still adamantly denying Soviet involvement in the Katyn massacre, Wiesenthal's book laid the prime responsibility for the massacre on the Red Army. The book only fuelled Communist antagonism towards Wiesenthal, but in today's Poland it has become a much-respected work and may be turned into a film.

Wiesenthal's second 'docu-novel', *Max and Helen*, published in 1981, is a love story with a twist that portrays the author in an uncharacteristic mode. It is based on an experience that he had already described in *The Murderers Amongst Us*, and tells the story of an ill-fated trio – Helen and Max, both Jewish Holocaust survivors who had become separated during the war, and Schulze, an SS commandant, who protected Helen but fathered her child. After the war, Wiesenthal found Schulze and searched for witnesses. But when Helen told him that she wanted to protect her son, who knew nothing of his father, he decided against trying to secure Schulze's indictment. It was, Wiesenthal claims, the only time he consciously decided to let a criminal go.

In a revealing passage in *Max and Helen*, Wiesenthal writes of a priest, who came to see him in his office because

he felt that I was exerting myself in vain in my efforts to bring criminals to face an earthly judge. The unvarnished truth would never come to light anyway in such lawsuits. 'Leave these criminals to the justice of God,' he advised. I replied that for those who did not believe in God and feared only earthly justice, this would be a neat solution. He felt that my answer was mockery and left me churlishly. But who knows, there may be a judge waiting for Schulze in the hereafter. At least we can hope so.

The real Schulze died in a motor accident.

Wiesenthal has called the last of his quasi-fictional reconstructions of wartime tragedies *Flucht vor dem Schicksal* (*Flight from Destiny*). Its plot ranges more widely than the two earlier ones, and more of its characters are fictional.

In a throw-back to Wiesenthal's consuming interest in Columbus, the book's central pair of characters are a Jewish father and daughter of Spanish origin with the name of Torres – the same as Columbus's interpreter, Luis de Torres. The plot centres on their experiences after they are forced from their home in Vienna in 1939. It describes the persecution of Jews in Austria, and the action then moves to concentration camps in Poland, temporary escape to the Ukraine, capture by the Germans, incarceration in the Janowska camp and escape with the help of the Polish underground to Romania, where they board a Jewish transport for Palestine. They do not, however, reach the promised land. The overcrowded boat is torpedoed and sinks.

The book distils many of Wiesenthal's own experiences and attitudes. His bitterness towards the Vatican is highlighted in a long dialectic with a priest whom Torres meets in Romania before boarding the boat:

'A half truth is a half lie,' Camillo Torres tells a priest. 'And silence is the easiest lie of all. A murder industry has been installed and the Church is silent ... the Jews are disappearing; but millions of you Christians are alive. Yet, with a few exceptions, you say nothing.'

'We pray,' the priest replies.

'We need your voices more than prayers. To bring hope to despairing people requires more. What the Nazis are doing is beyond the comprehension of ordinary people; but the Vatican knows what is going on. Why are the murderers not being threatened with excommunication? The church cannot allow itself to wait until the storm abates. Its duty is to stand by those who are threatened. If we escape it is our duty to break the silence.'

Justice Not Vengeance, first published in America in 1989, ranks together with *The Sunflower* and *The Murderers Amongst Us* as his best-known books. It is another memoir, intended as a summation of a lifetime's activism. Like its predecessors, it uses incidents in Wiesenthal's life to illustrate the lessons that he has drawn from his experiences. The book's title emphasises the underlying message which is also carried throughout the text. It stresses again and again that justice must be done and the lessons of the Holocaust remembered for all time. But the book also gives Wiesenthal's side of his confrontation with Austria's Chancellor Bruno Kreisky, which cast a shadow over his life for close on two decades. Wiesenthal's bitter dispute with the WJC over Austria's President Kurt Waldheim was far from over when *Justice Not Vengeance* was written, but enough had been said for Wiesenthal to include a detailed account of the reasons that led him to conclude that Waldheim, although a liar, could not be charged with mass murder.

The book seesaws backwards and forwards in time, to the war, to the search for Mengele, Braunsteiner and many others. But it also portrays Wiesenthal as a campaigner for human rights, arguing that the Nazi persecution of the Gypsies must be recognised and speaking up for their recognition as an embattled minority. He describes his efforts to establish the truth about the Swedish diplomat Raoul Wallenberg's fate and his involvement with the Sakharov Hearings to secure the Russian dissident's freedom.

Joseph Wechsberg was no longer alive to help with the writing. This time Wiesenthal had his friend, Peter Michael Lingens, to help with the text and write a biographical sketch. Wiesenthal's own preface is brief:

> My publishers have urged me to write my memoirs. I don't know if it is a correct description of this book, because what it contains about my private life is uninteresting. I am married, I have a daughter, I have grandchildren – they mean everything to me; but they are of no interest to the general public. Of interest alone is my life in relation to Nazism. I have survived the Holocaust and I have tried to preserve the memory of the dead. At the age of eighty, I am one of the last surviving witnesses. It is solely in this function, as a witness, that I write now.

As with most of the previous books, *Justice Not Vengeance* was published in several languages – even in Japanese. By now Wiesenthal's name and fame were so firmly established that the book was heavily promoted, widely reviewed and sold in satisfactory numbers. The royalties were a welcome, but far from massive, addition to Wiesenthal's income.

Wiesenthal did not envisage that he would write any more books – certainly no more memoirs or novels. The only extensive work he still had in mind was to compile a volume on 'the death of Jewish humour'. There he would recount the bitter jokes that Jews made up about the Nazis and the Communists. The stories are all stored in his head, but to commit them to paper takes more time than he can find. However, he can and does use them to regale his friends.

[17]
Paulinka Marries

S imon Wiesenthal never ceased to be haunted by the fact that his parents and all his relations were decimated by the Nazis; or that his wife's family suffered the same fate. The tiny nuclear family he was able to create assumed a giant's proportions in his mind and in his emotions. He always cherished his wife, suffered for her when her nerves gave out, and protected her from intrusion. But it is his only child, his daughter Paulinka, who has managed to combine loyal love for him with interest, insight and understanding for his work. Her three children, now adult, have given him his greatest happiness of all. Through them, he was given assurance of a future, of continuity; and though he is obviously not unique in being sustained by such deep feelings, without his daughter, and her children in the background, the essential loneliness of his existence might have become unbearable. The family and their love, their understanding and their respect have given him a quality of reassurance that no other source can provide. Regardless of his critics, what matters most is that all are wholly convinced of his integrity and that his life and achievements have earned him a place in history.

As a much-loved child, Paulinka was bright and always with an enquiring mind. She was born in 1946, when her parents were still trying to adjust to each other after their wartime traumas. They were living in Linz, in straitened circumstances. Her hyperactive father was consumed by his work and often absent. When she was little, she could not understand why, unlike her schoolfriends, she had no grandparents, no aunts or uncles or cousins. She could not be shielded long from knowledge of the Holocaust, 'although I don't remember as a child that my father deliberately set about to explain it to me'. It was, however, always around her in Linz. 'My father took me to his Documentation Office, to the displaced persons camps, and while he worked with ORT – the Jewish organisation for rehabilitation and technical training – to the camps for the Hungarian and Czech refugees. There was the odd word here or there and no need to ask questions.' She was less aware in Linz of his commitment to Nazi-hunting and the determination to vindicate the dead by making the world aware of their suffering.

It was only after the Eichmann trial, when she was already in her teens, that she gained a more complete understanding of his sense of mission. Wiesenthal gave her Anne Frank's diary to read; and he talked with her often and long, and taught her to be proud of being a Jew. But as with Cyla, he stopped short of telling Paulinka about his day-to-day work. When the threatening telephone calls came, and letters addressed to 'the Jewish pig' were thrown through the letter-box, he reassured Paulinka that these were sent by cranks, madmen, people who deserved only to be ignored. The family must not allow themselves to feel threatened.

But his work took him more and more frequently away from Vienna. The tense atmosphere at home, alone with the overprotective Cyla, must have been oppressive. Paulinka found welcome freedom as a student in Vienna, where she registered for courses in journalism and on the history of the theatre. She also became active in student organisations. On the eve of a student conference in Stockholm, she met her future husband, a psychology student. Left alone at the railway station with luggage belonging to her group from Vienna, Paulinka asked the tall stranger, obviously another student, to help her watch over it until her companions returned. 'He has taken care of her ever since,' Wiesenthal fondly says of his son-in-law. He was Jewish, from Holland, and in December 1965, when Paulinka was only nineteen, they married. She moved to Holland and switched her studies to English and psychology. Eventually, they moved to Israel. He works as a clinical psychiatrist; she works mainly with Dutch survivors of the Holocaust. Unlike her parents, Paulinka and her family are practising Jews, who keep a Kosher home and follow their religion diligently.

Physical distance from Vienna in no way diminished her love for her parents, or her loyalty. On the contrary, she probably needed it, both to make her own life and to gain a closer insight into her father's character. She comes to Vienna two or three times a year and phones almost daily; the whole family normally meets for an annual holiday in Switzerland. Cyla and Simon usually go to Israel at least once a year.

Though Paulinka's departure from Vienna left a huge gap at home, Wiesenthal seems to sense that Paulinka is always close to him. As he beavers away, it is as if he is telling her about his work and thoughts without, in any way, having to explain or justify what he is doing.

Paulinka is slim, attractive, vivacious and looks much younger than her age. She shares her father's intensity, and her mother's insistence on privacy. She is passionate in defence of her father's integrity, but also brings an almost clinical, psychiatrist's detachment to her judgment. 'He has always been able to confront the Holocaust rather than suppress it,' she says. 'He cannot suffer injustice. It goes straight to his heart. What makes him so effective is that he also possesses ingenuity, a fantastic memory and patience.' Many others point to his legendary patience, which has enabled him sometimes to wait for years to accomplish a task. Paulinka doubts that it was some inborn quality. Wiesenthal could be patient, mainly because he has always been involved simultaneously in so many projects. 'Otherwise he would not have been able to wait.'

In another life, she believes, her father would assuredly also have taken up a cause, and whatever project engaged his mind, he would have applied all his formidable energies to it. She regrets that he chose against settling in Israel, and believes that he would have been able to work just as effectively from there. 'Now he will only come to Israel to retire, and since he will never retire, he will never make his home here.'

Paulinka describes her father as a deeply principled man, who would never have been able to countenance a policy of liquidation applied as vengeance against Nazi criminals. 'My father has established his standards, and he will never hesitate to criticise others if he believes they act against them.'

She has no doubt that he is a man whose rigidly held principles can make others uncomfortable. She recognises that he often operates unconventionally and is often misunderstood. She admires his mastery of the media, and is frank: 'He manipulates them as a tool' – but quickly adds that it is always for good purposes.

Few people in Israel are aware that Paulinka is Simon Wiesenthal's daughter, and she has never publicly involved herself in the disputes about her father, especially over his role in the Eichmann hunt, that have surfaced in Israel from time to time. Privately she is tough in her defence of him, but she has always avoided the limelight. Quietly, she draws a picture of her father, who has 'in a careful, low-key way helped Jews to overcome the sense of guilt that they allowed themselves to be drawn, sheeplike, to the death camps'. By exposing the mass murderers and the extermination machine they had devised, he had shown that the victims had no chance to resist. 'He has helped to restore Jewish self-respect.'

Wiesenthal often talks angrily about the way the WJC has sought to minimise his achievements and denigrate him personally. However, it takes his daughter to talk of the 'sleepless nights, the deep anguish it has caused him; and not so much because it is directed against him personally, but because it is a quarrel between Jews'.

'My father is highly intelligent and intuitive. He is widely read, he researches his books like his cases, thoroughly, and handles his material well.' But Paulinka agrees that he is no intellectual. She knows that he has a big ego and how much he appreciates public recognition and treasures the honours he has been awarded. 'And yes, he does enjoy meeting the famous. But after all, here is a man from an obscure *shtetl* in Galicia, who worked in obscurity for years, was often disappointed, had little feedback, was driven only by his ideas and his beliefs. So when he is honoured, he deserves to enjoy it.'

Yet some of the worst trashing Wiesenthal had to suffer came at a time in his life when he thought that he had already earned himself sufficient renown to be accepted at his own worth. In 1975, when many of his major quarries had already been traced, the big battles with Kreisky still lay ahead, and his reputation was to be further demonised during the worldwide controversy over Kurt Waldheim's war guilt.

However, none of the bitter controversies that have surrounded Wiesenthal could ever distract him from the stubborn pursuit of human rights causes of his choosing. Outstanding among his human rights concerns has been his defence of the Gypsies. Another major Wiesenthal preoccupation has been to secure posthumous justice for Raoul Wallenberg, the Swedish diplomat who saved so many Hungarian Jews from the Nazi death camps, by establishing what really happened to him in the hands of the Soviet Union.

[18]
The Human Rights Champion

Justice has been Simon Wiesenthal's watchword since the day of his liberation at Mauthausen. First and foremost, he uses the concept as a way of expressing his determination to find the Nazi criminals and bring them to trial in a court of justice. But Wiesenthal has also developed much broader concerns for human rights. His conscience dictates recognition of the 'righteous gentiles', the men and women who actively opposed the Nazi system and helped the victims to escape extermination. Even his first list of war criminals, compiled within days of being freed in Mauthausen, drew specific attention to a handful of SS men, whom, he remembered, behaved well and therefore did not deserve prosecution.

But Wiesenthal is convinced that of all the heroes he could name, there was no one who has demonstrated better the potential for good in mankind than the Lutheran Raoul Wallenberg, the Swedish diplomat – with a mother of distant Jewish descent – who may have saved as many as 100,000 Jewish lives in Budapest in 1944, when Eichmann was in the city to organise the mass deportation of Hungary's Jews to the concentration camps. Wallenberg disappeared mysteriously when the Soviet authorities arrested him after they captured the Hungarian capital in January 1945. Why the Soviets took him; what happened to him; how long he remained alive in Soviet prisons; why the Swedish Government and the senior members of the Wallenberg family did not do more to try and extricate him, has been a matter of impassioned debate for decades.

Wiesenthal joined that debate, and for a while considered himself Wallenberg's leading champion, seeking to break down the walls of silence and to shame the West into action to compel the Soviet Union to own up. He blames successive Swedish Governments for failing to act decisively and also faults the Wallenberg family for putting their business interests with the Soviet Union before the interests of securing the truth about Raoul. He has not been alone in reaching such conclusions.

The available evidence points to the likelihood that Wallenberg remained alive until the mid-1970s, well after Wiesenthal was first invited to interest himself in the case. He was neither the first nor the last seeker after the truth about Wallenberg. His contribution has to be placed alongside that of others. He failed, as did everyone else, to persuade the Soviet Union to release Wallenberg while he was still alive; and even the publicity with which he tried to surround the case failed to establish the full facts about the circumstances of Wallenberg's detention; or even exactly why he was detained in the first place.

Wiesenthal did not take the initiative to involve himself in the Wallenberg case. He was recruited by Wallenberg's mother. She died in 1979, and he has always remained grateful that she turned to him. Wiesenthal considers Wallenberg as both an agent and also as a symbol of goodness and courage in a morass of evil, and he says that the search for the truth about Wallenberg became for him almost as much of an obsession as the search for Adolf Eichmann. He saw it as a human rights cause, an aspect of his work that was becoming increasingly important to him.

No doubt there was also an element of gratification that he should be invited to join the search for Wallenberg, proof that his credentials were now securely established. Besides, the Wallenberg case satisfied Wiesenthal's exhibitionist instincts. By pitting himself against the Kremlin, against the Swedish Government, against the influential Wallenberg family and against powerful men in the US administration who did not want to jolt US–Soviet relations, Wiesenthal turned it into a classic case-study of the Saint George and the Dragon phenomenon – except that he never wholly vanquished the Kremlin conspirators determined to maintain the wall of silence around Wallenberg's fate.

Raoul Wallenberg had done heroic work in Budapest, risking his life while he organised travel papers and snatched Jews away from Eichmann and the SS, even from some of the transports that were taking the victims to Mauthausen and Auschwitz during the last months of the war. After President Roosevelt had ordered that the US War Refugee Board should do everything possible to save Hungary's Jews, Wallenberg was acting on behalf of the Americans. But the risks he took and what he achieved went far beyond anything that the Americans had anticipated.

On 17 January 1945, with the Germans at last in flight from Budapest, Wallenberg went to the Red Army High Command at Debrecen, near Budapest, to plead for help for some of 'his' Jews hiding in city cellars. The Russians were suspicious, and they detained him. He was not seen again. Initially, the Soviets tried to put it about that he had been one of their agents. For a long time they denied that they were holding Wallenberg. It took twelve years before Foreign Minister Andrei Gromyko was brought in to 'certify' that Wallenberg had been in Moscow's Lubyanka prison in 1947, but had collapsed and died, probably of a heart attack, and had been cremated without an autopsy being performed.

In Sweden, a Wallenberg Committee was set up and Wallenberg's family urged the Swedish authorities to demand more information. But their willingness to pursue the Wallenberg case was tempered by reluctance to antagonise the Soviet Union, Sweden's powerful neighbour. Similar calculations appeared to dictate the actions of most members of the Wallenberg family itself. The Wallenberg empire's extensive commercial interests in the Soviet Union were at stake. Raoul's mother was virtually alone among the senior members of the family to speak out publicly, calling for greater international pressure to discover the truth about her son's disappearance. When President Truman, in 1947, personally offered to help extricate Raoul from Soviet custody, Marcus Wallenberg, the head of the family and Raoul's uncle, turned the offer down, telling the US President that 'Raoul is probably dead by now.'

Marcus had lived in London during the war while his brother Jacob remained in Stockholm. The two brothers had been important contact points for the anti-Hitler resistance in Germany. Marcus in particular had acted as intermediary for the German underground's efforts to bring about a separate peace deal with the United States and Britain. Even though nothing came of this, Marcus must have realised that the Soviet Union had little love for the Wallenberg name. It might have affected their treatment of Raoul. Certainly it would do little good for Marcus himself to campaign on his nephew's behalf. In fact, Marcus waited until the late 1980s to speak out publicly. Only then did he say that 'a great power must have the courage to admit that it made a mistake'.

Many years earlier, in April 1971, Wiesenthal had opened a letter from Stockholm, signed by Mai von Dardel, Raoul's mother's maiden name. Having read *The Murderers Amongst Us*, she wrote of her admiration for Wiesenthal's work in tracking down Nazi criminals:

I have reflected on what possibilities there may still exist of clarifying what happened to my son after the time, when, according to witnesses, he was still alive. I have asked myself whether you might find it possible, using your far-flung network of contacts, to discover any information. ... Over the past few years there have been repeated Swedish inquiries about my son, but the Soviet Government initially denied any knowledge. Then in 1957, they claimed he had died in Lubyanka prison on 17 July 1947. Yet a number of persons who have returned from Soviet prisons have testified to being in touch with him after July 1947. The last information about him dates from 1961, when the Soviet doctor Myasnikov told a colleague that Raoul was in a psychiatric institution.

If you could find Eichmann, surely you can find my son.

Wiesenthal was not one to resist such a challenge. He also felt that irrespective of whether Wallenberg was still alive, it was crucially important for the facts about his fate after January 1945 to be known. 'Historical truth is valuable in itself. Only a regime that admits to historical truth can learn from the past.'[1]

Wiesenthal was already familiar with the rough outlines of the Wallenberg case in so far as it was known. His first instinct was to consider what could be done to secure more eyewitness accounts of Wallenberg sightings. He hit on the idea of asking one of his former collaborators, who had moved on to work on Israel's Russian-language programme, to put out a broadcast about Wallenberg. Wiesenthal calculated that this might be heard by one of the Soviet Jews who had been in Soviet prisons and might remember the tall Swede. If he could collect convincing proof that Wallenberg did not die in the Lubyanka in 1947 and was seen later in other prisons, then he would target the Swedish and US Governments to confront the Soviet leadership with the evidence.

The next step was to map out a campaign for intensifying pressure on the Soviet authorities to tell the truth about Wallenberg. 'I realised that a case such as this could only be cleared up if it became known worldwide,' he wrote in his book, *Justice Not Vengeance*. The most obvious move was to mobilise the influential among Wiesenthal's friends. Another useful avenue was to publicise the case through the Documentation Centre's annual bulletin, which had, by the beginning of the 1970s, garnered 20,000 sub-scribers around the world. 'We consider it a matter of honour for the Jewish people to help solve the mystery around this outstanding man,' he wrote. 'We therefore request readers of our bulletin to ask their acquaintances who have come from the Soviet Union if they know anything about Wallenberg's fate and to relay it to us.'

An unorthodox idea was to try and persuade the novelist, Leon Uris, to write a novel based on the Wallenberg story. It was typical of Wiesenthal's fondness for dramatising events to interest the general reader in his causes. Wallenberg's mother liked the notion, but Uris could not be persuaded.

Then Wiesenthal took to direct lobbying. He proposed the establishment of Wallenberg Committees in the United States and in as many other countries as possible. That way, Raoul's memory would be kept alive. In California, he recruited Congressman Thomas Lantos and his wife, who had both been saved by Wallenberg. They became close friends of Wiesenthal. In New York, Senator Daniel Moynihan's wife presided over a Wallenberg Committee and Elizabeth Taylor, at that time married to Senator John Warner, gave a dinner for Wiesenthal, where he again urged the administration and Congress to act on behalf of Wallenberg. But Henry Kissinger, the US Secretary of State, refused to tax the Soviet Union with the Wallenberg case. Building a framework for better superpower relations was too important to allow for such diversions. Olaf Palme, Sweden's Prime Minister, also refused to take it up with the Soviet leadership. His view of the case was '*Utagerad*', Swedish for 'settled' or 'taken care of'.[2]

Wiesenthal wanted to increase the pressure and sought the establishment of a 'World Committee for the Discovery of the Truth about Wallenberg'. He hoped that Marcus Wallenberg, as head of the powerful family, would chair it, and sent him a memorandum to explain his proposal. He also explained that he did not have the funds to staff such a committee, and urged the Wallenberg family to assume financial responsibility for the project. Money would have been no problem for the Wallenbergs: the cost of the small staff that Wiesenthal had in mind would have been small change in their fortune. However, Raoul's mother was alone in putting her faith in Wiesenthal's power to break Soviet silence. The other family members seem to have thought of Wiesenthal as an unwelcome intrusion and saw no reason for backing his activities. Marcus did not even reply to Wiesenthal's letter.

Another project that came to naught was Wiesenthal's proposal that Wallenberg should be nominated for the Nobel Peace Prize. This died on the vine because the Nobel Committee required proof that Wallenberg was still alive.

Unwilling to abandon the Wallenberg cause, Wiesenthal turned to others more willing to help him stage an 'International Wallenberg Hearing'. It was held in Stockholm in 1981, two years after Raoul's mother had died. There were many luminaries of the Jewish world in attendance, including Gideon Hausner, the prosecutor in the Eichmann case. In his keynote address, Wiesenthal stressed that the Hearing was not intended as an anti-Soviet meeting, but was designed purely to 'free an innocent man from undeserved imprisonment, a man to whom thousands owe their lives'. Challenged to say whether he believed Wallenberg to be alive, Wiesenthal retorted that 'Wallenberg will be alive until the Soviets supply us with credible proof of his death.' The phrase virtually guaranteed Wallenberg his immortality, since even the opening of the Soviet archives after the collapse of the Soviet Union has failed to produce a full account of what happened to him.

In the United States, Wallenberg's friends helped to secure another sort of immortality for him: Lantos persuaded the Reagan administration and the US Congress that Wallenberg should be given honorary US citizenship. Next to the Nobel Peace Prize, there could have been no greater recognition for Wallenberg's place in history, Wiesenthal thought; perhaps it was even one better. Wiesenthal's own role in keeping the Wallenberg cause alive was recognised, and he was invited to Washington for the ceremonies to welcome the Swedish diplomat into 'the American family' *in absentia*.

Wiesenthal's involvement with the Wallenberg case sparked interest in the Nazi-hunter's attitude to Stalin's gulags, and to human rights violations under his successors in the Kremlin. Wiesenthal's primary concern for so long had been the Nazi mass murderers. Because he had consistently preached that the Nazi Holocaust was unique in its targeting of Jews and other minorities, he was often criticised for his apparent lack of concern for Stalin's gulags. He has always defended himself against such charges, and cites one of his press conferences in 1961 in Jerusalem during the Eichmann trial as evidence of his longstanding recognition of the immensity of Stalin's crimes. On that occasion, Wiesenthal had a heated exchange with Dr Friedrich Kaul, an East German observer, who claimed that the Eichmann trial was the result of a conspiracy between Israel and Bonn to indemnify all other war criminals from prosecution.

An angered Wiesenthal told Kaul that GDR spokesmen had forfeited all right to speak in public while they tolerated past and present human rights crimes in the Soviet Union. 'Today we know about Stalin's crimes – perhaps not yet everything, but enough to realise that just as with Hitler, he had thousands of henchmen, who, as members of the secret police, extorted confessions, and there were secret tribunals which handed down sentences of long years of punishment without as much as having seen the accused. . . .' Yet, Wiesenthal, on that day in 1961, stopped conspicuously short of charging Stalin with mass murder, even though the amount of evidence already available could lead to no other conclusion.

Nine years later, in 1970, Wiesenthal became one of the founder members of the Brussels-based Committee for Human Rights in the Soviet Union. He told the Documentation Centre's friends that, 'as victims of the Nazi regime, we feel we are under an obligation to fight human rights violations all over the world'. This was followed in the spring of 1975 with an invitation to Wiesenthal to join the committee of the newly formed International Sakharov Hearings, whose aim was both to secure freedom for Professor

Andrei Sakharov, the best-known Soviet dissident and human rights campaigner, and also to raise awareness of human rights violations in the Soviet Union.

As a nuclear scientist Sakharov had worked on the development of the Soviet Union's hydrogen bomb. After he broke with the Soviet authorities, he and his wife, Elena Bonner, used their links with the West and with the Western media in Moscow to campaign for human rights in the Soviet Union and to publicise the plight of Soviet dissidents. Sakharov was prevented from leaving the Soviet Union even when he was awarded the 1975 Nobel Peace Prize and was eventually consigned to internal exile in Gorki, where he remained until 1986, when Mikhail Gorbachev finally gave him full freedom.

By keeping Sakharov's plight in the forefront of international attention, the International Sakharov Hearings certainly helped to convince Gorbachev, newly installed as President, that his credibility in the West demanded freedom for Sakharov as one of the early moves of his Presidency.

The establishment of the Sakharov Hearings had been prompted by the 1975 Helsinki Declaration, which included a code of conduct to protect individual human rights and recognised the international community's right to concern itself with violations of the code within the territory of any of its signatory countries. Helsinki Watch Committees were set up in several Helsinki Declaration member states, and it was in this context that the first Sakharov Hearing was held in Copenhagen in October 1975. Several former prisoners who had been in Siberia testified. There was a further Hearing in 1977, in Rome, which Wiesenthal was invited to chair. He told the meeting:

> National Socialism was a crime in theory and in practice. Communism is a crime only in practice. When the world learned about the crimes of the Nazis, it was too late to help the victims. Today it is not too late to help the thousands of innocent people who are held in the camps and the prisons of the Eastern bloc.

By now, Wiesenthal acknowledged that 'Stalin may have been responsible for the deaths of even more people than lost their lives in Hitler's concentration camps'.[3] But he has never abandoned the view that the Holocaust was unique, in part because it deliberately targeted racial groups and other minorities, and in part because the Final Solution became a highly organised industry for extermination. Stalin, he argues, may have targeted certain classes, and subjected millions to the cruellest of conditions in his gulags, which led to the death of all but the strongest, but the Soviet Union had no gas chambers, no crematoria. Stalin's killing was 'unsystematic'.

There was a further refinement to Wiesenthal's views on the Communist countries' human rights record after the war: his starting-point, invariably, was anger that they were doing very little to deal with the Nazi criminals in their own ranks, while simultaneously attacking the Federal German Republic for failing to denazify. This suggests that he was less concerned with the handling of their own political prisoners, and far more with their failure to tackle their own Nazi legacy. When the Communist bloc countries mounted their attacks on Wiesenthal's integrity, he became more vocal in exposing their human rights shortcomings. But even then he remained reluctant to join in wholesale condemnation of Stalin's gulags. That was not because he failed to understand and to condemn the enormity of what had taken place in Stalin's Soviet Union. If he held back, it was principally because of the German 'historians' quarrel' over Holocaust denial. He wanted to avoid at all cost giving any ground to the group of German historians who asserted that Hitler's concentration camps were nothing compared to the slaughter in Stalin's gulags; that the whole sequence of killing had started with the Soviet Union and that Hitler was just following Stalin's example.

Wiesenthal became much more outspoken on wider human rights issues after the fall of the Berlin Wall in 1989 and the collapse of the Communist bloc. The old regimes were gone. Now he could feel free to stress the universality of human rights. In addressing young people, he began to offer a simplistic, but to him wholly realistic, message that 'human rights is the only ideology that deserves to survive'. After decades of 'false isms', future generations, he asserts, must look to the defence of human rights as the principal plank of any political programme.

In practical terms, this meant, among much else, that there had to be far greater respect for the rights of the Roma and Sinti – for the people known as Gypsies. This is not a novel conclusion for Wiesenthal; not one that he has reached with the ripeness of age or as part of a post-Communist embrace of a wider human rights spectrum. The Romas have been extremely close to his heart since the mid-1950s, when he was given his first inkling that the Nazi had targeted them for extermination just as much as the Jews. From then on, he resolved to collect every scrap of documentary evidence he could find about the suffering inflicted on the Gypsies. This led him to champion the rights of the Gypsies and to argue that Jews must recognise the Gypsies as victims who had shared the same fate in the Holocaust.

This was not a popular cause, and certainly went counter to the predominant view among those Jews who championed the uniqueness of Jewish suffering at the hands of the Nazis. In particular, it was one of the issues that put Wiesenthal on a collision course with Elie Wiesel; even though ironically, in more recent times, Wiesel has himself adopted a much broader human rights platform, which includes Gypsies amongst other embattled minorities.

Like the Jews, the Gypsies had also been targeted for genocide by Hitler almost from the moment he came to power. The 1935 Nuremberg laws, designed to protect 'the purity of German blood', classified the Gypsies, along with Jews and blacks, as elements posing a threat to racial purity. This sealed their fate. In December 1938, Himmler announced that he intended to deal with the Gypsy question 'in the aspect of their racial purity'. They were required to register with the police for 'racial identification', and anyone with Gypsy blood and no settled abode was forbidden to acquire any kind of technical qualification. An Office for the Fight against the Gypsy People – *Reichszentrale zur Bekämpfung des Zigeunerwesens* – was set up, attached to the State Criminal Police. By now, the Nazis had decided to get rid of the Gypsies, and bolstered their arguments for racial purity with the assertion that Gypsies were possessed of inborn criminality. They were now marked out for slaughter on a scale that the nomadic Gypsies had never before encountered.

As a first step, the regime ruled that the Gypsies were to be rounded up and transported to Poland, mainly straight into concentration camps, and in some instances into the Jewish ghettoes. As the Germans captured new territory in Central Europe, more Gypsies were taken to Poland. After the German invasion of the Soviet Union in 1941, *Einsatzgruppe D* had orders to annihilate all Gypsies in the Ukraine and Crimea.

The documentary record of where and how they were killed, and how many were involved, is far less complete than is the case with the Jews; but it is enough to establish beyond doubt that Gypsies were taken to all the main extermination camps, including Auschwitz, Bergen-Belsen, Belzec and Mauthausen. Dr Mengele experimented on Gypsy twins just as he did on Jews. Quite possibly the archives that have been opened up in recent years in Russia and the Ukraine will shed still more light on the killing of Gypsies. But after the war, virtually nothing was done to make a systematic record of the accounts of Gypsy survivors. The Allied occupying powers were not especially interested, and the Gypsies themselves had no Wiesenthals to urge Gypsy witnesses to come forward. What little information there was came from Jewish survivors, who had seen the Gypsies in the camps with them.

During the war years, Wiesenthal acknowledges that he was only dimly aware of the presence of Gypsies in the concentration camps. In Linz after the war, he paid little attention to their fate. It was only in 1964, when the Czech authorities had invited him to authenticate the mass of Nazi documents they claimed to have found in a lake in southern Bohemia, that they also showed him archives left by the Gestapo in Moravska-Ostrava in Bohemia. The documents showed that Adolf Eichmann had organised Gypsy transports to the death camps. Wiesenthal copied all the material he found about the Gypsies and resolved to dig deeper. This convinced him that the Gypsies had been the victims of genocide, and that those responsible must be brought to justice.

In 1965, Wiesenthal sent all the material he had collected to the Central Office for War Crimes Investigations at Ludwigsburg to add to their dossiers against Nazi criminals. In the Documentation Centre's annual report for 1965, he wrote that

> the extermination of the Gypsies is one of the least known chapters of the Nazi crimes, and was hardly dealt with until now. We succeeded in discovering a number of documents concerning the whole organisation . . . we have been able to discover that SS *Haupsturmführer* Walter Braune had to carry out this action. The case is now being investigated in Ludwigsburg.

But few of the investigations led to prosecution: the German authorities appeared to have even less interest in holding to account those responsible for the Gypsy killings than those responsible for the genocide against the Jews.

Simultaneously Wiesenthal went down his customary media route, showing some of the Gypsy documents to friends at the *New York Times* and other newspapers, all with the object of putting an end to public indifference mingled with widespread prejudice against the Gypsies. But Wiesenthal was even more concerned to educate the Jews. It affected him deeply that Jews, especially Jewish survivors, had so little understanding or sympathy for the Gypsies, and that they had even manoeuvred to prevent them receiving restitution payments for property sequestered by the Nazis in Austria. His strictures did nothing to endear him to Jewish leaders, who were already critical of him as a lone ranger who was forever inserting himself into controversial Jewish affairs.

Undaunted, Wiesenthal attended an international convention of Gypsies in West Germany in 1981, where he made an impassioned plea for greater awareness and concern for the losses suffered by the Gypsies at the hands of the Nazis. He brought with him leaflets documenting how the Final Solution had applied to Gypsies as much as to the Jews, and demanded that their murderers too must be brought to trial. He expressed regret that the prejudices against the Gypsies had not ended with the collapse of the Third Reich and appealed to the Western democracies, especially the Federal Republic, to abrogate their anti-Gypsy legislation.

The intervention was widely reported, but had little practical effect. In the Documentation Centre's report for 1982, Wiesenthal noted that

> the tragedy of the Gypsies has not ended . . . again and again, there are complaints about the discrimination to which they are subjected. In order to improve the situation of this hard-hit people, the Documentation Centre has repeatedly intervened with the German authorities.

In 1985, the Central Council of Jews in Germany held ceremonies to mark the fortieth anniversary of the liberation of Bergen-Belsen. The Gypsies' Central Council of Roma and Sinti asked to join in the commemoration in memory of the Gypsies who had suffered the same fate as the Jews. This was rejected by the Jewish organisers. Wiesenthal insisted that this was wrong and called for the personal intervention of German Chancellor Helmut Kohl, with whom he had already formed a firm friendship. Since the Roma and Sinti had been refused a platform by the Central Council of Jews, would the Chancellor please pay tribute to them when he addressed the gathering at Belsen. Kohl obliged 'and spoke in a moving way', Wiesenthal remembers.

While these campaigns were going on in Germany, Wiesenthal was also in pursuit of greater recognition for the Gypsies from the Jewish power-houses in the United States. The US Holocaust Memorial Council had been set up in Washington. Its aim was to ensure that the victims of the Holocaust would not be forgotten. Elie Wiesel, America's foremost writer on the Holocaust, was President of the Council. Polish, Russian and Ukrainian representatives served on it. Wiesel was approached to include a representative of the Gypsies. When this was ignored, the 'Society of Threatened People' asked Wiesenthal to intervene on the Gypsies' behalf.

Wiesenthal made representations to Wiesel. The reply only came after several weeks. It advised Wiesenthal that appointments to the Holocaust Council could only be made by President Ronald Reagan. So the Central Council of Roma and Sinti wrote to Reagan, who in turn sent the correspondence back to Wiesel. Wiesenthal wrote again to Wiesel, this time adopting a far sharper tone and arguing that it was essential to end 'this shameful state of affairs' by giving Holocaust Council representation to the Roma. Wiesel did not reply. Wiesenthal's revenge was to report on all this in his Documentation Centre report, and to urge readers to write to Wiesel on behalf of the Gypsies – another one of his postcard campaigns.

On this occasion it only served to deepen the tensions between Wiesel and Wiesenthal – which came to a head in 1986, when both men were proposed for the Nobel Peace Prize. There was a prospect of a joint award. Wiesenthal's name had been put forward from several quarters, most notably by Chancellor Kohl. Wiesenthal, who had made no secret of his eagerness for the Prize, learned that the Roma and Sinti intended to come to Oslo to demonstrate on his behalf. Fearing that this would only further antagonise Wiesel, and would do little to advance his candidacy, Wiesenthal cautioned against such a show of solidarity.

There was no Gypsy manifestation. Nor was there a joint Peace Prize award. Wiesel was the sole recipient. Chancellor Kohl thought then, and continues to think, that a mistake was made. 'I consider it very wrong that Wiesenthal has still not received the Nobel Peace Prize. I am absolutely on his side. He is far more than a Nazi-hunter. He is a visionary, who has understood that neither the individual nor a people can live without a system of moral co-ordination.'[4] With bravura, Wiesenthal shrugs off his disappointment that he failed to secure the Prize. Even if such protestations are taken at their face value, there is no denying that Wiesenthal has found it hard to reconcile himself to the fact that Elie Wiesel came out the winner in the contest for the international community's most treasured peace accolade.

Wiesenthal has remained convinced that the WJC, fired by the ever-growing dimensions of the dispute over Kurt Waldheim's wartime record, intrigued to dissuade the Nobel Committee from making a joint award in 1986. The WJC has been just as adamant to deny any involvement in the politicking that always surrounds the Nobel Peace Prize. 'Even had we wanted to oppose Wiesenthal's candidacy, we would not have had that kind of influence with the Nobel Committee,' one of the WJC's senior officials contended. But he added that Edgar Bronfman, President of the WJC, had endorsed Elie Wiesel's Nobel candidacy – though 'probably not in any formal way'.

Whatever the reason for Wiesenthal's failure to gain the Nobel Peace Prize, at least he was finally given satisfaction with respect to the claims of the Roma and Sinti to be given official standing in the Holocaust Memorial Council. When the membership of that body was renewed in 1986, Wiesel had altered course and was prepared to ensure Gypsy representation, and from that time on has embraced their cause with some of the fervour that Wiesenthal had brought to it years earlier, when he had been a lonely voice crying out against making the Holocaust a purely Jewish tragedy.

Wiesenthal himself has continued to fight for the rights of the Roma and

Sinti. After the establishment of the Simon Wiesenthal Centre in Los Angeles, Wiesenthal insisted that its Museum of Tolerance must emphasise that Jews were not the only group targeted for the Final Solution. He wanted a display to explain how the Gypsies also became victims of genocide, and why it was so important to show respect and racial tolerance towards the Roma and Sinti. Wiesenthal's wishes were respected. The plight of the Gypsies, taken to the gas chambers with Jews and other 'deviants', is graphically portrayed in the Museum. It brings nobody back from the dead. But Wiesenthal believes his work on their behalf has brought the Roma and Sinti forward towards being accorded the dignity and standing they deserve.

1970: The Start of the Kreisky Wars

'Kreisky attacked me and hurt me as no other individual had done since the Nazi period. He accused me of using the methods of a "political mafia". Even though he knew that it was hard to survive [during the Holocaust], he had information that my relationship to the Gestapo was different and that I lived in freedom etc. Naturally the journalists built this up. In the end, he retracted.'[1]

With these few, awkward phrases, Wiesenthal summed up his version of brutal warfare between giants that began in 1970, and continued with occasional respites until Kreisky's death in 1990. It has left behind a gnawing legacy of bitterness among Wiesenthal supporters, while in the Kreisky camp, there is regret and occasional embarrassment over what they prefer to regard as an aberration, a character flaw that mars an otherwise impressive statesman's record.

The story is Byzantine in its twists and turns and ramifications. It involves two men representing fundamentally different strands of Jewishness, who were totally unable and unwilling to understand each other, and eventually fell into a deep trough of mutual hatred. Wiesenthal saw Kreisky as a man who betrayed both his heritage and also the Holocaust, and who was power-hungry enough, if it was politically useful, to work with members of the former Nazi Party.

For his part, Kreisky painted Wiesenthal as a meddler and a hypocrite, bent on undermining Austria's Socialist Party, using his Documentation Centre to interfere in Austria's domestic politics to secure the fortunes of the conservative People's Party. But Kreisky's drive against Wiesenthal also reached deep into his own psyche and related to his need to distance himself from organised Jewry, to his unease with Zionism and to a determination to prove that his Jewishness would never stand in the way of his loyalty to Austria.

Kreisky's popularity meant that for most of his period in power, from

1970 until 1983, Austrian public opinion sided with the Chancellor and that Wiesenthal, already something of an enigma to Austrians, was made a virtual outcast. Since then, Wiesenthal's star in Austria has steadily risen and Kreisky's political heirs have come to treat him with great respect, brushing aside the former Chancellor's efforts to destroy him as an unfortunate episode in Austria's domestic politics.

The key triggers that launched and recharged the battles between Kreisky and Wiesenthal are relatively few and easy to identify. The ramifications are far more complex. The first skirmish occurred in April 1970, when Kreisky announced the members of his first Government. Wiesenthal promptly pointed out that four out of the eleven members of the cabinet had belonged to the Nazi Party, and that one of them had been an officer in the SS. Kreisky countered with slurs against the Documentation Centre, describing it as a secret star chamber and Wiesenthal as a 'Jewish Fascist'.

The war became far more serious in 1975, when it emerged that Kreisky had negotiated with Friedrich Peter, leader of the far-right FPÖ Party, as a possible coalition partner. Wiesenthal reacted with allegations that Peter had served in one of the SS brigades, whose involvement in the mass extermination of Jews was well documented. Kreisky, standing firmly behind Peter, responded with a fresh battery of attacks on Wiesenthal's reputation, crowning them with the claim that Wiesenthal had only survived the war because he had collaborated with the Gestapo. The Chancellor asserted that he had evidence to prove his allegations.

A flurry of slander actions resulted: Wiesenthal versus Kreisky; Peter versus Wiesenthal; Kreisky versus Peter Michael Lingens over the journalist's news magazine articles in defence of Wiesenthal. The Lingens case trailed through the courts until 1986. Peter withdrew his case in 1982. The potentially explosive court confrontation between Kreisky and Wiesenthal was averted after Kreisky was persuaded, in December 1975, to retract his Gestapo allegations against Wiesenthal.

But this was only an uneasy cease-fire. Sniping continued. Twice more, in 1981 and 1986, Kreisky returned to the charge that Wiesenthal had been a Nazi collaborator. Again Wiesenthal sued for slander, and, after three years, finally won a judgment against Kreisky, who was ordered to pay him substantial damages. But even this was a pyrrhic victory. Kreisky was dying and the fine was never paid.

The latent antagonism between Kreisky and Wiesenthal goes back way before the first public eruptions in 1970. Wiesenthal refers to an occasion in the 1950s, when he was still living in Linz, but had come to Vienna to discuss government restitution for synagogues burned down during the

Nazi era. Kreisky was then State Secretary in the Foreign Office. Wiesenthal and his colleagues ran into him in the Ballhausplatz, where the Chancellery and Foreign Ministry are housed, and Kreisky immediately said to them: 'I hope you are not coming to see me.' Wiesenthal adds: 'He always wanted to avoid contact with Jews.'

Wiesenthal pinpoints the real break in their tenuous acquaintance to a brief encounter in 1963. He and Kreisky had been invited to watch a television programme about the Arab–Israeli conflict, which included separate interviews with each of them. Wiesenthal berated Kreisky, who was by now Foreign Minister, for employing double standards, arguing that Kreisky was prepared to do more for the Palestinians than for his own countrymen from South Tyrol: 'I told Kreisky that "you want more for the Palestinians than you were able to secure for the South Tyrol". That constituted a *casus belli* between us. We never spoke to each other again after that incident.'

Until then they had only met occasionally, casually. They had exchanged correspondence, but there was no natural affinity. Far from it. The two men came from radically different backgrounds and drew fundamentally opposed lessons from their wartime experiences. Wiesenthal brought all the outsider's baggage of the Galician Jew from the *shtetl*, whose primary loyalty was to his Jewishness, and who believed that Jews who had survived the Holocaust had a moral duty to build bulwark defences – whether it be war crimes trials or support for Israel, or simple solidarity with other Jews – to preserve and strengthen the position of Jews wherever they happened to live. Kreisky had little understanding or sympathy for such deeply held views and was dismissive; he saw Wiesenthal as a typical product of what he described as the 'warped' mentality of the *Ostjude* – the Eastern Jew.

Kreisky's own comfortable, middle-class family came from Czecho-slovakia; his father from southern Bohemia, his mother from southern Moravia. His parents had spent most of their life in Vienna. Their son, Bruno, was born in 1911 into a prosperous, settled home, where assimilation was the accepted way of life and loyalty to the Hapsburg firmament was taken for granted. As he grew up in the unstable times of the post-war period, the young Kreisky soon became politicised and found his natural home in the Socialist camp. The labour movement was headed by Otto Bauer, a Jew who believed in assimilation as an historical imperative and argued against Zionism as a concept that would only serve to strengthen Jewish ghetto mentality and thereby reinforce anti-Semitism. Kreisky, from the outset, seems to have accepted the view that assimilation was the safest weapon against anti-Semitism.

By the age of sixteen, Kreisky had joined the Association of Socialist Secondary School Students. This was an essentially middle-class grouping, more concerned with Marxist theory than with Socialist activism. Kreisky, already concerned to distance himself from the accident of his Jewish birth and to mark his total identification with Austrian social democracy, moved over to the Socialist Workers Youth – SAJ – movement, and took part in demonstrations and other proscribed activities. In 1936, he was tried and convicted for illegal activities and was given a twelve-month sentence.

His cell mate was a Nazi, Sepp Weniger. They had many tough arguments, and on political issues, there was no meeting of minds. Nevertheless, closeness also bred loyalty. Kreisky probably saved Weniger from a much heavier sentence, when he reacted to an unexpected body search by swallowing an incriminating note that his Nazi cell mate had asked him to smuggle out of the prison. This seemingly insignificant reflex action may have been decisive for the course of Kreisky's – and Austria's – future: two years later, after the *Anschluss*, Kreisky was again in prison. He was badly beaten and in imminent danger of being sent to a concentration camp. It was then that Weniger, repaying his debt, intervened to testify to the solidarity that Kreisky had shown him and other Nazi inmates. This almost certainly saved Kreisky.

Kreisky, in a written appeal for freedom, told the Gestapo that during his previous incarceration, he had 'shown solidarity towards my National Socialist prison mates and frequently passed messages for them; it would never have occurred to me to do otherwise'.[2] Interrogated by the Gestapo soon afterwards, he was told that they had been made aware of his helpfulness to party comrades while in prison in 1936. In recognition of his behaviour, the Gestapo ruled that Kreisky, instead of being sent to a concentration camp, would be allowed to emigrate to a 'distant' country. A few days later, he was released; but rather than go to Bolivia, the country he had indicated to the Gestapo, he went to the safety of Sweden. He made a point of persuading himself that he was forced into emigration because of his political views, and not because he was a Jew.

Kreisky did not forget his debt to Weniger. After the war, Weniger was tried as a war criminal and executed – but not before Kreisky, still in Sweden, had intervened to plead for clemency.

Insufficient attention has been paid to the curiously symbiotic relationship between Kreisky and his Nazi mates while they were locked up together. But there has always been speculation among those closest to Kreisky that Weniger accounted at least in part for Kreisky's pragmatic attitude towards Nazis, and also for his willingness to draw a line under the past and work with them. The appreciation of what he owed to Weniger may have weighed more heavily with him than the fact that twenty-one members of Kreisky's family perished during the Holocaust.

But even without Weniger, there was the simple arithmetic of the road to political power in Austria after 1945. Kreisky not only fought his way up the ladder of the Socialist Party to be elected its chairman in 1967, but also became the first Jew this century to head a government anywhere outside Israel. It was no accident that he came to be referred to as the '*Kaiser*' (Emperor). Like Kaiser Franz Joseph, Kreisky sought stability and consensus, and to create a united nation. Principles had to be bent to achieve such pre-eminence in a country that had at least half-a-million ex-Nazi Party members in a population of seven million – a far higher percentage than in Germany. Kreisky could never have made it to the top without participating in the SPÖ's manoeuvres to secure political respectability for the FPÖ, the far-right party that had become the natural home for the former Nazis. From the 1950s on, the SPÖ gave financial support to the FPÖ, and followed this up later with Kreisky's decision to sponsor changes in the electoral law so as to give the FPÖ a greater number of seats; hence also Kreisky's decision to consider them as coalition partners.

Kreisky's calculated effort to disassociate himself from all matters Jewish may have been less decisive in his progress to political pre-eminence, but it certainly was a vital ingredient in the creation of the *Kaiser* image. In Kreisky's *Memoirs*, based on conversations with the French journalist, Manuel Lucbert, there are revealing passages which explain Kreisky's reluctant acceptance of his Jewishness, his problematic relationship with Israel and his dislike of Wiesenthal. The edited version is to be published in October 1996 as part of the third volume of Kreisky's *Memoirs*, but the full, unpublished transcript is even more revealing.

It confirms that Kreisky could not accept the notion of a united Jewish people, and believed that the idea of Israel as the Jewish home was a romantic delusion, which could never eradicate anti-Semitism. Assimilation, he held, was the only credible solution for Jews. Having ruled out the concept of a Jewish 'race', or the view that all Jews originally came from Palestine, he argues that Jews have far more in common with the cultures of the environment in which they live than with their co-religionists elsewhere. He insists on the wide gulf between the East European Jews from the *shtetls* of Galicia and the far more assimilated Jews from Central and Western Europe. They were driven together into what he calls an 'artificial unity' only through Hitler's anti-Semitism.

Expanding on his antipathy for Zionism, Kreisky argues that Zionism exploits anti-Semitism by arguing that Jews can only find security in Israel. He assumes that Israel, perversely, has less reason to object to anti-Semitism, because this helps to maintain a steady influx of Jews and strengthens the Jewish home. 'All this has an important bearing on my attitude towards Jewry. There is no single solution.'

Some Jews only feel themselves free in Israel; whereas some of the orthodox consider that persecution is part of their destiny and consider it a sin to live in Israel. 'But again others consider their life amongst other people as perfectly natural. ... I myself come from a family that never suffered from persecution before Hitler came to power. My family was in every respect integrated and had no awareness of persecution.' He questions whether Fascism was inherently anti-Semitic, and tries to prove his point by arguing that Mussolini was relatively benign to Jews.

> I have never understood my own emigration as the consequence of my Jewish origin. I would have been persecuted [by the Nazis] just as I had been four years earlier, for purely political reasons. This means that I cannot share the experiences of those Jews who consider themselves racially persecuted.

Being an agnostic, Kreisky also lacked all sense of a common religion. 'What then remains of my relationship to Jewry?' The answer:

> Primarily a strong feeling that one must not deny one's origins, or be ashamed of them. This is all the more important if one comes from a community that others consider inferior, or because one could be exposed to other kinds of unpleasantness. To sum up, one should no more deny being a Jew than deny being a German, or being the offspring of a prostitute. Emphatically, one should never deny that one comes from a socially inferior background; all the more so if one does not consider oneself to be inferior. The fact that I have a Jewish origin in no sense means that I consider myself the inferior of my Christian co-citizens.

But again Kreisky writes: 'Beyond the feeling that one neither can nor should deny one's origin, I have no real sense of belonging to Jewry.' Israel means no more and no less to him than any other state: 'I feel that Sweden, where I lived for twelve years, is my second home, and is certainly much closer to me than Israel. Zionism is based on racism, and this is something I cannot accept.'

Kreisky believes that his attitudes, and his kind of commitment to reconciliation, achieved far more than Wiesenthal ever did 'to convince people of the dangers of anti-Semitism'. Claiming that Wiesenthal has always applied 'the methods of permanent hatred', he adds that this can never persuade people to draw the correct lessons from the Holocaust. Ignoring that Wiesenthal lost his entire family in the Holocaust, Kreisky claims that, 'I at least have behind me the sacrifice of my nearest relatives, and I have an intensely deep sense of family. I understand the psychology of people. With unpleasant methods, you cannot convince people of wrongdoing.'

Kreisky reinforces his argument against Wiesenthal by claiming that 'he is not sufficiently qualified morally to fulfil this task [of convincing others of wrongdoing]'. And finally, 'the methods he employs stand in contravention with our democratic legal system. To declare people guilty before the courts have found them guilty. . . .'

Kreisky, who entered government as a junior State Secretary in 1953, was a member of the various ÖVP majority–SPÖ minority coalitions until 1966, when the conservative ÖVP won an outright majority. Party fortunes were reversed at the next general election in March 1970. With Kreisky at the head of the SPÖ, the Socialists won the largest number of seats, but not an overall majority. Kreisky became Chancellor. It took him almost seven weeks to form a government. The party debated long and hard whether to form another grand coalition, but the ÖVP, unaccustomed to the role of junior partner, posed conditions which the Socialists considered unacceptable.

Coalition with the far-right FPÖ was similarly ruled out, being politically unacceptable to a large faction of the Socialist Party. It was also considered unworkable by the FPÖ's leader, Friedrich Peter, who emerged badly from the 1970 election and was on the verge of being ousted from the FPÖ's leadership. But, in a dramatic stroke soon after the final count on election night of 21 April 1970, Kreisky invited Peter to an unexpected midnight meeting. Kreisky told Peter that the SPÖ would try and survive as a minority government. He went on to ask for a promise of support from Peter's FPÖ and, in exchange, offered an irrevocable commitment that the SPÖ Government would amend the electoral law in the FPÖ's favour to increase its opportunity to win more parliamentary seats in future elections. Peter says that his party was stupefied by this turn of events, and for the time being, his position as party leader was again secure. The SPÖ kept its word about electoral reform.

When Kreisky's cabinet list was published on 21 April 1970, Wiesenthal checked the ministerial credentials and quickly established that four members of the new cabinet had been Nazi Party members. One of them, the Minister of Agriculture, Hans Öllinger, had even risen in the ranks of the *Waffen* SS to become *Untersturmführer*. Otto Rösch, the new Minister of the Interior, came from a strong Nazi background and had been tried in 1948, during Austria's brief period of denazification, for helping former

Nazis to escape criminal prosecution. (It turned out that Rösch had been doing this at the instigation of an SPÖ minister, who was even then trying to find ways of enticing former Nazis into organising a new, separate party.) It was the first time since 1945 that the Government included Nazi Party members. Wiesenthal ensured that his findings about the Nazi past of Kreisky's cabinet found their way into the Austrian press, and not long afterwards also into the influential German weekly, *Der Spiegel*. Newspapers in many other countries followed up the story. Wiesenthal was readily available for comment.

Kreisky did order an investigation into Öllinger's past. Though it confirmed that no evidence of Nazi crimes had been found against him, and Kreisky defended him strongly, Öllinger soon resigned on time-honoured grounds of ill-health. He was succeeded by Oscar Weihs. Wiesenthal claimed that this minister too had been a member of the Nazi Party.

Kreisky grew apoplectic with fury from the moment Wiesenthal went public with his revelations. In his inaugural address as Chancellor, Kreisky vehemently insisted that every citizen must be allowed to have the right to reconsider his political views in the light of later experience and knowledge, including those held during the Nazi period. He believed that Wiesenthal was deliberately setting out to undermine Austria's first Socialist Government. He was determined to hit back.

During the Socialist Party's Congress in June 1970, the first of many slurs were cast at Wiesenthal: 'How much longer can we tolerate the Documentation Centre, this secret star chamber with its *"feme"* [slander] methods for avenging the past?' the Minister of Education, Leopold Gratz, declaimed. Wiesenthal, he asserted, was organising a private inquisition, 'a nest of spies and informers', who had outlived their usefulness and should not be allowed to continue on Austrian soil. Kreisky thundered that 'even a member of the Nazi Party or the SS must be permitted to hold political office in Austria as long as he cannot be convicted of a criminal act'. Wiesenthal was convinced that the Austrian Government would seek to close down the Documentation Centre – if by no other means than by intimidating Wiesenthal and his family to such an extent that he would no longer be safe to continue his activities.

Worse was to come from Kreisky a few days later. In an interview with a Dutch journalist, Martin van Amerangen, Kreisky spoke of Wiesenthal as an 'extreme reactionary'. As if that was not enough, the Chancellor added, in a poisonous aside, that 'you must of course understand that Wiesenthal is a Jewish Fascist'. Amerungen's article highlighted this phrase, though it had not appeared in the transcript of the interview that was submitted to the Chancellor's office for checking before publication. Dr Ingo Mussi, Kreisky's press secretary at the time, has confirmed this. Not that Kreisky's aides ever doubted that he had made the remark; it certainly represented his sentiments. For them, the only question has always been whether it had been on the record, or off the record and therefore not intended for the published interview. Amerungen's newspaper, *Vrij Nederland*, then produced photostat copies of the transcript that included the 'Jewish Fascist' charge. Mussi believes that there had been some mysterious doctoring; all the more so since the original did not surface again and was reportedly burned in a fire in Amerangen's office, ten days after the interview with its contested phrase was first published.

Where Wiesenthal was concerned, none of these mysterious goings-on made one iota of difference. To have the Documentation Centre's integrity questioned and to be personally insulted as a Jewish Fascist cemented Wiesenthal's resolution for an all-out fight against the Jewish Chancellor and his colleagues. Perhaps, if Kreisky had ordered a more energetic pursuit of war crimes trials, Wiesenthal would have been more tolerant towards the ex-Nazis in the Government. After all, he never attacked German Chancellor Konrad Adenauer for appointing several former Nazis to his immediate entourage. Wiesenthal insists that his refusal to castigate Adenauer had nothing to do with any personal political leanings, just because Adenauer was a Christian Democrat – while Kreisky was a Socialist. He felt able to show greater generosity towards Adenauer, Wiesenthal says, only because the German leader had taken a forceful attitude to bringing Nazi criminals to justice. Maybe also because Adenauer showed considerable respect towards Wiesenthal for his Nazi-hunting activities.

In Austria, Wiesenthal's first move against Kreisky and his colleagues was to launch a slander action against Leopold Gratz. He also described Kreisky as a 'renegade', and loudly complained that twenty-five years after the war, Austria was still protecting former Nazis and was trying to turn the tables on those who were seeking to expose this state of affairs. It seemed that the Nazis were innocent, while he, Wiesenthal, could be slandered with impunity.

Wiesenthal strenuously denied that he was conducting a vendetta against the Socialist Party. In a letter to Dr Rudolf Kirchschläger, the new Foreign Minister – and later Austria's President – Wiesenthal insisted that it was 'totally false to assert that I have intentionally created difficulties for the Socialist Party, while seeking to protect the Austrian Peoples Party, the ÖVP'. In support of his argument, Wiesenthal recalled his 1966 memorandum in which he had hit out at the slow pace of war crimes trials and the failure to denazify. At that time, Austria had an ÖVP Government; yet the Chancellor, Josef Klaus, 'in no way interpreted this as an attack on his party; instead, they made a serious effort to respond to my memorandum. I want to declare categorically that I do not belong to any political party and that my antagonism to the present government does not have an ideological basis.'

Going further on the offensive, Wiesenthal urged Jewish organisations, and his supporters around the world, to bombard Kreisky with protests about his attempts to discredit the Documentation Centre. 'You have certainly read in the papers about the heavy attacks and defamations against me and the Documentation Centre,' Wiesenthal wrote in a letter that was even read into the US Congressional Record.

> Our friends abroad sent telegrams of protest to Chancellor Kreisky and to the Socialist Party. We know very well that the Socialist Party needs the votes of the former Nazis to reach their majority. . . . In the present Austrian Government, there are several ministers with a Nazi past. Considering this, the Documentation Centre did not dare to let that pass without pointing to it. Our friends in Austria understood the Minister threatened to have the Documentation Centre closed. Presently we are the only ones to be active against the Nazis. If you think the Centre must not be silenced, please cable your opinion to Chancellor Bruno Kreisky, or to the Socialist Party of Austria.[3]

Soon, the Documentation Centre was able to compile a booklet, *Reactions from around the World*, consisting of protests against its 'threatened closure'.

But even though the support from abroad far outweighed Wiesenthal's local difficulties, there were also reservations. Israel's priority being to establish good relations with the new Austrian Government, it distanced itself from Wiesenthal and refused to join in official condemnation of the inclusion of former Nazis in the Kreisky cabinet. In a carefully nuanced interview, Israel's Ambassador, Zev Shek, stressed that the Israeli Government had no connection with Wiesenthal, but that Israeli Jews took a vivid interest in the work of the Documentation Centre because Jews around the world were concerned with the just punishment of war criminals.

Max Riegner, head of the European office of the WJC, as always uneasy over Wiesenthal's actions, questioned Wiesenthal's assumption that the Austrian Government meant to drive the Documentation Centre into closure, and doubted that the attacks on Wiesenthal warranted an international campaign of support from Jewish communities. In a memorandum that Riegner sent to top officials of the WJC, including the President, Nahum Goldmann, on 29 July 1970, he argued that, while the accusation of running a '*feme*' organisation was certainly a serious matter, I doubted personally whether this alone warranted an international concerted action by Jewish communities. It was my feeling that this rather was a matter to be handled by Jewish and non-Jewish institutions in Austria. ... It seems that Mr Wiesenthal wants to give the impression to the outside world that there is an imminent danger that the authorities will close down the Documentation Centre. On the basis of information available, this seems rather exaggerated. The public polemics about the Centre alone do not really support such apprehensions. But should the authorities proceed to any concrete action against the Centre, we may have to reconsider our position.

Wiesenthal became deeply depressed by the vitriolic nature of the domestic Austrian attacks against him. Kreisky's popularity in Austria was such that Wiesenthal was treated almost as a leper.

Among the public I had the image of an implacable avenger who eats some poor innocent little Nazi for breakfast every day. ... Now I was being attacked not just by anybody, but by Bruno Kreisky, who could say all the things against me that were normally said against me only by the extreme right-wing press, because he was immune by virtue of his Jewish birth.[4]

Even though Kreisky insisted that he would not allow himself to be pressurised by protestations from Wiesenthal's friends abroad, he was led to clarify the Socialist Party's, and therefore also his government's, position with respect to the Documentation Centre. Letters were sent out from Socialist Party headquarters to Wiesenthal's supporters, promising that there would be no interference with the Centre, provided it operated within the law. It was easy enough for the SPÖ to give such an undertaking – there had never been any serious intention to act against the Centre. There was no legal case for it and Kreisky knew it. Besides, it would have been politically hazardous; not least because of the outcry that would have been generated in the United States and other countries, where Austria's Socialist government was keen to establish its credentials.

But if Kreisky could not act against the Documentation Centre, his intransigence where Wiesenthal's person was concerned only grew stronger. He would not be pressured into dismissal of the former Nazis from his cabinet. 'Mr Wiesenthal, who combines a strong sense of justice with a highly developed gift for publicity, should not imagine that he is tabu when he intervenes polemically, as active Conservative and opponent of the Social Democrats, in Austrian domestic politics,' the SPÖ's Secretary, Franz Fischerlehner, wrote.[5]

Kreisky's spokesman, Ingo Mussi, was instructed to reiterate that it was time to draw a line under Austria's Nazi past. True enough,

> during the turbulent thirties, many Austrians became Nazis in good faith, because they expected an improvement in the situation. But, given that sufficient time has elapsed since the Nazi regime, and in order to put an end to the wholesale condemnation of anyone who belonged to the regime, the Chancellor has held for years that those who committed no punishable crimes, have distanced themselves from their past, and have committed themselves to democracy, should not now be disadvantaged.

The letter went on to deny that any member of the Kreisky Government had held a high position in the Nazi regime, and ended with the admonition that 'the federal government energetically rejects the attacks and rumours inspired by certain quarters'.[6]

By the summer's end, the battle between Kreisky and Wiesenthal turned into an uneasy truce. Wiesenthal buried his depression in still more work and took ever more pride in his growing international standing. Even if he was suspect in Vienna, he could walk tall in Washington, London, Paris, the Hague and even in Germany. The Stangl trial, in which he had an especially close interest, continued until close to the end of 1970; he was trying to secure Hermine Braunsteiner's extradition from the United States; he was chivying the German authorities to accelerate war crimes trials; he was fending off the attacks against him from Poland and the GDR; he was lecturing in several European countries, appearing on television, giving press conferences, promoting his books and planning new ones.

But none of this was too much for him to let Austrian matters rest. In November 1970, he wrote a letter to the Minister of Justice, Christian Broda, in which he referred to his 1966 memorandum on denazification and complained that still not enough was being done to bring Nazi criminals to trial. He demanded 'decisive measures' and blamed the Ministry of the Interior for negligence. There was no ministerial reply.

The Chancellor was otherwise preoccupied. Kreisky was beginning to implement his ambitious domestic programme, including tax reform, new economic and education policies, and extensions to the welfare system. In November 1970, the government went ahead with its promised reform of the electoral system, which until then had been weighted against the smaller parties and had put the FPÖ at a disadvantage.

Even so, early in 1971, it was becoming glaringly obvious that Friedrich Peter would not be able to carry his FPÖ members to support Kreisky's new budget. The Socialists decided on a new general election to aim for an absolute majority. It was held on 10 October 1971. The wager paid off. Kreisky had his first overall majority. It was a small one – only three seats over the combined ÖVP and FPÖ. Had he failed to win outright, Kreisky would have been prepared to invite the FPÖ to form a coalition.[7] If Wiesenthal had been aware of Kreisky's shift, the mother of all battles between Wiesenthal and Kreisky would have occurred much earlier. But these are the hypotheticals of history. As matters turned out in 1971, Kreisky's tiny majority held out long enough for him to remain in power until the next election in 1975, and Wiesenthal saved his heavy guns for that occasion.

[20]

The Peter Affair –
and Beyond

On 4 October 1975, the SPÖ won its second outright victory. Again Kreisky only had a precarious majority of three in Parliament. But as in 1971, it was enough to form a government, and there was no need for Kreisky to consider coalition with the FPÖ. Five days later, Wiesenthal dropped a bombshell.

At a press conference, he produced a damning dossier about Friedrich Peter, the leader of the FPÖ. It exposed Peter as a member of the 1st SS Infantry Brigade and asserted that he had served in Company 5 of the 10th Regiment, an extermination squad that was held responsible for large-scale civilian killings in Nazi-occupied Poland and Russia in 1941 and 1942. Wiesenthal had also established that Peter had later been awarded the Iron Cross for bravery and completed his career with the SS as *Obersturmführer* (lieutenant).

Wiesenthal was accusing Peter of having failed to disclose his full military record by omitting service with the 1st SS Infantry Brigade in his official biography, but expressly stopped short of charging him with war crimes: 'He was a member of a murder brigade, but I regard guilt as individual and not collective; and I had to admit that I had not found any conclusive proof of his individual guilt.' Peter acknowledged that he had indeed been with the 1st SS Infantry Brigade, but denied that he had participated in its atrocities, or had been aware of them, having been on sick leave in an army hospital during the brutalities that Wiesenthal had cited. Wiesenthal retorted at the time that he would leave it to others to draw their own conclusions.

Shortly afterwards Dr Adalbert Rückerl, head of Germany's Central Office for the Investigation of War Crimes at Ludwigsburg, confirmed that they had found no case for charging Peter with war crimes. Peter now says that he numbered all his wartime letters to his then future wife, and that there was one written from an army hospital which proves the accuracy of his statement that he was absent from his SS unit during the period of its excesses. While he still has a copy of that letter, the original is missing. No matter whether Peter's affirmations of non-involvement are accurate, in 1975 Wiesenthal's disclosures caused an unwelcome scandal with extensive and long-term repercussions on Austria's international standing. They also spelled the beginning of the end of Peter's political life.

Peter comes from a family with impeccable SPÖ credentials. But as a young man in the late 1930s, he frequently went to Germany and admits that he joined the *Waffen* SS – but not the Nazi Party – with 'unrestrained enthusiasm'. However, after the war he underwent a conversion to become a committed democrat and insists that his main objective as leader of the FPÖ had been to shift its membership away from Nazi influence. 'Wiesenthal and I should have worked together,' he says.

Wiesenthal had come across Peter's name in the SS *Kriegstagebuch* shown to him several years earlier in Prague, and subsequently published in Austria in 1965. He had noticed Peter's name then as a member of the *Waffen* SS, but claims that he attached no particular significance to it until a few weeks before the 1975 general election. 'Around the middle of September, I found among my papers a list of men from the 1st SS Infantry Brigade with candidates for further training. Amongst the twenty names was Friedrich Peter's. That was for me a great surprise, since he had never mentioned his service with that brigade, which had continued for twenty months. If I had known sooner, I would most certainly not have kept it to myself. But until that September day in 1975, I had only known of his connection with the *Waffen* SS, but not that he had been with that particular murder brigade.'

Wiesenthal says that he had toyed with going public about Peter's past immediately, even though Austria was on the eve of an election where, once again, Kreisky was negotiating with Peter to form a coalition in the event of the SPÖ's failure to win an outright majority. Finally, Wiesenthal decided to wait with his disclosures about Peter until after the election. Otherwise, he reasoned, he would be laying himself open to the charge of interfering in the election campaign. Wiesenthal decided to give an advance warning of his intentions by presenting his Peter dossier to President Kirchschläger on the eve of the election, but only to go public a few days after the election.

On 9 December, he wrote to his close friend and supporter in the Netherlands, Professor Sijes, that 'now I realise that my timing was a mistake, and that I should perhaps have waited 3–4 weeks after the elections. But such speculation is based on hindsight, now that Peter's political significance is greatly diminished, because Kreisky no longer needs him.'

Peter's own version of the sequence of events, which he only detailed many years later, in 1994, differs markedly from Wiesenthal's. According to him,[1] Wiesenthal had known his full wartime record since 1971. By implication Wiesenthal would have been biding his time to seize an opportunity where it would have maximum impact on Austrian politics. Peter declares that Kreisky came to him one day in 1971 and told him that Wiesenthal's Documentation Centre had asked for Peter's SS file from the war archives stored under US control in Berlin. 'This file can only be handed out with the consent of the diplomatic representation of the concerned person's country,' Kreisky said, and went on to ask whether Peter had any objections. Peter replied that he had none. According to Peter, Austria's Consul-General then obtained the SS file from the Berlin archive and sent it to the Foreign Minister — then still Kirchschläger. Peter was given a copy, as were other party leaders. Wiesenthal received his copy.

Peter's account continues:

> Then [in 1975], on the Thursday before the election, Wiesenthal takes his file to Kirchschläger — now President. He should have refused to receive it, and told Wiesenthal to go to the government prosecutor. Then, after Wiesenthal's post-election press conference, Kirchschläger gave me the Wiesenthal dossier, which was, in effect, the same file that Kreisky had already handed to me in 1971 ... and so, *tempi passati.*

All this would be beyond challenge, but for one little-known fact: Wiesenthal was among the few who had access to files in the Berlin archive without first securing the consent of their country's government. Austria would not necessarily have known of Wiesenthal's request.

In any event, Peter adopted a low-key response to Wiesenthal's charges and did not rush into a slander action against his tormentor. It took a month before he acted against Wiesenthal, and then only at the FPÖ's insistence. The conflict never became as personalised or as virulent as the conflict between Kreisky and Wiesenthal. Peter believes he merely served as a surrogate for Wiesenthal's true target, which was of course Kreisky. 'I often told myself that it was Wiesenthal's right to act as he did. On the rare occasions when we run into each other, we are always able to exchange a few polite sentences.' Wiesenthal concurs; he harbours no rancour towards Peter even though he still disbelieves that the former member of the *Waffen* SS has told the full truth about his wartime activities.

Irrespective of who had known what and when about Peter, it is indisputable that Kreisky's anger with Wiesenthal over the Peter disclosures rose several decibels, and took him well beyond rational thought. If his language had been careless in 1970, now it overstepped all bounds of reasonable discourse. On 10 October, the day after Wiesenthal's press conference, the *causa* Peter became the *causa* Kreisky–Wiesenthal. Kreisky sprang to Peter's defence not only by proclaiming his complete confidence in the FPÖ's leader, but also by insisting that Wiesenthal was bent on destroying him personally. 'He is trying to commit character assassination,' thundered Kreisky at the beginning of a stream of tirades. It was an organised campaign 'to bring me down', and not only Peter.

Wiesenthal's Documentation Centre was 'well-known for the ruthlessness of its methods'. Kreisky had no illusions 'how this gentleman operates. He manipulates by resorting to trickery.' He further insulted Wiesenthal with frequent references to him as 'allegedly a graduate engineer' with its insinuation that possibly Wiesenthal was making false claims to his professional qualifications.

Undeterred, Kreisky continued to goad Wiesenthal. During a lengthy, often rambling and confused press conference, directed in its entirety against Wiesenthal, the Chancellor repeatedly questioned Wiesenthal's good faith and insinuated collaboration with the Nazis during the war. 'Perhaps we don't know everything about Wiesenthal. ... Maybe then he would not have obtained his Austrian citizenship', followed by the charge that Wiesenthal was using 'Mafia methods' to destroy the reputations of Austrian citizens.

Then came the most damning insinuation:

> Wiesenthal co-operated with the Nazis, and thus lacks any moral qualification to point an accusing finger at others. I know of witness reports from people in Germany and Austria who can testify that he worked as a Nazi agent. ... Herr Wiesenthal, I maintain, had another relationship to the Gestapo from mine. Yes, there is proof. Can I say more? Everything else I shall say in court. My relationship with the Gestapo is unambiguous. I was its prisoner, its detainee. I was interrogated. His relationship was different – I believe I know this.

Kreisky wanted the media to reflect that

> Herr Wiesenthal lived [during the war] in a Nazi sphere of influence free from persecution. Yes? And he lived openly without being persecuted. And those who know about such things, that there should be no misunderstanding, he was not hidden or underground, but in public. ... That I think is enough. There were so many openings to be an agent, without having to be a Gestapo agent. There were many other possibilities to render service.

He made similar charges in other interviews, and amongst his numerous assertions said that 'I only know Herr Wiesenthal from secret service reports

[*Geheimberichten*], and these are bad, very disagreeable. . . .' Kreisky was basing his allegations on the Polish and East German propaganda campaign against Wiesenthal, which sought to portray him as a wartime Gestapo collaborator. The Chancellor chose to ignore warnings, given even by some of his closest collaborators, that these were fabrications without credibility to which he should not be lending any credence. Yet he persisted: 'This man has for years maintained a very pernicious attitude towards Austria, pretending it is a haven for anti-Semites and war criminals. . . . This man must disappear.'[2]

He had decided to act, he said, because

Wiesenthal's methods, this constant scandal-mongering, these accusations without proof, cannot continue. I consider it very dangerous, and somebody must finally have the courage to finish with this man — to launch a quarrel with him. As anyone, not of Jewish origin, risks being accused of anti-Semitism, and since I do not have to confront that risk, I have decided to act. It is a matter of justice that someone like him is not allowed to assume a moral authority in such a matter. Because he has none.[3]

After all this, Wiesenthal promptly instructed his lawyers to file a complaint for slander against the Chancellor. His suit focused primarily on Kreisky's allegations of collaboration with the Nazis, 'which are wholly untrue'. Wiesenthal's good name had been damaged and he therefore applied for Chancellor Kreisky's diplomatic parliamentary immunity to be lifted so that the case could be heard.

Unstoppable, Kreisky flailed out against Wiesenthal on a second track, alleging that the Nazi-hunter was acting on behalf of a 'small circle of people' who were disgruntled with Kreisky's policies towards Israel. There was a vendetta against him for failing to deliver the kind of pro-Israeli policies that Wiesenthal and his friends had expected from a Jewish Chancellor. He accused Wiesenthal of ill-disguised racism and a 'posthumous assumption of Nazi ideas in reverse'. As a subtext, there were suggestions that Wiesenthal had been urged on by the ÖVP leadership as a manoeuvre to undermine Kreisky's popularity. Kreisky again questioned whether Austria had been justified in granting Wiesenthal his Austrian nationality. Wiesenthal decided to issue a second complaint for slander.

Meanwhile, Kreisky summoned the Israeli Ambassador and demanded to know Israel's attitude towards Wiesenthal. At the time, it was strongly rumoured that, during the meeting, the Chancellor threatened to interrupt the transit facilities that Austria was providing to Soviet Jewry on their way to Israel. There is no conclusive evidence that this was actually said, or that the Israeli diplomat really feared that the exodus of Jews through Austria might be affected by Israel's stance with respect to the Kreisky–Wiesenthal dispute. But, as in 1970, Israel's Ambassador distanced himself and replied that his country regarded the Kreisky–Wiesenthal conflict as an internal Austrian affair.

Wiesenthal felt let down and thought that Israel had made a big mistake. It was morally wrong. But more immediately, it was as if 'Israel had given Kreisky the green light for a shoot-out against Wiesenthal'.[4] Moreover, if Kreisky was reckless to paint Wiesenthal as a Nazi collaborator, he also demonstrated poor judgment by depicting him as a symbol for Zionism, perhaps even as an agent of Israel. Wiesenthal was critical of Kreisky's policies towards Israel and his attempts to neutralise his Jewishness, but he had never been a fanatical Zionist and had been far too independent-minded to be close to Israeli governments.

Kreisky, however, refused to let go of his fixation with Zionist interference and his assertions that Wiesenthal was part of a deep plot against Austria. He became more and more careless in his speech. Interviewed by an Israeli radio journalist, Zeev Barth, Kreisky insisted that Wiesenthal had done more harm than good and repeated that 'the man must disappear'. Angrily refusing to explain why he had accused Wiesenthal of using Mafia methods, Kreisky countered that Jews were trying to persecute him. Then, as a parting shot, which Kreisky intended as a witticism, he remarked that 'if the Jews are a people, then they are a *mieses* [wretched] people'. Barth passed this story on to *Der Spiegel* – one of Wiesenthal's consistent media allies – and on 17 November the mass-circulation magazine splashed it under the provocative headline: '*Kreisky: Die Juden sind ein mieses Volk*' ('Kreisky: The Jews wretched people'). The article was accompanied by an unflattering photograph of Kreisky, which enhanced his Jewish features.

Kreisky now had a new enemy target. He complained vehemently to Rudolf Augstein, publisher of *Der Spiegel*. Augstein replied with a telegram declaring that 'I knew nothing of the article. Find the headline factually incorrect and also unfair.' In its next number, *Der Spiegel* published a letter from Kreisky, headlined 'professional [*ordentlicher*] journalism', in which he complained that his views had been distorted, but added disingenuously that 'a professional journalist would not have used my private asides, without at the least checking back with me'. There were shades of the Amerungen incident in 1971, when he had made his off-the-cuff remark about Wiesenthal being a 'Jewish Fascist'. Now, in 1975, he told *Der Spiegel* that since he did not believe that the Jews are 'a people', it followed that he could never label the Jewish people as 'wretched': 'Wretched individuals exist among every people – but they exist without distinction as to their origin, race, religion and community of fate.'[5]

By now, not only Austrians, but the outside world was avidly following each turn of these vicious tantrums. In Wiesenthal's Rudolfsplatz office, the telephone did not stop ringing. Media organisations from around the world wanted to know what was going on. Major international newspapers wrote about the conflict, expressing great puzzlement over Kreisky's treatment of the much-admired Nazi-hunter. Why had the normally hard-headed Kreisky seemingly lost all reason?

Kreisky, always ready to think the worst of Wiesenthal, even suspected that his antagonist had somehow tried to use his brother, Paul, in Israel to embarrass him just before the election. He suspected that Wiesenthal's friends had abducted his brother. Paul Kreisky had never fully recovered from a childhood accident. Bruno felt responsible for him, but always kept him out of the way. In the summer of 1975, Paul, without his brother's knowledge, had gone to Germany, apparently in pursuit of an affair of the heart. Kreisky did not know of his whereabouts. Rumours began to circulate that Kreisky was not taking financial care of his brother and was neglecting him.

The whole affair was a mystery and seems more likely to have been part of a disinformation campaign against Austria's Socialists promoted by the right-wing tabloid *Bild-Zeitung*. Kreisky however seized on his brother's temporary disappearance – he was soon located in Germany – to implicate Wiesenthal in yet another plot against him. He called in political friends and showed them documents which proved that he had been transmitting monthly cheques to his brother in Israel since the 1950s. Kreisky added that he suspected Wiesenthal either of fuelling insinuations against him that he had left Paul to struggle in poverty, or worse, of spiriting Paul away from Israel, and in any event scheming to use Paul to give Bruno a bad name.

At the time, Kreisky refrained from saying any of this publicly, and though there was the usual spate of rumour, the story only came into the public domain in 1981,[6] after Kreisky had referred during judicial proceedings to alleged threats and attacks by Wiesenthal against the Kreisky family. Wiesenthal responded with a rare letter to Kreisky's son, Peter, declaring that 'naturally neither I nor my friends kidnapped your uncle or have ever threatened your family'. He explained that when he had first heard of Chancellor Kreisky's suspicions, he had asked the Israeli Embassy to find out the circumstances under which Paul Kreisky had left Israel in 1975. He learned that a Jew from Frankfurt had provided Paul with a ticket to fly to Germany to meet the man's widowed sister. A few days later, Paul returned to Israel, still a bachelor. 'I thought at the time it was an amusing anecdote,'

Wiesenthal told Peter Kreisky.[7] Wiesenthal flatly denies any connection whatsoever with Paul Kreisky, and says that he has never even met him. Kreisky's allegations, Wiesenthal thought, were just one more manifestation of his campaign to discredit him.

In Austria, Kreisky had public opinion and important sections of the press, including the virulently anti-Semitic, mass-circulation tabloid, the *Kronenzeitung*, solidly on his side. Vienna's Jews felt caught in the middle. Old animosities involving Wiesenthal resurfaced within the politically divided *Kultusgemeinde*. They were disturbed, worried about the future and unwilling to back Wiesenthal.

However, the Austrian Resistance Movement, and the popular weekly *Profil* – edited during that critical period by Wiesenthal's former assistant, Peter Michael Lingens – as well as one of the Austrian dailies, the *Kurier*, sprang to Wiesenthal's defence. Lingens accused Kreisky of going beyond the bounds of political opportunism, describing his behaviour as 'immoral, monstrous and undignified'. He quoted a long string of witnesses and even contacted Heinrich Günthert, the head of the OAW in Lvov, where Wiesenthal did forced labour during the war.

'What do you think of the allegation that Wiesenthal was a Gestapo collaborator?' Lingens asked the former Nazi, who had treated his prisoner, Wiesenthal, reasonably well, for the simple reason that he needed his expertise to keep the vital railway yards functioning. Günthert replied: 'I can only laugh at the idea.'

Lingens wrote that Kreisky's Minister of the Interior, Otto Rösch, had stored many of the Polish allegations against Wiesenthal for use against him at a suitable moment, even though it had long been clear that they were fabrications. Kreisky countered by suing Lingens for defamation of character and ordered an investigation into the magazine's affairs.

Among the plaudits from Germany, nothing gratified Wiesenthal more than testimony from Rolf Sichting, the Federal German Prosecutor. Sichting had been the prosecutor in the Stuttgart trials involving concentration camp guards from the Lvov area, and was familiar with Wiesenthal's wartime life. In a lengthy statement, published in *Profil* as part of Lingens's defence of Wiesenthal, Sichting said that

> there were more than 200 witnesses who had testified about the events in Lvov, and not one had even minutely doubted that Wiesenthal had been a prisoner. ... The accusations against Simon Wiesenthal, that he was a collaborator of the Gestapo, are infamous. I stand by this word. I will answer for it. No other word would be appropriate.

Wiesenthal thanked Sichting profusely:

> It was a wonderful feeling to read your remarks [he wrote]. I am now living through my most difficult stage since 1945. I have to reckon with an opponent who is not selective about his methods, and who believes that he is responsible to no one for the words he pronounces. . . . In this confrontation there are only losers: Austria's good name, the Jews, Kreisky and I – irrespective of how all this ends – we will all be losers. The play that is unfolding can only serve those who want to hide the truth.

None of this affected the way Wiesenthal was routinely treated by the Austrian public. People shunned and insulted him. They spat at him in the street. Threatening letters piled up at his Rudolfsplatz office. The other tenants became anxious. Wiesenthal was asked to move out, but found equally cramped and shabby quarters nearby – ironically on the site of the former Hotel Metropol, the Gestapo headquarters in the Salztorgasse, where Kreisky had been interrogated in 1939.

Wiesenthal had to look over his shoulder wherever he went. His wife, Cyla, grew more nervous by the day. In *Justice Not Vengeance*, he wrote:

> In point of fact, the next six weeks were the worst time I have experienced since the war. I was a leper in my new home, and only the thought that I had survived Hitler prevented me from emigrating. It should be realised that Bruno Kreisky exercised an absolutely magic attraction for the public. Even critical intellectuals hung on the lips of the 'Sun King' as though he were offering a revelation.[8]

All through November Wiesenthal and Kreisky were flexing their muscles preparing for their days in court. Wiesenthal, the advocate of law and justice, was determined to have his good name and reputation affirmed by a judge, and to have Kreisky's allegations repudiated. Kreisky was equally set on having his say in court and wanted his parliamentary immunity lifted. He said he would even be prepared to resign if that was the only way. At the same time, he was calling for a parliamentary investigation into Wiesenthal's 'Mafia methods' and his connections with the state police. Kreisky was hinting darkly that some of Wiesenthal's friends in the Interior Ministry had passed him confidential information to which he had no right. Heinz Fischer, Kreisky's close SPÖ colleague, recalls that the Chancellor was so emotional about the conflict that it was virtually impossible to raise it with him.[9]

But alarm bells were nevertheless beginning to ring in both camps. On 24 November, Wiesenthal was warned by his lawyer, Dr Hans Perner, that he did not have a foolproof case against Kreisky. Perner pointed out to

Wiesenthal that the Chancellor's 10 November press conference, which formed the basis of the alleged slander, contained a series of contradictory statements. Towards the end, Kreisky had tempered some of his most damaging remarks about Wiesenthal's Gestapo links. It was possible, Perner argued, that the court 'would come to the conclusion that Kreisky's qualifications at the end of his press conference practically withdrew the damaging accusations made at the beginning'.

Going beyond juridical considerations, Perner also reminded his client that his 'activities in various East-bloc countries, notably Poland, had long been a thorn in Kreisky's eyes' – a reference to Kreisky's fear that the polemics between Wiesenthal and the Communists hindered his policy of building improved relations with the Warsaw Pact countries. Perner feared that Kreisky might use the slander proceedings to tar Wiesenthal with 'evidence', 'which does not correspond to the facts, but might be hard to refute'.

Wiesenthal's opponents were also worried. Kreisky's SPÖ colleagues were beginning to fear for the Government's political future. The conflict was getting out of control, they reasoned. Kreisky was rapidly destroying the fruits of the party's recent election victory. The Government's future and the Socialists' ambitious programme were at risk. Towards the end of November, Fischer and other prominent party members finally summoned the courage to confront Kreisky. They wanted an end to the affair, and to stop Wiesenthal's slander case from being fought out in court. They informed Kreisky that they would use the SPÖ's parliamentary majority to reject his request to have his parliamentary immunity lifted.

Kreisky's close friend, former Chancellor Willy Brandt, also weighed in with advice to halt the campaign against Wiesenthal. He telephoned, urging Kreisky to accept that damage-limitation had become imperative. 'Anyone who knew Kreisky well, would have realised the situation had to be defused,' Fischer recalls. 'Kreisky didn't ask any of us to act. But we could tell he was uncomfortable.'

The time was ripe to open backroom channels to find a compromise under which Wiesenthal might be persuaded to drop his charges against Kreisky. It was self-evident that Kreisky would have to make a formal statement of retraction. The President of the *Kultusgemeinde* in Vienna, Dr Ivan Häcker, sounded out Karl Kahane, a wealthy businessman, who was one of Kreisky's close intimates and backers. Fischer had a long discussion with Peter Michael Lingens.

The upshot was that on 2 December, the SPÖ formally announced that it had rejected Kreisky's request for parliamentary immunity. On the following day, Wiesenthal withdrew his slander action against Kreisky; the proposal for a parliamentary investigation into Wiesenthal's affairs was dropped, and Kreisky, still refusing to make a formal apology, limited himself to declaring that he had never described Wiesenthal as a Nazi collaborator. 'Only with the greatest difficulty, a most unpleasant chapter, burdened with many psychological implications involving our recent history, was removed from the fire just in time to prevent an explosion,' wrote Heinz Fischer.[10]

In later years, Wiesenthal doubted whether he should have yielded. Had his wife agreed to go to Holland, where his daughter was then living with her Dutch husband, he would perhaps not have given in. But with his wife refusing to leave, and Wiesenthal in the eye of the storm, he felt he had little choice. Vienna's Jewish community, his wife, Israel, all were closing in on him. He does not admit to being influenced by his lawyer's cautions. In *Justice Not Vengeance*, he has written of his wife's pleas to put an end to the conflict; added to that, 'the intolerable strain on the whole Jewish community in Vienna',[11] which feared that Kreisky's attacks would reverberate on them. Furthermore, the Israelis believed that Kreisky really would close Austria as a transit route for Soviet Jews. 'Thus it came about that both my Viennese friends and my friends in Israel implored me to make a compromise and come to some sort of truce with Bruno Kreisky.'[12] Much later, he confessed to his disappointment that Vienna's Jewish community did not close ranks behind him: 'I have never demanded support from Jews. But I expected it. ... While I had to submit to Kreisky's attacks against me, I expected that the Jews, especially those who were members of the Socialist Party, would adopt a common stand to back me.'

In his letter to Professor Sijes in Amsterdam, written on 9 December 1975, Wiesenthal gave a more detailed explanation. Coupled to Kreisky's accusations, there were the continuous attacks in the *Kronenzeitung*, with banner headlines such as 'Wiesenthal insults Austria abroad'.

Vienna's Jews began to fear pogroms, and I came under a certain pressure from those quarters. On Kreisky's part interventions were made to lower the temperature, and it is clear that even I had no interest in a further escalation with unforeseeable consequences. ... Once the Socialists had decided not to lift Kreisky's immunity, my legal case became worthless. My decision to withdraw the case was also influenced by Kreisky's explanation that he had not described me as a Nazi collaborator – although I could not secure a retraction of his 'Mafia' pronouncements against me. But this was less important than the Gestapo allegations.

During the thirty years since the war, I have had to make many personal sacrifices in the interests of my work [the letter continues]. I had to act in this sense now, all the more so since Cyla suffered terribly from the situation, and I was under continuous pressure not only in the office, but also at home.

He goes on to express concern that a parliamentary investigation into the Documentation Centre could have ended badly for him. It might dredge up a whole series of old complaints, often made by people who were no longer alive; it might last two years and divert him from his normal work, and the ultimate findings might go against him – 'even though there was nothing to hide', but quite simply because the Socialist majority in such a commission would not have dared 'to say that their chief, Kreisky, was wrong'.

'For two months, I have not had a single peaceful hour. Hundreds of letters have piled up. I even ask myself why I still run this office. ... It therefore became clear to me that I could not carry this burden. ... Hopefully this is now the end of the whole affair.' He erred; it was only a respite until the two protagonists had regathered their forces.

Wiesenthal added a postscript to his letter: 'New material has been found about Friedrich Peter, which would in any normal country end his political career. I hope that this will happen peacefully during the time still left to me to work.' Peter's slander case against Wiesenthal lingered on, but court proceedings never materialised, and the case was withdrawn in 1982.

Peter's political career did indeed go slowly downhill, and in 1983 he was forced to give up the chairmanship of the FPÖ in favour of the younger Norbert Steger. Popular sentiment against Peter even prompted him to turn down the chairmanship of the FPÖ's parliamentary group. Peter's political demise is usually attributed to a new mood in the FPÖ in the late 1970s and early 1980s to neutralise its Nazi antecedents, and by establishing a more liberal image to move closer to the centre of the political spectrum. Peter insists that this had also been his own objective and that he was misunderstood. Had he survived politically, he believes he might have been able to prevent the emergence of Jörg Haider, the FPÖ's widely feared new populist leader. If Peter's conjectures are accurate, Wiesenthal's intervention in 1975 has had unforeseen consequences and badly misfired.

At the end of 1975, an 'annus horribilis' for him, when Wiesenthal marked his sixty-seventh birthday, he no longer doubted that 'the conflict cost Kreisky far more than it cost me. He has lost credibility, especially among the intellectuals, on whom he always likes to lean.'

Soon afterwards, Wiesenthal set off on a lecture tour to the United States, where his morale rose further. He gave fourteen lectures, attended by close on 15,000 people. He was given a certificate of merit by Jewish war veterans and survivors. He was widely fêted, culminating in 1980 with a reception in the White House and his much-treasured award of the Congressional Gold Medal.

Kreisky was not impressed by Wiesenthal's fame abroad. If anything, he resented it. Even though he had undertaken to put a brake on his direct attacks on Wiesenthal, he continued the fight by proxy by persisting with his slander actions against *Profil* and Lingens. In March 1979, he scored a minor, although only temporary victory, when Lingens was fined 20,000 schillings, but Kreisky was awarded no damages. Both sides decided to appeal. In 1981, the judgment was confirmed, but the fine reduced. Lingens then moved his case to the European Court of Justice, which took until 1986 to deliver a verdict in his favour. The Austrian Government was ordered to pay Lingens damages of 284,000 schillings.

During the court hearings in 1981, Kreisky returned to his allegations that Wiesenthal had been a Nazi collaborator. Challenged by Lingens whether he considered it moral to have tarred Wiesenthal in 1975 with allegations of Nazi collaboration without offering any proof, Kreisky replied that he would not withdraw any of his remarks. When these quotations were published in *Profil* and the *Kurier*, Wiesenthal again sued Kreisky for slander, asserting that Kreisky had broken the undertakings he had given in December 1975. But the case was not pursued.

Theoretically at least, there should have been a small window of opportunity for reconciliation between the two men in 1986, when each of them, from their separate lairs, defended Austria's good name against outside charges that an alleged war criminal, Kurt Waldheim, was being allowed to stand for the Presidency. But it was not to be: the Waldheim affair did not bring Kreisky and Wiesenthal any closer.

On the contrary, in April 1986, shortly before the Presidential election, Kreisky – in retirement since 1983 – reopened the battle against Wiesenthal. In an interview in *Profil* on the 21st, Kreisky was asked once again about the aspersions he had cast on Wiesenthal in 1975. His response was unrepentant. Yes, he could have proved his case against Wiesenthal in a court of law, 'but I simply was not in the mood at that time to stand before a judge and depend on former Nazis as my witnesses'.

Wiesenthal sued once again. Parliamentary immunity no longer counted, as Kreisky had retired. But he was a sick man spending most of his time in his modest house in Majorca, and excused himself time and again from court hearings on the grounds of ill-health.

Kreisky's lawyers filed circumstantial evidence against Wiesenthal, yet again referring to the discredited Polish charges against him as a Gestapo agent, and twisting Wiesenthal's own account of his war years to insinuate that this demonstrated special treatment which could not be explained otherwise than that he had been a collaborator.[13] It was the same old tedious story. Wiesenthal found it 'grotesque'.

In March 1987, Kreisky put in a court appearance. He claimed that he had been provoked by *Profil* journalists during the previous year's interview into repeating his charges against Wiesenthal. He regretted that he fell for the provocation, but he still refused to withdraw his allegations against Wiesenthal: he remained convinced now, as ever, that he had been right. The judge then asked Kreisky whether he was prepared to make a full apology. Kreisky replied: 'No, a few years away from death, I refuse to give any more *Ehrenerklärungen* [full apologies].'[14]

The case continued until October 1989, when the court found Kreisky guilty of slander and fined him 270,000 schillings, the largest amount ever awarded in a libel case in Austria. In explanation of the verdict, the judge found that Kreisky had failed to produce concrete evidence to substantiate his charges against Wiesenthal. Given the circumstances, allegations that a Jew had been a Nazi collaborator were bad enough. 'But in a case where the charge was made against a well-known Jewish personality by another Jew, a politician equally well-known at home and abroad, there could be no doubt of intent to destroy his good name. ... The incriminating text was designed to achieve that.'

Under Austrian law, the fine did not have to be paid, because Kreisky had no convictions during the previous three years.

Kreisky died a few months later. Wiesenthal left the battlefield, deeply scarred, but head held high and determined to soldier on to defend his stand for justice – even though it took him into new, bloodier and perhaps even more painful encounters, where his integrity was questioned yet again: this time by the WJC, which painted him as a traitor to his own cause for failing to denounce Kurt Waldheim as a war criminal.

Vienna and Los Angeles:
A Marriage of Convenience

Simon Wiesenthal's demon forces him to work as a one-man band; almost, but not quite. In earlier times, there was Peter Michael Lingens. But since 1975, there has also been Rosemarie Austraat, his secretary and Girl Friday. Devoted and discreet, she has made herself indispensable. She has become a kind of second skin, who knows 'the boss's' mind, can help write his speeches, can put order into the chaos of his archives and knows where to find even the most obscure letter or document. As he has grown older, she makes sure that he does not overwork; she chauffeurs him when he needs to visit doctors; she takes him shopping when his raincoat has become too old and shabby, or when he needs a well-cut, new suit for the growing number of award ceremonies. In her practical, matter-of-fact way, Rosemarie Austraat has not only helped to make Wiesenthal's small office function smoothly, but has also given him the kind of back-up that makes it easier for him to take care of his wife Cyla.

Rosemarie had not anticipated any of this when she answered an advertisement for a part-time secretary. There was no name, just a telephone number to ring. When she called, Wiesenthal explained that his was a Documentation Centre, occupied with Jewish affairs. Would that bother her? The answer was 'No – provided you can work with someone who is not a Jew.' Blonde, slim, fond of neat, figure-flattering clothes, she went to meet him in his old Rudolfsplatz office. There were no curtains, no heating. She told him that her husband was Norwegian, that they had three young children, and that she was out of practice as she had not worked for nine years. She knew only a little about Wiesenthal's work, but had been to an Auschwitz exhibition and thought that she was 'conditioned towards Wiesenthal's preoccupations'.

As they talked, Wiesenthal produced photographs of his three grand-children. She showed him pictures of her sons. They bonded. Wiesenthal offered her the job. She accepted, little realising that she was taking on a responsibility that is set to last for the rest of Wiesenthal's life. Rosemarie Austraat went to work for him just as his confrontation with Bruno Kreisky was approaching its climax. Soon afterwards, demonstrations against him forced Wiesenthal to move from the Rudolfsplatz office to a marginally less cramped and dismal building in the nearby Salztorgasse. Only the presence of a policeman on the narrow stone staircase on the second floor suggests something out of the ordinary. Wiesenthal's Documentation Centre occupies a dingy, three-room flat. He uses the smallest room. His door is almost always open. When he needs something, he shouts for Rosemarie. When he is dictating letters, he sits on the edge of an ancient chair near her cluttered desk next door. From the window of his room, all he can view is a well between anonymous buildings; no glimpse of the outside world, which looms so large in his mind's eye. Bookshelves line two of the walls; framed citations and awards fill the wall behind his desk, which is permanently buried in paper. A huge map of 'Germany under Hitler's dictatorship', showing the concentration and extermination camps, hangs menacingly at the far end of the room above a red plush sofa, its springs gone long ago, that serves as yet another repository for magazines, books and articles. Two worn-out armchairs covered in faded red velveteen stand in the centre, one for visitors and one for Wiesenthal. Between them is one of those small, round, Moroccan brass coffee tables that more usually grace the rooms of impoverished students, barely leaving enough room for Wiesenthal to navigate his way from door to desk.

Rosemarie and a part-time colleague work from a larger room, with wall-to-wall shelves filled with box-files. Typewriters used to be the only concession to modernity; now there is also a word-processor, a fax and a duplicating machine. More framed awards, and above all Wiesenthal's much-prized Congressional Gold Medal citation, illuminate the dark passage from the front door of the office to the third room, euphemistically known as the library. Here there is enough space for Wiesenthal to address small groups of visitors, often school classes, who want to meet the great man to hear him talk about his work. A part-time student whose job it is to keep track for Wiesenthal of neo-Fascist publications and articles has a desk in this room. But here, too, much of the space is taken up with yet more files and books.

Nobody can ever replace Wiesenthal at the Documentation Centre. But he decided back in the 1970s that, when the day came to dismantle it, even the rickety furniture would not be consigned to the knacker's yard. Instead, he wanted it dispatched to Los Angeles and reassembled for view in the Wiesenthal Center's Museum of Tolerance. Wiesenthal's Vienna office would become one of its permanent exhibits, placed there as his legacy and as a continuous exhortation for people to comprehend the facts about the Holocaust and to remain alive to the dangers of anti-Semitism and of racism.

It was the promise of a dynamic institution, anchored in the experience of the past but geared to the education of future generations, which had led Wiesenthal to allow his name to be used for the Wiesenthal Center in Los Angeles, a new organisation dedicated to Holocaust studies and the fight against anti-Semitism.

The initial contacts between Vienna and Los Angeles were not especially auspicious – more of a comedy of errors than an instant meeting of minds. It was the summer of 1977; a typical day in Wiesenthal's office routine. As usual, Rosemarie was fielding a steady flow of telephone calls. In mid-afternoon, she told him that a Rabbi Marvin Hier was on the line from Los Angeles. Wiesenthal had no idea who this could be, but picked it up. The Rabbi started off with a reminder that they had casually met on two occasions. He had just begun to explain that his purpose in contacting Wiesenthal was to invite him to a fundraising banquet, when the Nazi-hunter broke in: 'No, no, I already have plenty of honorary doctorates.' Hier quickly clarified that this was not about a doctorate, but about something much more important. 'I told him it was something to do with creating an active Holocaust centre concerned with Nazism and anti-Semitism.'

Hier's principal reason for contacting Wiesenthal was to persuade him to allow his name to be used for the new project. He also proposed that Wiesenthal should leave his archives to the Los Angeles venture. Wiesenthal already had an extensive, well-established following in the United States. Hier, who possessed all the instincts of a born fundraiser, knew that a 'Wiesenthal' imprimatur would gain respect for the venture, would allow him to speak out on public issues, and would be a major selling-point to secure grassroots financial support. But it was not all cool calculation. Efraim Zuroff, who has worked for the Wiesenthal Center in several capacities – he now runs its outpost in Israel and is much involved in Nazi-hunting – says that 'Simon was a genuine hero to Hier. And there weren't many Jewish heroes. We had Elie Wiesel. But he is a hero of suffering. And we had Wiesenthal. He is more like the John Wayne of the Jews. So it seemed like the perfect match with Rabbi Hier.'

Hier felt that he would fail in his objective if he tried to explain his purpose over the telephone. So, 'I said that I wanted to come to Vienna with a small group of backers to lay out what we had in mind.' Hier guessed that Wiesenthal would need strong persuasion to be associated with the venture. Hier arrived, accompanied by Mark Belzberg, a wealthy young Canadian Jew, and two or three other founder members.

The idea, at that point, was fairly modest – to open a study centre, a *yeshiva* school that would concentrate not only on traditional Jewish religious studies but also on broader Holocaust themes. With Belzberg's generosity, they had bought a property on Pico Boulevard in Beverly Hills. 'Wiesenthal was impressed with the delegation I brought,' Hier says. They were young, and he had never met any Americans interested in this kind of project who were not themselves survivors. 'He told me that if my group had been similar to the people he had experienced before, he would have said "no" to us immediately,' Hier recalls. Wiesenthal wanted a dynamic institution; not a museum where archives and pictures would merely gather dust. After three days of thrashing all their ideas around, it was agreed that the project would be known as the 'Wiesenthal Center', that Wiesenthal would be kept closely informed of its activities, but that the Vienna Documentation Centre, headed by Wiesenthal, would retain its separate character and independence. For both sides, it was a marriage of convenience, based on mutual respect, but blemished by bursts of competitiveness and jealousy.

When they first made their compact, 'we had no idea that we would expand beyond Pico Boulevard', Rabbi Hier acknowledges. 'I guess Wiesenthal thought it was nice to have a local organisation in Los Angeles named after him.' They had not yet envisaged that the Wiesenthal Center would become a well-funded national and even an international human rights activist institution, with a steeply rising membership curve mounting towards the 400,000 figure. And they had certainly not imagined that their *yeshiva* would sprout the Museum of Tolerance, a multi-media educational and research tool, equipped with the best of modern information technology; or that they would themselves assume the mantle of Nazi-hunting, and act as a grassroots vigilante group against manifestations of anti-Semitism throughout the world.

Wiesenthal's detractors like to allege that he sold his name to Hier against the promise of a substantial income from the Wiesenthal Center. He denies this, and Hier himself is adamant that 'Wiesenthal did not get a cent from us before 1984'. That year Wiesenthal told Hier that the help he had been receiving from the Dutch Wiesenthal Foundation had been reduced to a tiny trickle. 'It was difficult for him to cover the expenses of his office, and he was no longer a spring chicken who could jump on to planes twice a week to earn lecture fees.' Hier was asked whether the Wiesenthal Centre was prepared to give a little help; and so it was agreed that he would be sent $5,000 a month. Since 1994, this has been increased to $7,500 a month.

These are modest sums by the standards of the Wiesenthal Center's resources, and Wiesenthal could, had he asked for it, have had more. But he jealously guards his independence – including the independence to criticise the Wiesenthal Center, even threatening the withdrawal of his name, if it acts against his views or advice.

Few people had a proper measure of Rabbi Hier when the project first took shape in 1977. Certainly, Wiesenthal did not realise how formidable Hier would prove to be – or the extent to which the Los Angeles organisation would manoeuvre to take over his mantle even in his own lifetime. The Wiesenthal Center likes to foster the Wiesenthal legend. But it is less respectful of the living, activist Wiesenthal, who wants to assert his primacy for as long as he remains around, and does not wish to be confused with the Wiesenthal Center.

Hier is a New York Jew from the Lower East Side, born in 1938, the son of a Polish immigrant lamp polisher. At the age of only twenty-two, he was appointed rabbi to Vancouver's leading orthodox synagogue. There he discovered a gift for communicating with young people, which he used successfully to bring Jews back to orthodox observancy. Among his disciples was Mark Belzberg, son of Sam Belzberg, a successful Jewish Canadian business tycoon, who had recently settled in Vancouver. Though the Belzbergs had not been orthodox, when they met Hier, they became close to the rabbi. Hier was outspoken in Vancouver in defence of human rights and Soviet Jewry, and went out of his way to attract publicity.

But in 1975, he took a sabbatical year in Israel, studying at a fundamentalist-oriented *yeshiva*, the Or Same'ach. On his return to Canada, Hier told Belzberg that he wanted a larger stage for his activism and that he had hatched a plan for a dynamic Jewish centre in Los Angeles, which would be fertile ground because of its considerable Jewish population. Hier and Belzberg flew to Los Angeles and bought the Pico Boulevard property with help from another Canadian millionaire. Then Hier together with Rabbi Cooper, another friend from Vancouver, opened the West Coast branch of Or Same'ach. An orthodox college was established, the Yeshiva University of Los Angeles, an affiliate of New York's Yeshiva University.

The college continues, but has been overshadowed by everything else that Hier, in close partnership with Cooper, has undertaken. The defining moment which decided Hier to branch out into much broader activism, came, he says, when he sat in a barber's chair and noticed in pride of place on the salon's wall a signed photograph of Hitler. He saw it as graphic proof that Nazism was alive and well, and that there were Californians who were no doubt capable of denying that the Final Solution had occurred and might infect generations with their evil philosophy. So the Holocaust Center was conceived as a place where all Jews, orthodox or otherwise, could meet with non-Jews to discuss the issues surrounding Nazism and the Holocaust, and would learn how to fight against any recurrence.

It was a new hybrid that had not been attempted before. 'You have to understand that Hier in terms of his ability to perceive trends, media, public opinion, is a genius,' Zuroff says. To complete the equation, Hier needed Wiesenthal. He soon had proof that his judgment, in associating Wiesenthal with his project, had been correct. When Hier and Cooper organised their first big banquet in Los Angeles, several of the large Jewish organisations, suspicious, or jealous from the outset, stayed away. Yet the occasion was oversubscribed with more than 1,700 people present. 'I could see that there will always be a directly inverse proportion between Wiesenthal and his work: between the support from his grassroots and the lack of support from the structured Jewish leadership. The outpouring of emotion that night of the people embracing their hero was quite outstanding,' Rabbi Cooper recalls.

The Wiesenthal Center concept took off like a rocket. Yet Hier and Cooper knew that they still had a great deal to learn about political activism and lobbying. They took professional advice. But in the early days, Wiesenthal's innate feeling for courting public opinion was crucial. Germany's statute of limitations was due to expire in 1979, and Wiesenthal was lobbying hard to secure an extension. On a visit to Los Angeles early in 1978, Wiesenthal said that the Center that bears his name should mobilise US support to lobby the German Government. Rabbi Cooper, 'naïvely' as he admits, thought that by writing a background paper and addressing it to Jewish organisations, he could advance the cause. He was wrong. Reactions were polite, but off-putting. The Wiesenthal Center was told that this was not a cause for American Jews. As ever, organised Jewry in the United States was not keen on a cause with which Simon Wiesenthal was associated.

Then Wiesenthal came up with the idea of the postcard campaign. The Center placed a full-page advertisement in *Time* magazine, and it was quite taken aback at the outpouring of requests for postcards to be forwarded to Helmut Schmidt, the Federal Republic's Chancellor. 'It was a real education for us,' Cooper says. It was a clear message that the populist approach worked best for Wiesenthal and for the Center. 'We learned that if we are going to carry the name of Simon Wiesenthal, we have to live up to his promise. And we learned that there are many people out there ready to help in a traditional way; but if you are going to wait for committees and Jewish Federations and others, there is no way we are going to attack the issues fast enough.' The Wiesenthal Center had reached political maturity.

It has moved from strength to strength. Rabbi Hier, working on the 'people-to-people' principle, developed a strategy for recruiting individual families as members, and encouraging small-scale as well as larger donations. Even those who are not wholehearted admirers say that Rabbi Hier ranks among the most effective fundraisers in the United States – quite a compliment in a country where fundraising has become a sought-after profession.

Being well-funded, the Wiesenthal Center has been able to monitor anti-Semitism worldwide, to initiate educational programmes, to issue alerts capable of attracting public attention and to use modern technology to track down the dying breed of Nazi criminals. Like Simon Wiesenthal himself, the two Rabbis realised from the outset that efficient use of publicity and access to the media were the keys to effectiveness. But with the money at their disposal, they have been able to use far more sophisticated methods than Wiesenthal himself has employed. He has always been at his best through the personal approach – though he relished the 'faction' films and documentaries that have been made about him. The two rabbis have commissioned their own television films, such as *Genocide* and *Liberation*, working with the Hollywood professionals, including Ben Kingsley, Whoopy Goldberg and Steven Spielberg, and using established authors like Martin Gilbert to do some of the writing. They employ public relations experts to help with their overall projects. Hier's critics within the Jewish establishment contemptuously say that it was no accident that the Center is in Beverly Hills, close to Hollywood. It is, they say derisively, made for 'central casting', just a stage set for artificially constructed activism; more and more Disneyland, and less *yeshiva*.

The Wiesenthal Center can afford to ignore such barbs. Offices have been established in New York, Paris and Jerusalem. On occasion Rabbi Hier flies in to lobby governments. Much to the confusion of the uninitiated, who are often unaware that they do not constitute one organic whole, the Wiesenthal Center is not averse to operating on Simon Wiesenthal's turf and capturing the limelight from its patron. Not least, the Center often voices protests on human rights issues that Wiesenthal likes to consider his particular preserve. Wiesenthal was particularly upset when Hier intervened in Britain to lobby for war crimes trial legislation, without first informing, let alone consulting, him.

Tensions between Wiesenthal and the Wiesenthal Center were inevitable. Some are more about protocol and about ego than about substance: for example, while Wiesenthal had the good sense to realise that it had modern technology and resources for searching out the last remaining war criminals which he could never match, he insisted on being closely informed of the Center's projects and major initiatives. When reporters turned to him for explanations of the Wiesenthal Center's actions, he did not want to be caught out for lack of being fully briefed.

Wiesenthal's most abrasive quarrel with Rabbi Hier has been over the Wiesenthal Center's role in the Waldheim affair. Though both sides claim to have restored cordial relations, Wiesenthal felt betrayed. He is too emotionally involved in the Waldheim controversy to forgive or forget.

Martin Rosen, forever trying to smooth relations between Wiesenthal and Rabbi Hier, insists that divorce would be against the interests of both. 'I say to Simon, if Rabbi Hier didn't have you, he could never have accomplished all that he does; and if you didn't have him, there would never have been the educational facilities to perpetuate your work. You two make a great team.'

Wiesenthal himself knows perfectly well that his differences with Hier pale behind the importance of the Wiesenthal Center's Museum of Tolerance. Its Hebrew name, *Beit Ha'Shoah*, has a different meaning: The House of the Holocaust. Wiesenthal could not have wished for a more vibrant way of perpetuating the lessons of his own life's work. The name alone – English and Hebrew versions combined – says it all, Wiesenthal often tells his audiences.

The two rabbis, Hier and Cooper, began to plan for the Museum in the early 1980s. Initially, they envisaged a more conventional Holocaust museum, but then they began to see it Wiesenthal's way: that the fundamental problem to be tackled was the eradication of hatred. It had to be memorial and museum and living institution, an organic whole that engaged the emotions, the sensibilities, the mind and the imagination, and which carried a universal message accessible to people of different backgrounds and experience.

It was a tall order and a costly $50 million undertaking. Unlike the big federal subsidies for the Washington Holocaust Museum, the only public support for the Wiesenthal Center's project came from the state of California, which voted $5 million towards the project. Even this was not achieved without controversy: the Anti-Defamation League, a Jewish organisation, opposed it on the grounds that it was unconstitutional, that such a grant would breach the separation between church and state. The ADL intervention failed. But it was typical of the resentment which the established Jewish organisations have regularly displayed towards the Wiesenthal Center.

They see it as a populist upstart, siphoning off money that might otherwise go to them.

It took until 1993 to complete the Museum. Wiesenthal, beaming with pride and a sense of fulfilment, was guest of honour at the dedication ceremony. Here was a modern marvel reaching beyond the twentieth century; light years away from his Vienna Documentation Centre, but fulfilling the same purpose. The Museum makes the horror and brutality of the Holocaust come alive through a series of tableaux that illustrate the origins of the Final Solution and go on to show how killing was turned into a remorseless industrial enterprise. It also has a separate multi-media research section with extensive archival material on the Second World War and the Holocaust.

The Museum achieves far more than words alone, or even eyewitness testimony, can do. It is not designed for the idle wanderer; there are few glass-encased exhibits. Visitors must follow a set path, a non-denominational progression along the stations to the Cross. This is a museum about participation, about involvement, about connections – past, present, future – and about conscience.

Its wealth of computerised, high-tech displays comes straight from California's silicone valley. They are used to underpin and dramatise, and to involve visitors enough to confront their own prejudices. The Museum forces them to become voyeurs in hell, almost participants in the Final Solution. It chills, it bombards the conscience, it aims at the senses and not only the brain. But it is not a morgue only preoccupied with the victims of the Holocaust. It is, foremost, an educational complex, a tool that also confronts visitors with contemporary human rights challenges, and forces them to learn that intolerance, hatred and bigotry are evils that affect all people, not only Jews; and harangues them to understand that such phenomena must be quashed before they can undermine present or future generations.

Reaching out through the full eight storeys of the building is a Tower of Witness, with hundreds of photographs recovered from the concentration camps. But then comes the active display. It begins with a corridor lined with scenes of the America of dreams and myths, where everybody is happy and at ease with family, neighbours and fellow citizens of all persuasions. Next the visitor enters the whisper gallery, where the hiss of racial and sexist epithets envelop the passer-by. 'Guess who has moved next door', or 'These people, they live like animals', or again, 'Sure I wouldn't want my daughter to marry ...' says an Asian, a white, a Hispanic, with voices, mumbling racial slurs about blacks, Hispanics, whites, all of them familiar in the contemporary world.

After this comes the 'Tolerance Workshop', a large hall filled with a jumble of video screens, programmed both to lay out the anatomy of events such as the 1992 Los Angeles race riots, and to enter into a dialogue with the visitor to explore the individual's racist attitudes. In the 'global situation' space, the monitors are programmed to provide information on contemporary human rights violations worldwide. Down the hall, a multimedia film of the civil rights movement with the voice of Martin Luther King, and images of the segregated world he sought to end, leads away from the cacophony to two doors. One is for the 'unprejudiced'; the second says 'prejudiced'. Visitors are asked to choose. Most tend to opt for the first door – only to find that it is locked. The moral is obvious: no one is perfect. Everybody must go the uncomfortable way into the vortex of the Holocaust. As they enter, visitors receive a 'passport card' with the name and photograph of a child caught up in the Holocaust. At various stages of the tour, the passport is updated with more information about the child. At the end, there is a brief biography that includes information about the child's fate – most of them did not survive.

Visitors have to move on in groups, led by an invisible guide speaking from a script written by Martin Gilbert, author of probably the most authoritative account of the Holocaust. Gilbert's commentary steers the visitor from one self-contained dramatised tableau to the next. This is not for the claustrophobic. At each stage the doors, behind and forward, are silently closed. An early tableau shows the easy-going café society of Berlin in the 1920s. As the carefully sculpted wooden figures chat, most of them are oblivious to the signs of nascent anti-Semitism and dismiss the Hitler phenomenon. Another tableau has the Nazis, still in their early days and not yet in power, but already pronouncing that 'the Jews are our misfortune'. The 1942 Wannsee conference is portrayed with words taken from Adolf Eichmann's testimony at his Jerusalem trial. It depicts the participants as they discuss the plan for the Final Solution, adopt the blueprint for action, celebrating their decisions with a self-congratulatory round of drinks.

Soon, the soft carpeting gives way to rough concrete. The tour has reached the Holocaust. The bravery, yet futility of Jewish resistance is described with exhibits from the Warsaw ghetto. For a few minutes, the visitors are made to experience the forces of evil that rendered resistance so futile. The tour continues through a replica of the gates at Auschwitz. Welcome to a death camp. The space is darkened, but the entrance to two tunnels is visible. One is labelled for the 'able-bodied' – meaning that they are suitable material for slave labour; the second for 'women and others' – meaning instant death. But both tunnels lead to the same horror, a bunker designed to resemble a gas chamber. As the visitors sit on small stools in the dark, they are forced to watch horrific scenes. German soldiers throw babies out of windows; naked men and women are led to their death while a German officer mumbles reassuring words that they will not be harmed. Even if visitors are tempted to close their eyes, they cannot escape the horror as the room resounds to the matter-of-fact voices of survivors recounting their experiences in the camps.

As the visitors are led out of this hell, they are confronted with a placard asking 'Who was responsible?' Immediately afterwards comes a life-size portrait photograph of Simon Wiesenthal, who sums up the purpose of the pilgrimage they have just completed: 'Hope lives when people remember.'

[22]

Waldheim –
The Poisoned Chalice

Forgetfulness to the point of deceit is Kurt Waldheim's strongest trait. Self-deception comes easily; truthfulness is not overly pronounced in his character. That much is common ground between Simon Wiesenthal, the WJC, Beate and Serge Klarsfeld, the International Commission of Historians who investigated Waldheim's war record, a UK Ministry of Defence enquiry, a US Government investigation, a televised Waldheim mock trial and several books that dissect the Waldheim saga.

Beyond that, there is a miasma of violent disagreement over Waldheim's wartime activities and the direct responsibility that he bears for war crimes committed in the Balkans, while he was stationed in the region. Facts have been turned topsy-turvy, reasoned analysis has been debased and frequently replaced by an entirely disconcerting amount of mud-slinging. Wiesenthal has been demonised by fellow Jews for persisting with the contention that there was insufficient evidence to charge Waldheim with war crimes. Contentiousness and jealousies that regularly plague Jewish life have been put on display for all the world to see.

The Waldheim controversy snowballed to become a Wiesenthal controversy. At a point in his long life when Wiesenthal, acclaimed and laden with medals and awards, felt he was entitled to relax in the belief that at last his reputation was secure and his often lonely fight for remembrance of the Holocaust vindicated, he suddenly found himself under determined attack from the senior officers of the WJC in New York for failing to defrock Waldheim. They were eventually joined by a handful of people such as the former Mossad chief, Isser Harel, and the Nazi-hunting couple, the Klarsfelds, who bore long-term grudges against Wiesenthal. The onslaught was broadened beyond the Waldheim affair to challenge the worth of virtually everything that Wiesenthal had done since the Holocaust.

Kreisky had been the first notable Jew to undermine Wiesenthal's reputation. Where he left off, the WJC and its allies have taken over. The

Waldheim affair has become a convenient means of belittling Wiesenthal's legacy, while his rivals fight to secure their own position in history's ranks of committed Nazi-hunters.

Wiesenthal sees Waldheim as an opportunist, as a 'world-class liar' and a weak, deeply flawed character, who rightly deserves to be described as a Nazi collaborator. But this is still a far cry from accusing Waldheim of personal and direct involvement in war crimes, and still further from finding witnesses capable of sustaining a case against him in an Austrian court of law.

This refusal to include Waldheim in his gallery of war criminals has been used to accuse Wiesenthal of incompetence, of malpractice and a deliberate cover-up, of making false claims for his achievements with respect to Eichmann and several other proven Holocaust perpetrators, of hampering rather than promoting the search for mass murderers, of growing rich by fabricating his own legend. His detractors express self-righteous indignation to anyone who questions their conclusions about Wiesenthal. 'If you do not accept that Wiesenthal is a liar, there is no point in discussing his role in the Waldheim investigations,' says Eli Rosenbaum, head of the US Department of Justice's Office of Special Investigations.[1] He was General Counsel to the WJC during the 1986 drive against Waldheim's election as Austrian head of state, and is the co-author of *Betrayal*, a book that claims to prove Waldheim's guilt and portrays Wiesenthal as 'a pathetically incompetent Nazi-hunter', who chose to defend Waldheim in order to protect his own reputation. Elan Steinberg, Executive Director of the WJC, talks of Wiesenthal as 'my idol until I knew what he really was', accuses him of 'malpractice' and claims that he is 'fundamentally dishonest' and must therefore forfeit any pretensions to moral stature.[2] Wiesenthal's accusers act as if they were born-again Nazi-hunters, whose attitudes must be allowed to prevail.

The terms of the debate set by the WJC inevitably provoked Wiesenthal and his friends to mount a stubborn, no-fault defence of each and every move that he has made in the Waldheim affair. Wiesenthal is convinced that the WJC rekindled anti-Semitism and resentment against immigrants and refugees in Austria, and that this led to the emergence of the dangerous, ultra-nationalist Jörg Haider and the growing popularity of his reshaped, far-right FPÖ Party. He argues passionately that, far from deterring Waldheim's election, the WJC's efforts to destroy his candidacy bought him an extra half-million votes and ensured his victory.

Wiesenthal also believes that the WJC so readily picked on him as one of the villains of the piece because it saw this as an excellent opportunity to pursue what he regards as its long-standing drive to discredit him while simultaneously magnifying its own organisation's virtues and importance. Wiesenthal's emotional response had ample cause. It was the cumulative effect of the resentment towards the WJC's establishment that he had felt ever since the mid-1950s, when he had been snubbed by Dr Nahum Goldmann, over the Eichmann case. After the publication of *Betrayal*, only the high legal costs, and the length of time it would take to make its way through the US courts, have deterred Wiesenthal from adopting his normal practice of filing slander suits against those who, he believes, have wronged him. 'Legal action in the US would extend beyond my lifetime.'

Any attempt at dispassionate assessment of the rights and wrongs of Wiesenthal's handling of the Waldheim case is to venture into a lion's den. But for all the posturing by those who insist that there is irrefutable proof of Waldheim's culpability, most of the investigations into Waldheim's past have come to the same conclusion as Wiesenthal himself, and have reached a 'not proven' verdict. This assessment includes both historians who have analysed the available facts, and also career civil servants in Austria, some of whom ruined their chances of promotion by public opposition to the Waldheim Presidency. The only important exception to these findings has been the OSI's investigations, which found that Waldheim did indeed expedite, and probably ordered, a long series of war crimes and atrocities.[3] This probe involved some officials who were familiar with the views of Mr Rosenbaum, himself a former staff member of the OSI – and back there now as its Director.

That Waldheim constructed a massive cover-up, or in plain language that he lied about his wartime record, is accepted by all the investigators, Wiesenthal included. That this alone was more than sufficient to disqualify him from the Presidency, and that it dishonoured Austria to have Waldheim represent his country as head of state, is a conclusion shared by Wiesenthal and all others who demanded his resignation.

Whether Wiesenthal erred in not investigating Waldheim more assiduously after he was asked by Yad Vashem in 1979 to check on Waldheim's wartime record is debatable. With the wisdom of hindsight, the answer has to be in the affirmative; but whether it was true at the time is much harder to determine. Had he gone deeper into Waldheim's past when Waldheim was still UN Secretary-General, perhaps the omissions in his *curriculum vitae* would have been discovered earlier, and the question of standing for the Presidency in 1986 would never have arisen. Inevitably questions have been asked whether Wiesenthal would have pried more deeply in 1979 if Waldheim had been a Socialist Party member instead of belonging to the conservative ÖVP; and would he have been less rigorous in demanding proof of complicity in war crimes before levelling war crimes charges against Waldheim? Did he develop a blind spot, because Austria's Socialist Party, the SPÖ, was manoeuvring against Waldheim? Indeed, would he have displayed greater curiosity about Waldheim's antecedents much earlier on in 1971, when Waldheim made his first, unsuccessful stab at the Austrian Presidency? And did Wiesenthal's long-standing animosity towards the WJC lead him to suspect each and every move by the WJC against Waldheim, and deter him from following similar lines of investigation?

Wiesenthal has always adamantly denied that party political considerations played any part in his Waldheim researches. And he insists that, if there were prejudice, it was all one-sided from the WJC in New York. He argues that he applied the same principles of justice that have animated all his actions.

He does not like to think that his emotions can play tricks with honest self-appraisal. Yet it is impossible to ignore Wiesenthal's long and many-faceted feud with Austria's Socialists, or his natural leaning towards conservative political parties, including Austria's ÖVP. It does not in any way detract from the accuracy of Wiesenthal's conclusion that Waldheim was a liar and not a war criminal. But initially in 1986, Waldheim, being the ÖVP's Presidential candidate, may have benefited from Wiesenthal's reluctance to go for the jugular.

However, there can be no doubt that once Wiesenthal realised that Waldheim had been profoundly economical with the truth, his investigator's and his Holocaust survivor's instincts prevailed over every other feeling and consideration. He wanted to establish the facts, not to sweep them under the carpet. At the same time, he refused to accuse without sound evidence and was genuinely convinced that the WJC's campaign was irresponsible. His natural obstinacy on these matters hardened when the WJC entered the fray with a campaign which he judged to be signally counter-productive. Wiesenthal argued that the WJC campaign would fan Austrian anti-Semitism and xenophobia, which in turn would virtually guarantee Waldheim's re-election. But his critics in New York overreached themselves when they alleged that Wiesenthal's refusal to damn Waldheim as a war criminal was all part of a cover-up for incompetence. They went further and bracketed Wiesenthal with Waldheim as joint conspirators in the suppression of truth about the deportations of Jews from Salonika, and about other atrocities committed in Greece and Yugoslavia.

Kurt Waldheim was born in 1919 into a staunchly Catholic conservative family, steadily making its way through the teaching profession up Austria's bourgeois ladder. The young Waldheim planned on a career in law and diplomacy, but in 1936 decided to enlist in the army as a one-year volunteer. He received his army orders at the end of 1936 and was posted to an elite cavalry unit. At the end of 1937, having completed his year's service, he was put on the reserve list and won a scholarship to the Consular Academy in Vienna.

The ambiguities began soon afterwards. According to German army records, Waldheim enrolled in the Nazi Student League on 1 April 1938, three weeks after the *Anschluss*. Yet he has always denied that he joined this Nazi group, and made no mention of his membership in the personnel forms that he completed for his diplomatic career. Nor did he disclose the matter in the official biographies that he circulated during his candidacies for the UN Secretary-General's post and the Austrian Presidency.

The same omissions were made with respect to his membership of Hitler's Brownshirts, the *Sturmabteilung* (SA) stormtroopers. In the summer of 1938, Waldheim was recalled for a few months' training with his former army unit, which had been incorporated into the German *Reichswehr*. That autumn he returned to the Consular Academy. Yet not long afterwards, within days of the *Kristallnacht*, Waldheim's army record card shows that he joined the Nazi SA, serving in the SA cavalry. Waldheim however disputes that he became a Brownshirt and claimed that he never wore its uniform.

He has stood by the version that his SA unit had been an innocent riding group of students at the Consular Academy. Waldheim explains that having little money, and being a passionate rider, the only way to have the free use of a horse had been to join the SA riding club. He denies that the move had political import. In 1945, when he applied for his post in the Austrian Foreign Office, he made an entry, acknowledging that he had belonged to a Nazi riding corps, but failed to designate it as an SA stormtrooper unit.

These omissions, when they were uncovered decades later in 1986, reinforced the suspicion that Waldheim was deliberately hiding Nazi convictions that had made him far more pliable when it came to involvement in wartime atrocities. Waldheim served first in France and, promoted lieutenant, fought on the Russian front in 1941. In October that year, he was wounded in battle; for a while he limped from a bad leg wound and was allowed, temporarily, to resume his studies. Waldheim would have preferred the world to think that his active military duty ended at that point, that he was able to resume his studies, received his law degree in 1944 and began his diplomatic career in 1945, serving in the Foreign Office under Karl Gruber.

Nothing in his official résumé suggested that he had, as was the fact, been declared fit for service again and that he served from 1942 to 1945 under the notorious General Alexander Löhr in Yugoslavia and Greece, as an ordnance and intelligence officer, with the rank of second lieutenant. Löhr was condemned for his extensive war crimes and hanged by the Yugoslavs in 1947.

Until more information was pried from him in 1986, Waldheim always skimmed over his military service in the Balkans. In his Foreign Ministry application, he admitted service in France, Russia and the Balkans, but mentioned no dates. In the German version of Waldheim's autobiography, written after he left the United Nations, he refers cursorily to his service in the Balkans; but even that was scrapped from the English translation.

Aides, who have known Waldheim since the 1960s, say that he was quite open in conversations with them about the fact that he had served under General Löhr's command; but he never referred to it in public until he was forced by the investigations into his past to acknowledge his postings in Yugoslavia and Greece. Even then he maintained that he had only been there as an armchair soldier, principally working as a translator and benefiting from frequent leaves. He wanted the world to accept that he neither saw, nor heard, anything untoward and was unaware of atrocities carried out by his Army Group E, commanded by General Löhr. He claimed to know nothing about the killings in the Kozara Mountains and other massacres close to his quarters, or about the deportations of Jews from Salonika and elsewhere in Greece. Waldheim blotted out all acknowledgement that he knew of the evil and brutalities around him with the classic explanation: 'I was only doing my duty.'

At the end of the war, relations between Tito's Yugoslavia and Austria were tense in the extreme. Having suffered so much at the hands of Hitler's armies, the Yugoslavs saw the Austrians as Germany's accomplices – if anything, because they were neighbours, the sense of betrayal went deeper. Moreover, Tito, seeking to create a unified Yugoslav nation out of the polyglot amalgam of nationalities he had under his control, made territorial claims on Carinthia, the Austrian province adjoining the then Yugoslav republic of Slovenia. He also bitterly attacked the Austrians for having 'Germanified' the considerable Slovenian population of Carinthia. Yugoslavia wanted the occupying powers to be tough on Austria, to insist on stringent denazification and war crimes trials, and was strongly opposed to the West's perception of Austria as Hitler's first victim. Tito had no sympathy for Austria's first post-war regime as it struggled to re-establish democratic government and was angered by the fact that his brutal foes, the Ustachi, were able to use Carinthia as an operational base against Yugoslavia. All this meant that the Yugoslavs were on the look-out for opportunities to embarrass the Austrian authorities and force them into territorial concessions.

It is against this background that the controversial *Odluka*, the Yugoslav indictment of Kurt Waldheim as a war criminal, deserves to be seen. The Yugoslav State Commission for the Determination of Crimes Committed by the Occupying Forces and their Collaborators completed its case against Waldheim on 18 December 1947 and called for his extradition as a war criminal to Yugoslavia. This was the prelude to filing the *Odluka* with the UN War Crimes Commission (UNWCC) in London on 25 December 1947. Russia and its Western allies had been unable to sustain their co-operation on UNWCC, and with the organisation due to be dissolved in the spring of 1948, a 31 December deadline had been imposed for the submission of cases.

The seven-page Yugoslav indictment alleged that Waldheim had been involved in 'murder, slaughter, the shooting of hostages, deliberate destruction of property and burning of settlements'. He was held responsible for 'preparing, issuing and acting upon criminal orders while his group operated in Yugoslavia'. It cited no documents or other evidence to implicate Waldheim directly in such atrocities. The indictment described Waldheim as 'missing', even though the Yugoslavs were aware that he was working in the Austrian Foreign Ministry. They pressed hard, and finally succeeded in February 1948, to have Waldheim's name put on the 'A' list, reserved for war criminals against whom there was a *prima facie* case. In spite of that, UNWCC's committee 1, the body responsible for checking the facts and evidence submitted in connection with the case, never examined the Yugoslav allegations.

UNWCC did not initiate proceedings against Waldheim. When it closed shop in March 1948, its lists were transferred to the Central Registry of War Criminals and Security Suspects (CROWCASS) of the Allied Control Council in Berlin. Even though every name on CROWCASS was subject to extradition, Yugoslavia made no request for Waldheim. Later, the Waldheim file was transferred to the UN archive in the bowels of the UN headquarters in New York. These files can only be withdrawn at the request of a UN member government. Yugoslavia never made such a request.

The Yugoslavs had come across Waldheim's name during General Löhr's trial, when they had Army Group E's personnel list. Austrians, and indeed most of the experts who have studied the curious history of the *Odluka*, are convinced that the Yugoslavs deduced correctly that the man on Löhr's list was the same person as the young diplomat at the Austrian Foreign Minister, Karl Gruber's side, during the abrasive negotiations on Yugoslavia's territorial demands on Austria. They saw an opportunity to exploit their discovery: Yugoslavia had been unable to win any concessions from Gruber, who was strongly pro-Western. Perhaps if they could expose one of Gruber's aides as a war criminal, it might cast doubt on Gruber's integrity. It was useful that the Yugoslavs held a prisoner of war, Johann Mayer, a clerk from Army Group E, who had apparently turned informer and was prepared to substantiate accusations against Waldheim.

Clearly not everybody agrees that Waldheim was deliberately framed by the Yugoslavs. Those who believe Waldheim's guilt insist that the *Odluka* was drawn up on the basis of clear and damning evidence, and dismiss the conspiracy theory that the Yugoslavs would have had the motive to invent a tainted indictment against Waldheim in order to discredit the Austrian Government. That is certainly the conclusion reached by Eli Rosenbaum in his book *Betrayal*.

But historians with a more open mind about Waldheim's past are convinced that Tito, in 1947, had ulterior motives in accusing Waldheim, and support their argument by pointing out that the Yugoslavs made no attempt to follow up their indictment against Waldheim, made no formal requests to Austria or the Allies to have him extradited, and never made available the dossiers on which the *Odluka* was based. Mayer, the Yugoslavs' one witness supporting their claim, was allowed to be repatriated to Austria in 1948. In later years, Tito developed a markedly friendly relationship with Waldheim, first when he was Austrian Foreign Minister and again in his later incarnation as UN Secretary-General. 'For Tito, the power politician, it was useful to know about the *Odluka*; but faked evidence of past sins did not prevent him from cultivating a man he needed,' is the conclusion drawn by Professor Robert Herzstein, the historian who was originally commissioned by the WJC to research the ramifications of the Waldheim case.[4]

Tito's successors were not prepared to discuss the 1945 Yugoslav case against Waldheim, even after the existence of the *Odluka* was exposed in 1986. The Austrian government, apparently oblivious, or else feigning ignorance, of the charges against Waldheim, allowed him to move steadily up the Diplomatic Service ladder and to make a seamless transition into ÖVP politics.

Waldheim's introduction to the United Nations came in 1964, when he was appointed head of Austria's Mission to the world body in New York. Four years later, in 1968, the ÖVP Chancellor Klaus made him Foreign Minister, and in that capacity, Waldheim travelled several times to Yugoslavia and always had extensive, and by all accounts cordial, meetings with Tito. Even though the Yugoslav leader was aware of the *Odluka*, he apparently never spoke of it to Waldheim. In 1970, when Kreisky became Chancellor, Waldheim ceased to be Foreign Minister and returned briefly to New York as Ambassador to the United Nations. The following year, 1971, Waldheim, running as the ÖVP's candidate, lost at his first attempt to win the Presidency. At no point during that election campaign, either at home and still less abroad, did Waldheim's wartime record become an issue.

After the Presidential campaign, Waldheim again took his well-trodden path to the UN. Only this time with a big difference: he had Bruno Kreisky's support when he decided to lobby for the UN Secretary-General's post. Kreisky saw the UN as an ideal instrument to enhance Austria's world standing. What better way to achieve that goal than to have an Austrian elected as UN Secretary-General? Waldheim already possessed one useful attribute: as former Ambassador to the UN, he was well-known in the world body. Thanks to his pliable character, he had made few hostages to fortune. However, Waldheim was by no means a unanimous first choice for the Permanent Members of the UN's Security Council, who have a vital say in the Secretary-General's election. In 1972, Waldheim only won after the third Security Council ballot, but four years later he was re-elected for a second term. He sought a third term in 1982, but was blocked by China – not because of rumours about Waldheim's past, but principally because the Chinese wanted a Secretary-General from the Third World, and were backing Tanzania's Salim Salim. In the end, a compromise candidate was found, Peru's Javier Perez de Cuellar, and Waldheim had to make an ignominious withdrawal.

Brian Urquhart, the top civil servant at the UN during Waldheim's tenure as Secretary-General, has written:

Throughout his ten years at the UN, Kurt Waldheim's answer to questions about his wartime service was that he was wounded at the Russian front in 1941, convalesced, and left the German army to resume his law studies in 1942.

When, from time to time, there were unsubstantiated stories or allegations about his past, Waldheim invariably and strongly reaffirmed the story, even claiming that he and his family were anti-Nazi. For lack of evidence to the contrary, we all accepted this version and reacted strongly to those who questioned it.

Waldheim, it has now become clear, lied for forty years about his war record, presumably believing that the truth would stand in the way of his relentless pursuit of public position and office. This seems to me a far greater disqualification for public office than the available evidence of his doings as an officer in Hitler's army.

Waldheim, emerging as a living lie, has done immense damage not only to his own country but to the UN. ... Waldheim's blind ambition for public office showed an astonishing lack of self-respect and of concern for the UN. [But] the Waldheim episode is above all an indictment of the way in which governments, and especially the great powers, select the world's leading civil servants. Political differences dictate a search for a candidate who will not exert any troubling degree of leadership, commitment, originality or independence.[5]

Waldheim returned to Austria in 1982 with Kreisky still acting as his patron and encouraging him to adopt an elder statesman's foreign policy guru role. Indeed in 1985, when Waldheim's thoughts again honed in on the Presidency, the now retired Kreisky's first inclination was to advise the SPÖ to support him and for the two major parties to run him as a joint candidate. Kreisky's successor as Chancellor, Fred Sinowatz, would have none of it, and once Waldheim had officially declared his ÖVP candidacy, the SPÖ decided to field its own man.

During all the years of Waldheim's service at the UN, none of the wartime allies, even if they were aware of the original Yugoslav charges, ever openly raised any doubts about Waldheim's past, or questioned his suitability for high office. There are many unanswered questions why this occurred, and at least two diametrically opposed answers. Rosenbaum and the WJC assert that the Soviet Union had deliberately held back from exposing Waldheim, because it used the Yugoslav *Odluka* evidence, which had been passed on to it in 1945, to bend him to support its interests first as Foreign Minister and later as UN Secretary-General. On the other hand, Professor Herzstein reached the firm conclusion that the CIA established links with Waldheim after the war, and that successive US administrations felt obliged to protect him, and only dropped their guard after the WJC furore erupted in 1986. Waldheim's senior aides in the UN Secretariat have always believed that the Secretary-General was not being protected by any of the great powers; but that he acted as he did simply because he was nature's blotting paper, always doing what he assumed would best please the dominant voices in the UN Security Council.

In Austria itself, it did not go entirely unnoticed that Waldheim's account of his war years was singularly devoid of detail. Vienna is a prototype rumour mill, but nothing dire had emerged during the 1971 Presidential campaign. As Waldheim was clearly the underdog in that campaign and victory considered unlikely, his political opponents had little reason to cast around for incriminating facts against him. And once he was UN Secretary-General, Austrians were proud to have one of their citizens in that high post, and had no interest in rocking the boat by voicing doubts about his fitness for high office.

Until 1979, nobody had ever suggested to Wiesenthal that he should investigate Waldheim's past, and Wiesenthal himself had not until then interested himself in the matter. However, in Israel there was deep concern about the way Waldheim handled Middle East affairs. In place of the neutrality the Israelis expected from a UN Secretary-General, they saw in Waldheim's words and actions evidence of partiality towards the Arabs and disregard of Israeli concerns. Wiesenthal was in Israel for a meeting of Yad Vashem's international council, of which he was a member. There was a discussion whether Waldheim might have a Nazi past, which might explain his behaviour. 'My friends asked me to check it out.' This was an informal request; in no way, Wiesenthal stresses, was it an Israeli Government move.

The obvious place to look, Wiesenthal says, was the Berlin Documentation Centre, where the US Nazi archives were deposited. Using a short cut to a normally cumbersome procedure, Wiesenthal asked his friend, the German publisher Axel Springer, to make enquiries. He received two documents: one from the US archive, which had negatives marked against membership of any Nazi organisation, including the SA, and which therefore appeared to clear Waldheim of a Nazi past; the second was from the French archive – the *Wehrmachtsauskunftstelle* – in Berlin. This showed that Waldheim had been a member of Army Group E in the Balkans, and also gave enough details of his absences on sick leave to prove that he had in fact spent the larger part of the years between 1942 and 1945 on duty in the Balkans.

'As far as I was concerned the matter was closed. I called Yad Vashem and told them that Mr Waldheim had been neither a Nazi nor an SA man.' Pride does not allow Wiesenthal to think that he should have displayed more curiosity. 'The Army Group E was a large force. It would have made no sense, and would anyhow have been impossible, to investigate every one of the 3,000 officers in that group; service under Löhr's command did not automatically imply involvement in atrocities. And since the Berlin archive had not produced any evidence of Nazi Party involvement, there was no reason to pry deeper.'

Seven years later, in 1986, Wiesenthal's judgment that there was no justification for further investigation into Waldheim's war came to haunt him.

The detailed sequence of events in 1985 and 1986 is muddied. But what emerges is that after a dull beginning to the Presidential campaign, Waldheim was surging ahead of his Socialist rival in the second half of 1985. He was campaigning on his claims to world stature. 'Dr Kurt Waldheim, the Austrian the world trusts', the posters screamed. At the same time, certain markers hinting at a dubious Waldheim past began to surface: a *Stern* magazine report that Waldheim had been a member of the Nazi Student League; alleged remarks by former officers in Army Group E that Waldheim had been particularly close to General Löhr; rumours, hotly denied by Waldheim, that as Foreign Minister in 1968, he had sought to limit entry visas for Czech refugees; an article in the weekly *Profil* in January 1986, exposing that Waldheim had been on General Löhr's general staff. About then, two Socialist members of the Austrian Resistance movement came to Wiesenthal to ask whether he had any evidence against Waldheim. Typically, Wiesenthal countered by charging the SPÖ with lack of interest in Friedrich Peter's Nazi past, but he also again insisted that there was no dossier against Waldheim.

The sudden interest in Waldheim's past appeared to be part of a calculated whispering campaign by the SPÖ to beat its opponent by discrediting him. Now enter, centre stage, the WJC and a coincidence of interests. Late in January 1986, Israel Singer, the Secretary-General of the WJC, sent Eli Rosenbaum to Vienna to sound out the rumours that Waldheim had been an active Nazi.

As another illustration of the tangled accounts that beset the Waldheim story at every important juncture, there is no consensus about the genesis of the WJC's involvement. One version is that the information had been relayed to the WJC by Leon Zelman, a Holocaust survivor in charge of the Jewish Welcome Service in Vienna.[6] Zelman in his own memoirs refutes the commonly held view that the SPÖ leadership was the hidden hand behind the initiative to stir up interest in Waldheim's war record. He claims that Singer tossed back to Kreisky the information that Zelman had sent to New York, and that Kreisky then seized on it – later taking the credit for having scented that Waldheim's past deserved further investigation.[7]

Notwithstanding Zelman's belief that he was the first to have sounded the alert about Waldheim, the more conventional view – which Wiesenthal shares – is that a Viennese historian, Georg Tidl, had become suspicious about Waldheim late in 1985, did more research and took his findings to the SPÖ.

At the time, the SPÖ had no concern for the moral aspects of Waldheim's aspirations to the highest office in the land. In the heat of the Presidential election battle, it simply appeared a useful weapon to undermine Waldheim's appeal to Austrians as a world personality whose record had made him a by-word for integrity. Rather than directly challenging Waldheim and risk alienating former Nazis who might vote for the Socialist candidate, the SPÖ preferred to leak the Waldheim story to the WJC, and that is how Rosenbaum came to be sent to Vienna to find out more about Waldheim.

Rosenbaum pointedly failed to contact Wiesenthal during his initial probe in Vienna, and Wiesenthal, when he heard about the visit, felt deeply slighted. It was one more black point in his book against the WJC.

The WJC had little interest in Austria's domestic politics, but it seized on Waldheim as an opportunity to demonstrate the organisation's moral strength and worldwide net of influence. Both during the period of Nazi persecution before the war, and after 1945, when Europe was littered with survivors in search of a refuge, American Jews had been slow to recognise the plight of European Jews, or to help them financially and press the administration to open American doors to the survivors. Between 1945 and 1948, only 41,000 Jewish refugees were allowed into the US. However, in 1948, the US Congress adopted the Displaced Persons Act and during the ensuing four years, 400,000 refugees settled in the US.

None of this was enough to mask the fact that for many years after the war, the Americans had been reluctant to acknowledge that numerous Nazi criminals had been given asylum in the United States, or helped to safety in South America, and that Nazi scientists had been recruited to help the US military build-up against the Soviet Union. Now, a new generation of Jews had the opportunity, the WJC reasoned, to demonstrate its mettle to its European co-religionists. If it could force Waldheim to abandon his election campaign, it would strike a blow for justice and, at the same time, reinforce its credentials with world Jewry. The WJC did not foresee that, far from shaming Waldheim to stand down, it would embroil them in Austria's domestic politics, and provoke a major clash with Simon Wiesenthal.

While Rosenbaum beavered away in Vienna, Elan Steinberg was doing his own research and lobbying against Waldheim in New York. Steinberg noted the discrepancies between the information in the documents he was uncovering and Waldheim's autobiography, where he had neutered his war years and depicted himself as a victim of the Nazis.

By 4 March 1986, the WJC was ready to go public. Waldheim had a notorious Nazi past, the WJC proclaimed, and handed out documents that confirmed his membership of the Nazi Student League and of the SA riding club; though it could not yet reveal the explosive CROWCASS listing of Waldheim as a war criminal, which only came to light later in the month. On the same day, 4 March, the *New York Times*, referring to these documents, published an article headed, 'Files show Waldheim was a war criminal.' In

Vienna, where Hubertus Czernin, working for *Profil*, had been beavering away for some time to document Waldheim's past, an extensive exposure was also published.

Wiesenthal reacted by again insisting that he did not believe Waldheim guilty of Nazi crimes and considered his membership of the Nazi Party 'improbable'. But he was sufficiently disturbed to call on the Yugoslav Government to open its Waldheim archives, including the *Odluka* and any evidence it held to justify the indictment it had issued in 1945. The Yugoslav Prime Minister, Mrs Milka Planinc, happened to be on an official visit to Vienna. Her response was an adamant refusal, which she justified by declaring that Yugoslavia did not want to become involved in Austria's election campaign.

Wiesenthal, still wanting to show that Waldheim had to be judged on firm evidence, then turned to the UN Secretary-General, Perez de Cuellar, and asked him to prevail with the Yugoslav Government to make its files public. During a lengthy exchange in New York early in April 1986, Perez de Cuellar undertook to discuss it with the Yugoslavs; but nothing came of it until several months later, when Dusko Doder, the *Washington Post* correspondent in Belgrade, obtained a copy that was promptly passed on to the WJC. Professor Herzstein was shown the *Odluka* file in 1987. The WJC and Herzstein drew very different conclusions. The WJC was convinced it had found the smoking gun. Herzstein, however, was now convinced of 'the political nature of the *Odluka*' and concluded that it 'established beyond doubt the nature and aims of the abortive Yugoslav conspiracy against Waldheim'.[8]

Inevitably, the WJC disclosures and the *New York Times* article made a big impact. In Austria, the vociferous right-wing press instantly concluded that Waldheim was the victim of an SPÖ or of a Jewish conspiracy, or a combination of both. If he had been cleared to serve two terms as UN Secretary-General, it was manifestly malicious to insinuate a criminal record. The more independent-minded papers, like *Profil*, stepped up their investigations into Waldheim's past. Austria's President Kirchschläger condemned the attacks on his would-be successor as a 'political witch-hunt'. Wiesenthal was bombarded for comments, but refused to go beyond questioning Waldheim's truthfulness, and maintained that knowledge of war crimes was not to be confused with participation.

In New York, the WJC kept up a daily bombardment against Waldheim. One press release followed another. On 22 March, the WJC published its bombshell: the CROWCASS listing showing that Waldheim had been sought by Yugoslavia for murder, and that the UNWCC had listed him as a suspected Nazi war criminal. Clearly Waldheim had much to hide, the WJC thundered; though at that stage it still stopped short of a direct accusation of war crimes against Waldheim. It had not yet seen the entire *Odluka* file, but it considered that it already had enough damning material to request the US administration to have Waldheim put on the Watch List as an undesirable alien, prohibited from entering the US – or if the alien was already in the US, from remaining – under the terms of the Holtzman amendment. This bars persons from the United States, if they are found to have 'ordered, incited, assisted or otherwise participated in the persecution of any person because of race, religion, national origin, or political opinion'.

Wiesenthal himself had successfully made use of this provision when he was pressing for the deportation of Hermine Braunsteiner. But where Waldheim was concerned, he reacted fiercely against such a move, convinced that the WJC was exploiting the Holtzman amendment for its own devious purposes. He was dubious about the CROWCASS listing, and the supporting evidence that the WJC had dredged up. It was surely unable to understand the finer points of the documents and was not qualified to interpret their meaning correctly. That, Weisenthal contended, was the more benign interpretation of the WJC's wild accusations against Waldheim.

The WJC campaign to have Waldheim put on the Watch List achieved its aim in April 1987, several months after he was elected President. But from the outset, one of its by-products was to cause a deep rift between Wiesenthal and Rabbi Hier, the head of the Wiesenthal Center in Los Angeles. Wiesenthal was both surprised and then deeply angered when he learned that Hier had agreed to undertake a postcard campaign to add to public pressure to have Waldheim put on the Watch List.

The rabbis, using the same technique they had employed so successfully in full collaboration with Wiesenthal to extend Germany's statute of limitations, they now printed cards, addressed to President Reagan, juxtaposing a uniformed Lieutenant Waldheim in compromising circumstances in Yugoslavia with a sober-suited UN Secretary-General, and the slogan: 'America says no to Waldheim.' In an accompanying statement, on 27 May, Hier said:

> On 8 June, the Austrian people will decide whether or not they want Waldheim to represent them to the world for the next six years. That is their decision. But it is for the people of the US to decide whether we want Waldheim on our shores. ... It is important for the White House to know that the American people do not wish to reward Waldheim for a career built on forty years of deliberate deceit and lies.

Hier had told Wiesenthal that he was under pressure to support the Watch List drive, but not that the Center had decided on such active involvement. The next day, an infuriated Wiesenthal reacted with a curt letter to Hier: 'Why didn't you tell me the truth? What the Wiesenthal Center is doing? ... I am very angry because you seem to think I am an idiot who can only be told part of the truth. ... This kind of co-operation between me and the Center cannot happen without any consequences.' In a later letter, again criticising Hier's efforts to have Waldheim internationally ostracised, Wiesenthal voiced this reprimand: 'The Simon Wiesenthal Center does not have to be the first to attack, insult and speak up on the basis of unproven accusations. I did not fight for justice and truth for forty-two years in order to have my name disavowed by the Simon Wiesenthal Center and be doubted in my credibility.'[9]

Hier admits that the Wiesenthal Center adopted a much more strident posture than Wiesenthal himself; and he is unrepentant. But he also claims that Wiesenthal was grappling with a different legal issue. In the US, it was a relatively simple question of whether there was a case, under the Holtzman amendment, for keeping Waldheim out of America. For such a decision to be reached, there was no need for a trial to establish Waldheim's guilt. Wiesenthal, on the other hand, was concerned to establish whether there was sufficient evidence against Waldheim capable of securing a conviction in an Austrian court of law.

Under the Holtzman amendment, a suspected war criminal has to prove himself innocent to be allowed into the country. Hier's justification for distancing himself from Wiesenthal was that, 'As an American, heading an American organisation, here was a man who had lied to the world and said until 1986 that he had never even heard of the deportations from Salonika.' That demanded a robust position. 'But I guess it is easier for Americans to shout: put him on the Watch List. But there wouldn't be a war crimes trial in America. The trial would have to take place in Austria.'

Hier says he accepted the logic of Wiesenthal's argument that there was insufficient evidence to secure a conviction in Austria. Wiesenthal asked him: 'What do you think the judges will do if Waldheim is put on trial? On the basis of the available documentation, there is not even the slightest doubt that the judges will acquit him, because we have no witnesses against him. He is not talking, and the witnesses are dead.' And an acquittal would only lead to charges that the Jews fabricated the case against Waldheim.

Briefly, Wiesenthal was tempted to have his name taken off the Los Angeles Center. But he soon realised that it would be an empty gesture, and that the positive aspects of the Wiesenthal Center's activities far out-weighed the transgressions over Waldheim.

The drive to have Waldheim excluded from the US only served to reinforce the resentment in Austria against a Jewish organisation, purporting to speak for Jews worldwide, actively seeking to influence the outcome of its Presidential election. Far from turning against Waldheim, Austrian public opinion rallied defensively behind him.

Perversely, a combative interview with Israel Singer and Elan Steinberg, published in *Profil* on 25 March 1986, may have clinched Waldheim's election. The two WJC officials described Waldheim as 'a Nazi, a liar who has deceived the world for forty years'. And they warned of sanctions, declaring that if Waldheim was elected, every Austrian abroad would find himself 'under a cloud of mistrust', and Austria's position in the world 'would be no bed of roses'. Urged by the head of Vienna's Jewish community, Dr Häcker, to prevent a fresh outburst of anti-Semitism by mod-erating their language, Singer asked how many Jews were still living in Austria. Told that there were 7,000, he retorted: 'Then just let them emigrate' – a quip that Wiesenthal found unforgivably insensitive, and that endorsed his belief that the WJC leadership lacked understanding of the suffering European Jews had endured under the Nazis. In a further twist, Singer later declared that he had been misquoted. But Wiesenthal checked with the *Profil* journalists, who insisted on the accuracy of their article.

Austria's political establishment was now united in condemning the WJC. Wiesenthal's old foe, Bruno Kreisky, was similarly outraged, describing the WJC's actions as 'colossal vileness and an exceedingly stupid intervention'. He interpreted it as an attack not just against Waldheim but against the Austrian nation. Alois Mock, ÖVP party leader, condemned the WJC for its 'unprecedented manhunt'. Waldheim himself maintained his denials of wrongdoing, claiming that the WJC's accusations had been plucked out of thin air. He now had a new campaign poster. Defiantly it proclaimed that 'We Austrians will elect whom we want. Now more than ever: Dr Kurt Waldheim.'

Wiesenthal's main concern was the adverse impact of all this on the position of Jews in Austria. Public opinion polls were already showing a sharp swing towards those who said that Jews could not be accepted as Austrians, and who claimed that the Jews themselves were partly responsible for the fate that had befallen them under Hitler. Wiesenthal never had a moment's doubt that the WJC campaign would backfire to the detriment of the Jews. He warned that the WJC would 'make anti-Semites of young people'. Years of educational work to weaken the hold of anti-Semitism risked being undone, he argued. His own work in drawing a line between culpable Nazi criminals and fellow-travellers was being undermined.

Undeterred, the WJC's Vice-President, Kalman Sultanik, demanded that Waldheim explain why he had felt compelled to keep his war record hidden for all these years. He also questioned Wiesenthal's judgment, claiming that he had lied to the Israeli Government in 1979 by telling them that Waldheim had no criminal war record. 'Waldheim who sent Jews to the gas chambers is being defended by that prominent Jew, Simon Wiesenthal.' Wiesenthal retorted that he had never been asked by the Israeli Government to undertake any research on Waldheim. His only dealings had been with Yad Vashem.

However, Wiesenthal no longer had any doubts that Waldheim had lied about his war record. Even before the first round of the Presidential election on 4 May, Wiesenthal was expressing open reservations about Waldheim's credibility. He could not accept, he declared, Waldheim's protestations that he had been unaware of the deportations of Jews from Salonika. This provoked a telephone call from Waldheim, insisting that the first he had heard of the deportations was from newspapers. Wiesenthal repeated that there was no way Waldheim could have been ignorant of an action involving thousands of Jews, that continued for six weeks and took place only five miles from the *Wehrmacht* headquarters where he was stationed.

After Waldheim still refused to acknowledge the obvious, Wiesenthal's mind was made up. 'By his public attitude towards the deportation of Jews from Salonika, if for no other reason, Kurt Waldheim made himself unacceptable to me as a Federal President,' he wrote in *Justice Not Vengeance*.[10] Yet it took another two years before Wiesenthal publicly called on Waldheim to resign. And he has never changed his mind that calling him a liar was still a far cry from branding him a war criminal, and that is an allegation Wiesenthal has steadfastly refused to make.

The WJC's Siamese Twins:
Waldheim and Wiesenthal

Kurt Waldheim was elected to the Presidency after a second round of voting on 8 June 1986. He won fifty-four per cent of the popular vote. Wiesenthal declared the 'Jews were the real losers in this election' and has remained convinced that 'many voters elected Waldheim, not out of sympathy for his person, but in protest against foreign interference'. Wiesenthal maintained that Waldheim – as a proven liar – was unfit to act as Austria's head of state. Nevertheless, given the state of public opinion in Austria, he argued that any attempt to force Waldheim's resignation without an independent assessment of the allegations against him would turn him into a martyr. Already, Austrians were blaming the Jews for the fact that the campaign against Waldheim had made enough headway abroad to cause his ostracism by much of the international community. Austria's head of state was no longer considered fit to be seen in the company of other world dignitaries. Throughout his Presidency, only a handful of Arab states were willing to invite President Waldheim, and when the Vatican received him, it ranked high among Pope John Paul's more controversial decisions. Foreign leaders avoided visits to Austria as much as possible, and when they did come, shunned contact with Waldheim as much as protocol permitted.

Wiesenthal calculated that the only way to bring clarity to Waldheim's missing war years was to appoint an international commission of historians to make an independent evaluation of the available evidence. This proposal was immediately welcomed by Waldheim. Yet it took a year before the body was actually set up. In the meantime, Waldheim embarrassed Wiesenthal by seeking to meet him, and by showing that he had come to regard the Nazi-hunter as a valued asset in establishing his innocence. Wiesenthal did his best to rebuff him, refusing to talk to him privately and staging a conspicuous walk-out, when an uninvited President Waldheim turned up at a Catholic University students' gathering, with 'reconciliation' as the theme of their discussions.

There was no truce in the war of words over Waldheim after his election. The WJC sniped at Wiesenthal and continued to publish evidence against Waldheim. Rosenbaum drafted an article for publication in Wiesenthal's monthly, *Ausweg*, in which he wrote:

> The recent election of Kurt Waldheim has shocked the conscience of the entire civilised world. Nearly as shocking has been the unpardonable behaviour of Simon Wiesenthal. . . . There can be little doubt that it was Mr Wiesenthal who ensured the electoral victory of Dr Waldheim. Each and every time that damning evidence regarding Waldheim's lies and his activities in Hitler's armed forces was brought forward by the WJC or by others, the world's most famous Nazi-hunter was there with another 'explanation'.[1]

This text, later published in Rosenbaum's book, *Betrayal*, was apparently watered down before it was sent to Vienna. Even so, it was not published in *Ausweg*, but found its way into the Italian magazine, *Epoca*.

From Paris the Nazi-hunters, Serge and Beate Klarsfeld, saw an opportunity to sneer at Wiesenthal, insisting that 'the existence of Wiesenthal in Vienna is one of the reasons why nothing was done about Waldheim's past when he became UN Secretary-General'. And an Italian journalist, Fiamma Nierenstein, wrote that Wiesenthal had suppressed evidence in order to help Waldheim, a claim that Wiesenthal angrily rebutted as an unwarranted slur.

Wiesenthal himself, conscious that the Waldheim controversy had led to a loss of prestige among some of his admirers in the United States, wrote numerous letters, justifying his actions and claiming that the WJC had acted irresponsibly. He complained bitterly that he had been deliberately excluded from the activities of the US Holocaust Memorial Commission. He was also convinced that the WJC had intervened with the Nobel Peace Prize Committee to argue against awarding the prize to him jointly with Elie Wiesel. In a typical letter to an American acquaintance, Wiesenthal betrays his feelings in less than perfect English, noting that

> these people [a reference to WJC and Elie Wiesel] could not handle my popularity in the United States. . . . The fact that Waldheim did not say the truth and was the best-informed officer in the whole Balkans, still does not make him a criminal. . . . In the end it will be that Waldheim will resign under the pressure of the propaganda. He will become a martyr and the Jews will be the guilty ones, since everybody believes that the WJC speaks in the name of World Jewry, even as we know that is not true. . . . I have said that on the basis of the documents I have seen, Waldheim was not a Nazi. At once I was asked why I defended

Waldheim. At once the perception was such that when one wanted to correct the things that people falsely believe, it was seen as defence. . . . For forty-two years I have worked in a way I will not change now. No accusation without proof, for this way we will slide into a position where people will not believe what the criminals, the real criminals, have done to us.[2]

In the Vienna Documentation Centre's report for 1986, Wiesenthal also argued that the WJC's tactics not only went against Jewish interests, but also risked the devaluation of the whole war crimes trial process. For the WJC to call Waldheim a war criminal on the assumption that behind the lies he told about his war record they would find proof, was bad enough. To threaten Austria with ostracism if it elected Waldheim had been worse.

Collective threats are incompatible with Jewish ethics. They ignored the fact that for 2,000 years Jews had been victims of collective threats and collective accusations. . . . Anybody familiar with me knows that I only believe in individual guilt, and I share this opinion with the whole civilised world. . . . There is no justice without truth. During more than four decades of work, I have accused none if I did not have proof against him. For this attitude, I have secured my reputation, not only with the Jews, but also with the historians, the judges, the public prosecutors of many countries and in the public opinion.[3]

The five-man commission of historians from Switzerland, Britain, Belgium, West Germany and Israel, assisted by an expert from Greece, produced their Waldheim findings on 10 February 1988. The commission was given access to virtually all relevant archives. One notable exception was the OSI in Washington, which refused to turn over its own and the CIA's file on Waldheim, or any other evidence that had led to the decision to put the Austrian President on the US Watch List, excluding him from visiting the US. The historian's commission principal conclusion was that Waldheim had 'been exceptionally well-informed' and had known far more than he had ever admitted about the atrocities committed in the Balkans, but that 'he had had little practical possibility of influencing events'. He had certainly been 'involved in the process of knowledge and action', and had tried 'to let his military past pass into oblivion and, as soon as that was no longer possible, to make it harmless'.

Wiesenthal took these findings as his cue to insist that Waldheim could no longer lay claim to the moral stature required of a head of state, and demanded his resignation. Austrian Chancellor Franz Vranitzki indicated that he shared this view, and warned that he might not feel able to remain in office if Waldheim refused to go. A committee led mainly by Socialists and intellectuals, but actively supported by Wiesenthal, was now set up to campaign for Waldheim's resignation. But Waldheim played the innocent and brushed the historians' findings aside with his customary protestations of blamelessness and patriotism. There was no shred of remorse, and he accused his enemies at home and abroad of 'manipulations, lies and forgeries'.

Waldheim has never conceded that he lied. The only admission he has been prepared to make is that he had glossed over his time in the Balkans and that he had done this because his semi-invalid's status had disqualified him from front-line service. He believed that he had been fully justified in refusing to resign. 'Resignation would have been an admission of guilt. That would have disappointed my voters.' As it was, by holding 'bravely' on to office in spite of the campaign against him throughout his six-year term, 'I made it possible for an orderly succession, and the election of the new President, Thomas Klestil.' Waldheim says that he does not believe that 'Wiesenthal took a conscious decision to help me. He was wrong to accuse me of lying about my knowledge of the Jewish deportations from Salonika. But I value him, because he handled himself correctly.'[4]

In New York, the President of the WJC, Edgar Bronfman, chose to interpret the historians' findings as 'a devastating indictment' not only against Waldheim, but also against the Austrian nation, which must be further blamed for reluctance to admit responsibility for its part in the Holocaust. Waldheim was 'a liar and an unrepentant man, who was part and parcel of the Nazi killing machine. ... But the issue is not Kurt Waldheim. He is a mirror of Austria. If a nation cannot or will not admit its role, there can be no guarantee it will not repeat its crime.'

With the debate showing no signs of dying down, one of Britain's commercial TV networks, Thames Television, organised a mock Waldheim trial, a 'commission of enquiry' with a panel of five distinguished judges. Alan Ryan, the first head of the OSI, acted as chief prosecutor. During a four-hour programme edited from nine days of hearings, twenty witnesses were sharply questioned by senior lawyers. The judges' unanimous verdict, similar to the historians' commission, amounted to the conclusion that the evidence was not sufficient to accuse Waldheim of complicity in war crimes.

Britain's Ministry of Defence, which had conducted its own independent enquiry by a group of historians and retired senior civil servants into allegations that Waldheim had been involved in war crimes against British soldiers in the Balkans, again found a lack of evidence against him: 'At all material times, for the purposes of this review, the then Lt Waldheim was a mere junior staff officer. There is no evidence here of relevant delegated executive authority or of any causative, overt act or omission from which his guilt of a war crime may be inferred.'

The only authoritative investigation that came to a conclusion of criminality was undertaken by Neal Sher, in his capacity as Director of the OSI. The investigation was undertaken in response to pressure, above all from the WJC, to have Waldheim placed on the US Watch List. The OSI determined that Waldheim had ordered a long series of atrocities, but conceded that he had not personally killed or tortured anyone. It painted a classic picture of the type of war criminal that Wiesenthal depicts as 'desk murderers' – people who organised and gave the orders for atrocities, and therefore had to be considered as culpable as those who executed the policy.

Neal Sher invited Wiesenthal to send him all his information on Waldheim. This he did. He intervened on several occasions, seeking to convince the investigation that Waldheim should not be put on the Watch List. Wiesenthal felt that the OSI's views may have been coloured from the outset. He feared that the OSI personnel, even Sher, an official with whom he used to be on good terms, were far too close to Waldheim's accusers in the WJC. Eli Rosenbaum, who has since succeeded Sher as Director of the OSI, had also worked there previously. The WJC's Elan Steinberg also belonged to the close inner circle working on the Waldheim dossier. They were and remain in close touch over all matters pertaining to Waldheim and Wiesenthal, and it would be surprising if they did not share some of the pertinent information.

Sher's attitude towards Wiesenthal underwent a remarkable metamorphosis. On 11 May 1986, he had written a letter to the *Jerusalem Post* strongly defending Wiesenthal against detractors. The letter described him 'as an invaluable source of information and sound counsel' and stressed his 'lonely struggle' in 'search of evidence which would bring to light the horror caused by the Nazis and their willing collaborators'. Yet in 1990, after the confrontation over the Watch List, Sher's tone dramatically changed, and it seems as if he had become convinced that Wiesenthal was an incompetent.

Sher wrote to Wiesenthal, showing impatience over requests to investigate suspected war criminals living in the United States and was wounding in his comments:

> I can tell you that a few of your allegations have resulted in active ongoing investigations. The vast majority, however, were of little value: many 'suspects' were dead; as to others there is no record of entry into the US. .... The bottom line is that ... no allegation which has originated from your office has resulted in a court filing by the OSI.[5]

Wiesenthal had upset Sher with his insistence that the OSI's investigation on Waldheim was based on mistaken assumptions, which had led to a faulty analysis. Wiesenthal had also complained that the US investigators were judging the evidence within the narrow terms of reference of the US Watch List, and that this was not adequate to determine whether a *prima facie* case existed to bring Waldheim before a war crimes trial.

The OSI report, written in 1987, led to the decision to ban Waldheim from the US, and was used by the WJC to build up its charges against the Austrian President. Although widely circulated at the time, the OSI report was only published in full in 1994, after feelers had been put out by Waldheim to be allowed to attend the UN's fiftieth anniversary celebrations in New York. Given the OSI findings, the US would not waive its ban on Waldheim's presence on American soil.

Neither did the WJC – more specifically, Eli Rosenbaum and Elan Steinberg – want to leave the last word on Waldheim with the historians' commission, or with any of the other experts who had concluded that there was insufficient evidence for a war crimes prosecution. Rosenbaum decided to undertake more research, analyse all the available material and write his book, *Betrayal*, with its subtitle: 'The untold story of the Kurt Waldheim investigation and cover-up'. It portrays Waldheim and Wiesenthal linked as Siamese twins, and caught within a web of mutual lies and deceits.

Rosenbaum bases his indictment on the assertion that in 1979 an incompetent Wiesenthal steered the Israeli Government away from investigating Waldheim. Later, realising that he had crucially blundered, Wiesenthal camouflaged his own mistake by becoming the chief architect of the cover-up for Waldheim's wartime guilt. An added, but less decisive factor in Wiesenthal's handling of the Waldheim affair, Rosenbaum alleges, was his strong preference for Austria's ÖVP party.

While working on the book, Rosenbaum requested an interview with Wiesenthal, but was turned down. Instead he sent a lengthy questionnaire to Wiesenthal, who considered it intrusive and school examination-like, and hardly calculated to secure a helpful response. In fact, it merely served to convince Wiesenthal that Rosenbaum and his WJC friends remained consumed with a passion to destroy his reputation, and had come no closer to understanding the political forces at work in Austria.

Wiesenthal refused to submit to the Rosenbaum quiz, or even to write a detailed rebuttal of the charges that were implicit in the questions. 'A closer inspection of the questions makes it seem as if, in his upcoming book, I, as well as Kurt Waldheim, are the accused persons. Also I find most of the questions offending,' he wrote to his Washington lawyer, Martin

Mendelsohn. The main burden of his letter was to argue that the WJC had not grasped the powerful influence that Austria's former Nazis still exercised. By involving itself in the Waldheim candidacy, the WJC had become embroiled in Austrian domestic politics beyond its understanding. The letter also reiterated in the strongest terms that Wiesenthal never made accusations without conclusive proof of individual guilt; and repeated yet again that he had never seen such proof where Waldheim was concerned.

Rosenbaum pressed ahead regardless. Stumbling on an account that Wiesenthal had written of his 1979 enquiries into Waldheim's record, Rosenbaum thought that he had found the key to Wiesenthal's later behaviour. As Rosenbaum chose to read matters, Wiesenthal had erred in 1979, knew it, but could not bring himself to admit it. He no longer entertained any doubt that

> Wiesenthal's reputation as the world's all-knowing authority on Nazi criminals was now bound inextricably with Waldheim's desperate struggle to protect the secrets of his Nazi past. If Wiesenthal backtracked, or if Waldheim's pursuers succeeded independently, the Nazi-hunter would be forced to face the humiliation of having the Israelis know – or perhaps even make public – the fact that he had failed so horribly. Wiesenthal and Waldheim each had a secret, and their secrets would have to share the same destiny.[6]

He insists on depicting an equivalence of immoral behaviour in Waldheim and Wiesenthal:

> As detail after detail tumbled into the public arena, Wiesenthal was ever more hopelessly mired on the wrong side of one of the most sensational Nazi scandals of all time. But with his and Waldheim's reputation now linked forever, the man whose Congressional Gold Medal declares him 'the keeper of the flame of conscience of mankind' had defiantly begun to take one position after another that was contrary to everything he had espoused before. His bizarre conduct became fully understandable only now that I realised he was not just defending himself; he was defending Waldheim.[7]

He blames himself and others 'who knew for years that Wiesenthal was pathetically ineffective as a Nazi-hunter' for not exploding the myth much sooner: 'Our silence has dishonoured the memory of those who were murdered.' In private discussion, Rosenbaum is even more scathing, self-righteously setting about demolishing the man he once revered as 'an idol' and now insists on describing as a 'liar, who has never been able to keep his story straight' and who, 'by supporting Waldheim, played politics with the Holocaust'.

While Rosenbaum was still writing *Betrayal*, Isser Harel re-entered the public arena to denounce Wiesenthal as a charlatan. Harel had long held a grudge against Wiesenthal for highlighting his role in keeping the search for Eichmann alive in the 1950s and tracing him to Argentina. On a lecture tour in the United States in 1989, Harel became deeply upset by constant questioning on why he had failed to acknowledge Wiesenthal's contribution to the Eichmann hunt. His exasperation led him to embark on a point-by-point demolition of any and every assertion about the search for Eichmann that Wiesenthal had ever made. Harel did not find a publisher for his manuscript. But on 7 May 1991, he gave an interview to the New York correspondent of the *Jerusalem Post*, in which he insisted that Wiesenthal 'had no role whatsoever' in Eichmann's capture, that the information he had provided was 'utterly worthless' and that he had, in reality, endangered the entire Eichmann operation and aborted the planned capture of Josef Mengele.

Wiesenthal, who describes Harel as a 'sick man', limited himself to saying that he felt 'sorrowful' about his statements. But Harel's remarks, reproduced in US and European newspapers, unleashed a furious controversy and revived the old debate over the 1954 Wiesenthal–Nahum Goldmann correspondence about Eichmann. Wiesenthal's detractors used Harel as useful ammunition.

It was no accident that the Harel interview coincided with a Plenary Assembly of the WJC in Jerusalem, where Harel was being honoured for the Eichmann capture. Harel's manuscript and assertions have been discussed in an earlier chapter, but, in 1991, it seemed as if Wiesenthal's critics were trying to square the circle. Those who were demonising him for his actions in the context of the Waldheim affair, now had an ally in the shape of the former Israeli intelligence chief, who was more than happy to support the thesis that Wiesenthal had been a fraud as a Nazi-hunter. Harel could hardly be considered an objective witness. Yet the WJC had no compunction about quoting Harel's interpretation of Wiesenthal's work as authoritative comment. Rosenbaum saw it as definitive proof that Waldheim had not been a one-off, but part of a pattern of bungling and cover-ups.

Wiesenthal's friends, including Michael Elizur, Israel's Ambassador in Vienna during the Waldheim election campaign, and the Dutch Foundation for the Fight against Anti-Semitism – STIBA – sprung stoutly to his defence. Gerhart Riegner wrote one letter which appeared to acknowledge the existence of Wiesenthal's letters to Goldmann, but followed this by a retraction, which is widely assumed to have been written at the urging of the WJC.

Betrayal was finally published in 1993 and endorsed by Elie Wiesel, who described the work as 'eloquent and well documented'. He later stressed that his remarks had been directed at the book's passages on Waldheim, and not at the references to Wiesenthal. However, a majority of the reviews highlighted Rosenbaum's attacks on Wiesenthal. 'Smashing the Wiesenthal icon', 'Waldheim's and Wiesenthal's shame', 'Throwing the book at a Nazi-hunter', 'The Devil's Advocate', were among the headlines provoked by the book.

Those who questioned Rosenbaum's thesis were met with furious rejoinders. When Professor Herzstein, the WJC's erstwhile collaborator, in a review for the New York newspaper, *Newsday,* defended Wiesenthal's actions with respect to Waldheim, Rosenbaum tried to stop the article from being syndicated. The *New York Times* review of *Betrayal* also led to an angry Rosenbaum rejoinder. Professor Jacob Heilbrunn, an expert on German and European Studies, concluded that

> the gleeful and mean-spirited tone of the book's passages on Mr Wiesenthal is chilling. Mr Rosenbaum does not shrink from drawing a moral equivalence between Waldheim and Wiesenthal. ... But whatever his faults, and they are legion, Mr Wiesenthal is not a Nazi. He is a survivor of the death camps. In annulling the distinction between victims and perpetrators, Mr Rosenbaum obscures the true story of the Waldheim affair.

Rosenbaum immediately protested that, 'regrettably, the review, while allowing that Mr Wiesenthal's faults are "legion", does not address the book's numerous and exhaustively documented disclosures about Mr Wiesenthal's outrageous conduct in case after case'.

Wiesenthal is profoundly bitter in his comments about *Betrayal*. He considers the attacks against him so unwarranted and malicious as to be unforgivable. He believes that the book is a distortion of everything for which he has always stood for. It is an attack on his integrity, a quality on which he has always prided himself. As he sees it, it is a continuation of the WJC's vendetta against him. He fears that outsiders, who know little about him, might be influenced by the book.

Whatever its pretensions as an indictment against Waldheim, '*de facto,* it is a book against Simon Wiesenthal, dictated by hatred and larded with assumptions and suspicions,' Wiesenthal wrote to the Friends of the Documentation Centre.[8] In a letter to the *New York Times,* he underlined that he had not personally troubled to read *Betrayal,* but knew enough about its contents to realise that it was written with prejudice and recycled old accusations against him. He summarised and defended his investigations into Waldheim's wartime activities, and pointed out that 'The WJC finds it difficult to accept the findings of the International Commission of Historians, formed at my initiative in Vienna.' Kalman Sultanik, WJC Vice-President, fired back to the *New York Times* that Mr Wiesenthal was once again, just as with respect to Eichmann, seeking 'to conceal his failures'.

In November 1993, Wiesenthal was in the United States lecturing to university audiences, who received him with customary enthusiasm, and meeting with a wide range of friends, who went out of their way to show that their judgment was in no way affected by Rosenbaum's charges. He comforted himself with the thought that those who knew his true worth would not be influenced by the adverse comment; while those who listened to Rosenbaum had probably been prejudiced against him all along. The confrontation between Wiesenthal and Rosenbaum had become so prominent that the popular talk-show host, Larry King, invited both men to appear on his programme; but Wiesenthal turned down a face-to-face meeting with his antagonist, and agreed to take part in the show only on condition that the interviews were conducted separately. Larry King agreed. Inevitably both men repeated their well-rehearsed arguments, but Wiesenthal persuaded himself that he had scored a victory.

In any event, back in Vienna, he found to his gratification that his reputation had risen to an all-time high. The political classes as well as grassroots opinion felt that Wiesenthal had earned his laurels with his handling of the Waldheim affair. He had acted with understanding, as a patriot. President Klestil awarded him one of the country's highest decorations, the first of many new honours to come his way; Socialist Chancellor Vranitzki led the chorus of worldwide congratulations on his eighty-fifth birthday. And, crowning a lifetime of achievement, shortly before Wiesenthal's eighty-seventh birthday, the Vienna City Council overwhelmingly voted to make Wiesenthal an *Ehrenbürger* – an honorary citizen – a high honour, awarded only to a handful of people. Only the far-right FPÖ voted against the move. Wiesenthal was relieved, feeling that the FPÖ's opposition gave the award maximum legitimacy.

More pleasing than any personal gestures towards him, Wiesenthal considered that his most worthwhile award came at the moment in 1994 when Vranitzki satisfied one of his most hard-fought-for endeavours: the Austrian Chancellor declared that he was at last prepared to lead the Austrian nation to accept that it must share responsibility for the Holocaust. He told the world that Austria could no longer hide behind the claim that it had itself been a victim nation. In a private letter to Wiesenthal, Chancellor Vranitzki referred 'to the numerous useful discussions with him, which 'had contributed' to the Government's new posture, and to the formulation of his government's declaration on Austria's Nazi links.

Wiesenthal had urged for close on fifty years that Austria must come to terms with the past. Better now than never. But he will believe for the rest of his days that Austria would have been shamed into admitting its true complicity in Hitler's 'Ostmark' much sooner if it had not been pushed on to the defensive by the WJC's Waldheim campaign.

[24]
Fifty Years On

It is late evening, 26 April 1995. The scene is Vienna's Heldenplatz (Hero's Square), the parade-ground outside the Hofburg, and witness to many of the great historic events in the life of the Austrian nation. There is a punishing downpour, drenching the many thousands of people who have come here to celebrate the fiftieth anniversary of Austria's second republic, the country's liberation and subsequent renewal after eight years as Nazi Germany's *Ostmark*. On the balcony where Hapsburg emperors, and Adolf Hitler, have waved down to enthusiastic crowds, stands an old man, an umbrella protectively held over his balding head. It is Simon Wiesenthal.

In strong and steady voice, he makes a brief speech, not more than a minute or two, and distils the conclusions of a long lifetime's battle into a Utopian vision of a world 'without dictators and without ideologies', dominated only by a commitment to human rights and individual liberty:

> During the Nazi period, I saw young people, who betrayed their conscience and performed unimaginable cruelties. They were drugged into believing that 'The *Führer*' – Hitler – was thinking on their behalf, and all they had to do was to follow his orders.
>
> But after our terrible experiences, all mankind must adopt one guiding principle: no individual must ever again allow his or her conscience to be twisted or misused by any movement, any party, or any one person. . . . By recalling the liberation fifty years ago, and the Nazi era, the new generations will come closer to realisation of the human rights ideal.

This receives thunderous applause; he has struck a deep and responsive chord. The whole evening's proceedings are televised. Afterwards, Wiesenthal is told that his ovation was longer than any other speaker's. Not even in his wildest dreams had he imagined that one day, an Austrian Government would invite him to speak in the same place where, in 1938, Hitler had surveyed his cheering new vassals; or that an Austrian crowd, composed in

313

the main of young people, would show him so much respect. How far he has travelled; not only in time and place, but in public esteem. It raises his spirits, but he also thinks that he is receiving no more than what has long been overdue.

Wiesenthal has never been deeply introspective. He is a passionate man in search of justice, who lives by his emotions as much as by brain and calculation. Fifty years after the war and after his liberation from Mauthausen, the eighty-six-year-old Wiesenthal might have been tempted into a searching assessment of his achievements. But this has never been his way, and now, in old age, he prefers the absolutes: at one extreme, to revel hugely in the medals, the titles and the doctorates, the recognition and the esteem he is earning; at the other extreme, either to accuse his detractors of malice or else to dismiss them as unstable and blindly prejudiced. By this simple accounting, he is confident that history will be on his side, marking him out as a doughty fighter for justice who has paid his dues to the millions of victims of the Holocaust.

He is less sure about the magnitude and durability of his achievement beyond his own lifetime. He likes to think that his constant stress on the need to hold mass murderers to account has made a significant contribution to the growing acceptance of war crimes trials as a way of protecting a universal code of human rights. But in his heart of hearts he recognises, however reluctantly, that much will depend on how the two Rabbis, Hier and Cooper, at the Wiesenthal Center in Los Angeles will handle his legend and his legacy.

A Jewish hero? A moralist who gives human dimensions to the great issues of our times? A messenger to future generations? A footnote to history? A human rights fighter? A populist philosopher? A man of unswerving principle? A visionary trapped in a tunnel? A politically conservative activist? A Nazi-hunter? A sleuth? A writer? An intellectual? A charismatic personality? A great communicator? An obsessive outsider? A walking, talking, breathing computer? An uncomfortable conscience? An egomaniac? A Don Quixote? An avenging angel? A manipulator? A liar? A hypocrite?

All these and endless more questions recur in any discussion of Simon Wiesenthal's life and meaning. He could be any one of these manifestations, or a jumble of several. For some, he can do no wrong; he is the personification of integrity and trustworthiness. For others, everything about Wiesenthal is bogus; to them he is an egomaniac who has lost sight of honesty and straightforward action. On the whole, people who dismiss him tend to be incapable of recognising any positive qualities in him; while those who value him as an outstanding achiever perceive Wiesenthal as very much a human being with inevitable failings as well as great virtues.

Academics with a focus on Holocaust issues fall in various degrees between these two extremes: Wiesenthal is not widely perceived as an intellectual, and there is a reluctance to accept his writings, even *The Sunflower*, as major contributions to Holocaust literature. This has led some members of the intellectual community to underestimate the significance of Wiesenthal's activism and the moral tenets that drove him on.

A notable exception is former German President, Richard von Weizsäcker, who has long preached that 'those who are blind to the past cannot see the future'. As a leader who successfully combined politics and academia, he has always been deeply preoccupied with the German people's struggle to come to terms with the Holocaust. Von Weizsäcker describes Wiesenthal as a singularly important phenomenon, even perhaps a lodestar. Though the two men have only met fleetingly, von Weizsäcker thinks of Wiesenthal as a kindred spirit. Comparisons about 'ownership' of the Holocaust are invidious. Even so it is striking that von Weizsäcker believes that he has understood more about the Holocaust from Wiesenthal's way of applying his personal experiences to wrestle with the past than from Elie Wiesel's searching questions and abstractions about the nature of evil.

'Wiesenthal challenged established ethical concepts, and addressed the issues of memory, guilt and forgiveness as they relate to the Holocaust with a singular intensity that few others have matched,' von Weizsäcker says. Both men reject the argument that memory and guilt are two sides of the same coin, so that the past can be forgotten once the sin has been absolved. Memory must always be kept alive, and related to the present and to the future.

Chancellor Helmut Kohl, who otherwise has little in common with von Weizsäcker, also says that Wiesenthal has illuminated his understanding of the Holocaust in a particularly meaningful way. They seem an unlikely pair to have become close personal friends. Yet Kohl affirms that 'the chemistry between us worked from the beginning'. They meet at least once a year for extensive brainstorming sessions and telephone frequently. 'He is an historic figure, a great man of passion and for justice, open-minded and without built-in prejudices. But he is also a genuinely modest person.' Kohl, whose enjoyment of good food is self-evident, also warms to Wiesenthal as a person who possesses the wholly admirable quality of love for culinary excellence.

Swanee Hunt, the Clinton administration's Ambassador to Austria, has understood better than many scholars that Wiesenthal is driven by an instinct that is more powerful than any calculated application of carefully defined moral principle. The Wiesenthal phenomenon can only be defined as 'raw goodness crushing raw evil', with Wiesenthal himself 'stumbling into circumstances of greatness'.

Rabbi Albert Friedlander, who has written extensively on Judaism and Jewish history, also seizes on Wiesenthal's instinctive integrity. He speaks of Wiesenthal as 'a moralist and a fanatic for justice – a troubler of humanity, of institutions and of consciences'. While scholars might dismiss Wiesenthal for being outside the circle of Jewish intellectuals, he deserves to be credited with the all-important fact that he has acted in the Socratic tradition and has posed the enduring question whether a just society can be allowed to forget evil. Friedlander feels

> compassion for Wiesenthal, because the life he has led was his response to the experience of the concentration camps. Others might have walked away. But he has brought the camps with him and carried them all his life. His message is not to forget and to be just. It is hard to be such a messenger, because you are alienated from those who want to forget.

Professor David Cesarani, former head of the Wiener Library in London, now at Manchester University, and a close student of the denazification process and of war crimes trials, is more dubious about Wiesenthal's credentials as a major Holocaust figure. He argues that Wiesenthal 'has become a peg on which the world can hang its conscience, because the world always needs figures of great certainty'. Yet he considers him parochial, narrowly focused, deliberately working in small offices with few staff, 'in a kind of spider's web and leading a cramped life. It's as if he is constantly hitting against a brick-wall.'

Professor Robert Wistrich of the Hebrew University in Jerusalem is another prolific author on Holocaust-related matters and an expert on Central Europe. He has first-hand knowledge of Wiesenthal's working methods and portrays him as a memory bank, as a man driven to use his own life to illuminate remembrance, justice, Jewish history. 'In his roughshod way, he represents integrity.'

While researching Wiesenthal's life, I had my first encounters with Wiesenthal's confirmed detractors. There were two kinds. Among retired diplomats, there are those who dealt with Wiesenthal in the displaced-persons camps in the immediate post-war period, but could never quite bring themselves to trust him, partly because they suspected his politics, but also because they felt uneasy with his personality. Among the Nazi-hunters, there were Isser Harel, who passionately insists that Wiesenthal is a thorough fraud, and Tuviah Friedman, who considers himself betrayed by Wiesenthal.

The extreme reactions to Wiesenthal were never more apparent than in the United States. To his lawyer, Martin Rosen, he is, warts and all, quite simply a great man. Elan Steinberg of the WJC and Eli Rosenbaum, author of *Betrayal*, portray Wiesenthal as an individual who has often subverted the truth and has betrayed the victims of the Holocaust.

I had few preconceptions about Wiesenthal when I began to map out his life. Now that I have come to know him, I recognise that he is not without his faults. But I have become convinced that he is a man of deep and genuine integrity. This places me firmly in the pro-Wiesenthal camp.

It would be absurd not to question the wisdom of some of Wiesenthal's actions – undoubtedly there have been glaring mistakes, occasional distortions of memory and displays of quite irrational cussedness. It would be equally foolish to ignore Wiesenthal's weaknesses, especially his need for approbation and the blind spots in his thought processes. Single-mindedness can easily lead to obstinacy, and this undoubtedly clouded Wiesenthal's judgment at crucial times in his life, most notably in his long-drawn-out battle with Bruno Kreisky, in his attitude to the WJC and his handling of the Waldheim affair.

Wiesenthal's seeming ability to recall the whole film of his life in minute detail is singularly impressive. That is why it is at the very least puzzling to find accounts of his war years that differed in certain aspects from the way he told it later, and that there are omissions in his earlier versions, such as the important *Sunflower* saga, which he afterwards described as seminal experiences.

It is obvious from all that is known about Holocaust survivors, as I pointed out in an earlier chapter, that memory plays exceptional tricks on men and women who have suffered so much, and Wiesenthal is no exception. Some experiences have a symbolic importance out of all proportion to what may really have taken place, and are distorted, glorified, in their remembrance. Others may be glossed over as they recede from the actual events. But in its essence, Wiesenthal's story has remained unaltered, and I am fully convinced that all the attempts to blacken Wiesenthal's good name by hints of wartime collaboration with the Gestapo, or with the Communists, were smear campaigns orchestrated from Warsaw Pact countries and, when it suited, taken up by Wiesenthal's critics, including Bruno Kreisky. Indeed, the more I have talked with Wiesenthal, observed him and learned about him, the more I have become convinced of his honesty and commitment.

In my encounters with people who have known Wiesenthal from far and near, one common denominator emerged: the fact that he regularly provokes strong reactions. This is understandable to the extent that he is a forceful personality operating in a deeply disturbing sphere of human experience and suffering. But to demonise or to trivialise him merely betrays a lack of will to understand him or to evaluate his importance. Some of Wiesenthal's most fervent admirers, however, are not much less misleading when they portray him as the James Bond among Nazi-hunters.

The image created by films such as *The Odessa File* romanticises him to excess. It is obvious that he takes great delight from some of these portrayals; but they are distortions, which can and do lead to sterile and often acrimonious arguments about Wiesenthal's true role in tracing Eichmann or Mengele, or any of the other war criminals with whom his name is associated.

His sleuthing was never on the grand scale. He can store a phenomenal range of information in his memory bank and is expert at reading and interpreting Nazi records, and deducing clues to the whereabouts of his quarries. However, there was only a brief period in the early aftermath of the war when Wiesenthal, working with the Americans, was a fieldworker, fanning out with them and directly engaged in Nazi-hunting operations. And yes, he tried to track Eichmann in Austria, working with the local police; but he never went to South America, where so many of the Nazis he sought had fled, and he never attempted to set up his own network of investigators in search of war criminals. Instead, he relied on his own powers of deduction, his data, his memory and the co-operation of friends in far-off places.

Though he likes to claim that he simply lacked the funds for bigger operations, it is fair to say that this serves more as a convenient excuse than as justification. Even if Wiesenthal had had the means, he would have lacked the ambition to set up sophisticated machinery for detective work.

Wiesenthal's true worth is simple enough yet extends far beyond the scope and efficacy of his Nazi-hunting. His singular achievement has been to force political leaders and public opinion alike to confront the memory of the Holocaust as a means of cleansing the moral fabric of present and future generations. Idiosyncratic and individualistic, he has by turns bullied, cajoled and massaged; but he has never veered from his conviction that an essential part of the process of coming to terms with the Holocaust is to catch the mass murderers and give them fair trials. The Holocaust's poison would only spread deeper if society allowed itself to take the law into its own hands. He deserves credit for the fact that public opinion has become so receptive to the establishment of tribunals for war crimes in Bosnia and

Rwanda, and to the growing public pressure for some kind of UN permanent machinery to bring mass murderers to justice.

There are three key aspects to Wiesenthal's struggles. First, there is his sense of mission, honed by his wartime experiences, and reinforced by an innate romanticism, which convinced him that his survival could only be justified by dedicating himself to keeping alive the memory of the victims. Second, standing virtually alone during the 1950s and part of the 1960s, he nevertheless managed to keep alive the pressure to bring the Nazi criminals to justice at a moment in history when the Western allies, preoccupied by the Cold War, had put the lid on war crimes trials and had no desire to reopen this aspect of the post-war agenda. Moreover without him, an Israeli state, which was more interested in consolidating its security, might never have been shamed into capturing Eichmann in Argentina and putting him on trial in Jerusalem. These are achievements that have surely guaranteed lasting stature.

Third, there is Wiesenthal the charismatic communicator. His ability to use the media to further his own ends is out of the ordinary. It hugely multiplies his impact. As I pieced together the episodes of Wiesenthal's life since he opened his Vienna Documentation Centre in 1961, I was struck time and again by his extraordinarily effective use of press and television, and even of novelists like Frederick Forsyth. He possesses an instinctive ability to dramatise the points he seeks to make and give them tangible human dimensions. He recognises the need to target and cultivate journalists, and his sense of timing has often been exquisite. That is how he secured such high name recognition, and how, for example, he helped to smoke out people like Hermine Braunsteiner and Eduard Roschmann, or to campaign for the extradition of war criminals from Latin America and the United States. But he is more than a good showman. He has been able to establish himself as a moral leader. He would never have come very far if he had not been so convinced of his cause, and not been able to impress others with his unswerving commitment to justice coupled with a determination to reject vengeance as a motor for disposing of mass murderers.

Wiesenthal's ability to communicate goes beyond his links with the media. Most of his books have been written to attract support and understanding for his fight to sustain the memory of the Holocaust, and he has always known how to illustrate his thesis with vivid accounts from personal experience. He has made himself an agile and effective political lobbyist – as his campaigns against the statutes of limitations have shown. He has taught himself to be a good lecturer capable of holding the attention of varied audiences. But I have found nothing more moving than to observe Wiesenthal with children listening raptly as he tells them how he found and identified the policeman who arrested Anne Frank, and speaking to them of his hopes and fears for the future – teenagers and an old man together, identifying with each other, instinctively trusting each other.

A missionary, a campaigner, a communicator: this is the context for evaluating the three great controversies – Eichmann, Kreisky and Waldheim – that will swirl around Wiesenthal to the end of his days.

Wiesenthal's compulsive need to establish that Eichmann was alive, and then to find him and have him brought to trial, is self-evident from his own published accounts and from the way he has continued to speak of him decades after his execution. Justly, I am convinced, Wiesenthal has always insisted that his initiatives in the late 1940s and early 1950s proved crucial in preventing Eichmann from being declared dead and thus halting the search. I also have no doubt that, by a quirk of circumstance, Wiesenthal knew as early as 1954 that Eichmann was in Argentina, and that the information he had assembled about Eichmann was sent to Nahum Goldmann, President of the WJC. Why the WJC denies the existence of this correspondence, of which there are copies elsewhere, is a mystery, and is bound to reinforce my impression that the WJC is motivated by deep animosity against Wiesenthal.

Wiesenthal has never claimed that he had anything at all to do with Eichmann's capture by Israel's Mossad in 1960. His book, *I Hunted Eichmann*, is only concerned with the years up to 1954; and though it undoubtedly distorts – and romanticises – some of Wiesenthal's initiatives in Austria, its theme throughout is that he merely kept the flame alive for others to pick up. But, of course, he was less experienced in dealing with the media in 1961 than he became later; and was probably overly impressed by the warm reception he was given in Jerusalem during the Eichmann trial. While he was free in 1961 to talk about his Eichmann sleuthing, the Israeli Government forced the Mossad operatives to maintain closed lips until 1975. By the time Isser Harel was allowed to give his own account, he had, for reasons that had little to do with the Eichmann case, become a sad and lonely figure, bearing grudges against life itself.

Harel's unpublished diatribe against Wiesenthal has convinced me that he is wide of the mark, and is an unreliable witness to the events described in Wiesenthal's Eichmann book. It is arguable that the book's title, *I Hunted Eichmann*, can be construed as mildly misleading; and also that at the time of its publication Wiesenthal did little to dispel the impression that he had been hunter right up to the climax, and not, as the book itself explains, only one of the early runners.

But in retrospect, even that hype can be seen to have been employed in a good cause. The book after all, became his first passport to fame; it enabled him to launch the Vienna Documentation Centre and to develop his crusade against Holocaust forgetfulness. In later years, Wiesenthal became much more careful to underline his limited – though emphatically crucial – role in bringing Eichmann to justice.

Between Wiesenthal and Kreisky there was a ready-made inflammatory brew of two different schools of Jewish tradition. But above all, their battles have to be judged in the context of Austria's chequered political history between the two world wars and during the Nazi era, and the country's post-war reluctance to submit itself to a thoroughgoing denazification process and to abandon the myth of having been Hitler's first victim and not his willing ally. Wiesenthal felt that Austria was beyond redemption when he realised that Austria's Socialist party, and Bruno Kreisky in particular, dallied with former Nazis, helping them back to political respectability and power. It confirmed his long-standing suspicions that, for virtually their entire history, Austria's Socialists had been unprincipled in their attitude to Fascism. His hypercritical attitude towards the SPÖ went deeper: notwithstanding his denials, it is obvious that Wiesenthal's political conservatism, apparent since his student days, influenced his attitude towards the governments of post-war Austria and Germany. Nothing illustrates this better than Wiesenthal's tolerant attitude when Christian Democrat Chancellor Adenauer appointed former Nazis to positions of influence in his governments.

Both Wiesenthal and Kreisky acted with dangerous irrationality in their mutual attacks. Kreisky was irresponsible and unjust in using Communist propaganda against Wiesenthal to smear him as a Gestapo collaborator. Wiesenthal, for his part, was off-balance and lost sight of his precept, 'Justice Not Vengeance', in the way he handled himself in his allegations that Friedrich Peter, the leader of the FPÖ, had been on active service with an SS killer brigade. Perhaps it is a mitigating circumstance that Wiesenthal's venom was directed less against the person of Peter himself than against Kreisky because of his readiness to work with Peter's far-right FPÖ.

The fight between Wiesenthal and Kreisky ended only with the latter's death. They had become used to hating each other and could not let go. Throughout the whole sorry saga, Wiesenthal exploited his media connections to the full. To some extent it distracted him from more important work. Certainly it hardened his prejudice against the SPÖ, so that when the SPÖ's footprints were detected on the eruption of charges against Kurt Waldheim in 1986, Wiesenthal was already conditioned to interpret it as yet another case of Socialist duplicity. As he saw it, their wrongdoing was compounded by the fact that they had turned to his arch-enemy, the WJC, to aid and abet them in their attempts to discredit Waldheim and prevent his election.

This does not mean that Wiesenthal obstinately set his face against any possibility that Waldheim had been a war criminal. But it certainly made him far more determined to look at every nook and cranny of Waldheim's wartime record before deciding whether there was conclusive evidence against him. He insists that Waldheim's political affiliation would never have made a difference to the way he conducted his research; but there will always be the tantalising question whether Wiesenthal would have adopted a less purist or less uncompromising approach if the SPÖ and the WJC had not been involved, or if Waldheim had been the Socialist Party's candidate when the allegations were first levelled against him.

In any event, Wiesenthal was surely wholly justified in arguing that the WJC's intervention in Austria's election campaign was ill-judged because it was bound to trigger a new wave of anti-Semitism and also strengthen the FPÖ. Jörg Haider, the current leader of the Freedom Party – whose liberal wing deserted him to found a new party – is a far more formidable politician than Friedrich Peter or any of his predecessors at the head of the FPÖ. Haider's xenophobic nationalism is widely feared as a threat to the comfortable fabric of Austria's post-war democracy. It is impossible to quantify how much Haider's emergence and popularity owes to the anti-Waldheim campaign, but it is accepted wisdom in Austria that it was a contributory factor.

It is beyond dispute that Wiesenthal's behaviour throughout the Waldheim saga – from his refusal to accuse without proof to his call on Waldheim to accept the consequences of his lies and resign the Presidency – combined to increase his stature in Austria and extend the circle of his admirers for the first time to the political left. This did give him satisfaction. Yet, not even Chancellor Vranitzki's actions in admitting Austria's complicity during the war, and honouring Wiesenthal's personal achievements, have been able to dissipate in their entirety the unease that Wiesenthal feels towards the SPÖ.

In the United States, Wiesenthal's refusal to accuse Waldheim of war crimes has blemished his reputation. It may also have led to his failure to secure the Nobel Peace Prize. These are deep disappointments to a man who never sought material wealth, but always yearned for recognition and loves the accolades that modern society confers on its heroes.

They are disappointments he did not deserve. He may have erred with

Waldheim by over-scrupulousness, but he did behave honourably through-out. Judged by his lifetime's record, the Nobel Peace Prize would have been well-earned. Even without it, Wiesenthal will surely be remembered, as he would have wished, as a man who dedicated his life to the victims of Hitler's Final Solution and gave his all to create a memory bank of the Holocaust's ravages that will act as a forewarning to new generations. There is surely a direct link between Wiesenthal's unremitting drive to bring the perpetrators of the Holocaust to justice and the growing acceptance that contemporary manifestations of genocide must be countered by the establishment of war crimes tribunal machinery.

Wiesenthal has been an exemplar, and yes, it has been a hero's life: not just a Jewish hero's, but a hero of our epoch.

Notes

Unless otherwise stated, the quotations from Wiesenthal are taken from the author's numerous conversations with him.

1: Poland 1994 – A Survivor's Return
1. Pery Broad, *KZ Auschwitz: Reminiscences of Pery Broad, an SS Man in the Auschwitz Concentration Camp, p. 71*

8: The Search for Eichmann Begins
1. *The Murderers Amongst Us*, p. 99
2. *Ibid.*, p. 100
3. Interview with Eric Silver, 26 May 1994
4. *Ibid.*

9: Eichmann Escapes to Argentina
1. *Meine Suche nach Eichmann* (1960), p. 8, Wiesenthal archive
2. *I Hunted Eichmann*, p. 43
3. *Meine Suche nach Eichmann*, p. 9
4. *The Murderers Amongst Us*, p. 123

10: Six Years in the Margins
1. Interviews with the author, 1993 and 1994
2. Telephone interview with the author, 14 November 1995
3. *The Murderers Amongst Us*, p. 124
4. Interview with Eric Silver, 1 March 1995
5. Letter from Wiesenthal to Dr S. Roth of the WJC, 12 June 1962
6. Telephone interview with the author, 14 November 1995
7. Interview with the author, May 1994 and November 1995

11: Wiesenthal Moves to Vienna
1. Robert Knight (ed.), *Die Wortprotokolle der Österreichischen Bundesregierung von 1945–52 über die Entschädigung der Juden*
2. Franz Olah, *Die Erinnerungen*, pp. 232–60

12: 'Moral Duties Have No Terms'
1. Interview with the author, 8 December 1994
2. Richard A. Stein, *Documents Against Words* (published under the auspices of STIBA, 1992)
3. Interview with the author, 22 November 1994

13: The Sleuth at Work
1. *Daily Express*, 23 December 1970
2. Efraim Zuroff, *Occupation – Nazi-Hunter*, p. 124
3. Documentation Centre's Annual Report, 31 January 1986
4. Interviews with the author, April 1994 and November 1995
5. Interview with the author, November 1995
6. Lucette Matalon-Lagnado and Sheila Cohn Dekel, *Die Zwillinge des Dr Mengele*, p. 211
7. Zuroff, *op. cit.*, pp. 123–43
8. *Der Spiegel*, 22 July 1991
9. Letter from Wiesenthal to Dr Oscar Karbach of the WJC, 24 April 1961

10. *Jüdische Lebenswege* (Fischer Verlag, Frankfurt-am-Main, 1992), p. 107; 'Witnesses of the Century': interviews with Nahum Goldmann, Simon Wiesenthal and H. G. Adler, first broadcast on German radio (ZDF)

14: The Two R's
1. *The Murderers Amongst Us*, p. 249

15: Attack and Counter-Attack
1. *Verjährung-Nein*, p. 8
2. '*Die Gleiche Sprache – Erst Hitler, dann Ulbricht*' (Rolf Vogel, Berlin, 1969), p. 5
3. Gunther Bohnsack and Herbert Brehmer, *Irreführung* (Carlsen)
4. '*Simon Wiesenthal ging den Weg der Espionage und des Verrats*', in Wiesenthal's Stasi file
5. Stanislaw Stratynski, 'The Two Faces of Simon Wiesenthal', in Wiesenthal's Stasi file
6. 'More about Wiesenthal's network', *Zycie Lieracke*, 25 October 1970
7. 'Polish emigrants in Wiesenthal's network', *Zycie Lieracke*, 18 October 1970

16: Of Books and Films and Fame
1. Interview with the author, February 1994

18: The Human Rights Champion
1. *Justice Not Vengeance*, p. 195
2. Katie Marton, *Wallenberg*, p. 208
3. *Justice Not Vengeance*, p. 199
4. Interview with the author, 18 March 1994

19: 1970: The Start of the Kreisky Wars
1. *Jüdische Lebenswege*, p. 99
2. Kreisky letter, 23 June 1938
3. US Congressional Record, 14 August 1970
4. *Justice Not Vengeance*, p. 299
5. Letter to *Verband demokratischer Wiederstandskämpfer und Verfolgter* (Union of Democratic Resistance Fighters and the Persecuted), Landverband Schleswig-Holstein, 24 August 1970

6. Letter to the *Federation Mondial des Resistants et des Deportes Juifs* (World Federation of Resistance Fighters and Jewish Deportees), Tel Aviv, 3 August 1970
7. Heinz Fischer, *Die Kreisky Jahre 1967–83*, p. 81

20: The Peter Affair – and Beyond
1. Interview with the author, October 1995
2. *Die Presse*, 4 December 1975
3. Transcript of Kreisky press conference, 11 November 1975
4. Wiesenthal letter to Professor Sijes, 9 December 1975
5. *Der Spiegel*, 24 November 1975
6. *Die Presse*, 2 April 1981
7. Wiesenthal letter to Peter Kreisky, 14 April 1981
8. *Justice Not Vengeance*, p. 299
9. Fischer, *op. cit.*, p. 147
10. *Ibid.*
11. *Justice Not Vengeance*, p. 302
12. *Ibid.*, p. 303
13. Kreisky papers filed with the courts, 24 March 1987
14. Letter from Dr Hans Perner to Wiesenthal, 27 March 1987

22: Waldheim – The Poisoned Chalice
1. Interview with the author, 19 November 1994
2. Interview with the author, 2 February 1994
3. 'In the Matter of Kurt Waldheim', Office of Special Investigations, 9 April 1987
4. Letter from Professor Herzstein to Wiesenthal, 17 September 1987
5. Brian Urquhart, *A Life in Peace and War*, p. 227
6. Eli Rosenbaum, with William Hoffer, *Betrayal*, p. 2
7. Leon Zelman, *Ein Leben nach dem Überleben*, p. 195
8. Robert Herzstein, *Waldheim: The Missing Years*, p. 246
9. Letter from Wiesenthal to Rabbi Hier, 29 June 1987
10. *Justice Not Vengeance*, p. 319

23: The WJC's Siamese Twins

1. Rosenbaum, *op. cit.*, p. 300
2. Letter from Wiesenthal to Leon Wells, 22 May 1987
3. Documentation Centre Annual Report, 31 January 1987
4. Interview with the author, March 1994
5. Letter from Neal Sher to Wiesenthal, 18 April 1990
6. Rosenbaum, *op. cit.*, p. 462
7. *Ibid.*
8. Documentation Centre Annual Report, 31 January 1994

Sources and Bibliography

As befits the biography of a living person, Simon Wiesenthal has been a prime source for much of the material in this book. I have quoted from many hours of conversations with him over a period of almost three years from 1992 to 1995. Where relevant, I have also quoted from his books – notably *I Hunted Eichmann, The Murderers Amongst Us, The Sunflower* and *Justice Not Vengeance* – from his speeches and from the annual reports of Wiesenthal's Documentation Centre in Vienna.

I have also had access to Wiesenthal's files and correspondence, to an oral history that Wiesenthal dictated in 1961 for the archives of Yad Vashem, to the Wiesenthal file assembled by the US Counterintelligence Corps, and to papers that have emerged from the archives of the former GDR's Stasi file on Wiesenthal. Other unpublished material, on which I have been able to draw, includes Isser Harel's manuscript on Wiesenthal's handling of the Eichmann case, Zvi Aharoni's manuscript on the capture of Adolf Eichmann and the search for Josef Mengele, and the third, still unpublished volume of Bruno Kreisky's *Memoirs*.

The Austrian weekly *Profil* has been a mine of contemporary information on the chequered history of Wiesenthal's relations with Bruno Kreisky and with Kurt Waldheim. Articles, notably those by Dr Oliver Rathkolb, in learned journals, together with newspaper cuttings from around the world, provided additional source material for the whole range of Wiesenthal's activities.

It would have been impossible to write Wiesenthal's story, or assess his significance, without the opportunity to interview those who have come into contact with him, and others who hold strong views about him, even if they do not know him personally. Many of those who agreed to be interviewed have already been named in the acknowledgments at the beginning of this book.

The list of books that have a bearing on Wiesenthal's background and his life is long; below are those that proved most helpful.

BOOKS BY SIMON WIESENTHAL

(Author's note: German and English versions are listed separately, but most of Wiesenthal's books have also been published in other languages.)

1946 — *KZ Mauthausen* (Ibis Verlag, Linz)
1947 — *Gross-Mufti: Grossagent der Achse* (Ried Verlag, Salzburg)
1961 — *Ich Jagte Eichmann* (Bertelsman, Gütersloh, Germany)
1965 — *Verjährung-Nein* (Europäische Verlagsanstalt, Frankfurt-am-Main)
1967 — *The Murderers Amongst Us* (McGraw-Hill, New York)
     — *Doch Die Mörderer leben* (Drömer-Knaur Verlag, Munich)
1969 — *Die Sonnenblume* (Opera Mundi, Paris)
     — '*Judenhetze in Polen*' (Rolph Vogel, Bonn)
1970 — *The Sunflower* (Schocken Books, New York)
1971 — *Segel der Hoffnung* (Walter Verlag, Olten, Switzerland)
1975 — *Krystyna: Die Tragödie des Polnischen Wiederstands* (Ullstein, Berlin)
1981 — *Max und Helen* (Ullstein, Berlin)
1982 — *Max and Helen* (William Morrow & Co., New York)
1984 — *Segel der Hoffnung* (revised version — Bleicher Verlag, Gerlingen, Germany)
1986 — *Livre de la memoire Juive* (Laffont, Paris)
1988 — *Jeder Tag ein Gedenktag* (Bleicher Verlag, Gerlingen, Germany)
     — *Recht nicht Rache* (Ullstein, Berlin)
1989 — *Justice Not Vengeance* (Weidenfeld & Nicolson, London)
1990 — *Jeder Tag ein Gedenktag* (Ullstein, Berlin)
     — *Flucht vor dem Schicksal* (Ullstein, Berlin)
1991 — *Sails of Hope* (Robert Laffont, Paris)
     — *Segel der Hoffnung* (2nd version — Ullstein, Berlin)
1995 — *Denn sie wussten was sie tun — Zeichnungen von KZ Mauthausen* (reissue of 1946 *KZ Mauthausen* — Deuticke, Vienna)
Bulletins of the Documentation Centre, 1961–95

Amerungen, Martin von, *Kreisky und seine unbewältigte Gegenwart* (Styria Verlag, Graz, 1977)
Arendt, Hannah, *Eichmann in Jerusalem* (Viking, New York, 1965)
Aridjis, Homero, '*1492*' (André Deutsch, London, 1992)
Ariel, Ehud, *Open the Gates* (Weidenfeld & Nicolson, London, 1975)
Bark, Dennis L., and Gress, David R., *A History of West Germany* (Basil Blackwell, Oxford, 1989)
Bauer, Yehuda, *Flight and Rescue: Brichah* (Random House, New York, 1970)

Beckermann, Ruth, *Die Mazze Insel, Juden der Wiener Leopoldstadt* (Löcker Verlag, Vienna, 1984)

Bedford, Sybille, *As It Was (Auschwitz Trial)* (Sinclair-Stevenson, London, 1990)

Beller, Stephen, *Vienna and the Jews, 1867–1938* (Cambridge University Press, Cambridge, 1989)

Berenbaum, Michael, *The World Must Know* (Little, Brown & Co., Boston, 1993)

Bierman, John, *Righteous Gentile: The Story of Raoul Wallenberg* (Viking, New York, 1981)

Bigley, Louis, *War-time Lies* (Picador, London, 1992)

Black, Ian, and Morris, Benny, *Israel's Secret Wars* (Hamish Hamilton, London, 1991)

Blum, Howard, *The Search for Nazis in the US* (Quadrangle/NY Times Publishing Co., New York, 1977)

Blumenau, Ralph, *A History of the Jews in German-Speaking Lands* (University of the Third Age, London, 1995)

Bolchover, Richard, *British Jewry and the Holocaust* (Cambridge University Press, Cambridge, 1993)

Bower, Tom, *Blind Eye to Murder* (André Deutsch, London, 1981)

Bower, Tom, *Klaus Barbie* (Michael Joseph, London, 1984)

Bower, Tom, *The Paperclip Conspiracy* (Michael Joseph, London, 1987)

Brix, Emil, *Simon Wiesenthal in Polen, Ein Weg* (Österreichisches General-Konsulat, Cracow, 1995)

Broad, Pery, *KZ Auschwitz: Reminiscences of Pery Broad, an SS Man in the Auschwitz Concentration Camp* (Panstwowe Museum, Oswiecim [Auschwitz], Poland, 1965)

Buber, Martin, *Zwiesprache* (Schocken Verlag, Berlin, 1932)

Buber, Martin, *Erzählungen von Engeln, Geistern und Demonen* (Schocken Verlag, Berlin, 1932) ·

Buber, Martin, *Erzählungen vom Hassidim* (Manesse, Zurich, 1949)

Bullock, Alan, *Hitler and Stalin* (HarperCollins, London, 1991)

Cantor, Norman, *The Sacred Chain* (HarperCollins, London, 1995)

Cesarani, David, *Justice Delayed* (William Heinemann, London, 1992)

Clare, George, *Last Waltz in Vienna* (Macmillan, London, 1981)

Dohrn, Verena, *Reise nach Galizien* (Fischer Verlag, Frankfurt-am-Main, 1991)

Fischer, Heinz, *Die Kreisky Jahre 1967–83* (Löcker Verlag, Vienna, 1993)

Forsyth, Frederick, *The Odessa File* (Hutchinson, London, 1972)

Friedlander, Albert H., *Riders Towards the Dawn* (Constable, London, 1993)

Gaiswinkler, Albrecht, *Sprung in die Freiheit* (Vienna, 1937)

Gilbert, Martin, *Auschwitz and the Allies* (Michael Joseph, London, 1981)

Gilbert Martin, *The Holocaust* (Collins, London, 1982)

Goldmann, Nahum, Wiesenthal, Simon, *et al.*, interviews, *Jüdische Lebenswege* (Fischer Verlag, Frankfurt-am-Main, 1992)

Gruber, Karl, *et al.*, *Wir über Waldheim* (Böhlau Verlag, Vienna, 1992)

Gutman, Roy, *Witness to Genocide* (Element Books, Dorset, 1993)

Hammer, Katarina, *Glanz im Dunkel – Die Begegnungen von Kunstschätzen in Salzkammergut* (Vienna, 1986)

Harel, Isser, *The House on Garibaldi Street* (André Deutsch, London, 1975)

Haumann, Heiko, *Geschichte der Ostjuden* (Deutscher Taschenbuch Verlag, Munich, 1990)

Herzstein, Robert, *Waldheim: The Missing Years* (Arbor House/William Morrow, New York, 1988)

Hitler, Adolf, *Mein Kampf* (Franz Eher Verlag, Munich, 1925)

Hudal, Alois, *Römische Tagebücher* (Leopold Stocker Verlag, Graz/Stuttgart, 1976)

Joffe, Joseph, 'The Battle of the Historians', *Encounter*, June 1975

Kahane, David, *Lvov Ghetto Diary* (University of Massachusetts, Boston, 1990)

Kenneally, Thomas, *Schindler's Ark* (Hodder & Stoughton, London, 1982)

Knight, Robert, (ed.), *Die Wortprotokolle der Österreichischen Bundesregierung* (Athenaeum, Frankfurt-am-Main, 1988)

Kreisky, Bruno, *Erinnerungen aus fünf Jahrzehnten* (Siedler Verlag, Berlin, 1986)

Kreisky, Bruno, *Erfahrungen eines Europäers* (Siedler Verlag, Berlin, 1988)

Laqueur, Walter, and Breitman, Richard, *Breaking the Silence* (Simon & Schuster, New York, 1986)

Langbein, Herman, *Against All Hope* (Constable, London, 1994)

le Chene, Evelyn, *Mauthausen: History of a Death Camp* (Methuen, London, 1971)

Levi, Primo, *If This Is a Man* (Abacus, London, 1987)

Levin, Ira, *The Boys from Brazil* (Michael Joseph, London, 1976)

Levy, Alan, *The Wiesenthal File* (Constable, London, 1994)

Lifton, Robert Jay, *The Nazi Doctors* (HarperCollins, London, 1986)

Lingens, Ella, *Eine Frau im Konzentrationslager* (Europa Verlag, Vienna, 1960)

Marton, Katie, *Wallenberg* (Random House, New York, 1982)

Malin, Peter, and Stein, Harry, *Eichmann in my Hands* (Muller Random Century, London, 1990)

Matalon-Lagnado, Lucette, and Cohn Dekel, Sheila, *Die Zwillinge des Dr Mengele* (Rowohlt, Hamburg, 1994)

Mayrhofer, Alois, *Künstler im Ausseerland* (Styria Verlag, Graz, 1985)

Miller, Judith, *One by One, Facing the Holocaust* (Touchstone, New York, 1990)

Mitten, Richard, *The Politics of Antisemitism* (Westbrook Press, Colorado, 1992)

Nicholas, Lynn H., *The Rape of Europa* (Macmillan, London, 1994)

O'McCagg, William, *History of the Hapsburg Jews* (Indiana University Press, Indiana, 1989)

Olah, Franz, *Die Erinnerungen* (Amalthea, Vienna, 1995)

Portisch, Hugo, *Österreich*, vols I and II (Kremayr & Scheriau Verlag, Vienna, 1989)

Posner, Gerald, and Ware, John, *Mengele: The Complete Story* (Macdonald, London, 1986)

Pulzer, Peter, *The Rise of Political Antisemitism in Austria* (John Wiley, London, 1964)

Rathkolb, Oliver, *Verdrängte Schuld, Verdrängte Sühne* (Verlag für Geschichte und Politik, Vienna, 1986)

Rathkolb, Oliver, *Die veruntreute Wahrzeit – Hitler's Propagandisten in Österreich* (Müller, Vienna, 1988)

Rathkolb, Oliver, *Es ist schwer jung zu sein – Jugend und Demokratie in Österreich* (Verlag Jugend und Volk, Vienna, 1991)

Roberts, Frank, *Dealing with Dictators* (Weidenfeld & Nicolson, London, 1991)

Rosenbaum, Eli M., with William Hoffer, *Betrayal* (St Martin's Press, New York, 1993)

Roth, Joseph, *Juden auf der Wanderschaft* (Verlag der Schmiede, Berlin, 1927)

Roth, Joseph, *Radetzky Marsch* (Rowohlt, Hamburg, 1953)

Rückerl, Adalbert, *NS Verbrecher vor Gericht* (Müller, Heidelberg, 1982)

Ryan, Alan J., *Quiet Neighbours* (Harcourt Brace Jovanovich, New York, 1984)

Schönfeld, Joachim, *Holocaust Memoirs* (KTAV Publishing House, Hoboken, 1988)

Secher, Pierre, *Bruno Kreisky* (Dorrance Publishing Co., Pittsburgh, 1993)

Sereny, Gitta, *Into that Darkness* (André Deutsch, London, 1974)

Sereny, Gitta, *Albert Speer* (Macmillan, London, 1995)

Silver, Eric, *The Book of the Just* (Weidenfeld & Nicolson, London, 1992)

Singer, Isaac Bashevis, *In My Father's Court* (André Deutsch, London, 1980)

Singer, Isaac Bashevis, *The Golem* (André Deutsch, London, 1985)

Smith, Bradley, *The Road to Nuremberg* (Basic Books, New York, 1981)

Stein, Richard A., *Documents Against Words* (STIBA [Foundation against Anti-Semitism], Rotterdam, 1992)

Steiner, Herbert, and Sporrer, Maria, *Ein unbequemer Zeitgenosse* (Orac Verlag, Vienna, 1992)

Stern, Fritz, *Dreams and Delusions* (Knopf, New York, 1987)

Szulc, Tad, *The Secret Alliance* (Pan, London, 1991)

Tusa, Ann and John, *The Nuremberg Trial* (Macmillan, London, 1983; reissued by BBC Books, London, 1995)

Urquhart, Brian, *A Life in Peace and War* (Weidenfeld & Nicolson, London, 1987)

Waldheim, Kurt, *In the Eye of the Storm* (Weidenfeld & Nicolson, London, 1985)

Waldheim, Kurt, *Im Glass Palast der Weltpolitik* (Econ, Düsseldorf/Vienna, 1985)

Weidenfeld, George, *Remembering My Good Friends* (Harper Collins, London, 1995)

Weinzierl, Erika, *Zu wenig Gerechte – Österreicher & Judenverfolgung* (Styria Verlag, Graz, 1969)

West, Rebecca, *A Trail of Powder* (*The Nuremberg Trials*) (Virago, London, 1984)

Wiesel, Eli, *A Beggar In Jerusalem* (Sphere, London, 1971)

Wiesel, Eli, *Night* (Penguin, London, 1981)

Wistrich, Robert, *Who's Who in Nazi Germany?* (Weidenfeld & Nicolson, London, 1982; new edition, Routledge, London, 1995)

Wistrich, Robert, *Between Redemption and Perdition* (Routledge, London, 1990)

Wistrich, Robert, *The Jews of Vienna in the Age of Kaiser Franz Joseph* (OUP, Oxford, 1990)

Wistrich, Robert, *Weekend in Munich* (Pavilion, London, 1995)

Wodak, Ruth, et al., *Wir sind unschuldige Täter* (Suhrkamp Taschenbuch, Frankfurt-am-Main, 1990)

Zelman, Leon, *Ein Leben nach dem Überleben* (Kremayr & Scheriau, Vienna, 1995)

Zuroff, Efraim, *Occupation – Nazi-Hunter* (KTAV Publishing Inc., New Jersey, 1994)

Index

To John,

Happy reading!

Colin August '67.

The Reivers

The Reivers

The Story of the Border Reivers

ALISTAIR MOFFAT

BIRLINN

First published in 2007 by
Birlinn Limited
West Newington House
10 Newington Road
Edinburgh
EH9 1QS

www.birlinn.co.uk

ISBN 13: 978 1 84158 549 9
ISBN 10: 1 84158 549 1

British Library Cataloguing-in-Publication Data
A catalogue record for this book is available from the British Library

Typeset by Hewer Text UK Ltd, Edinburgh
Printed and bound by Creative Print and Design, Wales

I have spent many happy months filming in the Borders, making the series on the Border Reivers for Border Television, and this book is for all those who helped me do it and have had such a grand time doing it. I hope that Fiona Armstrong, Terry Black, Annie Buckland, Chris Buckland, Paul Caddick, Livvy Ellis, Valerie Lyon, Louise Maving, Paddy Merrall, Eric Robson, Eric Scott-Parker, Allan Tarn and Ken Wynne all enjoy the book as much as I've enjoyed working with them.

Contents

List of Illustrations

Acknowledgements

First I want to thank Hugh Andrew of Birlinn for asking me to write this. I have greatly enjoyed working with him and his team. Too rare in publishing, they are dynamic, business-like and cheery. Birlinn makes authors feel good, even important, even if they're not particularly. And that's also too rare a trick in publishing. Thanks to Graeme Leonard for a brisk and painless edit, and to all my patient readers. Walter Elliot had something of a family interest in this one. And finally my thanks to lovely Liz Hanson for her superb photographs. They are an adornment – as ever.

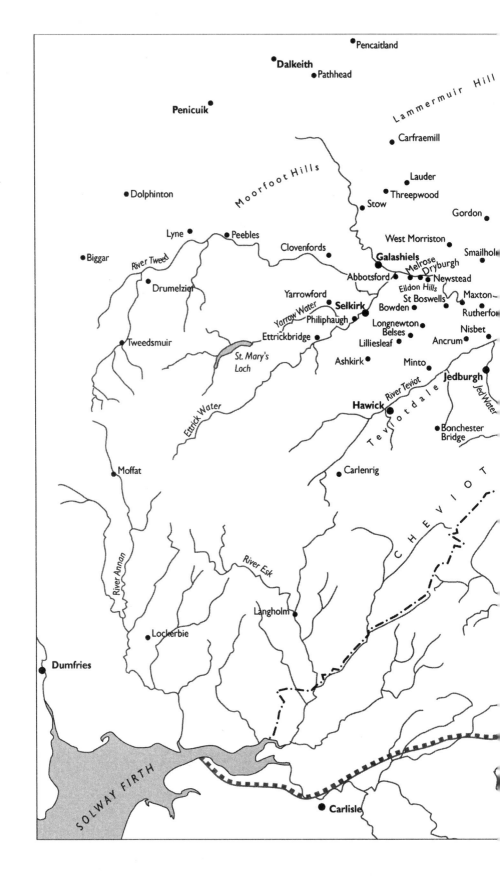

St Abbs

Coldingham

Eyemouth

Abbey St. Bathans

Burnmouth

Chirnside

Duns

Berwick Upon Tweed

Marchmont

Tweedmouth

NORTH SEA

Swinton

Eccles

Lindisfarne

Hume

Coldstream

Pallinsburn

Farne Islands

Ednam

Wark

Carham

Branxton

River Till

elso

Sprouston

Milfield

Bamburgh

Caverton Mill

Kirk Yetholm

Eckford

Town Yetholm

Yeavering

Chillingham

Linton

Morebattle

Gateshaw

River Aln

Alnwick

L L S

Alnmouth

Carter Bar

River Coquet

River Rede

R e d e s d a l e

Otterburn

Wansbeck

Hadrian's Wall

Newcastle
Upon Tyne

River Tyne

0   5   10   15   20   25 kilometres

Part I

1

Moonlight

The night wind whistled out of the west, sudden squalls spattering the ramparts, keeping the sentries moving, stamping their feet against the November chill. When the clouds scudded away into the formless mirk and the sky cleared, the moon lit the pale winter landscape. Bewcastle Waste stretched away to the north of the old fort, and beyond it lay Liddesdale, Teviotdale and trouble.

Leaning on their spears, the sentries peered into the darkness, searching the horizon, scanning the dark heads of the fells. Sometimes a shape seemed to move but another pair of eyes saw it was nothing. The cold and the wet – and the sleepless hour – could numb the senses and make a fool of the most experienced soldier. The Captain had set four troopers on the night watch but allowed only one brazier between them. While two warmed themselves, the others walked the rampart, watching for raiders, for horsemen who might appear out of nowhere, from any direction. But it was a foul night, surely even the most desperate thieves on the Border would stay snug by their fire.

Ten miles to the north, silently snaking through the hills, they were coming. Walter Scott of Buccleuch led 120 riders up over the pass at Whitrope, their ponies looking for the glint of the burn and the narrow path beside it. There was none of the martial jingle of heavily armed cavalry as the column wound its way quietly down through the willow scrub to the mosses of Liddesdale. Sodden now, but much better than nothing, cloaks were wound tight against the midnight chill. Looming out of the darkness, off to their right, Scott and his captains could see the black shape of the castle at Hermitage. No lights showed and if there was a watch, it was only nominal and probably looking the other way. The riders stayed on the east bank of the burn and moved silently on. No patrol would come out of the castle gate but it would not do to embarrass the Keeper by making the presence of a passing raiding party obvious. Only a short way downstream Whithaugh and the tryst with the Armstrongs were waiting.

At the end of September, having left them out on the fells as late as he dared, Willie Routledge and his herd-laddies had ingathered their cattle for the winter. The high summer pastures of the Bewcastle fells had begun to die back and the ground around the sikes and burns had churned to clinging clatch. After cropping for winter hay, Routledge's inbye fields had recovered and his cows would keep their summer condition on through the turn of the year and maybe beyond, if only the incessant rains of last winter would hold off. And his prized ponies were fat and sleek, swinging big grass-bellies in their winter coats.

All four sentries heard it. Each looked up and out to the north. And then at each other. Birdcalls in the dead of a winter's night? Only when their roost is disturbed. Was it a fox – or something more? The sentries waited for clouds to clear the full moon, holding their breath for another shriek from out in the waste, straining to focus in the formless dark. The Captain slept warm in his chamber; who would be bold enough to rattle down the rickety wooden stairs and wake him because a bird had called? Moments passed. No other alarm. Whatever it was had moved on, nothing of any moment. It came on to rain, again.

Sim's Jock Armstrong was in no doubt. Simplest was best, particularly on a filthy night like this. The old reiver wheeled his pony to come alongside Scott's, his eyes were hooded by the dripping rim of his steel bonnet but his rasping voice was clear enough. Scott and his riders should cross the border at Kershopefoot and then strike directly south towards the Bewcastle Fells. And they should come back on exactly the same track. The ponies would find their own scent and their own hoofprints in the dark. And once they had regained the Scottish side, everything should be left to the Armstrongs. They would be waiting, and not even Scott would see them as he passed. It was their ground and they knew its every brake and bush. By early morning all would be done, one way or another, and it would be done well, would it not? Sim's Jock and his riders would earn their cut. Walter Scott smiled and nodded. The board was set – let the game begin.

In the hay barn, the Routledge's dogs dozed in their own body-warmth, cocking an occasional ear as rats scratched and scuttled in the rafters. Bielded from the breeze by the farm steading, most of the ponies were quiet, some sleeping on their feet, all waiting patiently for the night to pass. And the black cattle snuffled in small groups, nosing around the inbye fields, nibbling now and again at the cold and bitter winter grass. One or two splashed across the burn to the farther pasture. The beasts at night somehow seemed peaceful to Willie Routledge, their steaming warmth consoling, their herding instincts a comfort. He and his boys had had a good summer with plenty of calves to sell on at Brampton Market and some to keep through the winter. Up on the shielings, the summertowns, the sun had shone and the good grass grown up through the yellow tussocks of the old. Next year would be even better. If only they could get through the long dark winter stretching out before them.

Towards midnight mist crept over the moonlit landscape, muffling sound, its damp chill seeping through the sentries' warmest cloaks. Beyond the ramparts the world slept, cold and still under a grey blanket. Only wakefulness kept the men warm; it was easy to lean on a spear and nod into a doze. But to allow that was to numb the bones for the rest of the long night. Activity, doing their duty, was what helped and after all Bewcastle Fort had been built and regularly repaired for good reason. It guarded a well-trodden byway into the west marches of England. To its south were vulnerable farmsteads, valuable herds and poorly defended villages.

They were in England now. Nothing could disguise their purpose as Scott's riders kicked their ponies on up the rising ground above the Kershope Burn. They would circle well to the west of Bewcastle Fort. Its new Captain, Steven Ellis, was his name, was reckoned to be more than usually anxious to please his masters in London, old Francis Walsingham and the rest. No courtly fawner or sponger, he was a professional soldier who saw his posting to Elizabeth's northern frontier as an opportunity to distinguish himself in action rather than words, to become part of what the Warden of the East Marches, Robert Carey, called 'a stirring world'. Ellis' troopers were also newcomers to the Border and none had yet compromised their loyalty. Time would surely change that, but for the moment Walter Scott would be cautious, not wishing to alert the Bewcastle garrison and have them clatter out of the fort and after him. Willie Routledge's cows were what he and his men wanted, and anything else they could carry off besides.

Scouts reported back. Dismounting, tying their ponies in the thickets down by the burn, they had crept up a ridge above the farm, seen no light, no watchers, noted that the herd was grazing the inbye fields and noticed some handsome nags in amongst them. Speed and stealth now. Scott's men were well armed, bristling with swords, daggers, pistols and spears. They wore steel caps and thick padded jerkins while their captains and a few others were protected by backs and breasts armour. It was not Willie Routledge and his sons who worried the riders but the long road home and the real possibility that the Bewcastle garrison would give chase and that they might have to cut their way through to the border and beyond.

Despite carrying 18 to 20 stone of kit and man, the ponies moved nimbly over the tussocks towards the farmhouse, keeping it between them and the cattle. Suddenness would unsettle the beasts and raise the house. Scott had split his force. Most waited to round up the cows and oxen and catch the ponies while a dozen dismounted. With Scott leading, they crept towards the thatched farmhouse like foxes.

Too experienced and too wily for needless drama, Scott lifted the latch and tiptoed inside. By the glow of the dying fire his men could see the sleeping family become restive – until their leader woke them by holding his pistol to Willie Routledge's head. A moment's uproar was immediately suppressed by some rough handling. All were quickly dragged and bundled into a corner of the room as Scott went out to supervise the roundup. The men raked around the farmhouse for valuables as Routledge swore and cursed at them. One pulled out a cowering, squealing daughter by the hair, forced her to kneel by the fire and held a dagger to her throat to encourage her father and terrified family to keep quiet.

Out in the fields the raiders caught up the ponies in halters and gathered the cattle into a tight pack. Once they were ready to move off, Scott's men tied up all of the Routledges and doused their fire. Let them shiver and make no signal. Anything to slow down the likely pursuit. Across rough ground and in the winter dark, cows were slow to drive and one or two would slip through the screen of ponies and need to be herded back.

All had been managed quickly and with scarcely a raised voice. No sound carried as far as the ramparts at Bewcastle, its sentries saw nothing amiss in the November night. But news was travelling. Young Edward Routledge had wriggled free of his bonds, untied the others and while his father and his brothers began quickly to build a beacon to blaze and raise the countryside, he ran, stumbling and falling, over the moorland to the soldiers and their fort.

Scott did not delay, riding up and down, hurrying his men. They had lifted about 40 head of cows and oxen and 20 ponies, most of them mares. The Routledge farm had yielded little in the way of valuables and no man was over-encumbered. But goading and whacking the lowing cows into a trot was difficult – and noisy. At this pace the border was perhaps an hour away, the dawn another hour beyond that.

Pinpointed in the distance, Edward saw the sentries' brazier and began breathlessly to holler and whoop. By the time he had scrambled over the old Roman ditches and ramparts and reached the outer gate at Bewcastle Fort, its Captain was awake and buckling on his breast-plate. Over to the west the Routledge's beacon crackled into life and lit the night sky. Within a few minutes 40 troopers were in the saddle and Edward on his way back to the farm with spare mounts. It was Scott they were after. Routledge knew for certain, and he would most likely be on the trail to the Kershope Burn and the Scottish side.

Even though those leading the stolen ponies could make better time, Walter Scott knew that his raiding party needed to keep all its strength together. If caught up, he would turn and fight while some of his riders kept the cattle from stampede. If they scattered into the darkness and the unfenced moorland, what was the point? Scott rode at the rear, often turning and straining to listen, screening out the grunt and low of the beasts as the herd moved northwards, nearer to Scotland and safety. Not that the frontier itself would protect him, government officials on both sides had the right to pursue raiders across it regardless of jurisdiction. Scott wanted to reach the Kershope Burn because the Armstrongs waited there, well hidden.

Captain Ellis and his troopers hurried along the trail, not far behind and not waiting for Routledge and his boys or anyone else. The rain was holding off, the moon glowed pale as it set and the ponies would somehow find good enough ground to trot. Often they could make out the hoofprints of cows and horses in the muddy sikes. They were gaining, closing fast on the raiders.

Willie Routledge and his sons followed on quickly through the half-light, hoping to catch up the Captain's troop before they engaged with Scott and his men. Willie hated the taunt, 'a Routledge – every man's prey', and was determined to show his family was no soft touch.

Against the paler blue of the dawning sky, on the ridge above the Kershope Burn, Ellis could make out the silhouettes of the raiding party and the cattle clearly. And just faintly he could hear them. The captain would catch them all, red-handed, as they stumbled downhill and across the water. His men spurred on.

Scott could hear them coming. Some of the Bewcastle troopers had booted their ponies into a canter. Silly. Could easily break a leg. But they might be lucky and be upon them soon. The leading raiders were skittering down to the burn, and breaking his silence, Scott roared for support to come up to him on the ridge. The cows splashed over the burn, riders whacking them on. It was difficult to know how close Ellis was. When all were across safely and moving into the woods on the Scottish side, Scott turned his men downhill and followed. At that moment the Bewcastle troop burst out of the mirk, only 40 yards away. Now at the banks of the burn, Scott's men scrambled over. But as Ellis' troop found the level ground, scores of riders erupted from nowhere. The Armstrongs had broken cover. Four Bewcastle men were immediately shot out of the saddle. Many others were badly wounded and the troop routed before their Captain had time to rally them to him. Careless of the grey light and the uneven ground, his men scattered in all directions.

Scott turned in the saddle to look back at the melee. The Armstrong ambush had been expertly sprung, the cows and horses were theirs and a good night's work had been done. On the high ground above the Kershope Burn Willie Routledge and his sons sat on their ponies and watched. If only the young Captain had waited, Willie would have told him why the raiders had returned on the same road. He could have warned them what was waiting.

These things happened. In November 1588 Walter Scott of Buccleuch rode out of his stronghold of Branxholme, near Hawick, with 120 reivers. He had made a tryst with the Armstrongs of Whithaugh in Liddesdale. Here is the full text of the complaint later made:

> Captain Ellis and the surname of the Routledges in Bewcastle complain upon the said Laird of Buccleuch, the Laird of Chesame, the Laird of Whithaugh and their accomplices to the number of 120 horsemen arrayed with jacks, steel caps, spears, guns, lances and pistols, swords and daggers purposely mustered by Buccleuch, who broke the house of Willie Routledge, took 40 cows and oxen, 20 horses and mares, and also laid an ambush to slay the soldiers and others who should follow the fray, whereby they cruelly slew and murdered Mr Rowden, Nichol Tweddle, Jeffrey Nartbie and Edward Stainton, soldiers; maimed sundry others and drove 12 horses and mares, whereof they crave redress.

The raid is the core of this story. It is the essence of all the extraordinary events which took place from the fifteenth to the early seventeenth century on either side of the border between England and Scotland. Thousands of raids like Walter Scott's foray to Bewcastle were run, often several on one winter's night. They formed the focus of a unique criminal society. Over an enormous area of Britain, perhaps a twelfth of the landmass of the island, there existed a people who lived beyond the laws of England and Scotland, who ignored the persistent efforts of central government to impose order, who took their social form and norms from the ancient conventions of tribalism, who invented ever more sophisticated variants on theft, cattle rustling, murder and extortion – and gave them names, like 'blackmail'. And they spoke and sang beautiful, sad poetry and told a string of stirring, unforgettable stories.

In the modern historical period, the tale of the Border Reivers is a tale without parallel in all of western Europe.

2

The Lords of the Names

Queens were executed, monasteries swept into oblivion and a Reformation forced upon his people by Henry VIII of England in his desperation to father a male heir and continue the Tudor line. And once Prince Edward had been safely delivered, this most brutal of English kings began to cast around for a bride for his boy. When James V of Scotland died in 1542 leaving his baby daughter, Mary, as queen, negotiations were soon underway. By July 1543 the Treaty of Greenwich had contracted a marriage between Prince Edward and Queen Mary. She was not yet one year old.

Almost immediately it began to unravel. The Scottish Parliament rejected the terms of the treaty and the nobility divided into pro- and anti-English factions. Henry VIII responded with what Walter Scott called 'the rough wooing'. Punitive expeditions rampaged through the Border countryside, burning and killing across a wide swathe, and in September 1547 a powerful English army drew up in battle order at Pinkie near Musselburgh. The Scots were no match; ten thousand were said to have been slaughtered, fifteen hundred taken prisoner and those who wisely fled the field were pursued up to the gates of Edinburgh.

As is often the case, it was a battle which need not have been fought. Although the English had vastly superior numbers, that fact was fast becoming their most pressing problem. Quartermasters were having great difficulty in supplying such a large army in the field and some historians believe that if the Scots had simply skirmished around them, harrying their communications in classic reiver fashion, then the English would have been forced into a humiliating retreat after only a few days. But rashness, and the urging of Scottish priests (who did not wish their national church to come under the control of York or Canterbury), drove the Scots captains into fighting a pitched battle they were odds-on to lose.

Borderers and their heidsmen must have understood all of this and it no doubt informed their actions. They fought on both sides, and it appears that the Scots contingent manoeuvred themselves opposite the English. A sharp-eyed observer noticed that in addition to their crosses of St Andrew and St George, both sets of Borderers wore a great deal of extra identification; kerchiefs tied like armbands and letters embroidered on their hats. Worse, their national badges were sewn on so loosely that 'a puff of wind might have blown them from their breasts'. But most embarrassing was the discovery that, standing within a spear's length of each other, in the midst of a furious battle, Scots and English Borderers were talking to each other. When they realised that they had been observed, both lots made some show of running at each other and 'they strike few strokes but by assent and appointment'.

It must have been a remarkable sight. Amid the din and clatter of battle, as others fought and died around them, two groups of nominally opposing soldiers making a pantomime out of deadly warfare. People who knew each other well had turned up at Pinkie to be seen to do their duty for the opposing sides but were actually determined to get through the battle, whichever way it went. For the truth is that it was not their fight.

Foreign policy, the aspirations of Henry VIII and the ambitions of the anti-English party in Scotland mattered very little to these men. Names were everything, nationality came a long way behind and loyalty to factions within a nation an even more distant third.

HENRY AND THE CLAP

Syphilis made landfall in Europe at Barcelona in 1493, having travelled across the Atlantic as an early import from America on board the *Nina*, one of Christopher Columbus' ships. It spread like wildfire and at some point in his extended amorous adventures, Henry VIII of England almost certainly caught it. The disease made it difficult for him to father an heir (and contributed to his dynasty's barrenness) and propelled Britain into all sorts of political convulsions. Not the least of these were the tremendously destructive punitive raids of the 'rough wooing'. The sixteenth-century epidemic of syphilis made sexual puritanism popular – as a matter of self-preservation. Previously popular in all gender combinations as a form of greeting, kissing on the lips was replaced by the safer handshake, and the fashion for wigs was encouraged. Sufferers from syphilis often lost all their hair.

Names were what made the Border Reivers who they were – in all important senses. Armstrongs, Elliots, Kers and Maxwells gave unhesitating loyalty to their surnames, what was a huge extended family in some cases. On the English side the Carletons, the Fenwicks, the Forsters and the Robsons felt greater affinity with the Scottish riding families than with those who lived to the south of them. And governments in Edinburgh and London may have done as they pleased but where the heidsman of a name led, those who had the same name saddled their ponies and followed.

These were powerful instincts. Few fought fiercer than family bands. When fathers and sons, brothers and cousins rode side by side, none turned aside and many found courage when the names of their blood needed them at their back. Astute commanders understood these bonds and in battles or skirmishes they always set the older and more experienced men in front, believing that honour and valour flowed down the generations to the younger men behind. Pitched battles between surnames were always the cruellest and bloodiest fights. When the Maxwells were cut to pieces by the Johnstones at Dryfe Sands near Lockerbie in 1593, the slaughter was unrelenting. More than 700 Maxwells were killed and Robert Johnstone of Raecleugh bloodied his lance on that terrible day. He was 11 years old.

Robert must have been a big laddie for his years, able to wrap long legs around his pony's belly and direct it, and also to couch the butt of his lance without being knocked out of the saddle on impact. 'If he's big enough, he's auld enough' is a comment still heard in Border rugby dressing rooms when a young player is brought into the team. And on 6th December 1593 the Johnstones needed every young lad, every rider they could muster. In pursuit of a deadly feud between the two names, the Maxwells had summoned a huge force. Two thousand horsemen rode with their heidsman, Lord Maxwell, and they came to lay siege to the Johnstone tower at Lochwood.

When news of the advancing army – for that is what it was – reached James Johnstone, he moved quickly and determined to fight like the reiver he was. He knew no other way to prevent the extermination of his name. Able to put only four hundred men in the saddle, Johnstone could not confront Maxwell in open country. His riders would be outflanked and rolled up and fatally surrounded. Instead, he laid a reiver's ambush. At a narrow place on the road, with plenty of cover on each side, the Johnstones hid themselves. When enough of the Maxwell vanguard had trotted into the trap, it was suddenly sprung. Roaring their war-cries, the Johnstones spurred their ponies and tore into their enemy's flanks. So furious was the charge that it drove the leading Maxwell riders backwards, forcing them to turn into the midst of the main party following them. Ponies reared and kicked, men were bucked off, weapons dropped, tangled and trampled and a murderous scrummage of confusion turned Maxwell's two thousand into a formless, panicking rabble.

As the Johnstones charged again and again, the battle became a rout and riders poured into the streets of Lockerbie, fighting as they went. Maxwells were trapped in narrow places, hacked at, killed and ridden down. Blood ran in the gutters, spattered on the faces of the living and the dying. Men screamed as they were cornered and skewered by lance and sword-thrust or their limbs were cut off and their bodies butchered unrecognisable. The Johnstones fought like furies for more than their lives – the very existence of their name was at stake on that awful December day. Extermination was what they desperately feared – and to visit it upon the Maxwells if they could.

Dryfe Sands was one of the last battles to be joined in the Borders and one of the most ferocious. And it was fought for the sake of a name, the very bedrock of reiver society.

LOCKERBIE LICKS

When horsemen fought each other head-on, troops of cavalry charging straight towards each other, it was a combination of resolve, numbers and heavier horses which usually won the day. The armies of Islam swept through North Africa and up into Spain and southern France in the eighth century. When the Arab cavalry reached the River Loire in AD 732, they came up against a new enemy. Charles Martel, the Mayor of the royal palace, had gathered a squadron of big horses, what became known as heavy cavalry. Bracing themselves in their stirrups, they charged the lighter Arab cavalry and knocked them off their feet. Islam was driven back to the Pyrenees and eventually across the Straits of Gibraltar. The small Arab ponies were tough, fast and nimble but entirely unsuited to pitched battle on good ground. Just like the Border Reivers. They too were light horsemen, what were known as 'prickers', good at harrying, skirmishing and wearing down a more cumbrous enemy, always fighting shy of taking them on upfront. On a broken battlefield Border horsemen were deadly, pouring through gaps in the line, quickly creating a melée of close-quarter fighting. At the Battle of Dryfe Sands the Johnstones got in amongst the Maxwells and inflicted terrible casualties, particularly on those fighting on foot. 'Get in amongst them!' is still shouted from the terracing at Border League rugby matches. Even on small Galloway Nags a horseman was always crucially higher than an infantryman, slashing downwards with a sword or using the pony's momentum to drive a lance forward. Many at Dryfe Sands suffered bad head and facial injuries from what became known as 'Lockerbie Licks', a passing backhanded cut at an opponent on foot – delivered with great venom.

The tribal surnames and their feral power were very old, reaching back across millennia into the mists of prehistory. When pioneer family bands came north after the end of the last ice age, and hunted, trapped and gathered a wild harvest, they probably enjoyed customary rights over wide swathes of the ancient wildwood. As farming pinned growing populations to more defined areas on the early map of the Borders, the beginnings of the surnames slowly began to form. DNA studies show tremendously long lineages, particularly in rural areas and many Border families of the sixteenth century had been on their land since a time out of mind. Of course, new people came, others moved or were removed but the balance of the human landscape stayed much as it was for a hundred generations or more. When men fought hard to keep or protect their land, they fought with all their courage for their history, and their name. They were seen as indivisible, the one impossible without the other.

Very early in the history of the Borders an old fault-line repeatedly divided communities. Hillmen and plainsmen had long led different styles of life. How the shepherd and the ploughman grew their food was shaped by geography and climate, but the distinctions were rarely absolute. Almost all farmers cultivated the ground and husbanded some beasts and the shepherd likewise. It was a question of degree. But the ploughmen of the flat and fertile plains of Berwickshire and the middle Tweed Valley saw themselves as different from the shepherds of Liddesdale in many ways – and they complained about them. In 1569 the lairds of the eastern and middle marches asserted that while they themselves were peaceable, the thieves of the western ranges were not. In a memorandum to the Scottish Privy Council they insisted that they must be controlled and made to behave like civilised men. And in case anyone missed the point, they supplied a *black list* of the surnames of the worst of them. And there were a few – all Armstrongs, Batesons, Bells, Crosiers, Elliots, Glendinnings, Hendersons, Irvines, Johnstones, Nixons, Routledges and Thomsons. In all this there is more than a whiff of superiority, the sense that the men of Liddesdale, Ewesdale, Annandale and Eskdale were little more than savages.

LIONEL AND TONY

Recent research suggests that men who bear the same surname are likely to be relatives. Lionel Blair and Tony Blair? Analyses of DNA testing of pairs of British males with the same surname shows that 25 per cent are direct if distant relatives. The Y chromosome passed from fathers to sons is the genetic link. The rarer the surname the greater the chance of men bearing it being related. Border Reivers knew all this anyway – but probably would have been appalled that the police plan to use the data to track down criminals.

For their part the hillmen found their lives more defined and constrained by geography. Over the valuable and accessible lands of the eastern plains the winds of social change might more easily blow. But in an upland valley, with one track in and one track out, there was less traffic of every sort and the year was shaped by the movement of flocks and herds, the time-hallowed journeys of transhumance. The communities of the hills were more conservative, perhaps closer-knit and more intimately tribal than those down in the valley bottoms and the broad fields of the east.

The herdsmen who moved their beasts around the flanks of the Cheviots and the hills and moors north of the Hexham Gap had more in common with each other than with the plainsmen who farmed the lower ground. The distinction between English and Scottish mattered much less. This is an important facet of the story of the Border Reivers. Since the earliest records were kept, the tribes of the northern Pennines and of the Cheviots and Southern Uplands allied themselves against the Roman invader. The Brigantes and the Selgovae and their satellites united their warbands in an attempt to keep some independence. Part of the reasoning behind Hadrian's Wall was to drive a firebreak between them, prevent them from reinforcing each other along the hill trails which were so dangerous to patrol. Fifteen hundred years later, when the governments in Edinburgh and London tried to exert control, the instincts of the hillmen were little changed.

FOUR AND TWENTY

Until well into the nineteenth century Cumbrian shepherds counted in Old Welsh: yan, tan, tedderte, medderte, pump (1, 2, 3, 4, 5 in English, or Arabic). When sheep were being accounted for on the high fells, Welsh was still shouted against the wind. Different valleys had slight variations; Coniston shepherds shouted tedderte while Borrowdale used tethera. It is an astonishing survival showing the deep conservatism of hill communities. And it is unlikely to have survived only in Cumbria. Mostly unlettered men, the shepherds of the Border hills probably counted as their ancestors did – and for many centuries after English was spoken in the valleys below. Like all Celtic languages Old Welsh used 20-base arithmetic. It reckons 2 × 20 for 40, 4 × 20 for 80 and so on. Memories of this habit lasted on into the twentieth century when old people used a Celtic word order. Instead of 24, they would say 4 and 20. The origins of 20-base counting are obvious and straightforward – the number of human fingers and toes. With their Vs and Xs Roman numerals look as though they might have a different derivation – but they do not. I is the simple symbol of one finger held up, V is from the notch between thumb and forefinger when a whole hand of five is shown and X is when two forefingers are crossed to signify all ten fingers and thumbs linked.

There are some similarities with the society of the Highland clans to the far north. Heidsmen in the Borders appear to have exercised great authority, not unlike the autocratic rule of clan chiefs. Some surnames, like the Moffats, sometimes had no heidsman, and perhaps for the avoidance of dispute, chose to acknowledge another. At the time of the Battle of Dryfe Sands the Moffats saw James Johnstone as their superior and no doubt horsemen of that surname hacked and killed Maxwells in the lanes of Lockerbie. There were many 'graynes' or branches of the Scott family, but Scott of Buccleuch was their unchallenged leader. And when Lord Maxwell summoned his small

army of 2,000 riders in 1593, by no means all bore his name –
although they were related. Other graynes, such as the Crichtons and
the Douglases, often rode in his forays.

These bonds of the blood were reciprocal. In return for unquestioningly saddling his pony and buckling on his sword at a moment's
notice, a man might expect to work his land as a secure tenant and
enjoy the protection of his heidsman. In fact men who found themselves outside these interlocking relationships, for whatever good
reason, could enter into a contract with a heidsman. Known as
manrent, this arrangement was not common but it did demonstrate
the power of the name. And a name was not something to be without
in the hills and valleys of the sixteenth-century Border country.

The sense of belonging, of pride and confidence in being an Elliot, a
Turnbull, a Selby or a Bell peeps through the records of the time again
and again. The Captain of Berwick, the great Elizabethan fortress-
town guarding the east coast road, complained that the local recruits
for his garrison were 'mutinous and insubordinate to their constables,
who are little above their own rank. Being of great clans and
surnames, this encourages their obstinacy'.

When obstinacy shaded into excess, heidsmen could threaten the
ultimate sanction. They could condemn men to be disnamed, to be
removed from the surname and cast into outlawry. In the Border
country disorder became so chronic in the sixteenth century that central
government was forced to rely upon heidsmen controlling their people
directly. By making solemn promises and sometimes giving up hostages,
the lords of the names retained an independent ability to enforce good
behaviour amongst their people. And if their people continued to
misbehave and promises and pledges (the term most often used for
hostages) were repeatedly broken or forfeited, then the heidsmen were
compelled to disname the persistent offenders. The process sometimes
called 'putting to the horn' involved a public declaration that certain
men were no longer who they used to be or might claim to be. They had
lost their name and become 'broken men' or outlaws, that is, outside the
laws of Scotland and, more importantly, the laws of their heidsman. So
great was this loss that many broken men formed gangs, thereby
creating a surrogate surname. 'Sandy's Bairns' was one such gang of
thugs and they mounted raids on both sides of the border in the 1590s.
After he had been cast into outlawry – no mean feat for an already
lawless surname, Kinmont Willie Armstrong appeared at the head of a
notorious gang known as 'Kinmont's Bairns'.

BALEFIRE

'Bale' in Old English originally meant pain or woe, and a balefire burned at the death of a leading person, a chieftain, even a king. They were lit on hilltops so that the message of an important death could be quickly transmitted. The modern meaning is related to 'ball' and describes a bundle, normally of hay or straw. In an unexpected way these two quite separate meanings combined at the time of the Border Reivers. As early as the fifteenth century there existed a sophisticated warning system for the lighting of balefires. Here is a set of instructions in early Scots. Some of the words sound an echo of fifteenth-century Border dialect:

A baile is warnyng of their cumyng, quhat power whatever thai be of. Twa bailes togedder at anis, thai cumyng in deide. Fower balis, ilk ane besyde uther and all at anys as fower candills sal be suthfast knowledge that thai ar of gret power and menys.

in English:

The [burning] of a bale is warning of their coming, whatever size [the force] might be. Two bales [burnt] together at the same time means that they are certainly coming. Four bales, each beside the other and [burnt] all at once like four candles are a sign of certain knowledge that they are of great power and menace.

It could all go horribly wrong. The balefire system was revived in 1803-4 when Napoleon Bonaparte threatened to invade Britain. At Hume Castle a lookout was certain he could see one blazing near Berwick. In a state of high excitement he fired his bundles, and all over the Borders other balefires crackled into life. As in an episode of 'Dad's Army' volunteers pulled on boots and uniforms and hurried to their muster-points, no doubt grabbing their muskets as they scrambled out the door. The countryside was in uproar and at any moment Napoleon's cuirassiers were expected to come clattering along the Berwick road, tricolours flying. They did not. No one did. It was all a ghastly mistake. What the hapless lookout on Hume Castle had seen was the everyday work of some Northumberland charcoal-burners. One of their mounds had burned out of control, flames licking into the night sky. What happened to the lookout is not recorded, but he will not have been popular and never allowed to forget what happened.

Broken men could be bold. So many regularly met in the streets of Hawick that government troops made their way south from Edinburgh to deal with them. The Earl of Mar's men surrounded the town. A proclamation was cried from the mercat cross pointing out to the inhabitants that it was a capital crime to harbour broken men, and in a short time more than 50 were rounded up. Mar did not delay and while six of the more important prisoners were sent for trial in Edinburgh, 18 were bound hand and foot and dragged down to the banks of the Teviot. There, wriggling and kicking, they were held under the water until drowned. Cheap and quick, and a dire warning.

James VI and I learned the power of disnaming in the Borders. In 1604 he applied it to the Highland clans and in order to cure the MacGregors of their love of cattle stealing, he banned their name entirely. It simply became illegal to be called MacGregor and any man bearing that ancient surname could be hunted and killed. The whole social and military structure of the clan was undermined. Alasdair MacGregor, the chief of the name, and five of his leading men, were hanged at the mercat cross for the crime of refusing to give up their name. Clan Gregor scattered. Some took to outlawry in the mountains, others adopted pseudonyms like Gregory, Grant, even Campbell. It is more than a lexical coincidence that the Gaelic 'clann' for clan translates directly as children or bairns – as in 'Sandy's Bairns' or 'Kinmont's Bairns'.

The year after the disnaming of Clan Gregor, James VI and I applied the same principles in the Borders. One of the most persistently infamous of the reiving families were the Grahams of Eskdale and the Solway mouth. While the royal courts did not ban the name of Graham, the king's officers did their utmost to extirpate it. Wholesale deportations to Ireland were backed by hangings and press-gangings into armies to fight in European wars. These draconian measures broke the power of the name, but did not remove it. Grahams found their way back to their native places – if not their old reiving habits.

Those who kept their names in the Borders were rarely known by them. As in Wales and the Scottish Highlands, Borderers used a relatively small stock of surnames. There existed many Scotts, Armstrongs, Robsons and Ridleys at any one time, most of them living in the same small area. The mists of confusion thickened when little imagination was used in the giving of christian names; the same handful recur down the generations and also sideways to cousins and uncles. It seems that scores of Walter Scotts, Gilbert Elliots,

Robert Kers, Andrew Forsters and Thomas Carletons lived in the sixteenth century, many of them at the same time.

Mistaken identity is more of a danger for historians than it was for the reivers. Scots and English borderers seemed to know exactly who was who, especially when it came to the collection of blackmail (of which more later) and the fact that these men could recognise each other in the smoke and confusion of the Battle of Pinkie is extraordinary.

They had help. Until the recent past Border farmers were often known by the name of their farm rather than what appeared on their birth certificate. The same thing happened in the sixteenth century. When Walter Scott of Buccleuch rode with Walter Scott of Harden to rescue Kinmont Willie Armstrong from Carlisle Castle in 1596, the shorthand ran that Buccleuch and Harden saved Kinmont's skin.

Blood ties bound tight in the Borders, and how people chose to address each other often remembered that closeness. Not only to avoid confusion in the mosaic of similar names but also to remind everyone of the precision of relationships, patronymics and occasionally matronymics were used. As with the Highland clans, a father's name was added to his son's, and men called 'Sim's Jock', 'Dick's Davie' or 'Sandie's Gib' are all to be found in the records. If any unclarity remained names could run to a third generation with the like of 'Gibb's Geordie's Francis' or 'Sandie's Rinyon's Archie'. Where a father was not available, mothers stepped in for 'Kate's Adam', 'Peggie's Wattie', and 'Bessie's Andrew'.

Further refinement could be added by the application of a nickname. These are very colourful and often eloquent. Like 'Nebless Clem Crozier', 'Halflugs Jock Elliot' and 'Fingerless Will Nixon', some had stories to tell and how Clem lost his nose, Jock part of his ears and Will his fingers would add real pungency to the dry recital of dates and places and people. Other nicknames were mercilessly observational. John Armstrong squinted and was 'Gleed John', Will Armstrong had a twitch and was 'Winking Will' and Jerry Charlton had a tuft of hair sticking up and was 'Topping'. A dark nature conferred 'Ill Will Armstrong' and 'Evilwillit Sandie'. Perhaps 'Unhappy Anthone' met them both on a particularly bad day.

Sexual preferences were unblushingly caught in the web of nicknames. 'Dand Oliver the Lover' was bland enough and Dand obviously enjoyed female company. More direct are 'Dog Pyntle Elliot' and 'Wanton Pyntle Willie Hall'. 'Pyntle' is Border Scots for 'penis'.

More surprising is the clear recognition of homosexuality. Gay reivers such as 'Davy the Lady Armstrong', 'Buggerback Elliot' or 'Mistress Kerr' are unexpected even though the image is hard to reconcile. Buggerback and Dog Pyntle were brothers (although scarcely able to compare notes) and Davy the Lady was the younger brother of Sim the Laird Armstrong, one of the most feared heidsmen in the Border hills.

Some nicknames are impossible to parse, their meaning long fled. What prompted 'Sweet Milk' or 'Hen Harrow' or 'As It Looks' to be applied is now mysterious – and very intriguing.

What is so attractive about these nicknames is that they sound a faint echo of how the reivers spoke and dealt with each other. They suggest a boisterous, grimly humorous society where men called a spade a shovel and enjoyed a good laugh at others' quirks and preferences.

Boisterousness often shaded into something darker. And a rare documented example of a Border Reiver talking is dark indeed, the testament of a cruel, ruthless but ultimately honest man. The surname of Burn (sometimes rendered Bourne) held land to the south of the Teviot, in the old Jedforest which grew on part of the Scottish slopes of the Cheviots. They were a hard-bitten, violent bunch, acknowledging Robert Kerr of Cessford as their leader, and even though he was a government official, the Warden of the Scottish Middle March, they enjoyed his open patronage and protection.

On a September night in 1596 Jock and Geordie Burn were returning from a routine raid across the Cheviot tops. Driving cattle before them, the Scots reivers were very unlucky. Riding through the gloaming they were intercepted by Sir Robert Carey, the Warden of the English East March, who was out on patrol with 20 troopers at his back. Hopelessly outnumbered, Geordie Burn, his uncle and their two henchmen fought ferociously. One escaped, two were killed, and Geordie was overpowered and taken prisoner.

Probably at Harbottle Castle, Carey had Burn quickly tried, convicted and condemned to death. But sentence was delayed while the news of the reiver's capture was allowed to reach the ears of his patron, Sir Robert Kerr of Cessford. Perhaps there would be an advantageous negotiation, perhaps an attempted reprisal which might deliver more prisoners to Carey. In the event there was silence. No word came over the hill trails and Geordie Burn realised that he had been abandoned and was likely to hang.

Sir Robert Carey's curiosity was stirred. It is said that the warden disguised himself and with two companions went to Burn's cell to talk with the condemned man. The swagger had gone, and in his resignation, the reiver reviewed the life he had led. Carey later wrote down what he remembered. It amounts to the only authentic testament left by a Border Reiver:

> He voluntarily of himself said that he had lived long enough to do so many villanies as he had done; and told us that he had lain with about 40 men's wives, some in England, some in Scotland, and that he had killed seven Englishmen with his own hands, cruelly murdering them; that he had spent his whole time in whoring, drinking, stealing, and taking deep revenge for slight offences. He seemed to be very penitent, and much desired a minister for the comfort of his soul.

This is fascinating, a catalogue of thuggery, rape, murder, larceny and excess freely confessed – and regretted. Faced with the hangman's rope, Burn was anxious to bargain with his maker as he owned up to all his sins and asked for a minister to advise him. The transaction has an old-fashioned ring, the medieval arithmetic of damnation. Perhaps like their patrons, the Kerrs of Ferniehurst, Burn's family had kept their catholic faith, such as it was, for a generation after the establishment of Reformation Scotland. The enumeration of 40 rapes (it is hard to believe that Burn was referring to extra-marital affairs) and the murder of seven Englishmen sounds like a request for other offences to be taken into consideration. He had been taken by Carey for cattle stealing and having been condemned to die had no need to confess to anything else. It sounds as though the reiver was asking to see a minister to enquire after the tariff operating for the fires of hell. What could he expect for 40 rapes and seven murders? Geordie offers no mitigation except penitence, he just wants to know how bad it will be.

The listing of all these crimes and the tone in which Carey records them also has a routine ring. The Burns were not especially notorious and no more than normally active as reivers. The likelihood is that each Border district had a quota of gangsters doing much the same thing. If that is so, then these were grim times. Observers noted that even in pursuit of their daily duties – working the land, herding beasts – many Borderers went about armed, or with a weapon of some sort close at hand. No wonder.

THE PENRITH PLAGUE

In 1598 God's Punishment tore through Cumberland and West-morland. An inscription on the wall of the parish church at Penrith records an astonishing figure. Apparently 2,260 perished in an outbreak of the plague. Around 640 died in the town, half the population, and a further 1,800 from the farms and villages of the Eden Valley. At almost exactly the same time in Carlisle 1,196 died in unspeakable agony from the same disease. It is a forgotten epidemic. In their 'Return of the Black Death', Susan Scott and Christopher Duncan show that no such thing happened. The epidemic was not a return of the Black Death. What ripped through these horrified communities was in fact a lethal virus not unlike ebola, and it was transmitted not by infected fleas living in the fur of rats but directly from person to person. All they had to do was breath. For this reason the disease spread like lightning, and with their housing huddled close and overcrowded, towns were perfect vectors. Entering Britain through the port of Newcastle, this version of ebola travelled west across Stainmore to Penrith and then made its deadly way north to Carlisle before crossing the border to reach Dumfries. It was an appalling illness, its victims vomiting blood and tissue, haemorrhaging internally and burning with fever. Mercifully many died quickly and their bodies were flung in plague-pits without any ceremony. They also died alone because it became too risky for a minister to give them the last rites and families fled for fear of becoming infected. Curiously this phenomenal outbreak is noted by few historians or many contemporary commentators – even though it presented a much greater threat than any Border Reiver.

Just as Geordie Burn's confession offers a momentary glimpse of a life of reiving, so the following tells how the law-abiding majority saw these thugs. The Bishop of Carlisle wrote to Cardinal Wolsey in London in the 1520s. He was even-handed:

> there is more theft, more extortion by English thieves than there is by all the Scots of Scotland . . . for in Hexham . . . every market day there is four score or a hundred strong thieves; and the poor men and gentlemen also see those who did rob them and their goods, and

dare neither complain of them by name, nor say one word to them. They take all their cattle and horse, their corn as they carry it to sow, or to the mill to grind, and at their houses bid them deliver what they have or they shall be fired and burnt.

Defiant, confident in the numbers and fearsome reputation, the outlaws regularly rode into town – all over the Borders. Like Tombstone, Dodge City and other notorious locations in the Wild West, the law-abiding folks of Hexham, Carlisle, Hawick and Berwick had much to abide. Those gangsters who lifted their cattle during the week could glare shamelessly on market days at the farmers they had impoverished – and in turn the farmers were compelled to scuttle about their business, heads down, avoiding eye contact, mouths shut. On the wild frontier the rule of law had fled.

THE TIME OF OUR LIVES

In the sixteenth century few knew what time it was, at least in the sense that we mean it now. No one owned timepieces and the only institution which cared enough about the time of day to mark it was the church. In order to summon monks to say the offices of the day – vespers, compline and so on – bells tolled the canonical hours and the day began to divide into more than simply dark and light. To Americans the term 'fortnight' is meaningless. It is a relict of the way in which ordinary people used to count the days – or rather the nights. Fortnight is short for fourteen nights and the obsolete 'sennight' for a week was in common use in the sixteenth century. Except for Sunday most normal weekdays merged into each other. People did not work hours, they did tasks which finished when they finished. Turning points of the seasons were prominent – like Michaelmas, Lammas, Whitsun and so on, as were saints' days. The names of these days often survive in the calendar but the meaning has been lost. Christianity used to have many dietary laws (fish on Friday and abstinence in Lent are the only popular survivals) and periods of restriction were usually preceded by a 'carnival'. It literally means 'farewell to meat' and Shrove Tuesday was when Christians ought to have been shriven – or confessed their sins to a priest. Few Border Reivers will have bothered.

Jedburgh may have been an exception, at least for part of the sixteenth century. The town government was thrawn, assertive, independent and willing to fight for its rights, sometimes against unwise odds. In the early 1570s Scotland was riven with dissension between catholics and protestants, between the influence of France and England, and the focus of the former was Mary, Queen of Scots and of the latter, Elizabeth I of England. These alignments were further complicated by the increasingly complex position of Mary's son and heir, James, and his claims to the throne of England.

Jedburgh stood firm and sure for the protestant cause while the loyalties of Border heidsmen were split. Scott of Buccleuch and Kerr of Ferniehurst were catholic supporters of Mary and Kerr of Cessford had fallen in with Elizabeth and protestantism. When Queen Mary's party sent a royal herald to read out a proclamation at the old mercat cross at Jedburgh, matters quickly became explosive – and somewhat theatrical, even farcical.

When the herald had dismounted to climb up the steps to the base of the cross, the provost, his bailies and no doubt a substantial crowd had gathered around. Proclamations were of prime importance and the means by which government directives were popularly transmitted. But when the herald unrolled his parchment and read in a loud voice that all men should obey Queen Mary only and ignore all others, the provost stepped forward to call a halt. The herald was taken hold of and forced to eat his parchment. Piece by indigestible piece, it was stuffed into his mouth. That was bad enough, but things were about to get much worse for the poor man.

A hurdle was found and the Queen's herald was 'caused to loose down his points'. In modern parlance, his trousers were pulled down around his ankles. The Jedburgh men then forced him to bend over the hurdle and with a horse's bridle, they spanked his bare backside.

It was an appalling humiliation for a royal officer and when the man sat carefully on his horse to take the road back to Edinburgh, no one doubted that retribution would quickly come the other way. Scott of Buccleuch and Kerr of Ferniehurst (whose tower lies only a little over a mile south of Jedburgh) mustered more than 3,000 riders and descended on the town. But the provost and the townspeople were ready, having laid in six days of provisions and sent urgent messages for aid from Robert Kerr of Cessford. Immediately he rode to the rescue and reinforcements of musketeers and cavalry hurried south. Buccleuch and Kerr of Ferniehurst were compelled to abandon the siege but the latter continued to burn with indignation and he pursued the feud against Jedburgh energetically. The Kerrs tormented the town with 'riots and murders', and the close proximity of Ferniehurst hung like a constant black cloud.

KERRY MITTS

There is a persistent Border tradition that the family of Kerr were left-handed. The example always cited is the spiral staircase in their towers. Other surnames built theirs turning clockwise so that if they had to fight a retreat up the stair (always a strong possibility in the second half of the sixteenth century), they could keep their un-guarded left side to the outside wall and swing a sword blade downwards with their right hands. With the left-handed Kerrs the stair ran anti-clockwise, confusing everyone except them. In the Borders lefties are still called 'kerry-mitted', or 'kerr-handed' or 'corry-fisted'. Interestingly, but probably coincidentally, the Scots Gaelic word for 'left' is 'cearr' with a hard 'c'. It also means 'wrong' or 'a wrong un' and derives from an ancient Celtic root word 'kerso'. Perhaps it is all true. The Kerrs were certainly aggressive and recent sociological research had shown a high correlation between left-handedness and skill in combat, or at least a liking for a fight. In tribal societies in Africa and Polynesia statistics suggest strongly that those with a high proportion of lefties also have a high proportion of violent crime. This research solved a conundrum for the principles of natural selection. Generally speak-ing left-handedness is a disadvantage and yet the number who are is not diminishing. The reason may be that lefties are good at combat – possibly because of the element of surprise and awkwardness. This translates into modern versions of single combat – such as tennis. The proportion of successful tennis players who are left-handed is much higher than the incidence in the general population.

Feud between a surname and an entire town was unusual, but blood-spattered, long-running vendettas between families were not. Throughout the sixteenth century the Border country was disfigured by serial, often interlocking feuds and as momentum built there were more and more raids, assassinations and even full-scale battles such as Dryfe Sands. By 1596 25 English surnames and ten Scottish were at feud in some way or other. The effect was to render the Borders even more lawless. Redress or legal retribution was paralysed because of the high risk of sparking yet another feud, and as a consequence reivers could ignore the law with increasing impunity. Robert Carey's execution of Geordie Burn was a brave exception.

The Maxwells and the Johnstones sustained what was probably the longest and bloodiest feud in British history. It began in the early sixteenth century and like many arguments, large and small, its origins were soon forgotten.

More important were the dynamics of local politics. At stake between the Maxwells and the Johnstones was control of the Scottish west march. It stretched from the watershed between Langholm and Hawick at Mosspaul, north to the Tweedsmuir Hills and away west to the River Cree in Galloway. A huge domain, it was the jurisdiction of its warden, and both the Maxwells and the Johnstones coveted the office.

Although it is likely to have smouldered for a long time beforehand, the feud first comes on record in 1528. As often an English government official reported on events on the Scottish side of the border (this is a recurrent theme – the English records are much better than the Scots, and the effect is to make Scots reiving appear more frequent and widespread, whereas in fact, population statistics suggest the opposite to have been the case). Given what was going on, it is hardly surprising that the Scottish records are more scant than usual. By 1528 the feud had crackled and sparked over much of eastern Dumfriesshire, so much so that the Warden of the English West March, Lord Dacre, was moved to write to the London government. He told Cardinal Wolsey that burnings, killings and swift reprisals had been very destructive, almost to the point where farmers and herdsmen saw little point in working their land.

REFORM TIME

By the middle of the sixteenth century, the calendar compiled by Julius Caesar's Roman clerks had got badly out of phase. So that Easter could be held at the traditional time and the Christian festivals which dated from it could fall back into a sensible sequence of dates, Pope Gregory XIII decided to reform the Julian calendar drastically. Catholic countries adopted it immediately but it took Britain nearly 200 years to have the same date as most of Europe.

The problem was that the Gregorian reform involved losing 11 days, something many people found deeply suspicious and worrying. By 1752, the British government decided to fall into line with Europe at last, and 3rd September became, magically, 14th September. There were riots. In several cities crowds called 'Give us back our eleven days!' The problem was that leap years had been throwing the calendar out, and at the turn of the century they had to be divided by 400 otherwise they could not have their extra day. Other drastic changes followed. Until 1752 Britain had celebrated New Year's Day on 25th March, but after that year, it fell on 1st January. Some communities still celebrate Christmas and New Year old style, that is, 11 days after the rest of us. And at the crying of the fair at Langholm Common Riding (when a man stands on the hind quarters of a horse so that he can be both seen and heard) the date is still counted 'auld style', i.e. as it would have been before 1752.

Nevertheless, it often suited English foreign policy to foment the Maxwell/Johnstone feud. It kept the Scottish west march weak and protracted internecine warfare presented no threat to England or English Borderers. In fact Lord Wharton, Warden of the English West March, took a hand in occasional policing in Dumfriesshire, imprisoning either Maxwells or Johnstones or both whenever his government's interests could be served by altering the balance of power.

The Johnstones suffered from a simple and perennial disadvantage. Holding lands primarily in Annandale (the Maxwells' power base lay further west, in Nithsdale and beyond) and allied to smaller surnames such as the Irvines and the Moffats, their fighting strength was always outweighed. The Maxwells were usually able to put many more men in the saddle – in fact it is a tribute to the Johnstones' tenacity that such an unequal feud lasted so long. Because of this weakness, they keenly sought the office of March Warden. As a government appointee a Johnstone warden could call for reinforcements from Edinburgh to keep order, which often meant little more than defeating the Maxwells. As a result the wardenship of the west march was always manipulated in either surname's interest, and the office changed hands with dizzying frequency. Between 1577 and 1588 there was a different warden almost every year, some incumbents lasting only a few months.

This was the period when the feud intensified. Each time a Johnstone was appointed as warden, the Maxwells and all their followers refused to recognise his authority. This made it easier for them to attract outlaws and chronically lawless surnames like the Armstrongs to their cause. Dumfriesshire was descending into anarchy.

In 1584 a Johnstone was made provost of Dumfries. The town lying in the midst of Maxwell lands, the office had traditionally been in their gift, and when the new provost attempted to have himself installed, he was barred from the town. Between July and October that year John Johnstone was unable to enter Dumfries. How the affairs of the burgh were conducted without a provost is not recorded. It was harvest-time and in retribution for his exclusion, Johnstone peruaded the English surname of Graham to come raiding and they burned the crops standing in the Maxwell fields. Dumfries was therefore neither fed nor governed.

National politics sometimes played in what had degenerated into a near-seamless cycle of raid and reprisal. The Maxwells suffered an Achilles' heel. They were a steadfastly catholic family (famously refusing to expel the old abbot and monks of Sweetheart Abbey until well into the seventeenth century) and as the supporters of King James VI grew more and more convinced that he might one day become the I, blatant catholicism needed to be suppressed. As his son and grandson were to discover to their immense cost, England expected a protestant prince and a well-known catholic family doing as it wished in the Borders was not an encouraging advertisement for James' credentials.

In 1585 John Maxwell, the heidsman of the name, was outlawed and as March Warden, John Johnstone was instructed to make an arrest. It appears that he failed, dismally. Maxwell and his allied surnames attacked Johnstone villages and burned Lochwood Tower, killing six of its defenders. Despite some retaliation the momentum of destruction wreaked by Maxwell built relentlessly. With a huge force, 1,700 riders, he raided Moffatdale and upper Annandale, stealing 3,000 head of cattle and burning everything in his path. By the end of the summer of 1585 the Maxwells were in complete control of the west march, every tower and castle was in their hands and John Johnstone was their prisoner. James VI and his advisers had been outplayed by sheer military muscle and aggression. They were forced to accept the unacceptable. Realpolitik allowed John Maxwell to assume the wardenship and do as he pleased in south-west Scotland.

John Johnstone died in 1587, and although consistently compromised by his catholicism, Maxwell held onto power. Raids on both sides stuttered on into the 1590s. It seemed as though the old feud might just fizzle out. But a minor event began a succession of escalating events which led to the battle at Dryfe Sands. Over a stolen horse, the Johnstones attacked the Crichtons, Maxwell allies, and killed 15 of them. It seems an extreme reaction but the slow-burning resentments of 70 years of feuding were easily fanned into flames. Maxwell demanded that the Johnstones surrender to him. He was of course rebuffed and the bloody road to the slaughter in the streets of Lockerbie began.

The battle was certainly vicious, but not decisive. The feud continued on into 1608, even after the March Wardenries had been abolished. James Johnstone agreed to a meeting with Lord Maxwell. There was only one item on the agenda – how to bring to an honourable end almost a century of appalling suffering and destruction. Maxwell had an answer. After tempers flared he shot James Johnstone twice in the back.

Strangely enough it was an answer of sorts. Maxwell fled to France and to exile. On his return, four years later, he was betrayed, arrested and executed. And with that last death, the feud ended.

ST GEORGE

A Roman soldier originally from Cappadocia in Asia Minor, St George was martyred in Palestine in the early 300s. Apparently he tore down the edicts of the Emperor Diocletian because they insisted that the pagan gods of Rome be worshipped. George may have been a cavalry officer for he quickly came to be identified with horsemen, and was also seen as the protector of flocks and herds. In Greece, 6th May, St George's Day (23rd April in England), was the traditional date for the journey to the high summer pastures. He was the ideal saint for the Border Reivers, had they been that way inclined, but after the middle of the fourteenth century, George became England's patron saint. Because of his popularity in Palestine (and Greece where he is also patron saint), it is thought that his cult was spread to England by returning crusaders. The cross of St George, England's flag and now increasingly in evidence on sporting occasions, certainly supports that notion. A red cross on a white field, it was the crusaders' symbol.

At the same time as the Johnstones and Maxwells were attempting to assure each other's mutual destruction, the Scotts were at feud with the Kerrs of Cessford (a dispute which touched on events at Jedburgh), and with the Elliots, who in turn were sworn against the Pringles and also the English surname of Fenwick. Cross-border feuds were less common, perhaps because it was usually the local control of land and political favour which were at stake. The Selbys conducted a vicious war with the Collingwoods after Sir Cuthbert accused Sir John Selby of treason. In 1586 an ambush was sprung on the Newcastle road near Morpeth. Sir Cuthbert and Lady Collingwood were travelling with their son-in-law, Robert Clavering, when the Selbys surprised them and held them at pistol-point. Despite Lady Collingwood falling to her knees and begging for mercy, Clavering's brother was killed and Sir Cuthbert badly wounded. The ground was laid for the beginning of a long and vicious feud, but for once matters played out somewhat differently. Three of the Selbys were arrested and convicted of murder and the Claverings accepted cash compensation for their loss, an old-fashioned blood-price. In this way feud was avoided and the affair quickly and cleanly resolved. But the enmity between the Selbys and the Collingwoods festered on and did flare into intermittent feud.

James Hepburn, Earl of Bothwell, later to be husband of Mary Queen of Scots, Keeper of Liddesdale and master of Hermitage Castle discovered a good reason to fear the visceral power of Border surnames. In 1566 he held high hopes to become the King Consort, the most powerful man in Scotland. Bothwell's ambition was un-bounded, he rode to Liddesdale in his pomp, planning to bring order to that nest of feuding thieves. And then he ran into Little Jock Elliot.

Bothwell's troopers swept into Liddesdale and his captains rounded up a few of the more available Elliots, the usual suspects. They were taken to Hermitage Castle and locked up. An aggressive, even head-strong, man, Bothwell was determined to stamp his imperious author-ity, show that he was worthy to be a warrior-king. When he encountered Little Jock Elliot of the Park, a leading Liddesdale reiver, he challenged him to single combat. Shooting Elliot out of the saddle, Bothwell seemed to have quickly settled matters. But then he made a bad mistake. Having dismounted to deliver the coup de grace, the Earl failed to notice that Elliot was not quite done for, and that he had a drawn dagger concealed under his body. In an instant the reiver sprang up and stabbed Bothwell in the face, chest and his hands, as he tried to protect himself. Badly hurt, pride dented, the Earl was laid out in a cart and trundled back to Hermitage Castle. Where the Elliot prisoners had overpowered their captors and taken control. After some negotiation, the bleeding Bothwell managed to regain the sanctuary of his castle. None of this was what he had in mind when he rose that morning.

The incident became famous, not least because of a famous Border ballad and a phrase which has entered the Scottish psyche. The following verse sums up something at the essence of the extraordinary story of the Border Reivers – the power of the name. To inspire fear, respect, and a sense of history, all Little Jock Elliot has to do is state it:

'I've vanquished the Queen's Lieutenant,
And garr'd her troopers to flee:
My name is Little Jock Elliot,
And wha daur meddle wi' me?'

3

The Landscape of Larceny

The see of John Leslie, the Bishop of Ross, lay almost as far from the Borders as it was possible to be in mainland Scotland, and yet he understood perfectly how the reivers executed their longer-range raids. Leslie must have spent time in the Cheviot Hills for the description he included in his *History of Scotland* (1572–6) is difficult to better. Here is part of it:

> They sally out of their own borders, in the night, in troops, through unfrequented by-ways, and many intricate windings. All the day time, they refresh themselves and their horses, in lurking holes they had pitched upon before, till they arrive at the dark in those places they have a design upon. As soon as they have seized upon the booty, they, in like manner, return home in the night, through blind ways, and fetching many a compass [taking circuitous routes]. The more skillful any captain is[,] to pass through these wild deserts, crooked turnings and deep precipices, in the thickest mists and darkness, his reputation is the greater, and he is looked upon as a man of an excellent head.

The landscape of the Borders was superbly suited to the dark needs of horse-riding thieves. And it is perhaps appropriate that all those lurking-holes and intricate windings first came about through violence, as a result of an ancient geological collision. Unimaginably long ago, about 450 million years BC, the crust of the Earth was still forming, massive continents were moving, vast oceans filled and drained. What was to become southern Scotland lay on the leading edge of a huge landmass while northern England was on the rim of another. Between them stretched the Iapetus Ocean. When the two super-continents collided, they shoved up the bed of the ocean, corrugating and buckling it as the harder rocks of Scotland ground and scraped up over the softer stones of northern England. Geologists can see the deposit of all that prehistoric drama when they compare the granite rocks of Galloway with the coal and iron-bearing seams of West Cumbria. They are very different and what ultimately became the political frontier between England and Scotland was something much more profound, the most fundamental geological division in the British Isles.

This is no mere scientific curiosity. Geology shapes the landscape and determines its nature. And the landscape forms the character of the people. Perhaps more obviously the old collision affected the direction of history because of the angle at which southern Scotland and northern England met. It was not head-on but more glancing and it made our geography run from north-east to south-west. Most of the hill ranges – the Southern Uplands, the Cheviots – are set on that compass bearing, strung out on parallel lines with the Midland Valley of Forth and Clyde, the Highland Line and the Great Glen. The Tweed, the Teviot, the Tyne, the Liddel, the Esk and the important little River Irthing run their courses in broadly the same way, while the shorter rivers of Galloway, Cumbria, Northumberland and the Borders flow down from the watershed ridges.

A journey from the banks of the Tweed to the Tyne is instructive. All that ancient geology had a surprising, counter-intuitive effect. A traveller takes the road winding up out of the fertile and green Tweed Basin, through the woodland by the banks of the Jed and up to the border at the Carter Bar. Those who take the time to park and get out of the car to look at the long vistas to the north and south see something unexpected. The valleys they left behind are patterned with the homely geometry of farming. Green fields and edging shelter belts lead the eye into the distance, as far as the Eildon Hills on a clear, crisp day. To the south there are twenty miles and more of moorland to be crossed before the road descends at Kirkwhelpington and goes on through a gentler landscape to Belsay and the beginnings of the western Northumberland plain. In the east and middle marches, much of the English side of the border is bleaker, more windblown and desolate.

The western ranges of the Cheviots merge with the hills of the Southern Uplands. The old road from Hawick to Langholm and Carlisle beyond it threads through one of the very few passes in these steep-sided hills, the narrow cleft below Mosspaul. Bleakness and hard living extended equally on both sides in the west march. And all of this geology had its effects as history flowed back and forth over the hills and what would become a frontier zone.

SIKES, DEANS AND BUCHTS

The names of places can be very old, often the oldest words in common speech. That they originally meant something has often been lost. Few now talk of sikes or deans even though they are generic words. The Border landscape is full of ancient descriptions now masquerading as proper names. Here are a few;

Bucht: a sheepfold
Cleuch: a deep, wooded valley, sometimes a cliff
Cote: a house or cottage
Dean: a small valley or defile, sometimes shortened to 'den' as in Dryden or Frogden
Gill: a ravine with a stream running at its bottom
Haugh: an open, often flattish parcel of land, sometimes by a river or stream
Hope: a hollow found amongst the hills
Knowe: a knoll or hummock
Mains: from the French 'demesne' (originally from the Latin 'mansio'), meaning home or central farm
Rig: a ridge, but also used for old-style cultivation areas and often found in farm names
Shaw: a flat piece of ground at the foot of a hill
Sheils: a permanently occupied hill farm or holding
Sheilings: temporary huts for shepherds
Swire: a steep pass between two hills, as in Redeswire
Sike: a marshy bottom where several small streams rise

After these valleys had been scoured and bulldozed into their modern form by the glaciers of the last ice age which flowed east and south from the ice-dome over Broad Law, the land began to green. Tundra gave way to grassland and as the climate continued to improve a vast wildwood carpeted the landscape, stunted trees and scrub even reaching up to the windy summits of Cheviot and the Carter Ridge.

As the first pioneers paddled up the rivers and made this temperate jungle their home, they began to make clearings, often using fire. When these peoples adopted farming as a staple way of life, forest clearance gathered pace and the optimum temperatures of the later prehistoric period allowed settlement up in the Border hills. Towards the end of the first millennium BC there appears to have an organised migration into the eastern ranges of the Cheviots. In the Bowmont Valley, south of Kelso, archaeologists have recognised the contours of terraces created for hillside cultivation and even a degree of soil erosion as a result. Some long forgotten central power based in the Tweed Valley probably forced communities to move upcountry, almost certainly as a consequence of overpopulation. But the weather was better then, the growing season longer and warmer and corn would ripen at those altitudes. Perhaps the wind was also less relentless.

The ancient wildwood survived in memory for a long time. As late as 1538, only five centuries ago, the antiquarian John Leland remembered it when he complained that 'the great wood of Cheviot' was 'spoyled now and crokyd old trees and scrubs remayne'. The reality was that the clearance had continued into the historic period and evidence of high altitude cultivation, particularly in the Lammermuirs, is not hard to find. On the beautiful, winding road between Duns and Gifford an evening sun will often show up a pattern of folded rigs on the flanks of the bare hills.

The uplands were attractive not only because of the kinder climate, they were dry in another sense. Before the agricultural improvements of the eighteenth and nineteenth centuries the Borders landscape was much more boggy. Valley bottoms were often very difficult to negotiate after the rains of winter. Many old roads preferred the dry and draining ground of the hills and the network of medieval and early modern drovers' tracks through the Moorfoots and the Cheviots remember that. In lower lying ground mosses could be dangerous, sometimes bottomless, and it was important to know exactly which way the track turned. Badly herded beasts sometimes blundered into bogs to be sucked under, thrashing and bellowing in wide-eyed panic.

In short, there existed a vigorous prehistoric and medieval upland community in the Borders. These were people who cultivated crops on the high plateaux, who reared animals on good grassland and who animated places we now think of as bleak and remote, places where almost no one now lives. In many important ways the hill country of the middle ages was a good place to live – but it was not to remain so.

In the early fourteenth century the climate began to change radically. The year after the battle at Bannockburn, 1315, saw a dreadful summer. From the end of June it seemed to rain incessantly (King Robert I was forced to abandon the siege of Carlisle because his engines stuck fast in the mud) and the harvest failed. There was another failure in 1316. This was a prelude to what scientists call 'the little ice age'. For approximately five hundred years, up to *c.*1850, the Earth's climate grew harsher. Average mean temperatures fell and a cycle of 30-year periods of bad weather began. Severe winters were followed by wet summers. In Europe the paintings of Dutch and Flemish masters recorded the long, icebound months. Particularly memorable is Pieter Breughel's *Hunters in the Snow*. Two periods of poor weather appear to have occured in the sixteenth century, one prompting reports of extreme, extended spells of rain in the 1570s, the other producing cold, sunless summers into the 1590s.

SLIPSHOD

Animals undertaking a long journey, usually to market, needed to be shod. Hooves used to grass and particularly to damp or soft ground were themselves soft, and since some travelling would be over hard, firm tracks, protection was necessary. Sharp stones could cut an animal's foot and make it lame, slow and doomed. There are many phrases and expressions deriving from the ancient craft of farriery or blacksmithing, but 'slipshod'is apposite here. It originally referred to a loosely nailed shoe. Other animals, apart from ponies, were shoed. Geese were made to waddle through hot pitch or tar, then into a patch of grit and sand, and finally into a mill pond to cool and fix the mixture. Tough grass and straw socks were knitted for pigs and their tender trotters, while halved pony shoes were nailed onto the harder cloven hooves of cows. It was impossible to get cattle to cooperate in the same way as ponies, and so they were upended and roped to keep them still. When the reivers lifted cattle, sheep or horses, they had to make a long journey whatever the condition of their feet, and more than a few must have gone lame and been left hobbling by the wayside.

Bad weather was rarely reported directly, as something noteworthy in itself. Periods or incidents influenced, often decisively, by storms or floods are what helps build a pattern. The terrible raids into Roxburgh-shire led by Henry VIII's generals, the Earl of Surrey and Lord Dacre, were much inhibited by a series of sustained rainstorms. Even though it had not been designed to resist the sort of artillery trundled up by the English bombardiers, Cessford Castle held out against Surrey's siege – because of the weather. The defenders had dug an earthwork, a 'vaw-mure', around the central stone tower, the donjon of the castle. This was likely a deep ditch topped by a massive earthen bank formed from the upcast, so thick that gunstones or cannonballs could not breach it. And the ditch probably presented attackers with, literally, insurmountable problems. The pouring rain must have turned it into a slithering quagmire, its sides too treacherous to be scaled.

When Sir Andrew Kerr, the lord of Cessford, at last came to negotiate, he offered to give up the stronghold if he and his men could leave unmolested with 'bag and baggage'. The Earl of Surrey was much relieved, believing that in the dreadful weather, he could not have hoped to take the castle.

It rained for much of the summer of 1523 and on into the autumn. By October the Scots were retaliating by attacking Wark Castle, an ancient fortress on a height above the south bank of the Tweed. Positioning his guns on the north bank, the Scottish Regent, the Duke of Albany, hoped to bring down the new polygonal artillery block-house built at Wark by the master mason at Berwick. Again the rain intervened. Whether it made ranging and aiming the cannon difficult or the setting of them in a sound footing in a battery impossible is unclear. What is certain is that in 1523 the heavens opened often and for days on end.

When the Earl of Sussex mustered his forces to pursue rebel catholic noblemen into Scotland in August of 1570, it rained so heavily and for so long that the expedition had to be seriously delayed. In 1573 a *tempest* of rain raged for eight days and nights without abating until a long stretch of Berwick-upon-Tweed's medieval walls was washed away and the bridge across the river badly damaged. They had stood since Edward I's time, built in the early 1300s.

Snow fell often in the sixteenth century and heavily, cutting com-munications for long periods. And when the thaws came, streams roared into torrents and the fords across the Tweed became impass-able for many days. In November 1570 a ferocious winter set in and storms blew regularly until the following February. The historian, William Camden, wrote that it was not only frequent periods of warfare which had made Borderers tough, the cruel weather had also 'hardened their carcasses'.

Many of the government officials appointed by Elizabeth I to posts in the Borders came from the south of England, and while complaints about the rain and the cold might have been expected, their comments are not routine grumblings. Some were vehement. The wonderfully named Peregrine Bertie, Baron Willoughby d'Eresby, was a reluctant Warden of the English East March. He hated the Border weather with a passion:

> If I were further from the tempestuousness of the Cheviot Hills, and were once retired from this accursed country, whence the sun is so removed, I would not change my homeliest hermitage for the highest palace there.

Appropriately he died of a heavy cold in 1601.

Notwithstanding Peregrine Bertie's exceptional unhappiness, there is a persistent note of misery at the worsening climate in the 1570s and the 1590s. And it can be no coincidence that this was the time when reiving wound up to its most extreme pitch, when theft was probably less a matter of greed and more a question of survival. In the weeks and months of rain, grass at least grew and hardy cattle, sheep and goats could feed and put on condition, and present themselves as coveted targets for thievery.

Poetry is a risky source of historical evidence, but despite the licence, it can supply atmosphere and make a basic point effectively. Walter Scott of Satchells wrote a famous verse which understands an essential fact of sixteenth-century life in the Border hills:

> I would have none think that I call them thieves.

> The freebooter ventures both life and limb
> Good wife and bairn, and every other thing;
> He must do so, or else must starve and die,
> For all his livelihood comes of the enemy.

Leaving aside the rights, wrongs, truths and half truths, Scott's verse does state the economic circumstances bluntly. The consistently bad weather of the second half of the sixteenth century and its sustained effect on the hill peoples of southern Scotland and northern England must have greatly fostered the creation of a criminal society.

AYE IN COMMON!

To people who depended utterly on what it can produce, the question of the ownership of land and the right to it were of the first importance. And yet in the sixteenth-century Border hills, it can be unclear to a historian. To contemporaries it could not have been vague. Around the Border towns and larger villages, there were common lands where the indwellers had customary rights. They could graze their beasts, and cut turf, peat and bracken. Some of the commons were huge – at its zenith Selkirk had 22,000 acres. But what happened in the hills? Where religious houses had been landowners, there was usually great precision. For example, the monks of Kelso Abbey owned much of the beautiful Bowmont Valley which leads close to the foot of Cheviot itself. In a series of documents they set down their boundaries and rights very clearly. It must be assumed that the windblown wastes of the watershed ridges were similarly precisely apportioned. But the historical documentation is hard to come by. The upland society of the Borders remained Celtic in many ways and the old practice of 'gavelkind' (which almost destroyed the medieval economy of Wales) still held, especially in Tynedale and Redesdale. A landowner divided his property equally amongst all his sons – until the individual legacies became so small as to be unviable. (Some historians believe that the poverty created by generations of gavelkind let directly to reiving.) In important ways the surnames of the Borders behaved like Highland clans – did their people have a similar relationship to the land owned by those names and their chiefs, or heidsmen? Sir Robert Bowes, at one time Warden of the English Middle March, seems to have seen the ownership of the valley of the North Tyne as surname-based:

> The country of North Tynedale which is more plenished with wild and misdemeaned people, may make of men upon horseback and upon foot about six hundred. They stand most by four surnames, whereof the Charltons be the chief. And in all services or charge impressed upon that country the Charltons and such as be under their rule, be rated for one half of that country, the Robsons for a quarter, and the Dodds and Milburns for another quarter.

The upcountry was never heavily populated; the quality of the land simply could not support dense settlement. But in the sixteenth century many more people lived in the likes of Liddesdale than do now. Aside from Carlisle, Berwick and Dumfries, towns were really villages and villages hamlets. Borderers lived overwhelmingly on the land, close to what they sowed and reared.

Working in the 1580s and 1590s, a well-known cartographer called Timothy Pont drew a detailed map of Liddesdale. When set beside even the largest scale modern Ordnance Survey for the same area, the differences are striking. Pont's map is closely speckled with place-names, most of them farm-steadings, some of them two or three variations on a single name, many lining the banks of streams and rivers. By comparison the modern map is sparse, the place-names have faded from history, the old cottages and barns reclaimed by the grass. Around Hermitage Castle a dozen farms clustered when Pont plotted his map at the end of the sixteenth century. Graistonhaugh Tofts, Ginglenwells, Rispeylaw, Faskenn, Byresteads and Reddadenn have all disappeared, leaving only shadowy contours in the grass only visible when they are lit by a late evening sun.

EATS AND SHOOTS

Grass is a remarkable plant. Not only is it an excellent coloniser, able to take over large areas very quickly, it also thrives on being cropped or cut. Unusually it grows from the bottom upwards and so when it regularly grazed, it becomes more dense and grows ever more abundantly. What farmers call 'sheep lawns' can be seen over the Border hills. These are places where constant cropping has produced a green, carpet-like effect, the sort of thing suburban gardeners dream of. They should consider renting some sheep – because it appears that most grazing animals like very short grass and bite it close to the roots. Perhaps it tastes better, is more juicy. Two general sorts of grass grow in Britain. Most sheep graze hill pasture, which is entirely natural and full of herbs and other beneficial nutrients. The other kind is sown grass. Its use came about when crop rotation began to demand that fields previously sown with corn or a root crop be returned periodically to grass. It was also a good way of moving animals around to fertilise the ground with their droppings. Most hay is taken from sown grasses such as cocksfoot, timothy or ryegrass, but where a farmer can cut a crop from high summer pasture or a meadow which has never been ploughed, he can command a hefty premium for it.

That relative density of settlement meant a landscape much more intimately detailed, its every resource used and given a name. Small, dyked inbye fields clustered around low-built farmhouses made from material close to hand and which blended so seamlessly with the native colours of the landscape that they could easily be missed by a modern eye. Outbye was likely more casually wooded than it is now (leaving aside the massive modern forest planting which has seen many hillsides disappear under a blanket of sitka green) with copses and thickets left standing to bield (shelter) beasts and supply a source of windfall firewood. Peat was cut from dark brown banks which are now mistaken for erosion, and of course no roads existed. People and ponies walked along tracks little more than a foot or two wide and which followed the grain of the land closely. More like sheepwalks on a hillside than anything we might now call a road.

There were ancient exceptions. Well into the medieval period the old Roman roads through the Borders were regularly travelled. Wide, able to take wheeled vehicles and with hard bottoming in place, they had weathered the rains of more than a thousand winters. At the beginning of the fourteenth century Edward II led his invading armies north on Dere Street and the tramping soldiers and their baggage train were strung out for 20 miles as the old road snaked up through the Cheviot Hills, passing the tumbled-down ramparts and ditches of the marching camps dug by the legionaries at Chew Green. The Roman road then aimed arrow-straight at the ancient army depot of Trimontium, the three Eildon Hills clearly visible to the north, rising up out of the Tweed Valley. Sometimes called the *Gamelspath* (an early Anglian personal name, perhaps a powerful landowner), Dere Street was used by drovers and their great herds making the long trek to southern markets in the eighteenth and nineteenth centuries, and in the sixteenth century by large and confident bands of Border Reivers driving herds which rarely belonged to them.

Further east, towards the huge, grey-green hump of Cheviot itself, runs an even older road also frequently used by reivers running forays. Clennel Street originally led from Kelso up to the head of the lovely Bowmont Valley, south of Yetholm, up over the Windy Gyle and down the English side to Harbottle and the winding River Coquet. It was certainly busy and important enough for Henry II of England to order the building of a substantial castle to guard its southern terminal. Possibly another personal name, or a description whose meaning is lost, Clennel Street was sometimes marked on maps as 'The Ermspeth', and that means 'The Eagles' Road'. The more usual name first comes on record as 'Clenhill' in 1242 but it may have been trodden in prehistoric times, perhaps when better weather and longer growing seasons allowed cultivation in the valleys on either flank of the Windy Gyle. Clennel Street was certainly used by large raiding parties whose strength made stealth irrelevant. Still, their ponies would have glad of the sure and solid footing. Wheeled traffic could also use Clennel Street and up in the hills stands a lonely eighteenth-century milestone with 'Kelso 15' on one side and 'H11' on the other for the distance to Harbottle. On the latest Ordnance Survey the name has been half-forgotten and the old thief road is now simply marked as 'The Street'.

Mosses could be very dangerous. Not patches of puddled, soft ground spiked by clumps of marsh grass and dotted with willow scrub, but places where a stumble or lost footing would at best result in a bad soaking or at worst a drowning in deep, black pools and their cloying, sucking mud. Fords rather than bridges were where rivers and streams were crossed and if heavy rain made a spate then that was that – until the level dropped. The difficulty – to say nothing of the dangers – of travel kept most peaceable people snug at home in the winter and willing to go only as far as they had to in the summer.

COUNTRY ROADS

While farm workers tended to stay put, travelling only to local markets and little further, medieval roads could nevertheless be busy. Merchants, itinerant craftsmen, pilgrims, nobility and royalty were often on the move. Roman roads such as Dere Street and prehistoric tracks like Clennel Street remained in use well into the eighteenth century. In England, where the Roman province lasted for nearly four centuries, the road network was much more extensive and in the twelfth century, Watling Street, Ermine Street, the Fosse Way and the prehistoric Icknield Way (which travelled along the tops of the watershed ridges) were all named as royal roads and brought into the king's protection. They were metalled, or paved, and had to be wide enough to allow two carts to pass each other, or sixteen armoured knights to ride abreast. This last sounds more like a formula than anything practical. The ancient roads lasted a long time. In the Borders the documents relating to Kelso Abbey talk of a 'via regis' between Roxburgh and Berwick, but despite the royal label, it was likely little more than a track by the banks of the Tweed. The 'Military Road' running to the south of Hadrian's Wall must have been well used. However, water routes were always prefered where possible and if rivers were deep enough, rafts and barges were towed down them. And in the west the Solway was busy.

The Cheviot landscape was changing. Because growing seasons were shortening in the second half of the sixteenth century and the weather generally deteriorating, farmers were abandoning cultivation, what contemporaries called 'tillage'. They were turning over more and more land to pasture. When the Earl of Hertford led a large army through the Borders in 1544 on a tremendously destructive and punitive raid, he remarked that the Borderers in his ranks (for there were plenty) 'will not willingly burn their neighbours' [corn]'. They knew how precious it was and what misery would follow the ruin of a subsistence crop. Stealing cows and sheep was one thing – they might be replaced or retrieved – but burnt corn was a disaster for which there was no remedy.

The gradual movement away from cultivation to pastoralism in turn led to depopulation and impoverishment, trends which showed up in the formal musters of men obliged to render military service which were occasionally held in the English marches. In 1580 and 1584 men who turned up complained that too much land was being given over to the grazing of beasts, and in 1597 the Dean of Durham Cathedral was anxious that the church's holdings in the Borders were too little cultivated. Although no one could be aware of it at the time, it looks very much as though climate deterioration was driving these changes.

BRIGANTIUM

When the Roman invaders pushed north into Yorkshire, they fought King Venutius and the nation of the Brigantes. In AD71 the legions won an important victory at Stanwick and their historian, Tacitus, hinted that they had been up against a confederacy of hill peoples and that Venutius 'had help from outside'. He meant warriors from the northern Pennines, the Cheviots and possibly the Southern Uplands. The Selgovae and the Brigantes were of the same stock as well as on the same side. The most famous Brigantian queen was Cartimandua and her name means 'Sleek Pony'. Letters written from the Roman fort of Vindolanda, near Haltwhistle, confirm a horse-riding society, noting that the natives 'had very many cavalry'. The Brigantian confederacy was a frequent source of trouble, rebelling several times, notably in 138. One of the reasons for Hadrian's Wall was that it cut through their territory, dividing a disruptive people. A horse-riding culture, a persistent threat to central authority – sounds familiar.

Liddesdale still looks like a reiver valley – despite the power lines, the abandoned railway and the tarmac road up to Whitrope and Hawick. A hard place that used to breed hard-bitten people and still a bleak place to live through a bad winter. In the sixteenth century there were likely as many people living in the valley (some historians believe more) as do now. Newcastleton is much bigger, an expanded, planned village which absorbed the old Armstrong place at Whithaugh. But by comparison the modern hinterland is empty, nothing like as densely settled as it was in the time of the reivers.

The Armstrongs rode out of Liddesdale and were a constant cause of trouble, particularly in the English middle marches. The royal officer appointed as warden to protect Elizabeth I's English subjects from Scottish raids (and each other) was Robert Carey and he left a memoir. It is eloquent about how Borderers understood and used the countryside they knew so well.

In June 1601 the Armstrongs mounted a destructive, punitive raid on the little English town of Haltwhistle, near Hadrian's Wall. They attempted to burn it down, 'running up and down the streets with lights in their hands'. But only ten houses were set on fire and after being driven off, the Armstrongs swore they would be back in greater strength to finish the job.

Robert Carey was forced to take decisive action and he laid his plans carefully. So that he could strike quickly against Liddesdale, his men built a stockade on the frontier above Bewcastle and it was garrisoned with 150 troopers. The Armstrongs immediately countered by abandoning their strongholds and farms in Liddesdale and melting away into the landscape. Taking their valuables (and presumably their herds and flocks), the reivers entered the wilderness of Tarras Moss. It lay to the west of Liddesdale in the high valley between Tinnis Hill and Whita Hill. There is a single track road from Newcastleton to Langholm which winds around the edges of what was Tarras Moss and it is a stern, wild and windswept waste. In 1601 it was an impenetrable maze and a place of impregnable refuge for those who knew its tracks. 'It was', wrote Robert Carey in his memoir, 'of that strength and so surrounded by bogs and marshy ground, with thick bushes and shrubs, that they fear no force nor power of England or Scotland.'

On the islands in this inland sea of treacherous mire the Armstrongs believed they could outlast the garrison in Carey's 'pretty fort' on Bewcastle Waste, and all they had to do was wait for the winter to chase away the soft southerners. Carey recorded a message from the defiant reivers:

> They sent me word that I was like the first puff of a haggis, hottest at the first, and bade me stay there as long as weather would give me leave; they would stay in Tarras-Wood 'till I was weary of lying in the Waste, and when I had had my time, and they no whit the worse, they would play their parts, which should keep me waking the next winter.

It was an insolent, cocky but broadly correct analysis, and Carey too knew that winter was no time for large-scale operations in Liddesdale, to say nothing of Tarras Moss. In early July his plan began to unfold. Under cover of darkness the warden sent ahead 150 troopers to circle the moss and bottle up the three safe exits to the west and the Scottish side. His captains were guided by an anonymous traitor, 'a moffled man not known to any of the company, no doubt someone with a grudge'.

The Armstrongs had set lookouts on the high ridges above Tarras but none of them saw the government troopers moving through the half-dark. Once his men had set their ambushes at the exit-paths, Carey moved quickly. With 300 troopers and 1,000 footmen, he attacked the moss. Just as dawn crept over Tinnis Hill, his men surprised the Armstrong camps and with much clang and clamour drove them towards the western exits. Where the ambushes were sprung. Important prisoners were taken but when others saw what was happening, they turned back into the wilderness and disappeared. And none of Carey's men made the mistake of following them.

Robert Carey was an outstanding officer, probably the most effective March Warden appointed by Queen Elizabeth, and the flushing of Tarras Moss was a superbly planned and executed operation. But it was also an exception. Border reivers knew their country intimately and almost always used it to advantage. Agricultural improvement, widespread (and very ugly) forestry planting and effective drainage have combined to change the character of this ancient wilderness almost beyond recognition, making the Armstrongs' use of Tarras Moss and other inaccessible places difficult to visualise. But it was true, there were trackless, uncharted wastes where only natives dared venture, and the reivers really were kings of a wild frontier.

PECORINO

One of the most delicious European cheeses is made from ewes' milk and sold in Italy. Pecorino comes in delicate flavours, from sweet to salty, and can be fearsomely expensive. Border reivers liked it. In their buchts the ewe-milkers of the hills made a variety of very hard, white cheese which they called 'whitemeats'. It kept for a long time without spoiling but was so hard that it had to be soaked and sometimes beaten with a hammer before it could be safely chewed and digested. On long-range raids, riders would take a hunk with them, and also a small amount of oatmeal. This habit was noticed by a French diplomat, Jean Froissart, who visited the Borders in the 1360s: 'Under the flaps of his saddle, each man carries a broad plate of metal, behind the saddle a little bag of oatmeal . . . they place the plate over the fire, mix with water their oatmeal, and when the plate is heated, they put a little of the paste upon it and make a thin cake like a cracknell or biscuit, which they eat to warm their stomachs.' An oatcake remains the best accompaniment to cheese.

Since a time out of mind, back into the deep prehistoric past when the land was even less tamed, the farmers of the Border uplands had in fact been herdsmen who only cultivated crops where they could. They drove cattle and sheep and also lived off a wild harvest of roots, fruits and berries as well as what game they could trap and catch. The earliest name attached to these people was 'Selgovae', meaning 'the Hunters', and in the medieval period the hunting dogs bred and trained by their descendants were famous throughout Europe. It was a persistent tradition. When Border reivers disappeared into their maze of hill valleys, mosses and byways, their pursuers sometimes used hunting dogs, what were called 'slewdogs', or scent-hounds to find their trails. Working on a leash with a handler urging them on, the slewdogs were also known as 'rauchs' in the Borders. They were trained not to bark or become excited when they closed in on their quarries. These animals were very valuable and raiders stole them whenever they could.

BEST FRIENDS

Dogs were domesticated very early in the prehistoric period, possibly from stray wolves who joined a human 'pack'. At first they appear to have been used as guard-dogs, warning of dangerous or unknown approaches by barking or perhaps howling. When wolves still prowled the Border hills looking to take lambs or old and weaker ewes, pastoral dogs warned the shepherds who would try to beat off an attack. When that threat receded in the middle ages (when Border sheep-rearing was radically commercialised by the abbeys of Kelso, Melrose, Dryburgh and Jedburgh), the dogs developed other skills, particularly in herding, what is known as 'the gather'. Border collies (the name seems to derive from 'coaly' or black) were first bred in the late nineteenth century by a Northumbrian farmer, Adam Telfer. Small, compact and very quick over short distances, collies have a keen intelligence and an expressive eye. Their owners of course claim that they are the smartest dogs to be found anywhere. Most ewes would reluctantly agree.

The beasts reared in the sixteenth century, their breeds of cattle and sheep, were much smaller and more hardy than the animals grazing on modern farms. They lived out, watered by streams running down hillsides and sheltered by the natural contours of the land. Mostly black in colour and also dark in nature, cattle were much less domesticated than the big bullocks we see now. In winter their coats grew shaggy and the animals sometimes deliberately rolled in mud to make them matted and therefore better able to keep out the biting wind. This must have made them difficult to see on the hillside on a grey day. When it was stormy, cows could be good indicators of the direction of the prevailing wind. They turn their backsides towards it and drop their heads to use their own bodies as a windbreak. The reivers' cattle will have seemed wild to us, the bulls very dangerous, and difficult to manage with their sharp horns and an instinct for open country.

NOWT, OUSEN AND KYNE

Even the fatter editions of the Oxford English Dictionary make no mention of these words, though they are liberally sprinkled through sixteenth-century reports of reiving. They are all words for cattle and were still in use in the Borders at the end of the twentieth century. 'Ousen' is a variant on oxen (which is an older word for a castrated bull-calf or bullock) as is 'nowt', sometimes written as 'nolte'. The latter can also mean specifically black cattle. 'Kyne' or 'kye' is a general term for cows, but can also mean a milker. All appear to derive from Anglian words first introduced into Scotland in the seventh and eighth centuries. 'Stirk' is used to mean a yearling – either a bullock or a heifer, it appears in no dictionary and yet is still in general use in the Borders. Sheep also had a nomenclature. Wedders were castrated lambs, bred for meat. Gimmers were barren or infertile ewes and a 'tup' is a Border word for a ram, and when fertile ewes had been 'tupped' lambs were expected to follow. Entertainingly 'tup-heidit' means 'a stupid, obstinate man'. Many Border shepherds pronounce it 'tip', and no doubt have come across a few tip-heids. Out on the hills sheep breeding is difficult to control and some farmers in the high valleys above Liddesdale still use an ancient method of contraception. 'Breeking' the ewes involves shepherds sewing a square of stout cloth over the animal's rear end to prevent the tups from mounting them successfully.

Pastoral dogs were slowly losing their prime function as defenders against the wolf-packs which roamed the Cheviots until the middle ages and becoming handy as sheep and cattle herders. More timorous, less aggressive and much smaller than cows, sheep were also more useful, giving both milk and wool. But cattle retained their ancient status as the prime measure of a man's wealth and the herds seem to have been the principal object of most reiver raids.

In springtime herdsmen drove their beasts up to the high summer pastures. As the weather improved and new grass poked through, cattle and sheep were rounded up and the herd-laddies whacked, pushed and roared them onto the old hill-trails. Many pastures were distant from what was known as the wintertown, the home farm, and often sheilings were built at the summertown. These were flimsy structures designed to keep out little more than light rain and wind. Most herd-laddies expected to sleep out through the long, light nights of the summer. No upstanding shielings are to be found nowadays in the Border hills but survivors can still be seen on the Hebridean island of Lewis. On the Barvas Moor, near Stornoway, corrugated iron, wood and sometimes brick huts dot the horizon.

Memories of warm summer nights flit through some of the Border ballads and even in the place-names found in the hills. Up from the wintertown, lassies came to the 'buchts' to milk the ewes, perhaps to make cheese. There was plenty of 'laughin' an daffin' at the yow-milkin'' and probably much else besides. And around the evening crackle of firelight, stories were told. The great tradition – unparalleled elsewhere – of the Border ballads was fostered on these summer nights up on the high grazing. Their written form (for all were held only in memory for many generations), collected by Sir Walter Scott just as they were waning, reflects something of where and how they were recited. Some ballads had dozens of verses, telling long and dramatic stories, and both to involve the listeners (who most likely knew the words anyway) and give the reciter time to remember what came next, the use of the chorus developed. Repeated between each verse, in the same metre, it jogged recollection and kept the tale moving along.

BALLADRY

Following a widespread European tradition, the Border ballads had a standard form of four line stanzas driven by a strong narrative. What distinguishes them is their antiquity. The subject of one of the oldest is the Battle of Otterburn and it was fought in 1388. The opening is classic – and stirring;

> It fell about the Lammas tide
> When muir-men win their hay
> The doughty Douglas bound him to ride
> Into England to drive a prey.

Memorable and with a driving metre, a spoken recital can keep an audience spell-bound. But what is often forgotten is the music. These ballads were originally sung and in his 'Minstrelsy of the Scottish Border', Walter Scott set many of the melodies alongside the text. American musicologists have argued that the ballad tradition transfered to the black communities of the south and they used the form to pass on stories. These often took a blues form, like 'Frankie and Johnny'. But the tradition is not yet dead in the Borders. It appears to be thriving. Collecting ballads and poems composed after Scott published in the early nineteenth century, the historian and poet, Walter Elliot, has compiled a New Minstrelsy of the Scottish Border.

Herds stayed out for as long as possible on the summer pasture. Their absence allowed the inbye fields around the wintertown to recover and be cropped for hay. Those left behind, the women and usually the older men, could use the break to clear up after the clatch and dark of the winter in what Borderers still call 'the redd'. Dykes were repaired, turf cut for roofing and what arable crops there were could grow, safe from beasts breaking in to devour them.

Fattened, glossy with good autumn condition, the herds came down off the hills when the weather began to close down and the year turned around the solstice. These weeks also saw the beginning of the raiding season. Dispersed over the hill pasture (and needing to feed and improve their condition in any case), the cattle and sheep were not a feasible target for reivers in the summer. Far better to come for them where they were handily corralled in the inbye fields and fat and fit enough to make a long journey when they had been lifted. The reivers did not choose to run forays in the winter. The going and the weather was much more difficult (although hard frost could make solid and passable ground out of normally boggy areas), it was the ancient cycle of transhumance which forced them out on rain-swept November nights.

What delivered a party of reivers to their quarry, what indeed made their entire way of life possible was an animal too little remarked upon by historians, the remarkable pony known as the Galloway Nag.

JOCK AND JACK

In sixteenth-century England the more than faintly derogatory term for 'a man of the common people', what we might more kindly term 'a bloke', or 'a fella', was a Jack. The phrase 'Jack of all trades' is a relict. In Scotland the accepted version was 'Jock' and by the seventeenth century, the diminutive 'Jockie' came to be applied to grooms working in aristocratic stables. Later it was also used to describe horse-dealers. By the time horse racing began to organise and enjoy widespread popularity, 'jockeys' had become the name for professional riders hired by owners to sit on their horses. The horses were valuable and had names and well-researched breeding, but their riders were all lumped under one category – wee Jocks.

Also known as 'hobblers' or 'hobbys', they were small, and at only 13 or 14 hands high, would now be thought much too small to carry adults comfortably and suitable only for children learning to ride. But these little ponies were powerfully made, their musculature compact and outline foursquare. In Galashiels, rearing up outside the old town hall, there is a beautifully made bronze sculpture of a fully armed reiver on his Galloway Nag. The rider's feet dangle well below the pony's belly and with his rig-out and weapons, he looks far too heavy, likely to exhaust his mount quickly. Sadly there is now no way to discover if indeed these neat little horses could have managed to bear such a burden. The Galloway Nag became extinct in the nineteenth century – but not before their famous prowess had been noticed by both William Shakespeare and Sir Walter Scott. Here is a second-hand description of the last of them, written in 1858 by William Youatt, an authority on horses and horse-breeding:

> A horse between thirteen and fourteen hands in height is called a Galloway, from a beautiful breed of little horses once found in the south of Scotland, on the shore of the Solway Firth, but now sadly degenerated, and almost lost.

The pure Galloway was said to be nearly fourteen hands high, and sometimes more; of a bright bay or brown, with black legs, small head and neck, and peculiarly deep and clean legs. Its qualities were speed, stoutness, and surefootedness over a very rugged and mountainous country.

Professor Edward Low understood something of the historical role and origins of the Galloways and was also at some pains to point out that nag was not a pejorative term, it simply denoted a small riding horse:

> They exceeded the pony size and were greatly valued for their activity and bottom . . . Besides this part of Scotland [the south] was a country of forays during the rude border wars of the times, when a more agile race than the ordinary pack-horse was naturally sought for; and all along the borders of the two kingdoms, a class [breed] of similar properties existed. Many of the true Galloways of the western counties were handsome, and their general characteristic was activity, and the power of enduring fatigue. Some raids were run over immensely long and difficult distances. Round trips of 100 miles were not uncommon and one daring and celebrated Scottish raid penetrated as far south as Blaydon, across the River Tyne, only a mile or two west of Newcastle. As well as furious, the owners of the stolen cattle must have been amazed. And the ability of the Galloways to deliver their riders to a destination – and then be used to cut out and round up cattle, and after that perhaps expect to be ridden as a cavalry pony in a skirmish or something worse – this was astonishing. They were unique little horses and it is sad that none now live to show how the reivers rode and how they sustained their way of life.

MY LITTLE PONY

The Celtic people of the Borders valued their horses. Calling them 'snow-maned', 'galloping, high-stepping', the seventh-century cavalry warriors of the Gododdin rode out from their fortress on Edinburgh's Castle Rock to challenge the invading Angles in AD 600. On their way south, they stopped at Kelso to be reinforced by Border riders and their prince, Catrawt of Calchvyndd. At Catterick in North Yorkshire, 'the retinue of Gododdin on rough-maned horses like swans, with their harness drawn tight' charged into the ranks of the Germanic invaders and their allies. And were decisively defeated. Their culture and language faded into half-forgotten stories but they did leave intriguing legacies. The Celts of Britain and Europe worshipped a complex and highly localised pantheon of gods. But one fertility goddess was widely revered. She was 'Epona', a mare, and from her the word 'pony' probably derives. Less attractive but equally possible is a Scots-French origin. 'Powny' may come from an obscure French word, 'poulonet' for a little foal, which in turn came from the Latin 'pullus' meaning the same. Eighteenth-century dictionaries defined ponies as 'little Scotch horses' and as the word travelled south it was rubbed smooth into 'pony'. Border Reivers used several names for their riding horses and they may just have coined this one.

Picking their way down steep and slippery hillsides, finding steady footing amongst tussocky bogs, winding their way between boulders and across stoney fords, one of the Nag's greatest qualities was its surefootedness. Much of this was done in darkness, often pursued or pursuing, and although horses have good night vision, the degree of sheer athleticism – to say nothing of trust – between pony and rider is to be marvelled at. Perhaps because the Galloways were small and a man could wrap his legs around its belly to squeeze and thereby give many signals, or shift his seat in subtle ways to change direction, the partnership may have been very close, almost intuitive. One Galloway was celebrated in verse;

> Wat Tinlinn from the Liddelside
> Led a small and shaggy nag
> That, through a bog, from hag to hag,
> Could bound like any Billhope stag.

Often carrying a weapon in one hand and holding the reins in the other, it would have taken no more than a touch on the neck from a good rider to wheel the pony. And in a skirmish where positioning was everything, speed of reaction and nimble footwork of a horse could mean life or death for its rider. A pony able to fiddle its feet to recoil from a blow or launch forward to deliver one was a valuable animal.

Stamina was as prized as agility and although no recent examples exist to confirm that the Galloways could carry a raiding party up over the Cheviot ranges and a long way down the other side – and back – there is an attractive and affectionate memoir from an eighteenth-century Scottish doctor called Anderson which recalls their great depth of staying power:

> In point of elegance of shape, it was a perfect picture; and in disposition was gentle and compliant. It moved almost with a wish, and never tired. I rode this little creature for twenty-five years, and twice in that time I rode a hundred and fifty miles at a stretch, without stopping except to bait [eat], and that not for above an hour at a time. It came in at the last stage with as much ease and alacrity as it travelled the first. I could have undertaken to have performed on this beast, when it was in its prime, sixty miles a day for a twelvemonth, running without any extraordinary exertion.

JOCKS AND GEORDIES

Uncomfortably for some, there is no question that Scots is a dialect of English. To distinguish it from Gaelic and Norn, Scots was known as 'Inglis' in the middle ages. Did the reivers on either side of the border speak in the same way, in the same dialect? Probably. When the Anglian warbands overran the Tweed Basin in the seventh and eighth centuries, their version of Old English gradually came to be spoken across what is now North Yorkshire, Durham, Northumberland and right up to the foothills of the Lammermuirs – and beyond. The Battle of Otterburn was fought in fading light and then under a full moon. The late fourteenth-century Westminster Chronicle records 'the darkness played such tricks on the English that when they aimed a careless blow at a Scotsman, owing to the chorus of voices speaking a single language, it was an Englishman that they cut down'. Shared dialect words between Geordies and Jocks (which are of course much more Geordie than Jock in origin, the direction of linguistic spread being from south to north) re-member that common language – the likes of 'bairn', 'canny', 'hoose' and 'bonnie'. On the western side of the border the dialect map is less clear but likely to have been similar. The language of the ballads shows some differences between Scots and English, but they are not striking. Andrew Boorde, an English doctor who practised in Scotland in the 1540s, reckoned that 'English and Scots doth follow together in speech' and in a late sixteenth-century play a dramatic device requires a Redesdale man to be mistaken for a Scot.

It was the Reformation which began to divide the dialect. In the second half of the sixteenth century independent and reformed English and Scottish churches were created and as a result different education systems began to divide the community and polarise the way in which Borderers spoke. Which, bonnie lad and lasses, is a shame.

In an age of motor transport we easily forget that in the centuries before cars and buses, most people could ride, probably as many as can drive nowadays. In the upland communities of the Borders, ponies were central to their lives. They carried herdsmen out into the hills behind their beasts and took them on all sorts of peaceful errands. Young herd-laddies probably threw a cloth and a bridle onto a long-suffering old pony and learned to ride the hard way, no stirrups and roaring and yelling across the heather.

A LOAD OF BOLLS

Units of measurement have changed regularly throughout history. Since around the 1960s we have moved gradually from imperial weights and quantities to metric. The process began officially with the creation of a decimal coinage in 1970 and will end when we talk of kilometres rather than miles.

a boll: 140 pounds
2 bolls: 1 sack
a hand: 4 inches
a cubitt: 18 inches
a military pace: 2 feet, 6 inches
a rod, pole or perch: 5 feet
a truss of straw: 36 pounds
a truss of old hay: 56 pounds
a bushel: 8 gallons.

Turned out to graze when not in use, the Galloways grew shaggy in winter, their thick coats protecting them against the worst of the weather. Good ponies were much prized and while out on a raid, reivers always stole them when they could. English legislators went so far as to control the sale of horses into Scotland very strictly. As much as weapons, they were regarded as instruments of war and criminality. English bloodstock and their taller stallions were wanted because, as one observer noted 'the Scots ponies were full of spirit and patient of labour but very little'. Race-meetings were popular along the border, and they provided very plausible cover for illicit horse dealing. A notorious reiver, Kinmont Willie Armstrong, is thought to have come regularly to Langholm Races for much more than sport and he often bought up big English horses for resale in Scotland.

It was a tribute to their central role that when the era of reiving came to an end at the beginning of the seventeenth century, it was specifically forbidden to own a pony over a certain value – in other words a good Galloway Nag.

What this rapid historical sketch – racing back and forth across millennia – serves to show is only that the landscape looked different in the time when the reivers rode and that the hills and upland valleys where they lived were not the windblown wastes they are now. They could be infinitely more dangerous and intimately better known. But much of that ancient knowledge has passed into memory and the community of the hills has almost entirely fled. It is difficult now to believe that only four centuries ago more than 2,000 horsemen could ride out of Liddesdale. But they did.

4

The Condition of Men

Officially Sir Thomas Carleton was Deputy Warden of the English West March, a royal official charged to ensure good order and the rule of law, but by nature he was an expert cattle thief, a talented, well-organised reiver. Under the unconvincing guise of furthering government policy, he plundered deep into Dumfriesshire in the winter of 1547. Needing a base for operations, he led his riders up Annandale to the Johnstone stronghold of Lochwood Tower. One of the reiving freelances in his party, Sandie Armstrong, had told him that although it was immensely well built and appointed, the tower was garrisoned by only a handful of men and some female servants. It was too good an opportunity to miss, and Carleton determined to take it. And very unusually he left a record of what happened.

Lochwood's first line of defence was the treacherous moss which surrounded it. Carleton chose a party of his best men, had them dismount and follow him carefully and silently through the boggy ground. It was late on a dull March afternoon, enough light in the sky to find the path but too little for Lochwood's defenders to pick out the shapes of the reivers creeping closer and closer to the barnekin, the outer wall. When darkness fell Carleton and a dozen men slipped over and into the outer courtyard. They 'stole into the house within the barnekin and took the wenches and kept them secure in the house till daylight'. The serving girls must have been terrified as they were gagged, bound and perhaps worse. Without doubt information was speedily extracted. Locked in the tower were only two men and one kitchen maid. They slept sound, oblivious of the danger waiting below.

As first light crept over the Moffatdale Hills the reivers hid quietly in the courtyard house, squinting out of the windows for signs of life in the tower. They knew that if a sudden alarm was raised and the doors were not opened from the inside that even against only two defenders and a servant, they would not take Lochwood easily. Eventually the reivers saw a man appear on the wall-walk up at roof level. Dressed only in his shirt, no doubt yawning and stretching in the cold morning air, he could see nothing amiss and called inside for the serving lass to go down and open the outer doors. There were two: an iron grill inside to keep out attackers and a wooden one on the outside of the door passage to keep out the weather. When the maid rattled back the bolts 'our men within the barnekin broke a little too soon'. She saw them running towards the doorway and very nearly got the wooden door shut and bolted before the first reiver slammed into it. Shouldering it ajar and with others forcing it open, they clattered inside and raced up the spiral stairs before any more internal defences could be closed against them.

It was a close-run thing and as soon as the stronghold was taken Carleton manned it with a substantial garrison. While they raided the countryside around, Lochwood Tower remained in English hands for three years.

Often called 'peel' towers, many of them patterned the Border landscape. In times of near-anarchy they were focal points of refuge for those heidsmen and local lords who could afford to have one built. Lochwood is ruined now but a very well preserved example of a peel tower occupies a commanding site near Kelso. Perched on a rocky outcrop and looking over wide vistas on every side, Smailholm Tower belonged to the surname of Pringle, and it was well made and very strong.

The term 'peel' tower comes from the barnekin wall described by Thomas Carleton. Many were rebuilt in stone but the original peels or 'pales' were wooden stockades. Inside them animals could be safely corralled and servants housed, as at Lochwood. Often ditches had been dug around the barnekin and the stakes of the stockade driven into the upcast – an ancient practice stretching back millennia to the prehistoric hillforts of the Borders. Thick thorn hedges were sometimes planted around to make an approach more awkward and slow down an assault.

PALUS

Each Roman legionary carried a 'palus', a cut and sharpened stake, in his backpack. It must have been an awkward burden on occasion, but a necessary one. When the Romans tramped into the Cheviots in

AD 79, they built marching camps right on the watershed at Chew Green. When Border reivers walked their ponies that way, they will have been able to make out the clear rectangular lines of ditches and ramparts. And around the sixteenth-century fort at Bewcastle, the wide encirclement of the Roman camp was obvious. As a matter of routine, legionaries always dug a camp each time they stopped overnight for they had learned through bitter experience always to defend themselves in hostile country. In only a couple of hours they will have dug a ditch (to a standard plan) and piled the upcast on the inside. Into the banked up earth they drove their sharpened stakes to create an instant stockade. Archaeologists have debated how this worked. A paling fence style with the stakes driven in vertically might have been easily pushed over by charging attackers. Perhaps they made caltrops, tying the sharp stakes together in spikey star-shapes and setting them on top of the upcast. The 'palus' has hung around in English. Not only has it supplied the derivation of paling, as in paling fencing, it has also given us the phrase 'beyond the pale'. This originated in Ireland. When the Elizabethans were attempting to colonise the country, they built a long stockade around Dublin – to keep the natives beyond it.

At Smailholm the view from the short wall-walk at the foot of the roof-pitch is sweeping. Watchers could see far to the south, away to the foothills of the Cheviots and the valley-mouths out of which many raiding parties rode. If English reivers came in strength or a government raid such as Sussex' invasion of 1544 came from the east, on the road up the Tweed from Berwick, Smailholm could see the approach from a long way off. This gave the Pringles precious time to make a decision – to stay and negotiate or gather up valuables and flee into the hill country and moorland to the north.

At the end of the wall-walk there is a stone seat for the lookout. It nestles against the chimney breast and on the long winter nights of the reiving season, whoever was on watch will have shivered and been grateful to whoever thought of that. Beside is a recess for a small lantern. It was useful for light, but even more as a means to set fire to the bundled balefire that lay close at hand in an iron crucible. When it blazed on Smailholm's top, half the Tweed Valley will have seen it.

Like Lochwood, there are two doors. The inner iron grill was known as a *yett* and in Border Scots the phrase 'steek the yett!!'

for close the door is still roared on a windy winter's night. Lintels were also often set low, forcing even smaller people to stoop under them, and designed to check anyone rushing to force a way in. Above Smailholm's outer door a slit is cut through the thick wall. Far too narrow to be breached or even easily fired on, it was used to rain arrows, crossbow bolts, and later, bullets on those trying to batter down the door or set fire to it.

The walls of peel towers were very thick, sometimes more than two metres. This was as much an architectural necessity for these tall buildings as for any defensive purpose. Solid and wide founds were needed for what were often the highest buildings for miles around. Certainly thick masonry helped to discourage attackers who might attempt to mine their way in (a tried and favoured method, used to get into Carlisle Castle when Kinmont Willie was rescued, was to remove those stones into which a bolt was slid at a doorway) but it would not have detained an artillery battery for long. That was not their purpose. Border towers aimed to repel fast-moving raiders and not armies trundling cannon around the countryside.

Windows were small and always set high up in the walls, never at ground level. Even on bright days it was very dark inside. The ground floor was lit only by a door, and frequently barrel-vaulted; it was used as a store and occasionally to house beasts rather than human beings. In emergencies milking cows and the best ponies would be quickly led into these 'pends' and tethered with some hay shoved in a handy rack. Measuring an average of 10 by 13 metres, they could accommodate many animals. In the sixteenth century farmers packed their cows and horses together tightly and perhaps as many as 40 might be squeezed into a pend and the yett and outer door secured behind them. It will have been a dark, steaming, smelly and noisy place as the animals sensed the danger outside. Neighing and lowing, they will have splattered the floor in their fear. Ventilation holes were cut in the barrel vault and often a trapdoor led to the first floor.

GUNNERY

Guns, gunpowder, canon and pistols were a feature of European military history for a long time before they became influential. Well into the sixteenth century generals prefered the simple and effective technology of archery to the chancy but spectacular power of artillery. At the siege of Roxburgh Castle James II of Scotland stood too close to a huge canon which 'flew in flinders and a part of it struck him in the thigh', and he bled to death. Experienced bombardiers stood well behind and, for some unknown reason, to the left of their pieces after they had lit the fuse. Reivers carried 'daggs', a pair of single-shot pistols, but many prefered a cheaper and very effective crossbow called a 'latch'. It could be fired with one hand while the other clutched the reins of a pony. It also had a more rapid rate of fire, was just as deadly and not likely to go off by accident. Also, raiding parties much preferred the quiet whoosh of bows and arrows to the loud crack of gunfire – which announced their presence for a mile or two in all directions. But in contrast, the great attraction of set-piece artillery was the noise and the explosive flash. It scared defenders of castles and towns in particular, and huge gunstones (canonballs were expensive) could inflict damage at long range. As fortification developed to keep pace with the technology of artillery, three degrees of defensive capability were recognised. The most formidable could withstand 'a siege royal', that is, the whole power of a king or queen's army to bombard a target. There was a more limited medium-sized fortress, and then at the bottom of the scale, a tower able to withstand 'an insult'.

Towers were essentially a stack of single rooms. Above the pend was a 'chaumer' or chamber with a fireplace set into one of the thick walls. The most accessible (and not least for the daily chore of carting up peats, logs and firewood), this room was where a lord or heidsman ate and transacted his business. And because it was warm in the winter, the place where people slept. These were not the houses of the wealthy, as we might imagine them, and there were few comforts. Benches and long settles rather than chairs, boards and trestles rather than tables and when the weather turned bad all was plunged into near-darkness as wooden shutters were closed over the open windows. Most of these had iron grills and very few contained glass. In fact it was considered such a luxury that there are records of noblemen taking their glass panes with them when they moved on to another tower or castle. Sometimes cattle skins were scraped thin, treated with linseed oil and used as windows. They were translucent and kept out the worst of the wind and cold. On the floor of the upper chamber serving lasses strewed heather and rushes on the floor along with some aromatic herbs – meadowsweet was popular – to keep the smell manageable.

Very little different from earlier medieval castles, Border towers were built for security (and for prestige – these buildings were what historians used to call 'a statement in the landscape') and not comfort, and we are inclined to forget that most people used to pass their lives out of doors, using their houses only for shelter, storage and as places to sleep. Indoors was in any case too dark for many domestic tasks. Darning, weaving, spinning and whatever needed precision and dexterity was brought outside if the weather allowed.

Rooms in these towers seem small to us, as do many in historic buildings. And in these days of hygiene, anxieties about body odour and general prurience, we also forget that until very recently people lived cheek by jowl, were concerned above all to keep warm and dry and cared much less than we do about washing. What would turn up our sensitive noses will scarcely have been noticed in a sixteenth-century Border tower.

Above the first floor chamber was another room, and then sometimes another on top of that, tucked under the eaves (and no doubt draughty). These were privy chambers, or private rooms, and they afforded a heidsman or a lord and his lady the occasional comforts of marriage. Many had beds and in the wills of the period a good bed was considered a valuable item. Downstairs, huddled close to the dying embers of the fire, the lesser people curled up on straw palliasses.

There was little privacy. All sorts of hints and unspoken under-standings surround sexual relations at this time and in this setting. With so many people sleeping in a communal space, it took a mixture of brazenness and urgency for a man and a woman to make love so close to others. Perhaps mores were very different, so different as not to be worthy of contemporary comment. Certainly the habit of removing all clothing in order to have sex is very recent. Most people used to remain, almost, fully clothed. But even when all that is born in mind it is difficult to imagine a society where sex was routinely listened to and even observed by others (some of them young), especially when the prudish-ness of the Scottish reformation began to take a strong hold after 1560. Couples certainly walked down lovers' lanes on a summer evening and records talk of children 'begotten in brake and bush'. Perhaps sex was something opportunistic, to be snatched at in passionate moments rather than a matter of routine. And in the chilly Border country, something of an outdoor pursuit.

Border society in the sixteenth century was ready to recognise illegitimacy as a fact of life, and there appears to have been little prejudice against bastard children. Allowances for them were made in wills and half-brothers and sisters were unquestioningly accepted into large families.

The old practice of handfasting persisted for a long time in the Borders, well into the nineteenth century. This was a form of conditional engagement. Couples could contract to live together for a period before being married by a priest or a minister, and if any children were born, they were provided for as part of the contract. Handfasted couples usually lived together for a year. Men and women kept the tradition going because it was sensible, both for the purpose of testing compatibility and also fertility. This last was very important. Farmers and farm labourers needed children to help with intensive agricultural work and right on into the modern period, men with large families found it easier to find a hire on a farm than bachelors. Handfasting was frowned upon by the kirk, but it lasted until the 1880s and 1890s in farm places in the Borders.

READING, WRITING AND REIVING

In Scotland one of the central tenets of the new protestant faith was literacy. More than cleanliness, it was next to Godliness. Believers had to be able to read the Bible, the sacred word of God, and understand it for themselves and shake loose the ancient and corrupting need for a priest to read and interpret it for them. All that mumbo-jumbo had to go. The 'priesthood of all believers' was how the congregations of the reformed church saw themselves. That meant a completely new education system was needed virtually overnight, especially after the removal of all of Scotland's monasteries and nunneries. Up to the middle of the sixteenth century such schooling as there was had been done by monks and nuns. Instead, there would be a school in every parish open to all. It was a hugely expensive undertaking for an impoverished economy but by the early seventeenth century more than 700 schools had been set up and by around 1700 universal coverage had been achieved. To meet a sudden and urgent need for schoolbooks, psalmodies and Bibles the Edinburgh publishing industry clacked into life.

Border towers and their barnekins were also farmhouses and upper rooms were often used for storage, and a simple toilet was placed on an outer wall of the topmost room. This was only used during a siege or when the nightime weather was so bad and the chamber pot so full that there was no option. At Naworth Castle, originally a tower, Lord Dacre organised the primitive plumbing to supply some grim amusement. The toilets drained into the dungeons.

Tower rooms were connected by a spiral staircase both for economy and for defence. Many had a 'trip-step', a riser which was higher than the others and designed to catch out an unwary attacker. When a large raiding party threatened a Border tower, the occupants often fled before them with pack-horses carrying their meagre goods. If they believed that their stronghold might be blown up with gunpowder, they filled the pend and sometimes the upper floors with smouldering peat. As it burned over a long period (it would have needed a great deal of water to put it out) it discouraged the use of gunpowder, which was much more volatile in the sixteenth century. Blackened with peat reek and in a terrible mess it might be, a tower was at least left intact by this tactic and quickly rehabitable.

When occupants chose to stay or were the victims of a surprise attack, they defended the barnekin wall first. This could be 5 or 6 metres high and a metre thick. Some had wooden platforms on the inside and these allowed missiles to be fired at the attackers. Beasts were corralled inside the barnekin and since they were usually the prize at issue, it was vital to protect them.

If defenders were driven back into a tower and they managed to get the doors locked, raiders sometimes used scaling ladders to fight their way up onto the wall-walk. Roofs were often made from split stone slabs, making them virtually fire-proof. But if attackers could reach the wall-walk, the game was up. Sir Robert Carey wrote that his preferred method of gaining entry to a tower was by lifting off the roof slabs and his men dropping down into the top chamber. Down on the ground, others would have tried to fire the door, and if they could gain access to the bottom of the spiral staircase, it allowed them a strangely named tactic. Scumfishing was what smoking out defenders was called and it appears to have been very effective. In 1545 Sir Ralph Eure's horsemen laid siege to Scott of Buccleuch's tower at Mosshouses on the moors north of Melrose. They hacked down the gate into the barnekin 'and got many nags and nolte and smoked very sore the tower and took thirty prisoners'.

Better than scumfishing or scaling ladders was surprise, and when Sir Thomas Carleton won Lochwood Tower, his diary could not hide his satisfaction at a job well done and a prize cheaply won.

Expense forced less wealthy farmers to seek alternative shelter against the frequent storms of anarchy, larceny and warfare. In Tynedale and Redesdale in particular the 'bastle house' was popular and more affordable than a tower. The name is probably from the French 'bastille' for a fort (although bastide seems more likely with its meaning of 'blockhouse') and examples are to be found mainly on the English side of the border. Some are virtually intact like those at West Woodburn and Tarset in Tynedale. Others have been adapted for use as snug modern houses like the one built inside the perimeter of the Roman fort at High Rochester in Redesdale. Better contructed than most, it benefited from a plentiful supply of squared-off Roman masonary readily to hand.

Bastles appear to have developed from wooden prototypes. In 1541 very strong houses constructed out of squared-off oak tree trunks were recorded. Closely bound together and roofed with turf and earth, they looked like the stout log cabins built in the woods of the eastern United States by early pioneers. Attackers found them very difficult to force or burn.

Stone-built bastles were intended to be equally fire-proof, designed to confound a small band of raiders with only their weapons and ingenuity to hand. Like towers they had a ground floor pend for beasts, probably most of what a smaller farmer owned might fit in, the remaining sheep or cattle driven off to safety. A ladder led to a door at first floor height and when trouble rode into view, the farmer and his family scrambled up and pulled it in behind them. Windows were again tiny. The concept of the bastle house was blunt and simple – it was designed to frustrate attackers into giving up and going home.

For most ordinary reivers home was even more basic, little more than shelters able to keep out the wind and most of the rain. It is often said that it took only a few hours to build one of these primitive houses and that those who had lived in them were not much inconvenienced if they were burned or cast down. Bishop Leslie asserted that they were only 'sheephouses and lodges . . . of whose burning they are not sore solaced'. This does not bear much examination. The destruction of a home, however mean and meagre, is never simply an inconvenience, particularly if the surrounding countryside has suffered the same fate, and the winter storms are blowing hard and children need to be fed and kept warm. Moreover the description of these farmhouses and cottages is familiar. Better documented sources suggest that they were little different from what was built elsewhere in Scotland, where regular burning and destruction was not a sad feature of life.

Even when they had been totally razed to the ground, sixteenth-century houses were usually rebuilt on the same footprint. Most were rectangular and about the same size, 8 or 9 metres long and 4 to 5 metres wide. This relative uniformity was dictated by the weakness of the construction methods, the need to keep warm in the winter and the habit of bringing beasts inside in bad weather. An A-frame was made from trimmed tree-trunks and the footing of the gables packed into postholes. A strong ridge-pole was slung between them. To make the walls, stakes were were driven into the ground, spaced at regular intervals. This was to allow freshly cut willow withies to be woven between them in what must have looked like a large set of hurdle-fences. So that they were supple and manageable, the withies had to be green and a good length. Once the walls had reached a height of at least a metre, they were slathered with mud, clay and even cow-dung, and then allowed to dry and harden. This covering gave the walls solidity and helped to keep out the wind and the rain. Sometimes a few courses of stone provided a more secure anchor for the wall-stakes. For more insulation turfs or peats were banked up against the wicker walls and to mitigate dampness a drainage ditch was dug around the house and filled with small stones. The faint outline of these ditches is sometimes the only trace of a long-disappeared house.

Adzed tree boughs were laid against the ridge-pole with a beam running along the wall-head. Tied with flexible pine roots (these are very strong, but home-made ropes were also used), they supported a roof of heather thatch or turf. This was usually weighted with boulders suspended on either end of long ropes slung over the pitch of the roof. Often, a scatter of these large boulders are all that remains for archaeologists to find. The doorway was generally set in one of the long walls and was often the only source of light, windows being awkward to fit into stakes and withies.

In the middle of a beaten earth floor (clay was best) lay the down-hearth. This was little more than a jigsaw of flat stones encircled by a sill of edgers, some with raised flat surfaces for a simmering pot to sit on. The fire was indeed the heart of the house, used for cooking, heat and light, the smoke curling up into the roof and seeping out through the thatch or turf. Because there was no chimney and sometimes not even a smoke-hole, the upper section of the house was constantly smokey (fires were lit at all seasons of the year) and everything smelled of it. Peat was often burned and at night smoored over to ensure that it could be nursed back into life in the morning. Kindling could be hard to come by and moreover it was bad luck to let a fire die. In the hills wood was scarce but peat-banks usually available on the moorlands. In the common land around towns and villages in the Borders the right to cut peat was well protected.

Most people ate potage – every day. What we might call thick soup bubbled at the side of every down-hearth, constantly being replenished by whatever was available; cereal certainly, water, bones, a wild harvest of roots and fungi, and occasional catches of small animals and fish. Nothing remotely nourishing was ever thrown away, it went straight into the pot. Hedgehogs, squirrels, and small birds made for some variety and wet clay was slapped around them and baked in a hot part of the fire. Sheep which had died from disease or drowned were also a welcome addition to the daily diet. The meat was known as 'braxie'. And while the body flesh was considered very acceptable, the head was not wasted either. Singed in the fire, it was added to the pot to make 'sheep's heid kail'. This was tasty and nutritional and still eaten in the borders up until the mid-twentieth century. Flat stones around the down-hearth and the hot sides of a potage skillet were handy for making unleavened bread, something like modern Greek pitta bread or Asian nan bread. Better-off families owned an iron girdle and oatcakes were well made on those, and some had a cauldron suspended from the ridge-pole by a chain.

THE LANGUAGE OF SOUP

When an older generation of Borderers used to make potage or the thick vegetable and meat stock soup known as 'kail' (after the fibrous plant introduced by the agricultural improvers in the eighteenth century), they always talked of it in the plural, even occasionally addressing it directly. 'They're guid efter the secint day, better on the third, ir ee no?' Kail did not do anything as posh as simmer, it 'seethit', and a 'spurtle' was used to stop it sticking to the bottom of the pan. Eaten with a 'boney spin', they, the soup, was often made with 'ket' mutton, certainly cheap and probably from an old ewe past her lambing days. The meat was not eaten with the spin but lifted out from them, the soup, and cut up and set over boiled tatties. At that point it became singular, and it was guid. When all was done, the spin and the bowl ('bowel') had to be 'sained oot' at the sink. Kail stuck to the utensils as well as the ribs.

Inside the house, but not directly over the fire, awnings were sometime hung when the weather was wild. They caught the sooty drips from a leaking thatch and kept the earth floor from becoming sticky under its covering of rushes, grasses and herbs. These houses might be described as vermin-infested hovels but if they were properly built and had a few three-legged stools, a settle and some decent bedding, they could be snug enough.

On a long winter's night, undisturbed by raiders, and with a warming bowl of potage inside them, Borderers sat in the circle of firelight and listened to stories. And they were wonderful stories, magical, unexpected and utterly memorable.

At the end of the eighteenth century, just as they were beginning to fade from history, Walter Scott listened to these stories and wrote them down. They were the *Border Ballads*, and they have much to say about the lives of the people who made them.

Since they existed only in the memories of older people, many of them women, the ballads had to be discovered and collected. One rendition led to another and with the help of John Leyden, James Hogg, Robert Shortreed and others, Scott made seven 'raids' into the likes of Liddesdale, Teviotdale and Annandale. As these old Borderers sat by their fires and sang the verses to him, Scott wrote down an immense tradition, stretching back into the fourteenth century and perhaps even earlier. Some ballads were very long, and 80 verses was not unusual. Others carried long sections of dialogue, many had crucial variations.

The old songs (all the ballads were originally sung or chanted and *The Minstrelsy of the Scottish Border* reproduces many tunes) often have big, dramatic themes. Warfare, cattle raids, tragic love all animate the action. But there is an overwhelming sense of melancholy, of bad and sad ends. Here are some verses from 'The Dowie Dens o' Yarrow':

> At Dryhope lived a lady fair,
> The fairest flower in Yarrow,
> And she refused nine noble men
> For a servan' lad in Gala.

> Her father said that he should fight
> The nine lords all tomorrow,
> And that he that should the victor be
> Would get the Rose of Yarrow.

The servant-lad was killed and his body flung into the Yarrow Water.
His lover rode the hills looking for him:

> But she wandered east, so did she wast,
> And searched the forest thorough,
> Until she spied her ain true love,
> Lyin' deeply drowned in Yarrow

She pulled him from the water and took his body back to Dryhope.
Her father was not sympathetic and assured her that she would wed
well:

> Haud your ain tongue, my faither dear,
> I canna help my sorrow;
> A fairer flower ne'er sprang in May
> Than I hae lost in Yarrow.

> I meant to make my bed fu' wide,
> But you may make it narrow,
> For now I've nane to be my guide
> But a deid man drowned in Yarrow.

> And aye she screighed, and cried, Alas!
> Till her heart did break wi' sorrow,
> And sank into her faither's arms
> 'Mang the dowie dens o' Yarrow.

Walter Scott's motives for compiling his collection were unabashed.
Prompted, inspired and embarrassed by the popularity of Thomas
Percy's *Reliques of Ancient English Poetry*, published in 1765, he
wrote in the introduction of *The Minstrelsy of the Scottish Border*: 'By
such efforts, feeble as they are, I may contribute somewhat to the
history of my native country; the peculiar features of whose manner
and character are daily melting and dissolving into those of her sister
and ally.'

This laudable patriotism was harmless enough, but it did skew the ballads slightly and the history of the Border Reivers a great deal. Nationalism intruded where all that really mattered was surname and the advantage of one surname against another. For example, in historical reality Johnnie Armstrong of Gilnockie was a vicious thug but Scott's instincts and ability to reshape a traditional ballad turned him into a Scottish hero who only raided in England, and was good to his people in his own way. Rough and tough, but just.

THE STRANGER-GAELS

In 1500 more than half the landmass of Britain and Ireland did not speak English or any of its dialects, such as the Scots of the Border ballads. They spoke Celtic languages; Irish Gaelic and Scots Gaelic, Manx, Welsh and Cornish. By 1100 the aristocracy and people of Galloway had become thoroughly Celtic in nature, and west of the Nith, a dialect of Gaelic was spoken. It seems that new immigrants from Ireland and the Hebrides brought a new language and Galloway itself gets its name from them. They were called 'the Stranger-Gaels', or the 'Gall-Gaidheil'. Across the Solway Firth, Cumbria is also a Celtic name and it derives from 'Combrogi' which was rubbed smooth into 'Cymru', the Welsh word for Wales. It means something like 'Land of the Fellow Citizens' and it is a memory of the Roman Empire. Galloway Gaelic was still spoken in the sixteenth century and many of the Dumfriesshire surnames were bilingual. When pilgrims travelling to the shrine of St Ninian at Whithorn crossed the Nith at Dumfries, they were entering the wild realm of the Stranger Gaels.

Walter Scott also had personal, romantic reasons for wishing to collect the ballads before they were lost to memory. As a boy, he had heard them sung by his grandfather, Robert Scott, his Auntie Janet and an old farm-hand, Sandy Ormiston. When very young, Scott had contracted a wasting disease, probably a strain of poliomyelitis, which had left him lame in his left leg. To recuperate, the 'wee sick laddie' was sent from Edinburgh into the fresh air of the Border countryside, to Sandyknowe Farm. The farmhouse lies near the crag which carries the ruins of Smailholm Tower. It was not the present tidy, two-storeyed house with long views to the Cheviots, but a small stone cottage now built into the old farm steading lying a little to the west. Scott never forgot his time by the hearthside at Sandyknowe and his young imagination was fired by the ballads and the tales of his grandfather, his auntie and the old cow-bailie, Sandy Ormiston. He whispered stories of raids and reivers to the wee laddie as they sat at the foot of the old stronghold:

> And still I thought that shatter'd tower
> The mightiest work of human power;
> And marvell'd as the aged hind
> With some strange tale bewitch'd my mind,
> Of forayers, who, with headlong force,
> Down from that strength had spurr'd their horse,
> Their southern rapine to renew
> Far in the distant Cheviot blue,
> And, home returning, fill'd the hall
> With revel, wassel-rout, and brawl.
> Methought that still with trump and clang,
> The gateway's broken arches rang;
> Methought grim features, seam'd with scars,
> Glared through the window's rusty bars,
> And ever, by the winter hearth,
> Old tales I heard of woe or mirth,
> Of lovers' slights, of ladies' charms,
> Of witches' spells, of warriors' arms;
> Of patriot battles, won of old
> By Wallace wight and Bruce the bold;
> Of later fields of feud and fight,
> When, pouring from their Highland height,
> The Scottish clans, in headlong sway,
> Had swept the scarlet ranks away.

That passage from *Marmion*, published in 1808 and phenomenally successful, recalls the power of the old ballads as they worked on the imagination of the wee sick laddie. And as he sat in the warmth of the farmhouse kitchen at Sandyknowe entranced by his Auntie Janet's voice, he was only doing what generations of Borderers had done before him. The ballads are best when simplest, when the four line stanzas sound out the steady rhythm of hoofbeats, of soldiers riding down to England to drive a prey, of drums beating as the gallows rope swings, of hearts beating as widows weep and lovers drown their tragic losses.

Many of the most famous ballads, 'The Battle of Otterburn' or 'The Outlaw Murray' and others take the grand themes and some span long stretches of historical time – and at 80 verses or so, take their time in telling it. Others fly in the faery realm, the supernatural world which lay beyond the flicker of the down-hearth, out into the fell night air and black-darkness where witches, warlocks and elven queens work their spells. Some of these are very old, 'Thomas the Rhymer' was probably composed before 1400 and was added to and changed over the centuries. Here are the first five verses:

> True Thomas lay on Huntlie bank;
> A ferlie he spied wi' his e'e;
> And there he saw a lady bright
> Come riding down by the Eildon Tree
>
> Her skirt was o' the grass-green silk
> Her mantle o' the velvet fine;
> At ilka tett o' her horse's mane,
> Hung fifty siller bells and nine.
>
> True Thomas he pu'd off his cap
> And louted low down on his knee
> 'Hail to thee Mary, Queen of Heaven!
> For thy peer on earth could never be.'
>
> 'O no, O no, Thomas' she said,
> 'That name does not belong to me;
> I'm but the Queen o' fair Elfland,
> That am hither come to visit thee.
>
> 'Harp and carp, Thomas' she said,
> 'Harp and carp along wi' me;
> And if ye dare to kiss my lips,
> Sure of your bodie I will be.'

With their grand martial themes and fey prophesies, the Border ballads were ripe for the further manufacture of romance. And Scott's rendition of them, some improved, others changed, was meat and drink for the romancing of the Border reivers. It began with a patriotic wish to memorialise their stunning musical and poetic culture, grew into a nationalistic urge to see them as Scotland's bulwark against anglicisation and ended with the historical suppression of the over-whelmingly dark side of what happened along the frontier in the sixteenth century. Accounts of the rescue of Kinmont Willie remember its daring and elan, but forget what a deeply unsavoury criminal he was. But then history is often untidy, the loose ends of paradox and contradiction hang everywhere. And if we have Sir Walter to thank for romancing the reivers we must also be grateful that he saved their wonderful ballads.

RIGHT HAND MEN

Most men are right-handed and most battles were fought by men who stood and fought next to each other in a tight line, at least at the outset. This combination of factors has led to persistent and interesting traditions. Because right-handed men carry a weapon in that hand and a shield in the other, they leave themselves vulnerable when they raise their weapon to strike a blow. They cannot cover their own body with their shield and therefore depend on the man standing to their right to protect them with his shield. When the Highlanders charged at Culloden in 1746, the government troops were instructed to bayonet whoever was run-ning at the man on their left. His weapon would be raised and in a disordered charge, his right side was unlikely to be protected by a man running to his right. Right? Right. This was both risky and counter-instinctive. Perhaps some disciplined redcoats did it. The life-or-death importance of a right hand man in battle has led to the use of the phrase for a trusted lieutenant and is also the reason why a best man stands to the right of a bridegroom at a wedding service. He is trying to protect him.

Poetic licence has seeped into other parts of Border history. Those partial observers who reported martial victories, skirmishes won, and raids punishingly executed, are wont to exaggerate the numbers involved. It is almost a tradition to overestimate the opposition army and their enormous losses at the hands of the smaller and braver force who defeated them with surprisingly few casualties. But when English sources claim huge Scottish raiding parties clattering over the border, the numbers simply do not add up.

Reliable historians have compared twentieth-century census figures with estimates of the population in the sixteenth-century Border country and come up with consistent and credible figures. On the English side of the border, in the three marches under the control of wardens, 120,000 people lived. And in the three marches in Scotland there were about 50,000. That imbalance, almost two and a half to one, was weighted by the fact that the only two genuine sixteenth-century towns in the Borders, Berwick and Carlisle, were both English.

What these overall figures show is something stark. On the Scottish side there can have been only 15,000 fighting men at the very most. Discounting half the population because women did not turn out to fight, at least not in a raiding party or an army, and a further 10,000 who were too old, too young, too infirm or disqualified for some other reason, that leaves 15,000. Even if riders as young as Robert Johnstone of Raecleuch are counted, it still feels like an overestimate.

So, when Walter Scott of Buccleuch counted 3,000 lances when he mounted a huge raid into England in 1532, 20 per cent of the total fighting capability of the *whole* of the Border country rode with him. And more, when he called on these men to follow him, Teviotdale must have all but emptied. It seems unlikely.

A comparison between the English and Scottish numbers is also instructive. With the odds so heavily stacked against them, Scottish raiders did well to maintain a balance of power. Even bearing in mind that the amount of Scottish raiding appears exaggerated because it was recorded by English sources (the traffic in the opposite direction was not necessarily less, just under-reported in scanty Scottish sources), it is surprising that Annandale, Teviotdale and the Tweed Valley were not constantly overrun and impoverished more than they were. Geology had also made the northern valleys broader and more fertile – and attractive to raiders – than the long miles of moorland to the south.

Perhaps the Scottish surnames were tighter bound, better organised and more motivated by need and greed. This was not often a national stand-off, with the size of opposing armies set relative to population. Raids and raiding were usually conducted by much smaller groups and this had the effect of rendering this discrepancy redundant. It simply did not matter to a party of 20 reivers picking their way down off the Cheviot tops to lift cows in Coquetdale.

Carlisle was the largest town, and by some distance. The population is estimated at 5,000 for the period between 1584 and 1600. Since the Roman period Carlisle had been an urban centre, its size fluctuating with the tides of history. When Hadrian's Wall was built after 122, a fort was built on the site of the castle and it became a command centre for the whole wall garrison. Parts of the city walls were originally Roman and they survived well into the sixteenth century and beyond. Medieval historians noted the ancient paved streets laid down a thousand years before and William of Malmesbury wrote of an arched building which carried an inscription to Mars and Venus. Carlisle had the history and feel of an ancient city. It still does.

The castle was the headquarters of the Warden of the English West March and the place where justice was dispensed. For Border reivers this could be summary and after sentence had been handed down, their hands were tied behind their backs and they were carted a mile down the London road. At Harraby Hill many had a first and last encounter with the Christian church when they *sang neck-verse* at the busy gallows south of the city. There the condemned tottered on a stool while they listened to a priest or a minister recite the Miserere or the 51st Psalm. As the hangman pushed them, a view of Carlisle was the last thing many reivers saw.

CRUEL JOKES

In the sixteenth century cruelty was thought to be amusing, even hilarious. At the midsummer fair in Paris cat-burning was very popular. The organisers set up a grandstand so that a large crowd could have a good laugh as they watched a net full of screaming cats lowered slowly into a large bonfire. In the Borders smaller-scale cruelties were routinely featured on saints' days and at festivals. Cock-fighting was enjoyed and if a bird was insufficiently aggressive, it would be tied to a stick and people had fun stoning it to death. When St James' Fair was held near Kelso each August, cats were tortured for amusement, set on fire and knocked about in a barrel. The fair has been revived, but not with all its original sideshows. Public cruelty to people was of course common with regular and well advertised executions at Harraby Hill in Carlisle and elsewhere. Best attended were the executions of those found guilty of treachery. Lengthy and horrific affairs, they involved the appalling fate of being hung, drawn and quartered. So that all dignity was removed and the crowd could delight in his involuntary defecation, a victim was usually stripped, his hands bound behind his back and a rope tightened around his neck. It was then slung over a beam and the hangman and his helpers pulled hard to lift the choking, wriggling, retching man in the air. It was then that he pissed and shat himself. Hangmen were expert judges and just as the victim was about to lose consciousness and choke to death, they suddenly let go of the rope and he crashed down onto the wooden scaffold. Revived by buckets of water, the man was dragged to a butcher's table and tied to it. Then he was slit from neck to groin and his intestines pulled out. If he had not died of shock, the victim could watch as his insides were thrown onto a sizzling brazier. And then, mercifully, he was dragged to a block and with the executioner's foot on his back, beheaded. The four quarters of his butchered body were set on display as a grim reminder. Simple hanging was also more sadistic. The knot in a rope was not designed to break the neck and there was no long drop to provide fatal momentum. The condemned were expected to choke to death slowly and noisily, supplying amusement as they did so. 'Dancing a jig' was a common euphemism. It is said that friends were allowed to bribe the hangman who then let them pull on the victim's legs in order to bring his agony to a merciful end. This is said to be the origin of the phrase 'hangers-on'. Sixteenth-century society could be almost unimaginably cruel, but what is striking is the public's delight and perverted fascination with extreme and long drawn-out rituals of cruelty. It speaks of a very different view of the world.

Berwick-upon-Tweed was smaller, but unusually there exists a sixteenth-century census. In June 1565 it was reckoned that 3,511 people were living in the town. Of these more than 2,000 were soldiers, labourers or tradesmen. The focus of their work still exists – a spectacular circuit of sixteenth-century walls.

Berwick was seen as a bastion of English foreign policy and the notoriously mean Queen Elizabeth I finally spent a staggering £128,648 on the construction of impregnable walls. Terrified at the thought of Mary, Queen of Scots as the linchpin of a strategic catholic alliance between Scotland and France (and with Spain to worry about after her sister's marriage to King Philip), she was determined to hold on to Berwick. In 1558 Calais had fallen and with it England's last foothold in continental Europe. With its new and mighty walls, Berwick would be a Border Calais – except that it would not be taken. The town could be easily supplied by sea, and as her father had shown in the terrible raids of the 1540s, it was a handy base for military action against southern Scotland.

Work on the fortification of Berwick had begun in the reign of Mary I but it was accelerated in 1558 for another reason. That year Mary of Guise, the Queen Regent of Scotland, had dispatched French soldiers and engineers to rebuild the promontary fort at Eyemouth, only a few miles up the North Sea coast from Berwick. An unmistakable, threatening gesture, the fort was erected quickly and using the latest Italian techniques to counter artillery attacks. The Berwick garrison tried to halt the work but were beaten back.

More permanent retaliation came with the arrival of Sir Richard Lee in Berwick. A notable military engineer, he immediately set to work. Town walls were very vulnerable to artillery and in Berwick's case from guns at sea as well as on land. The old medieval walls were crumbling and in any case enclosed too great an area. New plans circled the town with massive walls, in some places nine metres across. Stout stone retaining walls were built and infilled with rubble and earth. Artillery fire could certainly hope to damage such a wall but never breach it. Five arrowhead bastions were constructed along the land walls and the guns placed on them had a wide field of fire over the ditching dug in front of them. One of the many problems with sixteenth-century artillery was its lack of manoeuvrability. When attackers managed to advance inside its range and get close to the walls, it was difficult to depress the angle at which cannon fired or move them quickly to cover another area. With the help of an Italian military architect, Giovanni Portinari, Sir Richard Lee solved this by creating artillery positions which fired parallel with and along the length of his massive walls, raking any who tried to lever up scaling ladders or rush through a damaged section. And so that Berwick's guns did not shoot at each other in these places, he angled the retaining walls slightly. The ground in front of them was cleared of housing (some of it has remained open parkland) and these flankers completed total coverage of any attack.

By 1570 Berwick's walls were complete, and despite complaints from the garrison commanders about maintenance, they made the town virtually impregnable. The ingenious design was never put to the test. And in 1603 when James VI became the I, the new walls became politically irrelevant.

DAEMONOLOGIE

The Scottish Reformation brought many social as well as religious changes, but it also engendered a horrific habit of mind which gathered momentum towards the end of the sixteenth century over much of northern Europe. John Knox and his followers wished to create a 'godly commonwealth' of believers, a commonwealth which required to be continually purged of all pollutants. Witches began to be hunted – and with great enthusiasm in the Borders. (Although it must be said that in Germany it became a hysterical epidemic – in 1585 in Trier 118 women and two men were burnt at the stake because 'the prolongation of winter was the work of their incantations'. A grisly example of cultural and climate change coinciding.) In Scotland this vicious obsession was much encouraged by the king's personal interest. In 1597 James VI had published a treatise on witches called 'Daemonologie', and he himself was sometimes present at the interrogation of hapless victims. It was a terrible, disfiguring and lengthy episode, something of which succeeding generations of Borderers ought to be profoundly ashamed.

Houses in Berwick and Carlisle were nothing like as solidly built. Their construction differed little from the wall-stakes and withies of the countryside. Stone was more in evidence and space at a much greater premium. Most houses were built gable end-on to a street and with a narrow lane leading down to the door and the backlands beyond. These alleyways were still in evidence in the centre of Carlisle until a new shopping centre was built in 1984, and some can still be seen in Berwick.

In their long backlands town householders usually kept a milker cow and perhaps some chickens. Like the other Border burghs, Berwick and Carlisle had common grazings and most people led their animals out in the morning and back at night to be milked. Excavations in Perth have turned up the remains of drains and their noisome contents show where animals were kept overnight. Cross-contamination of their droppings and human sewage with a town's water supply often led to a rapid spread of diseases such as typhoid. Because of rising damp in their insubstantial walls, most townhouses had a limited life, perhaps only twenty years. Fires were frequent and sometimes devastating as dry thatch was set alight by little more than sparks from a vigorous cooking fire, and because people in towns lived cheek by jowl, fire always spread quickly. Infectious diseases did the same and when the ebola-like epidemic burst into Carlisle in 1597 it carried off more than a fifth of the population.

TYPHOID TEA

Water-borne diseases and poor sanitation combined to keep urban populations small in the sixteenth century. Frequent visitations of typhoid and other scourges carried off many and it seemed that there was an upper limit beyond which cities were unable to grow. More people, more sewage, more disease. In the eighteenth century improved water supply and better plumbing helped the great industrial cities of the north to expand, but tea also played an important role. At the same time as the fires of the Industrial Revolution began to roar into life, tea became a popular drink and cheap enough to be drunk by many. And the incidence of water-borne disease began to decline markedly. It used to be thought that the business of boiling water to brew tea was responsible for this, but the effect was much aided by the nature of tea itself. In the Far East it was seen as a tonic drink with many health-giving properties of its own. Tea turned out to be good for you.

Modern towns like Hawick, Galashiels, Duns, Kelso, Melrose, Jedburgh, Selkirk and Peebles were little more than villages, their houses clustered around the road that led to an abbey or important castle. Like Carlisle and Berwick most had weekly markets where the necessities of life could be bartered or bought. In the middle ages the Border economy had been energised by the wool trade and the entrepreneurial acumen of the great abbeys and their business-like monks. But with the Wars of Independence, the deterioration of the climate and the depredations of the Border reivers, wool growing and trading had declined dramatically. When the natural port for export and import at Berwick was detached from its hinterland in the Tweed Valley and briskly incorporated into England, further and lasting damage was inflicted. The Reformation finished off the declining and half-ruined abbeys and the great monastic sheep-ranches were broken up and shared out amongst aristocratic families. By the late sixteenth century Borderers lived in a subsistence economy – in a good year.

TRUNK ROADS

Wagga, a man who could fairly claim to have been Carlisle's first mayor, was very proud of the town's water supply. He was the 'reeve' (related to sheriff or 'shire-reeve'), the royal official sent by the Northumbrian kings to rule over the old Roman city and when Bishop Cuthbert visited in 685, Wagga showed him a gushing water fountain. Then he took the saintly bishop on a tour of Carlisle's Roman walls. Nearly 300 years after the end of Roman rule in Britain, a municipal water supply was evidently still in working order. That implies plumbing and the continuing ability to bring water into the city from a distance, and from higher ground. Perhaps there was an upstanding aqueduct somewhere. Clean water of course remained important but when the old Roman plumbing broke down, native tradesmen no longer had the skills to make replacement lead and ceramic piping. To keep the water flowing, they used wood, hollowed-out sections of tree trunks. These often ran by the side of a main road – which is where the phrase 'trunk road' originated.

Market days and saints' days (these took a long time to fade, despite the preachings of the protestant church) supplied welcome variety in the long months of day-in, day-out labour. These were often enlivened by sporting events. 'Baw' or 'handbaw' (pronounced 'baw' but spelt 'ba') was played in most Border towns and villages for centuries, and up until the 1930s games were held in Hawick, Ancrum, Selkirk and St Boswells. Reivers reckoned themselves good players: Willie Armstrong 'the best at thievecraft and the ba, and the Earl of Bothwell was a robust player. Six-a-side matches were organised and Mary, Queen of Scots is said to have watched one played on the river-meadow below Carlisle Castle. The style of play and the rules are blurred but the ba of the sixteenth century does have a lineal descendant, a match played in the old style twice a year. And it does have rules, apparently.

At Candlemas on 2 February and Fastern's E'en (Shrove Tuesday in England – 40 days before Holy Saturday, usually the end of February or the beginning of March, depending on when Easter is that year), the men of Jedburgh play at the ba, what they call handba. Players gather at the mercat cross and divide into two teams. The

'Uppies' team consists of men born in the town south of a line drawn from the car park at the end of the Friars in Exchange Street to the mercat cross and on the Deans Close in the Canongate, as well as those born outside of Jedburgh who first entered the town by a southern road, from Newcastle, the Dunion, Oxnam or Lanton. The same precision applies to the 'Doonies' who must have been born north of the line or first entered Jedburgh by the Edinburgh road, the Monklaw road, or the Ulston road. The size of the teams is limited only by the male population of the town and hundreds have been known to take part.

Aside from common sense on safety, to the outsider there appear to be no rules. At least none are published and everyone taking part seems to know what they are, which suggests that none actually exist. To start the game a leather ba, slightly bigger than a tennis ball and decorated with ribbons, is thrown high in the air. Then it disappears into an immense scrummage. Bodies heave and squeeze, the occasional expletive rising above the melée. Sometimes a runner squirts out of the pack and hares off with the ba. Occasionally someone hares off without the ba to set up a decoy chase while a team member slinks off in another direction with it stuffed up their jumper.

Scoring is a little less opaque. Goals or 'hails' are the object of the game and for the Uppies these are won when the ba is thrown over the railings surrounding Jedburgh Castle grounds. The railings to the left of the main gates, that is, before they turn into a stone wall. Where hails were scored before there were railings is lost in the mists of ancient games. Doonies' hails are more mysterious. They are won when the ba is rolled across an invisible stream. Under one of Jedburgh's streets, the Skiprunning Burn makes its hidden way towards the Jed and if a ba crosses it, on the ground, a hail goes to the Doonies. There is no time limit to the game but darkness late on a February afternoon usually sees the welcoming lights of Jedburgh's public houses twinkle in the gloaming.

FITBA AND HANDBA

On the front page of 'The Southern Reporter' for Thursday 2 March 2006 there is a photograph of a man making a football. He is stuffing it with moss. Rodger Hart is a saddler to trade and he has been hand-sewing and stuffing these little leather footballs for 25 years. He makes ten at a time (they are larger than tennis balls but

smaller than normal footballs) for use in the old Handba game
played at Jedburgh twice a year. The Earl of Bothwell was evidently
a keen footballer – and robust. There are reports of rough play,
disputes and a suspected broken leg. And the tale runs that after a
particularly vigorous match, the score was two dead and thirty
taken prisoner. The rules are hazy and the distinction between
handba and fitba blurred. That unclarity remains. When Border
rugby teams kick a ball over the crossbar, the crowds shout 'Goal!'
and rugby is often called fitba. All of that mythic nonsense about a
boy called William Webb Ellis having a brainstorm at Rugby School
when it suddenly came into his head to pick up the ball and run with
it obscures a much more interesting evolution from the games of
handba and fitba played by the Border Reivers and their contemporaries all over Britain.

Jethart handba is very old – and magnificent to watch. It has been
played with undimmed passion since the days of the reivers and
probably long before. And that passion continues. After the Fastern's
E'en game of 2006, a ba legend retired. At the age of 70, after 61 years
as a player, Ian Aitchison announced that in future he would become a
spectator. After an (accidentally) grazed chin and a cut wrist, the
veteran said: 'I'll not be doing this next year. I'll just watch instead.'
However, some time later, he went on to qualify his remarks: 'In 2007
I might be tempted to jump in now and then. I'll just have to wait and
see how I feel on the day.'

In the 1490s a righteous Hawick priest by the name of Robert Irland
warned the local lads against another absorbing game. 'Lang bullets'
or road-bowls was very popular and a lot less muscular than the ba.
Irland was anxious that his flock were ignoring mandatory archery
practice and spending far too much time throwing balls along the
High Street and the road leading out of Hawick.

Sixteenth-century Borderers loved horse-racing and just as the
Jethart handba is largely unchanged, so too are the informal meets
held at the summer common ridings. Called 'flappers' (perhaps on
account of the all-action riding style) these races are run on grass
tracks with only the most rudimentary layout. Betting was and is
integral and a good deal of horse-trading also went on. Winners were
awarded bells rather than cups and the oldest Carlisle bells are kept in
Tullie House Museum. At the Peebles common riding a bell is still the

most prestigious trophy. The races were also important places of business for Border reivers and it is said that the plans for the daring rescue of Kinmont Willie Armstrong from Carlisle Castle were laid when Walter Scott of Buccleuch met interested parties at Langholm Races. On an April Saturday in 1596 he was seen talking to the Grahams, probably negotiating safe-conduct through their territory, and also giving instructions to his go-between, Willie Kang Irvine.

THE BA FRONTIER

The border between England and Scotland is often said to run from the Redden Burn near Kelso down the midstream of the Tweed to below Paxton House where it turns north and inland to form the Berwick Bounds. This is not quite true. Between the villages of Wark and Cornhill there is a blip. On the Ordnance Survey the border line is shown to dip across the Tweed and take in two or three acres of the south bank. Why? There is no building, settlement or unusual feature. All that the curious can see over the hawthorn hedge is a flat riverside meadow. On closer inspection, a rectangular area, once enclosed by an ancient line of fencing (there is a tell-tale ridge suggesting a ditch lost in modern ploughing) lies close to the riverbank. Adjacent is a post which appears to have no purpose or significance except that it lines up with one on the Scottish bank opposite. What was this? An unlikely tradition might answer. This parcel of land is known locally as the 'Ba Green' and it is said that each year the men of Coldstream played a version of the ba or handba against the men of Wark. Whoever won kept the piece of ground for a year. And in this way it often alternated its nationality. Eventually Coldstream grew much larger than the beautiful little village of Wark and the Scots began to win every match. Whereupon no contest was declared and the Ba Green stayed in Scotland – a decision apparently recognised by the Ordnance Survey. It might just be a true story.

In all these sporting events and excitements women are rarely mentioned. Like Mary Queen of Scots they probably watched the handba, the bowls and the races, but they certainly never took part and the record is largely silent about the general role of women in sixteenth-century Border society.

The earlier ballads are more aristocratic in tone, like 'The Battle of Otterburn' with its protagonists, James, the Earl of Douglas and Sir Henry Percy, and when women are mentioned, they are cast as stereotypes and very definitely in supporting roles. As in 'The Dowie Dens o' Yarrow', they are often beautiful, romantic and ultimately tragic. Later ballads are more earthy, sometimes dealing with the lower orders in the sixteenth-century Border country, the working (or reiving) classes rather than earls or kings. But still women only appear as adjuncts to men, as objects rather than subjects.

Given the profound influence of the teachings of the church and the legacy of evil, tempted Eve and St Paul's unequivocal Letter to the Ephesians, 'Let wives be subject to their husbands because a husband is head of a wife, just as Christ is head of the Church', the lowly status of women is hardly surprising. In a normal household of the time even a widow was subject to her eldest son.

Evidence from European sources suggest that prostitution was part of rural life as well as urban, and that it was common. Many farm-workers, shepherds and lairds will have made their eager way to Carlisle and Berwick to buy the services of a whore. Both towns supported garrisons and the soldiers will have ensured a lively trade. In the early sixteenth century the Scottish king famously paid for sex. James IV's clerks recorded several cash sums to the account of Janet Barearse.

Contraception of some sort was undoubtedly practised, but was probably a matter left to women. There is evidence that breast-feeding was prolonged – for two years and sometimes three so that women could remain infertile.

BROGUES

Borderers with long memories can recall a time when shoes were a luxury, or at least only seasonal. Boots were worn in the snow and ice of the winter, but at Easter time bare feet became the norm. In the sixteenth century boots were much prized and often stolen on raids, passed on in wills or looted from the dead on a battlefield or after a skirmish. At Flodden, fought in the September rain, Scottish soldiers kicked off their footwear and hoped for better purchase on the boggy ground in bare feet. Most people wore brogues, boots being more expensive. These were not the clumpy, decorated (derby-fronted or bow-fronted are usually the options) brown or black men's shoes of the twenty-first century, but a much simpler ancestor. A piece of leather was cut and shaped to the foot and then tied over the top with thongs. Sometimes these came up to the ankle like espadrilles. This habit persists in the way that brogues worn with kilts are still laced up to the calf. Sixteenth-century brogues were pierced with holes so that water could easily run out of them. Not meant to be waterproof, their main purpose was to protect the feet from sharp stones. The holes are also still imitated in modern fashion with a standard pattern of tooling on brogues.

Children were expected to work almost as soon as they could walk and talk. On farm places many chores could be managed or made easier by a child with a stick who could roar at beasts and daily jobs like the collection of eggs or berry-picking in season could become adventures. Ploughing with the 'auld Scotch ploo' (made from wood tipped with iron and nothing like as efficient as the swing plough which was invented in the eighteenth century) required a family to work together. On late winter mornings someone had to lead the ox-team or horses while father guided the plough, and behind him women and children pulled out the worst of the weeds and bashed down the big clods. Children certainly grew up much faster and boys were expected to behave like adults when they attained their teenage years and girls sometimes married when they were 12 or 13. Life expectancy was also much shorter, and with a few exceptions society will have looked much younger.

On 9 September 1513 King James IV led the Scottish army to Flodden field and his nation to disaster. The outcome of that terrible day would turn the history of the Borders in another direction and set a fertile ground for the century of disorder which followed. As much as any single political act, the battle at Flodden made the Border reivers possible.

The battlefield lies only a mile or so over the English border, near the village of Branxton. It is an unremarkable place, part of a series of folded ridges rising up to the eastern end of the Cheviot range. When the sky is overcast it can be difficult to pick out the memorial to all those who died on that autumn day in 1513. But the fields themselves have an atmosphere, a stillness, perhaps a memory of fear, of ancient slaughter, of an immense, oppressive sadness. In a translation of a

Gaelic phrase, it is possible at Flodden to hear the music of the thing as it happened.

The alliance with France against Henry VIII had persuaded James IV to invade. Perhaps aspiring to be a player in international politics, he fulfilled an obligation he could easily have ignored and assembled a huge host, the largest army a Scots king had ever put in the field. But the English reacted quickly and the old warrior, the 70-year-old Earl of Surrey, raised a force of 20,000 and pulling out the banner of St Cuthbert from the nave of Durham Cathedral, he hurried north to meet the Scots. They faced each other across Flodden field.

Formed up in four battles, or battalions, on each side, 52,000 men – a huge number – stared across this undulating landscape, knowing that they were about to fight toe-to-toe for their lives. Close enough to see into the eyes of their enemies, close enough to smell the sweat and blood, close enough to feel the fear and panic. Medieval armies fought in ranks, packed dense, and usually their lords and captains led from the front, their standards snapping and fluttering in the breeze.

Gripping their pikes tight, endlessly checking their gear, fidgeting, glaring at their enemies across the shallow valley, men stood side by side, told each other to stand fast, encouraged their comrades around them. In the days before the army mustered, the older men will have listened again and again to mothers and sisters implore them to look out for their boys, to bring them home safe.

It is said that Flodden was a battle waited upon in silence, the usual barrage of insults and taunts were not exchanged between the Scots and the English. Only the roar of artillery and the blast of trumpets broke the tense quiet. But in the moment before the battalion of Borderers and Highlanders moved forward to begin the fighting, many men will have been literally sick with fear, retching and gagging, unable to stop it. Some will have undoubtedly soiled themselves.

Lords Home and Huntly and their captains in the front rank will have seen it all before and shouted over their shoulders to their men to stand fast and keep their courage. Before the first drum sounded the advance of the battalion of Borderers and Highlanders, it is likely that the Gaelic-speaking clansmen did a unique thing, something which will have baffled their enemies opposite. They began to recite their genealogy. Men could go back 20 generations: 'Is mise mac Iain, mac Rhuraidh, mac Dhomnaill. I am the son of John, the son of Rory, the son of Donald.' They did it to remember who they were and why their chiefs had brought them to Flodden to fight. And they roared their war-cries, the names of their places – 'Dunmaglass! Loch Moy! Glassaraidh!' – before they tore into the ranks of terrified English soldiers. Opening fatal gaps in the line, they were followed by Home's Border pikemen and the English battalion was knocked down. Most turned and ran for their lives. At first Flodden shaped to be a Scottish victory.

But when the battalion led by the Earls of Errol, Crawford and Montrose and that of King James IV advanced, matters began to go against the Scots. They were badly disordered by the boggy ground and the stream at the bottom of the hill. Crucial momentum was lost, their 17-foot pikes became unwieldy and the English began to work their shorter bills and poleaxes to deadly effect. Even though King James' battallion pushed the English back 200 yards, he was quickly surrounded and the slaughter began. In medieval warfare men were rarely killed outright, or even quickly. When a heavy blow or a cutting stroke was taken, it was vital to stay upright and often men wounded in this way would charge the man opposite and like a wrestler or tired boxer, use him as a support. When lines of battle engaged at close quarter, they often began to wheel round, like a rugby scrum. Because men are mostly right-handed and held their shields in their left hands and forearms, their inclination was to shove to the left – and this made the whole line tend to wheel to the left. Many battles were a matter of who pushed, shoved and hacked the hardest.

When a man was knocked down, the opposing ranks trampled over the top of him, cutting and kicking at him as they went. Often it was the second or third rank who bludgeoned a man to death or un-consciousness. Most died much later of wounds and the consequent blood loss. When fighting had stopped and the enemy put to flight, the exhausted victors found themselves masters of a battlefield strewn with the dead and many who were dying slowly, their lives bleeding away in a horrifically extended agony. Screaming and moaning men lay all around Flodden field in the awful aftermath. Plunderers and scavengers always carried daggers so that they could despatch the wounded and pillage their war gear and anything else of value.

JACKS

Border reivers rode in a fairly standard kit. Those who could afford them wore high, thigh-length riding boots and spurs. Wound around the legs of their breeches were lengths of wire or light chains, enough to turn a blow. On their heads most men wore a 'steel bonnet'. These caps could be elaborate with cheek-pieces, wide brims and high combs. But perhaps the most interesting item was a reiver's jack. This was not expensive to have made and men wore them over their torsos. A jack was made from layers of quilted cloth, sometimes leather, which had metal scales or even bits of hard bone sewn onto it. The wearer had far more freedom of movement than someone wearing armour and it reduced the burden on a pony. Jacks have a surprising history. In the medieval period the Lords of the Isles kept disorder to a minimum by despatching mercenary forces to fight for the warring local kings in Ireland instead of each other. It was a policy adopted a little too late in the Borders. These men were called Gallowglasses (from 'Gall-Oglaigh' for 'foreign warriors') and they developed as heavily armoured infantry able to repel and defeat cavalry. Their strategy was simple; the ranks of their regiments bristled with long spears and had the iron discipline to stand fast when cavalry charged. What helped that resolve was their jack. Sufficiently cheap for each man to afford one, they were the ancestors of what the reivers wore. Gallowglasses' jacks were long, stretching down to their knees. Below them they wore heavy boots which became known as 'jackboots'. And when the jack was adopted by horsemen it needed to be cut shorter and this coined the term 'jacket'.

When it became clear that Flodden was lost, many Scots turned and ran for their lives. These were mostly the men in the rear. King James' battalion was so large that it had 20 ranks but those at the back were usually poorly armed and had no captains to lead them. When they saw the Scottish pikes and standards going down in front of them and the beginning of a terrible slaughter, they scattered. Very few prisoners were taken at Flodden – only 400 – and very many died, perhaps more than 10,000 in total. Chroniclers thought it a cruel battle, worse than any fought at the time.

The day after the slaughter Lord Home led his Borderers back to Branxton, and it may be that they circled the English encampment, offering to continue the fight. Whatever their motives, they were driven off by artillery fire. Because of the terrible carnage and the fact that so many English soldiers had fallen or were badly wounded, Home might have thought Flodden could still be won.

Bands of other Border horsemen were waiting. Gathered on the ridges above the battlefield, keeping their distance, the so-called 'banditti' of Teviotdale and Tynedale were watching for an opportunity, biding their time. They later attacked the exhausted English camp and managed to carry off some plunder and a few head of horses. And as the defeated Scots were retreating northwards, the bandits shadowed them up the weary road to Soutra but eventually withdrew without launching an attack. These incidents were a prelude to what was to come in the sixteenth-century Border country. The dark days of the Border reivers were dawning.

Part II

5

Before Flodden

The night of 19 March 1286 was a night for feasting. A rainstorm had blown in from the North Sea, and the waves whipped up white tops out on the Firth of Forth. In the great hall of Edinburgh Castle King Alexander III of Scotland was drinking with his cronies. At the end of the evening, no doubt flushed with wine, he announced that he wanted to see his new, young wife. A few months before, Alexander had married the beautiful Yolande de Dreux. But the only difficulty was that she was in Fife, at the royal manor of Kinghorn. It was a foul, wild late winter's night, but the king would not be dissuaded. Clattering across the cobbles of Edinburgh Castle, he galloped through the sleeting rain to the Queensferry. Spindrift was spraying off the Forth and at first the ferryman refused to take the king across. It was dark, and far too dangerous a night to be out on the firth. At his insistence, and perhaps after some royal gold, the king got his way and the crossing was made. On the Fife shore the burgesses of North Queensferry implored the king to accept their hospitality and break his journey with them until morning. But he would not, and spurring his horse through the puddles of the coastal path, Alexander made his way to Kinghorn and the warm bed of his beautiful young wife. In the mirk and deafening wind, the king lost sight of his escort but did not stop and wait for them to catch up. Instead he kicked his mount on along the clifftop path on the headland at Pettycur. Perhaps he could see the lights of his manor house twinkling in the darkness. A sudden gust of wind buffeted them – the horse spooked and lost its footing and Alexander was thrown out of the saddle. He plunged two hundred feet though the darkness onto the rocks below.

When search parties found the king at first light, they picked up the lifeless body of the last of the macMalcolm dynasty. Alexander's only heir was a little girl who lived in Norway. His impetuosity had left

Scotland a kingless kingdom and it placed the Borders in the front line of almost three centuries of terrible and destructive war with England.

On the opposite shore of the Firth of Forth, entirely oblivious of the political catastrophe overtaking Scotland, the Earl of Dunbar and March sat by a roaring fire. His castle rose dramatically out of the sea, clinging to a rock by the ancient harbour of Lamerhaven, at Dunbar. Outside the wind whistled and big seas rumbled and crashed against the walls. It was a night for the fireside and Earl Patrick had gathered some of his captains and tenants for supper. Also summoned was a man of much lower status, a man who would also become more famous and revered than any of the noblemen who had dined in the castle hall. Thomas of Earlston, better known to history as Thomas the Rhymer, was probably a bard, a singer and poet whose role was not only to entertain but also to record important events in what he sang. Thomas and the other bards attached to noble households in Scotland could recite genealogies, historical ballads and tales which set his better born listeners in a glowing light. But on the night of 19 March 1286, Thomas would simply amaze them.

After supper Earl Patrick turned to his bard to enquire if the morning would bring anything interesting, a notable or important event. The chronicler, Walter Bower, reported a characteristic note of sarcasm in the earl's question but Thomas soon wiped the smirk off his face:

> 'Alas for tomorrow,' he exclaimed, ' a day of calamity and misery! Before the twelfth hour shall be heard a blast so vehement as shall exceed those of every former period – a blast that shall strike the nations with amazement – shall humble what is proud, and what is fierce shall level with the ground! The sorest wind and tempest that was ever heard of in Scotland!'

The terrible news arrived at Dunbar Castle at noon the following day. The king's death and the immediate proving of his prophesy made Thomas Rhymer famous. His sayings and writings were endlessly repeated and eventually printed over the coming centuries. Before Walter Scott and James Hogg made their marks, Thomas was the most widely known Borderer in history. Prophesy was part of the fabric of politics, taken very seriously and what he foretold was applied, reinterpreted and reapplied to explain, predict and even justify events. For example, the Rhymer's role was transformed from prophet to redeemer amongst the Celtic peoples of Britain, and the Highlanders in particular heard many resonances in what True Thomas uttered. Renamed Tomas Reumhair by the Gaelic bards who whipped up support for the 1715 Jacobite Rebellion, they claimed he had predicted victory, and in 1745 the army of Bonnie Prince Charlie was known as 'the Rhymer's Children'. Famous now only for the sweetened up and watered down ballad of Thomas the Rhymer, he was a powerful influence on Scottish politics for the best part of five hundred years.

The prophet may have been wrong about Culloden, or at least his Gaelic interpreters were, but he correctly predicted the outcome of the battle of Flodden and a score of other bloody defeats across the war-torn Borders landscape. The death of Alexander III was a disaster for the people of the Tweed Basin, Annandale and England north of Hadrian's Wall. With only short respites Borderers would watch a dismal procession of armies tramping across their fields, stealing their corn and cattle, molesting their women and killing their menfolk. For nearly three centuries they lived in a war zone and learned the arts of survival. The international politics of the late thirteenth and early fourteenth centuries laid a fertile ground for the rise of the reivers and a society based on fear, crime and feud. And after the Union of the Crowns in 1603, politics would destroy it.

Frontiers were different in the middle ages. Far more porous and less formal, they also depended on local relationships as much as national, either with individual lords or corporations like the great abbeys. And the Anglo-Scottish border made less sense than most. It divided people who were essentially similar, spoke the same language, farmed in the same way and for centuries had formed part of the old kingdom of Northumbria. It was the magnetic ambitions of the Gaelic-speaking kings in the north and the dynasties to the south which had pulled this polity apart and eventually drew a frontier line along the Tweed and the Cheviot tops.

The battle of Carham in 1018 is seen as a convenient watershed for the history of the border. In a bloody fight by the Tweed near Kelso, the spearmen of Northumbria were cut to pieces by Malcolm II of Scotland's axemen. The Scottish annexation of the Tweed Basin was never seriously in doubt after that date and even though all sorts of anomalies (to say nothing of long-term English occupation in the future) remained, kings in the north gradually asserted themselves over the Borders.

In the later eleventh century William the Conqueror and his sons had difficulty in gaining control of the north of their new kingdom. It lay far from their power-base around London and still attracted the ambitious attention of the Scandinavian dynasty which had ruled England in the first half of the eleventh century. But the Norman kings moved to meet the expansiveness of the macMalcolm dynasty and William Rufus reclaimed Carlisle, making it a plantation town. Communities of Flemings, Normans and Irish settlers were given land in the old Roman city, the castle was rebuilt and the walls repaired. At the eastern end of the Hexham Gap, on the site of the fort on Hadrian's Wall known as Pons Aelius, William Rufus' brother, Robert Curthose, built a new castle. Rising on the high ground to the north of the Tyne Gorge, the Newcastle protected the lowest crossing point over the river. In this way Northumberland and north Cumberland were also understood as potential areas of dispute and conflict. This status was confirmed throughout the twelfth century by the macMalcolm kings' claims on both areas. Often they were successful (due in large part to English distraction and weakness) and David I controlled much of the north of England. In 1153 he died in Carlisle Castle. But by 1157 the northern counties were back in English hands.

Control on either side of the border depended on a series of interlocking relationships of obligation. The church played a clear and progressively determinant role in drawing the Borders into Scotland and the northern counties into England. The bishops of St Andrews and Glasgow claimed independence from the Archbishops of York by maintaining pressure on the papacy in Rome, and they insisted on making all the important ecclesiastical appointments in the Borders. The jurisdiction of the Prince-Bishops of Durham extended right up to the Tweed (and in places beyond it) and they built a powerful castle at Norham to protect what they owned. As much as any other agency the church helped make the border a political reality.

In 1235 Alexander II married Joan, sister of Henry III of England. Two years later he agreed to the terms of the Treaty of York. In return for lands in Cumbria and the right to hang on to the old Liberty of Tynedale (as vassals of the English king), Alexander surrendered all of his claims to the earldom of Northumbria. The line of the Anglo-Scottish frontier was at last settled on the Tweed in the north-east and the Cheviot watershed, the Liddel Water and the little River Sark in the south-west.

This consolidation persuaded kings and their counsellors to organise. To cope with wrongdoing by Englishmen in Scotland and vice versa, the neighbouring jurisdictions needed a special legal mechanism. In 1248 six Scottish knights met with six English knights to discuss the formulation of what became known as the 'laws of the marches', and the following year these were codified and promulgated. In essence they insisted on the return of fugitives from justice, the recovery of debt and the regular production of accused parties at the ancient trysting places on the border line. Some of these, like the Reddenburn near Kelso, were well established and well known. Between 1249 and 1596 the laws of the marches were reviewed and recodified eight times.

Broadly the central transaction was simple. If an Englishman committed a crime in Scotland, for example a robbery, the Scot who had been robbed complained to the Scottish authorities. They in turn passed on the case to their English equivalent, who then investigated. If the charge was found to have substance, the English authorities were bound to produce the accused at a trysting place to answer for it. When it was followed through, this principle could work well and fairly. But it was not always followed through.

This comparatively civilised spirit of international cooperation did not last long. After the death of Alexander III's only close heir, the little Maid of Norway, and the harassed and miserable reign of King John, war clouds began to gather over the Borders. In 1296 Edward I arrived on the banks of the Tweed at the head of a huge army, probably the largest to invade Scotland since Agricola's legions marched north. While English armoured knights took Berwick in a matter of hours, riding right over the top of flimsy defences, no more than 'a ditch and a barricade of boards', a Scottish army mustered at Caddonlea near Galashiels. Less than half the size of Edward's force, the Scots had no intention of moving east to confront him. Instead they adopted a strategy which would become standard. In their council of war at the camp at Caddonlea, the seven earls who led the Scots decided to attack England's western frontier, advancing as far as Carlisle, and – redoubling the misery of ordinary Borderers – to burn, steal and kill in the countryside around. There was no escape, it seemed.

Between 1296 and 1328, what became known as the Wars of Independence trailed destruction in their wake, and on both sides of the border as armies crossed and recrossed. After the dreadful summers of 1315 and 1316 and the failure of the harvests, and the frequent passing of rapacious regiments of soldiers, ordinary Borderers must have despaired. These 34 years of destruction, the span of almost two generations, were another turning point, a time when the fundamental nature of society changed – and for the worse.

What did farmers and their families do in the face of an approaching army or raiding party? The sources are scant, almost silent. Chroniclers recorded the burning of dozens (sometimes hundreds) of farms, villages and towns, the beseiging of castles and the outcome of battles, but they have little or nothing to say about the people caught in this incessant crossfire. They must have fled. When Edward I returned to Berwick in 1298, it was said that the town was deserted, and when the Scots were mustering to raid into north Cumberland after Bannockburn, the English king's officers assisted in moving farmers and their stock south and out of the way. This was almost certainly a general pattern. Quickly gathering up what was valuable and portable and driving their beasts before them, farmers and their families must have retreated to remote places and hid and sheltered as best they could. Perhaps they made for the summer sheilings up on the high pasture. Foraging parties will have found some but at least there was a chance of survival.

HAY FEVER

Seasonal allergic rhinitis is the posh name for hay fever, a condition which has nothing to do with hay. Airborne pollen from grasses, weeds and flowering trees causes about 20 per cent of the population of Britain (more than 12 million and rising) to sneeze in May and June each year. Hay fever is new, the first cases were only reported in 1819. Warmer winters and wetter springs have been causing plants to flower earlier and produce more pollen to be blown around in early summer breezes. One of the few advantages of living in the period of the little ice age was that you were very unlikely to suffer from sneezing and eye irritation. It was too cold and wet for hay fever to present much of a problem.

In 1308 Edward II was at York, ordering his sheriffs of Northumberland, Cumberland and Westmorland to raise 'posses' to repel and pursue raiders, but not lead their men into Scotland unless absolutely necessary. This was most likely a measure to discourage the desperate, bands of riders looking to lift cattle after their own had gone.

Government papers carried reports that English borderers were forming criminal alliances with Scots raiders, becoming 'their companions and guides', and sharing in plundered goods and stock. Simmering under the surface was a question of loyalty. Were Borderers more likely to be loyal to their surnames and their neighbours than to their nationality? It seems so.

In November 1315, after the first sunless summer and its unripened harvest, Edward II wrote to the Bishop of Durham asking that he forbid his tenants on the border from making local truces with their Scots neighbours. So that some sort of subsistence agriculture could go on, it appears that landowners had been reaching accommodations with each other, people they knew well. 'The calamitous and helpless state' of the people had driven them to ignore the state of war between England and Scotland and ignore their king's wishes. And no wonder.

Famine had one thing to recommend it. It had at least prevented Edward II from reinvading Scotland in pursuit of revenge in the year following Bannockburn, but it probably encouraged more raiding across the border. Edmund de Caillou, the Captain of Berwick and a Gascon serving in the English army, led an expedition up the Tweed as far as the mouth of Teviotdale and Jedburgh. Returning with many head of cattle and much plunder, he was intercepted by Sir James Douglas. As a deliberate tactic the Scots commander sought out the Gascon and fought him in what amounted to a single combat. Douglas' force was much smaller and he needed to decapitate the English raiders if he could. And he did.

HEATH PEA

The first pioneer bands of hunter-gatherers who colonised northern Britain at the end of the last ice age lived off the land, the sea and the seashore. Their skills and lore were never lost, and in times of famine were especially valuable. Those who knew where to find mushrooms, raspberries, hazelnuts and crab apples might stave off starvation a little. There was a wide range of what we might now call weeds which could also supply much needed sustenance. Silverweed has a carroty, crunchy root which can be boiled or dried and ground into a sort of flour. It was so commonly used in the Highlands that the Gaels called it 'an seachdamh aran', or 'the seventh bread'. In 2006 it seems that these nutritious plants are back on the menu. Dietitians are investigating the properties of Heath

Pea. Its roots have an aniseed flavour and were said to give those who chewed them the ability to perform superhuman feats of strength and endurance. Highland armies apparently munched Heath Pea on the way to victories at Prestonpans and Falkirk in 1745 and 1746. However, all that may be, but 21st-century society is of course investigating the humble pea not as a source of nutrition but as a means of facilitating weight loss.

A familiar pattern of raid and reprisal began to establish itself. Sometimes it baffled outsiders – and locals. In July 1317 two Italian cardinals were sent by the new Pope, John XXII, to England and Scotland to attempt to broker a peace and gather support for a crusade. Travelling through Northumberland, John de Ossa and Luca de Fieschi were ambushed by 'banditti'. When confronted by two urbane Italian princes of the church in their scarlet skullcaps, the 'banditti' were somewhat nonplussed. Of course they robbed them of everything worth having, but failed to see the potential for a large ransom. Instead they abducted two local lords and left the cardinals, no doubt dazed but relieved, standing in the road.

No medieval community could survive a perpetual state of war and after another abortive English invasion in 1319, the terms of a truce were hammered out at Newcastle. Local contact between English and Scottish borderers was forbidden but the general heads of agreement look very much like a restatement and reinstatement of the laws of the marches. For the first time the appointment of officers to administer them is recorded. Known as 'Conservators of the Truce', two were drawn from Cumberland and Westmorland and four from Northumberland. They were bound to hear complaints about truce breakers, investigate them and seize and detain whoever was believed to have serious charges to face. So far so familiar. But 1319 saw an early organisational structure created to complement the old laws of the marches. These Conservators sound very like versions of the later March Wardens, the royal officers who would become central figures in sixteenth-century reiver society. No record of matching Scottish appointments survive, but for the reciprocal arrangements to work at all, these were likely to have been in place.

The arrangements did not work in 1322 when the truce was shattered by Edward II and his invading army. His men wasted the countryside as far north as Leith, but a year later negotiations resumed. Contact between Scots and English was again expressly forbidden – although one concession was made to practicality. The Conservators might meet their opposite numbers and hold 'truce days' to transact business. These could be held at the ancient trysting places along the border – at Kershope, Carter Bar and Reddenburn and elsewhere. By 1327 a famous name appeared on the scene. Henry de Percy was appointed as 'the Principal Keeper of the Truce' and paid 1,000 merks to maintain 100 men-at-arms and their 'hobelars' or ponies. The institutions of reiver society were slowly taking shape.

Another famous Border name emerged in the early fourteenth century. The Douglas family had been steadfast supporters of Robert de Bruce and tradition holds that the red heart in the centre of their coat of arms represents the great king's. After his death from leprosy in 1328, Bruce's heart was cut out of the hideous, decaying corpse and taken on crusade against the Moors in Spain by the Douglases. For many years the king had been under sentence of excommunication for his murder of John Comyn at the altar of Greyfriars Church in Dumfries, and even in death it seems that Bruce's remains were employed in penitent works.

After Bannockburn, the Douglases received more material rewards, taking over ownership of the forests of Selkirk, Traquair and Ettrick in 1321-22. By the end of the fourteenth century, they had built up a wide patrimony which included estates in Teviotdale, Eskdale, Lauderdale and around Kelso. Over in the west a closely related branch of the family became powerful in Wigtownshire, the wonderfully named Archibald the Grim taking the old title of Lord of Galloway. This was all a deliberate but dangerous royal policy. To buttress the border, Scottish kings needed bulwarks, concentrations of substantial military capability, and so on the Scottish side, the Douglases grew mighty – and as war rumbled wearily on they became mightier still.

Robert de Bruce and his immediate successors were forced to contend with a serious dynastic complication. Edward Balliol had a legitimate claim to the throne of Scotland, and as the son of King John, it was in some ways a better claim than Bruce's. After the hideous murder of his father, Edward III of England and his counsellors took over the simmering war with Scotland, and they found Edward Balliol a very handy political pawn. And because of geography and Balliol's own claims to family property, much of this fascinating political sub-plot was played out across the Borders landcape.

THE MEN WHO WOULD BE KING

At least three different sorts of royal claimants were important in fourteenth- and fifteenth-century politics. A rival claimant such as Edward Balliol, or Edward I of Scotland, presented a serious threat to the Bruces who felt their own royal status in constant need of bolstering. Across the Scottish nobility there were several families who had grounds for believing themselves as royal as the king's. But none had a father who had actually been crowned King of Scots. The second sort was the straightforward imposter. Far from being one of the princes in the Tower (escaped), Perkin Warbeck was not a legitimate claimant to the throne of England but evidently a Frenchman, born in Tournai. His position was perhaps the weakest. The most mysterious claimant was the man known as 'The Mammet'. This was the strange name (it may simply mean 'imposter') given to a man claiming to be Richard II. After having been deposed in 1399 by Henry IV Bolingbroke, Richard was said to have escaped from prison in London and sailed to sanctuary in the Western Isles. He was immediately taken under the protection of the Regent, the Duke of Albany, who paid him a handsome pension. Richard's presence in Scotland was a useful political counter, especially when the king of England was so clearly a usurper himself. The Mammet died in 1419 and was accorded a royal funeral in Stirling. Modern historians now believe that he was no imposter. In an age long before photography or the mass production of printed images, what mattered was not so much likeness as manner and knowledge. If the Mammet behaved like a king and had plausible personal recollection of his part in the major events of his reign, such as the Peasants' Revolt, then many will have bowed to him as Richard II of England.

With the death of the old warrior-king, Robert I, Scotland faced shifting phases of political uncertainty. The new king was a four-year-old boy, David II, and his Regent, Donald Earl of Mar, had only a shaky grip on power. Encouraged and funded by the English, Edward Balliol sailed out of the Humber Estuary in the summer of 1332 at the head of an expeditionary force. Known as 'the Disinherited', the invaders sought to reclaim the estates they believed were rightfully theirs. Many had been driven out of Scotland by Robert I, their lands seized and given to the king's supporters in the Wars of

Independence. Others were English magnates who had lost their Scottish holdings.

At Dupplin Moor, on the River Earn near Perth, the Disinherited unexpectedly defeated the Earl of Mar's larger army. Balliol had not the resources to grasp outright control and set about subduing the rest of Scotland, but he did understand the great power of symbols. A month after his victory at Dupplin Moor, Balliol's supporters had organised a traditional coronation ceremony at Scone. In the footsteps of ancient kings from Kenneth I onwards, he climbed the 'hill of faith' and had himself anointed by a bishop and crowned Edward I of Scotland by the time-honoured kingmaker, the Earl of Fife.

The coronation created a political mess which promised nothing but problems for those living on either side of the Anglo-Scottish border. Balliol granted the sheriffdoms of Roxburgh and Berwick to his sponsor, Edward III of England, 'for all time coming', and the two major towns and castles passed into English occupation. Roxburgh was lost to the Scots between 1334 and 1460 (with one short break) while Berwick was never recovered. Stranded far to the north of other population centres in Northumberland and cut off from its natural hinterland in the Tweed Valley, the town remains a historical anomaly. Lying to the north of most of the Border country, like an island unto itself, it is neither Scots nor convincingly English.

Two kings in Scotland and a powerful and expansionist king of England ensured that the economy of the Borders could not recover its former vigour. Based on the growing of wool, its sale at Roxburgh's markets and export through the port at Berwick, trade had been busy, international and lucrative. The great Border abbeys survive as monuments to God but also to all those business transactions with Flemish and Italian merchants on the quays at Berwick and in the shadow of Roxburgh Castle. But with the frequent tramp of soldiers keeping cartloads of woolpacks and hides off the roads into Scotland, and the long-term presence of English garrisons, the medieval sheep ranches in the Cheviots, Lammermuirs and the uplands never regained their scale and output. And with the customs revenues at Berwick and Roxburgh going to the royal treasury in London, Scots kings had little motivation for the reconstruction of the local economy and the wool trade. In this way fourteenth- and fifteenth-century politics sowed more seeds for the growth of the criminal society of the sixteenth century.

Edward Balliol's triumph lasted only a few months. Having arrived to celebrate Christmas at the town of Annan, part of the family's extensive estates in Dumfriesshire, the royal retinue was attacked by a thousand-strong force of David II's supporters. After his brother, Henry, had been killed, Balliol only just managed to escape. Scrambling onto the back of a horse, wearing nothing but a shirt, and hanging desperately onto its mane, he splashed bareback across the Solway sands to the English shore and was given refuge by Lord Dacre in Carlisle Castle.

By July of the following year Balliol was back in Scotland, this time with Edward III and a huge English army. And this time wearing his crown and riding under his royal banner. By-passing (temporarily) Scots-held Berwick, the invaders plundered their way far to the north, reaching Perth and all the while supplied and supported by a large fleet off the North Sea coast shadowing their advance and putting in at convenient harbours. When Edward III and Balliol returned to Berwick, they found the siege still in progress, and despite the cruel tactic of hanging two Scottish hostages (including the sons of the governor, Sir Alexander Seton) each day in full view of the walls and their defenders, the town held its nerve and held out.

When a relieving army finally arrived under the command of Sir Archibald Douglas, the English took up a powerful position on Halidon Hill, a mile north of Berwick and offered battle. The slaughter was unrelenting. As the Scots fought their way up the hill, they fell under a murderous hail of arrows. Echelons of English archers stood in the new 'harrow' formation which allowed them to fire to their flanks as well as directly in front. Able to loose at least ten arrows a minute from their tremendously powerful longbows (more than 6 foot long and with a draw weight of between 80 and 120 pounds) and send them prodigious distances, his archers won the battle at Halidon Hill for Edward III. Their technique of firing high into the air to harness gravity to the terrifying impact of the arrows brought down rank after rank of Scots foot soldiers and cavalry. Casualty estimates for medieval battles are usually unreliable, but thousands were shot dead or fatally wounded and many noblemen died on the bloody slopes of Halidon Hill, at least five Scottish earls and their commander, Sir Archibald Douglas.

Berwick fell the following day, and in its castle Edward I of Scotland established his puppet court. In reality his master seemed determined to leave him little to rule over. Edward III allowed his soldiers to plunder and burn over wide areas of Scotland south of the Forth. Unlike his grandfather, who sought to subdue by installing a pro-

English party in government, Edward opted for scorched-earth brutality instead of politics. His garrisons in the castles of the Borders terrorised the countryside around, creating a wasteland instead of cultivating a profitable colony – and thereby failing to gather support for Balliol.

ARMOUR PIERCING

From the early experiments at Halidon Hill through to the unexpected triumph at Agincourt, English archery dominated the battlefields of Britain and France. Scots kings tried hard to create similar skills in the north and several Border towns have streets which remember the practice areas for bowmen: the Butts, the Bow Butts. But it never happened. The immense hitting power and accuracy of English (and Welsh) archers, their ability to fire rapid volleys and also to send very long and heavy arrows into the air was unparalleled. Often an arrow might pierce plate armour but use up so much of its energy in so doing that it could not quite get through a mail shirt and pierce the abdomen of a charging knight. Recent tests at Kelso showed a different effect – which was almost as disabling. When an arrow pierced outer armour and mail and its sharp tip was wedged in place and touching the skin, the movement of riding a horse made it impossible to keep the armour on. As a knight moved, the arrow scratched and lacerated his skin until the agony forced him to dismount, if he could in the midst of battle, and tear off his breastplate. At Agincourt so many French knights dismounted and disarmoured that the lines behind them piled up into mounds of screaming men and horses.

In the years that followed the defeat at Halidon Hill, the regency of David II and ultimately the young king himself developed the policy of building up powerful local lordships along the English border. Douglases, Scotts, Humes and Kers grew accustomed to acting on their own initiative when trouble came north, and instead of a remote, often absent and weakened central royal authority, their more immediate ability to protect the countryside and its people fostered strong local loyalties around them. Some began to manipulate international relations to their own ends. Sir William Douglas of Liddesdale had cleared Teviotdale of English occupation by 1343 and began to call himself

Warden of the Scottish Middle Marches, a very early use of the office and title. His neighbour, Sir Alexander Ramsey, Warden of the Scottish East Marches, was made Keeper of Roxburgh Castle and Sheriff of Teviotdale by David II's government. Douglas was outraged. His men attacked Ramsey as he presided over a sheriff court at Hawick and bundled him off to Hermitage Castle. Confined in a filthy cellar, he was starved to death.

David II was allegedly furious. Sir Archibald Douglas calmly withdrew into 'the inaccessible wilds of the Border' and opened a correspondence with the court of Edward III of England. Within months he was restored to favour and granted the keeping of Roxburgh Castle. A familar political pattern was developing.

More military disasters waited for the hapless David II. While Edward III was embroiled in France in the early exchanges of the Hundred Years War, the Scots had recaptured much territory and were attempting to establish royal authority. But in 1346 the young king over-reached himself. At Neville's Cross near Durham, English archery again proved decisive and David II was badly wounded in the face by an arrow. Worse, he was taken prisoner.

The way at last seemed open for Edward Balliol and he immediately moved 'to recover his realm'. At first he tasted dramatic success, overrunning southern Scotland and reaching as far west as Glasgow. But always seen as an agent of the English king, his support remained slight and despite five years of guerrilla warfare, Balliol was never able to take a firm hold of his realm.

In 1349 his subjects had other, much more pressing concerns than rival claims to the throne. At Caddonlea near Galashiels, the traditional muster-place for the Scottish host, soldiers pitched their tents by the stream and waited for their captains to make plans for an invasion of England. Their purpose was to take advantage of the devastation in the south caused by the arrival of what they called 'the foul English pestilence'. Hundreds of thousands had died, communities were reeling at the impact of what historians came to call the 'Black Death'. Bizarrely, the Scots believed that it was a disease which respected nationality and frontiers, only affecting the English. The Tweed had been used as a cordon sanitaire, the fords and bridges closely guarded and the ferry boats pulled up on the northern bank.

When the disease suddenly erupted around the campfires at Caddonlea, the soldiers panicked and the army scattered. And thereby spread the plague much more quickly throughout Scotland. The contemporary chronicler, John of Fordun, believed that a third of all Scots died in 1349. Later historians estimated a quarter. By either reckoning it was a cataclysmic event, reducing the population from around a million to 750,000 or even less in a matter of weeks. Far more devastating than any military campaign or famine, the Black Death changed medieval Scotland radically, and for the worse. Around 30 per cent of the agricultural labour force disappeared, literally overnight, and the remainder lived in terror of following their agonising fate – at any moment. The economy must simply have ruptured and the rural cycle left badly damaged.

GROSS, GRIM, BLACK AND A LOSER

The Douglas family attracted nicknames like no other. Perhaps as a result of using the same Christian names in succeeding generations, the genealogies sprout soubriquets like Archibald the Tyneman (the Loser), Archibald Greysteel (fought well at the Battle of Ancrum Moor in 1545) and the splendid Archibald the Grim (fought well most of the time). There was also James the Gross (fat but long-lived) and – surely the worst of many Douglas nicknames – that attached to Hugh, Lord Douglas, who lived from 1294 to 1342. He has gone down in history as Hugh the Dull. In the early 1600s, the Border historian, David Hume of Godscroft, set the seal on Hugh's dismal reputation: 'Of this man, whether it was by reason of the dullness of his mind, we have no mention at all in history of his actions.' Oh dear. But perhaps the most extravagant transition was that of Charles the Wellbeloved, King of France until 1422. Because he began to lose his mind, attacking his courtiers without warning, he first became a tentative 'Charles the Silly' and then, after he had killed four of them – only desisting when his sword broke, definitely 'Charles the Mad'. Perhaps his wife drove him to it. Queen Isabella's great bulk and even greater sexual appetite conferred the title 'The Great Sow'.

In the Borders, as elsewhere, those who caught the disease were left to die a lonely and excruciating death. Priests were not allowed to administer last rites and families forbidden to sit by the beds of the dying. Those who recovered – and around 40 per cent did – must have been in danger of dying of thirst and starvation as they were left to their miserable fate. In a very short time thousands were thrown into mass graves, houses gutted and the possessions of the dead burned on huge pyres. It was a holocaust.

Here is John of Fordun's account of what happened:

> For, to such a pitch did that plague wreak its cruel spite, that nearly a third of mankind were thereby made to pay the debt of nature. Moreover, by God's will this evil led to a strange and unwonted kind of death, insomuch that the flesh of the sick was somehow puffed out and swollen, and they dragged out their earthly life for barely two days . . . Men shrank from it so much that, through fear of contagion, sons, fleeing as from the face of leprosy or from an adder, durst not go and see their parents in the throes of death.

In the weeks following the arrival of this lethal illness few people travelled unless they had to and market days must have been sparse and trade doubtless declined sharply. A labour shortage soon took hold and while it benefited those who were left, the economic downturn was bad for everyone. Food prices rocketed, land values fell and cultivation shrank back. After the dismal effects of climate change from 1315 onwards, this new calamity only added more momentum to the decline of the Borders in the fourteenth century. The plague returned regularly and outbreaks were reported as late as the eighteenth century.

Edward Balliol was a tough old bird and his ambitions survived, but support in England was waning. The captured David II was much more valuable to Edward III if he was recognised as the legitimate sovereign of Scotland. As the Hundred Years War absorbed more and more resources, a king's ransom became very attractive to the English. They needed the money and Balliol became expendable.

In January 1356 Edward III held court in his castle at Roxburgh and summoned Edward I of Scotland into his presence. For the times Balliol by then was a very old man indeed at 76. But 'like a roaring lion', wrote the chroniclers, he tore the crown of Scotland from his head and with the symbols of earth and water, he gave them up to Edward III. And having resigned his kingdom and all his Scottish possessions, he was awarded a pension so that he could retire to his family estate at Bailleul in northern France, as his father had done. A remarkable man – who might have been king – he died almost ten years later at the immense age of 85.

By the terms of the Treaty of Berwick, concluded in 1357, the

English finally got their money. David II was ransomed for 100,000 marks, a vast sum whose payments further crippled the economy. Officially the treaty also stipulated that there be a 20-year truce between the kings of England Scotland. But not necessarily between Borderers. The Scots in particular ignored it and before the ink was dry and the wax had set on the new treaty, the reconquest of Berwickshire and Roxburghshire began.

Nibbling at the margins of English occupation, local lords re-imposed themselves and forced English garrisons to stick close to their castles. By 1364 the Chamberlain at Berwick was reporting that no rents could be collected at Hawick because of the actions of Scots lords, and in 1369 the Earl of Dunbar and March repossessed his old estates around Earlston. Two years later the Chamberlain was accounting only for rents paid within a 5-mile radius of Berwick – the minimum effective range of regular patrols.

In Roxburghshire the English held onto the powerful castles at Jedburgh and Roxburgh itself, and controlled the countryside in a ten-mile corridor between them. Attacks on these strongholds were likely to sting the English into large-scale military action and the new king, Robert II, was in any case bound by the terms of the treaty which released his predecessor. But privately the first Stewart king condoned what the Border lords were doing and he rewarded them.

The fourteenth century saw the consolidation of the 'Auld Alliance' between Scotland and France against England. Edward III, his son 'the Black Prince', and successor, Richard II, pursued territorial wars against the French for more than 60 years. It was in Scotland's direct interest to give aid to her enemy's enemy and vice-versa. But this only rarely worked in any practical way, although it did force the English into a mindset of fighting a war on two fronts. And when a truce had been declared or the war had gone well in France, the English kings could turn their attention northwards.

In the early 1380s the Earls of Douglas had been active on the border, retaking Wark Castle and even extending control over parts of north Northumberland. Richard II of England retaliated with vigour. At the head of a huge army of 14,000 men, the largest to march north since Halidon Hill, he led a full-scale invasion of Scotland. Once again the Borders suffered. At Hoselaw near Kelso the English pitched camp, their banners snapping in the breeze, their 'thousand fires' twinkling in the night sky and sending a chill of terror around the countryside. Many Border lords and prelates hurried to make their peace.

As Richard II pursued Douglas and his supporters, the Scots scorched the earth in front of his huge army. Quartermasters sent out foraging parties but there was little to be gleaned. Perhaps out of frustration, the English king ordered the destruction of Melrose and Dryburgh abbeys. He also tightened his hold over Roxburghshire and Berwickshire.

A repeating, highly destructive and depressing pattern of raid and retaliation had become entrenched and for fully four generations fire, rack and ruin had blighted the Border country.

Born in 1316, two years after the sensational victory at Bannockburn and while his grandfather was in his martial pomp, Robert II was an old man when he succeeded to the throne of Scotland. Fifty-five was a venerable age in the fourteenth century. By the 1380s Robert had attracted an unflattering nickname. Known as 'Auld Bleary', he clung to kingship long enough to frustrate the ambition of his eldest son, John, the Earl of Carrick. In 1384, exasperated, he orchestrated a palace coup which removed the old king from the effective exercise of power and forcibly retired him to Dundonald Castle on the family estates in Ayrshire.

TAILZIE

Disputed successions to kingdoms, estates, titles or privileges were a continuing source of conflict in medieval Scotland and England. One solution was the mechanism known as 'entail' in England, and it essentially nominated an alternative line of succession should the principal line fail to produce heirs. In Scotland it was called 'tailzie' (the original meaning was 'a slice of meat') and it worked in much the same way. So, when David II failed to produce an heir, an agreed tailzie meant that the children of Robert the Bruce's daughter, Marjorie, could pick up the succession to the throne. This sort of sideways move could be problematic but it caused less dissent than the old Celtic principle of tanistry which operated in Scotland until the mid-twelfth century. Tanistry broadened the succession very much more by including all those whose great-grandfather had been a king as possible heirs. It certainly guaranteed the line of succession but also sparked endless, vicious, blood-spattered incidents. Unknowingly, William Shakespeare dealt with the consequences of tanistry in 'Macbeth'.

Auld Bleary lived long enough to see his son punished for his presumption. Badly injured by a kick from a horse, the Earl of Carrick was left so crippled that he could take no active part in warfare. It was as much a blow to prestige as a practical matter for a medieval magnate. This allowed his younger brother, Robert, Earl of Fife, to take up the reins of authority and become Guardian of Scotland. One of his earliest acts was to organise a huge raid over the border into England which culminated in the famous battle at Otterburn.

This was not an invasion in pursuit of political advantage or the annexation of territory: the campaign of 1388 bore all the marks of a raid, plain and simple, and it owed much more to the growing habit of reiving than to the policies of Robert I or Edward III. And its climactic battle was fought in moonlight.

The events of that summer were exceptionally well recorded. Jean Froissart, the French chronicler, had spoken to two Gascon esquires who had fought for Sir Henry Percy at the battle at Otterburn, Jean de Castelnau and Jean de Cantiron. Their conversation took place only a year later and memories must have been sharp. And like a good historian, Froissart sought a balanced view. Also in 1389 he interviewed a Scottish knight and two esquires who had fought for the Earl of Douglas. In addition, seven other medieval accounts survive and these are further supplemented by one of the best and very earliest of the Border ballads, 'The Battle of Otterburn'. It is a strange and significant story, and the seeds of much of what was to come lay at its core.

When the Earl of Fife mustered the Scottish host in the high valley of the Jed Water, retaliation was much on his mind. Richard II of England's invasion of 1385 had achieved few strategic purposes but it had been tremendously destructive. Borderers in particular responded to the new Guardian's call to arms and many joined him in the Jedforest in the summer of 1388. They had suffered at the brunt of the English advance and had scores to settle. Under the command of James, Earl of Douglas, many surnames came. Led by their heidsmen, both Johnstones and Maxwells rode in from the west, and there were Kers and Humes from the eastern marches. The opening stanza of the ballad and its hunting metaphor bears repetition for it makes it very clear what was being planned around the campfires in the old forest – a raid:

It fell about the Lammastide
When muir men win their hay,
The doughty Douglas bound him to ride
Into England to drive a prey.

Fife and Douglas decided to divide their forces. From Southdean Kirk, the larger division made for the Larriston Fells and the head of Liddesdale. The Guardian and Sir Archibald Douglas would lead them down towards Carlisle and the fertile farms of the English west march. They had no siege equipment and would make no attempt to take the town and its squat, well-made castle. James Douglas sought his prey by moving his troopers up over the Carter Bar and down into Redesdale and then on to Tyneside. The strategic intention may have been to tie up English defenders on both sides of the north Pennines and thereby disable any flanking incursion into Scotland.

Both divisions moved with lightning speed. On the morning of 28 July Douglas crossed into England and late the same day his small army camped only a few miles north of the Tyne. By midday on the 29th they were across the river and raiding almost as far south as Durham. The Earl of Fife and Sir Archibald had made 40 miles on their first day and driven many to take refuge behind the stout walls of Carlisle.

What made this medieval blitzkrieg possible was something simple. These armies travelled on horseback. Carrying little or no baggage, their troopers lived off the land and their ponies ate the summer grass. Jean Froissart reported that these huge raiding parties could strike over a range of 60 or 70 miles in a day and a night and since they were pulling no baggage carts, they could move quickly over the hill trails, avoiding towns, their garrisons and delaying trouble until they reached their objective.

The western division bypassed Carlisle on 3 August and rode up the Eden Valley, plundering and raiding as they went. They burned the town of Appleby and advance parties reached as far as Brough before wheeling their ponies northwards again.

Douglas had been busy in the east and by 1 August his men were driving hundreds, possibly thousands of head of stolen cattle across the Tyne fords at Prudhoe. The bridge at Ovingham may still have been standing. From that moment on, the campaign took on all the lineaments of a classic raid. Douglas further divided his forces and sent on a party with all of the plunder to make as much haste as possible up the line of Dere Street and on towards the border. The old Roman road turned down into Redesdale at Otterburn and Douglas and his chosen men would rejoin them there.

Once their plunder had begun to move north, the remaining Scots rode east along the north bank of the Tyne. Much of Hadrian's Wall was still upstanding in 1388 and the military road which paralleled it enabled Douglas to reach the great West Gate of Newcastle's walls in little more than an hour, probably on the afternoon of 3 August. There was no intention to make any attempt to break into the city. The Scots had come to stall, to play for time. While their comrades made slow progress with all those cows up the Roman road, Douglas would bottle up the English behind Newcastle's walls, buying a precious day or even two to allow his men to get as far north as possible.

Sir Henry Percy, made famous by Shakespeare as 'Harry Hotspur', no doubt knew exactly what was going on. Froissart and others relate a tale of single combat between the two commanders outside the West Gate. Perhaps it is true. Douglases had done it before. Hotspur's soldiers certainly sallied out of the city to harass the Scots and it may be that he himself challenged the Earl of Douglas. Single combat took place before Bannockburn and Halidon Hill, and notions of chivalry were very fashionable at the end of the fourteenth century. Here is Froissart's account:

> The Scots returned to Newcastle and rested and tarried two days, and every day they skirmished. The Earl of Northumberland's two sons were young lusty knights and were ever foremost at the barriers to skirmish. There were many proper feats of arms done and achieved: there was fighting hand to hand: among others there fought hand to hand the Earl of Douglas and Sir Henry Percy, and by force of arms the Earl of Douglas won the pennon of Sir Henry Percy, wherewith he was sore displeased and so were all the Englishmen.

Whatever the truth, it all wasted time, and by the morning of 4 August it was enough. Defenders looked out from the West Gate and saw nothing. The Scots had gone before dawn. Two days was judged to be sufficient for the plunder to have reached the rendezvous at Otterburn.

Douglas led his riders and their surefooted ponies through the grey hour before first light, and when they reached Ponteland, they overran the sleeping village and its castle. Both were torched and the local lord, Sir Raymond Delaval, captured and carried off for ransom. Without any more delay the Scots remounted and hurried up the north road to Otterburn.

Percy had sent scouts to shadow Douglas and when they reported a much smaller force than he had assumed, it was resolved immediately to give chase. Hotspur would earn his nickname. Otterburn and Redesdale lie more than 30 miles north of Newcastle and Percy knew that only a mounted force had any chance of catching the Scots before they could slip over the Carter Bar and down into the Jed Valley and safety. A muster-call rang around the city and some time around mid-morning Sir Henry Percy's banner dipped under the Pilgrim Gate and his men spurred their ponies into a canter. Douglas may already be climbing the winding road up to the Carter. No time to be lost.

While they waited for their comrades to arrive from Newcastle, the Scots attacked Otterburn Castle. But having travelled light with no siege equipment in tow, they made little impression and the defenders held the castle described by contemporaries as 'tolerably strong and situated among marshes'.

Elsewhere the Scots had used the boggy ground to their advantage. A large corral had been built for their plundered cattle, probably on the higher haughland still visible in a loop of the River Rede. Work-gangs of servants had improvised a stockade of sorts with cut branches and brushwood, and watered by the river, bitten by the midges, the cows were protected by the surrounding treacherous marshes. Froissart wrote of the stockade being 'at the entrance to the marsh on the road to Newcastle'. This was significant for what was to take place later. Just as Otterburn Castle was well defended by its surrounding marshes, the Scots' cattle corral made use of the undrained land, keeping the animals in and attackers out.

Meanwhile, Percy's troopers kicked their ponies on up the north road, passing the charred and smoking houses at Ponteland, on up to Belsay and beyond. As the terrain rose after the Scots Gap, the English commanders no doubt sent ahead a screen of scouts. Ambush was a favourite tactic and there were several likely places. By the afternoon Sir Henry Percy's mounted army, perhaps 4,000 strong, was climbing up past Kirkwhelpington onto the moorland above Redesdale. Dere Street and its wide, hard roadway lay well to the west and his troopers will have had to trot along much narrower paths. Sometimes no wider than sheepwalks, the hill trails of the middle ages may have forced

Percy's horsemen to travel in single file in places. This slowed progress tremendously and would later have sore consequences. But it was the Scots who would make the first mistake.

Probably convinced that it was far too late in the day for Percy or any other pursuer to be approaching, Douglas' scouts may have made their way down off the hills to the camp at Otterburn by the early evening. Perhaps the English outriders took care to conceal themselves well. As afternoon shaded into evening, the Scots unbuckled their kit, lit cooking fires and gathered round them to sit, talk over the excitements of the last days and take their ease.

Peace was shattered when a rider tore into the camp at full gallop, whooping and hollering that a huge English force was closing fast. Seven standards fluttered in the breeze, according to the ballad, as Percy spurred on towards Douglas and his thieving band. A day's hard riding – and he had caught them!

Chaos crackled through the Scottish camp as men fell over themselves to buckle on their armour, fiddle with fastenings, pull a mail-shirt over their heads and find their weapons. Many managed to lay hands on only part of their war-gear as their captains screamed at them to stand to. The Earl of Moray fought without his helmet, the Earl of Douglas without much of his body armour, others were without gauntlets, greaves, some had spears but no dagger, others went barefoot across the heather. But the Scots did not lose their composure or forget their common sense.

Henry Percy did. The sun was setting fast, and as soon as Sir Matthew Redman's vanguard arrived at Otterburn, they attacked the Scots' cattle corral. When Percy's horsemen galloped up out of the village, they dismounted and massed for an immediate attack. Without waiting for all of his long column to gather and quickly pushing his men into a line, Percy became Hotspur and led his men over the moorland. His fatal problem was organisation. Not enough time had been allowed for his captains to form up their men into battalions. Most of the heavily armoured men-at-arms bunched together at one end of the line while at the other lightly armed archers found themselves unsupported and very vulnerable. According to the Westminster Chronicle they 'straggled into action in irregular order'.

As the light faded, the Scots scrambled into a much better drilled battle formation. Seeing that Percy's front was badly unbalanced, they quickly wheeled and attacked him on his flank, driving their spears into the company of archers and knocking them down before they could begin firing. As Percy's late-comers arrived and dismounted, they rushed into the battle piecemeal, making no dramatic difference. By contrast the Earls of Moray and March calmly rallied their contingents as a strategic reserve and waited for their moment.

The battle soon became a bloody scrummage as the two lines locked together in the hacking, shoving and kicking of close-quarter fighting. In the midst of all that intimate fury James, Earl of Douglas, was felled and, incompletely armoured, done to death by wounds to his body. Few noticed in the melee. Few could see further than what was at their front and immediately beside them. As darkness descended and the big harvest moon rose over the moor, Percy's men began to tire. They had ridden all day to fight at Otterburn while many of their enemies had rested. After the failure of the disordered first charge, their chances of victory hung in the balance.

Then Sir John Swinton broke the line. A tough, battle-hard soldier from Berwickshire who had fought in English armies for pay and plunder in the Hundred Years War, he hacked his way through Percy's men-at-arms and turned them. The chroniclers reported that the death-blow followed quickly when the Earls of March and Moray and their reserves drove into the dying battle and all in a moment Otterburn became a rout.

English soldiers threw down their weapons, turned and ran for their lives. Many noblemen, exhausted in their heavy body armour, held up their hands, yielded and were captured for lucrative ransoms. One of these was Harry Hotspur, Sir Henry Percy. And it was then that Sir Walter Scott's strange, (and, of course, retrospective) prophesy for James, Earl of Douglas, came true:

> But I hae dreamed a dreary dream,
> Beyond the Isle of Skye;
> I saw a dead man win a fight,
> And I think that man was I.

Late in the afternoon of 5 August, the likely date of the battle, the Prince-Bishop of Durham left Newcastle with several thousand soldiers (almost certainly not the 10,000 claimed by Froissart) to reinforce the impetuous Percy. But they had not gone far before they met streams of fugitives from the disaster at Otterburn. So many of the Prince-Bishop's men turned and fled with them to the safety of Newcastle's walls that his force was reduced to fewer than 500. So rather than face the pursuing Scots, the wise prelate realised he had no choice and he retreated through the Pilgrim Gate.

Having recovered their self-possession by the following day, Durham's soldiers mustered and rode hard for Otterburn. This time the Scottish scouts were alert. They warned their commanders of a second approach and this time they set to strengthening their temporary fortifications. When the Prince-Bishop and his captains rode into view, the Scots taunted them from behind their barricades, blew trumpets and issued dire threats. It was enough. Durham retreated and Douglas's men eventually made their way over the Carter Bar. What was perhaps the greatest raid in the long story of reiving ended profitably – but with the death of their captain, the Scots had paid a heavy price for all that plunder.

Archibald the Grim gained most. After a perilous crossing of the treacherous Solway fords with the Earl of Fife, he returned from the western raid to Cumbria to discover that he would inherit vast tracts of land from the dead Earl James. To add to his Galloway estates between the Cree and the Nith, the new Earl of Douglas became master of Douglasdale, Eskadale, Lauderdale, the old royal Forest of Selkirk and many farms and villages in the Tweed Valley. It was an immense and valuable domain – but almost all of it lay in a war zone.

Archibald the Grim got his nickname for an apt quality. Said to be grim, or in its older meaning 'merciless', in battle, the English also called him Archibald the Black. The latter tag came to apply to his descendants and that branch of the family were known as 'the Black Douglases'. This distinguished them from the Earls of Angus who were called 'the Red Douglases', very much junior cousins.

DUKES PUT UP

Towards the end of the fourteenth century English and Scottish kings began creating dukes and dukedoms, probably in imitation of the French. In 1398 the Duke of Albany was first north of the border, but the title lapsed on the execution of his son, Murdoch, in 1425. It passed through various royal hands until it finally became extinct in 1917. Leopold, the Duke of Saxe-Coburg and of Albany was a German and like Duke Murdoch he was forced to forfeit the title. Dukedoms were created as a pinnacle for the aristocracy and only kings could make them. The word derives from the Latin 'dux' meaning a leader. Richard II created his uncles Duke of Buckingham and Duke of Cambridge at Hoselaw near Kelso in the course of his invasion of Scotland in 1385. Little good it did him. Dukes have precedence over all other aristocratic titles. They are followed by Marquises, then Earls, Viscounts, Barons, Knights, then Esquires and finally Gentlemen. Titles like these go before names and letters after. And the letters which have precedence over all others are VC.

The year after Otterburn, Earl Archibald and George Dunbar, the Earl of March, mustered their soldiers to raid into England and exploit the weakness of Richard II's administration, but their plans were thwarted when a French envoy arrived in Edinburgh. A three-year truce between the kings of England and France had been concluded, and as partners in the Auld Alliance, the Scots were bound by its terms. Robert II's sons forced the Douglas/March army to disband. Furious, the two earls began to enter into private arrangements with the English, and these were designed to deliver advantage to their families and their possessions in the Borders. International relations and the wider cause of Scotland as a whole came a very distant second.

Auld Bleary finally died in 1390 at his retreat at Dundonald Castle. He was 74 and 'broken by age'. His eldest son, John Earl of Carrick, who had been broken by accident, took the regnal name of Robert III. He and his counsellors wished to avoid the issue of the legitimacy of King John Balliol's short reign. The names 'John I' or 'John II' both had baggage attached. The former would have denied Balliol's existence and the latter recognised it and also the claims of Edward Balliol and his descendants. Dupplin Moor lay only two generations in the past.

Robert III was anxious to prolong the truce of 1389. He and his family needed time and the opportunity to exert their authority inside Scotland and not allow themselves to be distracted or destabilised by war across the border. And just as important, the powerful southern earls of Douglas and March must not be given the chance to become more powerful.

On 11 March 1398 Scots and English commissioners met at Hadden Stank near Kelso. Like the nearby Redden Burn it was a customary trysting place on the line of the border. David, Earl of Carrick and heir presumptive, arrived with a bishop, another earl, a baron, two clerks, two knights bachelor, and a squire. This carefully compiled list was balanced by a deputation of exactly equal rank on the English side. It was led by the Duke of Lancaster and Guyenne, John of Gaunt, the king's uncle. Known by contemporaries as 'Days of Trewe' or Truce Days, these were the ancestors of the sixteenth-century meetings held by March Wardens or their deputies.

With royal dukes and earls in charge and great magnates in tow, the deliberations at Hadden Stank would have been formal, showy affairs. Heraldic standards, pavilions, perhaps fanfares, announcements, processions, oaths and the fixing of waxen seals. If the March weather was unusually benign, it must have been an impressive spectacle.

The grander business of state was speedily concluded (having been agreed beforehand) but the grit of cross-border relations took more time. Complaints from Scots about alleged English wrongdoing and vice-versa had already been lodged. In a stark geographical quirk, English bills of complaint were handed to the Sacristan of Kelso Abbey and Scots bills to the Governor of Roxburgh Castle – which lay just across the Tweed, less than a mile distant. Such were the awkward realities of everyday life in the eastern Borders. At Hadden Stank these bills were heard and adjudicated upon. The old term of 'Conservators of the Truce' was used and deputies appointed to see that the peace was kept.

It was not. The Truce Day of 11 March 1389 failed, despite its high-born cast list and its high-flown language and intentions. Truce-breaking of all sorts went on and another meeting was scheduled for the autumn in an attempt to bring criminals to justice. Certain customs were reaffirmed and the second Truce Day of 1389 heard mention of what became known as 'hot trod', the right to pursue 'with horn and hound' thieves and stolen goods from one realm into another without impediment.

The following year all was thrown into even greater confusion when Richard II of England was deposed and the usurper, Henry Bolingbroke, assumed the crown and called himself Henry IV. Henry Percy, Earl of Northumberland, and Ralph Neville, Earl of Westmorland, both supported the new king and were confirmed by him as Wardens of the East and West Marches respectively. Immediately they found their hands full as Scottish reiver lords took the opportunity to raid into England. In Coquetdale a band of reivers were happily rounding up cattle when they were attacked and taken prisoner by Sir Robert Umfraville. One of the Scots was John Turnbull, known as 'Out With The Sword', a very early example of a classic reiver nickname.

DUEL OR NO DUEL

Deals were sometimes done over long-term sieges. They were expensive and an early resolution was welcomed by both parties. Defenders would calculate how much food, water and resolve they had left and occasionally negotiate surrender by a certain date if no relieving force had arrived before then. This happened at Berwick and Roxburgh. The quid pro quo was usually an agreement that lives would be spared and property respected. In the aftermath of a battle at Humbleton Hill near Wooler, Harry Hotspur laid siege to the tower of Cocklaws in the Scottish Border. When it held out, he agreed that it should surrender by 1 August 1403 if neither the Duke of Albany or Robert III came with an army to relieve it. Albany raised an army, and Percy did the same. A victory on the scale of Bannockburn was promised. The Scots army marched south to relieve Cocklaw – but the English did not turn up. Percy had been raising his army to fight Henry IV at Shrewsbury and the whole thing was a ruse. In 1394 Sir William Inglis briefly took Jedburgh Castle for the Scots but lost it soon afterwards to Sir Thomas Strother. Over some now lost point of honour the two men agreed to fight a duel with the winner taking the castle. At Rulehaugh, a flat piece of ground nearby, an audience including the Earls of Northumberland and Douglas gathered. After a furious fight lasting no more than a few minutes, Inglis killed Strother. But for some reason Jedburgh stayed in English hands and Robert III compensated Sir William with the old barony of Manor, not far from Peebles.

One of the heroes of Otterburn, the Earl of March, was anxious to make contact with Henry IV and involve him in a serious domestic dispute. In exchange for a large sum in gold, Robert III had agreed to give his eldest son, the Duke of Rothesay, in marriage to March's daughter, Elizabeth Dunbar. Archibald the Grim immediately outbid him and the old king changed his mind, and promptly added injury to insult by refusing to repay March his handsome dowry.

The earl did not waste time or mince his words. In a letter to Henry IV, he invited the new English king to take sides in a family feud in Scotland. In exchange for his support, March would immediately defect and throw his weight behind English ambitions in Scotland. By midsummer the Duke of Rothesay had married Archibald the Grim's daughter and March had been joined by the Percies in raiding in the Borders and East Lothian. Thus the winner and loser of Otterburn disregarded national politics and combined in pursuit of family interest. Like true Borderers.

Henry IV then invaded Scotland, laid siege to Edinburgh Castle, issued a few irritated letters, marched up and down and then hurried south to Newcastle. Nothing was resolved and a year later a peace conference assembled hopefully at the village of Kirk Yetholm, near the border. Prior diplomacy had not prepared the way and when the English commissioners trotted out the tired old formula which stretched back into the mists of myth-history and which – self-evidently – proved that Scottish kings had in fact been subject to English kings since the time of Athelstan of Wessex and likely long before, the reaction was less than polite. When arbitration on the matter was suggested, the Bishop of Glasgow replied with a question. Would Henry Bolingbroke's claim to the English throne also be subject to the same scrutiny? In such an atmosphere, there was nothing to be achieved.

In any case Henry IV had more pressing problems elsewhere. In 1400 he had been forced to abandon his siege of Edinburgh Castle and lead his army south to Wales to deal with a serious rebellion. Owain Glyn Dwr and his men had attacked the hated English towns in the north and burned Oswestry and Welshpool. His cousins, Gwilym and Rhys ap Tudur took Anglesey and were strong enough to confront Henry IV and drive him behind the walls of Beaumaris Castle. The gold dragon-standard of Uther Pendragon was unfurled in all its ancient glory and it led Owain Glyn Dwr to many victories over the Sais, the despised English, between 1402 and 1404.

English distraction, whether in France or in Wales, usually encouraged the belligerent Border lords into bouts of military opportunism, and amid the labyrinthine complexities of Scottish domestic politics, the seemingly ever-present need to raid into England was at least a constant. It was becoming a habit of mind, and for those who had to suffer its dismal consequences, a fact of life, year in year out.

THE WOLF OF BADENOCH

Alexander Stewart, the Earl of Buchan and brother of King Robert III, became notorious in the 1380s as 'the Wolf of Badenoch'. Having abandoned his wife and taken 'a concubine' known as

Mairead, Stewart began to turn himself into what he saw as a Highland chieftain. When the Bishop of Moray reproved him for his adultery, the Wolf destroyed the town of Forres and burned the episcopal cathedral at Elgin. Alexander Stewart, most certainly not a Gael, did much to develop the reputation of the Highlands as a lawless, savage society. It was a description soon to be applied to the Borders. What compounded the actions of the Wolf was a grisly affair known as 'the Battle of the Clans'. To settle a territorial dispute, two groups, probably Camerons and Mackintoshes, met near Perth to fight to the death. Thirty men stood on each side. They were not allowed to wear armour – this was to be a decisive encounter – and carrying Lochaber axes, dirks and crossbows, they were watched by grandstands crammed with a specially invited audience. There was to be no quarter and no mercy. At the end of this appalling spectacle only two Camerons and ten Mackintoshes were left standing. All the others had been hacked to pieces. Every Scottish chronicler reported this, as did many English.

Archibald the Grim died in 1400, but his son, also Archibald but not yet grim, continued a close alliance with his father's old reiving partner, the Earl of Fife. He had lately been elevated with the grand title of Duke of Albany.

As King Robert III's grip on power slackened, Albany's grew tighter. Douglas supported him and in return was allowed to plunder into Northumberland despite the fact that a truce was theoretically still in place. In June of 1402 a party of Scots raiders were driving their spoils up the old Roman road of Dere Street. As they crossed the River Teviot, north of Jedburgh and near the hamlet of Nisbet, they were ambushed by the renegade Earl of March. Several notables were killed and others captured for ransom. In itself this incident was part of the small change of Border politics but it did sting Douglas into action and was the first move in a fascinating sequence of events.

In August 1402 he entered England at the head of a large force and raided down as far as the Tyne. Somewhere, somehow, more booty was found and the Scots made their way north by the low road, the trail which skirted the eastern end of the Cheviot ranges. To their astonishment, Douglas and his captains ran into a substantial English army arrayed directly across their route north, barring the way up the valley of the River Till. There was no way round, and Harry Hotspur and the Earl of March were sitting on their ponies in the front rank, itching for revenge.

Encumbered by loot and fearful that they were badly positioned the Scots panicked themselves into a bad mistake. Seeking higher ground, they rushed to occupy the site of a prehistoric hillfort, Humbleton Hill, its grassy old ramparts still visible. Hotspur and March moved quickly to entrap the Scots and – as at Otterburn – the former showed that he had learned nothing and advocated an immediate charge. March calmed Hotspur and instead brought forward the lethal companies of English archers. As the Scots cowered powerless on the hillfort, they fell in their hundreds under the incessant, murderous whoosh loosed on them from below.

That hard-bitten old campaigner, Sir John Swinton, was sheltering under his shield amongst the carnage and he knew that if the Scots made no move, they would be cut down where they stood. Protecting themselves as best they could, his 'chosen lances' climbed into the saddle. Kicking their terrified horses into a gallop, yelling their war-cries, he led them in a desperate downhill charge towards the ranks of archers and English men-at-arms. The archers lowered their aim and firing heavy bolts more like small javelins at the Scots' horses, they brought down most of them before they could engage. It was said that some bolts could pierce plate-armour at close range. Old Sir John disappeared into the ruck of the fighting, going to ground with his horse to be trampled and hacked to death.

Along with four other earls and a hundred or so knights, Archibald Douglas was captured at Humbleton Hill. Soon after the battle he acquired a nickname very different from his father's. Douglas became known as 'the Tyneman', a Scots word meaning 'the Loser'.

SOLDIERS OF FORTUNE

The Hundred Years War greatly encouraged the use of professional soldiers, or mercenaries. Campaigns fought in France were not attractive to an amateur English medieval host mustered to do its mandatory military service. The logistics did not work for part-timers. Back home crops needed to be sown, harvests led in and winter ploughing done. Bands of battle-hardened fighting men evolved, usually under the command of English knights. Sir John Hawkswood had pursued a successful career with his 'White Company' fighting in Italy for one city against another. The

Florentines gratefully remember him as 'Giovanni Acuto' and he sits on a prancing warhorse in a fresco on the wall of their great cathedral, the Duomo. But he could see more lucrative work across the Alps in France and he led his company northwards. Sir John Swinton has no similarly splendid memorial but he was engaged in the same business, fighting for the English kings in the Hundred Years War. Mercenaries were supremely realistic and when they saw which way a battle was going, the last thing they wanted to do was fight to the last man. In the midst of the din and chaos of battle opposing commanders would have no hesitation in holding up their right hand (the accepted signal of surrender) and making sure it was seen – and sometimes they were quickly hired by the winning side. Daft amateurs must have worried mercenaries most.

The nationalism so robustly evident at Bannockburn and in the masterful person of King Robert the Bruce appeared to have fragmented into family factionalism by the end of the fourteenth century. The Earl of March's defection to the Percy power complex gave rise to a blood feud with the Douglases. In the opening decade of the fourteenth century this sort of rivalry blurred the idea of the border. The extent of a noble family's reach seemed as important as the limit of more formal jurisdictions.

In 1403 a remarkable meeting in North Wales took place, an occasion later given vivid form by William Shakespeare in his play *Henry IV Part One*. Owain Glyn Dwr, Henry Percy and Edward Mortimer, the grandson of Edward III, each signed an agreement known as 'the Tripartite Indenture' at Bangor. They resolved to topple the fragile and illegal regime of the usurper King Henry, replace him with Mortimer (whose claim was legitimate) and divide England and Wales between them. Percy was promised all of the north beyond the Trent for his family fiefdom and, to bolster his position, he abandoned George Dunbar, Earl of March and drew Archibald the Tyneman into the conspiracy.

His ill-luck was contagious. Percy and Douglas met Henry IV at Shrewsbury, Glyn Dwr failed to turn up and the battle went badly wrong. The Tyneman lost yet again, was captured and spent five years under arrest before returning to Scotland in 1408. Percy was killed in the fighting and Glyn Dwr retreated into the mists of the Welsh mountains to bide his time.

These events seem to be outlandish, to run against the grain of history. But in the political reality of the time, they certainly did not. The great magnates of the borders – Percy and Douglas – had huge ambition and would not have hesitated to remove a crowned king if their family's interests were threatened. Henry IV was weak, broke and his regime very unstable. If Percy had not perished at Shrewsbury and Glyn Dwr's Welsh archers had come to the fight, it might all have fallen out very differently. And the Tyneman might have lost his reputation and his family might have waxed even more powerful even more quickly in Scotland.

The intensity of cross-border raiding begs a difficult question. Where did all that loot come from? In the late fourteenth and fifteenth centuries the same territory was continually plundered, year after year, but there are no indications of the law of diminishing returns. Surely the same beasts did not trek wearily over the Cheviots only to trek back where they came from the following year. Perhaps they did.

More likely was the operation of a vicious downward spiral. As Border society gradually descended into organised criminality, it became progressively poorer. And its governing dynamic turned from production to larceny – which bound it to become poorer still.

Economic indicators, such as they are, support a darkening picture of the Border countryside in decline. The appalling devastation that followed in the wake of the Black Death of 1349 was compounded by repeated visitations. Between the first outbreak and 1420, there were eight 'plague years' in Scotland. Eight times the virus cut its way through communities and mortality rates could sometimes be as high as 10 per cent.

For the fifteenth century, records of rural life in Northumberland are better than those for Cumbria, Galloway, Dumfriesshire and the Tweed basin and they show a general retreat from cultivation. Some of this was a consequence of the Black Death and labour shortages but contemporaries cite raiding as the prime cause. Farmers who worked the land in a frontier zone could occasionally expect to see foraging parties of soldiers stealing their crops, but it happened year after year; some felt forced to give up their tenancies. This trend was certainly recorded in Northumberland but it was probably widespread over the whole Border region, perhaps so common it passed without comment.

In the Tweed basin the shifting political map had a direct impact on the local economy. The levels of customs revenues measured import and export activity and before the Wars of Independence Berwick-upon-Tweed's volume of trade had been very substantial. Ships from north-western Europe landed a colourful array of cargoes on the quaysides at the mouth of the Tweed. Thousands of gallons of wine, spices, exotic foods, high-value metal goods and much else arrived in the holds of merchant ships. These were refilled with bulging wool-sacks for the continental textile factories and hides for the leather trade. In 1286 the customs revenue for Berwick was £2,190 compared with £8,800 for the whole of England.

What made all of this trade possible was a hinterland. Reaching 70 miles westwards up the Tweed Valley, an immensely productive and well-organised rural hinterland grew all that wool and leather for export through Berwick. But when the town became a political prize, batted back and forth between English and Scots occupation, the trade gradually evaporated. When in English hands, as it was for most of the late middle ages, Scottish kings did not want to see Tweed and Teviotdale wool exported through Berwick and supplying their enemy with customs revenue. Instead they promoted Edinburgh, and despite the difficult upland routes over Middleton Moor and Soutra Hill, such Border wool as could be harvested did go north.

To the English kings, Berwick was not only a northern Calais, it was also an opportunity to make money – if they could gain control of its productive hinterland. If the garrisons at Roxburgh (the main inland wool market) and Jedburgh could only extend their power over the whole area then trade would boom once more. It was eminently possible in more politically stable circumstances. English kings and magnates had made fortunes from the wool trade in the stable south. If only they could incorporate the Tweed basin into England, much needed revenue would flow.

As it was, neither side gained anything – and between the two the Border economy suffered badly. From the 1370s to the 1450s the total Scottish customs revenue declined sharply – by around 70 per cent, from £9,000 per annum to only £2,500. This decline undoubtedly created the conditions and led to the causes of crime.

One of the prime engines of economic growth in the twelfth and thirteenth centuries had been the great Border abbeys. Only magnificent ruins survive now, but in their time they were majestic churches. A description of Kelso from 1517 talks of a huge cathedral-like structure with a double crossing and 12 side-chapels each with its own altar. It was an opulence made possible by the wool trade.

The Border abbots had been princes of the church, influential in national politics. But in the fourteenth and fifteenth centuries little is heard from these men. Their surnames suggest that some were certainly local, probably minor aristocrats. Few made any impression beyond their abbey precincts and religion and the influence of its wealthy prelates appeared not to mitigate the developing criminal atmosphere of the times.

ROXBURGH

Perhaps the most dramatic – and poignant – casualty of the bloody centuries of cross-border warfare and raiding is now completely invisible. Across the Tweed from Kelso lies a green and empty park studded with mature trees and grazed by sheep and cattle. Twice a year race-horses thunder around a point-to-point track. It is now known as Friar's Haugh and the Fairgreen, but in the middle ages it was the site of a large medieval town. It has entirely disappeared, right down to the foundation stones of its many houses and churches. Nothing at all remains of Roxburgh – despite the fact that for at least 200 years it was one of the most vibrant and prosperous places in medieval Scotland. It served as the inland market for the profitable wool and leather trades, the prime destination for the shepherds and stockmen who drove their flocks and herds down from the high valleys and the western ranges. Roxburgh's hinterland was huge and as an animal processing centre on an industrial scale, it brought together primary producers and merchants, and many of the latter were European. With its port of export at Berwick, Roxburgh was the axis of a busy and booming economy. Dominated by its tremendous castle, the town had at least three major streets: King Street, the Headgate and Market Street. There were four churches: Holy Trinity in the centre of the town, St James to the north, near the Tweed, the Friary of St Peter to the south, and inside the castle walls, the Chapel of St John. One of Scotland's very earliest schools was set up and a royal mint turned out currency. Yet it has all gone. After 350 years of ruin and war, the town is entirely effaced. By 1649 St James Church had only six communicants and in the nineteenth century its ruins were removed to make way for a racecourse. Roxburgh gave its name to a county and a ducal title but the ghost-town has seen no sensible archaeology and the site remains essentially mysterious, an inland Atlantis lost under the grass.

The Synod of St Andrews in 1400 published a list of prohibitions which shed a glancing light on the church and its community at the outset of the fifteenth century. Most of all the synod was anxious that priests should understand their role clearly, be able to say mass correctly and minister to their communicants in a proper manner. This was extremely important in a society which believed absolutely in Heaven and Hell. And with the growing importance of the idea of Purgatory (where sins were, literally, purged) in the middle ages, the church reached into the afterlife and became an active agent in the transit of souls.

The horrors of the Black Death had sharpened perceptions immeasurably and the starkness of Heaven and Hell had softened. Purgatory was not eternal, it offered the chance to cleanse earthly sins and the living took part directly in influencing this process. The chapels in Kelso Abbey saw many masses said and sung for the souls of the dead in Purgatory. The more the better, and the shorter the time spent in the cleansing fire. In return, the dead spent their time in prayer and this lightened the burden of sin on the living. It was a straightforward spiritual transaction with clear outcomes, and the Synod of St Andrews attempted to deal with any abuses by forbidding priests from accepting cash payments from those with recently dead relatives to celebrate several masses a day.

MYSTERIOUS MASS

The chantries in the Border abbeys and churches where mass was sung for the souls of the (wealthier) departed were busy. The word for them comes from the Latin 'cantana' meaning 'a place for singing'. It was no doubt very beautiful and very atmospheric. Some early Irish churches sang what was called the 'Laus Perpetuus', or 'the eternal praise' when monks worked in relays around the clock so that the music never stopped and the building was never silent. Mass was intended to be mysterious and until the modern era, it was celebrated behind a screen (often called a rood screen because it was topped by a rood or cross) and the laity could not see the service. The word 'mass' is from the dismissal, also mysterious, which runs 'Ite, missa est', or 'Go! It is sent.'

The more sinful of the early Border reivers could also hope for another method of redemption, especially if they were wealthy and willing to endow the church. An ancient belief persuaded people that the place of burial was very important. The more sacred the ground, the more effective the soil itself would be in purging the body of sin. This is why many aristocratic tombs are to be found inside churches, often as close to the altar as possible or even under it. When James Douglas' body was brought back from Otterburn, it was interred close to the high altar in Melrose Abbey. This was thought to be one of the most deeply sacred places in the Borders because of the association with St Cuthbert and others. Some noblemen went to the trouble of becoming novice monks towards the end of their lives (almost always they endowed the abbey with gifts at the same time). This guaranteed burial inside the precincts, in the cleansing soil.

The St Andrews synod also demanded that priests should behave with more dignity. They should not visit brothels and also put away their common-law wives. They should not go about armed, at least not with long (and obvious) daggers attached to their belts.

Other prohibitions occasionally strayed into what seems to be excessive solemnity. The church was at the centre of community life in the middle ages and a regular focus for social events. At festivals, such as Whitsun, special cakes and ale were taken in the churchyard and games often played. Perhaps handba was, they certainly had hurling in Cornwall and Wales. But the Synod of St Andrews set a ban on dances in the churchyards and also on wrestling and other sports, which must have made the world a duller place.

In other ways life for ordinary Borderers in the later middle ages was unchanging. As an overwhelmingly rural society, the turns of the year dominated. In the hungry months of late winter and spring, most subsisted on grey rye bread, porridge and dairy products such as butter, curds and cheese. Replenished by root vegetables and onions, potage always bubbled by the hearth-side and meat was rare. Summer saw fruit, mostly apples and pears, and beer was drunk by all ages, not so much for its alcoholic nature (although that was no doubt welcome) but for the calories. Made from barley or oats, it was very nutritious. Historians have reckoned that the daily intake was three pints.

By 1406 Robert III had died, and it seems his passing went unlamented. Even at a distance of six centuries there is a palpable atmosphere of personal misery and political failure around the early Stewart kings. An oft-repeated quote sets the tone. When Annabella, his Queen, asked Robert III what arrangements he had in mind for his tomb and a suitable epitaph, this mournful reply came back. It was reported by Walter Bower, a contemporary chronicler:

> I have no desire to erect a proud tomb. Therefore let these men who strive in the world for the pleasures of honour have shining monuments. I on the other hand should prefer to be buried at the bottom of a midden, so that my soul may be saved on the Day of the Lord. Bury me therefore, I beg you, in a midden, and write for my epitaph: 'Here lies the worst of kings and the most wretched of men in the whole kingdom.'

It reads like a passage of invented dialogue, but rings true as a general judgement which appeared to be current at the time. But they are extraordinary sentiments from a King of Scotland.

With the same sort of miserable luck which dogged his father, James I had been made a prisoner by the English. Sent away to France allegedly for the furtherance of his education but more likely for his safety, the young prince's ship had been boarded by 'pirates' off Flamborough Head. They handed James over to Henry IV and commodious and secure lodging was found in the Tower of London. When news of his heir's capture was brought to Robert III, 'his spirit forthwith left him, the strength waned from his body, his countenance grew pale, and for grief thereafter he took no food'. Three weeks later the king was dead.

His brother, the Duke of Albany and former Earl of Fife, was made Governor of the Realm. In the continued absence of James I and the consequent lack of a coronation, Albany ruled over 'a kingless kingdom'. And he did so in quasi-regal style, occasionally attaching the phrase 'by the grace of God' to his title.

As Governor, Albany encouraged the annual meetings at Hadden Stank and even entertained discussions of a more lasting peace. All of this diplomatic talk was interspersed with sporadic incidents of Anglo-Scottish violence. Ships were seized and anchorages raided, and on 7 May 1409 Jedburgh Castle was at last prised from the grip of its English garrison. The successful assault was led by 'mediocres Thevidaliae', literally, 'the middling people of Teviotdale'. Some historians have mistranslated this into the peasants of Teviotdale being swept along on a rising tide of Scottish nationalism and storming Jedburgh castle to evict the hated English. In reality the 'mediocres' were lesser lairds, younger sons and the like, and were led by Sir

William Douglas of Drumlanrig, who would have been affronted to be thought a peasant.

The middling sort and their impetuosity were perhaps preferred to anything more formal or deliberate because they were deniable in the event that Henry IV of England planned a hefty response. These things just happened in the less lawful frontier zone. In any case, Albany stepped in quickly to order that Jedburgh Castle be entirely effaced. At only 8 miles from the border up on Carter Bar, it was too exposed to leave standing, and its removal erased any argument over reoccupation. An early nineteenth-century county jail now stands on the impressive site.

Berwick and Roxburgh still remained in English hands and the latter began to come under increasing threat. In 1410 the Douglases and the Dunbar families (now on speaking, or at least raiding terms) broke into the town of Roxburgh and set it on fire, and retreating across the bridge over the Tweed to Wester Kelso, they pulled it down.

BRING BACK BERWICK

In 2003 a group of Border Scots hatched a plan to offer to buy back Berwick. No one was sure about where a cash offer should be made and it was suggested that a donation might go to the League of St George. A press release was issued and amongst the world's media, the story caught fire. As far away as New Zealand, it was reported that the Scots were about to march over Berwick Old Bridge and retake the town. Perhaps they would occupy the Guild Hall, or somewhere. TV crews arrived, the Vicar of the Parish Church offered to mediate, and eventually – nothing happened. It was all a jolly PR stunt designed to highlight the attractions of the Borders and persuade tourists to come back after the devastating epidemic of foot and mouth disease. But such is the strange position of Berwick, out on a limb, that the story was just credible enough to be widely believed. Some in Berwick supported the initiative. No wonder. Sociologists from Edinburgh University have carried out a scientific and systematic survey of attitudes to nationality in the town. Lying so close to the Borders Berwickers were expected to embrace an English identity more enthusiastically – for precisely that reason. More than 100 household interviews showed that Berwickers were ambivalent, preferring to take on a local identity rather than an English, or even Scottish, one.

When Henry V ascended the English throne, he seemed determined to revive the Hundred Years War, and as the heir of Edward III, he claimed the crown of France. His expedition of 1417 across the Channel sparked events in the Borders. Archibald the Tyneman attacked Roxburgh Castle, but true to his nickname, failed to make any impression. This despite a survey of the fabric in 1416 which discovered that much of the old stronghold was crumbling. Sections of walls and towers were thought to be on the point of collapse and the timber shoring down the shaft of the castle's well had completely rotted. Roxburgh even lacked iron gates. Yet the immense strength of its position between Tweed and Teviot was enough, and the English held on. Twenty miles to the east the Duke of Albany attacked Berwick and was also repulsed. Considering the absence of the English king and his army in France, it was a feckless episode.

When James I returned from captivity in 1424, he quickly neutralised the power of the Albany Stewarts and began to show himself as a determined, courageous, perhaps even tyrannical king. After the pitiable miseries of Robert III, it was a shock to the Scottish political system.

James was ruthless. In order to divide the great magnates he offered preference and support to the Douglases and had Albany's son (the Duke had died in 1420), his two sons and his 80-year-old father-in-law, the Earl of Lennox, arrested and tried at Stirling Castle. They were all dragged out onto the esplanade and publicly executed. Nothing like this had been ordered by a Scottish king for more than a century and it signalled the arrival of a Stewart resolved to rule without opposition from a powerful nobility.

In 1436 James mustered the royal host and marched on Roxburgh Castle, where and it all promptly went wrong. Queen Joan arrived in the camp with news of a conspiracy against the king. Surrounded by his nobility and all their soldiers, James suddenly felt uncomfortable, squabbled with his captains, and to the amazement of the garrison watching from Roxburgh's battlements, abandoned the siege and made his way back north. A year later it all came true. In the Dominican Priory in Perth, hiding in the sewers, James was found by assassins and stabbed to death. Members of his own household were involved and had left doors unbarred and without servicable locks.

James I left a surprising legacy. Despite his ruthlessness and blood-spattered end, he was one of the best educated of Scottish kings, having passed much of his 18-year imprisonment in England in reading, music-making and writing. *The Kingis Quair* (from 'quire', a gathering of leaves of paper) is a long poem composed by James in English and much influenced by the work of Geoffrey Chaucer. It also contains several identifiable Scotticisms and along with the work of other poets and writers, it signals the increasing use of Scots and the retreat of French as the language of the court. This process was clearly underway when the Earl of March wrote to Henry IV in 1400. He apologised for not writing in French, and he did so because 'the English tongue is more clear to my understanding'.

At that time Scotland was a patchwork of speech communities. While the court and most people living in central Scotland spoke a form of Scots, the Church wrote and celebrated mass in Latin, and most official documents were also set down in Latin. In the north and west Gaelic was widespread and a dialect of Irish Gaelic was the speech of Galloway and Carrick. It is said that King Robert the Bruce was fluent in it. In the Northern Isles Norse predominated, and in the Borders it is likely that the same dialect of northern English was spoken on both banks of the Tweed. This apparently caused confusion at the battle of Otterburn in 1388, but it must also have bound English and Scottish borderers together. The ancient tongue of Old Welsh had long fled from the lowlands but pockets of use may have survived in isolated upland communities.

MERLIN AND THE ASH TREES OF MEIGION

Owain Glyn Dwr, Edward Mortimer and Harry Hotspur Percy drew up an agreement in 1403 known as the Tripartite Indenture. It set down the three-way partition of England and Wales for each man who attached his seal to it. So that there could be no possibility of forgery, the document was divided up by a zigzag or indented line to produce jagged edges. This meant that only the genuine pieces would fit together. So called because of this procedure, indentures were made like this up until well into the nineteenth century. Owain Glyn Dwr wanted a substantial share and his 'Greater Wales' reached far into England. Like most of his countrymen, he knew that Old Welsh had been spoken all over Britain, especially in southern Scotland – the place known as 'Yr Hen Ogledd' or 'the Old North', and that Welsh kings had once ruled in London. Owain believed in prophesy and especially in the words of Merlin. Under the command of the mighty King Cadwallon the Welsh had won a great victory at the Ash Trees of Meigion, and Merlin said that they would win there once more. Owain insisted that the boundaries of Greater Wales should reach Meigion. To their amazement, Percy and Mortimer agreed. The Ash Trees of Meigion lay in the Peak District, deep in the heart of England. But this old attachment was not as odd as it sounds. The Peak District is one of the most Celtic areas of England. Ancient and pagan customs like well-dressing, where flowers are arranged around the many natural springs of the district, survive and on the Ordnance Survey many Old Welsh places-names are plotted.

James II was seven years old when his father was assassinated in Perth. A fractious elite of the most powerful noble families, including the Douglases contrived somehow to run Scotland, but immediately there was disaster to contend with. The plague returned. And Archibald, Earl of Douglas, was one of its victims. Concerted periods of bad weather in the spring and summer of 1437 meant the harvest failed. In 1438 it failed again and the countryside was gripped by famine. It must have been a miserable time for ordinary people.

Power politics scarcely missed a beat and James II and his counsellors entered upon an aggressive campaign against the Black Douglases. In 1440 what became known as 'the Black Dinner' was held in Edinburgh Castle. The king invited the young Earl William of Douglas and his brother to join him in a banquet. In a memorable moment of melodrama, the king's chancellor, Sir William Crichton, placed a bull's head on the table. The Douglas boys were arrested, tried on trumped up charges and decapitated on the executioner's block on the Castle Hill.

The effect of this outrage was surprisingly muted. James the Gross became earl and did much to restore his family's position. By 1448 the Douglases were back raiding in north Northumberland. In the tit-for-tat warfare of that time Percy and Neville incursions into the west march was balanced by attacks in the east. A system of warning beacons was set up in Dumfriesshire.

In 1452 James II summoned the Earl of Douglas to Stirling Castle Reassurances were sought and given by means of a safe-conduct. A discussion of the Douglases' alliance with the Earl of Crawford and Ross quickly grew heated. The king lost his temper with the earl and 'did stert sodanly till him with ane knyf and strake him in the collar and down in the bodie'. The wounded Douglas was immediately stabbed to death by Patrick Gray, James II's bodyguard, and others.

It was a sensational and utterly outrageous act, a second earl murdered after some royal deception. The Douglases found themselves themselves under the command of a new earl, James, and he led 600 men into Stirling. After denouncing the king, he had the worthless safe-conduct issued to Earl William tied to a horse's tail and dragged through the muddy streets. It was a declaration of civil war. But instead of seeking to create an alternative to James II's tyranny, the Douglases burned the town of Stirling. It was not good politics.

James II was more adroit and carried hostilities to appropriate targets. He mustered the royal host and marched into Douglas territory, attacking Peebles, Selkirk and Dumfries. By means which remain unclear some sort of reconciliation was effected whereby Earl James forgave the murderers of Earl William and promised to dissolve the contentious alliances with other magnates, and for his part the king gave assurances of fair treatment. The Douglases guaranteed that they would defend the Borders and honour the truce with England. None of it lasted.

In 1455, presumably when he felt strong enough, the king went on campaign against the Douglases, bombarding their castles, raiding their territory, especially the Forest of Selkirk. In what seems to have been a failure of nerve, the earl capitulated very quickly. James fled to England while his three brothers were caught near Langholm by a band of Johnstones, led by their heidsman. Two were killed and the third escaped to join Earl James in exile in England. The Johnstones sent the severed head of Archibald Douglas to the king. No doubt he was pleased to see it.

Within only three months the immensely powerful and resilient dynasty of the Black Douglases had been utterly defeated and James II ruled unchallenged in his kingdom.

A parliament convened in August 1455 and waved through acts of formal disinheritance of the Douglases. Much of their territory and most of their castles (Threave in Galloway was the most famous and it had been a model in its time. Archibald the Grim's massive fortress was much admired and widely copied) passed into the hands of the king. James II's annual income increased substantially and the royal domain now reached far down into southern Scotland.

In local government a longer-term effect of the fall of the Black

Douglases slowly became apparent. Such was the grip of the earls on the Borders and Galloway and so great were their resources that they were able to keep order amongst the lesser nobility. But when their leadership was removed – virtually overnight – a patchwork of names, small lordships, old resentements and budding ambitions replaced it. Kers, Pringles, Humes, Scotts, Johnstones, Maxwells and others emerged – and began to compete, squabble, and eventually feud with each other in the power vacuum left by the departure of the Douglases.

James II was determined to use the profits of suppression to cement his own kingship. Instead of the great magnates, he would provide effective central government. Parliament passed ordinances on the defence of the Borders. Fords were to be watched and a system of warning beacons maintained. Three companies of troops (spearmen and archers, both mounted) would be paid for by the royal exchequeur and deployed to the three Scottish marches.

In 1456 the king mustered the host and marched into the small enclave controlled by the English garrison of Roxburgh Castle. With no attempt to lay a siege and in what seems to have been no more than a show of force, he then moved on to encamp on the Kale Water, near Morebattle and not far from the northern terminal of Clennel Street. English envoys arrived and for reasons which are unclear, James was induced to retreat from what was shaping to be an invasion of northern England. Two months later the army was marched south again, and this time they crossed into Northumberland on a raiding expedition. A year later Berwick was unsuccessfully assaulted. Business as usual for the long-suffering farmers of the Borders.

It may be that the royal council decided at that point to take a more considered approach. In the toppling of the Black Douglases, James II had used artillery to deadly effect and he was evidently fascinated by cannon and how they worked. Materials for cannon-founding were bought from European specialists and arrangements for the manufacture of gun carriages put in train.

DOE OR DIE

The rise of the Douglas family has left a small legacy in a Border town. The motto of Kelso High School is 'Doe or Die' and it encircles a representation of a heart. Both are taken from the Douglas coat of arms and the local association is with the beautiful Springwood Estate near the town. It belonged to the Douglas family

and looked across the Teviot to Roxburgh Castle, which is historically very appropriate since in 1314 Sir James Douglas captured the
stronghold from the English in a daring assault. He fulfilled Robert
the Bruce's dying wish that his embalmed heart should be taken on
crusade against the Moors. The promise of such pious actions, even
after death, were important to the king as his life slipped away.
After his murder of John Comyn at the high altar of the Greyfriars
Kirk at Dumfries, Bruce had been excommunicated by the Pope and
he must have feared the fires of Purgatory. When fighting against
the Moors at Teba de Andales, it is said that Sir James Douglas
threw the casket containing the king's heart deep into the ranks of
the Unbelievers and challenged his men to cut their way through to
rescue it. They were forced to 'doe or die', and they did, both.
Recently Bruce's heart was found buried at Melrose Abbey, the site
of the fourteenth-century Douglas tombs.

When Henry VI was captured in 1460 by the Yorkist faction in one of
the many twists of the Wars of the Roses, James II believed that an
opportunity had presented itself. Once again he summoned the royal
host and this time substantial artillery pieces were trundled down Dere
Street to Melrose. The target was Roxburgh Castle, and the aim to
remove the English garrison. It had become nominal but remained
irksome, and was sustained by the defensive excellence of the site of
the ancient fortress. Much strengthened and expensively maintained,
the fabric of the mighty ramparts was in good repair and an immense
effort would be needed to breach them. James and his bombardiers
dug in their guns on the north bank of the Tweed, below where Floors
Castle now stands. The trajectories were plotted, the elevations
calculated and the king spent much time fussing over his elaborate
artillery battery.

On Sunday 3 August, Queen Mary of Gueldres arrived to support
her husband in what promised to be his hour of triumph, a success in
the place where his father had so humiliatingly failed in 1436. To
welcome his queen, James ordered a salvo on the castle walls. He
stood by one of the largest guns, known as 'the Lion', and:

King James hauing sik plesure in dischargeng gret gunis past til a
place far fra the armie to recreat him selfe in schuiting gret pieces,
quhairof he was verie expert, bot the piece appeiringlie, with ouer

sair a chairge, flies in flinderis, with a part of quhilk, strukne in the hench or he was war, quhairof (allace) he dies.

It seems likely that the king bled to death. But such was the unity he had welded together, Mary of Gueldres was able to rush her nine-year-old son across the Tweed to the great church of Kelso Abbey and in the assembled presence of all of Scotland's great magnates, have him crowned as James III. Thereafter, the royal host remained sufficiently resolved and purposeful to complete the siege of Roxburgh success-fully. After more than 160 years of enemy occupation the great fortress was once again in Scottish hands.

It all came too late for the once-thriving town. With the loss of much of the lucrative wool trade and the continuing occupation of its port at Berwick, Roxburgh had shrivelled into little more than a village. It was a spectacular casualty of international politics since 1296 and the Wars of Independence. Now, nothing at all remains to be seen, not a single stone stands above ground.

Immediately after the siege Roxburgh Castle was 'doung to the ground'. Like Jedburgh Castle it lay close to the frontier and would have presented a tempting target for English re-occupation. By 1488 it had become a place of such small importance that 'the castle and the place called the castlested' could be granted to Walter Kerr of Cessford, heidsman of a reiving surname.

Queen Mary of Gueldres was the dominant influence at court after 1460 and as she and Bishop Kennedy of St Andrews dabbled for advantage in the Wars of the Roses, armies tramped regularly back and forth. Berwick was retaken and then quickly lost. Eventually James III grew into his period of personal rule and he began to alienate sections of his magnates. In the process of all this, the Humes of Berwickshire became embroiled in dynastic politics. Because they objected to the appropriation of the ancient church at Coldingham by the crown, Lord Hume gathered an army of Borderers about him. The dispute was allowed to spiral rapidly into a civil war. The disaffected heir apparent, James Duke of Rothesay, joined Hume's forces while his father mustered an army. They met at Sauchieburn, near Bannockburn, in 1488.

The royal standard flew on both sides. James III had rallied support from the north of Scotland, including detachments of Highlanders, while at his back Prince James had men from Galloway, the Borders and the Lothians. In the confusion and din of battle the king became detached from his bodyguard, fell off his horse and was probably injured. Isolated, and in mysterious circumstances, it seems that he was stabbed to death by a priest. Young Rothesay found that he was James IV well before his time and in penance for his part in his father's death he went often on pilgrimage to saintly shrines and wore an iron belt during Lent.

Those Borderers who had helped the new king overthrow his father were rewarded, and the rise of a new aristocracy in the aftermath of the fall of the Black Douglases was consolidated.

Although James IV was only 15 years old at Sauchieburn, he was determined there would be no faction-ridden regency and that his personal rule would begin on the morning after the battle. Like most young men he could be headstrong and in 1495 James welcomed the pretender to the English throne, another young man called Perkin Warbeck. It was an ill-advised, potentially dangerous friendship. Warbeck claimed to be the son of Edward IV, one of the murdered princes in the Tower. Despite the fact that he was an imposter, the claimant had gathered support. Enemies of the Tudors, such as the Irish earls and the Holy Roman Emperor, Maximilian, had even supplied him with troops. For his part, James IV gave help, a base for operations into his usurped kingdom of England and also a Scots wife. The board seemed set for yet more cross-border conflict.

Henry VII of England was a canny politician, and when Warbeck's pretensions fizzled out after an abortive invasion of the West Country, the king imprisoned him in the Tower of London. It was only when he attempted to escape in 1499 that Warbeck found himself on the scaffold at Tyburn with a rope around his neck.

Meanwhile Henry and James had agreed a peace treaty 'of perpetual amity', sometime also known as the 'Treaty of Perpetual Peace'. When this was consummated in 1503 by a marriage between Margaret Tudor, Henry's daughter, and James, Borderers must have breathed a collective sigh of relief. Perhaps the long, weary years of near-constant warfare were at last drawing to a close. The royal houses of Scotland and England were uniting and both kings seeking cooperation rather than conflict.

But it was a false dawn. A hundred bitter years would have to pass before the marriage of Stewart and Tudor could change the course of history for the better. And it would be a century of unprecedented slaughter, violence and waste along the whole length of the border. It would be the century of the Reivers.

6

The Wild Frontier

Hob the King and his brother, Dand the Man, had cheek. Nicknamed like the Chicago gangsters they so closely resemble, the Elliot brothers had forayed far out of Liddesdale in the winter of 1502. The charge-sheet recorded that they had led a raiding party 'beyond Tweeddale and Lauderdale', probably up into the Lammermuir Hills above Edinburgh and there they had lifted nine score sheep. And it seems that they did it with impunity. Halbert Elliot and Andrew Elliot – to give them their Sunday names – appear never to have answered for their crimes, or at least not that one. All that contemporaries could do was record who had done what and approximately where. They could not catch them or bring them to any sort of justice.

The raid was audacious, even reckless. Stealing livestock within sight of Edinburgh's Castle Rock, the traditional seat of royal government, and removing them southwards down Lauderdale, Tweeddale, Teviotdale and home to Liddesdale without let or hindrance – it must have galled James IV as he attempted to assert himself over all of his kingdom. Even more galling was the fact that Hob and Dand's raid was only remarkable because it brought the chronic problems of lawlessness in the Borders so close to Edinburgh. Raiding was growing rife and one family became particularly hard-riding – 'ever-riding' according to one contemporary historian. When the king was in Jedburgh on the 5 and 11 November that year, he had heard grievous complaints against the Armstrongs of Liddesdale, Elliot allies and neighbours. Edmund Armstrong and his brothers were commanded to appear before James and defend the charge that they had burned Borthwickshiels near Hawick, the property of the Scotts of Buccleuch. They were also accused of stealing 300 sheep, 60 oxen and cows, 20 horses and mares, and goods to the value of 100 merks. More Elliot allies and neighbours, the Crosers or Crosiers, were also named as horse-riding thieves at the Jedburgh Assizes. Whether or not any of them turned up to hear the charges is less clear. It is unlikely.

It was a weary, dreary roster of disorder, what had become a way of life for many Borderers, both perpetrators and victims (who could easily exchange roles). The use of such clearly criminal names as 'Hob the King' and 'Dand the Man' in official records speaks of unwelcome familiarity. As James IV prepared for his marriage to Princess Margaret Tudor, these unchecked raids were an embarrassment. Such an obvious inability to control the Border country through which his bride was to travel did not say much for the king's ability as an effective ruler. A solitary consolation was that lawlessness seemed at least as substantial a problem on the English side.

MARGINAL DISORDER

Scottish kings had difficulties asserting themselves in the north and west of their kingdom as well as in the south. Their nominal subjects had no hesitation in making alliances with the English. In 1462 Edward IV signed the Treaty of Westminster-Ardtornish. If James III of Scotland could be deposed, then the co-signatory, John Macdonald, Lord of the Isles and King of Man, would take over half of the kingdom, that part lying to the north of the Forth–Clyde line. From his castle at Ardtornish, on the mainland opposite southern Mull, John ruled an Atlantic principality. He could command 10,000 soldiers, but more important, a navy of 250 galleys. The Stewart kings had some success in 'the daunting' of the isles but the threat from the west remained constant in the first half of the sixteenth century. By 1545 Donald Dubh, the Clan Donald heir of John, rallied the Highlanders and Islesmen to his banner, and at a Council of the Isles on Islay, he and his allies negotiated with the agents of Henry VIII. The gathering rebellion only fizzled out when Donald unexpectedly died of a fever in Ireland. The Border surnames never presented an equivalent political threat even though they could muster highly mobile cavalry armies at lightning speed. They were too busy squabbling amongst themselves ever to consider unifying against the crown.

Relative distance also allowed James IV a course of action usually denied to the Tudor kings based in London. He could personally lead punitive expeditions to the Borders and use all his royal authority to press hard on the worst of the reiving families. More than eighty such expeditions tramped south from Edinburgh in the sixteenth century and they generally met with only temporary success. But James IV's marriage contract, the 'Treaty of Perpetual Peace' was at least optimistic, containing clauses about curbing lawlessness in the Borders.

The Armstrongs shrugged their shoulders at all this breezy diplomacy, and by the early 1500s they had forged themselves into the most feared of the riding families. With the Elliots, Nixons and Crosiers, they had made Liddesdale their redoubt and last resort. When royal expeditions commanded the heidsmen of the Armstrongs to appear and answer for their crimes, the summons was routinely ignored. Seventy of the name were listed as outlaw. This meant a good deal more than it does now, basically a synonym for criminal. In the sixteenth century to be branded an outlaw, that is to say, placed beyond the protection of the law, could be very dangerous and exposed. Any man, an officer of the law or not, could attack and kill an outlaw with impunity, perhaps even receive a reward. In addition, his dependants and property were similarly fair game. But in the Border country the effects of outlawry were much mitigated by membership of a large and aggressive family like the Armstrongs and also the general – and widespread – reluctance to do anything which might spark a deadly feud.

In 1509 the political weather changed. Canny Henry VII died and was succeeded by the very different character of his son, Henry VIII. Headstrong, bellicose and initially highly able, he plunged into the maelstrom of European war, alliance and intrigue. The loss of England's possessions in France still smarted and Henry was anxious to set about reclaiming them. An immediate diplomatic difficulty was his brother-in-law. James of Scotland was close to the French, and while the terms of the Treaty of Perpetual Peace carefully allowed both England and Scotland to give aid to their respective allies, it looked in reality as though they were set on a collision course.

Momentum began to gather on both land and sea. Scotland's new naval capability was challenged by Henry VIII's captains and Scots ships were boarded and seized. James' naval commander, Andrew Barton, was accused of piracy and died in English captivity. On the border, a long-running dispute flared into significance. At a truce day, probably in 1509, Sir Robert Kerr was presiding as Warden of the Scottish Middle March. For reasons now lost he became involved in a fatal scuffle with three Englishmen. They were Lilburn, from near Wooler, a man called Starhead and the splendidly described John Heron, the Bastard of Ford. After Kerr had been killed, the Scottish contingent rallied and managed to lay hands on Lilburn, but the Bastard Heron and Starhead escaped. It was all very embarrassing – and the incident is said to have enraged James IV. Kerr had been a close courtier, principal cup-bearer to the king and master of the royal artillery.

The Bastard Heron's half-brother, the legitimate Lord of Ford, was Warden of the English East March and he was either persuaded or felt compelled to act honourably. He therefore gave himself up to be a hostage for the Bastard and with Lilburn was detained in Fast Castle on the Berwickshire coast north of Eyemouth. Lilburn then died, but far from giving himself up and thereby freeing his half-brother, the Bastard Heron was reportedly seen desporting himself in public, and even worse, was sending raiding parties over the Tweed into Scotland.

Meanwhile two associates of Andrew Kerr, the son of the murdered Sir Robert, had been busy. The brothers Tait had been on the trail of the third wanted man, Starhead, and they found that he had fled to York. Following him – and showing the long reach of deadly feud – they murdered the man in his house and then hacked off his head, put it in a sack and rode back to Ferniehurst with grisly proof that the hit had been made. Such was the intricacy of serial violence in the sixteenth-century Border country.

THE GREAT MICHAEL

Between 1505 and 1511 James IV spent huge sums to create a Scottish navy. Its most impressive ship was The Great Michael, and it was huge, far outstripping Henry VIII's Mary Rose or any other contemporary craft then afloat. At Newhaven, near Edinburgh, an immense keel was laid down: it measured between 150 and 180 feet and on it the skeleton of The Great Michael was slowly built up. At 1,000 tons, it could carry 27 cannon and needed a crew of 300 to sail it. The cost was staggering at £30,000 Scots. The huge ship took five years to build, but it never fired its guns in anger. Only three years after the launch, the battle of Flodden changed everything and The Great Michael was sold to the French for only £18,000. Eventually it was left to rot to pieces in Dieppe harbour.

The feud between the Herons and the Kerrs would grind on for another sixty years, but more immediately its beginnings gave James IV ample excuse, as he and his counsellors saw it, to ignore the Treaty of Perpetual Peace if and when it suited them. However, more straightforward causes for war were soon on hand.

Perhaps prompted by the Bastard Heron, an English raid struck deep into the Scottish east marches, carrying off many beasts and successfuly driving across the Tweed. The fords were no doubt running low in the summer of 1513. Under the command of Alexander Home, the Lord Warden of all the Scottish Marches, the response was rapid and designed to be stunning. Hume put at least 3,000 men in the saddle and hurried over the Border. With such a large force, there was no need – or indeed possibility – of stealth. Seven villages were torched in north Northumberland and much plunder taken. Given that most herds and flocks would have been out summering on the hills, the most attractive and readily available prize for Hume's raiders was horses, and very many were herded together and driven north.

Sir William Bulmer mustered a small force of Northumbrians and in a classic reiver tactic, rode around and ahead of the slow-moving Scot, their plunder weighing down and delaying them. When the English riders reached the Milfield Plain, Bulmer chose a place by the track where broom bushes had grown thick and gave good cover. It was probably somewhere near where the modern A697 skirts the foot of the Cheviot Hills, not far from Flodden Hill. Bulmer had archers with him, and when the Scots rode into the ambush, they let fly. The volleys were deadly. Perhaps 500 Scots fell and 400 were captured. Home lost his banner and only just escaped.

Known as 'the Ill Raid', it took place only a few days before James IV finally decided to call on the royal host of Scotland to muster, before he took the first step down the road to disaster at Flodden.

At first all went well. Sieges were laid at Wark, Etal and Ford castles, and at the strongest of the Border keeps, at Norham, James's army scored a brilliant success, breaking through the solid defences in only five days. Harrying the north Northumberland countryside, carrying off plunder, and the king even finding time to dally with Lady Heron at Ford, the Scots expedition behaved at first like a raiding party, albeit one of gigantic proportions. But that cannot have been James' main purpose. United behind him, the Scottish magnates sought battle, the chance of a signal victory over the English and a degree of freedom of action in the north not seen since the days of the Bruces. James seemed ambitious to make himself a player in European politics, and he advanced into England as an ally of France. No one reckoned with the old warrior, Surrey, and his tactical brilliance on the day of battle.

Historians often aver that the English army could not exploit their stunning victory by invading Scotland because they themselves had taken heavy punishment at Flodden. The walls frantically thrown up to protect Edinburgh were never needed, and, short of provisions, the Earl of Surrey was forced to turn his army south and disband it. Historians of the Borders see the aftermath of Flodden quite differently.

In command of a small but battle-hard troop of mounted soldiers, Thomas Lord Dacre, Warden of the English West March, was instructed to bring fire, sword and plunder to the Borders. And he did it with a vengeance. In the winter of 1513/14 plumes of black smoke billowed on the chill winds as Dacre's men burned hundreds, perhaps thousands, of Borderers out of their homes, and as families hid in the damp woods or sought refuge in the sheilings of the grey upland valleys, they waited for the fires to die. When they straggled back to their farmsteads, many saw that the English troopers had rounded up their livestock and driven it away. And not just English riders. In Dacre's small army were four hundred Scots, 'outlaws . . . which should be under the obeisance of Scotland'. No doubt many were Armstrongs, and no doubt their intelligence reports and advice settled many an old score with the help of English spears. It must have been a desolate, freezing and hungry winter in fire-blackened farms and villages of Tweeddale, Teviotdale and Annandale.

TOE-ROPE

A military historian once wrote that the invention of the stirrup was 'the most significant development of warfare between the taming of the horse and the invention of gunpowder.' Alexander the Great and Julius Caesar and all their cavalry rode without stirrups. Until around AD700 military riding techniques in western Europe were completely different: troopers held on with their legs and one hand on the reins to guide their ponies. That of course meant that they could only fight with one hand, and that in turn restricted the range of weapons they could use. Stirrups changed all that. They were invented in India around 200 BC, initially as a method of mounting the horse. They were called 'toe-stirrups' at first and the word derives from the Old English 'stigan', meaning to climb up, and 'rup' is a near-synonym for 'rope'. When Attila and his Huns tore through Europe in the fifth century AD, their devastating success came from the ability to control their nimble ponies with their legs and feet – secure in stirrups. This left both hands free to fire arrows while moving very fast around the battlefield. Border Reivers were also adept as using weapons with both hands, and like those of the Huns, their little ponies responded readily to leg-aids, able to stop, move and change directions without a pull on the reins.

Sometimes Dacre's men met resistance. While raiding around Hawick, a troop of riders was intercepted at Hornshole, two miles east of the town. Tradition holds that they came from Hexham and that the Hawick callants not only won the skirmish but also carried off their banner. Much of the Hawick Common Riding is founded on this incident and the 'banner blue' held up high by the Hawick Cornet is said to be a replica of what fluttered in front of the Hexham men at Hornshole.

The most ancient of the Border common ridings have strong traditional connections with the battle at Flodden. And however real or imagined these may be, it is significant that the common ridings at Selkirk and Peebles first come on record in the early sixteenth century (and when those at Hawick and Lauder are first noted in the early eighteenth century, they seem to be already very old). The central purpose was to walk or ride around the boundaries of the common land belonging to the town. Surrounding lairds sometimes encroached on the common or pastured their beasts on it without permission. The procession of townspeople was led by a principal, in the shadowy beginnings probably the provost, and then later a young man when ceremony gradually replaced necessity. They carried a flag and the principals of the ancient common ridings, with one exception, are all called 'Cornets', a term for a cavalry officer first used in the seventeenth century. Flags were centrally important and the Hawick Cornet may indeed have plundered his in 1514 from a detachment of Lord Dacre's men.

Flodden threw Scottish politics into a dizzying, faction-ridden spin in which Border heidsmen were intimately involved. James V was an

photographs taken by Liz Hanson. The lonely farm of Ovenshank in Liddesdale, the quintessential reiver valley.

A hardy Galloway bullock in the foothills of the central ranges of the Cheviots.

The ruins of a tower house at Edgerston, at the head of the Jed Valley, below the Carter Bar.

Falside, in the central ranges of the Cheviots.

A hailstorm over Cheviot.

Carewoodrig Valley.

Late winter on Hownam Law in the Cheviots.

Sourhope at the head of the Bowmont Valley in the Cheviots.

The Cheviots just before a winter storm at the head of the Jed Valley.

The modern road from Langholm to Newcastleton through the Tarras Moss.

The Tarras Burn

Late spring on the high pasture of the Lammermuirs, in the Allan Valley.

Spring in Upper Teviotdale.

Late autumn, after the harvest in fertile Berwickshire with snow on the Cheviots to the south.

Wild country at the head of Annandale, the lair of the Johnstones.

The Devil's Beeftub at the head of Annandale.

Goldilands Tower in Upper Teviotdale, a Scott stronghold.

The ruins of Dryburgh Abbey near St Boswells.

River mist over Berwick-upon-Tweed.

Flodden's fertile fields as they are now.

Smailholm Tower and its commanding views over the Tweed Valley.

Even in a watery sunshine Hermitage Castle still looms.

The remains of the Hume's castle inside the walls of the folly now known as Hume Castle. Its exaggerated crenellation still dominates the Border skyline.

The Victorian Mercat Cross at Jedburgh, the site of the royal herald's humiliation.

Mary, Queen of Scots' House at Jedburgh.

Norham Castle standing guard over the Tweed.

Berwick-upon-Tweed and its walls.

Greenknowe Tower near Kelso.

Modern hill farming in Upper Teviotdale.

Limiecleuch Farm in Teviotdale shows how even in summer, the land looks inhospitable.

Evening at Priesthaugh Farm in the Cheviots.

Sunset over the Border Hills.

infant and frantic power-broking crackled incessantly around his cot. At first the Queen Dowager, Margaret, the sister of Henry VIII of England, claimed the right of regency and attempted to direct matters of state. In 'a triumph of passion over policy' she married the much younger Earl of Angus. This combination presented a clear threat to the Earl of Home and he began to encourage the entry of John, Duke of Albany, into the bitter intrigues whispering around the Edinburgh court. Educated in France, unable to speak English, he was nevertheless a legitimate candidate for the regency. As James V's cousin, he stood very near the throne in the male line of succession.

KING SAM

In the sixteenth century kings listened to various forms of address – 'Your Royal Highness', 'Your Majesty' or sometimes 'Your Grace'. Capital letters also seemed to be optional. Looked at with a lexical eye, these terms seem daft to us now, 'Your Majesty' literally meaning 'Your Bigness'. But in the late middle ages and beyond, the aristocracy insisted on their rank being recognised. Modern forms of address can be found in the excellent *Debrett's Review*. 'Madam' seems to cover most women (even the Queen – 'Ma'am' is only an abbreviation) and 'Sir' most men. One of the most complex entries in this fascinating and definitive list is for titled ladies who are divorced. Amongst the general tables of precedence and relative ranks in the armed forces is the order of succession to the throne. Sixteenth in line is a young man called Samuel Chatto. 'King Sam' has a certain ring to it but seventeenth in line, his little brother's name has even more of a resonance. His name is Arthur.

But it all went quickly wrong for Home. Courtiers – almost certainly those fluent in French – began to sway Albany away from supporting the interests of the Border heidsmen, and when Home persuaded the Queen Dowager and the Earl of Angus to abduct the infant king, the game grew very dangerous indeed. The plot failed and Home and the Anguses fled to the Borders. After more clumsy attempts to outmanoeuvre Albany, Home mustered a raiding party of seasoned riders. In November 1515, as the first blasts of the winter blew in off the North Sea, 'banditti of the borders' rode north over the Lammermuirs and plundered Albany's town of Dunbar. Shut up in the castle was a small garrison of French soldiers and also Home's captured mother. As a flourish of reiver power, the Dunbar raid appeared to have its effect and Home was forgiven his treasonable transgressions.

The outbreak of peace did not last. Trusting Albany's assurances of safe-conduct, Home and his brother, William, arrived at court in Edinburgh. They were accompanied by their fellow Border heidsman and ally, Dand Kerr of Ferniehurst. All were immediately arrested, the brothers forced to go through a farrago of a trial – in which Home was charged with treacherous inactivity during the course of the battle of Flodden – and on 11 October 1516, sentence was carried out. Home mounted the scaffold and was decapitated. A day later his brother was forced to kneel and lay his neck on the headsman's block. Seeing how bloodily politics was playing out and fearful of the same fate, Dand Kerr bribed his guards and rode hard for Ferniehurst and safety.

A few weeks later the Duke of Albany followed Dand to Jedburgh where a general assize was held to deal with the worst of the reiving families and their excesses. Then the Regent made a bad mistake. The glamorous Sir Anthony Darcy, styled 'Le Sieur de Beaute', was a Frenchman much favoured at court. With Home's execution, the east marches of Scotland lacked a warden and the man Borderers called 'Bawtie' was appointed. He did not prosper.

When the castle at Langton, near Duns, was unlawfully seized by William Cockburn, Bawtie gathered a small posse and rode out of Dunbar Castle to set matters to rights. Arriving below Langton's walls he instructed that the castle be returned to its rightful owner, Cockburn's young nephew. But what seemed to the Frenchman a simple, black and white business began to turn nasty when Sir David Home of Wedderburn turned up with a troop of horsemen. Not only was Wedderburn kinsman to the recently executed Home, whose job Bawtie had taken over, but he was also a close ally of William Cockburn. After a few harsh words, the Home horsemen made short work of the Dunbar posse. Bawtie turned tail and galloped northwards for his life, but not knowing the countryside, he found himself riding full pelt into a trackless bog, somewhere east of Duns. Frantically pushing his horse on through the maze of pools and tussocks, he was slowly surrounded by Wedderburn's troopers. One of them charged, with his sword flailing, and decapitated Bawtie where he stood. It was said that Wedderburn took the Frenchman's head by its fashionable flowing locks, plaited them and tied the trophy to his saddle pommel. Many centuries before, the same gory habit had been seen amongst the Vikings of the north of Scotland, and long before that amongst the Celtic cavalry warriors of western Europe.

Border heidsmen were utterly ruthless in pursuit of their family's interests, and when opportunities presented themselves, they rarely hesitated. On the desperate night following the battle at Flodden, Dand Kerr and his men broke into the Abbey of Kelso and claimed it and all its far flung possessions for their own. The king of Scotland lay dead on the field and his heir was an infant of only seventeen months. Who was to stop Kerr from throwing out the servants of Andrew Stewart, Bishop of Caithness? James IV had gifted the revenues of Kelso to his bastard son, but he too had fallen at Flodden and Dand Kerr knew a chance when he saw one. Before the high altar he had the small congregation of monks witness the installation of his brother, Tam, as the thirtieth Abbot of Kelso. When the mitre was placed on his head, the great monastery passed into the pastoral care of a local bandit.

Founded by David I in 1128, dominated by the immense church with its cathedral-like double crossing, Kelso had been one of the richest and most venerated abbeys in Scotland. Its abbots held the hard-won right to wear the bishop's mitre and their community was seen as a special daughter-house of the Holy See in Rome. But as news of the slaughter at Flodden spread like wildfire throughout the Borders, the Kerrs took advantage. Their descendants, the Dukes of Roxburghe, now control a wide patrimony based on the gifts of land made to Kelso Abbey during the middle ages. The glory of God became the pride of the Kerrs.

The Humes were similarly quick to see what was possible after Flodden. John Home had been installed by his brother, Alexander, as Abbot of the Augustinian Canons at Jedburgh, but when Lord Home was executed, John was forced to flee north of the Tay.

HUME, HOME, KERR AND CARR

The twenty-first-century descendants of the reiving aristocracy are sometimes slightly disguised. Homes became Humes – the confusion in pronunciation began early, in the twelfth century – and they became earls. But they were no longer based at Home Castle and are instead Earls Home, pronounced Hume, of the Hirsel, a very beautiful house near Coldstream. The Kerrs became Dukes of

Roxburghe, with an 'e' for some reason, and they say their name as Carr. Deborah Kerr, the demure Hollywood actress, also affected Carr. Ferniehurst Kerrs became Marquises of Lothian at Monteviot House, near Jedburgh while Elliots became Earls of Minto, near Hawick. Most widely landed of all, the Scotts graduated to Dukes of Buccleuch. Their house at Bowhill near Selkirk and their vast estates might be seen by the cynical as first prize for reiving. The largest and arguably most active reiver surname, the wild Armstrongs of Liddesdale, failed to keep up: dukedoms, earldoms and marquisates eluding them. They are even a headless surname, with no heidsman or chief. But at least they got to go to the moon.

While Thomas, Lord Dacre, had a clear commission from Henry VIII to stoke the fires of disorder in 1513, he also held the office of Warden of the English West March and was therefore responsible for keeping order. As such he kept a close eye on the riding families of Redesdale and Tynedale. Charltons, Robsons, Milburns, Storeys and others were every bit as thrawn and independent-minded as the Scottish surnames. In fact their reputation was bad enough to prompt the Merchant Adventurers Company of Newcastle to brand them as unemployable in an ordinance of 1554. They were expressly forbidden 'to serve. . . any who are born of brought up in Tynedale, Redesdale or any other such like places'.

In 1518 Dacre sent an expedition into the wilds of north Northumberland and it captured ten of the leading reivers. Determined to bring them quickly to trial, probably at Morpeth, Dacre's troop of eighty horsemen picked their way carefully down Redesdale, straight into an ambush. At a narrow place the warden's posse was trapped and attacked by a force from the Redesdale surnames of Halls, Headleys, Storeys and others. The captured reivers were immediately freed, the Bailiff of Morpeth killed and five others forced to travel north to Scotland, possibly to be held for ransom.

By 1520 the faction fighting at the Scottish court had paralysed government to such an extent that ambassadors could not be sent to England to negotiate a truce. Instead, Tam Kerr, Abbot of Kelso (styled 'Thomas') was instructed to treat directly with Lord Dacre and conclude a short-term agreement. This was no more than a recognition of the realities of power in the Borders. Bluntly, the Kerrs and the Dacres were in a better position to monitor and enforce an international truce than any in Edinburgh and London.

By 1521 Tam appeared to be sharing the office of abbot. According to contemporary records his brother Dand held an extraordinary combination of offices which recognised his family's dominance of mid Tweeddale. When he met Dacre at a truce-day at the ancient trysting place at Redden, Dand was simultaneously Abbot of Kelso, Warden of the Scottish Middle March and Heidsman of the Kerrs. It was local, not central authority which counted.

When the Duke of Albany returned from France in 1521 to take up the office of Regent once more, the truces negotiated by Dand and Tam Kerr were set aside. With the promise of French backing (a substantial force did arrive, but too late in the year to campaign), the Regent rekindled the smouldering war with Henry VIII's England. But the Scots were reluctant to invade – not only because of the risk of another Flodden but also because sympathies were divided. There were those who were uneasy at being a pawn of French foreign policy and others who believed that England would make a better ally than an enemy.

Where Albany did succeed was in provoking Henry VIII. And the Borders paid dear for his pro-French diplomatic posturing. In 1522 Dacre and the Earl of Northumberland made plans to have the village of Wester Kelso (most of it now invisible under the walls, lodge houses and policies of Floors Castle) burned but were anxious not leave any fingerprints. Here is Northumberland's letter to the king:

> I . . . have devised that, within these three nights, God willing, Kelso shall be burned, with all the corn in the said town, and then they [the Scots] shall have no place to lie any garrison near to the border. And this burning of Kelso is devised to be done secretly, by Tynedale and Redesdale.

The raid was aborted but wind of it reached whichever Kerr was Abbot of Kelso. He wrote to the Queen Dowager, imploring her to persuade her brother to desist, and Margaret passed on the plea: 'Also my Lord, the Abbot of Kelso has prayed me to write to you to be his good lord, and for my sake you will not let any evil be done to that place, which I pray you to do.'

The plea was ignored. A year later the Earl of Surrey and Lord Dacre rode into the eastern Borders in great strength, blazing another trail of terror and destruction. This time, however, it was systematic and very devastating. Some of its effects can still be seen.

HORSESHOE LUCK

Old and worn-out horseshoes were often nailed over a country doorway. They are believed to bring protection from bad luck as well as good luck and the origins of that belief turn out to be very old. An upturned shoe, making a u-shape, is thought to represent horns, specifically the horns of the Celtic god, Cernnunos. Despite the Christian appropriation of his headgear for the Devil, people persisted in believing that he could protect a house and the family in it. Horseshoes set in the opposite position, with the gap at the bottom, were thought to bring luck – and also to be protective. From the earliest prehistoric days of blacksmithing, it is likely that touching iron warded off evil, a bit like touching wood. And many touched the shoe as they entered and exited the doorway. The upside down position was protective because it resembled the shape of the female genitals. Just as over the entrances to medieval churches where carvings of female figures with exaggerated pudenda are found (known as 'sheela na gig'), the horseshoe was placed to distract evil spirits from coming into the house. However unlikely that might sound there exists plenty of evidence from several cultures to support the interpretation.

By the spring of 1523 Dacre was at Kelso, his men torching the wooden and thatched houses. What made this more than a raid was the time and trouble taken to inflict lasting damage: 'In the morning of the day which was yesterday, we set forward and we went to Kelso where we not only burned and destroyed the whole town that would burn by any labour but also cast down the Gatehouse of the Abbey.'

Dacre's men became even busier. They fired the abbot's house and then demolished the blackened ruin. In the great church itself the beautifully worked wooden stalls from one of the many side-chapels, the Chapel of the Blessed Virgin, were ripped out and burned, while the lead covering the roof was stripped, probably for use as artillery shot. By itself, that last action probably caused most damage. And so that the monks might endure as much discomfort as the townspeople, their dormitory was wrecked and burned to the ground.

What might have converted a sacred place like Kelso Abbey into a legitimate target was the Kerr takeover after Flodden. The Earl of

Surrey noted that Dand Kerr was Dacre's 'mortal enemy' and the ancient abbey was no more than another of his possessions. But piety, or the lack of it, likely made little difference. It was no defence ten years later when Henry VIII's commissioners dissolved and destroyed England's monasteries and nunneries.

Jedburgh fared little better. When the Earl of Surrey's forces reached the town, they saw a place they reckoned was twice the size of Berwick. In addition to its venerable and beautifully sited abbey, Jedburgh boasted six defensive towers. Perhaps they were the possessions of different families (possibly rivals, as in many of the northern Italian cities and towns of the same period), or perhaps they formed part of a fortified perimeter. In any case, the town was 'cleanly destroyed, burned and thrown down', though but only after bitter street-fighting.

While Jedburgh burned, Dacre led his small army south to nearby Ferniehurst, the stronghold of Dand Kerr. As now, the approach to the tower is thickly wooded, and in the early sixteenth century it was very vulnerable to artillery. When the English force trundled their guns within range, the Kerrs attacked them in the woods, desperate to prevent their deployment. The trees also prevented the much superior English numbers from being automatically decisive. Dacre's men joined what was said to have been a vicious fight. Ferniehurst eventually fell and Dand Kerr was captured.

As darkness came down the English picketed their horses, around 1500 of them, in the woods around the tower, but they failed to set a proper watch. No sentry heard the approach of a small force of Borderers and at dead of night, they cut loose the tethered horses and whacked and hallooed them into a stampede. Hurtling through the dark woods, they bolted, some racing through the burning streets of Jedburgh, others galloping over the river-cliffs by the Jed Water. The English lost half their mounts, and Dacre ascribed the attack to an appearance of the Devil. Dand Kerr must have smiled.

NIGHTMARE

Nightmares have nothing to do with female horses. 'Mare' is an Old English word for an incubus, an evil spirit which sat on the chests of women while they slept. Later it came to mean a Demon Lover who ravished women during the night, a handy explanation for unwanted pregnancies. The confusion with horses grew up in the

nineteenth century with a series of very popular engravings by the
Swiss artist, Fuseli. They show an incubus sitting on a sleeping
woman's chest while a strange, blind horse watches.

A year later the Duke of Albany returned to France. And with him
went most of France's influence on Scottish foreign policy. Peace
negotiations were soon underway. Here is a report sent from Berwick
to Cardinal Wolsey, the royal chancellor:

> The confirmation of the peace on the part of the Scots was brought
> hither by the Abbot of Kelso, the Headsman of the Kerrs of
> Teviotdale, well accompanied by honest men to the number of
> 60 persons to whom I made such cheer as I could that day at dinner.
> And forthwith we examined our commissions and made collation of
> the other of our greater writings. And so, at night we departed and
> kept our lodgings. And because the companions with the said Abbot
> were Borderers, I bid them to be well accompanied and good cheer
> to be made unto them. The said Abbot being a sad and wise man,
> brother to Dand Kerr of Ferniehurst.

With the conclusion of a temporary peace and the departure of the
Francophile Albany, power swung towards the pro-English party and
its leader, the Earl of Angus, first amongst the Red Douglases. As de
facto Regent, he led several punitive expeditions to the Borders, and in
1526 blundered into the convoluted tangle of local politics.

The young James V was effectively the prisoner of the Douglases,
but his agents were able to negotiate the help of Walter Scott of
Buccleuch. Plans were laid for the rescue of the king. When the Earl of
Angus rode south at the head of another expedition and stopped at
Melrose, the Scotts were waiting. With 600 riders they launched
themselves at Angus' force, somewhere near the Tweed fords. The
assault faltered, lost momentum and ranks closed around the king.
With the help of the Kerrs of Cessford and Ferniehurst, the Red
Douglas and his men beat off the Scotts. When the skirmish turned
into a panicky rout, Kerr riders galloped in pursuit. One of the Scotts'
confederates, an Elliot, wheeled his pony and turned to fight. Couch-
ing his lance, he charged at Dand Kerr of Ferniehurst and killed him.
The incident ignited a feud which lasted at least two generations.
Intermittent efforts were made to patch it up and a marriage was

contracted in 1530 between Walter Scott of Buccleuch and Janet Kerr, daughter of Dand. But bitter resentments still burned and in the High Street of Edinburgh, 26 years after the fight at Melrose, a gang of Kerrs and their allies set upon Walter Scott and stabbed him to death.

The late 1520s saw Liddesdale increasingly become the central focus of lawlessness, the Armstrongs, the Elliots, Crosiers and Nixons able to ignore and even publicly belittle an ineffectual royal authority in Scotland. Even though the Earl of Angus led two well-organised and powerful expeditions, in 1525 and 1527, which hanged several notorious reivers out of hand and captured Sim the Laird of the Armstrongs of Mangerton in Liddesdale (probably the high heidsman of the whole surname) and his brother, Davy the Lady, his efforts had little lasting impact. In fact his plundering of 4,000 head of cattle only prompted more retaliatory raiding.

Such was their collective disdain for national authority that the Liddesdale surnames began to make common cause with the reivers of Tynedale. The Armstrongs and Elliots rode with the Charltons and Dodds, mustering large bands of riders, not troubling to act in secret or with stealth, and flying their own standards as they scoured the Borders for plunder. This sense of a cocky, semi-independent principality of thieves flickered briefly into real substance in 1527.

Tynedale and Liddesdale reivers are recorded as mounting a concerted attack on Tarset Hall in north Northumberland. Soon after they became even more bold. When Sir William de Lisle, heidsman of a prominent English surname and a sometime ally of Liddesdale, was imprisoned in Newcastle, the Armstrongs and Elliots rode into town and freed him. It was an act of amazing audacity – and self-confidence. For much of 1527 Lisle led large bands of riders on either side of the border, and it appeared that no government official or force could check their excesses. A descent into anarchy seemed finally to have taken place, the Borders had become the badlands, a no-go zone of utter lawlessness.

Sir William de Lisle's brief but spectacular reign as the reiver-king of several allied surnames was brought to an end in early 1528. Rousing itself into action, the English crown appointed Henry Percy, Earl of Northumberland, as Warden of all the Marches and he quickly weighed in with a heavy hand. Forays were intercepted and raiders summarily hanged. When Percy threatened to invade Liddesdale, the Armstrongs saw that the game was up and without hesitation they surrendered de Lisle and his leading men to the English warden. They appeared before Percy with symbolic ropes around their necks and he wasted no time in converting the symbolism into brutal reality when he hanged the lot of them.

Across the border, the Armstrongs remained unpunished. For some forgotten tactical reason, they left their fastness of Liddesdale and chose to occupy the Debatable Land. This was an area of about 40 square miles in the western marches, lying between Gretna Green and Canonbie. As the name suggests it was disputed territory, neither English nor Scottish. In 1528 the Armstrongs moved in, claimed it and determined to defend themselves.

CLANS AND SURNAMES

Ancient Border surnames wishing to form themselves into societies in order to maintain their historical links and shared past have unfortunately taken to calling themselves 'clans'. There is a Clan Elliot, a Clan Armstrong, and for goodness' sake, a Clan Moffat. They are in fact nothing of the kind. The misappropriated Highland nomenclature has brought all sorts of misleading connotations: clan chiefs, clan pipers, clan tartan, gatherings and the whole biscuit-tin lid kit and caboodle. The central problem is that the use of 'clan' appears to establish a connection, to suggest that the Gaelic-speaking Highland families were somehow linked to the great Border surnames. They were not. Perhaps the only tangible contact was made by Walter Scott, who publicised tartan Scotland in the nineteenth century, and the Border textile mills who made most of it. The central difference was in relation to land. Highlanders of the same surname had an umbilical attachment with a particular place. This old notion of 'duthchas' is difficult to translate but it wraps up the way in which a clan had collective customary title to the glen or shoreline where they had lived since a time out of mind. Border heidsmen had tenants in the sixteenth century and sometimes even moved to take over different areas. What bound them together was the name itself and the loyalty it commanded. When Highlanders raised their broadswords to charge, they roared the names of their places: Loch Moy! Dunmaglass! When Borderers fought in battle, they shouted out who they were and rallied all of that surname to them. They were most certainly not clansmen and would not have been seen dead wearing tartan.

When William, Lord Dacre, the Warden of the English West March, heard of this flagrant annexation, he planned an attack. Mustering more than 2,000 riders, he advanced up the little River Sark, and into an ambush. The English surname of Storey had wind of what was afoot, warned their Armstrong allies who beat back Dacre with ease. A single surname had defeated a small English army.

In the 1520s the Border Reivers were becoming increasingly notorious across the north of Britain. News of their crimes and lawlessness had spread all over Scotland and much of England. They had become a national disgrace and were the target of a remarkable reaction from the national churches. Gavin Dunbar, the Archbishop of Glasgow, had been tutor to the young James V. When the king began his personal rule, free of the Red Douglases, Dunbar was appointed as Lord Chancellor of Scotland. Where military solutions had failed to make much impact on the perennial problem of the Borders, perhaps the spiritual power of the church might do better. It was certainly cheaper, and worth a try.

Some time in the late 1520s the Archbishop promulgated 'a monition of cursing' against the reivers. He did not hold back:

> I curse their head and all the hairs of their head: I curse their face, their eyes, their mouth, their nose, their tongue, their teeth, their neck, their shoulders, their breast, their heart, their stomach, their back, their belly, their arms, their legs, their hands, their feet, and every part of their body from the top of their head to the soles of their feet, before and behind, within and without.

And that's not all:

> I dissever and part them from the Church of God, and deliver them alive to the Devil of Hell, as the Apostle Paul delivered Corinthian. I interdict the places they come to for divine service, the ministrations of the sacraments of Holy Church, except the sacrament of baptism only, and forbid all churchmen to shrive or absolve them of their sins, until they be first absolved of this cursing.

Because they are nothing but

> common traitors, reivers, thieves, dwelling in the south part of this realm, in Teviotdale, Eskdale, Liddesdale, Ewesdale, Nithsdale and

Annandale. They have been in several ways pursued and punished by the temporal sword and our Sovereign Lord's authority, and do not fear it.

The vehemence of the language is palpable – even at a distance of five centuries – but it should not be allowed to distract from the importance of Dunbar's actions. Not only were the reivers placed outside the temporal legal system, they were now also cast out of the church.

Excommunication was an extremely serious matter. Marriages could not be blessed or contracted, funerals would lack a priest, last rites could not be administered or a final confession heard and the sins absolved. The sole consolation was that the monition of cursing was very general, no individuals were named and many no doubt claimed that it did not apply to them.

English reivers did not escape. Perhaps as a deliberately timed complement, the Bishop of Durham delivered himself of a similar curse on the surnames of Tynedale and Redesdale, but again it was not practical to name specific names. Apparently Hector Charlton, a Tynedale reiver, held a communion where he himself took the service and served all those who attended with wine. In a time when – even on the eve of the Reformation – religion and the church played a central role in the lives of everyone, it was a surprising and shocking example of blasphemy.

When Gavin Dunbar determined 'to strike with the terrible sword of Holy Church', he probably struck harder than we can imagine in this Godless age. The curse was never lifted and the fell sentence of excommunication remained in force throughout the sixteenth century. When in 1596 Robert Carey listened to Geordie Burn's recital of all his crimes, it sounded like a confession which might have been made to a priest.

CARLISLE CURSES

When the Archbishop of Glasgow cursed the Border Reivers in 1525, he made it comprehensive, an invective which could easily have found its way into a Monty Python film. Carlisle City Council recently created an underpass and had it decorated by a pavement inscribed with many of the Border surnames. At the end of the underpass there is a polished, pink granite boulder with the Archbishop's curse beautifully carved around it. In 2001 a Christian group in the city petitioned to have it removed. They claimed that the curse was still working, nearly 500 years later. The outbreak of foot and mouth disease in 2001, the Carlisle floods of Christmas 2004 and the recent poor form of Carlisle United FC were all cited as evidence. Perhaps they have a point.

By the end of 1528 the three-year truce concluded after the devastating raids on Kelso, Jedburgh and elsewhere was about to expire. Official commissioners met at Berwick and agreed terms. At Alnwick an unofficial meeting took place between Sim the Laird, the Armstrong heidsman, and the Earl of Northumberland. If they could not agree, then the truce made at Berwick would not be worth the wax melted to seal it.

Northumberland was an appointed government official, Warden General of the English Marches and directly responsible to Henry VIII and the royal administration in London. Sim the Laird had no such status, and held no equivalent office of any kind in Scotland. The December meeting in Alnwick was the stuff of realpolitik, and it was fascinating. The heidsman of the Armstrongs, a surname riding high in its pomp, in some ways the successor of Sir William de Lisle as a reiver-king, the ruler of Liddesdale and many of the valleys round about, Sim was probably the most powerful man on the Scottish side of the frontier. It made every sort of sense for the Earl to talk directly to him. If they could do a deal, it would stick.

Very unusually some sense of what actually passed between the two was recorded. Northumberland's account may suffer a little from an English bias, and Armstrong's words may have been intended for effect as much as substance. But what he said was remarkable.

The fundamental problem of disorder in the Borders was caused not by the crimes of the riding surnames. No, that was only a symptom, an effect. According to Armstrong, the root cause was the ineffective rule of the Scottish kings. Neither James V nor his predecessors had been able to deliver justice properly, either in its administration or its enforcement. And those counsellors and regents who had ruled while the Stewarts were minors were no better. Sim could produce first-hand, convincing evidence for this governmental failure. He and his riders could raid unchecked over great distances, destroy churches and generally act with impunity. It was a scandal – and also a political version of Groucho Marx' view of clubs and his membership of them.

The best solution for the Borders was a radical one. The whole area should become part of England. If only Henry VIII were to replace James V as sovereign over the Scottish marches, then the rule of law would prevail. Presumably the Armstrongs would then lay down their spears, swords and pistols, yoke their ponies to the plough, become peaceable farmers and convert Liddesdale into an agrarian paradise. Possibly.

Sim the Laird's analysis must have been disingenuous, and Northumberland might have laughed, though he probably didn't believe it either. The Armstrongs' interests would have been ill served by the agents of a powerful monarchy, English or Scottish. His game may have been to play off one against the other. Sim knew fine that his words would be reported to London, and by indicating that the Armstrongs might be willing to become allies of the Tudor kings, he may have hoped to bolster his position against the Stewarts. Liddesdale was undoubtedly in Scotland, at least for the moment, but if its inhabitants aspired to be English, or threatened to, then that could only foster their ability to act independently. Three thousand riders galloped behind Sim the Laird. That fact alone persuaded London and Edinburgh to listen to what he said in Alnwick.

TAIN BO

One of the oldest stories in Europe survived in Irish Gaelic and takes cattle reiving for its theme. Some things never change. The 'Tain Bo Cuailgne', or 'The Great Cattle Raid of Cooley' is set in the north of Ireland and it describes prehistoric reiving and a society which existed in the first millennium BC. The boy-hero is Cuchulainn and he defends the cattle of Ulster single-handedly against the raiders of Connaught. Queen Maeve is after more wealth, and like the Borderers of the sixteenth century, she saw it as having four legs. When in bed with her lover, the queen talks of the measurement of wealth and they agree on its ultimate expression in a particularly fine bull. This habit of counting wealth in cows is culturally widespread and historically persistent. Sheep and goats are intrinsically more useful, versatile and easier to manage, but a man (or an Irish queen, or a Border Reiver) who owned cows was a man of real substance.

Nationality mattered in sixteenth-century Scotland, and England. After the Wars of Independence, and all the blood shed since, and especially after Flodden only 15 years before, Borderers had a keen sense of Scottishness. But when set against family loyalties, this appeared to slacken. The same was true in the north of Scotland, amongst the Highland clans. Family or clan came first, and if it was in the best interests of family to change national allegiance, then so be it. But it was no trivial matter.

English and Scottish Borderers were also often related. Major surnames such as the Nixons, Grahams, Bells and Halls had large branches on both sides of the frontier, and a weary Warden of the English West March noted that the Armstrongs were in the habit of intermarrying with their allies, the Tynedale families.

Even if distorted and exaggerated, Sim the Laird's remarks gave voice to actions and previously unspoken policies. In all they did, the Armstrongs and the other great surnames put their own interests before any other. And despite all the violence, the thieving and the feuds, such undying fidelity to family is not entirely unattractive.

Sim's opinions were probably also intended for the ears of James V and his allegedy feckless counsellors. They may well have been passed on directly by the Earl of Northumberland himself. He met the Earl of Moray, James V's bastard brother, at one of the trysting places on the eastern border only three months after the conversation in Alnwick. On the agenda at the Reddenburn near Kelso were the terms of the truce agreed at Berwick, but the meeting broke up in acrimony. Northumberland refused Moray's insistence that such meetings ought to take place in Scotland. If heated words were exchanged, some of Sim's assertions might have spiced the atmosphere.

In any event James V resolved to take firm action. The Borders would be tamed and the heidsmen brought to heel. Before a parliament convened in Edinburgh in May 1528, Scott of Buccleuch, the Kerrs of Cessford and Ferniehurst, Maxwell, Home, Johnstone, and other leading heidsmen were all summoned and then immediately imprisoned. William Cockburn of Henderland, in the Yarrow Valley, and Adam Scott of Tushielaw up Ettrick were both executed and their severed heads spiked on the Edinburgh Tolbooth. Scott must have been a notorious reiver for the records attach the label 'King of Thieves' to notice of his death. He was particularly accused of 'taking Blackmail', and his royal title may have stemmed from his central control of a widespread protection racket.

The heidsmen seem to have been detained to guarantee the submission and good behaviour of their surnames. Soon after their arrest James V embarked on yet another expedition to the Borders and it was important that all went forward well. Eight thousand strong, his men advanced quickly into Upper Teviotdale, above Hawick, to a place known as Carlenrig.

Black Jock had agreed to meet the king there. Better known as Johnnie Armstrong of Gilnockie, he was one of the most famous – and notorious – reivers ever to ride the marches. Plays were written about him – one of them is still much performed. *Armstrong's Last Goodnight* (1964) by John Arden has Johnnie as the central character. Songs and poems have also been composed about Black Jock and they paint him in romantic, even heroic, colours. He only raided in England, and, Robin Hood-style, robbed the rich to pay the poor. Just, in his own rough and ready way, and brave, Johnnie was the very epitome of reiver romance.

Most of what has been written about Black Jock (using the name conferred by contemporaries is salutary and places him properly alongside the likes of Hob the King and Dand the Man) is simply ahistorical. But there must have been something more, something which sparked the romance that swirls around him and no other reiver. Perhaps it was a dark glamour, a memory of style, manner and dash.

No Armstrongs had submitted to James V's parliamentary court in Edinburgh. It may be that Black Jock and his retinue of leading riders came to submit to the king at Carlenrig. Certainly some sort of assurance or guarantee must have been sought and received. Black Jock was a seasoned criminal and he cannot have willingly ridden to meet the king if he thought his life was in danger. But it most certainly was.

Carlenrig lies just off the modern A7, about 10 miles south-west of Hawick. A well-set kirk stands on one side of a narrow country road. Near the wrought iron gates into the kirkyard, the road widens considerably to allow space for ample parking – and not only for use on a Sunday. On the opposite side of the road there is a much-visited shrine. In a small, walled graveyard, which seems much older than the kirk, stands a monument to a notorious thief. Such is the power of Johnnie Armstrong's posthumous (and largely confected) reputation that someone guilty of many very serious crimes finds himself warmly remembered in a Christian cemetery.

Alongside the sober tombstones of generations of God-fearing farmers stands a defiant and even assertive memorial to one of the most rapacious and ruthless of all the Border Reivers. The raised and armed arm of the Armstrong emblem, designed to look as though it is about to strike, is much in evidence. No one appears to see any irony.

Why? The bare facts of what happened at Carlenrig offer little convincing explanation. That most discursive and informative of Border historians, the Rev. George Ridpath, wrote that the king caused '48 banditti to be hanged on growing trees' and that John Armstrong was one of them. That is all.

But stories began to elaborate the incident very soon after 1530. They told of trickery, bad faith and bitter exchanges between the king and Johnnie Armstrong before he and his men were strung up. The essence of the embroidered tale was that by some device, an invitation to join a hunting party or a promise of safe conduct, Armstrong and thirty or forty of his leading men were lured into the royal presence. Dressed in their flashy finery (the sixteenth-century equivalent of the sharp and shiny suits of Mafia mobsters), their cockiness seems to have offended the king. Here are the details from the ballad which described the event:

> John wore a girdle about his middle,
> Imbroidered ower wi' burning gold,
> Bespangled wi' the same metal:
> Maist beautiful was to behold.

> There hang nine tassles at Johnnie's hat,
> An ilk ane worth three hundred pound.
> 'What wants yon knave that a king should have,
> But the sword of honour and the crown?'

> 'O, where got thou these tassles, Johnnie,
> That blink sae brawlie abune thy brow?'
> 'I gat them in the field fechting,
> Where, cruel king, thou durst not be!'

The incendiary dialogue is obviously invented, but it does sound a small, faint note of authenticity. Perhaps insulting words were exchanged and a hot-tempered king ordered a summary execution.

The royal soldiers closed in around Johnnie and his retinue. Once he realised how perilous the situation had suddenly become, the reiver started talking, for his life. Border Reivers were renowned for their gifts of oratory – or at least persuasion, and the ballad gave Johnnie some eloquent lines:

> 'Grant me my life, my liege, my king!
> And a brave gift I'll gie to thee –
> All between here and Newcastle town
> Shall pay their yeirly rent to thee.'

But it was no use:

> 'To seek het water beneath cauld ice,
> Surely it is a great folie –
> I have asked grace at a graceless face,
> But there is nane for my men and me.'

The king turned his back and left Armstrong and his men to wriggle and choke on the end of a rope. It is a puzzling episode. An unmistakable odour of dishonour and betrayal drifts around the old trees at Carlenrig. Even though he was scarcely an honourable figure himself, there persists a powerful sense that Johnnie Armstrong was hard done by. And it might be true.

Amongst all those who report the incident, even the laconic Rev. Ridpath, one phrase is repeated. Historians record many executions in the long story of the reivers, but what was remarkable about that of Armstrong and his men is that they were 'hanged from growing trees' or 'growand trees'. Ropes were slung not over a gallows beam but over what was handy at that moment, the stout limbs of the mature trees around Carlenrig churchyard. This speaks of an impulsive act, of something unplanned and unexpected. Perhaps Johnnie Armstrong and James Stewart really did exchange insults. Like most of his royal ancestors, James V was apparently hot-tempered. And in 1530 he was only 17 years old. In the sixteenth century boys grew into men much earlier than they do now but even so there is more than a hint of youthful impetuosity in stringing up the Armstrongs from growand trees.

In any event, it would have made more sense to deal with a famous reiver in a considered way – the same way in which William Cockburn and Adam Scott had met their fate. Better to make a public spectacle of the dispatch of Johnnie Armstrong on a scaffold at the mercat cross of Edinburgh and spike his severed head on the Tolbooth walls for all to see. Or hold him in detention as a guarantee for the good behaviour of his surname. Killing him at Carlenrig looks like an indulgence and bad politics.

The role of Lord Maxwell in this business is also suggestive. Immediately after his death, within three days, Armstrong's goods and lands were made over to the Dumfriesshire family. The Maxwells and the Armstrongs had long been associated, and even after Carlenrig, remained close. But there is a hint that Lord Maxwell (even though he was probably still in prison in Edinburgh at that time) had had a hand in arranging the meeting of Johnnie and King James. Perhaps he guaranteed the reiver's safety. This only adds to the sense of a spontaneous altercation in the churchyard. Surely if Maxwell had played false a blood feud with the Armstrongs would have followed. Others had been pursued for much less.

THE REIVER TRAIL

The broadcaster and writer, Fiona Armstrong, owns a resonant reiver name and she is fascinated by all that history attached to it, good and bad. Fiona has helped create 'The Reiver Trail'. It begins at the bleak mass of Hermitage Castle and climbs west, up through a high valley where stock-rearing farms like Carewoodrig (still in the hands of Elliots) still run the tough little cows known as Galloways (not the big beef cattle called Belted Galloways – these are all black or sometimes brown with dense coats). These beasts did not look much different in the sixteenth century. The trail then joins the A7, takes in Carlenrig where Johnnie Armstrong was strung up and swings down to Langholm and the Armstrong Museum. It passes the beautiful tower at Hollows before turning east into Liddesdale, the quintessential reiver valley. The landscape looks different now, much less wild, cars whizz by and that hard-bitten life is long fled. But there are places on the trail, like the lovely, lonely road up to Carewoodrig, where the past rushes in with the swirling mists, where the whaups cry on the wind, and where at an early winter twilight no one would be surprised to hear the thump of hoofbeats on the grass.

The lynchings had little lasting effect. There is a tradition that King Henry VIII had asked James V to deal with Johnnie Armstrong. Evidently his surname had been overdoing their forays into England and causing mayhem. Perhaps there was concern at the alliances with Tynedale and Redesdale. This sort of intervention is unlikely on a number of levels. Especially against a background of hostility in the 1530s, one sovereign king would scarcely be anxious to take instruction from another in how to keep order in his own kingdom, unless there was a deal, and there is no evidence that there was. In any case Henry was usually happy to see the Stewarts in difficulty in the Borders. In fact, in 1532, the English were doing their best to foment disorder. The Warden of the English West March, Lord Dacre, was advised to encourage the men of Liddesdale to raid into Scotland 'as may annoy the King of Scots'.

The tradition of Henry VIII's involvement in the lynching at Carlenrig was later employed as shaky evidence to back the assertion that Johnnie Armstrong's demise was all the more unjust because he was some sort of rough and ready patriot who raided only in England and never so much as harmed a hair on any Scotsman's head. Simply not true.

Significantly, Sim the Laird, Johnnie's elder brother, was still at large and still active. If James V had hoped to inhibit the Armstrongs, he failed. More worrying for the Scots king was the escalation in the nature of cross-border raiding in the 1530s. The Douglas Earl of Angus, leader of the pro-English party in Scotland, had fled when James began his personal rule. In 1532 he was in Berwick mustering a large raiding party. In the October of that year, they rode into the eastern Borders with fire and sword. This was evidently in retaliation for a previous Scottish raid which had penetrated as far as Wooler. In the familiar sequence of hit and counter hit, the Earl of Northumberland also led 1500 riders into Teviotdale. The Scott stronghold of Branxholm, near Hawick, was burned and much plunder taken. Like the tower and dozens of farm steadings, deep resentment smouldered in the Borders. When it came, the retaliation was stunning, and on a new and extraordinary scale.

Buccleuch sought and received support from both the Cessford and Ferniehurst Kerrs. Together they mustered what amounted to a small invasion force of 3,000 riders. With no need for or possibility of stealth and concealment, Buccleuch led his huge raiding party over the Cheviots and down into Northumberland. Establishing themselves at a central location, the identity of which unfortunate village is uncertain, the reivers proceeded on a plan for systematic looting. Forces of two or three hundred detached themselves to attack and pillage the surrounding towns and returned to their base to pile up their gains. Despite local resistance, the Buccleuch raid was so imposing that when the area had been exhausted, his riders could return northwards without fear of serious attack. There were simply too many of them.

This pattern, the Big Raid, repeated in the following decade. It became a way of prosecuting an undeclared war between Henry VIII and James V, and the reivers were content to exploit the situation for their own reasons. Fuelled simultaneously by the inherited hurts of long-standing family rivalries and the turns of international politics, the Big Raids did immense and lasting damage. The older habit of running small forays with dozens or scores of riders was frightening enough, particularly during periods of special intensity, but when thousands of soldiers descended on a valley or a wider area, they stripped it like locusts and often destroyed its ancient fabric.

Royal prompting was unmistakable – and unwise for anyone to ignore. When King Henry wrote to his warden, Sir William Eure, requiring him 'to let slip as many under his rule as should do the Scots three hurts for one', he let them slip across the border in force and regularly.

BOOKS AND BORDER BOOKMEN

The occupation of southern Scotland by English troops had an unexpected and initially non-violent effect. Protestant literature spread around the countryside, and although it was forced underground by the alliance with catholic France, its circulation helped to turn people towards the reformed religion. A new printing industry had taken root in Edinburgh. Walter Chepman and Andrew Millar, both originally Borderers from Selkirk, had set up the first printing press in the Cowgate in Edinburgh. Dating to around 1508, Scotland's oldest surviving books were made by them. They are very small, only 15 centimetres tall, varying in length from 8 to 48 pages. Mostly poetry, and some prose, they appear to have been popular. Millar was a bookseller and Chepman a merchant, both well suited to making a business out of publishing, and they laid a fertile ground for the mushrooming of religious literature as the sixteenth-century Reformation gathered momentum.

By 1534 a truce temporarily halted the alternating cycle of big raids. The English king needed relief on his northern frontier. Henry VIII's continuing inability to sire a male heir to sustain the Tudor dynasty began to drive all his policy. While James V was busy hanging Johnnie Armstrong at Carlenrig, Henry had called what became known as the Reformation Parliament. Because the Pope would not grant a divorce from Catherine of Aragon (inconveniently, she was the aunt of the Emperor Charles V, the most powerful catholic prince in Europe) and allow the fertile Anne Boleyn into his bed, the king was preparing to change the church in England into the Church of England. And to kill anyone who stood in his way. The likelihood that Henry himself was the problem, probably becoming infertile as a consequence of bouts of syphilis, never crossed the mind of this most ruthless of monarchs.

In a series of parliamentary acts the church was disconnected completely from Rome and the Pope. As Henry himself was confirmed as the head of the new Church of England, all its revenues, appointments and properties came into direct royal ownership. Doctrinally there were few changes and worship carried on much as it had always done.

To retain the vital support of his aristocracy throughout all these upheavals, Henry and his brilliant Chancellor, Thomas Cromwell, devised a simple strategy. All of England's monasteries were to be dissolved – allegedly because they were nothing but nests of corruption – their monks and nuns expelled and their vast landed wealth become the property of the crown or sold at knock-down prices to the nobility. The strategy worked well and as England's ancient network of social and educational welfare was swept away, thousands of minor landowners became major ones – and also loyal supporters of good King Harry.

Except in the north. Rebellion stirred – but not very violently. In a strangely pious and passive atmosphere, the rising known as the Pilgrimage of Grace gathered momentum. Many were appalled that a vital part of Holy Mother Church was being summarily and sometimes brutally dismantled – and at dizzying speed. Drawing recruits from Carlisle, Cumberland and Northumberland, as well as Yorkshire and Lancashire, and marching under the banner of the Five Wounds of Christ, more than 40,000 pilgrims were led south by Sir Robert Aske. Henry VIII and Cromwell were terrified. The Duke of Norfolk was packed off to Doncaster to parley with Aske and told to concede whatever he wanted, except for the restoration of monastic lands. He did. The pilgrims immediately tore off their badges of the Five Wounds, rejoiced that the king had seen the light and rejected evil counsel, dispersed and rode home to the warmth of their winter hearths.

A year later Henry VIII repudiated all that Norfolk had agreed to, executed Sir Robert Aske and the ringleaders of the pilgrimage and set up the Council of the North. This was an extended arm of the ever-centralising government based in Tudor London and designed to deal with the unruly, disloyal and half-savage north. The pilgrimage had persuaded the royal administration to appoint March Wardens from anywhere except the Borders. Locals were not to be trusted or raised up too high and made powerful. Ignorance on the part of incomers was to be compensated for by more even-handedness and for the rest of the sixteenth century many of the English wardens were often highly competent, professional royal officers from the south.

The north almost certainly retained another suspect loyalty – to the doctrines of the catholic church, whatever the structural changes forced through by Cromwell and his king. Protestantism tended to thrive in the towns and in London, while the more conservative rural areas clung longer to the old faith. In the remote valleys of the southern ranges of the Cheviots such piety as there was (or was possible) remained predominantly Roman Catholic for generations. On the northern side of the frontier famous Scottish reiver surnames also stayed loyal. In Dumfriesshire the Maxwells kept their catholicism into the early seventeenth century, refusing to expel the Abbot of Sweetheart Abbey until 1607, long after Scotland's reformation had triumphed. The Kerrs of Ferniehurst also took some time to convert, but when the monastic houses of Scotland were also dissolved, they grabbed their share when the family came into possession of the abbey at Newbattle, near Dalkeith. Since the progressive emancipation of catholicism began in the early nineteenth century, other Border families have reconverted.

James V had matrimonial difficulties of his own, and when he married Mary of Lorraine, a French princess, Henry VIII was uncomfortable with the match. He himself had made overtures but after the execution of Anne Boleyn for the crime of giving birth to a little girl, few eligible aristocratic European women could have failed to notice the English king's high turnover of wives. Alliance between Scotland and France was also troubling, and diplomatic approaches were made. Would James of Scotland meet his uncle Henry at York?

Could the Scots be persuaded to embrace a similar reformation to England's? James finally agreed to talk. A date was set in 1541.

As was his habit, Henry VIII made an elaborate royal progress to York. Lavish preparations were made for the arrival of his Scottish nephew. And the king waited, and waited. Probably as a result of European diplomatic pressure and certainly influenced by his bishops who were determined to keep intact the hard-won independence of the Scottish church, James was persuaded not to keep the appointment. Humiliated, enraged and determined to use force where words had not even been given the chance to fail, Henry made his plans.

Despite at least two Scottish embassies, both laden with explanations and soothing excuses, there was scarcely a delay. Plenty of pretexts for action offered themselves to the English wardens. Liddesdale riders had attacked Bewcastle and killed seven Fenwicks during the course of the raid, and Scots families had illegally colonised the Debatable Land. The Tynedale and Redesdale riders were encouraged to set about their old allies in Liddesdale – but in a remarkable exchange they refused. Such a foray would only spark a debilitating feud. Instead the Charltons, Milburns and others proposed and carried out a raid on Teviotdale and the Scotts and Kerrs. In turn they retaliated and the familiar cycle began to spin.

DIPLOMATS

Ambassadors had been used by kings and prelates for many centuries, but they had generally returned home after their missions had been completed – or not. As the Tudor and other European states centralised in the sixteenth century, a need for permanent embassies grew. They could send back political, military and commercial intelligence. The growing Tudor civil service was able to process all this material and to act on it. As royal courts settled more or less in a principal or capital city, a diplomatic corps developed. It could sometimes be dangerous work and all sorts of reciprocal immunities and exemptions were devised and agreed. The Pope tried to claim that his nuncios were the most senior ambassadors and that all others should be ranked according to the date of their country's conversion to christianity. This was plainly daft, did not reflect contemporary power politics and squabbles broke out. In the Hague the retinues of the French and Spanish ambassadors confronted each other in the street, each refusing to let the other pass – since that would imply precedence. For a whole day they stood glaring at each other until the city authorities demolished a set of railings to make the street wider and therefore avert 'a diplomatic incident'.

In response to these routine raids, Sir Robert Bowes, the Warden of the English East March and Captain of Norham Castle, began to muster a large force. In August 1542 three thousand riders followed him along the southern bank of the Tweed. They were making for the easy, dry crossing of the border at the Reddenburn. The big raids were about to resume – and with a vengeance.

Hadden Rig lies to the east of Kelso, one of the gently folding ridges which climb out of the Tweed Valley and up towards the Cheviot Hills. It commands wide views to the north and sits astride an old track running south west through good farming country. Sir Robert Bowes thought it a handy base for his big raid. Only a mile or two inside the frontier and less than a day from his castle at Norham, the site had many advantages. Principally, Hadden Rig was an open place, on high ground, difficult to surprise.

Following the pattern of previous big raids, Bowes divided his forces. While a holding garrison camped on the high ground at Hadden Rig, two substantial sorties were despatched to raid in the Tweed Valley around Kelso. This was fertile farming country and decent pickings could be expected. Led by John Heron of Ford, the Redesdale and Tynedale families formed one group and the Berwick and Norham garrisons made up the other.

James V had sent George Gordon, Earl of Huntly, to do what he could; which turned out to be a great deal. Perhaps with local advice, certainly showing real awareness of the situation, he devised a simple plan. Even though it was always a dangerous tactic, the big raids depended for their success on a division of strength and Huntly focused on this. His riders manoeuvred themselves between Bowes' camp up on the rig and the sorties out in open country. And they attacked them as they returned with their loot.

The Earl of Angus had defected to the English at the time, and he later wrote down what he saw. Like the reivers they were, the Tynedale and Redesdale surnames did not hang about. Seeing that Huntly's attack was succeeding, they gathered together what plunder they could manage and cut and ran for the Cheviot Hills immediately to the south of Hadden. But once they had turned to flee, the English reivers were highly vulnerable, and as often happened, more men were killed when the retreat scattered into a rout.

At some point Lord Home arrived with 400 riders behind him and his sudden presence seems to have turned Hadden Rig from a defeat into a debacle. Bowes, his brother Richard and John Heron of Ford were all captured for ransom and several hundred horsemen were killed. Estimate vary – as they always do in war. Hadden was a comforting victory for the Scots, an encouraging example of good, thoughtful tactics winning out over superior numbers. But in truth it was not significant. Henry VIII had determined to invade Scotland in strength and the fell engines of war were rumbling into place. The Borders was about to suffer its most appalling period of devastation, and Scotland its most humiliating defeat in battle.

At York the Duke of Norfolk and his quartermasters made preparations for the muster of a large army. It was early October and very late in the year to be campaigning, but King Harry would have his way – the Scots were to be brought to their knees and humbled. Many of the 20,000 men who made their way to Norfolk's headquarters were mounted and it was an age-old dictum that cavalry only fought when the grass grew. Quartermasters complained immediately that they were critically short of provisions, especially beer. Even so, the English column eventually clattered out of the old Roman city and filed up Dere Street, the north road, the invasion route to Scotland. By 21st October Norfolk's troops had crossed the Tweed fords, and war had once more burst over the Borders.

After his victory at Hadden Rig, the Earl of Huntly's strength had been bolstered by reinforcments but was still no match for the English in open field. Knowing that such a large invading army could not expect to feed itself by foraging, especially in late October, and that it was forced to carry all it needed, Huntly was content to shadow the Duke of Norfolk's advance. If he could restrict their efforts to find fodder and food, then it could only be a matter of time before the English were forced to withdraw.

Before that day came, though, Norfolk's soldiers were busy. They left a trail of smoke-blackened devastation along the Scottish bank of the lower Tweed. Paxton, Ednam, Stichil, Nenthorn, Smailholm, Roxburgh, Kelso and Kelso Abbey were all ransacked and burnt. The invaders crossed the river, possibly rebuilding Roxburgh bridge (one of the stone piers is still visible) and then fording the Teviot just west of Kelso. The villages of Sprouston, Redden and Hadden were all fired. No attempt was made to control the countryside by anything other than brute force: what Henry VIII intended was systematic destruction. This was a punitive raid to teach the king of Scotland a lesson – but as usual it was Borderers who were forced to learn it.

HIRSELS HEFTED

Many modern Britons have an ignorant eye for farm animals. To us they all look the same, or at least very similar. Border Reivers and Border hill farmers of the twenty-first century knew and know their beasts well, and understand their habits. A hirsel, or small flock of sheep, become hefted to a hillside. In other words they become attached to a particular patch of pasture and do not often stray from it. Observant shepherds understand this mysterious process. Ewes create the heft. Before weaning, lambs stay very close to their mothers and even afterwards they graze with her on the same patches amongst the heather and bracken, often enlarging them. Eventually several generations, essentially families of sheep, have learned to crop a particular area of hillside. They will likely have scraped bields, places where the sheep can shelter from the worst of the winter weather, and where a good shepherd will find them in the deepest snow. Robert Elliot of Carewoodrig used to farm his Galloway cattle and sheep on the back of a pony. It could take him to places inaccessible for a quad bike and could sometimes help the dogs sniff out buried sheep. When Robert brought his pony into its stable after the last gather in 2005, an immense tradition was at last broken.

By the time Norfolk's 20,000 pitched camp at Fairnington, south of St Boswell's, not far from the line of Dere Street, supplies had dwindled alarmingly. If the army retreated to Berwick, the English captains argued, they could be supplied by sea and still sally out into Scottish territory to inflict more damage. If they remained in the Borders countryside, haunted by Huntly and with winter closing in, they could find themselves dangerously weakened. The duke took their advice and after only eight days on Scottish soil, and a swathe of terrible destruction, his soldiers marched downriver to pitch camp under Berwick's walls.

Meanwhile James V had been busy assembling an army. The muster was called to Fala Moor in Midlothian, on Dere Street. Recent historians have reckoned that only 15,000 to 20,000 soldiers came, less than half the number who marched to Flodden 30 years before. That dark memory was still fresh. And when news of Norfolk's retreat to Berwick reached Fala, there were widespread desertions. Perhaps a third of the army melted away.

James V had been a virtual prisoner of the Douglases for much of his young life and his consequent mistrust of the Scottish nobility had led to a general atmosphere of simmering dislike and disunity. Matters were not eased by the king's habit of promoting lesser lairds (who depended absolutely on his patronage) to high office and ignoring those powerful families who believed they had a traditional right to be involved in government. In November 1542 many magnates found excuses for staying at home – some may even have welcomed an English invasion which might remove a troublesome king – and when the royal host moved south to climb up Soutra Hill, it may have numbered only 12,000 to 14,000.

The usual strategy was adopted. With the main English strength lying in the east at Berwick, the Scots would avoid direct confrontation and attack in the west. Given the clear reluctance of the nobility and their captains, this traditional manoeuvre may have been all that was politically possible. Morale was not improved when James V became too ill to lead his army, and his household made its way to Lochmaben Castle to wait upon events. Lord Maxwell was Warden of the Scottish West March, and in the absence of the king, he may have assumed that command of the army would be his. He assumed wrong.

As the Scots threaded their way through the Southern Uplands, English scouts hurried down to Carlisle. The warden, Sir Thomas Wharton, knew how badly outnumbered he would be. A more timid man might have shut himself up inside Carlisle Castle and let North Cumbria burn around him. Others had done exactly that. But when he heard of the Scots' advance, Wharton gave orders to fire the beacons. They should blaze over the hilltops and summon 3,000 riders to their warden, far too few to face the Scots but enough to do some damage. Wharton could not possibly have imagined how much damage.

The invading army had formed itself into two battles or battalions, one based in Langholm, the other in Mortonkirk. They moved quickly south towards the border and in the gathering dusk of 23rd November, their skirmishers attacked the Debatable Land, firing its farm buildings and scattering those Grahams who had been bold enough to stay behind.

With orders to send on latecomers as fast as they could ride, Sir Thomas Wharton galloped north out of Carlisle with only two or three thousand horsemen at his back. He knew that the Scots would have to cross the Esk fords just below Arthuret (now Longtown) and pick a careful way along the edges of the great Solway Moss, a treacherous, shifting stretch of waterland at the mouth of the firth. With his captains, Wharton made for Arthuret Church and the heights above the sacred well of St Michael. From there he could see the sky lit red by the burning farmsteads of the Debatable Land, and in the grey hours of the early morning of 24th November the English riders watched the Scots battallions begin to splash across the Esk and make their way through the moss. If it had been a still October morning, Wharton would have heard men shouting and complaining their way through the chill water. Even though he was vastly outnumbered and his small force incomplete, Wharton saw that this was his moment.

As the Scots floundered across the river, full of winter rain, Sir William Musgrave charged down from Arthuret Heights and tore into the ragged flank of the army. The difficult fords and the moss restricted the ground and did not allow soldiers to turn in formation to face Musgrave's 'prickers'. The tactics of hitting and running, attacking ferociously and then retreating before the Scots could organise themselves began to spread panic. How many were they? Was an English force waiting up on the heights? And then panic was turned into pandemonium by a moment of signal idiocy from the absent James V.

Twenty miles to the north in Lochmaben Castle the king had a rush of blood to the head – an episode all too typical of the headstrong Stewart dynasty. Instead of appointing Lord Maxwell, an experienced Borderer able to demand loyalty, he sent a commission to Oliver Sinclair to take command of the army. Described as 'the king's minion', he had been born into the Sinclair family which held the wealthy earldom of Orkney, but more to the point he was good-looking and the king's favourite. 'Minion' is an odd description and it appears in several accounts of the battle. It did not carry the meaning of 'underling' or 'slave' in the sixteenth century. The word derived from the French 'mignon' and it meant 'sweet' or 'dainty'. Perhaps its repetition was a faint reference to the nature of Oliver Sinclair's relationship with the king, certainly it was not a set of characteristics likely to appeal to a force of hard-bitten soldiers on the point of invading England and who found themselves sore beset by determined Border horsemen. A sweet and dainty general? Perhaps not.

When Sinclair's commission arrived, he was raised up 'on pikes' so that all his captains and the men near him could recognise their new commander. The reaction was immediate. It is said that 'a general murmur and breach of all order ensued'. Little imagination is needed to guess what soldiers had to say when they saw Oliver attempt to take command. There almost certainly followed substantial desertion as the news of James V's madness spread like wildfire. The Scottish army began to implode.

All the while Musgrave's horsemen were attacking and wheeling away – and eventually breaking up the Scottish ranks and getting in amongst them, as reivers loved to do. Extraordinary scenes began to unfold. Most of those in the rear who had not crossed the Esk turned and fled north, others began to surrender en masse. Sometimes three or four Scots would throw down their weapons and surrender to one English rider. The army simply lost all its confidence. No one wanted to die fighting for Oliver Sinclair (including Oliver Sinclair – he surrendered like the others) or the royal idiot who had appointed him. Many were trapped at the Esk fords and did not lift a hand to resist. The list of aristocratic prisoners who would fetch good ransoms is long, and very eloquent about the battle which had become a debacle in moments. Opposite the names of Scottish earls and lairds are their captors, those who could claim the ransoms. In the main these were ordinary English borderers such as Wat's Willie Graham, George Pott, Willie Storey, and Oliver Sinclair found himself the prisoner of one Willie Bell. No doubt they were both as startled as each other.

Sir Thomas Wharton must have been astounded. As he watched from Arthuret Heights and marvelled at how easily the Scots army came apart, he had never seen classic reiver tactics succeed so brilliantly – and against a force many times larger. He did not have the manpower to pursue the Scots who were fleeing north. They fell prey to Scottish reivers, many of them glad of the chance to repay the king for his policy of vigorous suppression. James V joined his retreating remnant, and finally took to his bed in Linlithgow Palace a few days later. He died at the age of only 30, possibly of shame. Willie Bell, Willie Storey and their friends were no doubt amazed to find themselves heroes, and no doubt better pleased to discover that Henry VIII had promised them all 'ready money' for their unexpected prisoners.

ARTHURET

Fords were often the sites of important battles. When an army was forced to cross a substantial river, it immediately found itself in a weak position, its strength temporarily divided in three: a vanguard having crossed, those behind crossing, and those waiting to cross. Fords were predictable, places where generals were forced by nature to go. Solway Moss was not the first battle to be fought at the Esk fords near Longtown in Cumbria. In 573 the pagan king of Carlisle, Gwenddolau, fought the Christian kings of York at Arderydd, or Arthuret, the ancient name for Longtown and still the name of its parish. It is thought that the historical King Arthur fought battles in the north, some of them at fords in north Northumberland, on the River Glen near Wooler and the Rede, near the top of Redesdale. Like the men who won so spectacularly at Solway Moss, it is likely that he and his warband fought on horseback using similar equipment and similar tactics.

The dismal defeat at Solway Moss turned out to be little more than a prelude to even more misery for the Borders. English military capability was untouched by the battle. The ambassador from the court of the Emperor Charles V reckoned that only 700 or 800 of Wharton's riders had actually engaged with the Scots, and of those a mere seven were killed. A shameful statistic, something which helped persuade James V to turn his face to the wall.

With the king's death, the Stewart succession became shaky. The baby who would become Mary, Queen of Scots, was only a week old. Henry VIII moved quickly to take advantage of the uncertainty and betroth the infant to his son, Prince Edward, and a political wrangle began – and ended in the middle of 1543 with the Scots' withdrawal from the match and the resumption of the alliance with France. At one point in the negotiations the English considered a radical approach. They offered the hand of Princess Elizabeth to the son of the Regent of Scotland, the Earl of Arran. The proposed deal was cut and dried. If Arran agreed, he would be made King of Scotland 'beyond the Firth', meaning the Forth–Clyde line. It was an old judgement. After the Agricolan invasions of AD 79, Roman historians believed that if a conquest had to be undertaken at all then southern and central Scotland were the only bits worth having, the north being too wild, infertile and hostile. Despite Arran having royal lineage (he was the grandson of Mary, the sister of James III), the negotiations never moved past speculative talk. But it is worth a moment's pause to reflect on what might have happened if they had. Princess Elizabeth eventually became Queen Bess of Merrie England – and James Hamilton might have become King of Great Britain more than 50 years before James VI did.

Dynastic union was more than an undercurrent. The 1540s saw an aggressive English attempt to force it through in a series of episodes Walter Scott called 'the rough wooing'.

In the west Sir Thomas Wharton was busy extending his influence over much of Dumfriesshire. He encouraged Scottish surnames into feuds with each other. Armstrongs attacked Scotts and Kerrs while Elliots and Nixons raided in the countryside around Jedburgh. The policy was both simple and clever. Wharton supported the lesser surnames in their attacks on the greater, dangling the promise of the extensive lands of the Scotts, Kerrs and Humes as a reward for the likes of the Turnbulls, Pringles, Rutherfords and others. That way powerful and substantial support for the regency from the great Border families would be eroded without any obvious interference from the English king or any of his soldiers.

Wharton and his agents also furthered English policy in southern Scotland by non-violent means. Hundreds of minor lairds and aristocrats took 'assurance of the King of England'. In effect, they took his money. In return for an oath of allegiance to Henry VIII many Borderers were paid what amounted to wages or a pension from the London exchequer. Some were forced into this arrangement by their feudal superior or their heidsmen and as time went on it became more and more sophisticated. If an assured Scot found himself attacked or robbed by a neighbour who was not a fellow pensioner, or by the Edinburgh government, or even in some accidental way by English action, then he could make something very like an insurance claim. The network spread wide: from Berwickshire and the lower Tweed up to East Lothian and Fife. Considering the frequency and ferocity of English incursion into the Border 'taking assurance of the King of England' must have seemed no more than common sense.

In May 1544 the heavy hand of Henry VIII reached into Scotland once more with the first of the big raids of 'the rough wooing'. Two hundred ships appeared in the Firth of Forth carrying the Earl of Hertford's army and they attacked the port of Leith. Two ships and a valuable store of grain were captured but the army, more than 10,000 strong, failed to breach Edinburgh's city walls and had to content themselves with the looting of Holyrood Palace and the abbey. When the Provost of Edinburgh attempted to negotiate with Hertford, he was met with little more than invective, a speech which ended with a statement of the simple purpose of the expedition. The Earl declared: 'he was sent thither by the King's Highness to take vengeance of their detestable falsehood' (the rejection of the marriage treaty between the infant Mary Queen of Scots and Prince Edward of England), 'to declare and show the force of his Highness' sword to all such as should make any resistence unto his Grace's power'.

The English army turned south from Edinburgh and found the small villages and farmsteads of the Borders much easier prey. When the king commissioned Hertford, his instructions were indeed unequivocal: the Tweed Basin was to be 'tormented and occupied'. Kelso was considered as a base for operations and the immense strength of Roxburgh Castle noted. The summer of 1544 saw a nightmare come to haunt the Borders. The early sixteenth-century history of the area is littered with the language of war and misery, and it is difficult to attach adjectives which a carry sufficient sense of how awful life must have been for the mass of ordinary people. Suffice to say that in a place which had already suffered dreadfully, the worst came that year. As Hertford's men burned, killed, raped and looted, Sir Ralph Eure's troopers rode over the Carter Bar, descended on Jedburgh and burned it. It was the largest town in the Tweed Valley, save Berwick. Here is the report sent by the Earl of Surrey to Henry VIII:

> The town is so completely burned that no garrison, or anyone else, can be lodged there, until it is rebuilt . . . The town was much larger than I thought it was, for there are twice as many houses in it as there are in Berwick, and well built, with many honest and fair houses, sufficient to have lodged a garrison of a thousand horsemen. And there are six good towers there. But the town and the towers are completely destroyed, burned and thrown down.

In the same letter Surrey comments on the Borderers he fought:

> I assure your Grace that I found the Scots, this time, the boldest men, and the hottest that I ever saw in any nation. Throughout the expedition, upon all parts of the army, they continually skirmished.

I never saw the like. If they might assemble 11,000 men like that, instead of only 1,500 or 2,000, it would be a hard encounter to meet them.

The English had also come to visit hellish destruction on even the smallest of places. Ever thorough, Hertford's clerks listed every place on the trail of tears and sent it back to London to show how busy they had been. Exactly 192 towns, villages, farmsteads, towers and bastle houses were burned and razed. At Lessudden (the old name for St Boswell's east end) there existed a cluster of 16 bastle houses making the village more like an armed camp of blockhouses. All were cast down. In his excellent footnotes the historian, George Ridpath, adds to this:

> Scots slain four hundred; prisoners taken eight hundred and sixteen; nolt [cattle], ten thousand three hundred and eighty six; sheep, twelve thousand four hundred and ninety two; nags and gelding, two thousand, two hundred and ninety six; goats, two hundred; bolls of corn [a boll was 54 litres], eight hundred and fifty; insight gear [furniture] etc, in indefinite quantity.

Such lists are the litany of rape, the rape of a whole community and countryside. The effect of it all can only be imagined, or at best inferred. The record-keepers of Hertford and his fellow captains show no interest in the fate of those burned out of their houses, unless they were valuable aristocrats. These are no more than the habits of mind of the times. Scots raiding in Northumberland or Cumberland would have behaved no differently. As ever, ordinary people are left to suffer in historical silence. No doubt most fled before the gathering storm, but for a population of around 45,000, where was there to flee to? The summer shielings certainly but Hertford had 10,000 at his command and Eure and others rode with more. There can have been few hiding places – and little respite. The summer of 1544 probably saw only a meagre harvest, anything allowed to ripen being commandeered by English quartermasters.

The wealthy were also brought to the point of destitution. Lord Hume had been robbed so often and so thoroughly that he literally 'had no goods left undestroyed to furnish his castle'. As heidsman of major Border surname, he was not part of the English scheme of assurance and so the Scottish parliament granted him £300 in 1545. Henry VIII desired to torment the Borders, and there is no doubt that he did.

OLD BUITTLE TOWER

Near Dalbeattie, in Dumfries and Galloway, Jeffrey and Janet Burn live at Old Buittle Tower. At weekends they and their friends recreate the way of life of Border Reivers, and it is wonderfully well done. The tower itself has been sensitively restored, there is a blacksmith's forge, a medieval hall and a kitchen. But best of all are the ponies. The Galloway Nag being extinct, Jeffrey Burn has found its nearest relative in the fell ponies which live happily in his stable barn. In costume and with precisely remade sixteenth-century saddles and tack, Burn and his 'Borderers' group ride reiver-style for the visitors who gather in the paddock opposite the tower. And they are very accomplished horsemen able to control their ponies in the same way as the reivers did in the sixteenth century. The saddles are particularly interesting. With high cantles and pommels, they wedge a rider in and make impossible to rise in a conventional trotting style. But the ponies are so well schooled, strong, small and sensitive that the technique of riding with one or no hands is soon picked up, even by a novice. Simply laying the reins on a pony's neck will cause it to turn – immediately. Buittle Tower is fascinating – and the website with all the details of activities is easy to find.

As autumn began to turn to winter, it appears that the Earl of Hertford and many of his men returned south. But the raiding continued along the border. Winter was after all the traditional season amongst local families. Sir Thomas Wharton and Lord Dacre were joined by the assured Scots, the Earls of Lennox and Glencairn, in an attack on Dumfries. Once the town had been fired, the Nith and Annan valleys were looted and harried.

Over on the east coast, at Coldingham, there was fighting around the ancient church, once a possession of the Bishop of Durham. It had been desecrated and garrisoned by invaders. Allied to the English at Hadden Rig, the Earl of Angus had rejoined the Scottish cause and he fought bravely. It was said that Angus had been disgusted by the destruction of his family's tombs at Melrose Abbey and English attacks on his lands, but it may also have been the relentless destruction which persuaded Archibald Douglas to change sides. How would a wasteland benefit him and his family – especially when he owned a great deal of property in its midst? There seemed to be no long-term plan – only fire and sword.

In February 1545 Sir Ralph Eure and Sir Brian Laiton attacked Melrose and its abbey with 5,000 men. The town lay at the centre of Douglas country and the abbey was the last resting-place of Robert the Bruce's heart. Angus reacted quickly but rode out of Edinburgh with only 300 and was unable even to skirmish with the English. Instead he retreated to the higher ground south-west of the Eildon Hills and waited for reinforcements. After Walter Scott of Buccleuch and Norman Leslie, the Master of Rothes in Fife, had brought substantial companies of riders to join him, Angus and his allies laid their plans.

Having looted Melrose, Sir Ralph Eure and Sir Brian Laiton led their 5,000 south towards Jedburgh, down the old straight road, Dere Street. Using all his local knowledge and probably encouraged by Buccleuch to remember his reiver tactics, Angus overtook the plunder-laden English by riding around them. He took care to go quietly, avoiding any contact with the enemy. At Lilliardsedge, about a mile north of the village of Ancrum, he found good ground to set an ambush. No doubt believing that the sheer size of the army was sufficient protection, and believing that Angus had few riders at his back, Eure and Laiton failed to scout their route properly. At a place where the ground was boggy and treacherous on both sides of Dere Street (especially in winter), the Scots hid themselves and waited.

To bait the trap, Angus stationed a small force on the road, probably near where the modern A68 breasts a rise and reveals a stunning view of the Eildons and the middle Tweed Valley, somewhere they could be easily seen. When the English vanguard caught sight of what they assumed was a small party of riders, they gave chase – and were pulled into the ambush. When the Scots erupted from their cover and attacked on three sides, it became quickly clear that in the narrow corridor between the treacherous ground numbers would no longer count. The Borderers who had suffered in the terrible summer of 1544 fought like furies, spitting vengeance at those who had burned their homes, killed their relatives and stolen their cattle. Those Scots in the English ranks (either assured like the Olivers, Rutherfords, Nixons or Crosiers or merely mercenaries) soon saw which way the battle was moving and they tore off their badges of the cross of St George and turned on their comrades. Realising that they could expect no mercy, Eure and Laiton fought to the death, finally falling in the ruck of slaughter at the centre of the battle. Much blood flowed on Ancrum Moor as vengeance was taken.

Much was made of the Scots' victory, not only in Edinburgh but also amongst their allies in France. But in truth it did not represent more than a temporary reverse. Henry VIII had more rough wooing to do and Borderers were about to suffer second summer of terrible torment.

Muster points often have a long history. They have to be places known to all those called to arms, and for centuries prehistoric standing stones, some dating back to 3,000 BC, were often nominated. In the west march, reiving bands and national armies used the Clochmabenstane to rally. It is ancient and stands at the northern terminal of the Solway fords. In the east, the standing stone known as 'the King's Stone', lies not far from the battlefield at Flodden. It was where the Earl of Hertford's raiding army mustered in early September 1545, camping on the flat ground of Crookham Moor in north Northumberland. This time there was a plan, rudimentary, but something more thoughtful than more fire and more sword. There would be an attempt to hold what was overrun. Destruction would continue, certainly, but 1545 would see the establishment of a network of fortresses with garrisons to control the countryside around them. The Borders would become an English pale, a similar arrangement to what had been set up around Dublin by King Henry VII.

Hertford had 12,000 men. Numbers were swollen by mercenaries, some of them exotic like the Spanish arquebusiers, Germans, Frenchmen, Italians, even Greeks. Marching alongside this cosmopolitan force were troops of what the English and Scots considered semi-savages, the Irish 'kernes'. Lightly armed foot soldiers, these men had acquired a fearsome reputation during the Tudor wars in Ireland. With their long hair, their shrill Gaelic war cries and careless courage, the kernes probably terrified many who gathered by the old standing stone at Crookham Moor.

The English army made straight for Kelso – and immediately, and surprisingly met resistance. Heroic, if ill-advised, around a hundred men, including twelve monks, had barricaded themselves into the abbey church. Hertford had the York Herald demand surrender, but when they shouted out of the upper windows that they would not, he brought forward the Spanish arquebusiers. Fixing their blunderbuss-like guns onto tripods, probably just out of range of arrows and missiles, they took careful aim at the fabric of the old church. The intended effect may have been to frighten the defenders into quick submission with these loud, fiery and new-fangled weapons of war. When it failed, the English rolled up their cannon and began to pound and breach the walls. The bombardment drove the defenders into one of the towers of the abbey's double crossing. And as night fell, they had managed to hold on against heavy odds.

KERNES

In the sixteenth century those wishing to become professional soldiers had few opportunities in Tudor England. There was no standing army and only three permanent garrisons (this reduced to two when Calais fell in 1558). Two of these were in the Borders, at Carlisle and Berwick. These towns were defended by soldiers who were paid royal employees, and the English March Wardens often had professional military ambitions. In Celtic Britain the tradition of soldiering for pay was much better developed. In addition to the employment of Gallowglasses, Irish kings used foot soldiers known as 'kernes'. Some companies migrated to mainland Britain where they were greatly feared as savage, almost feral, uncontrolled fighters. They could work themselves up into what was known as a 'rage-fit' before an attack. Europe came to know the Irish kernes in the early seventeenth century when many were forcibly transported to fight in the armies of Gustavus Adolphus in the Thirty Years War. When the plantations began in the north of Ireland, 'wood kernes' or forest bandits became the stuff of nightmares – the wild men of the woods emerging from the shadows to attack the hated new settlements.

Whoever set pickets around the abbey will have heard a sharp word the following morning. A dozen defenders had let down ropes from the tower and slid down into the darkness, somehow finding their way through the English camp to freedom. When daylight came, the bombardment resumed and within hours, the English had broken into Kelso Abbey and killed those left behind.

Perhaps to discourage any more resistance, or to ram home very publicly and obviously his destructive mission once more, Hertford gave orders that the beautiful, cathedral-like church and the monastic precinct around it was to be destroyed. Engineers undermined the walls (as at many medieval monasteries, the foundations were often very shallow) so that much of the nave and the east end with the crossing over the altar was tumbled to the ground. Lead was stripped off the roof and 'all was overthrown'. It took a week for the bulk of the monastic buildings to be levelled, Hertford going to considerable trouble to destroy most of a famous landmark which had stood for centuries. None of the other three Border abbeys suffered as badly as Kelso did.

In 1545 the raider-army appears to have singled out churches. Melrose, Dryburgh and Jedburgh were also wrecked, as were the friaries at Roxburgh and Jedburgh. Once again a detailed list of destruction was compiled: 16 castles, towers and piles (large houses), 5 market towns, 243 villages, 13 mills and 3 hospitals (often used by pilgrims). It must have been heart-breaking to see the bone and sinew of Border life cut away so cruelly. The abbeys and churches had supplied what passed for social services and education in the sixteenth century, the market towns were central to the local economy and many of the 243 villages must have been burned for the second time within a twelvemonth. When the second half of the sixteenth century saw a spiralling rise in reiving – is it any wonder, given the pounding taken by Borderers in the first half?

Sir Robert Bowes, defeated and captured at Hadden Rig, left a very rare comment on the effect of the Hertford Raids on ordinary people. As he rode along Border tracks, he saw that there was no one left to fight, 'save only women, children and impotent creatures, who, nevertheless by night times and holidays work as they may to manure the ground and sow corn . . . so wretchedly can they live and endure the pain that no Englishman can suffer the like'. They had no choice, nowhere else to go.

The year 1546 seemed like a respite. No large-scale incursion loomed from the south, and while English-sponsored raiding flickered on, particularly in the west march where Sir Thomas Wharton continued to be very active, Border horizons saw few plumes of black smoke rising in the summer skies. People crept back to their villages and farms, and ever watchful, tried to grow food and repair their blackened and charred houses.

Some historians have reckoned that the number of Scots taken into assurance rose markedly that year, perhaps as high as 7,000. This seems unlikely, certainly very expensive, but if the total number in English pay, be it in kind or in cash, is counted, then it may be accurate enough. Wharton had hundreds of Scottish reivers riding under his banner, the Armstrongs were especial allies, avid to pay off old scores while in English service. But it could be a dangerous stratagem. As at Ancrum Moor, Border horsemen in it only for the money could change sides in a moment. In early 1548 Sir Thomas led a large Anglo-Scottish force up Nithsdale as far as Drumlanrig deep into Douglas country. His son, Thomas Wharton, rode with him and left a record of what happened. The Earl of Angus ambushed the vanguard and then attacked the main force: 'when the assured Scots with my father perceived the enemy coming, they took or laid hands on any Englishmen in my lord's company. I cannot tell whether my father or what others are taken or slain, but few or none came away'. In fact Sir Thomas did escape and regained the safety of his castle at Carlisle.

RUTTER

James V was curious about his kingdom. In 1540 his fleet sailed right around the Scottish coast, from the Firth of Forth to the Firth of Clyde. Piloted by Alexander Lyndsay, the expedition had scientific as well as political aims. The king not only wanted to see the troublesome Western Isles for himself and exact obedience from the Highland chiefs, he also wanted to collect the materials needed to make an accurate map of the coastline, all of the headlands, islands and inlets. Lyndsay's chart subsequently fell into the hands of English sailors who passed its details on to a French mapmaker, Nicholas de Nicholay. He produced the first recognisable, proportionate and reliable outline of Scotland – and with copies of his map, he accompanied the French fleet which sailed to besiege St Andrews Castle after the murder of Cardinal Beaton in 1546. The map is now known as 'the Nicholay Rutter' after its maker and a corruption of the French word 'routier', meaning 'way finder'. It was part of an 86-page handbook of directions for sailors, the sort of thing skippers used before the era of accurate instruments. Only a dozen copies of the Nicholay Rutter survive and they fetch high prices at auction.

Over the winter of 1546/7 King Henry VIII's health began to fail. He had been an active, dynamic ruler for nearly 40 years. On 28th January 1547, Henry died, leaving his ten-year-old son as Edward

VI. Scots – and none more than Border Scots – must have prayed for a change of royal policy. But after a palace coup had left the Seymour family in the ascendant, there was to be none. Hertford became Duke of Somerset and 'Lord Protector of the Kingdom and Governor of the King's Person'. And all powerful, and determined to bring Scotland and the Borders within his control.

The wording of the oath of assurance grew more elaborate. Those who accepted an English pension were made aware of exactly what they were getting into. They swore 'to serve the King of England, Edward VI, renounce the Bishop of Rome, do all in their power to advance the king's marriage to the Queen of Scotland, take part with all who served the king against his enemies, not assist the said enemies, and obey the Lord Protector, lord lieutenants and Wardens'.

However, the policy of assurance was beginning to crumble. The unrelenting destruction of the big raids had alienated many who had to live amongst their consequences and it began to drive some into the welcoming arms of the French. Aiming to keep Scotland in a catholic Europe and ever angling for a dynastic marriage for their king with the young Mary, Queen of Scots, the French began to pour men and money into Scotland, though not soon enough to save the south from one last visit from its nemesis, Edward Seymour, the new Duke of Somerset.

Preparations for war were put in hand and all summer long provisions laid in and plans made. The Scots waited. A chain of warning beacons was set up on the coastal high points in the east, between St Abb's Head, North Berwick Law, Arthur's Seat, Edinburgh Castle and Binning Crag, above Linlithgow Palace. Lookouts expected to see the sails of an English fleet coasting up from the south. Post horses were stationed in the event that the invasion force was first seen further inland.

Somerset came by both routes. At the end of August 1547, 18,000 troops tramped up the north road to Berwick, and they were shadowed by a fleet of 34 warships, 30 transports with supplies and a single oar-driven galley. The English had come in force – and this time to do more than burn and kill. If a pale was to be created, then strongpoints and garrisons were needed to hold it. At Eyemouth Somerset ordered the construction of a fort at the harbour mouth, and the castle at Dunglass, wisely surrendered by Matthew Hume, was demolished.

Meanwhile the Earl of Arran had successfully mustered a much larger army, perhaps 30,000, possibly even more. As the English approached Edinburgh, the Scots moved east to the line of the River Esk, near where it runs into the sea at Musselburgh. Using the line of the river to his advantage, Arran drew up his battle formations behind it, barring the road to the city. And then, as often seems to have happened, the Scots needlessly abandoned a strong position. Partly because the English fleet found it could reach his lines with a bombardment, and partly because he mistakenly believed Somerset had ordered a retreat, Arran allowed his army to cross the river and charge. Poor communications, an impression that the Earl of Huntly was about to desert and the distraction of the Highlanders by the promise of plunder all combined to disorganise the Scottish army. On both land and sea, Somerset's artillery had a murderous effect, and within a very short time, the battle had turned to a rout.

The day after, the English advanced to Leith to seek provisions from their ships. Somerset had planned a march down Dere Street, up and over Soutra and down into Lauderdale and the middle Tweed – far from the sea and the supporting fleet. Home Castle surrendered three days later and it was quickly stripped of most of its stores and garrisoned by Lord Dudley and 200 men.

From there the invaders moved to the site of the old burgh of Roxburgh, near Kelso, and camped on what is now known as Friar's Haugh. Otherwise detailed records make no mention of the ruins of the old town and it seems that by 1547 it was deserted. Somerset had come because he was anxious to exploit the massive mound of Roxburgh's ancient castle. Long and steep-sided, between the rivers Teviot and Tweed and controlling the crossings of both, it was 'as strong a place ever I saw in Scotland'. So enthusiastic was he that Somerset is said to have stripped off and joined the work gangs repairing the walls. The old fortified area on top of the mound is extensive, and the English engineers proposed to reduce the defences substantially. By digging transverse ditches and using the upcast to form broad, mounded banks, they created a square artillery emplacement out of an oblong medieval castle – which had been very vulnerable to bombardment. After the accidental death of James II below its walls in 1460, Roxburgh had been 'doung to the ground'. Now Somerset had made a modern fort out of the ruins and with its guns in place, given it a commanding presence once more. The outline of the Tudor banks and ditches can still be clearly seen amongst the tangle of fallen trees, nettles, brambles and willowherb which now clutter the magnificent ruin.

ROMAN ROXBURGH

At the west end of Roxburgh Castle's impressive mound there are a series of ditches and banks almost, but not entirely, obliterated by modern deep-ploughing. The mound itself also looks somewhat artificial, perhaps a natural eminence at first but then almost certainly enhanced by the back-breaking labour of mattocks and baskets of earth. The most concrete evidence of Roxburgh's great antiquity lies on the opposite bank of the River Teviot, which runs at the northern foot of the castle mound. In a flat field known as the King's Haugh archaeologists have found hundreds of Roman coins. Some are valuable, such as a gold aureus, but most are the small change of the Empire. Bronze radiates, they date to the late fourth century AD, very late in the life of Roman Britain, especially in the north. More clues as to what was happening at Roxburgh lie in old names. The ancient kinglists for the lost Celtic realms of southern Scotland include several men with Roman or Romanised names. Tacitus and Aeternus may have simply been leaders who took their names as a sign of their conversion to christianity (very closely associated with the Empire) or they may have been Roman or, more likely, Romano-British commanders of cavalry units based at Roxburgh. One of these was Paternus Pesrut, a name combining Latin with Old Welsh. It means 'Paternus with the red cloak', perhaps a serving Roman officer. The ancient name for Roxburgh itself (the present one, derived from 'Hroc's burh', dates from the seventh century AD and the Anglian takeover of southern Scotland) is 'Marchidun'. It means ' the Cavalry Fort'.

Somerset's captains followed his energetic example and the fort was finished in only five or six days. All the while local lairds and heidsmen rode to Roxburgh to make their submissions and to swear the oath of assurance. Kerrs, Douglases, Humes and many others promised the Lord Protector their support and loyalty. Sir Ralph Bulmer was appointed constable of the castle, given a garrison of 500, and then the main body of the army dispersed and its general returned to London.

The English Pale was strengthened and extended. To sit astride the main inland road of Dere Street, a fort was built at Lauder, and to keep a grip on East Lothian, Lord Grey moved to fortify Haddington and make it a base of occupation. A large garrison of 2,500 was based in the town.

Diplomatic talk of dynastic and political union echoed back and forth. Sharp-eyed observers in London will have noticed how sickly the young king Edward VI was and, however tuberculosis was diagnosed, it was understood to be ultimately fatal. But that did not necessarily hinder the notion of union – in any arrangement, England would inevitably be the senior partner. Somerset was in the ascendant, presiding over the flow of history, as it must have seemed to him.

The French were forced to respond. A bargain was struck. If the young Mary, Queen of Scots could be sent to France (thus virtually guaranteeing eventual union between the two royal houses), then an expeditionary force would be sent in the opposite direction. In June 1548 Le Sieur D'Esse landed at Leith with 6,000 troops and almost immediately marched to attack the English at Haddington. After some hard pounding, they found they could not breach the walls and were compelled to organise a blockade to starve the garrison into surrender. Relief came with the Earl of Shrewsbury and a large English army. After lifting the blockade, they marched south to the Borders and ravaged Teviotdale, treating those unable to escape with great cruelty. A company of 3,000 German mercenaries behaved savagely. Le Sieur d'Esse attacked when he could. It was said that when the Scots campaigned alongside the French, they bought English and German prisoners from them so that they could torture and kill them.

All of this marching and counter-marching was extremely expensive and draining, and with the departure of the young Scottish queen to France, England and Somerset's dreams of dynastic union were fading fast. The French began to spend huge sums in Scotland. In 1549 £1 million pounds Scots was poured in. Assured Scots replaced English with French gold (sometimes enjoying both simultaneously) and the political tide began to turn decisively.

Trouble flared elsewhere for Somerset. Far to the south on the invisible border between England and Cornwall, rebellion spilled over. The English Reformation under Henry VIII had at first been only political. Doctrinal change came with the Act of Uniformity in 1549 which abolished the wide diversity of religious observance which had been happily tolerated all over England and Wales. The new Book of Common Prayer was to be in English, the beautiful English of Archbishop Thomas Cranmer, and all of the services formerly said and sung in Latin were to be conducted in that English. The Cornish were outraged, and in East Anglia Robert Kett led a well organised insurgency sparked by the new liturgy, as well as a residual resentment at the dissolution of the monasteries. The latter was crushed by the Earl of Northumberland (his army stiffened by the company of German mercenaries who had terrorised the Borders) and he emerged as a serious rival to Somerset. By October, the Duke had been toppled and sent to the Tower of London accused of treason. With his fall, the policy of Henry VIII towards Scotland and the Borders collapsed. The strongholds of the English Pale were taken piecemeal and by 1551 a treaty between England and Scotland had been agreed and signed.

THE REBELLION OF THE PIOUS

As far from the Borders as it is possible to be in mainland Britain, Cornwall unwittingly interceded in Border history – for the better, and twice. In 1497 Henry VII had been voted heavy taxes by parliament so that he invade Scotland: James IV was unwisely harbouring the pretender and imposter, Perkin Warbeck. Suddenly, in the west a rebellion erupted in Cornwall. Led by the charistmatic Michael Joseph, a blacksmith (known by the Cornish name of 'An Gof'), an army raised in Cornwall marched clear across southern England to Blackheath, outside London, where they were mercilessly crushed by King Henry's army. Dragged upside down on a hurdle through the city, An Gof and his comrade, Thomas Flamanck, suffered the awful death of a traitor. In 1549 Cornwall rose again. This time it was to protest at the new reformed church liturgy in English. Archbishop Cranmer and the London government had forgotten something crucial. In the mid sixteenth century most of the Cornish did not speak English, and interspersed in the old Latin mass, priests had spoken and chanted Cornish to their congregations. They complained that the new service was 'like a Christmas game . . . we will have our old service of Mattins, Mass, Evensong and Procession in Latin as it was before. And so we the Cornish men (whereof certain of us understand no English) utterly refuse this new English.' Somerset was ruthless in suppressing the rebellion, his men draping so-called Popish items like rosaries and censers around the necks of priests and then hanging them from their bell towers and spires.

With Somerset's execution in Janury 1552, the period of the Borders' greatest suffering came to a close. Certainly war would crackle along the frontier more than once after that, but nothing like the devastation of the big raids led by Somerset would be repeated. But his death did not mark the beginning of a happier time of peace and fruitfulness. Far from it. The terrible international conflicts which rolled back and forth were a prelude to the most intense period of reiving, the second half of the sixteenth century. Violence and thievery might be more local, sometimes done by men well known to their victims, but it was violence for all that.

7

Riding Times

Buried deep in the darkness of Tinnisburn Forest, barely discernible in the tangle of brambles, sits a prehistoric monument. A group of small standing stones was raised on the southern slopes of Tinnis Hill around 5,000 years ago. Nearby are two long cairns which may be a little older but are certainly related. Before the vast, green, suffocating blanket of sitka spruce was planted after the Second World War, it might have been possible to understand something of the reasons why our ancestors laboured to erect their monuments on this hillside. Perhaps the views to the south and the Solway were long, perhaps the view of the stones and the cairns from afar was what mattered more. The Old Peoples who lived amongst the Border hills undoubtedly revered those who had gone before them and they may have dragged the stones upright to commemorate their forebears, and also visibly to assert their rights over the land itself.

Place-names sometimes sound faint echoes from a long past, and the little monument stands on the flank of Tinnis Hill, near the Tinnisburn. And it is an old place. 'Tinnis' is the local version of the Welsh word 'dinas' which now means a city but in the first millennium BC described a 'stronghold' or a 'place of refuge'. Near at hand is Tinnis Well, a useful as well as sacred place. Blown by the whistling west wind and carpeted by the sterile forest, Tinnis Hill was a place of power once, a place of forgotten significance.

By the eleventh century, the power had long gone but the significance of the standing stones had not entirely fled. When King William Rufus came north to subdue Cumbria and lay out a plantation town on the old Roman grid at Carlisle in 1092, he established a frontier with the ambitious and expansionist Gaelic kings of Scotland. It ran along the Esk and the Liddel Water. Two generations later it moved decisively south. David I macMalcolm took possession of Cumbria in

1136 and held it until his death, at Carlisle Castle, in 1153. To bind local magnates closer to the Scottish crown, he granted to the Cumbrian Lord of Liddel lands lying to the north, the parishes of Canonbie and Kirkandrews on Esk. After 1153 and Henry II's rapid retrieval of the north-west, the lordship straddled the border, part of it under Scottish jurisdictions, part English.

This sort of split happened elsewhere along the Border line and many great medieval barons held land from both the Scots and English kings. But after the battle at Bannockburn in 1314 and the rise of Robert the Bruce and a vigorous nationalism, such holdings became increasingly awkward. By 1318 the Scots had taken back the parishes of Canonbie and Kirkandrews. Animated dispute followed, and after 1349 the Lords of Liddel assigned their claims to the English crown in order to put more weight behind them. In this way what had been a private disagreement became an issue of national sovereignty. By the fifteenth century the 7,400 acres of the two parishes had become known as 'the Debatable Land'. Its northern boundary began at the standing stones on Tinnis Hill and 12 miles to the south it terminated on the Solway shore between the outfalls of the Esk and the little River Sark.

Over in the eastern Borders there were other debatable areas. On the fertile southern banks of the Tweed longstanding disputes went on over 100 acres at Carham, 300 at Haddenrig and 40 at Wark. In the sixteenth century several efforts at arbitration failed. As late as 1769 the ownership of these 'threiplands' was still unclear. And, surprisingly, the twenty-first-century frontier is by no means a fixture. Near Hadden is a substantial woodland of mixed spruce and birch which might be English – or Scottish.

But the Debatable Land was much the most extensive and valuable place of contention. It is described exactly as that, 'terra contentiosa' in the fifteenth century, and by the early decades of the sixteenth the activities of reivers had converted it into a political as well as a legal problem. An area of uncertain jurisdiction was a god-send for law-breakers on either side of the border, and the best, or rather the worst, of them happened to be near-neighbours.

The northerly segment of the Debatable Land, above the Esk and around the villages of Canonbie and Rowanburn, appears to have fallen securely into the arms of the Armstrongs. A strong tower had been built at Gilnockie (and almost certainly occupied by Black Jock, or Johnnie Armstrong) in the early sixteenth century and other fortified settlements existed nearby. In the south a famous English reiver family was dominant. The Grahams were much feared, called 'viperous', and were so cocksure that they nailed lists of those paying and owing them blackmail on the door of Arthuret Church, near Longtown. At their zenith, they held 13 towers in north and east Cumbria.

These two powerful families and their numerous allies further complicated the question of the Debatable Land. When they occupied it, the Armstrongs had the brute strength to beat off a small English army led by the Warden of the English West March. The Grahams became so ruthless and rapacious that at the beginning of the seventeenth century they found themselves deported from Cumbria and dumped in central Ireland.

Because there was no fixed jusrisdiction, customary law came to decree that there should be no fixed abode in the Debatable Land. Whenever any group looked like settling, their farmsteads were routinely burned and their beasts driven off. March Wardens on both sides did this. But the ban on settlement (and by implication a clear claim of ownership) cannot have been total. The village and priory of Canonbie (hence the canons and the place-name) was well established and other places in the north seem to have gone unchallenged. The reach of the Armstrong base in nearby Liddesdale probably discouraged dispute.

The southern area was different. At the mouth of the Solway much of it was moss, useless, treacherous bogland. As the land rises above the 30-metre contour, it becomes more fertile, more valuable. But it must be significant that south of Canonbie, between the Esk and the Sark, there are still no villages or even hamlets to be found. The area is still something of a blank. Across the Esk from Longtown the Ordnance Survey shows a huge factory covering much of the southern end of the Debatable Land. No name is attached by the mapmakers to this massive and mysterious complex. It is in fact DM Longtown, or Defence Munitions Longtown, and its eerie presence perpetuates the sense of a no-man's land.

THE DEVIL'S PORRIDGE

War continued to dominate the land around the mouth of the Solway even into the twentieth century. Between Longtown and Eastriggs, right across the southern Debatable Land and the Solway Moss, the largest factory in history was built. Nine miles long and two miles wide, it maufactured what Sir Arthur Conan Doyle called 'the Devil's porridge'. In the trenches of the First World War, artillery was dominant, but for the first two years of the fighting, Britain's was dangerously inadequate. High explosive shells were in short supply and the huge factory was quickly set up to make them. A mixture of gun cotton and nitroglycerin, 'the Devil's porridge' was the explosive ingredient in ordnance and 800 tonnes of bullets and shells were being turned out each week by 1917.

The factory was enormously extensive because its buildings needed to stand well apart so that any accidents could be contained. The Longtown, Gretna, Eastriggs site was chosen because of the excellent rail links nearby, its location well to the west and out of range of zeppelin attacks, and the handy source of coal from Canonbie and Sanquhar. At its peak, 30,000 worked in the great factory. Two towns, at Gretna and Eastriggs, were built to house the workers and because many of them were women, a unique women's police force was recruited. With 100 miles of water mains, 130 miles of internal rail track and 30 miles of roads, the scale was vast. And yet very little remains to be seen. Apart from a few enigmatic ruins, the world's largest ever factory has virtually disappeared.

As relations between England and Scotland warmed after the death of Henry VIII negotiations began. First, a treaty was agreed between France and England (with France doing most of the talking for Scotland) and then at Norham more specific issues were discussed and resolved. One of the heads of agreement concerned the Debatable Land. Since the Armstrongs and the Grahams had become more and more established there, diplomats on both sides were anxious to agree something on sovereignty. If it remained anomalous and unresolved more than local trouble might flare.

At first scorched earth was proposed – again. Both surnames were to be burned out. But it was persuasively argued that while such draconian measures might be dramatic, they had never worked in the past, or at least never had any lasting effect. Better surely to seek a peaceful, and cheaper, solution by agreeing on a territorial division. Commissioners were summoned, but apparently the air grew quickly heated when they convened. Before fighting could break out, a professional diplomat, in the shape of the French ambassador, took charge. Approximately where Graham influence collided with the Armstrongs, a straight line was to be drawn from east to west. Simple as that, 'mes amis'.

The Scots Dike (the majority usually confer names, and the majority in this case were English) runs for 4 miles from near the River Sark at a farm called Craw's Knowe. A generous gap round the end was probably left for access. Its eastern terminal is on a height above the River Esk, and again a gap was left. The busy A7 now rumbles through it. The dike itself is an earthen bank, the upcast from two ditches on either side. Around three metres wide and originally standing two and a half metres high, it must have been imposing – and unmistakable. A modern wood completely screens it now. Red sandstone markers were placed on either end and it was agreed that no buildings would be erected near it. One sharp-eyed historian has pointed out that a very similar frontier lies close by: the vallum constructed behind Hadrian's Wall.

SLIPPERY STONE

In the autumn of 2004 a television crew was filming a series about the frontier between England and Scotland. The Scots Dike is one of the most dramatic and important stretches of that frontier but it has no signs leading to it, no information board and no car park at its western end. It just looks like a long strip of woodland. As the film crew fought their way along the overgrown path to find the beginnings of the dike and its ditches, one of the presenters slipped on a large stone. After some scraping around, it was found to be the western terminal marker stone, although the royal arms of Scotland and England which had been carved on either side had long been effaced. But it was certainly what it seemed to be. Later the same day the film crew found that the eastern terminal stone was exactly the same. This was an important archaeological find. But who to contact? The stone had collapsed into the ditch on the English side, but the dike was surely a joint monument. Sadly English Heritage have still to return the phone call and Historic Scotland have shown no interest. Surely this fascinating stretch of the border deserves better. With the explosion of interest in walking, to say nothing of history, its restoration would prove an attraction. The Scots Dike is one of the most substantial and tangible memories from the age of the reivers.

The Scots Dike marked more than a boundary. It also signalled the end of an era, what had been an indescribably painful time for the Border country, especially the Scottish side. More trouble certainly lay ahead in the remainder of the sixteenth century, but no devastating invasion would cross the Tweed or the Esk until the Civil War brought troops tramping up the north roads. After the labourers had laid the last turf on the banks of the Scots Dike, it would be local rather than national or international politics which sparked violence and reprisal in the hills and river valleys. In fact reiving began to ratchet up to its most frantic pitch in the second half of the sixteenth century. These would be the years of the 'ever-riding' surnames, the decades known simply as 'the riding time'. The foundations, what a modern politician called the 'causes of crime', and the grim, hard-bitten attitudes of a society which lived by larceny had been laid in the fire and smoke of the 1520s and 1540s. If not quite every man for himself, it was definitely every surname for themselves.

And the weather grew worse. More reports of extreme conditions spatter the historical record, especially in the 1570s and 1590s. A period of relative peace did not bring a revival in farming, a string of bad summers and wet winters discouraged cultivation and led to a more widespread adoption of the less risky business of husbanding beasts. More herds of hardy cattle and sheep munched the green, well-watered landscape.

History often seems inevitable in hindsight, but at the time events might have turned in any direction. Astute Border heidsmen kept a weather eye on developments in Edinburgh and in London. In the closing decades of the sixteenth century it became increasingly likely that James VI of Scotland would become James I of Great Britain and Ireland. But anything could have happened to prevent that. James might have died young. Queen Elizabeth might have astonished everyone by contracting a late marriage and thereby altering the succession. But the heidsmen knew that the most likely outcome would involve the erasure of the border by a union of the crowns. And that would be bad for business.

Through the late 1580s and into the 1590s there was a gathering realisation that life would change radically – and sooner rather than later. Borderers must have listened intently for news. But like addicts, the reiving surnames kept at it, and as the old queen grew older there is a sense that they went at it harder. Instead of positioning themselves for change, they grabbed as much as they could before the party ended.

When the Scots Dike was being dug in 1552, most of these considerations lay far in the future. In Newcastle, in the middle of September, the new Deputy Lord Warden General of the English Marches summoned a council. Thomas Wharton had himself been the first appointment made by the Lord Warden General, the Earl of Warwick, John Dudley. It was an astute move. The victor at Solway Moss, Wharton was one of the most experienced, cool, wise and reliable royal officers on the frontier. Warwick's own appointment as Lord Warden General of the Marches was also politic. The garrisons at Carlisle and Berwick and the troops of horsemen stationed around the English border strongholds were the only professional soldiers in England and to gain control of them made Warwick even more powerful.

Edward VI was young, ill and rapidly failing. Only 15 years old, the king suffered attacks of smallpox and measles in 1552, and by the end of the year the deadly symptoms of tuberculosis had been observed. From that time onwards it was not a question of if but rather when the king would die. Warwick was the weightiest player at court and the dying young monarch relied on him to manage the succession and stave off a potential catholic revival led by his sister, Mary. Elevated to the dukedom of Northumberland, Warwick installed his son into the royal line by contracting a marriage with Lady Jane Grey.

The Lord Warden rode north to make his own first-hand assessment of the state of the marches, England's defences and their organisation. The chaos of the 1540s had seen the mechanics of law and order rust with disuse and abuse. Warden courts were convened at Alnwick, Newcastle and Carlisle as the new duke attempted to sort out the mess. He toured the fortifications along the border, stopping at Berwick where expensive new work was beginning. However, the fragility of the king's health discouraged long absences from court and after his summer inspection, the duke hurried south to London.

Wharton was left to get on with it. For reasons of prestige as well as good order, the administration of the marches needed to be shaken up. Wharton was the man to do it. At his council at Newcastle, he welcomed three men on whom he could rely: Lord Eure was to be Warden of the English East Marches, Lord Ogle the Middle and Sir Thomas Dacre the West. In addition the captains of all the strongholds on the frontier were in attendance along with about thirty of the most powerful local noblemen.

It was a lengthy meeting with a substantial agenda, and detailed records of what was decided have survived. The list of measures to discourage reiving and generally maintain good order are eloquent: they have a good deal to say by inference about what was being discouraged.

Most important to Wharton and his officers was information – and its rapid and effective transmission. Undetected raiding, until it reached its target, was a central problem. Watches had been kept before but it was a dreary and thankless business which could easily slip into laxity or worse. The Newcastle council ordered that between 1st October and 16th March watches would be resumed, and properly kept. These winter months were traditionally the time when raiding reached its peak.

River fords were seen as the most important places to set sentinals. And they all had to be watched. Every raiding party, particularly when the winter spates ran, was forced to use them en route to their quarry and on the way back as they drove plundered beasts before them. Two men were assigned to each of the fords over the Tweed and also, crucially, to those on its tributary, the Till. Notoriously deep and treacherous in places, this little river flows south to north and falls into the Tweed east of Cornhill. Its 39 crossing places were painstakingly listed and where it was not practical to set a watch (there are no large settlements along the river which might have supplied men), the ford had to be made unusable. This was done by damming the flow to create as deep a pool as possible where there had been shallows.

Landward passes threading in and through the Cheviot Hills also had to be watched. Equipped with a horn, men were charged to raise the alarm if they saw a party of raiders making their way down from the hills. How exactly they were expected to see them in the winter's dark is less clear. Perhaps ears were more useful than eyes. But the emphasis on the ready availability of good, quick ponies and a sound knowledge of byways and back tracks was probably not misplaced.

THE RAIDERS

One of the very best modern poems about the Border Reivers was written by Will H. Ogilvie. Born at Holefield, near Kelso, he lived a life almost as romantic as his verse. At the end of the nineteenth century, Ogilvie spent 12 years in the Australian outback, his horsemanship much admired by even most hard-bitten of the 'jackaroos', the cow hands on the remote cattle stations. Camped out in the bush, under the stars and with an audience around a campfire, Ogilvie honed his poetic talents – to excellent effect.

Last night a wind from Lammermuir came roaring up the glen
With the tramp of trooping horses and the laugh of reckless men
And struck a mailed hand on the gate and cried in rebel glee
'Come forth, Come forth, my Borderer and ride the March with
    me!'

I said 'Oh! Wind of Lammermuir, the night's too dark to ride,
And all the men that fill the glen are ghosts of men that died!
The floods are down in Bowmont Burn, the moss is fetlock deep;
Go back, wild Wind of Lammermuir, to Lauderdale – and sleep!'

Our spoke the Wind of Lammermuir, 'We know the road right
    well,
The road that runs by Kale and Jed across the Carter Fell.
There is no man in all the men in this grey troop of mine
But blind might ride the Borderside from Teviothead to Tyne!'

The horses fretted on their bits and pawed the flints to fire,
The riders swung them to the South full-faced to their desire;
'Come!' said the Wind from Lammermuir, and spoke full
    scornfully,
'Have ye no pride to mount and ride your father's road with me?'

A roan horse to the gate they led, foam-flecked and travelled far,
A snorting roan that tossed his head and flashed his forehead star;
There came the sound of clashing steel and hoof-tramp up the
    glen
. . . And two by two we cantered through, a troop of ghostly
    men!

I know not if the farms we fired are burned to ashes yet!
I know not if the stirks grew tired before the stars were set!
I only know that late last night when Northern winds blew free,
A troop of men rode up the glen and brought a horse for me!

Wharton understood the personal connections and networks constantly at play in Border politics, and he attempted to break the links
between the reiving families on either side of the Cheviots and the
Tweed. No man was permitted even to speak to a 'Scotchman', far less
associate with him. More ambiguously only those individuals known
to the watch were allowed to pass and if any raiders were allowed to
escape without a fight or a chase, then the watchers themselves would
be imprisoned as criminals. As well as deterrents, incentives were
offered. If goods were recovered, there was 'a price of rescue' on offer
with a clear tariff attached. And if there was an argument, various
resorts for settlement are described in some detail. Clearly arguments
regularly sparked.

Further up the social scale, Wharton insisted that wardens, captains
and the other royal officers of the marches had to be very carefully
chosen. Too many local lords had themselves been complicit in raiding
in the past to police it properly in the future. It was decreed that one
man could hold only one appointment and that he should stay 'in the
proper station'. This avoided any sense of these roles being seen as
honorary or ancillary. Whoever was Captain of Berwick stayed in
Berwick, commanded the garrison and did his job – himself.

The 30 noblemen at the Newcastle council were instructed to enclose
more of their land. Old-fashioned open pasture made it much easier for
reivers to operate and it was decided that hedges, or 'quickset', would
inhibit movement. The method was prescribed. Ditches were first to be
dug (five quarters wide [45 inches], six quarters deep [54 inches]), and on
either side quickwood (usually hawthorn, blackthorn, wild rose or crab
apple) was to be planted (at no less than a height of three quarters [27
inches]). Some of these thick sixteenth-century double hedges can still be
seen, and they are formidable barriers. There is a fine run near the farm at
Pressen Hill, not far from Kelso.

Finally, either Etal or Ford castles were to be repaired in order to
provide a residence for the Deputy Warden of the East March.
Wharton himself would be based at Alnwick. These government jobs
were no longer the prerogative of local lords but hands-on jobs for
professionals.

While a virtual state of undeclared war had obtained throughout
the 1540s, the cross-border truce days had, not surprisingly, fallen
into abeyance. Many complaints were long outstanding. A renovated
set of procedures was proposed at Wharton's council. Those living in
England who had been robbed or suffered in some other way at the

hands of Scots were to report complaints to their local wardens. They in turn would submit them at the next cross-border meeting where a jury of six Scots and six Englishmen would adjudicate. If they found a complaint justified, it was filed or 'fouled', and at the next meeting the guilty was bound to be produced. When it worked, it worked well.

In 1553 all manner of disputes appear to have been settled peacefully at truce days. Grazing rights were reinstated and compensation paid by those who had abused them. A fishing on the English side of the Tweed was returned to its rightful (Scottish) owner, stolen sheep were restored and the crime of tresspass clarified. The small change of Border justice was being exchanged once more.

Sir Robert Bowes, a wily old warrior, noted another traditional – and more immediate – response to theft: 'men may lawfully follow their goods either with a sleuth hound on the trod thereof, or else by such other means as they can best devise'. This was the pursuit well known as the 'hot trod', or hot trail. Those who had just seen their beast or goods, or both, stolen had the right to raise a posse and to follow hot upon the heels of the theives. Even if the latter made it over the border, a hot trod could be lawfully pursued in either direction. In fact Wharton set out a list of punishments for those neighbours who did not join in. The horseman leading a pursuit was said to have carried a burning peat on the end of his lance to lead the way and signify to all that a trod was in progress – but this sounds unfeasibly theatrical, a piece of highly unlikely romance. What is sure is that trods were often run. If a posse could not be rallied on the night of the robbery, or the theft not discovered until morning, then for six days after that a cold trod was permitted. Borderers were well used to taking the law into their own hands, and here was an institution which encouraged them to do exactly that, legally. Rewards or rescue money also supplied an incentive.

ON THE BOUND ROAD

Border towns like Selkirk, Hawick, Langholm and Lauder like to think of their common ridings as the oldest and most senior. But they are not. The central notion behind these annual events is to patrol the marches, the boundaries of the towns' common land. Encroachment from neighbouring landowners needed to be checked and vital customary rights maintained and asserted. This is exactly what was being done on the Berwick Bounds as early as

1438. Selkirk has the earliest records in the Scottish Borders and they go back only to the early sixteenth century. In 1438 the enclave around Berwick on the north side of the Tweed was agreed and the burgesses of the town immediately began to patrol what became known as the Bound Road. The major difference between the ancient perambulations which set out from the Border towns and those at Berwick is that its marches were also an international frontier. This made for more vigilance, and by 1550 the Captain of Berwick and the Marshall of the garrison (an office still filled every year) rode at the head of a troop of light cavalry. By 1604 ditches had been dug and marker stones set up. Some can still be seen. On the Coroner's Meadow, on the banks of the Tweed, an old-fashioned horse race, around a long course, is held as an assembled crowd roars on the riders and takes a little refreshment. Berwick's sister-city of Casey in Australia also rides its bounds each year in direct – and flattering – imitation and the Hotspur Trophy is awarded to the Champion Rider.

As ever English records have survived in relative abundance, and were in any case probably better kept than the Scots'. No equivalent refreshment of the Border laws seems to have taken place in Scotland. Indeed, with the assassination of Walter Scott of Buccleuch by the feuding Kerrs in the streets of Edinburgh in 1552, it seemed like grim business as usual. But the Queen Dowager, Mary of Guise, did manage to agree a practical measure with the Governor, the Earl of Arran. Border lawlessnes might be at least partly cured by a long holiday. The Kerrs and their allies, the Humes, were told to muster 500 of their most warlike horsemen and lead them into the service of the King of France in continental Europe. Perhaps they might never come back.

At the same time as Wharton was at Newcastle attempting to work out how to forestall and deter Scottish reivers from crossing the border, a man from Haddington was causing all sorts of trouble only a few yards from the castle, at St Nicholas Parish Church. John Knox had, astonishingly, survived two years' brutal imprisonment as a slave on a French galley. At one of the most dramatic incidents in the early phase of the Scottish reformation, the siege of St Andrews Castle, he had been captured and sent to what was reckoned to be certain death at the oars of a French ship. But Knox was released, found safe haven in Edward VI's determinedly protestant England and was accepted at St Nicholas in Newcastle as a lecturer, a preacher paid a stipend. From the pulpit he thundered so effectively against the Roman pope and all his works that thousands came to listen. Most were fellow Scots and John Dudley, the Duke of Northumberland, worried at such large gatherings of the very people Wharton was trying to control. The bishopric of Rochester in Kent was vacant and just at the point when the duke had begun to persuade all concerned that Knox was the best candidate, Edward VI died and sent the process immediately into reverse. The accession of his catholic sister, Mary, sent Knox fleeing out of the country and ultimately north to Scotland in 1555 as the reforming movement was gathering momentum. It was Rochester's loss.

One of Wharton's most pressing problems was the apparent seamlessness of disputes in the Borders. Few incidents, raids, reprisals, trials or simple enmities stood by themselves. There was usually a history attached, and this made reform and a decisive break with the past very difficult. At Newcastle the Deputy Warden General had insisted that particular care be taken over the appointment of royal officers. Far too frequently the local nobility, who expected to be given these jobs by right, were so entangled in the disputes they were expected to resolve that the workings of border justice, when they worked at all, had become impossibly labyrinthine. The years 1552 and 1553 were not easy for Wharton as he wrestled with the problems of asserting royal policy over local politics.

Cuthbert Musgrave would probably have shrugged his shoulders and got on with it. Very early on a July morning in 1552, as he climbed into the saddle, that was exactly what he was doing, getting on with it. Musgrave was Captain of Harbottle Castle, the stronghold guarding the southern end of Clennel Street, where the old road wound down from the Cheviots into the fertile fields of Upper Coquetdale and the Northumberland plain below. Five hundred riders had mustered under Musgrave's command and as he and his deputy, John Hall, led the huge raiding party north-west into the summer hills, there was no attempt at stealth. How could there be with five hundred men in the saddle on a July morning?

From later recriminations and defences, it looks as though Cuthbert Musgrave was out on legitimate business, believing that he had Wharton's commission to ride in strength up over Clennel Street and down into the Bowmont Valley and Scotland beyond it. The

English troopers made good time and by ten o'clock they had reached the villages of Yetholm and Kirk Yetholm. Sheep and cattle were briskly rounded up, many of them belonging to George Kerr of Gateshaw. His tower still stands near Morebattle, at the foot of the Kale Water valley. The livestock may have been Kerr's property, or it may not. Musgrave's men lifted a huge number: 3,500 sheep and 500 cows, and it seems likely that this well-reported incident was consequent on something unreported. Perhaps there had been a raid on the English side? When the Scottish warden complained, Lord Grey, the English deputy, refused to concede that anything illegal had taken place. Given the openness and scale of the Musgrave expedition, it looks very much as though the Captain of Harbottle Castle was going about the business of righting a prior wrong. In his opinion.

Some blatant chicanery did routinely take place – and was perpetrated by royal officers. Norham Castle looks across the Tweed at Scotland at a place where the river bends away northwards. There are deep pools where salmon feed and the fishing is reliable. Snaking out into the current are long breakwaters made from big stones known locally as 'yiddies'. They are very old indeed. Yiddies were probably first made by prehistoric hunter-gatherers to help create areas of slack water where fish could bask, away from the effort of constantly swimming against the strong currents. They also took fishermen away from the bank into the midstream where they could cast their nets cleanly, not risking fouling them on bushes and trees on the bank. The ancient pools all have names and opposite Norham Castle is the Halywell fishing, likely to have originally been the property of a nearby religious house, perhaps the Cistercian nunnery at Coldstream. By 1553 the Hume family owned it but their claim was hotly contested by Richard Bowes, the Captain of Norham Castle.

Bowes countered with his own assertion that Norham Castle had rented the Halywell from the Humes for many years. It was a convenient source of good food for the garrison. When Hume's men picked their way carefully out on the yiddies to cast their nets, they came within bowshot of the castle walls. It appears that the Captain had been ordering his men to fire on the fishermen. The dispute became so serious that the long-suffering French ambassador was summoned once more to arbitrate, and he found in favour of Hume. This bad-tempered little incident showed how sour cross-border relations could be, and how petty. The horrors of the 1540s had mercifully passed but the memory would take a long time to fade.

It also shows how royal officers were by no means above bending the law and legal process to their advantage. If Wharton was aiming to free the English frontier administration from all the corruptions and brokerage of the past, then to do that properly, the law had to be relied on. But if matters became strained over a few pounds of fresh salmon at Norham, the Deputy Lord Warden General had much bigger problems upriver at Wark. The English Captain of the castle was due at a Truce Day on 24th August 1553 to be held at the time-honoured trysting place near Kelso, right on the border at the Reddenburn. He saddled up early and with 120 men at his back rode hard up the side road to Hadden, where he had business to deal with. Bloody business, as it turned out, for the Captain and his men laid hands on Patrick Jameson and John Davidson and killed them.

The murder took place in the morning, only two hours before the Truce Day began at Reddenburn, a few hundred yards from Hadden. On the face of it, it was an incendiary act. Friends and relatives of the two victims were gathering at the Reddenburn where large groups of heavily armed Englishmen and Scots would face each other. However, if any reaction flared into violence, it was not reported. Which is very surprising. It may have been another case of offence and reprisal. There had been serious outbreaks of fighting at Truce Days on infinitely less inflammatory pretexts.

PRIORESS HOPPRINGLE

High religious office tended to stay in the hands of the aristocracy, often the family who were principal benefactors of a church, monastery or nunnery. In 1505 Isabella Hoppringle took over from her aunt, Elizabeth, as Prioress of the wealthy and important nunnery at Coldstream. March Wardens often met there and truce days were occasionally held. Everything changed on 22nd August 1513 when Prioress Hoppringle watched part of a huge Scottish army splash across the Tweed at the Coldstream fords, hard by the convent walls. When battle was joined at Flodden, only 3 miles away, the nuns could hear the roar of the cannon and the tumult of shouts, screams and war cries as men hacked at each other. When George Hume of Wedderburn was persuaded to leave the battle-field, being the sole heir to the family estates, Prioress Hoppringle (the name was later shortened to Pringle) rebuked him and he went back to the fighting, and to his death. The day after the slaughter, the nuns and their servants drove carts to Flodden to pick up the dead for burial, probably only the artistocratic dead. Two years later the Prioress gave sanctuary to Queen Margaret Tudor, James IV's widow and the Queen Mother. It was an astute gesture. Throughout the time of the English invasions of the 1520s and 1530s, the Queen Mother repeatedly wrote to the commanders of the English forces (often she knew them personally) asking them to spare Coldstream's nunnery, which they did. When Isabella Hoppringle died in 1537, her beloved priory did not outlive her for long. In the wake of the Reformation it ceased to exist. But in the 1860s traces of the graveyard were found (while digging for a gasometer), the place where Prioress Hoppringle had had some of the fallen at Flodden buried.

The way in which these regular border meetings was organised was formal, and the rigidity and predictability of the ritual was designed to reduce tensions. Truce Days were essential for any possibility of international justice working effectively. At the traditional trysting places along the border (most meetings seem to have been held at the Reddenburn, Cocklaw, at the top of Clennel Street, Redeswire on the Carter Bar, Kershopefoot in Liddesdale and at the Lochmabenstane near Gretna) the wardens and their parties of riders came together. These parties could be very large, sometimes more than a thousand men on each side and since the express purpose of the meetings was to discuss and settle grievances, the atmosphere could be volatile.

When Truce Days were held, the ground chosen was usually open. At the Reddenburn, the small stream which marks the frontier, before it joins the Tweed, has carved out a shallow declivity. The ground on either bank rises to form two ridges which face each other, more or less. When wardens and their men approached the trysting place by the side of the burn, they would halt on the ridges, presumably out of bowshot. Each side took time to appraise the other. No doubt men looked along the opposite ranks to see if either accused or accusors had turned up. And numbers mattered in any potentially explosive situation. If one group overwhelmed the other, then the smaller might be glad of the opportunity to retreat.

After a time it was the English warden, by tradition, who rode forward and crossed the burn into Scotland accompanied by a few of his lieutenants. He would ask of the Scots warden that the peace be kept until the following sunrise (or longer if the weight of business demanded more time). This was important because it allowed men time to get safely home. When it was agreed to uphold the peace, and hold the Truce Day, then both wardens held up their hands as a signal for the two groups of riders to come together. At the Reddenburn there is a flattish stretch of haughland by the Tweed and that was probably where the wardens got down to business.

The preliminary always first on the agenda was the appointment of a jury to hear and decide on cases or complaints. Using an elegant formula, the English side chose six Scottish jurors and the Scots chose the six Englishmen who would sit in balanced judgement with them. Some fine calculations must have been routinely made. Perjury had always been a problem and in 1553 a tariff of punishments was formulated. The most severe was not a fine or imprisonment but something many Borderers feared more. If a man was found guilty of lying under oath then his word would never be believed again and no testimony, promise or surety would be admitted or given any weight. It was a potentially profound humiliation in a society where honour of a visceral sort did operate, and where to be branded a liar was deeply shaming. As Geordie Burn confessed to Robert Carey, honour was something to be ruthlessly upheld, since he 'had spent his life taking deep revenge for slight offences'.

Major insults were often exchanged at Truce Days. The custom of 'bauchling and reproaching' raised the temperature as the men of one side literally pointed accusing fingers at someone in the ranks opposite. By blowing horns, name-calling and pointing lances at a man they reckoned to be guilty of an offence – even before any judicial process had had a chance to get underway – they could turn the already difficult atmosphere of a meeting into an impossible one. Fighting often broke out and wardens had to force themselves into the melée 'to stand together and make a quietness about them'.

In 1553 bauchling and reproaching was sensibly banned at Truce Days unless prior permission had been sought and granted by both the English and Scottish wardens, and if any broke the ban they were to be arrested by their own warden and handed over to the other side. Perhaps it worked occasionally.

James V's widow, Mary of Guise, became increasingly powerful in Scotland during the minority and then absence of her daughter, Mary, Queen of Scots. By 1554 the Queen Dowager had replaced the Earl of Arran as Regent, and a year later she was active in measures to deal with lawlessness in the Borders. On the castle mount at Roxburgh the fort built so quickly by Protector Somerset in 1547 was to be refurbished at the substantial cost of £20,000 and used as a base for government forces. Mary herself had probably visited the impressive old stronghold, for later in the summer of 1555 she held a council at Duns. A straightforward proposal to improve the policing of the border on the Scottish side was made. Like Lord Wharton, Mary's advisers wanted to disentangle frontier administration from local politics, and instead of depending on part-time soldiers and riders owing their allegiance to local lairds and heidsmen, they planned to employ mercenaries. These men would depend on central government and have no connection with the Kerrs, the Humes, the Scotts, Armstrongs or any of the other leading reiving and landowning surnames, who of course vigorously objected, particularly since it became clear that the cash to pay the mercenaries would come from taxation levied directly on them. The proposal was not adopted and strife and dissent continued to spark.

In the summer of 1555 there were two meetings at the Reddenburn and it appears that the numbers attending were growing tremendously large – never a good sign. At the Truce Day of 28 June an astonishing 2,000 turned up with the English March Warden, 1,000 complaints of trespass were made against the Scots in one march alone. This was not a matter of the illegal incursion into England of individuals, in the sense that we understand trespass now. The problem was that Scots were, allegedly, grazing their beasts on English ground (this is what might have been behind Cuthbert Musgrave's expedition to Yetholm) without permission. So that all the complaints could be properly heard, a double Truce Day was arranged at Norham, one session to take place at Norham Church, the other across the border at Lady-kirk.

One of Mary of Guise' most active supporters in the Borders was Patrick Hepburn, Earl of Bothwell. Having inherited a wealthy patrimony, and a handily placed castle at Crichton near Pathhead, he allied himself with the catholic Regent but was himself a protestant. Bothwell attended the Truce Days at the Reddenburn and later mounted expeditions to Liddesdale to quell the wild Armstrongs. But as the Rev. George Ridpath drily remarked in his *Border History* of 1848, 'the banditti had the advantage in two rencounters'. Nevertheless Bothwell was influential in the government of Mary of Guise, one of the few Scots to matter as the embrace of catholic France grew tighter, even suffocating, in the Scotland of the late 1550s. Most of the strategically important castles were garrisoned by French troops under their own commanders, and they of course did nothing but pursue the political interests of France.

Henri d'Oysel sailed to Leith to become Mary of Guise' chief military adviser, and in effective charge of French forces in Scotland. Although Edward VI's sister, the new Queen Mary of England, was a devout catholic and had married Philip II of Spain, this did not help create friendly relations across the border. In the balance of European power politics the match placed England against France, and as ever the French were anxious to use Scotland to force a threat if not a war on two fronts.

In 1557 d'Oysel rode south in strength to Eyemouth where, despite the provisions of the Treaty of Norham expressly forbidding it, he began to build a modern fortress on the headland, the northern wing of the harbour mouth. With the expertise of Italian engineers, defensive ditches and banks were thrown across the narrow neck of the peninsula. Two broad bastions were added and a state-of-the-art artillery fort created – only 6 miles north of Berwick and 4 from the English border. It was a deliberate provocation and the Berwick garrison tried to disrupt the work. D'Oysel's men beat off their attacks, but the episode did galvanise the London government. Mary Tudor ordered Sir Robert Lee to Berwick to begin work on building modern defences which could withstand artillery bombardments.

While these international tensions did not spill over into outright war, there was a constant state of alert along the border. Nicholas Ridley, Bishop of London, reflected on what life was like:

> In Tynedale, where I was born, I have known my countrymen watch night and day in their harness, such as they had, that is in their jacks, and their spears in their hands . . . And so doing, although at every such bickerings some of them spent [lost] their lives, yet by such means, like pretty men, they defended their country.

As the political temperature rose, Thomas Wharton's reforms began to wilt. The big raids resumed. The Scots crossed the Tweed in numbers and forayed in Northumberland, the English under Henry Percy penetrated Berwickshire and reived 4,000 cows, some nags and took a few prisoners. More marching, raiding, counter-marching and skirmishing followed, but when Henri d'Oysel brought the Scottish nobility and their soldiers to muster for a full-blown invasion, they would have none of it. At Flodden a Scots army had fought and died for French interests and the bitterness still festered on.

In November 1558 Mary Tudor died and was succeeded by her half-sister, Princess Elizabeth. A martyr-burning catholic had been replaced by a protestant conciliator anxious to see peace settled with Scotland. The diplomatic game changed quickly; French influence north of the border suddenly seemed even more problematic. Mary of Guise still held the reins of power and her daughter, Mary, Queen of Scots, had married Francis, the Dauphin of France, in April 1558. Dynastic union looked very possible because the marriage settlement agreed that in the event of Mary's death, Francis should become King of Scotland. But the growth of Scottish protestantism, followed by the accession of Elizabeth, made that outcome anything but certain. When Henri II died in July 1559 and Francis II and his Scottish Queen succeeded to the throne of France, arguably the most powerful in Europe, the pieces all moved again and history was poised to take any number of directions.

PLAY THE MAN

Unusually, a scion of a famous reiving surname became a bishop, and ultimately a martyr for his protestant beliefs. After an education at Newcastle and Cambridge, Nicholas Ridley became Bishop of London and contributed importantly to the liturgical revolution which created the Church of England. When the catholic Queen Mary came to power he was arrested, removed from his bishopric and put on trial at Oxford. A skilful and brave defence against catholic interrogation made no difference, and with Hugh Latimer, former Bishop of Worcester, Ridley was condemned to the hideous death of a heretic. When brought out into Broad Street and faced with his pyre, his nerve broke and the terrified man began to weep and shake uncontrollably. At his side, Latimer is said to have whispered consolation; 'Be of good comfort, Master Ridley, and play the man. We shall this day light such a candle by God's grace in England, as I trust shall never be put out.'

And it promptly did, taking an unexpected turn. Within 18 months of his accession, King Francis died from an ear infection. He was only 17 years old, and in contrast to what had been agreed for Scotland, Mary did not succeed him as sovereign of France.

In fact it became increasingly clear that Mary was left with no substantial role in her adopted country and that it was highly likely she would return to Scotland to begin her personal rule. The political picture was developing yet another layer of complexity. Since the burning of Patrick Hamilton outside St Salvator's Chapel in St Andrews in 1528 the Scottish reformation had stuttered, appearing by turns inevitable, impossible and often leaderless. Between Hamilton's death and 1558, twenty-one had suffered the awful fate of the martyr/heretic and many of the important figures in the reformist movement fled Scotland, or were removed, like John Knox. The brutal strategy of 'the rough wooing' in the 1540s had discouraged many from a closer relationship with England and the new faith. Meanwhile catholic France had poured men and money into Scotland.

While the Regent, Mary of Guise, was in France in 1558 attending her daughter's marriage to the Dauphin, catholic zealots arrested Walter Mylne. Accused of preaching protestantism in Dysart in west Fife, he was taken prisoner to St Andrews, tried for heresy, and after his refusal to recant, was condemned to death at the stake. Mylne was 82. There was widespread revulsion at the sentence. At first an executioner could not be found to carry out the gruesome ritual on the old man. But when the ashes were at last swept away and the smoke cleared, politics in Scotland had shifted again. Mylne would be the last martyr.

Protestantism flourished in the towns where better-off supporters kept 'privy kirks' in their homes. Preachers held the reformed communion in small rooms with families and their friends. Privy kirks were not routinely suppressed but discretion on both sides had kept Scotland from the worst excesses. In 1557 a faction of the nobility felt strong enough to combine formally as 'the Lords of the Congregation' and their avowed aim was the establishment of the reformed church. While Mary of Guise retained power and French garrisons controlled the country, the Lords' had to bide their time, but Walter Mylne's death seemed to quicken the pace. John Knox returned in 1559 and preached with great passion at Perth and St Andrews. Rioting followed and some churches were vandalised, especially those with ornate interiors.

As ever, political alignments ran alongside religious convictions. After the accession of Elizabeth to the English throne in 1558, her support for Scottish protestantism and the Lords of the Congregation gathered momentum. While Francis II lived and the marriage settlement with Mary held out the real possibility of dynastic union with France – to say nothing of their claims on the English throne – England could do nothing. But despite the events of the 1540s, support inside Scotland grew for Elizabeth. Protestants increasingly looked as if they wanted Scotland to retain its independence while catholics seemed to be ready to acquiesce in the nation becoming part of an enlarged French kingdom, little more than a principality.

Knox of course played hard on these connections, claiming that Mary of Guise was a much reviled Regent acting mainly in the interests of her native France. In 1560 the surprising sight of an English army arriving in Scotland to support the protestant cause brought the situation to a head. Discouraging rather than defeating French forces outright, the English intervention cleared a way forward for the Lords of the Congregation. Mary of Guise conveniently and unexpectedly died at the height of the crisis and a solution was forced on the French. By the terms of the Treaty of Edinburgh, Scotland was to be free of occupation by foreign troops. In August 1560 parliament met and, in effect, set out the legal basis for the Scottish Reformation. The mass was banned, the reformed confession of faith (written by John Knox) installed and papal jurisdiction removed. Scotland was no longer a catholic nation, at least officially.

In rural areas such as the Borders change happened only slowly, and was sometimes even humane. At Kelso Abbey the brothers were allowed to continue to live in the conventual buildings and enjoy some of the revenues of the old church until 1587 when 'the haill monkis of the abbay of Kelso ar decessit'. The pattern of change was patchy. By 1574 Scotland's 1080 parishes had almost all been taken over by protestant ministers or readers (there was an initial lack of men ordained in the reformed faith), but in the 1580s a third of the nobility still held to the catholic church. The proportion of heidsmen who had not changed allegiance was probably higher.

The domestic effects of the Reformation are difficult to detect in the Borders. No doubt some families were split, others indifferent. But the general political consequences were certainly beneficial. When the Treaty of Edinburgh removed foreign soldiers, it also reduced by many degrees the likelihood of cross border conflict. After the reigns of Edward VI and Mary I, Elizabeth found the royal treasury much depleted. Stability, she correctly judged, would produce prosperity and revenue for the crown, which was also what her subjects desired. Her policies allowed peace to descend over the borderlands.

But it was to be a guarded peace. Orders were issued for the massive defence works at Berwick to be carried on, troops of horsemen were stationed along the frontier and cash was made available to pay and feed them adequately. Remarkably, Lord Dacre received the queen's thanks for a foray he had made into the Scottish west march in the winter of 1559/60, but was also advised that it would have been more politic to have done nothing. The Scots were not to be provoked, and instead watchfulness was the word from London. On each side of the border garrisons were brought up to full complement and Lord Wharton's advice for proper administration of the English marches was to be followed. Elizabeth wrote to the Lords of the Congregation that there was not 'a better place betwixt the realms than ever was heard of in any time'. Not for long.

Soon after her return to Scotland, Queen Mary gave her half-brother, Lord James Stewart, a difficult commission. By whatever means were to hand he was charged to pacify the borders – and they were the usual brutal means. Levies were raised, and at Jedburgh the usual suspects rounded up and twenty of these banditti summarily hanged. Forty more were dragged off to Edinburgh to stand trial. At Kelso Lord James met Lord Grey, Warden of the English East March, and Sir John Forster, Warden of the English Middle March. They agreed to cooperate as best they could.

Forster and Grey were related and both leading men from powerful Northumberland surnames. Like the Scots, their loyalty was to family first and nation or crown second. Elizabeth I's civil servants had no illusions about this, and unlike the Scots, far fewer natives were appointed to the wardenries. Neutral southerners with no prior attachments were usually preferred. But Sir John Forster was exceptional in other ways. Making his debut appearance as Warden of the English Middle March in 1558, he held the office, off and on, for nearly 40 years. Living to an immense age, probably 101, Old Sir John was at the centre of Border politics for the whole of the second half of the sixteenth century. He was clearly a rogue, what might now be generously termed a pragmatist, in the period when reiving spread like an epidemic. But Forster was also attractive: clever, unscrupulous, kind, a spade-caller, and fiercely loyal, he might be described as the epitome of the age, a reiver's reiver.

Forsters were to be found mostly along the eastern marches, holding lands and tenancies north of Coquetdale, particularly around Aln-wick, Bamburgh and Belford, and the rolling farmland fringing the North Sea coast. Sir John was wealthy – and generous. With his long-standing mistress, Isabel Sheppard, he had several children whom he readily owned as his own, giving them the Forster surname. Nicholas Forster was much favoured and he appears in later records as a considerable landowner. With his long-suffering wife, Forster seems to have had two daughters, Grace and Juliana. Both married into the Northumbrian gentry, spreading family connections ever wider.

Since the rebellions of the late fifteenth century and because of their adherence to the old catholic faith, the Percy earls of Northumberland had suffered the stain of royal mistrust. Elizabeth I would tolerate them as great barons, but not allow them to recover their ancient power in the north which might make them even greater barons. Sir John Forster was an implacable and constant enemy of the Percys and at feud with their supporters, the likes of the Collingwoods who also held lands in north Northumberland. In the 1560s these tensions festered – and then burst into flames when rebellion broke. In 1569 Thomas Percy joined Charles Neville, Earl of Westmorland in what came to be known as the Rising of the Northern Earls. They were catholics and outraged at the execution of Henry Howard, Duke of Norfolk.

Late in the year, badly organised, panicked into precipitate action by the discovery of their plot, the rebels nevertheless looked dangerous – as a catalyst. The reiving families of Tynedale and Redesdale saddled up to join Percy's insurgents, and for a few weeks it seemed as though substantial support from southern Scotland's catholic surnames might ride over the border.

Sir John Forster was a puritan, at least in name, and he moved smartly to blunt the rebels' momentum. Taking Alnwick and Wark-worth castles back into royal hands, he also sent riders to block the hill trails and prevent more from joining Percy and Neville. Then he occupied the walled city of Newcastle. Word went out to the Forster network of alliances and connections, and rallying riders to him, Sir John skirmished and harried rebel forces. There was news of an army mustering at York for the crown, and more mobilisation in the south. Percy and Neville faltered, lost confidence and the Rising of the Northern Earls began to disintegrate. With Forster giving chase, the rebels fled into Liddesdale, in desperation trusting the Armstrongs to protect them.

Much relieved and ready to be grateful if not generous (she was famously penny-pinching). Elizabeth I summoned the triumphant Sir John to London so that she could thank him personally. The episode was the making of Forster and it was to forgive many transgressions, keeping him in office almost to the end of the century. The queen outlived him by a year.

Deal-making rather than rigid adherence to the law came to characterise the administration of the English middle march. Forster turned many blind eyes – when he was Captain of Bamburgh Castle, he allowed smugglers to unload contraband below the walls – but whenever anyone was awarded a favour, another will have been expected in return. Operating at the centre of a web of interlocking loyalties, Forster was more like a mafia godfather around whom the world seemed to turn rather than a royal official. 'He possessed all in Northumberland,' complained those excluded from the penumbra of patronage. It was an exaggeration, but only a slight one.

March Wardens were expected to communicate with the civil servants in London, their paymasters (Forster once boasted that he was wealthy enough and didn't need the money). The fact that they did so regularly is the main reason why English records are comparatively full. Forster's preferred approach was simple: he wrote frequently with good news. The border was quiet, all was well, thievery contained. Even more quietly the warden dealt with business in his own way, by constant brokerage, favour for favour, punishment meted out when obligations were not met. The question of lawbreaking was less important but Forster kept order of a sort. By 1568 his enemies had seen through the deceptions and complained to London directly, saying that the border was far from quiet, that the warden had done nothing about Scottish raiding, that he had too many Scottish friends and repeatedly failed to raise contentious issues at Truce Days. The Rising of the Northern Earls piled up credit at court in the nick of time.

BOOK HANDS AND CHARTER HANDS

Handwriting in the sixteenth century took two forms. Before the invention of printing (and for some time afterwards – in fact some bibliophiles would not have printed books in their libraries and commisioned manuscript versions), book hand was used for the copying of formal, important texts, like bibles. This involved what we might call lettering rather than writing. Several strokes could be used to make a letter, wide margins were often left, illuminations persisted and all was done on durable vellum. For less permanent work clerks or scriveners wrote a more cursive script, that is, one stroke of the pen was enough to form a letter and sometimes a whole line. The March Wardens used scriveners to compile reports to London in a charter or cursive hand. Often they developed idiosyncrasies which made forgery difficult. These could be highly original abbreviations, almost a code, or even consistent and deliberate mistakes. sixteenth-century charter hands can be very difficult to read because many were written at great speed, as though from dictation. When he was in a rage, it might have been difficult to keep up with Old Sir John Forster.

There was more where that came from. On 23rd January 1570 Lord James Stewart, by that time Earl of Moray and Regent of Scotland after his half-sister's abdication, was riding through the streets of Linlithgow. An assassin shot him out of the saddle and bleeding uncontrollably from a stomach wound, he died a few hours later. Lord James had managed to hold the Scottish Borders in check, but his sudden removal had an immediate effect. The day after, a huge raid was mounted by two of the largest surnames. Led by the catholic Kerrs of Ferniehurst and the Scotts of Buccleuch, it was run in support of Mary, Queen of Scots and the usual motives were spiced by politics. In addition to plunder, the Border lords intended severe provocation. After a diversion to burn the treacherous Hector of Harelaw's house in Liddesdale, they rode over the border to create havoc, hoping to let loose the dogs of war with England, to goad Elizabeth beyond endurance. Westmorland rode with the reivers, perhaps reflecting on how direct and uncomplicated their approach was – compared with his own dithering lack of resolve a few weeks earlier. They burned stores of corn at Mindrum and later raided as far south as Morpeth.

In February the Kerrs and Scotts rallied their men again in the cause of their catholic queen and aimed to link up with Leonard, Lord Dacre, and a small army of English sympathisers in east Cumbria. They had mustered under the ingenious pretext of banding together to protect the countryside against the Scottish raids. This conflagration promised to be even more dangerous than the rebellion of Percy and Neville.

Queen Elizabeth's cousin, Lord Hunsdon, had been appointed Warden of the English East March, and with Sir John Forster and his men, he rode quickly to Hexham. Before Dacre could be reinforced by the Scots, the wardens hurried on west. They met him south of Brampton on the banks of the River Gelt. And although outnumbered, Hunsdon and Forster's men had the better of a fierce little fight and drove Dacre and his riders into a panicky retreat. The queen was evidently delighted at the news, sending thanks to her wardens and her great gratitude and favour ensuring that Forster could continue to do as he pleased in the middle march.

A Truce Day was set for 7th July 1575 at the Carter Bar, the scene of an event which came to be known as the Raid of the Redeswire, the border name of the place where the River Rede rises. The border line runs down from the Carter Fell (now following the edge of a large forestry plantation on the Scottish side) and crosses the A68 on a small plateau. It is the watershed of the Carter Burn which runs north into the Jed Water and also of the Rede, which runs south. The view into Scotland is panoramic, the whole of the middle Tweed Valley unfolds to the three Eildon Hills far in the distance. Visitors who turn their gaze south see only moorland stretching down into England, the busy road running through a wide area of bleak hill country before it reaches the fertile green of the Northumberland plain.

The Redeswire is always given as the location of the Truce Day of July 1575, but it is incorrect. The meeting is commemorated by a stone set up on the north-facing slopes of the Carter Bar ridge, at least 200 yards into Scotland, above the watershed of the Jed. The reason for this is traditional. Truce Days were always held just to the north of the border because 'the Scots did always send their ambassadors into England to seek for peace after a war'. And the English ought to be prepared to cross into Scotland to parley. That sounds unlikely, like a later rationalisation by an English historian. But it might have vaguely mirrored the formulaic preliminaries to a Truce Day. The Scots warden usually rode into England to agree the peace with the English warden, and perhaps a habit developed of an equivalent recrossing of the line into Scotland for the meeting itself. Correct form was always important and occasionally had been the subject of argument when Truce Days were first held.

However all that may be, it appears that in 1575 there had been some awkwardness in protocol. The Scottish Warden of the Middle March, Sir William Kerr of Cessford, was for some unstated reason unable to attend. Perhaps he was ill. His deputy, Sir John Carmichael, also Keeper of Liddesdale, came to the Redeswire in his place. For England, Old Sir John Forster, the Warden of the English Middle March appeared and his deputy, Sir George Heron of Ford, accompanied him. There had been difficulty at a previous meeting between Carmichael and Heron and it may be that Forster himself turned up to sort things out. At the extraordinary age of 74, the ride up the steep and winding valley of the Rede would have been a business for Forster, and perhaps he only climbed onto his pony on that summer morning because he had to. The meeting also seems to have been unusually well attended, and that only happened when there were important complaints to be settled, issues affecting many families. The ballad composed afterwards noted the arrival of 'five hundred Fenwicks in a flock', but the attractions of alliteration might have triumphed over accuracy.

At first matters went forward as they should. Complaints were called from the roll by the clerks and dealt with. Then the case of the man recorded as Farnstein (this is very likely to have been a scribal error for Falstone, or Harry Robson of Falstone) came up. Old Sir John could not produce the accused as he was bound, and promised faithfully to bring him to the next meeting. Perhaps Farnstein/Falstone had also failed to appear at the last warden meeting, the one where Heron and Carmichael had argued. In any case the no-show at the Redeswire was not good enough for Carmichael. The temperature rose, maybe drink had been taken. Insults were traded. Drawing himself up to his full stature, Forster pulled rank on the young Scot. He had been the Queen's Warden for nearly twenty years and Carmichael was a mere deputy and knew nothing of the Border! The old man no doubt grew red in the face as he went on to cast more than aspersions on his parentage. The Scots rebuked Sir John: 'Fye Fye! Comparison, comparison.' And then the angry tumult suddenly got completely out of hand. The Tynedale contingent, including the flock of Fenwicks, loosed a volley of arrows; some of Carmichael's men were killed and wounded, and the Scots were driven down the slope, where they met the men of Jedburgh, late arrivals at the Truce Day. No truce being observed, and much reinforced the Scots fought back, killed Sir George Heron along with a handful of others and took Forster and a few English notables prisoner. While they were at it, the party rode down into Redesdale and reived 300 head of cattle.

It was all very embarrassing. The Scottish Regent, the Earl of

Morton, had the prisoners quickly released (the Scots claimed, probably truthfully, that they had only taken prisoners to protect them from a worse fate) and packed them off home with gifts. John Carmichael was offered as a hostage into England, and then released 'with honour'. A commission of inquiry was convened. The likely instigator of the fracas, grumpy Old Sir John, was interrogated at Berwick where it was made clear to him how furious Elizabeth I was. An entirely unnecessary diplomatic fuss at a time when relations between England and Scotland were delicately poised. Lord Killigrew, the queen's ambassador, reported that 'the English warden was not so clean in this matter as he could wish'.

Like himself, Forster's way of doing things was ageing, becoming obsolete. He had come across Carmichael, who was not a Borderer and owned no land in the area, who sought justice and good order more than personal advantage, and they clashed over a case whose details have long vanished from the record. But for some lost reason it particularly mattered to Forster and he resented the persistent, even dogged, interest of Carmichael. It was nothing to do with him! Old Sir John would fix it. Some historians have even gone so far as to suggest that the Farnstein/Falstone case was about to reveal something particularly incriminating about Forster and that he deliberately goaded Carmichael and his men into violence as a cover-up, and perhaps a way of having the Scots Deputy Warden removed. The significance of the Raid of the Redeswire, as it came to be known, was not military or even diplomatic. It signalled the beginnings of a long end for an old way of doing business across the border.

Forster's credit with Queen Elizabeth had not yet run out. She remembered his courage in the face of rebellion in 1569 and 1570 and left him in place as warden, with promises of better behaviour. Henry Hastings, Lord Huntingdon, had become president of the Council of the North and he kept a critical eye on Old Sir John, occasionally calling for his resignation. Well into his eighties, the warden increasingly suffered from what his enemies bluntly termed 'imbecility and weakness', but the ancient warrior had grown into an icon, buttressed by a supporting group of aides and family members, tightly woven into local loyalties by a seamless web of connections and obligations. In addition Forster was a puritan, of a sort, and Huntingdon's candidate to replace him as warden was Sir Cuthbert Collingwood, a catholic and former supporter of the Percy family. Both sides regularly wrote to London complaining about the other.

The feud came to a head in 1587 when Collingwood and Huntingdon's accusations were considered so numerous and plausible by the privy council as to merit investigation. Sir John was obliged to step down but he must have allowed himself a wry smile when he learned that his friend, Lord Hunsdon, the queen's cousin, was to replace him and make a report on his alleged crimes. The old man had been particularly censured for having too many Scottish friends, but it was Forster's preferred means of preventing even more trouble. If a working understanding, a modus vivendi, with the Kerrs, the Burns, the Elliots and other reiving surnames could be found then the ever-present threat of warfare would be averted. If the price for relative peace was a culture of raid and counter-raid, then it was worth paying.

Hunsdon's report to the privy council was unequivocal:

I find that mere malice [has been] prosecuted by Sir Cuthbert Collingwood of long time, and furthered and maintained by my Lord of Huntingdon. There is no man [Forster] so perfect and having so many great matters to do in so great a wardenry, and having to deal with so many perverse and malicious people as in this country

Sir John was duly reinstated in 1588 but the task grew ever more thankless, and a very old man by the 1590s it seems that he found it impossible to carry on as raiding intensified and ran out of even his control.

Lord Huntingdon kept up the pressure, and by 1595 he succeeded at last in having Forster dismissed from the Wardenship of the English Middle March. He had been shameless in his unconcealed understandings with the Scottish surnames – the criminal activities he had ignored 'would fill a large book'. He had allowed, it was claimed, more than forty Scots who deserved the gallows to go free. But the charges would not come to anything – he knew for certain that none would testify against him. A mafia-style omerta seems to have locked down any evidence. Here is the old godfather's reply to his accusers:

I am accompted a negligent officer, an oppressor, a man inclined to private gain and lucre, a destroyer and not a maintainer of the Borders, a bearer with Scots and their actions, and a maintainer of them against my native countrymen . . . God forbid that any one of them could be proved against me!

Despite outfacing his opponents, Sir John found himself suffering the indignity of house arrest under the jursidiction of the Bishop of Durham. His replacement as warden, Lord Ralph Eure, was forced to endure a torrid baptism. With little or no local loyalty to back him, and the undying antipathy of the Forster faction to contend with, he found himself virtually powerless to deal with Scottish raiding. Like most politicians coming into office, he blamed the past: 'Sir John has ruined this country.' But he also understood why he himself was so ineffectual: 'there is no gentleman of worth in Northumberland not near of kin or allied to Sir John Forster'.

In the Border country of the 1590s resentments did not die, they simply matured, and even though Sir John was in his late nineties, those bearing grudges were determined on revenge. In October 1597 a troop of Scottish riders came for him. Arriving under cover of darkness below the walls of Bamburgh Castle, they broke in and found the stair leading up to Forster's private apartments. As they scrambled up, Lady Forster came out onto the landing to see what the noise was, ran inside and got the door shut and bolted in the nick of time.

In 1602 the old warrior died in his bed. More than a hundred years old, he had seen it all, and done most of it himself. Sir Robert Carey had followed the hapless Lord Eure into the English middle march and he left a measured judgement on Sir John Forster:

[He] had been an active and valiant man, and had done great good service . . . [but] grew old, at length to that weakness by reason of his age, that the borderers, knowing it, grew insolent, and by reason of their many excursions and open roads [raids], the inhabitants of the march were much weakened and impoverished.

Lord Hunsdon had affectionately reckoned Old Sir John 'the fittest man for his time'. And it was true. For all his corruption, Forster remains an impressive figure, a long-lived paradigm for the story of the border in the second half of the sixteenth century, in many ways the worst of times. He was a quintessential reiver lord.

DEEP DNA

Several websites now offer loggers-on impressive services to help trace their DNA. Tests are easy to take, all they involve is spitting into a sample container (apparently not after having drunk a cup of coffee) and sending it through the post to analysts. Newcastle University prefers blood, and in particular they are looking for the descendants of Border Reivers to carry on a long tradition and spill some – their own. At the Border History Fair held at Hexham on 2nd December 2006, many people with the right qualifications came forward. These included being able to trace all four grandparents to the same area, either in Northumberland, North Cumbria, County Durham or the Scottish Borders. It also helped if subjects had reiver surnames such as Fenwick, Robson or Milburn. The Head of the Institute of Human Genetics at Newcastle University is Professor John Burn, a prime candidate who meets all of the criteria, although why he would actively seek a genetic link with the likes of Geordie Burn is less clear. And apart from sharing the same DNA, it would be entertaining to work out the precise connection between Old Sir John Forster and the delicate English novelist, E.M. Forster.

When Sir John's long career was only beginning, international politics pulled Borderers in various competing directions. Mary, Queen of Scots was a committed catholic and a focus for all those who continued to worship in the old faith in both England as well as Scotland. By itself that set her in opposition to the protestant Elizabeth I, who also worried over Mary's strong connections with catholic monarchs in continental Europe. The French-speaking young Queen of Scots had very recently been one herself. Further complications were added by Mary's profound wish and ambition to be named as the heir to the throne of England.

Because Elizabeth believed that Mary would ultimately prove hostile (no matter that they initially exchanged an elaborately affectionate correspondence, and hoped very much to meet and talk, although they never quite did), she was determined that her northern frontier would be well organised and well guarded. The new fortifications at Berwick continued to rise, soaking up vast sums from the London exchequeur. Henry, Lord Scrope of Bolton, was appointed Warden of the West March and instructed to summon a commission to sort out the administration of the border, just as Thomas Wharton had done a decade before. It was also in Mary of Scotland's direct interest to show herself at least as effective a sovereign as Elizabeth if she wished to succeed her, and her wardens cooperated in the commission. Meetings were held at Carlisle and Dumfries in 1563 with Scrope, Sir John Forster and Lord John Maxwell in attendance. The agenda shed more light on the condition of law and order – and life – on the border.

With the recent resolution of the matter of the Debatable Land, more confusion over jurisdiction was not to be tolerated. Severe confiscations would punish any Scots or English (the deliberations make it clear that it was mainly Scots involved) who pastured their cattle in 'the opposite realm'. A time limit of six hours was set by the commission. Inside that period, no offence was deemed to have taken place, but over it, then the beasts would be forfeit, seized by the landowner whose pasture they were illegally grazing. The Cheviot ranges and the lower lying valleys and watersheds were open, un-fenced country in the sixteenth century and cows and sheep had no idea where the border was. Therefore it made sense to allow shepherds time to turn straying beasts back to their own pasture.

Problems arose when the border was persistently ignored and Scots in particular were in the habit of attempting to establish customary rights to pasture which lay in England. One of the many complaints against Old Sir John Forster was that he turned a blind eye to this practice in the English middle march. Scots were apparently going so far as to build summer shielings in England.

Over in the west, the Grahams also drove their animals to grazings over the border, but in the other direction. After many years of doing this without hindrance, they were appalled when the Maxwells cited the laws of 1563 and seized their flocks and herds. In 1580 the Grahams fell foul again when they bought land in Scotland and simply moved over the border and settled down to sow and grow corn. There existed a general prohibition of cross-border cultivation – but the complaints about the Grahams seem like an extreme application of the law. But then they were Grahams.

Scrope, Maxwell, Forster and their clerks spent much effort on the problem of 'overswearing'. This was the sixteenth-century equivalent of an exaggerated insurance claim. When beasts had been reived and a complaint subsequently made to a warden, injured parties had got into the habit of overswearing. That is, they greatly inflated the value of what they had lost so that when fines were levied and compensation paid, they did very nicely thank you. Amongst farmers of the twenty-first century, this cultural habit may not have entirely died out. Back in 1596 Lord Scrope wrote to London with the extraordinary calculation that Borderers often claimed twenty times the value of goods lost. Some compensating increase was acceptable but this had become ridiculous. No doubt many imaginative scams were running – in both directions.

The commissioners of 1563 wished to hold Truce Days once a month, so heavy was the press of business. This proved impractical, but certain simple and draconian measures did at least clarify the legal picture and force the pace of justice. When a man committed the same offence three times, he was to be summarily executed. No doubt many were guilty, but how many answered with their lives is less certain. An unconscious note of irony ends the deliberations of the warden meetings of 1563. All should know and understand the content of what had been agreed, that is, the new laws made since the last period of 'amity and perpetual peace'.

That 1564 was considered a peaceful year on the border says much about the state of civil order. It was not as if an age of amity and perpetual peace had dawned, more that the year seems to have seen slightly less raiding and killing than usual.

The ever-canny Elizabeth I continued to strengthen her hand. After the death of Lord Grey, towards the end of 1563, she sent Francis Russell, Earl of Bedford, north to take over the wardenship of the east march. He was also made Governor of Berwick, a title with a decided colonial ring to it. On 27th March the earl arrived in the town and was much vexed to find the defences in a weak and vulnerable state, and the garrison little better, lacking in organisation. A census of 1565 counted more than 2,000 soldiers, labourers and tradesmen working at Berwick, and Russell immediately set about tightening up administration. As a second in command, he appointed a High Marshall, a Treasurer, a Chief Porter (to control traffic in and out) and a Master of the Ordnance. To set an example, Russell took his turn at doing sentry duty along the walls.

The Scots were also active, but in a very different way. In the west march the bloodfeud between the Elliots and the Scotts sparked into life. Led by Martin Elliot of Braidley, near Hermitage Castle, a party of 300 raiders made their way up Carewoodrig, over Mosspaul and descended on Scott territory around Hawick. Black smoke billowed into the air. Flooding into Liddesdale in great strength, the Scotts quickly retaliated, lifting many cattle and killing both Elliots and their close allies, the Crosers. Ill-matched, and almost overwhelmed by superior numbers, Martin Elliot was forced to play politics. Contacting Lord Scrope at Carlisle, he offered to deliver Hermitage Castle into English control and sought the protection of Elizabeth I. The Elliots would even change their nationality and become Englishmen. Scrope sensibly declined both suggestions, but he did agree to support the Elliots with cash, and if they needed occasionally to escape the Scotts by crossing the border, the warden would turn a blind eye. For all the surface talk of amity and perpetual peace, the privy council were happy quietly and ruthlessly to encourage mayhem in the Scottish borders. Sir John Forster, as usual, understood the situation better than most: 'the longer such conditions continue . . . the better quiet we shall be', meaning it was much preferable to see the Scots fighting amongst themselves than raiding over the border.

Despite the number of bloodfeuds (almost 40 were festering at that time on the middle and east marches), there is an increasing sense of raiding being seen as international rather than internecine. It may be an impression formed by the nature of the sources, but the Scots seemed to be directing their raids more towards England and vice-versa.

Feuds were different. Usually carried on amongst neighbours of the same nationality, they tended to be local affairs. In Northumberland the Herons feuded with the Carrs over the ownership of Ford Castle, and were said to wish to 'overthrow each other rather than face the enemy', and the Forsters were at odds with the Muschamps and with the Greys. By 1560 Lord Grey, Francis Russells's predecessor in the English east march, was complaining that everyday life was coloured by continual feuding: 'there is daily armour and weapon used both to the church, the market and the field, as in time of war: as no man here minds to deal in the matter, it is needful that some be sent from the Queen and Council to make an end hereof'.

Some brave, or foolhardy, people occasionally took matters into their own hands and intervened. When Bernard Gilpin was preaching at Rothbury Parish Church in Coquetdale in 1566, he noticed the Heron family in the congregation, fully armed, and also the Lisles and Ellerkers – with whom they were at feud. Paying little attention to the service, both sides glared at each other and appeared to be moving closer. Swords were drawn and then sheathed. When they were drawn a second time, Gilpin halted the service and his sermon, and he:

> came down from the pulpit, and stepping to the ringleaders of either faction, first of all he appeased the tumult. Next he laboured to

establish peace between them, but he could not prevail in that: only they promised to keep the peace unbroken so long as Mr Gilpin should remain in the church.

When it became clear that that was as much as he could achieve, Gilpin climbed back into his pulpit 'and spent the rest of the alloted time which remained in disgracing that barbarous and bloody custom of theirs'.

The commissioners of 1563 at Dumfries and Carlisle were anxious to revive and clarify the old practice of hot trod, which encouraged the immediate pursuit of stolen goods and thieves even if it involved crossing the border. One of the difficulties was an understandable fear of feud. Many law-abiding farmers relieved of their beasts believed that reprisals would follow any successful hot trod, or indeed a Cold Trod. It was simply not worth the risk, better to seek redress through the wardenries, or accept the loss. In this way feuding in an increasingly fearful society greatly hindered the administration of justice.

At Berwick the new defences spoke loudly of the possibility of war between Scotland and England. No one had ever seen such massive walls, and the ruthlessness which had demolished many houses on the north and eastern sides of the town to create open fields of fire underlined how seriously Elizabeth took that possibility. Even the medieval castle of Berwick, where Edward I had listened to claimants for the throne of Scotland in the 1290s, had been left outside the perimeter.

Nevertheless, diplomacy tried to keep pace with construction (to say nothing of the funding of the feuding Elliots in the west) and Francis Russell was directed to convene a meeting at Berwick to discuss the pressing matter of dynastic politics. Elizabeth was strongly suggesting her favourite, Robert Dudley, Earl of Leicester, as a suitable match for Mary, Queen of Scots, but as a rival queen, she felt that his rank was inferior, 'unequal and dishonourable', as one nineteenth-century historian remarked. For three days Russell, Randolph, the English ambassador in Edinburgh, and Lord James Stewart, Earl of Moray and William Maitland of Lethington, Mary's Secretary of State discussed the matter and arrived at no conclusion. Eight months later the young queen arrived at her own and married Henry Stewart, Lord Darnley, a sufficiently distant cousin. He was 21 years old, possessed of the Stewart good looks, the Stewart arrogance and the Stewart recklessness. Through his mother, he was also the eldest male descendant of Henry VII's eldest daughter which gave him as powerful a claim on Elizabeth's throne as Mary's.

The Darnley marriage hardened attitudes – on both sides of the border. Mary's half-brother, James, Earl of Moray, felt compelled to rise in the armed rebellion known as 'the Chaseabout Raid'. Battle was never joined and after only a few weeks, Moray was isolated. Most of the major surnames in the south, the Maxwells, both branches of the Kerrs and the Humes remained loyal to Mary. By September Moray was in Dumfries pleading for English support. Elizabeth sent £1,000 and the Earl of Bedford gave £500 on his own account. The English ambassador, Thomas Randolph, advised the privy council to maintain their subsidy to the Elliots so that they continued to raid the Humes in the east march 'and kept them at home'. Substantial bands of reivers began to ride again, and in the west march the Maxwell/Johnstone feud found some pretext or other to flare up into renewed bitterness.

THE CHEVIOT, THE LAMBS
AND THE BLEAK, BLEAK HILLS

Hardiness was and remains the basic quality of those sheep bred for meat in the Border hills. Lincoln rams and some Leicester bloodlines were used in the eighteenth century to improve the breed and generally produce larger animals. But it is their ability to live out on the windy hills and high valleys all year round which is reckoned to make their meat so dense and flavourful. Hay is only dropped for them when the snow is deepest and even the most determined ewe cannot scrape her way down to the bitter winter grass. Hill lambs mature late, having seen at least one winter, and the grazing they live on is entirely natural, with all its herbs and different varieties of grass, the very definition of organic. The older ewes are often sold to lower-lying farms where the climate is kinder and a longer productive life is possible.

Work at Berwick accelerated and the Earl of Bedford was encouraged both to promote discord, but quietly, over the border and also to hold his garrison in a state of readiness. The moment for action came when two of the Berwick captains led 800 riders to pillage the nearby villages of Chirnside and Edington, and to lift stock and take prisoners. The exchange of protests and protestations of innocence and misunderstanding which followed the raid was a classic passage of sixteenth-century frontier diplomacy.

When Mary, Queen of Scots' council complained and asked Elizabeth to reprimand Bedford for such a flagrant breach, they received a reply which was convoluted in its reasoning but, given the fondness of Borderers for punch and counter-punch, not altogether implausible. The English claimed that they had only attacked Chirnside because they themselves had been ambushed by a party of Scots some time beforehand. These Scots had captured a few Englishmen, who themselves were attempting to take prisoner other Scots (or possibly the same Scots who ambushed them in the first place) who had been robbing both Scots and English on either side of the border. So the expedition was not an unprovoked attack but rather a rescue attempt. And anyway there were only 400 riders in the party, not 800. In a master-stroke of po-faced hypocrisy, Elizabeth ordered Bedford to make sure the laws were respected and complaints properly heard. So there.

Despite all the diplomatic froth, 1565 saw the general atmosphere darken. Maxwell was attending to the state of his fortresses in the west, and James Hepburn, the Earl of Bothwell, had command of a troop of horsemen and was attempting to subdue the English-backed Elliots in Liddesdale, though with only mixed success. A year later Little Jock Elliot was to deal a hefty blow to Bothwell's prestige.

As part of their marriage settlement, Mary insisted that her young husband be recognised as 'Henry, King of Scots'. It all seems to have quickly gone to his head, and there were reports of near-insufferable swagger and arrogance. Darnley and Mary had been married by catholic rite, and although he had come to Scotland religiously neutral, the new king embraced the old faith when he attended mass at Christmas 1565. It was said that afterwards he strutted along Edinburgh's High Street announcing that with his reconversion all Scotland had come back to catholicism. Reaction to this found scandalous expression in the murder of Mary's Italian secretary, David Riccio, by a band of protestant lords. The fact that Darnley's was one of the daggers left in the corpse shows inconsistency at the very least and also substantial dashes of jealousy and rashness. At court and around Edinburgh the hotheaded King Henry was rapidly finding himself an excluded, almost irrelevant figure.

Nevertheless he did serve one vital dynastic purpose. Darnley fathered a son on his queen and in June 1566 the baby who would become James VI and I was born. Three months later Mary led a judicial expedition to deal with the ever-present problems of the Borders. Levies were summoned to muster at Melrose on 8th October, and from there the queen rode with her small army to Jedburgh. Assizes were put in session for six days. Apparently the trend was for offenders to be heavily fined – if they had the cash. The historian, Robert Lindsay of Pitscottie, reported that 'poor men were hanged and rich men were hanged by their purses'.

At some point during the assizes, Queen Mary heard that Bothwell had been attacked by Little Jock Elliot of the Park, and then carried in a litter, badly, maybe fatally wounded, back to Hermitage Castle. No doubt against all advice, to say nothing of common sense, Mary set out to ride from Jedburgh, through dangerous Elliot country, to Hermitage and back – in a day. It is not an easy journey from Hawick up the valley of the Slitrig to the bleak high pass over Whitrope and down into Liddesdale, and the fact that Mary could not be dissuaded from making it speaks of the play of powerful emotions. The round trip was nearly 50 miles on horseback, no mean physical feat for a fit man and a hardy, surefooted pony, and a tremendous challenge for a slight, 24-year-old woman only four months after giving birth to her first child. No other explanation for this rashness fits so well as the simple likelihood that the queen had fallen madly in love with Bothwell. Memorably described as 'a man sold to all wickedness', he was just that, a man, a vital, brave and dynamic man, and not a preening boy or a sickly French prince.

After spending only two hours with the wounded earl at Hermitage, Mary climbed wearily back into the saddle for the long journey back to Jedburgh. It was 16th October, a short autumn day. And it may have been that in the gathering gloaming, her little grey pony missed its footing and threw the queen headlong into a marsh. Probably soaked through, Mary and her escort trudged back to Jedburgh. The house where she lodged still stands; it had been lent by the Kerrs of Ferniehurst.

The day after her return, the queen fell gravely ill, possibly having contracted pneumonia as a result of her soaking. Fevered, fainting, Mary believed that her last hours and days had come, and when the illness allowed, she began to make her peace. For her nobility, or 'governors', unity was what mattered above all:

You know that by the division of governors, provinces and regions are troubled and molested, and contrariwise, by agreement and unity, they are stabilised, pacified and advanced. Therefore above all things, I require you to have charity, concord and love amongst yourselves.

To du Croc, the French ambassador, she asked:

Commend me to the king, your master: tell him I hope he will protect my dear son, and also that he will grant one year of my dowry, after my death, to pay my debts and reward my faithful servants: but above all, tell the Queen-Mother that I heartily ask her forgiveness for the offences I may have either done, or have been supposed to have committed against her.

Despite her conviction that the end would soon come, Mary's illness reached its crisis after six days and her doctors were optimistic: 'Her Majesty has been sick these six days past, and this night had some dwams of swooning, which puts men in some fear. Nevertheless we see no tokens of death.'

On 25th October the Earl of Bothwell was brought to Jedburgh after an uncomfortable journey on a horse-litter from Hermitage Castle. Lord Darnley arrived three days later when the queen was almost recovered but he was not well received by the earls and lords attending her, and indeed he may not have been permitted to see his sick wife. In any event King Henry stayed only one night, not lodging in the same house, but with Lord Hume in the High Street. The presence of his rival, the cause of all the alarm, cannot have made for conviviality, but all was clearly well with Mary by 30 October, when a messenger was dispatched to Edinburgh to buy and bring red silk, black taffeta and black velvet to make a new gown. She had survived but the business of bringing justice to the Borders had almost cost Mary her life. The remainder of her reign would turn out to be brief and the rest of her life nothing but a deepening disappointment, and she was sometimes heard during her long imprisonment to remark that she wished she had died in Jedburgh.

BUSTLE AT THE BASTLE

When Mary, Queen of Scots stayed in Jedburgh in 1566, she and her entourage of ladies took over a large house owned by the Kerrs of Ferniehurst. It had survived the terrible destruction of the English raids of the 1540s and been much added to since. Originally a near-indestructible bastle house, it was heightened, climbing to four storeys, although the windows remained sensibly and defensibly small. The staircase supports the theory of the left-handed Kerrs since it has the rope/handrail on that side. Rather as happens before modern royal visits, a new toilet was installed for the queen's use, and for her ladies. At Jedburgh Mary was attended exclusively by her identically named body servants, the famous Four Marys: Mary Seaton, Mary Beaton, Mary Fleming and Mary Livingston. Confusing. In 1987 the house was refurbished and opened to visitors. For some reason it was timed to coincide with the 400th anniversary of Mary's execution.

Fully recovered, the queen led her retinue eastwards to visit Hume Castle, and from there on to Berwick and Eyemouth. The frontier around the town encloses a substantial pale, a tract of good farmland sufficiently large to feed at least some of the garrison, and it is marked by the Bound Road. There Sir John Forster met Queen Mary, probably at Mordington Bridge, on the old road from Duns. Bothwell rode with her and Lord Hume and Walter Kerr of Cessford had 500 men in attendance. They made their way down to Halidon Hill, the site of the Scots' dreadful defeat at the hands of Edward III's archers in 1333 and a place where they could see the town of Berwick and its splendid new walls. Any sense of historical irony was not recorded. The Master of the Ordnance fired a volley from his cannon in salute, but as the queen dismounted she was kicked by Sir John's pony, and while managing to conduct a meeting on cross-border business, she grew very uncomfortable. In fact the pain and bruising were so severe that Mary was forced to abandon the planned visit to Eyemouth and retrace her steps to Hume Castle to rest for two days. Clearly the Borders was not a lucky place for her majesty.

As raiding grew into an ever more constant sore in the second half of the sixteenth century, ill luck struck many. At the end of a winding track in the high country on the southern flanks of the Ettrick Valley lies the remote farm of Dodhead. Walter Scott made it famous because he preserved and 'improved' a ballad which told the unlucky tale of the laird, 'Jamie Telfer o' the Fair Dodheid'. The people named in its verses were real and they set the action probably in the 1570s, possibly as late as the 1590s. It tells the sorry tale of the victim of a raid into Scotland, and tells it with verve – and even a happy ending. The Captain of the fort at Bewcastle, a government officer, raided the farm and lifted all of Telfer's cattle:

> There's nothing left in the fair Dodhead,
> But a greeting wife and bairnies three,
> And six poor calves stand in the stall.
> A routing loud for their minnie.

Even the least of the Border lairds had connections they could call upon in extremis, and Jamie immediately rode over the hills to Stobs in the Slitrig Valley, below Hawick. But Gibbie Elliot refused to join the hot trod after Bewcastle, telling Telfer that he should seek help from those to whom he paid blackmail. There are suspicious echoes of the Elliot links with the English March Wardens and their generous subsidies, and the local politics of the Elliot/Scott feud persuaded the persistent Jamie to ride down to Teviotdale. At Branxholm, Buccleuch promised to raise 'the water', meaning all of his people who lived by Teviot Water.

> Go warn the water, broad and wide,
> Go warn it soon and hastily!
> They that will not ride for Telfer's cows,
> Let them never look in the face o' me.
>
> Warn Wat o' Harden and his sons,
> With them will Borthwick Water ride,
> Warn Goldilands and Allanhaugh,
> And Gilmanscleuch, and Commonside.

The intended route of the hot trod was made clear by Walter Scott of Buccleuch's instructions. After mustering a party at Branxholm, Telfer and the Scotts planned to ride up Teviotdale to the watershed at Mosspaul, and then up over Carewoodrig and down into Liddesdale:

> Ride by the gate at Priesthaughswire
> And warn the Currors o' the Lee;
> As you come down the Hermitage Slack,
> Warn doughty Willie o' Gorrenberry.

But they caught them up much sooner than Buccleuch believed they would, coming on the Captain of Bewcastle and his stolen cattle making a weary way up the narrow pass carved by the Frostlie Burn. It was a classic example of fast-moving pursuers overtaking a party of thieves ponderous with too much plunder. It often happened, and was the reason why a hot trod was encouraged. Telfer and the Scotts first tried talking, but negotiations quickly failed. 'Set on!' shouted young Willie Scott and a furious fight ensued along the banks of the little burn:

> Then to it they went with heart and hand,
> The blows fell thick as bickering hail,
> And many a horse ran masterless,
> And many a comely cheek was pale.

First into the thick of the fray, Willie Scott was killed, and his kinsman (perhaps even his natural father), Auld Wat of Harden, was enraged. All the Scotts roared for revenge, led into the ruck of the fighting by the barrel-chested, bull-like old warrior:

> But he's taken off his good steel cap,
> And thrice he's waved it in the air;
> The Dinlay snow was never more white
> Than the lyart locks o' Harden's hair.
>
> 'Revenge! Revenge!' Auld Wat did cry,
> 'Fye lads, lay on them cruelly!
> We'll never see Teviotside again
> Until Willie's death revenged shall be.'
>
> O, many a horse ran masterless,
> The splintered lances flew on high,
> But before they won the Kershope Ford,
> The Scotts had gotten the victory.

Jamie Telfer had his cows back, but the cost had been heavy. As well as young Willie Scott, thirty of the Bewcastle troopers had been killed, and although in its triumph the ballad does not name them, more Scotts probably fell by the Frostlie Burn. The Captain of Bewcastle had been taken prisoner – and perhaps he might prove useful.

There was a price to be extracted for all that blood, and Auld Wat rallied his surname to him. In what might have been a pre-arranged plan, and what would certainly have supplied a motive, the pursuers turned into raiders and made their way down into Liddesdale. Their target was Stonegarthside Hall, an impressive house which still stands by the roadside south of Kershopefoot. It belonged to the Captain of Bewcastle and the Scotts intended to return the compliment by lifting his cows. Auld Wat probably reckoned to manage all without a fight, enough Scott blood had been spilled that day, by offering the captured captain in exchange for his beasts.

Recorded in a ballad much repeated and probably more than a little altered (in fact there is a version in which the Elliots did ride to help Dodheid – and it is true that Sir Walter Scott sometimes inserted the Scotts into unwarranted starring roles), the tale of Jamie Telfer o' the Fair Dodheid nevertheless carries the marks of authenticity. It feels as though it was composed soon after the event when memory was fresh and the details reliable. It was the small change of life on the frontier, a routine raid and counter-raid, conducted in part under the walls of Hermitage Castle and in the jurisdiction of the Keeper of Liddesdale.

In 1567 the Earl of Bothwell was not at Hermitage, but in Edinburgh, and although historians have argued the facts endlessly, it appears that he was involved in plotting the death of King Henry Darnley. At Jedburgh and elsewhere it was said that Mary, Queen of Scots had made it clear that she could no longer stand the sight of her feckless husband and in fact longed to be rid of him. Divorce was possible but that option might have compromised the legitimacy of her precious son and heir, Prince James. That left only one other course of action, but in the dark recesses of hatred, passion and boundless ambition, who knows if the queen said more?

In any event, gunpowder changed the political landscape spectacularly. In February 1567 Darnley's house at Kirk o' Field, which lay just outside the Flodden wall to the south of Edinburgh, was blown up. The strangled corpse of the young king was found in the garden. Who did it? Whatever the evidence and the actual truth of the matter, the Earl of Bothwell was widely suspected. Due process was required. The death of a king, albeit one only in name, had occurred and someone had to stand trial. Bothwell appeared in front of a jury on 12th April, and a well-armed troop of riders hung around near at hand to make sure the correct verdict was arrived at. It was. And the growing scandal began to gather momentum.

When Mary took the next step, even if it was with Bothwell's hand on her neck, by marrying him on 15th May, matters had gone beyond repair. The couple had lost the support of most of the nobility. Darnley had been a joke and his removal almost tolerable, but Bothwell as Mary's husband and potentially king-consort could be dangerous. And appearances were important. Mary had profoundly stained the institution of monarchy by seeming to have encouraged the murder of her husband, and then becoming the wife, willing or not, of the man suspected of that murder. Public opinion ran strongly against the queen and her lover, and her government of Scotland began to wobble.

FÊTE ACCOMPLI

The baptism of the infant James VI was marked by the staging of the first Renaissance fête ever seen in Britain. On the esplanade of Stirling Castle a wooden fort was built and defended in a mock siege. As fireworks crackled and flashed, 'wild Highland men' and other agents of anarchy (surprisingly, no Border Reivers are reported) were beaten back by Mary, Queen of Scots' valiant garrison. The fête was based on spectacles seen by the queen, and specifically on the lavish entertainments mounted on the French/Spanish border by the young French king, Charles IX in 1564-5. Like these, the Stirling extravaganza was intended to symbolise the power and durability of the Stewart dynasty while stressing the need for religious tolerance and friendship between England and Scotland. As in the French celebrations, a political message was made unmissable and explicit. The following was composed by Patrick Adamson, a Protestant minister.

Our leader has transposed Mars ablaze with civil war into peace in our time . . .

A powerful young woman, whose race was from the lofty blood of kings, controls by her rule the warlike Scots . . .

The importance of kingship is eternal; it will be in the power of the Stewart family; the crown of Mary awaits her grandsons . . .

The fates will grant you to extend the territory of your realm, until the Britons, having finished with war, will learn at last to unite in one kingdom.

Chased by Lord Hume and 800 riders, Mary and Bothwell fled from Edinburgh, first to Borthwick Castle in Midlothian and then to Dunbar. On 15th June the crisis came to a head when the Confederate Lords, the coalition formed to oppose the queen, met her forces in battle order at Carberry, south of Musselburgh. After a day of talking rather than fighting, Bothwell was granted a safe conduct into exile (he died in Denmark) and Mary was taken into the custody of the lords. When she reached Edinburgh, the mob chanted, 'Burn the whore! Burn the whore!'

There was to be a dramatic escape from the castle on Loch Leven and a losing battle to fight at Langside near Glasgow, but compromise at Carberry signalled the effective end of the reign of Mary, Queen of Scots. She abdicated in favour of her son in July 1567 and the little boy was crowned James VI at Stirling a few days later.

Meanwhile it was business as usual in the Borders. Turmoil at the heart of central government always encouraged the reiving families to saddle up, and as the autumn and winter of 1567 came on, they rode hard and often for plunder.

James Stewart, Earl of Moray, was named Regent again and he quickly determined to stamp on disorder in the south. A central difficulty faced by many large and well-advertised judicial expeditions was that the really hardened elements often ignored summons to appear before the court. In October 1567, Moray quietly gathered a small force with Lords Lindsay and Hume and the Earl of Morton, and suddenly descended on Hawick, hoping to surprise Liddesdale men in the town. The intelligence was good and 40 reivers were captured. Some were drowned in the pools where the Slitrig meets the Teviot, others were taken for trial in Edinburgh.

A year later, Moray was in the marches again, this time with 6,000 men in the west, making sure that Queen Mary's Maxwell supporters did not stir. On the English side Lord Hunsdon, lately made Warden of the East March, was dishing out summary justice to Teviotdale reivers, and with Sir John Forster he cooperated with Moray in keeping the Borders quiet.

Under house arrest in England, moved from Carlisle to Bolton Castle, Mary remained a focus for the catholic cause. Supporters proposed a marriage to the catholic Duke of Norfolk (with a clause insisting that Prince James would be betrothed to Norfolk's daughter), but it was pie in the political sky. To no one's surprise, Elizabeth frowned at the idea. Within months Norfolk found himself in the

Tower of London, indicted for alleged treason and certain recusancy. His execution shocked the predominantly catholic northern aristocracy and his brother-in-law, Charles Neville, Earl of Westmorland, began to ponder the removal of his queen, her replacement with Mary and the restoration of the old faith.

BRING BACK BOTHWELL

After the debacle at Carberry, James Hepburn, Earl of Bothwell, fled, ultimately to Denmark. Captured in 1567, he was imprisoned in grim conditions at Dragsholm Castle on the island of Zeeland. Apparently he spent the rest of his life chained to a stake half his height. This may have been a means of restraining him because it is said that Bothwell went mad. Cause and effect are difficult to disentangle. After ten years in the dungeon, Hepburn died and, surprisingly, his body was mummified and now lies in Faravejle Church, near Dragsholm. Tourists are encouraged to visit the last resting place of 'a Scottish king'. Bothwell's direct descendant, Captain Sir Alastair Buchan-Hepburn, is campaigning to have the body returned to Scotland. The Danes are unwilling – for the strange reason that they believe the mummy may not be the earl. Buchan-Hepburn has offered to have his DNA compared with it, and if there is a match, which there should be if it is indeed Bothwell, then it should be brought back to Scotland. Perhaps the Danes will relent.

Thomas Percy, Earl of Northumberland, had approached Lord Scrope, Warden of the English West March, when he had the Scottish queen temporarily in his custody at Carlisle Castle. He attempted to persuade him that protocol would be served if she was released into his keeping. Percy had remained a catholic, not thought reliable by Elizabeth I and Scrope wisely declined his kind offer. And so when the Earl of Westmorland looked for support in his rebellious plans, he did not have to look far.

With the help of highly talented and utterly loyal civil servants such as Thomas Cromwell, Robert Cecil and Francis Walsingham, the Tudors had built up an efficient, centralised administration which could be run from London. A vital function was the gathering of intelligence and its use in formulating policy. Walsingham and Cecil, men who depended entirely on Elizabeth I for their status and advancement and were not powerful hereditary landowners, created a network of informants whose tentacles reached into every corner of England – and many in Scotland, Wales and Ireland. In 1569 it was only a matter of time before London got wind of Westmorland and Northumberland's treasonable talk. Subsequent events showed considerable incompetence, and it seems likely that in formulating plans proper secrecy and discretion were not observed. The earls had been in touch with the Spanish for help, and written to the Duke of Alva, Governor of the Netherlands.

When Elizabeth sent word to Westmorland and Northumberland, summoning them to appear at court in Windsor, they flapped into a panic, believing that royal spies had discovered their plot. They probably had sniffed something, but Westmorland flew into precipitate – and pointless – activity. It was said that it took threats and cajolements to stir Northumberland into rebellion. No coherent plan of campaign appeared to exist, and when it quickly became clear that help was not on its way from the Spanish Netherlands (a fleet was expected at Hartlepool) or from catholic sympathisers amongst the Border heidsmen, the earls panicked even more and began to think of flight rather than victory. With Sir John Forster standing firm, having retaken the castles at Alnwick and Warkworth (without a fight) and fortified Newcastle, and the Regent Moray recently arrived in the Borders with soldiers at his command, options and time began to run out.

At Hexham the rebel army disintegrated and Westmorland and Northumberland ran for it. Their support now only a personal bodyguard of forty or so faithful men, the earls and Lady Anne, Countess of Northumberland, fled for shelter to Naworth, the house of Leonard Dacre, a local catholic lord. His door remained firmly shut, and at midnight on 20th December, in desperation, they took the only course remaining and rode into the nest of thieves and outlaws that was Liddesdale.

It was a headlong descent. Charles Neville, Thomas Percy and his wife, Lady Anne, were now entirely at the mercy of men like Jock o' the Side Armstrong and Black James Ormiston, one of the killers hired to stab David Riccio to death. Hoping that the rising would succeed, Mary, Queen of Scots had written to catholic sympathisers amongst the Border surnames, and so the arrival of the earls in Liddesdale was not exactly a surprise, even if the circumstances were certainly a disappointment. But Ormiston and Armstrong were ruthless reivers, thieves for whom everything – and everyone – had a price.

Through her agents Elizabeth I let it be known that she was willing to pay handsomely for the traitors, while on the Scottish side, the Regent Moray was similarly disposed, anxious not to offend England. Black Ormiston and Jock Armstrong must have rubbed their hands in glee at the thought of a lucrative auction. Sleeping on the earthen floors of what they certainly thought of as miserable, verminous, freezing hovels, changing their expensive and conspicuous clothes for the rough cloth of ordinary people, the earls and their countess no doubt looked at each other and pondered the high price of rebellion.

The Regent Moray wasted no time. Messages were got through the winter weather to the mercurial Martin Elliot of Braidley. He rode with three hundred to deliver an ultimatum to Black Ormiston. The earls could not stay in Scotland, their presence was a political embarrassment. They were to be gone in a day – or else. Ormiston acted immediately and moved the fugitives down the Liddel Water to Harelaw, the tower of Hector Armstrong. It lay only half a mile from the border. Westmorland and Northumberland had been stripped of all they owned. Countess Anne had been left behind in Liddesdale, her value as a captive probably the only thing keeping her from greater indignities at the grubby hands of Jock o' the Side and his crew of unwashed ruffians. The lady was a famous beauty, and will have no doubt been a sore temptation.

At Harelaw, Hector Armstrong managed somehow to detach Northumberland from Westmorland and those men who had stayed with him. Despite Armstrong 'having obligations' to the earl, he promptly sold him for cash to the agents of the Regent Moray. Westmorland attempted a rescue but Thomas Percy was hurried away to prison in the castle of Loch Leven, no doubt more secure than when it failed to hold Queen Mary.

Meanwhile the catholic Kerrs of Ferniehurst had saddled their ponies. Riding down into Liddesdale, they released Lady Anne and the feckless Earl of Westmorland and took them back to the comfort of warm firesides, clean clothes and some deference to their rank. Sir Thomas Kerr did not trouble to conceal his guests. When an English spy talked his way into Ferniehurst, he casually came across the Earl of Westmorland out walking, apparently unconcerned about security or that persons unknown to him might approach. Such laxness would soon cost Kerr dear.

The rebels were also looked after by the Scotts of Buccleuch at Branxholm before making their miserable way into exile in Flanders. Surprisingly the Border heidsmen appear to have acted solely out of fellow feeling for those who clung to the old faith. After a failed, shambolic attempt at rebellion in the north of England, there could be absolutely nothing in it politically for them, but their support showed how easy it was for powerful Borderers to ignore government policy and act independently. The English were sore displeased, and here is Lord Hunsdon's letter of 9 January to the Regent Moray:

> That notwithstanding his grace's direct proclamations against re-
> ceiving or aiding the queen's rebels anywhere in Scotland, yet the
> Earl of Westmorland and others were openly kept in Ferniehurst,
> and some others of them at Branxholm with Buccleuch, others of
> them with Bedrule, Andrew Kerr, and the Sheriff of Teviotdale. And
> upon Thursday night last, the Countess of Northumberland was
> brought by Ferniehurst towards Hume Castle, and was forced to
> stay by the way at Roxburgh, by the soreness of the weather (being a
> great storm), so as it was eight o' clock on Friday morning ere she
> came to Hume . . . The Regent well knew that the queen could not
> take this well at their hands, especially at Lord Hume's . . . and she
> [may] make him repent his folly.

A letter to the Earl of Leicester ends the sorry tale of the Rising of the Northern Earls with a footnote on the fate of Lady Anne:

> The Countess of Northumberland retired out of Scotland for very
> penury, being miserably treated there, and forced for her safety to
> move from friend to friend without rest, fearing always to be spoiled
> by these barbarous people.

Hunsdon's letter to Moray was imporant for more than political reasons. Unusually it mentions the weather; but then the weather in the 1570s was itself unusual. The great storm which delayed the Countess of Northumberland at Roxburgh was only one of many in that rainy and windswept decade. Elizabeth I's efforts to bring the rebel earls to justice were much hampered by severe weather in Yorkshire, and the Earl of Sussex was forced to delay his expedition into Scotland. Three years later 'a tempest' lasting more than a week washed away part of Berwick's circuit of medieval walls. In 1587 what was described as 'stormy and contagious weather' did at least have the effect of discouraging raiding for a few weeks. It must have been bad. The year after that the Spanish Armada famously suffered in terrible conditions around the coasts of Britain.

There are not many reports noting the weather in the late sixteenth century, but that fact in itself makes a concentration of them at the beginning of the 1570s all the more significant. It was also the period when the last and most intense period of reiving began, and these two facts cannot be a coincidence.

THE DEEP MIDWINTER

Perhaps one of the most popular winter scenes ever painted and reproduced on endless Christmas cards, Peter Breughel the Elder's *Hunters in the Snow* is more than a great work of art. It is also a historical document. The year it appeared, 1565, was the worst winter anyone could remember. Right across northern Europe the snow lay deep and crisp and even – for months. What Breughel's painting recorded was the dawn of a new phase in the little ice age. In the Alps glaciers creaked and groaned once more. Many moved down to the edges of the high valleys, overwhelming villages, scraping over and enveloping pasture, laying down sheets of thick ice on the fields. Near Chamonix, deep in the western ranges of the Alps, shepherds watched in horror as the huge 'mer de glace', the ice sea, slid even faster down the slopes of the Mont Blanc massif. Grinding down the mountain side, it seemed that the long-dormant glacier would obliterate all in its path. Priests brought out the images of saints and whole communities knelt in the snow to pray for God's help in stopping the river of ice. And it worked. The weather warmed enough to convert the glacier into a raging torrent – damaging, but disposable.

After the failure of Leonard Dacre's rebellion in early 1570 and the murder of the pro-English Regent Moray, Elizabeth I determined to suppress support for Mary, Queen of Scots, the catholic faith and the ever-present possibility of foreign invasion. And if the Scottish central government could not keep the Borders and the likes of Kerr of Cessford and Scott of Buccleuch under control, then she would do it herself. Commissioned by the queen to raise a punitive expeditionary force, the Earl of Sussex began his muster. Despite the weather, he managed to scrape together 1,000 horse and 3,000 foot soldiers. They would be augmented as he rode north. When news of the invasion spread – and it was no less than that, an invasion of Scotland by English troops – the Scots reacted. Cessford and Buccleuch sought a truce, which was rejected out of hand, ordinary Borderers 'threshed their corn [so that they could take it with them in sacks]', fled with their cattle and unthatched their houses, and in the west the catholic Maxwells began their own muster. No one knew it at the time, but the 1570 English invasions were not one more episode in an endlessly repeating pattern. This would be the last of them.

Moray's death at the hands of a sniper gave Elizabeth sufficient an excuse. The young James VI was being kept safe in Stirling Castle by its constables, the Eskine family. But over the rest of Scotland government was less secure. The regency passed to the catholic Earl of Lennox, Matthew Stewart, the father of the unfortunate Henry, Lord Darnley. Evidently Lennox was devoted to his wife, his chief counsellor and encouragement. On Moray's death, Elizabeth promoted Lennox enthusiastically for the regency but sought insurance for his good behaviour by keeping his beloved countess under house arrest in England. None of this mattered for very long, since in 1571 he was attacked in the streets of Edinburgh by a supporter of Mary, Queen of Scots and stabbed to death. The Earl of Mar stepped gingerly into Lennox' shoes. After two assassinations in quick succession, the regency was clearly a dangerous commission – and so it continued to prove. Mar lasted no time at all, succumbing, it was widely believed, to poison in 1573.

All of these fatal rounds of musical chairs were music indeed to the ears of the reivers. Kerr of Cessford and Scott of Buccleuch went largely unpunished by any of these short-lived administrations – but not by Elizabeth I. In April 1570 the Earl of Sussex' army tramped out of Berwick, and keeping to the southern bank of the Tweed, they crossed by 'the dry march' at the Reddenburn, near Kelso. At first, the force of 5,000 or so seemed to be moving fast, avoiding the obvious target of Kelso, pausing only to burn a Scott tower near Eckford and a Kerr stronghold near Crailing. At Jedburgh, where the provost and baillies were sound supporters of the young king and the protestant faith, Sussex made rendezvous with Old Sir John Forster who had led the men of the middle march over the Cheviot tops and down the narrow valley of the Jed. Once these two had met and made plans, systematic destruction began.

Z

There is frequent confusion and indeed some mystery about the occasional inclusion of a silent 'z' in Scottish words and names. Menzies, Kailzie and several more. Tailzie, for example, has a puzzling pronunciation. The French fashionable at the Scottish court of the first half of the sixteenth century seems to be the linguistic culprit. The 'z' appears in Scots borrowings to help render the double 'l' or 'yi' sound in French words. So 'tailzie', meaning entail, has the alternative spelling of 'tailyie' and it comes from the French 'taille' which freely translates as 'arrangement'. Sir Menzies Campbell, the Liberal politician, correctly calls himself 'Mingis', although, distressingly, the English tended to pronounce the silent 'z', especially when there existed a chain of newsagents of the same name. When at Jedburgh Mary, Queen of Scots sent to Edinburgh for 'abulziements', she probably asked her ladies to order 'habillements'. S'il vous plait.

An early target was the Scott town of Hawick. But when the English closed in, they could see a plume of smoke billowing on the western horizon. By the time their scouts breasted the ridge above the Teviot at Cavers, it looked as though the town was ablaze. The more experienced soldiers had an inkling of what had happened. Having had enough warning, the townspeople had pulled the thatch down off their roofs, piled it up in the streets and set fire to it. This removed the handiest means for pillaging soldiers to burn their houses. All that remained were rows of wood and stone skeletons – which would take some trouble to light, hopefully more trouble than Sussex' men had time for.

All the inhabitants had gone, taking every beast and scrap of food with them into the hill country around Hawick. Instead of starting them, the English soldiers were forced to put out the fires and to eat what small rations they had brought with them. All of the larger goods, furniture and the like, had been crammed into Drumlanrig's Tower at the west end of the High Street, by the bridge over the Slitrig. No mention is made of the stronghold being stormed. After decades of invasion, it seems that Borderers were at last becoming skilled at minimising the mess.

Teviotdale had a harder time. Farms were not easily defended and much and many will have perished in the flames. Ferniehurst Castle was badly knocked about but the English sappers failed to bring down all of its walls with gunpowder. Tunnelling was used instead, and with some effect. The rest of the Kerr country down towards Kelso was wasted, Sussex's men leaving 'never a house or tower unburnt'. Cessford and Lord Hume came to the English camp to plead for clemency, but when both declined to give hostages or to betray the rebels they had harboured, they were sent packing. Battered by artillery deployed on the heights to the north east, Hume Castle surrendered and was garrisoned by an English force.

At the same time, the Warden of the English West March, Lord Scrope, was moving through Dumfriesshire, burning as he went. United for once, Lord Maxwell and James Johnstone attacked a small force commanded by Simon Musgrave and very nearly gave them a hiding. Scrope rode hard from Cummertrees with reinforcements, arriving just in time to turn the battle. He had the help, almost inevitably, of Liddesdale Armstrongs and no doubt they extracted a good price from the English warden as well as settling some old scores in Dumfriesshire.

Elizabeth I's strategy worked well. During the shaky years of Moray, Lennox and Mar, her wardens rode often across the border, forcing the catholic heidsmen like Scott, Maxwell, Hume and Kerr to stay at home and defend their property as best they could. She allowed them no opportunity to unite with sympathetic lords in the centre and north of Scotland, and lend their considerable military muscle to Mary's cause. By the end of 1570, they had all made their peace with the English queen, pledging to become supporters of the young James VI. The game was up for the Earl of Westmorland, and from Aberdeen he took ship for Flanders, the Spanish, and political oblivion.

For the first few winter months of 1571 the Borders was quiet. Even though it was the favoured season for raiding, hoofbeats were rarely heard on the hill trails after darkness. Part of the reason was a series of devastating storms, one of which washed away several arches of Berwick Old Bridge. Civil war flickered in Scotland, but the Border surnames were rarely involved. James Douglas, Earl of Morton, began to establish himself as Regent, and he wisely took a pro-English position. One of his earliest actions was to sell the captive Earl of Northumberland to Lord Hunsdon, Warden of the English East March, for £2,000. The miserable prisoner was kept at Berwick, behind the newly completed walls. No attempt was made at a rescue, and a few weeks later, the earl climbed onto a scaffold at York and laid his neck on the headsman's block.

In 1573 the Regent Morton led several judicial expeditions to the Borders, and he appeared satisfied with their outcomes. But through inexperience, his officers seemed unaware of how little was actually achieved. Those accused of stealing sheep and cattle had become adept at passing them on quickly to 'privy friends' and thereby removing evidence. At least Morton's men caught up with Black James Ormiston, the betrayer of the rebel earls, and although his fate was not recorded, it may be imagined.

The Regent's diplomatic skills were tested by the Raid of the Redeswire in 1575. A firework rather than a conflagration, it nevertheless required careful handling. Most embarrassing was the killing of Sir George Heron of Ford, Deputy Warden of the English Middle March. After quickly releasing all the prisoners taken by the Scots up on the Carter Bar, Morton attempted some charm by sending gifts of hawks to influential courtiers. Some said that they had been given 'live hawks for dead Herons'.

Between 1575 and 1581 the Borders seems to have lain quiet. Either that, or the reporting of complaints was declining. In any event the Regent Morton exerted himself and maintained 'the amity' with England at almost all cost, and there was no reason for armies to cross the Tweed or the Cheviot tops. Reivers did but the number of reported incidents appears to have remained constant for the latter half of the 1570s.

James VI was growing up, and having spent much of his youth at Stirling Castle in the capable but unloving care of the Countess of Mar, he probably craved both freedom and some colour in his dull life. The promise of both arrived in 1579. Esme Stuart, Sieur d'Aubigny, landed in Scotland. Good-looking, dashing, sophisticated, ambitious, almost certainly gay, and catholic, he was an incendiary mixture of possibilities, few of them good. Barely 14 years old, highly impressionable, James was dazzled and seems to have fallen in love. The earldom of Lennox was in the possession of the Bishop of Caithness, but the king quickly persuaded his great-uncle to resign it in favour of Esme, who was after all a Stuart and a distant kinsman. Overnight d'Aubigny became very powerful at court.

Throughout 1580 the Earl of Morton tried to hang onto his office, but as seemed likely from the outset, beauty proved stronger than a big political beast. Morton had imported a new-fangled French contraption which dropped a heavily weighted and very sharp blade on a man's neck and sliced it clean off. It was a prototype guillotine known as 'the Maiden'. In 1581 the charge that Morton was deeply implicated in the murder of Henry Lord Darnley was trumped up, and the Maiden was erected on a scaffold in Edinburgh and used to part Morton's head from his body.

Esme was created Duke of Lennox, but his catholic leanings and his overweening influence on the infatuated young king were too much for native protestant aristocrats to bear. Amongst the charges were that the king's favourite had not only condoned but actually encouraged the Border surnames to raid into England and thereby inflame the international situation. Catholicism was thought to be baiting Elizabethan protestantism as the reivers lifted English cows, although most of them almost certainly could not have cared less about the wider context. Maxwell, the Ferniehurst Kerrs and the Humes were Esme's main supporters. In 1582 a coup was led by William Ruthven, Earl of Gowrie, the king was abducted, and forced to sign an order banishing his beloved Esme to France. The Duke of Lennox died a year later.

Meanwhile Gowrie had imprisoned the young king at Huntingtower, his castle near Perth, so that government according to the true religion could be taken forward. But in June 1583, while in St Andrews, James VI escaped, and after rallying support to him, he rounded on his traitorous captor. It seems that the Maiden was trundled out once more to 'kiss' Gowrie's outstretched neck.

King James was proving a canny politician, and he used the fact that his closeness to Esme Stuart had alarmed more than the protestant Scottish lords. The French dangled the possibility of a catholic alliance (and a generous pension for the cash-strapped monarchy), leaving Elizabeth I uncertain about which way Scotland would turn. Her concern was such that her chief minister, Francis Walsingham, arrived in Edinburgh in August for talks. Part of his commission appears to have been appraisal. His queen had never set eyes on James and she wanted some idea of his character and abilities. To the profound annoyance of the pro-catholic Earl of Arran and other powerful courtiers, Walsingham insisted on meeting the young king alone, but he found little immediate satisfaction on Border affairs, reporting that the reivers were, in his view, being used to annoy England rather than raiding on their own initiative. By the winter of 1583 disorder was growing and the surnames were to be 'set neither by prince nor warden'. Truce Days were not held with any regularity and the Tynedale families in particular rode into Scotland to carry off what they could.

STEWART BEAUTY

The atmosphere around Mary, Queen of Scots is fascinating. Many monarchs were and are esteemed beautiful as a matter of routine royal flattery, but Mary's arrival in Edinburgh appears to have caused high excitement, even a sensation because she was thought to be very beautiful. Standards have fluctuated wildly over time, for both genders, and it is difficult to judge from her portraits (also routinely flattering, although rather anaemic and characterless to our eyes), but the young queen seems to have been a looker – and got into a great trouble because of it. Many of her extended family were also lookers. Esme, Sieur d'Aubigny, was hailed as 'a fascinating Frenchman', and thought very handsome. 'La Belle Stuart', Frances Theresa, Duchess of Richmond and Lennox was described by Samuel Pepys as ' the greatest beauty' he had ever seen. She married family, a distant cousin, Charles Stuart, handsome grandson of Esme. She was said to have posed for the drawing of 'Britannia' which adorned British coins until very recently. And of course the Stewarts supplied the only heir to the throne ever to be popularly distinguished for good looks, Bonnie Prince Charlie.

When Anglo-Scottish relations were strained or simply uneasy, the heidsmen usually showed less inhibition, raiding whenever the opportunity arose and more disdainful of such forces of law and order as were operational. Contemporaries called this downward spiral 'decaie'. Especially on the Scottish side the warden system worked only intermittently. For those Truce Days that were held a massive backlog of crimes and complaints piled up. More were urgently needed to release it.

For midsummer 1585 on the middle marches another Truce Day was at last set. With their retinues and all interested parties (and there were many), the wardens arranged to ride up to the border ridge amongst the highest of the Cheviot Hills. Thousands appear to have mustered and filed up into the eastern ranges, following the 'Hexpethgate' (a version of 'Ermspeth' or Clennel Street). Old Sir John

Forster no doubt straightened his back and spurred his pony on when he saw the Scots gathering on the saddle between the high Windy Gyle and its neighbouring hill, the Butt Roads. Following the ritual, the old man rode forward into Scotland to meet the warden, Sir Thomas Kerr of Ferniehurst. They knew each other well. Proclamation was made that none would incite another 'by word, deed or look' and the two sides came together at this the most spectacular of all the trysting places on the frontier. From the highest point on ancient Clennel Street long views can be seen on all sides – to the east the massive hump of Cheviot itself rises with its two cairns guarding the ravine of the Henhole.

At first all went according to custom. Bills were exchanged and, given the great backlog, priority was probably given to the most important and urgent. What happened next is a matter of dispute and conjecture. Old Sir John wrote two very different accounts of the affair for Francis Walsingham, one following the other in only three days.

At first Forster claimed in a letter dated 28th July from his house at Alnwick that 'it chanced a sudden accident and tumult to arise amongst the rascals of Scotland and England about a little pilfering among themselves'. His son-in-law, Sir Francis Russell, had become involved and 'now rose and went aside from us, with his own men, and there being in talk with a gentleman, was suddenly shot with a gun and slain'. Before the Truce Day could boil up into a small battle, as it had at the Redeswire ten years before, Forster wrote that he and Kerr, his fellow warden, 'stood together and made a quietness'.

Three days after that version, Forster supplied Walsingham with a second. This was countersigned by 32 Northumbrian lords who had been with their warden at the meeting. What had really happened, said Forster, was much different. Led by Kerr of Ferniehurst, the Scots had evidently marched to the Truce Day on Clennel Street in battle order, flags flying and drums beating. Sir Francis Russell had been shot when the flagrant truce-breakers had charged the astonished English ranks. It had been 'a premeditated matter, devised before', wrote the warden.

What really really happened is that the needs of international politics almost certainly intervened in the three days between the first, and likely truthful, account and the second. The shooting of Russell probably had been an accident, a moment of hot-headedness. Mention was made of an argument over a pair of spurs, money owing, and a young Englishman called Wanless being accused. Forster's subsequent tale of what amounted to a Scottish army appearing over the ridge at the Windy Gyle is simply not plausible. Up on those blasted wastes it is very difficult to conceal thousands of men with flags and drums. It was also claimed that the Kerrs had come with the express purpose of killing Russell – but according to Forster himself, there was no certainty that the intended victim would be there. Attending 'for particular causes of his own', Russell had actually come to the Truce Day against his warden's advice. And a whole army to kill one man? Unlikely.

However, it suited Elizabeth and Walsingam to have the affair inflated into an international incident. The notion that the catholic-sympathising Kerr of Ferniehurst, probably in cahoots with the Earl of Arran, had attacked and killed a notable English lord helped them discourage James VI from following bad advice, as they saw it. The mayhem at the Windy Gyle seems like a good example of an old-fashioned Border scuffle being turned to the purposes of the London government.

The year 1585 also saw the Johnstone/Maxwell feud burst into flames once again. When Morton had found himself facing the blade of the Maiden in 1581, John, Lord Maxwell, rubbed his hands. He had been promised the forfeited earldom, and from soon after the date of the execution, he styled himself Morton, thereby confusing generations of historians. Ambition achieved, he began to behave less like the Warden of the Scottish West March and more like the reivers he was charged to suppress. Gathering a band which included Armstrongs, Grahams, and many broken men, he raided deep into the Ettrick Forest. When Morton/Maxwell refused to come to Edinburgh to answer for his crimes, he was deprived of the wardenry. It passed to James Johnstone of Dunskellie – and it proved a poisoned chalice.

A government force sent to help Johnstone was ambushed by Robert Maxwell, Morton's brother, at Crawfordmuir and slaughtered. The Johnstone tower at Lochwood was burned, along with 300 houses, and more than 3,000 beasts were lifted. James Johnstone attacked Dumfries twice and was only turned back by the dreadful weather of the 1580s. After a more successful series of murderous raids along the Nith, a group of Maxwell widows made a remarkable journey to Edinburgh. Taking the bloodied shirts of their dead husbands, they attempted to persuade the king and his council to act against the Johnstones, but they were refused an audience. The outraged women took to the High Street where they showed the gory sarks to the appalled citizenry. After the Edinburgh mob loudly demanded action, James VI was forced to order Morton/Maxwell (warden again by this time) to arrest James Johnstone of Dunskellie. It was the first step on the road to Dryfe Sands, perhaps the most vicious battle ever fought in the Borders.

By 1585 the English and Scottish sovereigns had convinced themselves and each other that their interests were best served by a peace treaty. The Border at first saw fewer raids, and the wardens called for Truce Days. Then trouble broke out suddenly from Liddesdale and also in Northumberland. It seemed that the situation was highly volatile, not following its usual pattern.

What might have detonated a war twenty, or even ten, years before passed almost without incident in 1587. On 8th February at Fotheringhay Castle Mary, Queen of Scots was at last beheaded for treason. After almost twenty years of imprisonment, apparently endless entanglements in catholic plots, and for continuing to serve as a willing focus for dissent in England as well as the rest of Britain, Mary went to the executioner's block. Her cousin, Elizabeth I, was ten years older and may have believed that the captive queen would outlive her to cause mayhem with what she dearly wished would be an orderly succession. The pretext, carefully managed by Walsingham and his network of spies, was the Babington plot, a feeble business involving only a dozen participants which aimed to free Mary and dispose of Elizabeth simultaneously.

When news of Mary's death reached Scotland, nothing much happened. James VI probably did not mourn the mother he had never known (although he made some show of irritation by refusing to see Elizabeth's messenger), and her removal certainly served to buttress his own position. Incessant rainstorms soaked the Borders in February and March 1587, making the burns and rivers into roaring and impassable spates. No one could even consider driving stolen cattle – or even riding out in darkness – in conditions like those.

Old Sir John Forster thought his march very quiet, and he took time to make his way to Newcastle to deal with accusations of misconduct and corruption. His enemies, Collingwood and Huntington, were attempting to have him removed from the wardenship. It was said later that 'he trusted all to a drunken, bastard son', probably Nicholas Forster. But from other sources, it seems that Sir John's description of a peaceful border was not a tactic to demonstrate his competence but an accurate assessment – at any rate for the winter months.

More wet and windy weather in the summer and autumn of 1586 had flattened the grain harvest so badly that the traditional 'hungry months' of May, June and July, when stores from the year before were running out, were worse than usual. On these long early summer days, much against the grain, raiding rose to new levels. Horsemen must have been forced to scour the hill pasture looking for herds and flocks sent out summering. They were desperate. In Forster's middle march the peace was shattered as 37 raids were counted at that time and the complaints listed 700 cows, 400 sheep, 80 nags and 30 prisoners taken. Lord Hunsdon was so taken aback by this unseasonal outbreak that he suspected that the Scottish reiving surnames might have been party to a deliberate distraction. James VI was being courted by Spain with an offer of wages for 30,000 soldiers for three years, a huge sum for a king mired in penury. But James knew that the great prize was England, and these diplomatic rumblings were probably designed to persuade Elizabeth I to commit to him as her heir.

John, Lord Maxwell, had difficulty committing to anything except his own surname's cause and his catholicism. After his brutal defeat of the Johnstones and reinstatement as Warden of the Scottish West March, he began to behave like an independent reiver-king, answerable to no one. Mustering a substantial band of riders, he again terrorised eastern Dumfriesshire and fortified a network of castles. But his contrariness caught up with him, and although the Johnstones were defeated, Maxwell found himself imprisoned for his faith and then driven into exile. Spain was his immediate destination. Returning to Dumfriesshire in 1588, he set about raising support for the coming invasion, the arrival of the Spanish Armada, known as 'the Enterprise of England'. Logistically it made good sense. A large fleet might sidestep English defences in the Channel and sail up through the Irish Sea to make landfall at the Solway ports, where Maxwell and his small army might make them most welcome.

Suddenly the Borders was more than the scene of internecine squabbles. James VI hurried south to Dumfries, took the Maxwell castles at Langholm, Lochmaben and Caerlaverock and after a chase, captured the rebel himself. Amazingly, Maxwell talked his way out of the hangman's rope, and by the early 1590s was once again warden.

Feuding in the Borders was so much a constant feature of life that little notice seems to have been taken of it. Out of sight, out of mind. When it spilled over into the streets of Edinburgh and claimed the lives of titled lords, that was different and the king became directly involved. Sir Robert Kerr of Cessford attacked and killed William Kerr of Ancrum. The reasons read like the usual genealogical tit-for-tat. Ancrum was a relative and a supporter of the Ferniehurst Kerrs, who were more or less at feud with the Cessford Kerrs for much of the sixteenth century. Because the Ferniehurst heir was only a little boy, his affairs were being managed by Ancrum, who had accused and secured the conviction of one of Cessford's men for raiding into England. Instead of bringing the complaint to the Warden of the Middle March, none other than Sir Thomas Kerr of Cessford, he took it to Edinburgh to be heard. So Cessford killed him. It all made sense at the time, and as always seemed possible with the families who held the Scottish wardenries, Cessford escaped, made himself scarce for a while, and after a great deal of contrition and compensation to the Ancrum Kerrs, he evetually got away with it.

Throughout the second half of the sixteenth century the differences between Scots and English wardens grew starker. Elizabeth I and her counsellors had retained a tight grip on appointments and tended to prefer men who had few, if any, local interests. Sir John Forster was the exception. On the Scottish side, the wardenships were more or less hereditary, sometimes alternating between two powerful families, such as the Maxwells and the Johnstones. They used the office to contend for control of the area. From 1557 the Humes were Wardens of the Scottish East March and their neighbours, except for one year when Sir Thomas Kerr of Ferniehurst held office, were an unbroken line of Cessford Kerrs in charge of the middle march. Despite his colourful criminal record, Sir Robert Kerr acted as deputy to his father from 1590 and probably took over in 1594.

These differences were important – and the source of much cross-border conflict in the 1590s. Robert Kerr rarely hesitated to mount raids, pursue feuds or murder an adversary. If these acts characterised the behaviour of the three principal officers of the law in the Borders, then it follows that there was no law at all. Or at least none that might be recognised as such.

What did exist was a broad code of behaviour and an under-standing of certain customary rights. Criminal societies are not necessarily anarchic: in order to function, they need some norms or standards. These were well demonstrated in one of the most famous, and dashing, incidents in reiver history, the rescue of Kinmont Willie Armstrong in 1596.

Through the rainswept darkness of the night of 13th April, Walter Scott of Buccleuch led a party of 80 raiders from Langholm to Carlisle. It was an elite force, the best and most daring men he could find.

Having swum their ponies across the swirling spate of the River Eden, they approached the glowering battlements in total silence, signalling directions to each other, looking for a small postern gate in the west wall. It would be locked from the inside, but Buccleuch's men quietly levered out the stone into which the bolt had been shot and crept like foxes into the courtyard of the castle. Guided by a sympathetic serving-lass, six of the raiders found Kinmont Willie's lodging, got him down and out through the postern, onto a spare pony and away into the mirk of the enveloping night. No one laid a hand on them and no pursuit dared to cross the swollen river. It was a brilliant coup, meticulously planned, perfectly executed, a stinging embarrassment to Lord Scrope, the English warden, and also one of the last great raids over the border.

Its immediate cause was the illegal capture of Armstrong at a Truce Day a month before, but the origins of the rescue stretch a long way back into the sixteenth century, and they can be seen as a paradigm for the development of the unique criminal society of the Border Reivers.

KINMONT CANVAS

In March 2006 Bonhams of London offered for sale at auction an interesting painting. By Richard Beavis, a Victorian artist, it purports to illustrate a moment in the rescue of Kinmont Willie from Carlisle Castle in 1596. Yet it looks more like a leisurely evening hack. Two steel-bonneted riders lead a cavalcade of similarly clad horsemen. The leaders, presumably Walter Scott of Buccleuch and one of his lieutenants, appear to be chatting and their horses walking, even dawdling. Beside them a hound strolls as if out for a walk, looking at the anonymous landscape. The only figure who shows any sense of urgency rides beside the column, wearing a rakish plumed hat (more seventeenth than sixteenth century – as are all the riders. They wear breastplates over shirts with wide lacy collars. Perhaps they were particularly well-dressed reivers who shared the same tailor) instead of a steel bonnet, he seems a little older and more portly than his companions, a little like the 'Laughing Cavalier'. The hat is different so that part of a head of white hair might be revealed, and this offers a clue to his identity. Auld Wat of Harden was noted for his 'lyart' locks, or grey hair, as well as his girth. The painting was sold for more than £7,000.

Like Old Sir John Forster, Willie Armstrong lived a long time, rode forays for more than 50 years and saw many things. At the time of the raid on Carlisle Castle, it seems likely that he was 66 years old, born in 1530, when the outrageous executions took place at Carlenrig kirk-yard. Along with Black Jock, Kinmont's grandfather, Ill Will Armstrong, was hanged from a 'growand tree'. The incident must have influenced the attitudes of the little boy, at the very least inculcating an almost genetic mistrust and distaste for authority. Ever independent-minded, the Armstrongs sided wherever their interests were best served and accepted pensions from Henry VIII as 'assured Scots'. Genealogists who have traced Kinmont's branch of the family tree believe that as a 12-year-old, he fought at the battle of Solway Moss – on the English side. In 1547 the boy rode with his father, Ill Will's Sandy, and 300 others to help Thomas Carleton take the Johnstone tower at Lochwood.

For three generations Kinmont Willie rode and raided the border on either side, family far more important than nationality. In 1581 he mustered 400 men and led a daylight foray down to Haydon Bridge on the South Tyne, and a year later was in North Tynedale lifting cattle, sheep, goats and horses. The first Lord Scrope of Bolton, father and predecessor of the warden in 1596, complained that justice would never be done because Armstrong and the Scottish warden were so often in each other's company. Maxwell was very unlikely to uphold any complaints against his friend for raiding into England.

Meanwhile Kinmont cemented other relationships. Having married the daughter of his neighbour, Hutcheon Graham, he arranged for his sister's betrothal to his wife's brother. Their daughter later became the wife of another Thomas Carleton, Deputy Warden of the English West March, and Constable of Carlisle Castle. A family connection which was to prove extremely useful.

When James VI came to Dumfries at the head of a small army to deal with the Maxwells, their ally, Kinmont Willie, suggested a classic Armstrong tactic. To avoid an unequal confrontation and likely capture, the Maxwells were led into that impregnable fortress, the Tarras Moss. It was a wise move. When the Maxwells were restored to the wardenship, the Armstrongs returned into favour with the Scottish king.

Over the border, brooding behind the walls of Carlisle Castle, Lord Scrope was growing old, bitter and testily impatient with the fact that Kinmont could ignore the law with regularity and impunity. Whenever a plan was formulated or an opportunity presented itself to capture him, the target seemed to melt away into the hills like a will o' the wisp. The reason was more prosaic – his son-in-law, Thomas Carleton, always leaked information in sufficient time. The old warden died in 1592, disappointed that one of the greatest reivers on the border had eluded him.

Thomas, Lord Scrope, succeeded to his father's office, determined to do better. In 1593 Kinmont, Will Elliot of Larriston and the Armstrong Laird of Mangerton ran a big daylight raid into Tynedale and drove nearly 3,000 beasts back to Liddesdale. Having received intelligence on the reivers' movements (after the raid), young Scrope instructed Carleton to set an ambush. Once again Kinmont and his associates vanished, and instead Thomas captured two English reivers – who managed to escape before they could be got to Carlisle. Furious, Scrope removed Carleton from the deputy wardenship.

Having made an enemy at his back, Scrope then proceeded to make another over the border. Instead of contacting his fellow law officer, Walter Scott of Buccleuch, the Keeper of Liddesdale, the English warden wrote directly to James VI. He asked the king to appoint 'an officer over against him to provide for quietness till the evil of the winter [i.e. the raiding season] be past'. Buccleuch was incensed.

Truce Days had been held only very irregularly, and the backlog of complaints must have been substantial. On 17th March 1596 at Kershopefoot in Liddesdale a rare meeting was set. Well attended, with a few hundred riders on each side, its business was done at the Tourneyholme, a flat field on the Scottish side of the Kershope Burn, where it runs into the Liddel Water. Neither Buccleuch nor Scrope attended, complaints being dealt with by Robert Scott of the Haining, his deputy, and Salkeld, the English deputy. Presumably because there were matters of interest to him on the agenda, Kinmont Willie came to Kershopefoot. In his sixties, hugely experienced, he would have known almost everyone there and was related to many.

After the meeting and while the Truce Day immunities were still in force, Willie rode home by the banks of the Liddel. What happened next goes to the very heart of the whole matter – but it was and is hotly disputed. It seems likely that a large party of English riders were making their way along the opposite bank. That stretch of the Liddel is not too wide and conversation across it would easily have been possible. Perhaps Willie insulted someone, perhaps the name-calling became heated, but it could all certainly have come to nothing. The

Truce Day immunity and the river would surely keep the English and the Armstrongs apart. They did not. Tempers frayed and snapped. The English riders splashed across, laid hands on Kinmont Willie and took him prisoner to Carlisle Castle. A tremendous diplomatic row began almost immediately.

Lord Scrope had been away when Kinmont arrived at his castle, but on his return, he could and should have cleared up the mess by releasing the old reiver without delay. Instead, however, he saw that at last he had his father's old adversary in custody. Let him stew for a while. Over the border Buccleuch acted with some restraint and wrote to Salkeld demanding that Kinmont be set free. No answer. Then a letter over Salkeld's head to Lord Scrope. No answer. Finally Buccleuch went over Scrope's head and wrote to Sir Robert Bowes, Elizabeth I's ambassador at the court of James VI. This time there was action. Apparently Bowes wrote to Scrope in the strongest terms, insisting that the prisoner be released ('enlarged') before matters got out of hand. This was a delicate time. The English queen was now very old and might die at any moment. If there was to be a smooth handover of power, incidents like this would not be helpful.

After the rescue, in his efforts at self-justification, Lord Scrope claimed that he wrote to Buccleuch saying that Kinmont had somehow broken the terms of the truce, that he was a notorious criminal who in any case deserved incarceration and that he offered to ask King James and Sir Robert Bowes to arbitrate in the dispute. If he did, no evidence of any of these approaches has survived.

All attempts at diplomacy having failed, Buccleuch felt that personal insult had been added to a flagrant breach of the law, and as a man of honour, albeit somewhat dubious, he had to act.

Carlisle Castle was one of the strongest in the north, and the last thing Lord Scrope would expect was an assault – which is precisely what was being planned. Not a frontal assault with all cannons blazing, but an assault made by a reiver, a leader well practised in all the arts necessary – speed, surprise, deception and sheer daring. All that Buccleuch needed lay to hand. This was not a dispute between England and Scotland, as it has sometimes been portrayed, or even between Scrope and Buccleuch. Rather, it was a contest between the old reiver society and conventional government forces of law and order and although no one who took part could know it, a contest between the past and the future. Kinmont Willie Armstrong was the quintessential representative of the unique criminal society of the sixteenth-century Border country, and it would rise up in one last glorious raid to break him out of the clutches of the London government.

On 7th April Thomas and his brother, Lance Carleton, met Andrew Graham, Kinmont's brother-in-law and two of his men. They rode to a rendezvous at Archerbeck, not far from Canonbie, where Buccleuch, his kinsman, Auld Wat of Harden and Gilbert Elliot of Liddesdale were waiting. From the very outset the raid on Carlisle Castle involved both Scots and English, all reivers to their blood and bone, combined against an outsider who had broken their code. It was an alliance which mirrored Kinmont's own web of contacts. Family and not nationality brought the conspirators together. Each had his own reasons, the Carletons in particular, for wishing to see Warden Scrope done down, and each brought the different elements essential for the success of any raid on his squat, dour but very secure castle.

Buccleuch argued for a small, experienced, elite force. Between them the western surnames could raise four or five thousand riders but no matter how large an army galloped up to Carlisle's walls, they did not have the equipment or know-how to break them down. Better to go with only 80 or so – the best of the Scotts, Wat of Harden as a vastly seasoned, unflappable lieutenant, a contingent of Elliots and there was no doubt that Kinmont's four sons could not be kept at home. That was enough. Surprise and stealth would be impossible if more came.

The Grahams would organise security. The raid would cross that part of the Debatable Land controlled by the surname, and they needed to keep it quiet, no blundering into other raiding parties, no possibility of a chance observer galloping to Carlisle to raise the alarm. In order to gain entry to the castle itself, Ebby's Sandy Graham had the necessary skills. Most important was the precise route to be taken once Kinmont Willie had been rescued. In places with good cover, ambushes needed to be set to trap any pursuers, and Willie Kang Irvine, a go-between trusted by Buccleuch, would let the Johnstones and his own surname know where. Scaling ladders were stored at Morton Rigg, Kinmont's own tower. It lay only ten miles from Carlisle and on the route the raiders planned to follow. Finally the Carletons agreed to look after intelligence. Evidently Armstrong was being held in a house in the lower courtyard of the castle, one of several built against the west wall. Next to it was an old postern gate which opened directly to the outside, and crucially, offered a way in which did not involve passing through any of the gates into the walled city of Carlisle. An Elizabethan map shows the arrangement very clearly. It was perfect.

After four hours of detailed discussion, the date was set. The raid would run on the night of Sunday 13th April, and the rendezvous arranged for the day before at Langholm Races. The crowds, the betting and the general hubbub would provide good cover for the muster. Secrecy was vital and to delay any longer, urged the Carletons, would be to risk discovery.

The day dawned, squally and wet as it often can be in spring in the Borders, and Willie Kang Irvine had come to Langholm to ensure that all was ready to go forward. Buccleuch ate with Hutcheon Graham at the castle, which stood immediately adjacent to the racecourse. When gloaming at last began to gather, the raiders saddled their ponies and slipped quietly out of the town on the Carlisle road.

Ever fearful of interception, Buccleuch took care to dispose his small force in military order. A screen of scouts swept the country in front of them, often moving off the road to look for ambushes. Right behind was a support group of about 40 riders. Then came Buccleuch and the handful who would break into the castle and find Kinmont. Pack horses carried ladders, crowbars and other gear. All were followed by a watchful rearguard.

While there was still a little light in the sky, the party splashed across the Esk, probably avoiding the fords at Longtown (where they might be seen), preferring the crossing lower down, near the outfall into the Solway. From then on it was vital to ride in silence: no warning whatsoever must be given. It was raining and very windy, and while that was uncomfortable, the bad weather might keep the curious indoors. Buccleuch wanted to approach Carlisle from the north so that his party would be hidden behind Stanwix Bank. In 1596 the River Eden ran in two channels on either side of the Sands, an island sometimes used for horse-racing and a good bridging point. The plan was to avoid it and make for a point on the riverbank a few hundred yards to the west, where the Eden turned out of sight of any sentries on the bridge. This crossing-point would also deliver the raiders directly below the battlements of the castle, to a piece of ground known as the Sauceries Flat.

But the Eden had to be negotiated first, and that would take some good horsemanship and some brave ponies. After a night of rain it may have been flooding: 'It happened to be very dark in the hindnight (after midnight) and a little misty.' Good cover but dangerous.

Soaked but safely over, the party divided on the Sauceries. Most took a position by the west wall, lances couched, where they could discourage any who sallied out of the Irish Gate and attempted to intervene. Buccleuch led perhaps six or eight up to the postern. Ebby's Sandy Graham set to work with crowbar and chisel to remove the stone by the gate which acted as the keeper for its bolt. It was a technique sometimes used to break into peel towers.

Once inside the lower courtyard Buccleuch might have expected resistance from the sentries, but there was none. In a lame excuse, Lord Scrope later claimed that the watch had either been driven inside by the rainstorm or they had fallen asleep. Or they had been bought by Thomas and Lance Carleton. In any case Kinmont was quickly found and shoved out through the postern, onto a pony and then into the Eden's freezing water for a soaking. Despite the hullaballoo described in 'The Ballad of Kinmont Willie' with all the bells of Carlisle ringing, there appears to have been no pursuit. Perhaps the operation went so smoothly it was not discovered until morning, perhaps none of the sleepy guards fancied a ducking in the midnight river, perhaps too many of the Carleton's coins jingled in their pockets.

A great deal is known of the detail of this incident because of the recriminations afterwards. Lord Scrope extracted information from the Grahams and others, and to placate an enraged Elizabeth I, Buccleuch was eventually forced to make statements about who did what. Despite the excuses and assurances, the raid was emblematic, a carefully planned, immaculately executed example of the craft of the reiver. All of those criminal skills were seamlessly employed as border society of the 1590s ignored nationality and combined to right what it saw as a wrong and defeat the forces of legitimate central government.

But at the moment of perhaps its greatest and most famous triumph, the world of the reivers was fading, and most of the men who rode through the storm to Carlisle sensed it. Elizabeth I was well into her sixties and it had been understood for some time that James of Scotland would succeed as king of a united Britain. That meant no border between separate jurisdictions, no ability to play off one sovereign and their representatives against another, and the more astute of the heidsmen began to turn their minds to the future.

Robert Carey called the last years of the border 'a stirring world', and he was witness to most of its signal events. The seventh son of Lord Hunsdon (said by many to be half-brother to Queen Elizabeth), he trained as a soldier and gained experience as a courtier and diplomat. In 1593 Thomas, Lord Scrope, appointed Carey as his deputy in place of Thomas Carleton, and the young man may have been in Carlisle Castle on the night Kinmont Willie slipped out of the postern gate.

Despite Carleton's well-earned reputation for duplicity and a likely resentment of his successor, he had occasion to give Carey some excellent advice. The new deputy warden was anxious to give the impression of diligence and also to assert his authority. When he learned of the flight of two murderers (they had killed a church minister) and their being harboured in a Graham tower, a troop of 25 was ordered to saddle up. Riding out of the castle in the early hours of the morning, Carey planned a surprise attack. Thomas Carleton came along – and it was just as well.

When the troop reached their target, they found the tower securely barred against them, 'and I could see a boy riding from the house as fast as his horse would carry him'. Carleton understood immediately what was about to happen: 'He will be in Scotland inside this half hour, and he has gone to let them know you are here, and to what end you have come, and the small number you have with you, and that if they make haste, on a sudden they may surprise us, and do with us what they please.' Carey reacted well and did something similar very quickly, a rider being sent the five miles to Carlisle to bring reinforcements.

After a time 400 Scottish riders cantered into view and halted some distance away. With his reinforcements, the deputy warden could probably have made a contest of it, but the Scots holed up in the tower had offered to negotiate and Carey prudently sent a messenger over to the Scots to ask them to withdraw. Which they did, no doubt to considerable relief – on both sides.

Lord Hunsdon died in 1596 after half a lifetime's service on the border and his son took over as Warden of the English East March. It was a plum job. Carey found himself in charge of not only north Northumberland but also the garrison at Berwick. For a professional soldier, it was a rare opportunity to command fellow professionals.

But Carey's satisfaction was short-lived. Because of the dismissal of Old Sir John Forster from the middle march and his replacement with the unhappy Lord Eure, a vacancy occured. Eure departed gratefully, and Carey was moved into the much more difficult job. And while he might have been flattered at such trust in a relatively young man, his memoir complains at how inconvenient it all was. The unfortunate Peregrine Bertie took charge of Berwick and the east march.

At least Robert was able to dodge what turned out to be an unusual, difficult and persistent problem, something the wardens well not well equipped to deal with. Pirates known as 'Dunkirkers' were attacking shipping off the Northumberland coast. Their fleet was large, with 24 substantial galleons, and their prey was crucial to the local economy. Off Berwick Roads they prowled, lying in wait for the corn and supply ships which plied in and out of the harbour, and further down the coast, they captured the colliers which ran coal from the Tyneside pits down to London. Such everyday, bulk cargoes might not at first seem attractive to pirates, but apparently the Dunkirkers drove the captured corn and coal ships to dock in European ports where they auctioned the contents, the crew and their craft.

The pirates returned in 1600 and again in 1601 when Peregrine Bertie manned and armed a warship at his own expense to deal with them. Fishermen had been complaining that they could not leave harbour. Some had been caught, stripped of their clothes and cast ashore to watch their boats being ransacked and sometimes sunk. Even more pressing for Bertie was the fact that the victualling ships supplying Berwick's garrison could not get through, the voyage having become much too risky. It all seemed to overwhelm the warden and, complaining about the Borders, Borderers, and Border weather, Peregrine Bertie caught a bad cold while waiting for the wind on his warship in Berwick Roads. On 25th June 1601, he died.

Suddenly border government on the English side began to look like the sort of family affair it had long been in Scotland. In the west Thomas Lord Scrope had taken over from his father, and in the east Robert Carey's brother, John, became warden. They all knew that their appointments were temporary, lasting only as long as their old queen lived. And astute as ever, Robert Carey reckoned that Elizabeth's death would not be long in coming.

In his entry for 1603, the historian, D.L.W. Tough wrote: 'There really is no more Border history.' In an important sense, he was right. That was the year the political border disappeared. When Robert Carey attended court in London in the winter of 1603, he sensed that Elizabeth had lost the will to go on and sought the release of death. And so he hung on, waiting upon events, and pondering a plan.

Philadelphia Carey, Robert's sister, was one of the old queen's body servants. When Elizabeth took to her bed and sent away Robert Cecil and her other advisers and courtiers, only she and her female companions stayed in the royal presence. It was only a matter of time. Meanwhile Robert organised a relay of good horses to be posted at intervals along the great north road from London to Edinburgh. If he was to hope for favour and preferment at the coming court of King James VI and I, it would do him much good to be the first to give the new King of Great Britain the news he had been waiting for all his life. Official royal messengers would take at least four days, maybe five in bad weather, to make the 400-mile journey. Carey believed he could do it much faster, in two or perhaps three days. He knew the road well. For a wager, he had once walked from London to Edinburgh.

When Elizabeth died in the early morning of 24th March, Philadelphia cut her coronation ring from the queen's puffy finger and rushed down to the courtyard where her brother waited. James VI would need a token that Carey's news was reliable. Hell for leather, he rode out of London on a clear spring day, kicking his first horse on while the rider was not yet tired. Doncaster was reached by nightfall, and then Northumberland by the following evening. Having slept at his house at Widdrington, Carey, no doubt still sore, saddled up, expecting to reach Edinburgh well before darkness fell, but on the road his horse spooked and threw him, somewhere south of Norham, and adding injury to insult, it accidentally kicked him in the head. The wound was bad, progress much slowed but Carey rode on doggedly through the gloaming along the East Lothian coast road, reaching Edinburgh late that night.

When he clattered into the cobbled courtyard of Holyrood Palace, Carey demanded that the king be woken. Bloodied down one side of his face, his cloak and boots caked in mud, the messenger knelt by James' bedside, gave him Elizabeth's coronation ring and acknowledged him as his king, the new King of England and Scotland. From that moment, there really was to be no more Border history; the days of the reivers were over.

Envoi

The end was brutal, and brief. It took only seven years for the new government of Great Britain to dismantle reiving society. As if to stiffen James I and VI's resolve, the Grahams, the Armstrongs and the Elliots took the death of Elizabeth I as their cue for an outbreak of concentrated, almost frenzied, foraying. In what became known as 'Ill Week', 5,000 cattle were lifted in Cumbria, and one band rode as far south as Penrith before reining in their ponies. It seemed like a reflex, a last tearaway gallop before the inevitable. As the Bishop of Carlisle watched from the ramparts of the castle, Hutcheon Graham led a company of reivers through the meadows by the River Eden. His men took their time, not troubling to conceal themselves. Perhaps they looked up at the bishop and made whatever gesture was the sixteenth-century equivalent of sticking up two fingers.

Even before he reached London, the new king left none of the heidsmen in any doubt about what was coming. When James' triumphant progress through his new kingdom reached Newcastle in April 1603, he paused from the celebrations to turn a withering westward eye on the reiving families:

> To his messengers, sheriffs and others, the late marches and borders of the two realms of England and Scotland are now the heart of the country. Proclamation is to be made against all rebels and disorderly persons that no supply be given them, their wives or their bairns, and that they be prosecuted with fire and sword.

From London, a few weeks later, a firm deadline was laid down, and the outset of a new era marked with the giving of a new name. The excesses of Ill Week were also noted:

Requiring all who were guilty of the foul and insolent outrages lately committed in the Borders to submit themselves to his mercy before 20th June – under penalty of being excluded from it forever . . . [the king] prohibited the name of Borders any longer to be used, substituting in its place Middle Shires. He ordered all places of strength in those parts to be demolished except the habitation of noblemen and barons; their iron yetts to be converted into plough irons and their inhabitants to betake themselves to agriculture and other works of peace.

Having erased the border line from the map in fact as well as name, and removed all means of avoidance or escape, the king and his counsellors set about enacting a series of measures which would solve a long-standing and profound irritation. There is a distinct impression that James himself had given the problem of the Borders a great deal of thought as he waited for Elizabeth of England to die.

He also had the example of the Highlands to draw on. At the same time as the suppression of the Border Reivers began, James was looking north, to his kingdom's other substantial locus of marginal disorder, the remote territories of the semi-independent Highland and Island clans. In 1608 royal agents tricked and abducted many of the important chiefs and held them as hostages for the good behaviour of their people. The Gaelic language was discouraged as 'one of the principal causes of the continuance of barbarity and incivility', and the elder sons of the chiefs were to be educated in English and in the Lowlands.

Compared with the Statutes of Iona, the treatment of the reivers was summary and savage. The March Wardenries and all of the march laws were first abolished: Borderers would be subject to the same laws as everyone else. In 1603 Lord Hume was appointed as Lieutenant of all the Scottish Marches and Sir George Clifford, Earl of Cumberland, held a matching commission for the English side. Both were supported by deputies who were professional soldiers, respectively Sir William Cranston and Sir Henry Leigh. The hangings began almost immediately.

Methods were not complicated. Known thieves were rounded up, charges trumped up or old ones cited and revived, and hundreds were executed without any or much legal preamble. It was the grisly beginning of what came to called Jethart Justice, a practice of hanging first and – maybe – asking questions later. Mass executions took place in Dumfries, Jedburgh and Carlisle. Hume himself witnessed '140 of the nimblest and most powerful thieves in all the Borders' choke to death on the end of a rope. Not sufficiently nimble to dodge a determined government offensive, the heidsmen could see that this was no routine purge. It was Judgement Day and history was moving.

Walter Scott considered absence a wise course and he mustered 2,000 riders, taking them off to fight in the 'Belgic Wars', the Dutch struggle for independence from Spain. When he returned, Buccleuch did not hesitate to join Hume and he turned on his own surname, those who had loyally ridden behind him to Carlisle Castle in 1596, and any others who appeared to resist.

In 1605 a Border Commission was set up in Carlisle Castle. Five Scots lairds and five English adjudicated on cases, but it seems that whenever Clifford, Leigh, Hume or Cranston or any of their officers referred a case, the same instructions were always issued – hang them.

As Scott and the other, more astute heidsmen lined up on the side of law and order, they were much motivated by the mechanism of dispossession. Whenever an alleged reiver was executed, his lands came up for grabs – and many large estates were grabbed after 1603. Some families were nevertheless unrepentant, too far gone in reputation and inclination. The Grahams were heavily persecuted, many were deported to Ireland, to settle in the landlocked county of Roscommon. Few stayed. The Armstrongs suffered badly, and it must be significant that no substantial aristocratic family bearing either of these feared and powerful names has survived in the Borders.

By 1610 the world had changed. Sporadic raiding still sometimes flickered on a winter's night, but society had moved on. Men were no longer permitted to go about armed, ponies worth more than £30 Scots were forbidden, saddles were to be replaced by work harness, well known thieves did not strut the streets of Hexham or Hawick – even iron gates were to be beaten into ploughshares. While the last sounds like a classical rhetorical flourish, there was nothing allusory about the effects of the Border Commission. In only seven years enough reivers had been hanged, deported or ennobled to alter radically what had been a thoroughly uncontrollable criminal society.

It was a savage and sad end to many old songs. The ballads romanticised the reivers impossibly, almost obliterating the grim historical truth, the killing, 'the deep revenge for slight offences', the rapes, the greed and the pain inflicted. But for all that it is not an entirely unattractive story. In addition to their manifold faults, the reivers had some virtues – or at least some humanity. Stowlugs Armstrong, Nebless Clem Crosier and Davey Bangtail Armstrong had a stoic humour about them, and the nicknames seem to bring them all closer. They were not a fanfare of big names and titles, but a collection of much more modest men and women. Ordinary people do not do what Willie Kang Irvine or Lancie Carleton did, but their otherwise everyday lives are somehow more accessible and not at all remote. They may have been thieves and blackmailers but their characters are pungent, alive, and oddly more attractive than the stiff formalities of kings, queens, bishops and aristocrats who usually people the pages of history.

The reivers also showed unmistakable dash and bravery, routinely risking their necks and sometimes even acting out of more than an immediate self-interest. In their disregard for central authority, constantly cocking a snook, the riding families readily find modern supporters, those who might condemn their actions but cheer on their independent cheek. Most of all they were tough, hard-riding and as durable as they windy hills they knew so well.

When the police action began in 1603, it became quickly clear that some surnames would certainly suffer while others might prosper if they switched loyalty from family to the state. The Grahams and the Armstrongs got nothing, the Elliots and the Johnstones and some of the upland Tynedale and Redesdale families very little. Such dour unwillingness to change seems somehow more admirable than all that jostling and jockeying done by the Kerrs, the Humes and the Scotts. At least the Grahams and the Armstrongs were unflinchingly consistent, unrepentant Border Reivers to the soles of their riding boots. No better than they should have been.

Family counted for everything in the reiving centuries, and in an alienated, fragmented urban world, that is also attractive. 'My name is Little Jock Elliot' was more than a boast, it described a way of life. It has almost all gone now, the riding surnames are only a unique and fascinating memory. The reivers have melted into the moonlit landscape, their grey shapes fading into the darkness of the past. But the names have endured, and Borderers have made other, better marks on history. All of these ancient qualities of bravery, dash, cheek and independent strength of will and mind seemed to coalesce in the greatest foray ever run. Neil Armstrong rode the moonlight like none of his reiving ancestors when he reached out and touched it.

Appendix 1

The Border Ballads

Despite much alteration, licence and the poetic needs of metre and rhyme, the Border Ballads are not ahistorical pieces of fancy. They offer atmosphere, emotion, a sense of how people thought 500 years ago and also what they believed at that time. Beliefs and attitudes inform motivation and that is what makes them integral to any understanding of our history. Here is a selection of five famous ballads. Some describe real events, with flamboyance, while others sing of the raids and the raiders.

(All ballads from *Minstrelsy of the Scottish Border*.)

The Battle of Otterburn

It fell about the Lammas tide,
When the muir-men win their hay,
The doughty Douglas bound him to ride
Into England, to drive a prey.

He chose the Gordons and the Graemes,
With them the Lindesays, light and gay;
But the Jardines wald not with him ride,
And they rue it to this day.

And he has burn'd the dales of Tyne,
And part of Bambroughshire:
And three good towers on Roxbergh fells,
He left them all on fire.

And he march'd up to Newcastle,
And rode it round about;
'O wha's the lord of this castle,
Or wha's the lady o't?'

But up spake proud Lord Percy, then,
And O but he spake hie!
'I am the lord of this castle,
My wife's the lady gay.'

'If thour't the lord of this castle,
Sae weel it pleases me!
For, ere I cross the border fells,
The tane of us shall die.'

He took a lang spear in his hand,
Shod with the metal free,
And for to meet the Douglas there,
He rode right furiouslie.

But O how pale his lady look'd,
Frae aff the castle wa',
When down, before the Scottish spear,
She saw proud Percy fa'.

'Had we twa been upon the green,
And never an eye to see,
I wad hae had you, flesh and fell;
But your sword sall gae wi' me.'

'But gae ye up to Otterbourne,
And wait there dayis three;
And, if I come not ere three dayis end,
A fause knight ca' ye me.'

'The Otterbourne's a bonnie burn;
'Tis pleasant there to be;
But there is nought at Otterbourne,
To feed my men and me.

The deer rins wild on hill and dale,
The birds fly wild from tree to tree;
But there is neither bread nor kale,
To fend my men and me.

Yet I will stay at Otterbourne,
Where you shall welcome be;
And, if ye come not at three dayis end,
A fause lord I'll ca' thee.'

'Thither will I come,' proud Percy said,
'By the might of Our Ladye!' –
'There will I bide thee,' said the Douglas
'My trowth I plight to thee.'

They lighted high on Otterbourne,
Upon the bent sae brown;
They lighted high on Otterbourne,
And threw their pallions down.

And he that had a bonnie boy,
Sent out his horse to grass;
And he that had not a bonnie boy,
His ain servant he was.

But up then spake a little page,
Before the peep of dawn-
'O waken ye, waken ye, my good lord,
For Percy's hard at hand.'

'Ye lie, ye lie, ye liar loud!
Sae loud I hear yr lie:
For Percy had not men yestreen,
To dight my men and me.

But I hae dream'd a dreary dream,
Beyond the Isle of Skye;
I saw a dead man win a fight,
And I think that man was I.'

He belted on his good braid sword,
And to the field he ran;
But he forgot the helmet good,
That should have kept his brain.

When Percy wi' the Douglas met,
I wat he was fu' fain!
They swakked their swords, till sair they swat,
And the blood ran down like rain.

But Percy with his good broad sword,
That could so sharply wound,
Has wounded Douglas on the brow,
Till he fell to the ground.

Then he call'd on his little foot-page,
And said – Run speedilie,
And fetch my ain dear sister's son,
Sir Hugh Montgomery.

'My nephew good,' the Douglas said,
'What recks the death of ane!
Last night I dream'd a dreary dream,
And I ken the day's thy ain.

My wound is deep; I fain would sleep;
Take thou the vanguard of the three,
And hide me by the braken bush,
That grows on yonder lilye lee.

O bury me by the braken bush,
Beneath the blooming brier;
Let never living mortal ken,
That ere a kindly Scot lies here.'

He lifted up that noble lord,
Wi the saut tear in his e'e;
He hid him in the braken bush,
That his merrie men might not see.

The moon was clear, the day drew near,
The spears in flinders flew,
But mony a gallant Englishman,
Ere day the Scotsmen slew.

The Gordons good, in English blood,
They steep'd their hose and shoon;
The Lindsays flew like fire about,
Till all the fray was done.

The Percy and Montgomery met,
That either of other were fain;
They swapped swords, and they twa swat,
And aye the blude ran down between.

'Yield thee, O yield thee, Percy!' he said,
'Or else I vow I'll lay thee low!'
'To whom shall I yield,' said Earl Percy,
'Now that I see it must be so?'

'Thou shall not yield to lord nor loun,
Nor yet shalt thou yield tome;
But yield thee to the braken bush,
That grows upon yon lilye lee!'

'I will not yield to a braken bush,
Nor yet will I yield to a brier;
But I would yield to Earl Douglas,
Or Sir Hugh the Montgomery, if he were here.'

As soon as he knew it was Montgomery,
He struck his sword's point in the gronde;
And the Montgomery was a courteous knight,
And quickly took him by the honde.

This deed was done at Otterbourne,
About the breaking of the day;
Earl Douglas was buried at the braken bush,
And the Percy led captive away.

Dick o' the Cow

Now Liddesdale has layen lang in,
There is na riding there at a';
The horses are a' grown sae lither fat,
They downa stir out o' the sta'.

Fair Johnie Armstrang to Willie did say –
'Billy, a riding we will gae;
England and us have been lang at feid;
Ablins we'll light on some bootie.'

Then they are come on to Hatton Ha';
They rade that proper place about;
But the laird he was the wiser man,
For he had left nae gear without.

For he had left nae gear to steal,
Except sax sheep upon a lee:
Quo' Johnie – 'I'd rather in England die,
Ere thir sax sheep gae to Liddesdale wi' me.'

'But how ca' they the man we last met,
Billie, as we cam owre the know?'
'That same he is an innocent fule,
And men they call him Dick o' the Cow.'

'That fule has three as good kye o' his ain,
As there are in a' Cumberland, billie,' quo' he:
'Betide me life, betide me death,
These kye shall go to Liddesdale wi' me.'

Then they have come on to the pure fule's house,
And they hae broken his wa's sae wide;
They have loosed out Dick o' the Cow's three kye,
And ta'en three co'erlets frae his wife's bed.

Then on the morn when the day was light,
The shouts and cries rase loud and hie:
'O haud thy tongue, my wife,' he says,
'And o' thy crying let me be!

O haud thy tongue, my wife,' he says,
'And o' thy crying let me be;
And aye where thou hast lost ae cow,
In gude suith I shall bring thee three.'

Now Dickie's gane to the gude Lord Scroope,
And I wat a dreirie fule was he;
'Now haud thy tongue, my fule,' he says,
'For I may not stand to jest wi' thee.'

'Shame fa' your jesting, my lord!' quo' Dickie,
'For nae sic jesting grees wi' me;
Liddesdale's been in my house last night,
And they hae awa my three kye frae me.

But I may nae langer in Cumberland dwell,
To be your puir fule and your leal,
Unless you gie me leave, my lord,
To gae to Liddesdale and steal.

'I gie thee leave, my fule!' he says;''Thou speakest against
my honour and me,
Unless thou gie me thy trowth and thy hand,
Thou'lt steal frae nane but whae sta' frae thee.'

'There is my trowth, and my right hand!
My head shall hang on Haribee,
I'll ne'er cross Carlisle sands again,
If I steal frae a man but whae sta' frae me.'

Dickie's ta'en leave o' lord and master;
I wat a merry fule was he!
He's bought a bridle and a pair o' new spurs,
And pack'd them up in his breek thie.

Then Dickie's come on to Pudding-burn house,
E'en as fast as he might drie;
Then Dickie's come on to Pudding-burn,
Where there were thirty Armstrangs and three.

'O what's this come o' me now?' quo' Dickie;
'What mickle wae is this?' quo' he;
'For there is but ae innocent fule,
And there are thirty Armstrangs and three!'

Yet he has come up to the fair ha' board,
Sae weil he's become his courtesie!
'Weil may ye be, my gude Laird's Jock!
But the deil bless a' your cumpanie.

I'm come to plain o' your man, fair Johnie Armstrang,
And syne o' his billie Willie,' quo' he;
'How they've been in my house last night,
And they hae ta'en my three kye frae me.'

'Ha!' quo' fair Johnie Armstrang, 'we will him hang.'
'Na,' quo' Willie, 'we'll him slae.'
Then up and spak another young Armstrang,
'We'll gie him his batts, and let him gae.'

But up and spak the gude Laird's Jock,
The best falla in a' the cumpanie:
'Sit down thy ways a little while, Dickie,
And a piece o' thy ain cow's hough I'll gie ye.'

But Dickie's heart it grew sae grit,
That the ne'er a bit o't he dought to eat –
Then he was aware of an auld peat-house,
Where a' the night he thought for to sleep

Then Dickie was aware of an auld peat-house,
Where a' the night he thought for to lye –
And a' the prayers the pure fule prayed
Were, 'I wish I had amends for my gude three kye!'

It was then the use of Pudding-burn house,
And the house of Mangerton, all hail,
Them that cam na at the first ca',
Gat nae mair meat till the neist meal.

The lads, that hungry and weary were,
Abune the door-head they threw the key;
Dickie he took gude notice o' that,
Says – 'There will be a bootie for me.'

Then Dickie has in to the stable gane,
Where there stood thirty horses and three;
He has tied them a' wi' St Mary's knot,
A' these horses but barely three.

He has tied them a' wi' St Mary's knot,
A' these horses but barely three;
He's loupen on ane, ta'en another in hand,
And away as fast as he can hie.

But on the morn, when the day grew light,
The shouts and cries raise loud and hie –
'Ah! whae has done this?' quo' the gude Laird's Jock,
'Tell me the truth and the verity!

Whae has done this deed?' quo' the gude Laird's Jock;
'See that to me ye dinna lie!'
'Dickie has been in the stable last night,
And has ta'en my brother's horse and mine frae me.'

'Ye wad ne'er be tauld,' quo' the gude Laird's Jock;
'Have ye not found my tales fu' leil?
Ye ne'er wad out o' England bide,
Till crooked, and blind, and a' would steal.'

'But lend me thy bay,' fair Johnie can say;
'There's nae horse loose in the stable save he;
And I'll either fetch Dick o' the Cow again,
Or the day is come that he shall die.'

'To lend thee my bay!' the Laird's Jock can say,
'He's baith worth gowd and gude monie;
Dick o' the Cow has awa twa horse;
I wish na thou may make him three.'

He has ta'en the laird's jack on his back,
A twa-handed sword to hang by his thie;
He has ta'en a steil cap on his head,
And gallopped on to follow Dickie.

Dickie was na a mile frae aff the town,
I wat a mile but barely three,
When he was o'erta'en by fair Johnie Armstrang,
Hand for hand, on Cannobie lee.

'Abide, abide, thou traitour thief!
The day is come that thou maun die.'
Then Dickie look't owre his left shoulder,
Said – 'Johnie, hast thou nae mae in cumpanie?

There is a preacher in our chapell,
And a' the live lang day teaches he;
When day is gane and night is come,
There's ne'er ae word I mark but three.

The first and second is – Faith and Conscience;
The third – Ne'er let a traitour free:
But, Johnie, what faith and conscience was thine,
When thou took awa my three kye frae me?

And when thou had ta'en awa my three kye,
Thou thought in thy heart thou wast not weil sped,
Till thou sent thy billie Willie ower the know,
To tak three coverlets off my wife's bed!'

Then Johnie let a speir fa' laigh by his thie,
Thought weil to hae slain the innocent, I trow;
But the powers above were mair than he,
For he ran but the pure fule's jerkin through.

Together they ran, or ever they blan;
This was Dickie the fule and he!
Dickie could na win at him wi' the blade o' the sword,
But fell'd him wi' the plummet under the e'e.

Thus Dickie has fell'd fair Johnie Armstrang,
The prettiest man in the south country –
'Gramercy!' then can Dickie say,
'I had but twa horse, thou hast made me three.'

He's ta'en the steil jack aff Johnie's back,
The twa-handed sword that hang low by his thie;
He's ta'en the steil cap aff his head –
'Johnie, I'll tell my master I met wi' thee.'

When Johnie wakened out o' his dream,
I wat a dreirie man was he:
'And is thou gane? Now, Dickie, than
The shame and dule is left wi' me.

And is thou gane? Now, Dickie, than
The deil gae in thy cumpanie!
For if I should live these hundred years,
I ne'er shall fight wi' a fule after thee.'

Then Dickie's come hame to the gude Lord Scroope,
E'en as fast as he might hie;
'Now, Dickie, I'll neither eat not drink,
Till hie hanged thou shalt be.'

'The shame speed the liars, my lord!' quo' Dickie;
'This was na the promise ye made to me!
For I'd ne'er gane to Liddesdale to steal,
Had I not got my leave frae thee.'

'But what garr'd thee steal the Laird's Jock's horse?
And, limmer, what garr'd ye steal him?' quo' he;
'For lang thou mightst in Cumberland dwelt,
Ere the Laird's Jock had stown frae thee.'

'Indeed I wat ye lied, my lord!
And e'en sae loud as I hear ye lie!
I wan the horse frae fair Johnie Armstrang,
Hand to hand, on Cannobie lee.

'There is the jack was on his back;
This twa-handed sword hang laigh by his thie,
And there's the steil cap was on his head;
I brought a' these tokens to let thee see.'

'If that be true thou to me tells,
(And I think thou dares na tell a lie)
I'll gie thee fifteen punds for the horse,
Weil tald on thy cloak lap shall be.

'I'll gie thee ane o' my best milk kye,
To maintain thy wife and children three;
And that may be as gude, I think,
As ony twa o' thine wad be.'

'The shame speed the liars, my lord!' quo' Dickie;
'Trow ye aye to make a fule o' me?
I'll either hae twenty punds for the gude horse,
Or he's gae to Mortan fair wi' me.'

He's gien him twenty punds for the gude horse,
A' in goud and gude monie;
He's gien him ane o' his best milk kye,
To maintain his wife and children three.

Then Dickie's come down thro' Carlisle toun,
E'en as fast as he could drie;
The first o' men that he met wi'
Was my lord's brother, Bailiff Glozenburrie.

'Weil be ye met, my gude Ralph Scroope!'
'Welcome, my brother's fule!' quo' he:
'Where didst thou get fair Johnie Armstrang's horse?'
'Where did I get him? but steal him,' quo' he.

'But wilt thou sell me the bonny horse?
And, billie, wilt thou sell him to me?' quo' he:
'Aye; if thou'lt tell me the monie on my cloak lap,
For there's never ae penny I'll trust thee.'

'I'll gie thee ten punds for the gude horse,
Weil tald on thy cloak lap they shall be;
And I'll gie thee ane o' the best milk kye,
To maintain thy wife and children three.'

'The shame speed the liars, my lord!' quo' Dickie;
'Trow ye aye to mak a fule o' me!
I'll either hae twenty punds for the gude horse,
Or he's gae to Mortan fair wi' me.'

He's gien him twenty punds for the gude horse,
Baith in goud and gude monie;
He's gien him ane o' his best milk kye,
To maintain his wife and children three.

Then Dickie lap a loup fu' hie,
And I wat a loud laugh laughed he –
'I wish the neck o' the third horse were broken,
If ony of the twa were better than he!'

Then Dickie's come hame to his wife again;
'Judge ye how the poor fule had sped!'
He has gien her twa score English punds,
For the three auld coverlets ta'en aff her bed.

'And tak thee these twa as gude kye,
I trow, as a' thy three might be;
And yet here is a white-footed nagie,
I trow he'll carry baith thee and me.

But I may nae langer in Cumberland bide;
The Armstrangs they would hang me hie.'
So Dickie's ta'en leave at lord and master,
And at Burgh under Stanmuir there swells he.

Johnie Armstrang

Sum speikis of lords, sum speikis of lairds,
And sick lyke men of his hie degrie;
Of a gentleman I sing a sang,
Sum tyme called laird of Gilnockie.

The King he wrytes a luving letter,
With his ain hand dae tenderly,
And he hath sent it to Johnie Armstrang,
To cum and speik with him speedily.

The Eliots and Armstrangs did convene;
They were a gallnt cumpanie –
'We'll ride and meit our lawful King,
And bring him safe to Gilnockie.

Make kinnen and capon ready then,
And venison in great plentie;
We'll wellcum here our royal King;
I hope he'll dine at Gilnockie!'

They ran their horse on the Langhome howm,
And brak their speirs wi' mickle main;
The ladies lukit frae their loft windows –
'God bring our men weel back agen!'

When Johnie cam before the King,
Wi' a' his men sae brave tae see,
The King he movit his bonnet to him;
He ween'd he was a King as well as he.

'May I find grace, my sovereign leige,
Grace for my loyal men and me?
For my name it is Johnie Armstrang,
And a subject of yours, my liege,' said he.

'Away, away, thou traitor strang!
Out o' my sight soon may'st thou be!
I grantit niver a traitor's life,
And now I'll not begin wi' thee.'

'Grant me my life, my liege, my King!
And a bonny gift I'll gie to thee –
Full four and twenty milk-white steids,
Were a' foaled in ae year to me.

I'll gie thee a' these milk-white steids,
That prance and nicker at a speir;
And as mickle gude Inglish gilt,
As four o' their braid backs dow bear.'

'Away, away, thou traitor strang!
Out o' my sight soon may'st thou be!
I grantit niver a traitor's life,
And now I'll not begin wi' thee!'

'Grant me my life, my liege, my King!
And a bonny gift I'll gie to thee –
Gude four and twenty ganging mills,
That gang thro' a' the yeir to me.

These four and twenty mills complete,
Sall gang for thee thro' a' the yeir;
And as mickle of gude reid wheit,
As a' their happens dow to bear.'

'Away, away, thou traitor strang!
Out o' my sight soon may'st thou be!
I grantit niver a traitor's life,
And now I'll not begin wi' thee!'

'Grant me my life, my liege, my King!
And a great gift I'll gie to thee –
Bauld four-and-twenty sisters' sons,
Sall for thee fecht, tho' a' should flee!'

'Away, away, thou traitor strang!
Out o' my sight soon may'st thou be!
I grantit niver a traitor's life,
And now I'll not begin wi' thee!'

'Grant me my life, my liege, my King!
And a brave gift I'll gie to thee –
All between heir and Newcastle town
Sall pay their yearly rent to thee.'

'Away, away, thou traitor strang!
Out o' my sight soon may'st thou be!
I grantit niver a traitor's life,
And now I'll not begin wi' thee!'

'Ye lied, ye lied, now, King,' he says,
'Altho' a King and Prince ye be!
For I've luved naething in my life,
I weel dare say it, but honesty –

Save a fat horse, and a fair woman,
Twa bonny dogs to kill a deir;
But England suld have found me meal and mault,
Gif I had lived this hundred yeir!

Sche suld have found me meal and mault,
And beef and mutton in a' plentie;
But nevir a Scots wyfe could have said,
That e'er I skaith'd her a puir flee.

To seik het water beneith cauld ice,
Surely it is a greit folie –
I have asked grace at a graceless face,
But there is nane for my men and me!

But had I kenn'd ere I cam frae hame,
How thou unkind wadst been to me!
I wad have keepit the border side,
In spite of all thy force and thee.

Wist England's King that I was ta'en,
O gin a blythe man he wad be!
For anes I slew his sister's son,
And on his breist bane brak a trie.'

John wore a girdle about his middle,
Imbroidered ower wi' burning gold,
Bespangled wi' the same metal;
Maist beautiful was to behold.

There hang nine targats at Johnie's hat.
And ilk ane worth three hundred pound –
'What wants that knave that a King suld have,
But the sword of honour and the crown!'

'O whair got thou these targats, Johnie,
That blink sae brawly abune thy brie?'
'I gat them in the field fechting,
Where, cruel King, thou durst not be.

Had I my horse, and harness gude,
And riding as I wont to be,
It suld have been tald this hundred yeir,
This meeting of my King and me!

God be with thee, Kirsty, my brother!
Lang live thou laird of Mangertoun!
Lang may'st thou live on the border syde,
Ere thou see thy brother ride up and down!

And God be with thee, Kirsty, my son,
Where thou sits on thy nurse's knee!
But thou live this hundred yeir,
Thy father's better thou'lt nevir be.

Farewell! my bonny Gilnock hall,
Where on Esk side thou standest stout!
Gig I had lived but seven yeirs mair,
I wad hae gilt thee round about.'

John murdered was at Carlinrigg,
And all his gallant cumpanie;
But Scotland's heart was ne'er sae wae,
To see sae mony brave men die –

Because they saved their countrey deir,
Frae Englishmen! Nane were sae bauld
While Johnie lived on the border syde,
Nane of them durst cum neir his hauld.

Kinmont Willie

O have ye na heard o' the fause Sakelde?
O have ye na heard o' the keen Lord Scroope?
How they hae ta'en bauld Kinmont Willie,
On Haribee to hang him up?

Had Willie had but twenty men,
But twenty men as stout as he,
Fause Sakelde had never the Kinmont ta'en,
Wi' eight score in his cumpanie.

They band his legs beneath the steed,
They tied his hands behind his back;
They guarded him, fivesome on each side,
And they brought him ower the Liddel-rack.

They led him thro' the Liddel-rack,
And also thro' the Carlisle sands;
They brought him to Carlisle castell,
To be at my Lord Scroope's commands.

'My hands are tied, but my tongue is free,
And whae will dare this deed avow?
Or answer by the border law?
Or answer to the bauld Buccleuch!'

'Now baud thy tongue, thou rank reiver!
There's never a Scot shall set ye free:
Before ye cross my castle yate,
I trow ye shall take farewell o' me.'

'Fear na ye that, my lord,' quo' Willie:
'By the faith o' my body, Lord Scroope,' he said,
'I never yet lodged in a hostelrie,
But I paid my lawing before I gaed.'

Now word is gane to the bauld Keeper,
In Branksome Ha', where that he lay,
That Lord Scroope has ta'en the Kinmont Willie,
Between the hours of night and day.

He has ta'en the table wi' his hand,
He garr'd the red wine spring on hie –
'Now Christ's curse on my head,' he said,
'But avenged of Lord Scroope I'll be!

O is my basnet a widow's curch?
Or my lance a wand of the willow tree?
Or my arm a ladye's lilye hand,
That an English lord should lightly me!

And have they ta'en him, Kinmont Willie,
Against the truce of Border tide?
And forgotten that the bauld Buccleuch
Is Keeper here on the Scottish side?

And have they e'en ta'en him, Kinmont Willie,
Withouten either dread or fear?
And forgotten that the bauld Buccleuch
Can back a steed, or shake a spear?

O were there war between the lands,
As well I wot that there is none,
I would slight Carlisle castell high,
Tho' it were builded of marble stone.

I would set that castell in a low,
And sloken it with English blood!
There's nevir a man in Cumberland,
Should ken where Carlisle castell stood.

But since nae war's between the lands,
And there is peace, and peace should be;
I'll neither harm English lad or lass,
And yet the Kinmont freed shall be!'

He has call'd him forty marchmen bauld,
I trow they were of his ain name,
Except Sir Gilbert Elliot, call'd
The laird of Stobs, I mean the same.

He has call'd him forty marchmen bauld,
Were kinsmen to the bauld Buccleuch;
With spur on heel, and splent on spauld,
And gleuves of green, and feathers blue.

There were five and five before them a',
Wi' hunting horns and bugles bright;
And five and five came wi' Buccleuch,
Like warden's men, arrayed for fight:

And five and five, like a mason gang,
That carried the ladders lang and hie;
And five and five, like broken men;
And so they reached the Woodhouselee.

And as we cross'd the Bateable Land,
When to the English side we held,
The first o' men that we met wi',
Whae sould it be but fause Sakelde?

'Where be ye gaun, ye hunters keen?'
Quo' fause Sakelde; 'come tell to me!'
'We go to hunt an English stag,
Has trespassed on the Scots countrie.'

'Where be ye gaun, ye marshal men?'
Quo' fause Sakelde; 'come tell me true!'
'We go to catch a rank reiver,
Has broken faith wi' the bauld Buccleuch.'

'Where are ye gaun, ye mason lads,
Wi' a' your ladders, lang and hie?'
'We gang to herry a corbie's nest,
That wons not far frae Woodhouselee.'

'Where be ye gaun, ye broken men?'
Quo' fause Sakelde; 'come tell to me!'
Now Dickie of Dryhope led that band,
And the nevir a word o' lear had he.

'Why trespass ye on the English side,
Row-footed outlaws, stand!' quo' he;
The nevir a word had Dickie to say,
Sae he thrust the lance through his fause bodie.

Then on we held for Carlisle toun,
And at Staneshaw-bank the Eden we cross'd;
The water was great and meikle of spait,
But the nevir a horse nor man we lost.

And when we reached the Staneshaw-bank,
The wind was rising loud and hie;
And there the laird garr'd leave our steeds,
For fear that they should stamp and nie.

And when we left the Staneshaw-bank,
The wind began full loud to blaw;
But 'twas wind and weet, and fire and sleet,
When we came beneath the castle wa'.

We crept on knees, and held our breath,
Till we placed the ladders against the wa';
And sae ready was Buccleuch himsell
To mount the first, before us a'.

He has ta'en the watchman by the throat,
He flung him down upon the lead –
'Had there not been peace between our land,
Upon the other side thou hadst gaed!' –

'Now sound out, trumpets!' quo' Buccleuch;
'Let's waken Lord Scroope, right merrilie!'
Then loud the warden's trumpet blew –
'*O wha dare meddle wi' me?*'

Then speedilie to work we gaed,
And raised the slogan ane and a',
And cut a hole thro' a sheet of lead,
And so we wan to the castle ha'.

They thought King James and a' his men
Had won the house wi' bow and spear;
It was but twenty Scots and ten,
That put a thousand in sic a stear!

Wi' coulters, and wi' fore-hammers,
We garr'd the bars bang merrilie,
Until we cam to the inner prison,
Where Willie o' Kinmont he did lie.

And when we cam to the lower prison
Where Willie o' Kinmont he did lie –
'O sleep ye, wake ye, Kinmont Willie,
Upon the morn that thou's to die?'

'O I sleep saft, and I wake aft;
Its lang since sleeping was fleyed frae me!
Gie my service back to my wife and bairns,
And a' gude fellows that spier for me.

Then Red Rowan has hente him up,
The starkest man in Teviotdale –
'Abide, abide now, Red Rowan,
Till of my Lord Scroope I take farewell.

Farewell, farewell, my gude Lord Scroope!
My gude Lord Scroope, farewell!' he cried –
'I'll pay you for my lodging maill,
When first we meet on the Border side.'

Then shoulder high, with shout and cry,
We bore him down the ladder lang;
At every stride Red Rowan made,
I wot the Kinmont's airns played clang!

'O mony a time,' quo' Kinmont Willie,
I have ridden horse baith wild and wood;
But a rougher beast than Red Rowan, –
I ween my legs have ne'er bestrode.

And many a time,' quo' Kinmont Willie,
'I've pricked a horse out oure the furs;
But since the day I backed a steed,
I never wore sic cumbrous spurs!'

We scarce had won the Staneshaw-bank,
When a' the Carlisle bells were rung,
And a thousand men, in horse and foot,
Cam wi' the keen Lord Scroope along.

Buccleuch has turned to Eden water,
Even where it flowed frae bank to brim,
And he has plunged in wi' a' his band,
And safely swam them thro' the stream.

He turned him on the other side,
And at Lord Scroope his glove flung he –
'If ye like na my visit in merry England,
In fair Scotland come visit me!'

All sore astonished stood Lord Scroope,
He stood as still as rock of stane;
He scarcely dared to trew his eyes,
When thro' the water they had gane.

'He is either himself a devil frae hell,
Or else his mother a witch maun be;
I wad na have ridden that wan water,
For a' the gowd in Christentie.

The Raid of Reidswire

The seventh of July, the suith to say,
At the Reidswire the tryst was set;
Our wardens they affixed the day,
And, as they promised, so they met.
Alas! that day I'll ne'er forgen!
Was sure sae feard, and then sae faine-
They came theare justice for to gett
Will never green to come again.

Carmichael was our warden then,
He caused the country to conveen;
And the Laird's Wat, that worthie man,
Brought in that sirname weil beseen:
The Armestranges, that aye hae been
A hardie house, but not a hail,
The Elliot's honours to maintaine,
Brought down the lave o' Liddesdale.

Then Tividale came to wi' speid;
The sheriffe brought the Douglas down,
Wi' Cranstane, Gladstain, good at need
Baith Rewle water, and Hawick town.
Beanjeddart bauldly made him boun,
Wi' a' the Turnbills, stronge and stout;
The Rutherfoords, with grit renown,
Convoyed the town of Jedbrugh out.

Of other clans I cannot tell,
Because our warning was not wide –
Be this our folks hae taen the fell,
And planted down palliones there to bide.
We looked down the other side,
And saw come breasting ower the brae,
Wi' Sir John Forster for their guyde,
Full fifteen hundred men and mae.

It grieved him sair, that day, I trow,
Wi' Sir George Hearoune of Schipsydehouse:
Because we were not men enow,
They counted us not worth a louse.
Sir George was gentle, meek, and douse,
But *he* was hail and het as fire;
And yet, for all his cracking crouse,
He rewd the raid o' the Reidswire.

To deal with proud men is but pain;
For either must ye fight or flee,
Or else no answer make again,
But play the beast, and let them be.
It was na wonder he was hie,
Had Tindaill, Reedsdaill, at his hand,
Wi' Cukdaill, Gladsdaill on the lee,
And Hebsrime, and Northumberland

Yett was our meeting meek enough,
Begun wi' merriment and mowes,
And at the brae, aboon the heugh,
The clark sate down to call the rowes
And some for kyne, and some for ewes,
Called in of Dandrie, Hob, and Jock –
We saw, come marching ower the knows,
Five hundred Fennicks in a flock.

With jack and speir, and bows all bent,
And warlike weapons at their will:
Although we were na well content,
Yet be my trouth, we feard no ill.
Some gaed to drink, and some stude still,
And some to cards and dice them sped;
Till on ane Farnstein they fyled a bill,
And he was fugitive and fled.

Carmichael bade them speik out plainlie,
And cloke no cause for ill nor good;
The other, answering him as vainlie,
Began to reckon kin and blood:
He raise, and raxed him where he stood,
And bade him match him with his marrows,
Then Tindaill heard them reasun rude,
And they loot off a flight of arrows.

Then was there nought but bow and speir,
And every man pulled out a brand;
'A Schafton and a Fenwick' thare:
Gude Symington was slain frae hand.
The Scotsmen cried on other to stand,
Frae time they saw John Robson slain –
What should they cry? the King's command
Could cause no cowards turn again.

Up rose the laird to red the cumber,
Which would not be for all his boast
What could we doe with sic a number?
Fyve thousand men into a host.
Then Henry Purdie proved his cost,
And very narrowlie had mischiefed him,
And there we had our warden lost,
Wert not the grit God he relieved him.

Another throw the breiks him bair,
Whill flatlies to the ground he fell:
Than thought I weel we had lost him there,
Into my stomack it struck a knell!
Yet up he raise the treuth to tell ye,
And laid about him dints full dour;
His horsemen they raid sturdily,
And stude about him in the stoure.

Then raise the slogan with ane shout –
'Fy Tindaill to it! Jedbrugh's here!'
I trow he was not half sae stout,
But anis his stomach was asteir.
With gun and genzie, bow and speir,
Men might see mony a cracked crown!
But up amang the merchant geir,
They were as busy as we were down.

The swallow tail frae tackles flew,
Five hundreth flain into a flight,
But we had pestelets anow,
And shot among them as we might.
With help of God the game gaed right,
Frae time the foremost of them fell;
Then ower the know, without goodnight,
They ran with mony a shout and yell.

But after they had turned backs,
Yet Tindaill men they turned again;
And had not been the merchant packs,
There had been mae of Scotland slain.
But, Jesu! if the folks were fain
To put the bussing on their thies;
And so they fled, wi' a' their main,
Down ower the brae, like clogged bees.

Sir Francis Russell ta'en was there,
And hurt, as we hear men rehearse;
Proud Wallinton was wounded sair,
Albeit he be a Fennick fierce.
But if ye wald a souldier search,
Among them a' were ta'en that night,
Was nane sae wordie to put in verse,
As Collingwood, that courteous knight.

Young Henry Schafton, he is hurt;
A souldier shot him wi' a bow:
Scotland has cause to mak great sturt,
For laiming of the laird of Mow.
The Laird's Wat did weel, indeed;
His friends stood stoutlie by himsel',
With little Gladstain, gude in need,
For Gretein kend na gude be ill.

The Sheriffe wanted not gude will,
Howbeit he might not fight so fast;
Beanjeddart, Hundlie, and Hunthill,
Three, on they laid weel at the last.
Except the horsemen of the guard,
I could put men to availe,
None stoutlier stood out for their laird
Nor did the lads of Liddisdail.

But little harness had we there;
But auld Badreule had on a jack,
And did right weel, I you declare,
With all his Turrnbills at his back.
Gude Edderstane was not to lack,
Nor Kirktoun; Newton, noble men!
Thirs all the specials I of speake,
By others that I could not ken.

Who did invent that day of play,
We need not fear to find him soon;
For Sir John Forster, I dare well say,
Made us this noisome afternoon.
Not that I speak preceislie out,
That he supposed it would be perril;
But pride, and breaking out of feuid,
Garr'd Tindaill lads begin the quarrel.

Appendix 2

The Names

There were many reiver surnames, great and small. Some repeat endlessly down the decades, others are mentioned only once or twice. All of them are listed below. Alliances shifted and some families gave up land in one place (or were moved) to settle in another. Others were represented on both sides of the border. Here is an alphabetical list of all who were involved in the riding times and in brackets are the principal locations of the name.

Aglionby (North Cumbria)
Anderson (North Northumberland)
Armstrong (Liddesdale, Annandale, Eskdale and North Cumbria)
Beattie (also Batey, Bateson, Dumfriesshire)
Bell (Annandale, North Cumbria, North Northumberland)
Bromfield (Berwickshire)
Burn (also Bourne, Teviotdale)
Carleton (also Charlton, Tynedale and North Cumbria)
Carmichael (Dumfriesshire)
Carnaby (North Northumberland)
Carruthers (Dumfriesshire)
Collingwood (North Northumberland)
Cranston (Teviotdale and Berwickshire)
Craw (Berwickshire)
Crichton (Dumfriesshire)
Croser (also Crozier, Liddesdale and Teviotdale)
Curwen (North Cumbria)
Dacre (North Cumbria)
Dalgleish (Berwickshire)
Davison (also Davidson, Teviotdale)
Dickson (also Dixon, Roxburghshire and Berwickshire)

Dodd (Tynedale)
Douglas (Liddesdale and Dumfriesshire)
Dunne (North Northumberland)
Elliot (Liddesdale, Ewesdale, Teviotdale)
Fenwick (Tynedale, North Northumberland)
Forster (North Northumberland)
Gilchrist (Teviotdale)
Glendinning (Dumfriesshire)
Graham (North Cumbria and Dumfriesshire)
Gray (North Northumberland)
Hall (Liddesdale, Teviotdale, Redesdale)
Harden (North Cumbria)
Hedley (Redesdale)
Henderson (Liddesdale)
Heron (North Northumberland)
Hetherington (North Cumbria)
Hodgson (North Cumbria)
Hume (Berwickshire)
Hunter (Liddesdale)
Irvine (Annandale and Eskdale)
Jamieson (North Northumberland)
Jardine (Dumfriesshire)
Johnstone (Dumfriesshire)
Kerr (Roxburghshire)
Laidlaw (Liddesdale)
Lilburn (North Northumberland)
Lisle (Dumfriesshire)
Little (Dumfriesshire)
Lowther (North Cumbria)
Maxwell (Dumfriesshire)
Medford (North Northumberland)
Milburn (Tynedale)
Moffat (Dumfriesshire)
Musgrave (North Cumbria)
Nixon (Liddesdale, North Cumbria)
Noble (North Cumbria)
Ogle (North Northumberland)
Oliver (Teviotdale)
Percy (Northumberland)
Potts (North Northumberland)

Pringle (Roxburghshire)
Read (Redesdale)
Redpath (Berwickshire)
Ridley (North Northumberland)
Robson (Tynedale, Liddesdale, Teviotdale)
Routledge (North Cumbria)
Rutherford (Roxburghshire)
Salkeld (North Cumbria)
Scott (Teviotdale, Ewesdale)
Selby (North Northumberland)
Shafto (North Northumberland)
Stamper (North Northumberland)
Stapleton (Tynedale)
Stokoe (North Northumberland)
Storey (Eskdale, North Northumberland)
Tailor (North Cumbria)
Tait (Roxburghshire)
Thomson (Liddesdale, North Northumberland)
Trotter (Berwickshire)
Turnbull (Roxburghshire)
Turner (Liddesdale)
Wilkinson (North Northumberland)
Woodrington (North Northumberland)
Yarrow (Tynedale)
Young (Teviotdale)

Appendix 3

Kings and Queens

Even as late as the sixteenth century regnal years were often preferred to the modern system of AD dating. That is, 1510 was counted as the twenty-second year of the reign of James IV, rather than 1510. For that reason and the confusing fact that both the Stewarts and the Tudors were fond of repeating the same Christian names, here is a short but handy list of English and Scottish sovereigns in the sixteenth century:

English
Henry VII: 1485 to 1509
Henry VIII: 1513 to 1547
Edward VI: 1547 to 1553
Mary I: 1553 to 1558
Elizabeth I: 1558 to 1603
James VI and I: 1603 to 1625

Scottish
James IV: 1488 to 1513
James V: 1513 to 1542
Mary I: 1542 to 1567
James VI: 1567 to 1625

Appendix 4

How the Ferniehurst Kerrs
Stopped Reiving and Became Part
of the British Establishment

Sir Thomas Kerr of Ferniehurst remained a catholic until his death in 1585. His son, *Andrew*, became Provost of Jedburgh and was created the *first Lord Jedburgh* in 1621. Sir Thomas' cousin, *William Kerr of Ancrum*, really advanced the family's fortunes out of a local context when he sent his son to join the large band of Scotsmen on the make which followed James VI and I to London in 1603. *Robert Kerr of Ancrum* was elevated to the *earldom of Ancrum* and became *MP for Aylesbury* in 1625. After the Civil War he was exiled to Holland where he died in 1655. His son, *William*, managed the shifting politics of Cromwell's Commonwealth very adroitly. Supporting the Covenanting cause, he became the *third Earl of Lothian*. Promotion came for his successor, *Robert, the first Marquis of Lothian* in 1701. He also inherited the Ancrum title from his uncle and became Chief of the Name. Five *Williams* followed as Marquises. They lived at Newbattle Abbey near Edinburgh and managed always to choose the right political options. *William, the fourth Marquis*, brought his own regiment, Kerr's Horse (of course), to fight in the government army at Culloden in 1746. His grandson, also William, caused the monument on Penielheugh to be built. Visible from almost everywhere in the central Borders, it commemorates the Duke of Wellington's victory at Waterloo. In the nineteenth century Marquises of Lothian sat as MPs and also developed an impressive habit of winning double firsts at Oxford University. *Schomberg, ninth Marquis of Lothian*, not only sported a Christian name which would have baffled his reiving ancestors, he was also one of the first Secretaries of State for Scotland, in office from 1887 to 1892. Having established Monteviot House, near Jedburgh, as their principal residence, the Kerrs continued to be involved in politics with *Philip, the eleventh Marquis*, being appointed to the key post of Ambassador to the USA from 1939 to 1941. His son, Peter, became a minister in three Conservative administrations. And his son, known as *Michael Ancrum*, is also a prominent Conservative politician, and like the first Earl, sits for an English constituency. It is a very far cry from Ferniehurst, but a remarkable story of making and taking opportunities.

Appendix 5

The Common Riding Year

Since the timing of the Border Common Ridings follows ancient rubrics such as 'the first Friday after the second Monday in June', it is wise not to attach specific dates. Here is the time-honoured sequence:

June

* Hawick Common Riding
* Selkirk Common Riding
* Peebles Festival
* Melrose Festival
* Braw Lads Gathering at Galashiels

July

* Jethart Callants Festival
* Duns Reivers' Week
* Kelso Civic Week
* St Ronan's Festival Innerleithen
* Langholm Common Riding

August

* Coldstream Civic Week
* Lauder Common Riding

Bibliography

Most historians list vast bibliographies, almost like battle honours. I have spent years writing Border history but instead of showing off and noting everything I have read, here is a very select bibliography, something for those who really do want to read further:

Armstrong, P. *Otterburn 1388*, Ospey, Oxford 2006
Bates, Cadwallader J. *History of Northumberland London* 1895
Barr, N. *Flodden*, Tempus, Stroud 2003
Bogle, K.R. *Scotland's Common Ridings* Tempus, Stroud 2004
Burnett, J. *Riot, Revelry and Rout* Tuckwell Press, East Linton 2000
Davies, N. *Europe – A History* Oxford University Press, Oxford 1996
Douglas, Sir G. *Roxburgh, Selkirk and Peebles* 1894
Durham, K. and MacBride, A. *The Border Reivers* Osprey, Oxford 1995
Fraser, A.F. *The Native Horses of Scotland* John Donald, Edinburgh 1987
Fraser, G. MacDonald *The Steel Bonnets* Barrie and Jenkins, London 1971
Lynch, M. *Scotland – A New History* Century, London 1991
McCulloch, A. *Galloway* Birlinn, Edinburgh 2000
Macdonald, A. *Border Bloodshed* Tuckwell Press, East Linton 2000
MacIvor, I. *A Fortified Frontier* Tempus, Stroud 2001
Marsden. J. *The Illustrated Border Ballads* Macmillan, London 1990
Meikle, M.M. *A British Frontier?* Tuckwell Press, East Linton 2004
Miles, D. *The Tribes of Britain* Weidenfeld and Nicolson, London 2005
Moffat, A. *The Borders* Birlinn, Edinburgh 2007
Nicholson, R. *Scotland, the Later Middle Ages* Oliver & Boyd, Edinburgh 1974
Ridpath, G. *Border History* Berwick 1848

Robson M. *Ride with the Moonlight* Newcastleton 1987

Scott, S. and Duncan, C. *Return of the Black Death* Wiley, Chichester 2005

Sprott, G. *Farming* National Museums of Edinburgh, Edinburgh 1999

Tabraham, C. *Smailholm Tower* Historic Scotland, Edinburgh 1993

Tough D.L.W. *The Last Years of a Frontier* Oxford University Press, Oxford 1928

Watson, G. *The Border Reivers* Hale, London 1974

Winchester, A.J.L. *The Harvest of the Hills* Edinburgh University Press, Edinburgh 2000

Index

NOTE: References to families are placed before references to individuals carrying that surname. A page number followed by 'box' indicates that the item will be found in a box on the given page.

BIRLINN LTD (incorporating John Donald and Polygon) is one of Scotland's leading publishers with over four hundred titles in print. Should you wish to be put on our catalogue mailing list **contact**:

Catalogue Request
Birlinn Ltd
West Newington House
10 Newington Road
Edinburgh EH9 1QS
Scotland, UK

Tel: + 44 (0) 131 668 4371
Fax: + 44 (0) 131 668 4466
e-mail: info@birlinn.co.uk

Postage and packing is free within the UK. For overseas orders, postage and packing (airmail) will be charged at 30% of the total order value.

For more information, or to order online, visit our website at **www.birlinn.co.uk**

Birlinn *Limited*
IMPRINTS: JOHN DONALD · POLYGON